Favorite Recipes of America

®

DESSERTS

including party beverages

FAVORITE RECIPES PRESS,
Louisville,

TABLE OF CONTENTS

FAVORITE RECIPES PRESS, INC. © MCMLXVI
Post Office Box 18324
Louisville, Kentucky 40218

INTRODUCTION

Cakes, pies, meringues, ice creams, tortes, souffles . . . the parade of desserts is almost endless. And there is nothing that Americans enjoy more than delicious homemade desserts.

Americans like desserts so much that as a nation we annually consume more sweets than any other country in the world. Adults, as well as children, need sugar to supply the energy that keeps them active.

Take your pick—you'll find desserts of every description in this unusual collection of FAVORITE RECIPES OF AMERICA. You'll find recipes that are a snap to prepare while others are more complicated and require more patience. Some are definitely not for weight watchers, while others are a blessing for the calorie conscious. You'll find recipes for desserts just like Grandmother used to make. Others have been simplified for the busy homemaker of today. The special section containing recipes for party beverages is an added attraction.

These recipes were selected from my files of more than 50,000 favorite recipes to represent the desserts that Americans like best. These favorite recipes were home tested by hundreds of American cooks just like yourself. Each recipe was personally endorsed by the homemaker whose name appears under the recipe. You'll find that these recipes, which came from North, South, East and West, can be used for family meals or special occasions when you have guests.

Once you have tried the many delectable dessert recipes in this "Desserts" edition of FAVORITE RECIPES OF AMERICA, you'll know just why they are favorite American recipes—for you'll find many that will become your favorite recipes, too.

Mary Anne Richards
Staff Home Economist
Favorite Recipes Press, Inc.

ABBREVIATIONS USED IN THIS BOOK

Cup .... c.
Teaspoon .... tsp.
Tablespoon .... tbsp.
Pound .... lb.
Ounce .... oz.
Gallon .... gal.

Large .... lge.
Package .... pkg.
Square .... sq.
Dozen .... doz.
Pint .... pt.
Quart .... qt.

MEASURES

3 tsp. = 1 tbsp.

2 tbsp. = ⅛ c.

4 tbsp. = ¼ c.

8 tbsp. = ½ c.

16 tbsp. = 1 c.

5 tbsp. + 1 tsp. = ⅓ c.

12 tbsp. = ¾ c.

4 oz. = ½ c.

8 oz. = 1 c.

16 oz. = 1 lb.

1 oz. = 2 tbsp. fat or liquid

2 c. fat = 1 lb.

2 c. = 1 pt.

2 c. sugar = 1 lb.

2⅔ c. powdered sugar = 1 lb.

2⅔ c. brown sugar = 1 lb.

⅝ c. = ½ c. + 2 tbsp.

⅞ c. = ¾ c. + 2 tbsp.

4 c. sifted flour = 1 lb.

1 lb. butter = 2 c. or 4 sticks

2 pt. = 1 qt.

1 qt. = 4 c.

A few grains = Less than ⅛ tsp.

Pinch = As much as can be taken between tip of finger and thumb

Speck = Less than ⅛ tsp.

SUBSTITUTIONS

1 tbsp. cornstarch (for thickening) = 2 tbsp. flour (approximately)

1 c. sifted all-purpose flour = 1 c. minus 2 tbsp. sifted cake flour

1 c. sifted cake flour = 1 c. minus 2 tbsp. sifted all-purpose flour

1 tsp. baking powder = ¼ tsp. baking soda plus ½ tsp. cream of tartar

1 c. bottled milk = ½ c. evaporated milk plus ½ c. water

1 c. sour milk = 1 c. sweet milk into which 1 tbsp. vinegar or lemon juice has been stirred; or 1 c. buttermilk

1 c. sweet milk = 1 c. sour milk or buttermilk plus ½ tsp. baking soda

1 c. molasses = 1 c. honey

CHOOSING A DESSERT

Apple pie . . . chocolate souffle . . . strawberry cream . . . meringue kisses . . . the choices of a dessert are endless. A dessert is an added attraction to any meal but must be chosen carefully if the meal is to end happily. The nutritional balance of the entire meal must be the major factor when choosing the proper dessert as well as a pleasant taste treat for rounding out the meal.

It's easy to choose a dessert if you'll remember this simple rule of thumb. A heavy dessert, such as pie or cake, goes with a light meal. But if the meal itself is heavy, serve a dessert such as fruit custard, gelatin, sherbet or something else that's light and not too filling.

Even Desserts Need . . .

. . . perking up sometime. With a simple garnish, you can change your ordinary Plain Jane dessert into an elegant culinary masterpiece—and all in a matter of minutes.

Now's the time to use your imagination. But—a note of warning—don't overgarnish your desserts. A garnish should add to and not detract from the food it is adorning. The garnish should never overpower the dessert. Stick with simple garnishes and not too much.

Frosted grapes . . .

. . . are extremely pretty and easy to do, too. Simply dip washed grapes into slightly beaten egg whites and then coat with granulated sugar. Place on waxed paper to dry. Sugared grapes are even easier . . . just dip wet grapes into granulated sugar and then refrigerate until needed.

Toasted, slivered almonds . . .

. . . are attractive on many desserts. Blanch whole almonds and remove the skins. Finely chop the almonds and put them on a cookie sheet. Pop into a slow oven to toast.

Crystallized flowers . . .

. . . will draw raves of admiration and delight. Wash fresh rose petals in sudsy water. Be sure to rinse well. Dip each petal into beaten egg white. Shake fine granulated sugar on the petals and place on waxed paper to dry. Treat whole violet blossoms in the same manner and put them into lemon sherbet just before it freezes. Use crystallized flowers as a garnish for desserts—they're simply beautiful and so elegant looking.

Candied orange peel . . .

. . . is another attractive garnish. Peel four oranges with a sharp knife. Cut the peels into quarters and scrape off any excess white portion and membrane. Place rack in pressure cooker. Add ½ cup water, ½ teaspoon salt and orange peels. Cook for 6 minutes at 15 pounds pressure. Cool, then cut peels into ¼-inch strips. Combine ½ cup water, 1 cup sugar and 2 tablespoons light corn syrup in cooker. Bring to a boil, stirring occasionally. Add peels and simmer, uncovered, for 12 minutes. Cool peels in syrup. When cool, reheat just enough to loosen peels. Drain strips on cake rack. Roll in granulated sugar and spread out to dry or shape into flowers. You can treat lemon peels in the same manner.

Tiny, decorative fruits . . .

. . . made of confectioners sugar add much to desserts. Use this basic recipe to make attractive fruits for garnishing pies, cakes and candies.

> 1 tsp. rum extract
> 4 tbsp. cream cheese
> 2 c. sifted confectioners sugar
> Yellow, red and green food coloring
> Whole cloves and cocoa

Blend rum extract, cream cheese and sugar; mold into a ball. Divide ball into four equal parts. Tint two parts yellow, one part orange and one part red. To make orange, mix red and yellow food coloring. After forming fruit, place on waxed paper-covered cookie sheet and chill overnight. Yield: about 45 pieces of fruit.

A. Yellow Part:

Apples—pinch off pieces and roll between palms to ½ to ¾-inch diameter. Insert cloves, upside down, into tops of apples for stems. Paint cheeks on apples using small water color brush and diluted red food coloring.

Pears—follow same directions as for apples, forming balls into pear shapes. Insert cloves and paint with food coloring.

Lemons—pinch off and roll pieces into small balls as for apples. Mold into slightly oval shapes with fingers. Paint a few strokes of green food coloring on the end of lemons.

Bananas—pinch off pieces and roll between hands as for apples. Mold into banana shapes with your fingers. Paint a few strokes along the length of bananas to simulate the brown areas of a ripe banana, using a little cocoa mixed with water.

B. Orange Part:

Oranges—pinch off pieces and roll as for apples. Insert whole cloves into tops of oranges for blossom ends.

C. Red Part:

Strawberries—pinch off pieces and roll as for apples. Mold balls into tapered strawberry shapes, wide at the top and tapered to a rounded point at the bottom. Dip top surface in granulated sugar before using.

Pictured below is a pie garnished with these lovely decorative fruits and candied peels.

DESSERT DEFINITIONS AND PROCESSES

DEFINITIONS:

A LA MODE . . . . . Served with a topping of ice cream

AU LAIT . . . . A beverage made and served with milk

BAVARIAN . . . . . . A dessert pudding made with a gelatin-cream base

BLANCMANGE . . . A rich frozen dessert, flavored and thickened with cornstarch, flour or gelatin, and usually shaped in a mold

BOMBE . . . . A frozen dessert of two or more mixtures such as ice cream or sherbet which are packed into a melon-shaped mold

BONBON . . . . A sweet made of or dipped into fondant

CARAMEL . . . . . . A burnt sugar syrup used for flavoring and coloring

CHARLOTTE . . . . A dessert made by lining a dish with strips of cake, ladyfingers or bread and filling it with fruit, whipped cream, custard or other filling

COBBLER . . . . . . A deep dish fruit pie made with a rich pastry or biscuit dough top

CREPES SUZETTE . A paper-thin pancake served in butter sauce flavored with orange, lemon and curacao and flamed in brandy

ECLAIR . . . . A small custard or whipped cream-filled, finger-shaped pastry

FONDANT . . . . . . A type of candy made from sugar syrup, which is kneaded to creaminess

ICE . . . . A sweet frozen dessert of fruit juice, water and sugar

KISS. . . . . A tiny dessert meringue

MACAROON . . . . . A small cake made from egg whites, sugar and ground almonds or almond paste

MARZIPAN . . . . . A confection of almond and sugar paste, shaped into miniature fruits and vegetables and tinted

8

MERINGUE	A mixture of stiffly beaten egg whites and sugar, used as a pie topping or baked and served as a dessert with ice cream, fruit or flavored whipped cream
MOCHA	A coffee or chocolate-coffee flavor combination used in beverages and desserts
MOUSSE	A sweetened, frozen whipped cream dessert with fruit and nuts
PARFAIT	A dessert of ice cream, fruit and whipped cream; or a frozen mixture of egg whites or yolks, cooked with hot syrup and combined with whipped cream
PETIT FOUR	A small tea cake that is usually frosted
PRALINE	A flat sugar candy containing nuts
SHERBET	A fruit juice, sugar, egg white, milk or water mixture which is frozen
SOUFFLE	A light airy dessert made most frequently with fruit or chocolate
TORTE	A cake or pastry made of many eggs, sugar and often grated nuts or dry bread crumbs instead of flour, and baked in a large flat form pan. Sometimes filled with jam and usually covered with frosting.

PROCESSES:

BAKE	To cook by dry heat in an oven
BEAT	To whip with a spoon, hand beater or electric mixer in order to combine food or incorporate air as in beating egg whites and whipping cream
BLEND	To mix ingredients until thoroughly combined
CANDY	To cook fruit and fruit peel in heavy syrup until transparent and plump
CARAMELIZE	To heat dry sugar or food containing sugar until light brown and caramel-flavored
COAT-THE-SPOON	To cook until a mixture adheres to the stirring spoon in a thin layer

9

CREAM	To work or beat shortening until light and fluffy. Sugar and/or flour and eggs may be creamed into the shortening
CUT	To combine shortening with flour and other dry ingredients by chopping it into the mixture with two knives or spatulas
DREDGE	To coat with flour or other finely divided food
FOLD	To combine ingredients by blending with a spoon or wire whisk, using an up-and-over motion
GLAZE	To coat with a thin sugar syrup that has been cooked to the crack stage; to cover with a thin icing
KNEAD	To manipulate with a pressing motion, plus folding and stretching
SCALD	To heat liquid to a temperature just below the boiling point. A thin skim forming over milk indicates sufficient heating
SIMMER	To cook in liquid that is just below the boiling point
WHIP	To incorporate air into a mixture by beating rapidly by hand or with an electric mixer

Cakes

RECIPE FOR MOCK POUND CAKE ON PAGE 58

Do You Remember . . .

. . . when you were a child and watched your mother bake a cake? Do you remember waiting to "lick the bowl"? The batter tasted almost as good as the cake itself.

Because so many people associate cakes with the good things in life, cakes have become an all-American favorite dessert. A cook's greatest moment of pride comes when she takes a perfect cake from the oven.

The varieties of cakes are endless. They are homey when served warm and plain with no frosting. When dressed with luscious frostings and fillings they become elegant and fit for a king.

All cakes fit into the following groups: 1) those made without shortening—angel and sponge cakes; 2) those made with shortening—quick mix or conventional cakes; and 3) combination angel and shortening types which include the chiffon cakes.

Although the cakes in these groups are different in the ingredients, method of mixing and the characteristics of the baked product, basic rules of cake making apply to all three groups.

Good Ingredients . . .

. . . are essential for a superior cake. A good cake must have fine granulated sugar. Use cake flour for sponge and angel cakes and those made with shortening.

The shortening, whether it be butter, margarine or vegetable fats, must be of high quality and at room temperature when used. Fresh eggs are essential. Let eggs reach room temperature, too, before using them—they are easier to beat.

Measure ingredients carefully and accurately, using standard measuring cups and spoons. Use level measurements unless specified otherwise in the recipe.

All ingredients are not measured alike. Follow these suggestions for accurate measurements every time.

Flour	Handle flour gently. Sift before measuring, but don't sift directly into the measuring cup. Instead, lift lightly with a spoon and place in a dry measuring cup. Don't shake or pack down. Fill the cup to overflowing and then gently level off.
Spices, Salt, Baking Powder, etc.	Dip measuring spoon down into the container holding the ingredient. Level off with a spatula or back of a knife.

White Granulated Sugar	Sift only if the sugar has lumps. Lift sugar lightly into a dry measuring cup and level off with the straight edge of a knife or spatula.
Confectioners sugar	Always sift before measuring. Press stubborn lumps through a sieve if they won't sift out. Unless the recipe calls for packed confectioners sugar, it should be lightly spooned into a dry measuring cup and leveled off.
Brown sugar	Sift before measuring if it's lumpy. Crush big lumps with a rolling pin. Unless the recipe specifies otherwise, brown sugar should be firmly packed into a dry measuring cup and leveled off. If it is packed firmly, brown sugar will hold the shape of the cup when turned out.
Molasses	Measure in a graduated dry measuring cup. The molasses will "round up" so it must be leveled off with a spatula. Remove all of the molasses from the cup with a spatula.
Solid Shortening	Firmly pack room temperature shortening into a dry measuring cup; level off. If less than ¼ cup is needed, pack into a measuring spoon in the same manner. Remove from cup or spoon with a rubber spatula.
Water Replacement Method for Shortening	Solid shortening may also be measured in this way. Use a liquid measuring cup. Subtract the amount of shortening the recipe calls for from 1 cup. Put that amount of water in the cup. For example, if you need ¼ cup shortening, fill a cup with water up to the ¾-cup level. Then add shortening until the water reaches the 1-cup mark. Be sure the shortening is completely covered with water. Drain off the water and remove the fat.
Butter or Margarine	Measure as for solid shortening. If stick margarine or butter is used, measurements may be made by the following estimates:

¼ stick = 2 tbsp.   ½ stick = 4 tbsp. or ¼ c.
1 stick = ¼ lb. or ½ c.   4 sticks = 1 lb. or 2 c.

Melted Fat	Measure before or after the fat is melted—it doesn't matter because the amount will be the same. Measure salad oil just as you would any other liquid.
Milk or Water	Use a liquid measuring cup. Place the cup on a level surface. Slowly pour the liquid into the cup while bending so the measuring line will be at your eye level.

13

CAKE PAN CHATTER

Bake your cakes in loaves, sheets, cupcakes, tubes or the ever popular layers. Many recipes can't be interchanged, however. If the recipe specifies a tube pan, for example, the cake must be baked in a tube pan for best results.

Cake pans are made of aluminum, heavy tin or ovenproof glass. Use the pan size recommended in the recipe. Check the pan size by measuring it across the top. Use bright, shiny pans. Discolored pans cause uneven browning. Avoid warped pans, too, for they cause uneven baking. If glass pans are used, follow the manufacturer's instructions. Glass usually requires a lower baking temperature.

A cake recipe calling for 2 cups of flour should be baked in two 8-inch round pans that are 1½-inches deep. A cake recipe calling for 2½ to 3 cups of flour should be baked in two 9-inch round pans that are 1½ to 2-inches deep, or in two 8-inch square pans that are 2-inches deep.

A recipe for two 8-inch layers will make:

Two 8-inch layers that are 1½-inches deep
One loaf cake that is 9 x 5 x 5 inches
One oblong cake that is 13 x 9½ x 2 inches
Two square layers that are 8 x 8 x 2 inches
1½ dozen large (3 x 1½ inch) cupcakes
2 dozen medium (2½ x 1¼ inch) cupcakes
2½ dozen small (1½ x ¾ inch) cupcakes

PREPARING THE PANS

Grease the bottom of baking pans for any cake made with shortening except chiffon types. Line the pan with waxed paper that has been cut to fit the bottom exactly. Grease the paper. Do not, however, grease the baking pans for sponge and angel cakes. If the pans are greased the batter can't cling to the sides of the pans as it bakes and the cake won't reach full volume.

FOR PERFECT CAKES

1. Follow the recipe exactly.
2. Measure accurately.
3. Be sure to use the size and type cake pans specified in the recipe.
4. Fill cake pans one-half to two-thirds full. Pour the batter into the pans, spreading to the sides and filling all corners so that the baked cake will be even. Tap the batter-filled pans lightly on the table to break up air bubbles that form.
5. Space oven racks so that the cake pans will be almost in the middle of the oven. Stagger layer pans so no pan is directly over another and they do not touch each other or the sides of the oven.
6. Bake in a preheated oven at the temperature specified in the recipe.
7. Test for doneness at the end of the minimum baking time. Don't peek at the cake before this time.
8. Let cake stand in pans for five minutes before removing. Loosen the edge of the cake with a knife and turn out onto a rack. Remove paper.
9. Cool cake completely before frosting.

COMMON CAUSES OF CAKE FAILURES

If This Happens	It May Be Caused By This in Butter-Type Cakes	It May Be Caused By This in Sponge-Type Cakes
CAKE FALLS	1. Too much sugar, liquid, leavening or shortening 2. Underbaking 3. Oven temperature too low 4. Not enough flour	1. Egg whites overbeaten 2. Egg yolks underbeaten 3. Greased pans were used 4. Too much sugar 5. Underbaking
CAKE CRACKS OR HUMPS	1. Overmixing 2. Oven temperature too hot 3. Too much flour or not enough liquid 4. Batter uneven in pan	1. Too much flour or sugar 2. Oven temperature too hot
HARD TOP CRUST	1. Overbaking 2. Oven temperature too hot	Same as for butter-type cakes
STICKY TOP CRUST	1. Too little baking 2. Too much sugar	Same as for butter-type cakes
HEAVY, COMPACT	1. Too many eggs 2. Too little leavening or flour 3. Too much mixing 4. Too much shortening or liquid 5. Oven temperature too hot	1. Egg yolks underbeaten 2. Too much mixing 3. Egg whites overbeaten
HEAVY, STICKY BOTTOM LAYER	1. Eggs underbeaten 2. Underbaking 3. Too much liquid 4. Undermixing 5. Shortening too soft	1. Not enough mixing 2. Too many eggs or egg yolks

HIGH ALTITUDE BAKING

Two problems develop in altitude cookery—boiling and leavening. The higher the elevation, the lower the atmospheric pressure. At sea level, water boils at 212° F. Each 500-foot increase in altitude causes a drop of about 1° F. in the boiling point. At very high altitudes, boiling water is relatively "cool". Since the heat, not boiling, cooks foods, more time is required for food to reach the desired internal cooking temperature at higher altitudes.

The oven temperature must be increased 25 degrees over the temperature required at sea level for altitudes of over 3,500 feet. For example, cakes baked at sea level at 350° F. should be baked at 375° F. at all altitudes over 3,500 feet. The faster baking "sets" the cell framework within the flour mixture and helps to prevent falling.

In high altitudes, flour may become excessively dry unless it is stored in airtight containers. More liquid than the recipe calls for may be necessary to bring a batter or dough to the right consistency. Some sea level cakes are delicate and defy adjustments to varying altitudes. In this case, choose a new favorite from altitude-tested recipes. Some other recipes are so well balanced that little if any adjustment may be necessary up to 5,000 feet. This is especially true of some of the commercial cake mixes. Keep a written record of any adjustments you make in your recipes.

Cakes Without Fat:

Air, incorporated in the beaten eggs, is the leavening agent in cakes without fat. The eggs should be beaten less at high altitudes, so less leavening power is given to the batter. In angel food cakes, beat the whites just until they form soft peaks; in sponge cakes beat the egg or egg yolks only until they are slightly thickened.

Cakes With Fat:

The emulsified shortenings available on the market today give good results in all altitude baking. Because the emulsifier enables the shortening to tolerate a larger amount of liquid, it is preferable for the "speed-mix" cakes with high sugar ratio.

Flour:

All-purpose flour is preferable in most recipes. Sift before measuring and make the following adjustments:

ELEVATION IN FEET	INCREASE FLOUR
3,500 to 5,000	1 tablespoon
5,000 to 6,500	2 tablespoons
6,500 to 8,000	3 tablespoons
8,000 and over	4 tablespoons

Eggs:

An additional egg may be added to prevent the cake from being too dry and too tender.

Leavening:

All types of baking powder and baking soda are treated alike in reductions for increased altitudes. When both baking powder and soda are used in a recipe, make the suggested adjustments in both ingredients. Accurate measurement of leavening is of increased importance as the altitude increases. The leavening adjustments begin with 2,000 feet elevation.

ELEVATION IN FEET	DECREASE LEAVENING
2,000 to 3,000	¼ to ⅓ teaspoon
3,500 to 5,000	⅓ to ½ teaspoon
5,000 to 6,500	½ to ⅔ teaspoon
6,500 to 8,000	⅔ to ¾ teaspoon
8,000 and over	¾ teaspoon

Decrease each teaspoon the lesser amount for lower altitude within each given range and the larger amount at higher altitudes within the given range.

CAKE CUTTING CAPERS

There's a satisfactory method of cutting each kind of cake. The factors to keep in mind are the size and number of servings and the cutting utensil to be used. The size and number of servings depends upon the size and number of layers in the cake. A knife with a sharp straight-edged thin blade is the most suitable for cutting batter cakes. To make a clean cut, dip the blade into warm water before cutting each portion and keep the blade free from frosting and cake crumbs.

Fruit cake, which also is a batter type cake, may be cut in the same way. Because of its richness, the size of fruit cake servings generally are smaller than those shown for layer cakes.

The following diagrams illustrate unusual ways of cutting cakes of various sizes and shapes. The average number of servings per cake are given.

LAYER CAKES

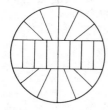
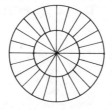
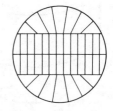

10-inch, 2-layer cake
Yield: 20 servings

12-inch, 2-layer cake
Yield: 36 servings

14-inch, 2-layer cake
Yield: 40 servings

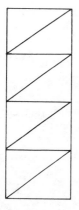
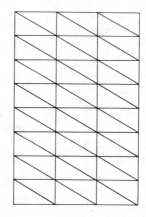

1 pound loaf cake
Yield: 8 servings

18 x 25-inch cake
Yield: 48 servings

TIER CAKES

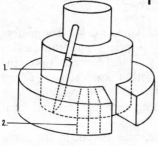

A. Cut vertically through the bottom layer at the edge of the second layer as indicated by the dotted line marked 1; then cut out wedge-shaped pieces as shown by 2.

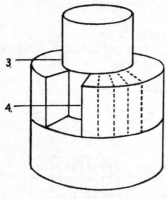

B. When these pieces have been served, follow the same procedure with the middle layer; cut vertically through the second layer at the edge of the top layer as indicated by dotted line 3; then cut wedge-shaped pieces as shown by 4.

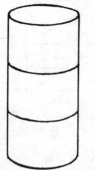

C. When pieces from the second layer have been served, return to the bottom layer and cut along dotted line 5; cut another row of wedge-shaped pieces as shown by 6.

D. The remaining tiers may be cut into the desired size pieces.

APPLE SCOTCH CAKE

½ c. butter
1 ¼ c. sugar
2 eggs
1 tsp. vanilla flavoring
1 c. applesauce
2 c. flour
1 tsp. baking soda
1 tsp. salt
1 tsp. cinnamon
½ tsp. cloves
⅔ c. butterscotch pieces

Cream butter; add sugar gradually. Beat well. Blend in eggs and vanilla flavoring; beat well. Add applesauce. Add dry ingredients and butterscotch pieces. Pour into a 9 x 13-inch pan. Bake at 350 degrees for 30 minutes.

TOPPING:
2 tbsp. butter
1 c. coconut
½ c. brown sugar
¼ c. cream
¾ c. nuts
⅓ c. butterscotch pieces

Mix butter, coconut, brown sugar, cream and nuts; heat until blended. Add butterscotch pieces; spread on cake. Place under broiler for 2 minutes, watching carefully to prevent burning. Yield: 20 servings.

Mrs. Loren Downes
Nashwauk, Minn.

DANISH APPLE CAKE

½ c. flour
1 tsp. baking powder
¼ tsp. salt
¾ c. sugar
3 tbsp. butter
1 egg
1 c. finely chopped apples
¾ c. nuts
1 tsp. vanilla flavoring

Mix dry ingredients; add butter, egg, apples, nuts and vanilla. Blend well. Bake at 350 degrees for 25 minutes. Serve hot with grated cheese for a coffee or cold with a scoop of vanilla ice cream for dessert. Yield: 6 servings.

Mrs. M. M. Motes
Richmond, Va.

DUTCH APPLE CAKE

CAKE:
2 c. flour
½ tsp. salt
¾ c. sugar
2 tsp. baking powder
4 tbsp. butter
1 egg, beaten

⅔ c. milk
6 to 8 apples, peeled and sliced

Sift all dry ingredients; add to butter. Mix well. Stir in egg, milk and apples. Pour into greased 9 x 12-inch cake pan.

TOPPING:
½ c. butter, melted
3 tbsp. flour
¾ c. brown sugar
¼ tbsp. cinnamon
½ c. chopped nuts

Combine butter, flour, sugar, cinnamon and nuts. Sprinkle over cake batter. Bake at 400 degrees for 1 hour.

Mrs. Keith Barkley
Gretna, Nebr.

GERMAN APPLE CAKE

1 tsp. baking powder
½ tsp. salt
1 ¼ c. flour
½ c. butter or margarine
1 egg
2 tbsp. milk
4 or 5 lge. apples, peeled and sliced

Mix dry ingredients and butter like pie crust until lumpy. Add egg and milk; mix well. Pat into 11 1/2 x 7 1/2-inch glass baking dish, pressing and spreading dough about half way up the sides. Spread apples over dough.

TOPPING:
¾ c. sugar
¼ tsp. cinnamon
1 ½ tbsp. flour
2 tsp. (heaping) butter

Mix all ingredients with hands; spread over apples. Bake at 350 degrees for 40 minutes or until apples are done. Yield: 8 servings.

Mrs. Hugh M. Elwood
Glenview, Ill.

RAW APPLE CAKE

2 c. cubed or sliced raw apples
1 egg
1 c. sugar
¼ c. oil
1 tsp. cinnamon
1 c. chopped nuts
¾ c. raisins
1 c. flour
1 tsp. soda
¼ tsp. salt

(Continued on next page)

19

Combine apples and egg; mix well. Mix in sugar; stir in oil. Combine all remaining ingredients; add to sugar mixture, mixing well. Pour into a square baking pan. Bake at 350 degrees for 45 to 50 minutes. Yield: 9 servings.

Mrs. Joanne Harker
Petaluma, Calif.

APPLESAUCE CAKE WITH BROWN SUGAR ICING

½ c. shortening
1 ½ c. sugar
2 eggs, beaten
1 c. thick unsweetened applesauce
2 c. flour
¼ tsp. salt
1 tsp. baking powder
½ tsp. soda
1 tsp. cinnamon
½ tsp. cloves
1 c. chopped seeded raisins

Thoroughly cream shortening and sugar; add eggs. Beat well. Add applesauce; add sifted dry ingredients. Beat until smooth; fold in raisins. Pour into a waxed paper-lined 8-inch square pan. Bake at 350 degrees for 45 to 60 minutes. Serve plain or frosted.

ICING:
2 c. brown sugar
⅓ c. butter
1 c. cream
½ tsp. vanilla flavoring

Boil sugar, butter and cream until a soft ball forms in cold water. Add vanilla; beat until of spreading consistency. NOTE: This cake will remain moist for several days in closely covered container.

Frances L. Hambsch
Galesburg, Ill.

APRICOT CAKE

2 c. sugar
2 c. flour
1 tsp. cinnamon
1 tsp. cloves
½ tsp. nutmeg
1 tsp. salt
1 tsp. soda
1 c. oil
3 eggs
1 c. mashed cooked apricots
1 c. pecans
1 c. sour milk

Mix all dry ingredients; add all remaining ingredients. Pour into a loaf pan. Bake at 325 degrees for 1 hour. NOTE: Prunes may be substituted for apricots if desired.

Mrs. Hazel Hill
Texas City, Tex.

APRICOT CRUMBLE CAKE

1 8-oz. pkg. cream cheese, softened
½ c. margarine
1 ¼ c. sugar
2 eggs
¼ c. milk
1 tsp. vanilla flavoring
2 c. sifted cake flour
1 tsp. baking powder
½ tsp. soda
¼ tsp. salt
1 12-oz. jar apricot preserves

Thoroughly blend cream cheese, margarine and sugar. Gradually add eggs, milk and vanilla. Add sifted dry ingredients, mixing until well blended. Pour one-half of the batter into a greased and floured 13 x 9-inch baking pan. Cover with apricot preserves; top with remaining batter. Bake at 350 degrees for 35 to 40 minutes.

TOPPING:
2 c. shredded coconut
⅔ c. (packed) brown sugar
1 tsp. cinnamon
⅓ c. margarine, melted

Combine all ingredients; spread on cake. Broil until golden brown. Yield: 10 servings.

Mrs. Ethel Ogburn
Camden, S.C.

BANANA-CREAM CAKE

2 ¼ c. sifted cake flour
1 ¼ c. sugar
2 ½ tsp. baking powder
½ tsp. baking soda
½ tsp. salt
½ c. shortening
2 eggs
1 ½ c. mashed bananas
1 tsp. vanilla
½ c. chopped nuts

Grease and line with waxed paper two 8-inch layer pans. Sift all dry ingredients. Drop in shortening and eggs; add 1/2 cup mashed bananas. Beat with electric mixer at low speed for 2 minutes, scraping bowl as necessary. Add remaining 1 cup bananas and vanilla; beat for 1 minute longer. Fold in nuts. Pour into pans. Bake at 350 degrees for 25 minutes. Cool in pans on wire racks for 2 minutes. Remove from pans; cool. Frost with Seven Minute frosting. Yield: 20 servings.

Mrs. Eva Etheridge
Americus, Ga.

BANANA-CREAM CAKE

1 angel food cake
2 pkg. banana cream instant pudding mix

(Continued on next page)

2 c. cold milk
1 c. heavy cream, whipped
1 banana, sliced

Split angel food cake to make 4 layers. Add pudding mix to cold milk; beat slowly for 1 minute. Let stand for 2 minutes. Fold into whipped cream. Spread between layers and on top. Chill. Place sliced banana on top. Yield: 12 servings.

Mrs. Thomas C. Piddington
Governors Island, New York

BLACKBERRY CAKE

1 c. butter or margarine
1 c. brown sugar
3 eggs
1 c. blackberry preserves
1 tsp. nutmeg
1 tsp. cloves
1 tsp. cinnamon
1 tbsp. soda
1 c. buttermilk or sour milk
2 c. flour

Cream butter and sugar; beat in eggs. Add preserves; stir in spices. Dissolve soda in buttermilk; add to batter. Blend in flour; pour into three 8-inch layer cake pans. Bake at 400 degrees for 30 minutes. Yield: 14 servings.

Louise Manning
Felicity, O.

BLUEBERRY CAKE

1 c. butter
2 c. sugar
3 eggs, beaten
½ c. milk
3 c. flour
1 ½ tsp. baking powder
⅛ tsp. salt
¼ tsp. mace
1 c. (or more) blueberries

Cream butter and sugar. Add eggs alternately with milk. Sift all dry ingredients; add to sugar mixture. Fold in blueberries. Bake at 350 degrees for 1 hour and 20 minutes in a turk head mold or tube pan. Yield: 10 servings.

Mrs. Warren E. Richards
Collingswood, N.J.

MELT-IN-YOUR-MOUTH BLUEBERRY CAKE

2 eggs, separated
Sugar
½ c. shortening
¼ tsp. salt
1 tsp. vanilla flavoring

1 ½ c. flour
1 tsp. baking powder
⅓ c. milk
1 ½ c. fresh or frozen blueberries

Beat egg whites until stiff. Add 1/4 cup sugar. Cream shortening; add salt and vanilla. Add 3/4 cup sugar gradually. Add egg yolks; beat until light and creamy. Set aside a small amount of flour. Sift remaining flour and baking powder; add alternately with milk to egg yolk mixture. Fold in beaten egg whites. Dredge blueberries in remaining flour. Fold into batter. Turn into a greased 8-inch square pan. Sprinkle top of batter lightly with sugar. Bake at 350 degrees for 50 to 60 minutes.

Mrs. Inez M. Campbell
Searsport, Me.

BUTTER CAKE

½ lb. margarine
1 ¾ c. sugar
5 eggs
1 tsp. vanilla flavoring
1 tsp. butter flavoring
1 tsp. rum flavoring
2 c. sifted flour

Cream margarine thoroughly; add sugar gradually. Add an egg at a time; mix well. Add flavorings. Add sifted flour, a small amount at a time; blend well. Pour batter into greased and dusted 10-inch stem pan. Bake at 325 degrees for 1 hour or until toothpick inserted into center comes out clean.

BUTTER CAKE ICING:
½ c. water
1 c. sugar
1 tsp. rum flavoring

Bring water and sugar to a boil. Cool; add flavoring. Use pastry brush and apply to warm cake. Yield: 24 servings.

Mrs. Mabel Helton
Livingston, Tex.

BUTTERSCOTCH CAKE

2 c. sifted flour
1 tsp. salt
3 tsp. baking powder
1 ½ c. brown sugar
½ c. shortening
1 c. milk
⅓ to ½ c. eggs
1 tsp. vanilla flavoring

Mix all dry ingredients, shortening and 2/3 cup milk; beat for 2 minutes. Add remaining 1/3 cup milk, eggs and vanilla. Beat for 2

(Continued on next page)

minutes longer. Bake at 350 degrees for 30 to 35 minutes. Yield: 12 servings.

Virginia Adams
Wichita, Kans.

BURNT SUGAR CAKE

2 c. sugar
½ c. hot water
¾ c. shortening
2 eggs
1 tsp. vanilla flavoring
1 c. cold water
Flour
1 tsp. soda

Brown 1/2 cup sugar until it smokes. Add hot water; boil until it makes a syrup. Cream remaining 1 1/2 cups sugar and shortening. Add eggs; beat well. Add syrup, vanilla and cold water. Sift flour three times; measure 3 cups. Add soda. Mix in one-half of flour; beat well. Add remaining flour; beat. Pour into three layer pans. Bake at 350 degrees until tests done.

ICING:
2 c. sugar
½ c. cream
½ c. butter
Vanilla flavoring

Combine all ingredients except vanilla in pan used to brown sugar for cake. Cook until it boils; remove from heat. Add vanilla. Beat until of spreading consistency. Spread on cake.

Mary Lou Furr
Camden, Ark.

CARAMEL-APPLE-PECAN CAKE

2 c. self-rising flour
1 ½ c. sugar
½ c. shortening
1 c. milk
1 tsp. flavoring
4 eggs
1 apple, finely chopped

Mix flour, sugar and shortening. Add milk and flavoring; beat vigorously. Add eggs; beat for 2 minutes. Flour apple; add to batter. Pour into two 8-inch greased and floured pans. Bake at 350 degrees for 30 to 35 minutes.

ICING:
3 c. sugar
2 sticks butter
¾ c. heavy cream
1 tsp. vanilla flavoring
1 c. finely ground pecans

Brown 1/2 cup sugar in saucepan. Combine remaining 2 1/2 cups sugar, butter and cream;

bring to a boil. Add browned sugar; cook until it forms a soft ball. Add vanilla and nuts. Spread between layers and on top of cake. NOTE: For white cake, omit egg yolks.

Millie Camp
Aberdeen, Miss.

POTATO-CARAMEL CAKE

2 c. sugar
¾ c. butter
4 eggs, beaten
1 tsp. soda
1 c. sour milk
1 c. mashed potatoes
1 square chocolate, melted
2 c. flour
1 tsp. cinnamon
½ tsp. cloves
½ tsp. salt
1 c. nuts

Cream sugar and butter; add eggs, soda and sour milk. Add potatoes and chocolate; add dry ingredients. Stir in nuts; pour into two 9-inch layer pans. Bake at 350 degrees until cake tests done.

Evelyn Morgan
Rosalia, Wash.

CARROT CAKE WITH CREAM CHEESE FILLING

1 ½ c. oil
2 c. sugar
4 eggs, well beaten
2 c. flour
1 tsp. salt (opt.)
2 tsp. cinnamon
2 tsp. soda
2 tsp. baking powder
1 c. broken pecans
3 c. grated carrots

Mix oil and sugar; beat well. Add eggs. Sift all dry ingredients two or three times. Add nuts; mix with sugar mixture. Add carrots, a small amount at a time. Bake at 350 degrees for 1 hour for loaf or tube pan or at 300 to 350 degrees for 30 minutes in three layer pans. NOTE: If desired, whole eggs may be added one at a time, beating well after each.

FILLING:
½ to 1 stick margarine
1 8-oz. pkg. cream cheese
1 box powdered sugar
2 tsp. vanilla flavoring

Mix all ingredients; beat well. Spread between layers or on cake. Yield: 12 servings.

Louise W. Talley
Leesville, La.

SPICY CARROT CAKE

1 ½ c. salad oil
2 ½ c. sugar
4 eggs, separated
5 tbsp. hot water
2 ½ c. sifted flour
1 ½ tsp. baking powder
½ tsp. soda
¼ tsp. salt
1 tsp. nutmeg
1 tsp. cinnamon
1 tsp. cloves
1 ¾ c. grated raw carrots
1 c. chopped pecans

Mix oil and sugar; add an egg yolk at a time. Add hot water. Sift all dry ingredients; beat into egg mixture. Add grated carrots; add pecans. Beat egg whites until soft peaks form; fold into batter. Pour into greased and floured 10-inch pan. Bake at 350 degrees for 1 hour to 1 hour and 10 minutes. Cool for 15 minutes; remove from pan. Frost with glaze frosting. Yield: 30 servings.

Irene Gray
Tulsa, Okla.

WALNUT-CARROT CAKE

1 ½ c. vegetable oil
2 c. sugar
4 eggs, well beaten
2 c. flour
2 tsp. cinnamon
½ tsp. salt
1 ½ tsp. soda
3 c. grated carrots
½ c. chopped black walnuts

Mix oil, sugar and eggs. Sift flour, cinnamon, salt and soda; add to egg mixture. Add carrots and nuts; mix well. Pour into a large 9 x 10-inch greased and floured pan. Bake at 350 degrees for 40 minutes. NOTE: Bake at 325 degrees if a glass pan is used.

ICING:
1 8-oz. pkg. cream cheese
1 box powdered sugar
1 tsp. vanilla flavoring
Cream (opt.)

Cream cheese well. Add sugar a little at a time. Add vanilla; continue stirring until fluffy. Cream may be added if too stiff. Spread on cake.

Mrs. Nancy Baron
Miami, Okla.

BLENDER SOUP-CREAM CHEESE CAKE

CRUMB CRUST:
16 graham cracker squares
½ c. sugar
½ tsp. cinnamon
¼ c. melted butter

Break 5 graham crackers at a time into blender container. Cover and blend on high speed for 5 seconds. Empty crumbs into bowl. Repeat until all crackers are crumbled. Add sugar, cinnamon and melted butter; stir until crumbs are moistened. Press into 5-cup mold or pan.

FILLING:
2 eggs
½ c. sugar
2 tsp. vanilla flavoring
1 ½ c. sour cream
2 8-oz. pkg. cream cheese, softened
2 tbsp. butter, melted

Put eggs, sugar, vanilla and sour cream in blender container. Cover; blend on high speed for 15 seconds. With motor on, gradually add cream cheese and butter. Pour into prepared pan. Bake in preheated 325 degree oven for 30 to 40 minutes or until set in center. The filling will be very soft, but it will firm up as the cake cools. Chill thoroughly before serving. Yield: 12 servings.

Mrs. William R. Brown
Brunswick, Me.

CHEESE CAKE WITH GLAZE

CRUST:
12 to 14 graham crackers, crushed
¼ c. sugar
4 tbsp. butter, melted

Combine all ingredients; press into bottom of a 10-inch spring form pan.

FILLING:
5 8-oz. pkg. cream cheese
1 c. sour cream
6 eggs
½ tsp. salt
1 tsp. grated lemon rind
1 tsp. vanilla
1 ½ c. sugar
3 tbsp. flour

Blend cream cheese and sour cream. Add eggs; beat well. Add all remaining ingredients; mix well. Pour into crust. Bake at 350 degrees for 1 hour and 30 minutes or until knife inserted comes out clean. Cool in pan; cake will fall.

CHERRY GLAZE:
1 1-lb. can sour red cherries, packed in water
¼ c. sugar
1 tbsp. cornstarch
1 tbsp. lemon juice
2 drops red food coloring

(Continued on next page)

Drain cherries, reserving 1/2 cup liquid. Combine sugar and cornstarch in a saucepan; add reserved cherry liquid, stirring until smooth. Bring to a boil, stirring, over medium heat; boil for 1 minute. Mixture should be thick and translucent. Remove from heat; cool slightly. Add lemon juice, cherries and food coloring. Cool thoroughly. Spread over cooled cheese cake. Yield: 18 servings.

Mrs. Louis Graziosi
Ellington AFB, Tex.

CHOCOLATE SWIRL CHEESE CAKE

CRUST:
1 ¾ c. plus 2 tbsp. graham cracker
  crumbs
½ c. sugar
¼ tsp. cinnamon
⅛ tsp. nutmeg
½ c. butter

Combine crumbs, sugar and spices; cut in butter until completely blended. Press mixture evenly on bottom and sides of heavily buttered 9 or 10-inch spring form pan. Chill.

FILLING:
1 square chocolate
2 8-oz. pkg. cream cheese
1 c. sugar
6 eggs, separated
1 tsp. vanilla flavoring
1 tbsp. grated orange rind
1 tbsp. orange juice
1 c. heavy cream

Melt chocolate over hot water. Blend cream cheese and sugar until creamy and light. Add an egg yolk at a time, beating well after each addition. Stir in vanilla, orange rind and juice. Beat egg whites until stiff but not dry; spoon onto cheese mixture. Whip cream; fold with egg whites into cheese mixture until blended. Spoon one-third of the filling into crumb-lined pan; trickle a little chocolate over surface and swirl lightly into filling with tip of knife. Repeat procedure twice, ending with chocolate. Bake in 300 degree oven for 1 hour. Turn off heat but leave cheese cake in oven with door closed for 1 hour longer. Remove from oven. Cool at room temperature; chill. When cold, loosen crust around sides with knife; release spring and remove pan. Yield: 6-8 servings.

Mrs. William A. DeLorenzo
Dover, N.J.

COTTAGE CHEESE CAKE

CRUST:
½ c. butter
⅔ c. sugar

1 tsp. cinnamon
1 box zwieback, finely crushed

Melt butter in skillet; stir in sugar, cinnamon and crumbs. Press mixture against bottom and sides of skillet, saving 1/4 cup of mixture.

FILLING:
4 eggs
1 ¼ c. sugar
½ tsp. salt
Juice of ½ lemon
1 ½ lb. cottage cheese
¼ c. flour
1 tsp. cinnamon

Beat eggs and 1 cup sugar until light. Add salt, lemon juice, cheese and flour. Press through a sieve. Pour into crust. Sprinkle cinnamon and remaining 1/4 cup sugar over top. Top with remaining crust mixture. Bake at 325 degrees for 1 hour and 30 minutes. Cool. Yield: 10-12 servings.

Mrs. Eula Brown Ackerson
Chattanooga, Tenn.

CREAM CHEESE CAKE

1 ¼ c. graham cracker crumbs
½ c. butter, melted
3 tbsp. sugar

Mix all ingredients. Line buttered 8 x 8-inch pan with mixture.

FILLING:
2 8-oz. pkg. cream cheese
⅔ c. sugar
1 tsp. vanilla flavoring
3 eggs

Combine all ingredients; beat until very smooth. Pour into crumb lined pan. Bake at 375 degrees for 25 minutes. Cool for 15 minutes.

TOPPING:
½ pt. sour cream
1 ½ tbsp. sugar
½ tsp. vanilla flavoring

Mix all ingredients. Spread over top of cake. Bake at 475 degrees for 4 minutes. Refrigerate overnight. Yield: 10-12 servings.

Ethel Edwards
Detroit, Mich.

NEW ENGLAND CHEESE CAKE

1 pkg. lemon gelatin
1 c. boiling water
1 c. sugar
1 8-oz. pkg. cream cheese, softened
1 ⅔ c. evaporated milk, chilled
½ c. butter
1 c. graham cracker crumbs

Dissolve gelatin in boiling water; add sugar and cream cheese. Blend until dissolved. Chill until slightly thickened. Whip milk until it stands in peaks. Fold milk into cream cheese mixture. Melt butter; mix with graham cracker crumbs. Press two-thirds of the crumbs into a 10 x 15-inch cake pan. Fill with cheese mixture. Top with remaining crumbs. Chill thoroughly.

Mrs. Arvid Hansen
Hampton, N.H.

NO-BAKE CHEESE CAKE

2 envelopes unflavored gelatin
1 c. sugar
¼ tsp. salt
2 eggs, separated
1 c. milk
1 tsp. grated lemon rind
3 c. creamed cottage cheese
1 tbsp. lemon juice
1 tsp. vanilla flavoring
1 c. heavy cream, whipped

Combine gelatin, sugar and salt. Beat egg yolks and milk; add to gelatin mixture. Cook in double boiler, stirring constantly, until gelatin is dissolved and mixture thickens. Remove from heat. Add lemon rind; cool. Stir in cottage cheese, lemon juice and vanilla; chill, stirring occasionally, until mixture mounds slightly when dropped from spoon. Fold stiffly beaten egg whites and whipped cream into chilled gelatin mixture. Chill in spring form pan until firm.

TOPPING:
2 tbsp. butter, melted
1 tbsp. sugar
½ c. graham cracker crumbs
¼ tsp. cinnamon
¼ tsp. nutmeg

Combine all ingredients; sprinkle over cake after removing from pan. Yield: 10-12 servings.

Mrs. R. C. Johnson
Georgetown, S.C.

PINEAPPLE-CHEESE CAKE

16 graham crackers, crushed
1 c. drained crushed pineapple
1 ½ lb. cream cheese
1 c. sugar
4 eggs
1 tsp. vanilla flavoring
1 pt. sour cream

Pat crumbs in bottom of large angel food cake mold. Top with pineapple. Cream remaining ingredients in order listed. Pour over pineapple. Bake at 350 degrees for 1 hour.

Mrs. R. E. Hammond
San Diego, Calif.

CHERRY CROWN CAKE

2 ¼ c. flour
1 ⅓ c. sugar
1 tbsp. baking powder
1 tsp. salt
½ c. butter
1 c. milk
1 tsp. almond flavoring
2 eggs
½ c. finely chopped walnuts
2 c. grated coconut
1 1-lb. 5-oz. can cherry pie filling, chilled

Combine dry ingredients; blend in butter and milk. Beat for 1 minute and 30 seconds on low speed of electric mixer or 225 strokes by hand. Add flavoring and eggs; beat for 1 minute and 30 seconds longer. Stir in nuts. Sprinkle 2/3 cup coconut in each of two 8 or 9-inch layer pans. Pour batter into pans; sprinkle top of each with 1/3 cup coconut. Bake at 350 degrees for 35 to 40 minutes; cool. Spread cherry pie filling between layers and on top to within 1 inch of edge.

BUTTER CREME FROSTING:
2 tbsp. flour
½ c. milk
½ c. butter
1 c. sifted confectioners sugar
¼ tsp. almond flavoring

Blend flour with milk in small saucepan. Cook over low heat until very thick, stirring constantly; cool completely. Cream butter, sugar and flavoring until light and fluffy. Beat in flour mixture until smooth. Frost sides and top edge of cake; refrigerate.

Ruth Caulfield
Marietta, Ga.

DUTCH CHERRY CAKE

2 c. sifted flour
2 ¼ tsp. baking powder
½ tsp. salt
1 c. sugar
2 eggs, separated
½ c. milk
⅓ c. butter, melted

(Continued on next page)

CHERRY, CHIFFON CAKES

1 No. 2 can unsweetened red cherries
3 tbsp. brown sugar
1 tsp. cinnamon

Sift flour three times with baking powder, salt and 3/4 cup sugar. Beat egg yolks; add milk and butter. Quickly stir into flour mixture just until batter is smooth. Beat egg whites until stiff; beat in remaining 1/4 cup sugar until stiff. Fold into batter with 1 cup well drained cherries, reserving remaining cherries and juice for sauce. Pour batter into a buttered baking pan which has been lined with waxed paper. Sprinkle top with brown sugar mixed with cinnamon. Bake at 400 degrees for 35 minutes or until browned on top. Serve hot or cold with sauce.

CHERRY SAUCE:
Juice from cherries
1 tbsp. cornstarch
3 tbsp. sugar
3 tbsp. boiling water
Pinch of salt
1 tbsp. butter
⅛ tsp. almond flavoring
Cherries

Heat cherry juice to boiling. Mix cornstarch and sugar; add boiling water, stirring to make a smooth paste. Add to hot juice. Cook over direct heat until sauce boils and thickens. Stir in all remaining ingredients. Serve with cake. Yield: 6-8 servings.

Barbara R. Sabatini
Bunkie, La.

PINK AZALEA CAKE

16 Maraschino cherries, finely chopped
⅔ c. soft mixed shortening and butter
1 ½ c. sugar
3 c. sifted cake flour
2 ½ tsp. baking powder
1 tsp. salt
¾ c. milk
1 tsp. vanilla flavoring
5 egg whites, stiffly beaten

Drain cherries, reserving 1/4 cup juice. Cream shortening and sugar until very light; add all dry ingredients alternately with milk, cherry juice and vanilla. Fold in egg whites and cherries. Pour into two greased and floured 9-inch pans or three 8-inch pans. Bake at 350 degrees for 30 to 35 minutes.

AZALEA PINK FROSTING:
2 ½ c. sugar
2 tbsp. light corn syrup
1 c. water
3 egg whites, stiffly beaten
1 tsp. vanilla flavoring
½ c. chopped blanched almonds
2 or 3 drops red food coloring (opt.)

Mix sugar, syrup and water. Boil to 242 degrees or until it will spin an 8-inch thread from spoon. Pour hot syrup slowly over egg whites, beating constantly. Add vanilla, nuts and food coloring. Beat for 2 to 3 minutes. Frost cake. NOTE: If desired, the almonds may be used as a garnish for frosted cake.

Amelia B. Ryan
Portsmouth, Va.

BLACK WALNUT CHIFFON CAKE

1 c. sifted flour
¾ c. sugar
1 ½ tsp. baking powder
½ tsp. salt
¼ c. cooking oil
3 egg yolks
6 tbsp. cold water
1 tsp. vanilla flavoring
4 egg whites
¼ tsp. cream of tartar
½ c. finely chopped black walnuts

Sift all dry ingredients. Make a well; add oil, egg yolks, water and vanilla. Beat with spoon until smooth. Beat egg whites with cream of tartar until very stiff. Pour egg yolk mixture over whites, gently folding until blended. Fold in walnuts. Pour into an ungreased 9-inch tube pan or 9 x 5 x 3-inch loaf pan. Bake at 325 degrees for 50 to 55 minutes. Invert; cool. Yield: 6-8 servings.

Mrs. John R. Barrowclough
Port Clinton, O.

MAPLE-NUT CHIFFON CAKE

2 ½ c. sifted cake flour
¾ c. sugar
3 tsp. baking powder
1 tsp. salt
¾ c. brown sugar
½ c. salad oil
5 egg yolks
¾ c. cold water
2 tsp. maple flavoring
8 egg whites
½ tsp. cream of tartar
1 c. finely chopped California walnuts

Sift flour, sugar, baking powder and salt into mixing bowl; stir in brown sugar. Make a well in dry ingredients. Add salad oil, egg yolks, water and flavoring; beat until satin smooth. Combine egg whites and cream of tartar in large bowl. Beat until they form very stiff peaks, stiffer than for meringue or angel cake. Pour egg yolk batter in thin stream over entire surface of egg whites, gently cutting and folding just until blended. Fold in nuts. Pour into an ungreased 10-inch tube pan. Bake at 325 degrees for 55 minutes. Increase heat to 350; bake for 10 to 15 minutes. Invert pan on

(Continued on next page)

funnel or tall bottle; cool thoroughly. To remove, loosen sides and around tube with knife; invert pan and tap edge sharply on table.

GOLDEN BUTTER FROSTING:
½ c. butter or margarine
1 lb. sifted confectioners sugar
½ c. light cream
1 to 1 ½ tsp. maple or vanilla flavoring

Melt butter in saucepan over low heat until golden brown, watching carefully so it doesn't scorch. Remove from heat; stir in sugar. Blend in cream and flavoring. Place pan in ice water; beat until of spreading consistency. More cream may be added if needed. Spread on cake.

Regina Murphy
Davenport, Iowa

ROYAL CHIFFON CAKE

2 c. flour
1 ½ c. sugar
3 tsp. baking powder
1 tsp. salt
½ c. corn oil
7 egg yolks
¾ c. cold water
2 tsp. vanilla flavoring
Grated rind of 1 lemon
1 c. egg whites
½ tsp. cream of tartar

Sift flour, sugar, baking powder and salt into bowl; make a well in the mixture. Add oil, egg yolks, water, vanilla and lemon rind; beat until smooth. Beat egg whites with cream of tartar until stiff peaks are formed; gradually add egg yolk mixture, gently folding in until blended. Do not stir. Pour immediately into 10-inch tube pan. Bake at 325 degrees for 55 minutes. Invert pan on funnel to cool.

ICING:
2 tbsp. shortening
1 tbsp. butter
¼ tsp. salt
3 c. sifted powdered sugar
½ c. crushed pineapple

Blend shortening, butter, salt and 1/2 cup powdered sugar. Add remaining 2 1/2 cups sugar and pineapple alternately. Spread on cake.

Cora J. McDowell
Chesapeake, Va.

SPICE CHIFFON CAKE

2 c. sifted cake flour
1 ½ c. sugar
1 tsp. salt
3 tsp. baking powder
2 tsp. cinnamon
½ tsp. nutmeg
¼ tsp. cloves
½ c. salad oil
¾ c. water
1 tbsp. lemon juice
7 lge. eggs, separated
½ tsp. cream of tartar

Have all ingredients at room temperature. Sift flour with sugar, salt, baking powder and spices. Make a well in mixture. Pour in oil, water, lemon juice and egg yolks. Add cream of tartar to egg whites; beat until they hold very stiff peaks. Beat flour mixture until smooth. Gently fold batter into whites. Do not stir. Pour batter into ungreased 10-inch tube pan. Bake at 325 degrees for 55 minutes. Increase heat to 350 degrees for 10 to 15 minutes or until cake tester in center comes out clean. Invert, removing pan, to cool.

MAPLE BUTTER FROSTING:
½ c. butter or margarine
¼ c. hot water
1 lb. confectioners sugar, sifted
¼ tsp. maple flavoring

Melt butter in saucepan over medium heat; cook until light golden brown. Add remaining ingredients. Beat until frosting cools and holds shape. Add a small amount of water if needed to make frosting of spreading consistency. Spread on cake. Garnish with nuts.

Catherine Kimmel
Atlanta, Ga.

WHITE CHIFFON CAKE

½ c. butter
1 c. sugar
2 tsp. baking powder
2 c. (scant) cake flour
⅔ c. milk
4 egg whites
1 tsp. vanilla flavoring

Cream butter; add sugar gradually. Beat until frothy. Add baking powder to flour; sift several times. Add milk and flour mixture alternately to creamed mixture. Beat egg whites, adding vanilla when partly stiff; continue beating until stiff. Fold egg whites into cake mixture. Bake at 325 degrees for 1 hour. Yield: 12-16 servings.

Margaret Riley
Mason City, Iowa

CHOCOLATE-CINNAMON CAKE

2 c. flour
2 c. sugar
1 c. water

(Continued on next page)

4 tbsp. cocoa
1 stick margarine
¼ c. shortening
1 c. buttermilk
1 tsp. soda
1 tsp. cinnamon
3 eggs

Sift flour and sugar into bowl. Combine water, cocoa, margarine and shortening; bring to a boil. Add to flour and sugar. Add all remaining ingredients; mix well. Pour into a greased and floured 9 x 18-inch cake pan. Bake at 350 degrees for 20 minutes.

ICING:
1 stick margarine
1 box powdered sugar
4 tbsp. cocoa
4 to 6 tbsp. milk
1 tsp. vanilla flavoring
½ tsp. butter flavoring

Mix all ingredients; spread on hot cake.

Helen M. Campbell
Longview, Tex.

CHERRY- CHOCOLATE CAKE

2 c. sifted flour
1 tsp. soda
¼ tsp. salt
½ c. butter
1 c. sugar
1 egg
1 tsp. vanilla flavoring
2 squares unsweetened chocolate, melted
1 c. thick sour milk
1 8-oz. bottle Maraschino cherries and juice
½ c. chopped walnuts

Sift flour three times with soda and salt. Cream butter; gradually add sugar. Add egg; mix well. Add vanilla and melted chocolate. Turn electric mixer to low speed. Alternately add dry ingredients, milk and cherry juice. Fold in sliced cherries and nuts. Pour into greased 9 x 13 x 2-inch pan. Bake at 350 degrees for 40 minutes or bake in a 9-inch tube pan for about 1 hour. Cool and frost. Yield: 24 servings.

Rosemarie C. Winkler
Dickinson, Tex.

BLACK BOTTOM CUPS

BASE:
1 ½ c. sifted flour
1 c. sugar
¼ c. unsweetened cocoa
1 tsp. soda
½ tsp. salt
1 c. water
⅓ c. cooking oil
1 tbsp. vinegar
1 tsp. vanilla flavoring

Sift all dry ingredients into mixing bowl. Add all remaining ingredients; beat until well blended. Fill lined muffin cups one-third full with batter.

FILLING:
1 8-oz. pkg. cream cheese
1 egg
Sugar
⅛ tsp. salt
1 c. chocolate pieces
Chopped almonds

Combine cream cheese, egg, 1/3 cup sugar and salt; beat well. Stir in chocolate pieces. Place a heaping tablespoonful of mixture on batter in each muffin cup. Sprinkle with additional sugar and chopped almonds. Bake at 350 degrees for 30 minutes. Yield: 24 servings.

Mrs. R. L. Persing
Washington, D.C.

CHOCOLATE SHEET CAKE

2 c. flour
2 c. sugar
4 tbsp. cocoa
1 stick margarine
1 c. water
½ c. cooking oil
½ c. buttermilk
1 tsp. soda
2 eggs
1 tsp. vanilla flavoring

Sift flour with sugar and cocoa. Combine margarine, water and oil in saucepan; bring to a boil. Pour over flour mixture. Combine buttermilk in which soda has been dissolved, eggs and vanilla. Add to mixture; beat well. Pour into 11 x 16-inch pan. Bake at 400 degrees for 20 minutes.

ICING:
1 stick margarine
⅓ c. milk
1 box powdered sugar
4 tbsp. cocoa
1 tsp. vanilla flavoring
1 c. nuts or coconut (opt.)

Heat margarine and milk; pour over all remaining ingredients. Blend well. Spread on cake.

Mae Deane Merriman
Pratt, Kans.

CHOCOLATE SUNSHINE CAKE

2 sticks butter
2 c. sugar
4 eggs
1 tsp. vanilla flavoring
4 1-oz. squares unsweetened
  chocolate, melted
3 c. sifted cake flour
4 tsp. baking powder
½ tsp. salt
1 c. milk

Cream butter and sugar until light and fluffy. Add an egg at a time, beating well after each addition. Blend in vanilla and melted chocolate. Sift all dry ingredients; add alternately with milk to creamed mixture. Butter and lightly flour three 9-inch cake pans; pour in batter. Bake in preheated 350 degree oven for 25 to 30 minutes. Cool for 10 minutes. Remove from pans onto cake racks; cool completely. Fill with orange glaze filling; frost with orange butter icing. Yield: One 3-layer, 9-inch cake.

ORANGE GLAZE FILLING:
6 tbsp. sugar
2 tbsp. cornstarch
½ c. water
1 c. orange juice
2 tbsp. lemon juice
1 tbsp. grated orange rind
3 tbsp. butter

Mix sugar and cornstarch in a saucepan. Stir in water until smooth; add all remaining ingredients. Cook, stirring constantly, for 5 to 8 minutes or until smooth and thickened. Cool. Set aside 5 tablespoons filling to be used in orange icing. Spread remaining filling between layers. Yield: Filling for a 3 layer, 9-inch cake.

ORANGE BUTTER ICING:
2 sticks butter
6 c. sifted confectioners sugar
5 tbsp. orange glaze filling
1 tsp. grated orange rind
Dash of salt
1 drop of red food coloring
2 drops yellow food coloring

Cream butter; gradually add confectioners sugar alternately with orange glaze filling. Beat until smooth and creamy. Blend in all remaining ingredients. Frost sides and top of cake. Yield: Icing for a 3 layer, 9-inch cake.

Photograph for this recipe above.

CHOCOLATE-COCONUT RIPPLE CAKE

1 ½ c. finely grated coconut
¼ c. water
2 squares semi-sweet chocolate,
  melted

(Continued on next page)

2 ¾ c. flour
3 ½ tsp. baking powder
1 tsp. salt
1 ⅔ c. sugar
⅔ c. shortening
1 ⅓ c. milk
1 tsp. vanilla flavoring
4 egg whites

Combine coconut and water; stir in chocolate. Sift flour with baking powder and salt. Add sugar gradually to shortening, creaming well. Combine milk and vanilla. Add alternately with dry ingredients to creamed mixture, blending well after each addition. Beat egg whites until stiff but not dry; fold into batter. Spoon tablespoonfuls of batter and small teaspoonfuls of coconut mixture alternately into two 9-inch round layer pans which have been well greased. Cut through with knife to marble. Bake at 350 degrees for 35 to 40 minutes. Cool; frost with a chocolate frosting.

Anne Townsend
Columbus, Miss.

GERMAN'S CHOCOLATE CAKE

1 pkg. German's sweet chocolate
½ c. boiling water
1 c. butter or shortening
2 c. sugar
4 eggs, separated
1 tsp. vanilla flavoring
½ tsp. salt
1 tsp. soda
2 ½ c. sifted cake flour
1 c. buttermilk

Melt chocolate in boiling water; cool. Cream butter and sugar; add an egg yolk at a time, beating well after each addition. Add chocolate and vanilla. Add sifted dry ingredients alternately with milk to creamed mixture. Beat until batter is smooth. Fold stiffly beaten egg whites into batter. Pour into three lined 8-inch pans. Bake at 350 degrees for 30 to 40 minutes. Cool; top with frosting.

COCONUT-PECAN FROSTING:

1 c. evaporated milk
3 egg yolks
½ c. butter or margarine
1 tsp. vanilla
1 c. sugar
1 ⅓ c. flaked coconut
½ to 1 c. chopped pecans

Combine milk, eggs, butter, vanilla and sugar; cook over medium heat until thickened, about 12 minutes. Add coconut and pecans; beat until thick. Frost top of cakes only.

Golden Ellis
Clark, N.J.

DEVIL'S FOOD CAKE

⅔ c. cocoa
2 ½ c. flour
1 tsp. soda
1 tsp. (rounded) baking powder
¼ tsp. salt
½ c. butter
2 c. sugar
3 eggs, separated
1 tsp. vanilla flavoring
1 c. sour milk

Dissolve cocoa in 1/2 cup boiling water. Sift flour, soda, baking powder and salt. Cream butter; slowly beat in sugar. Add beaten egg yolks, flavoring and cocoa. Add flour mixture alternately with milk, beating well after each addition. Fold in stiffly beaten egg whites. Pour into two greased layer pans. Bake at 375 degrees for 25 minutes.

SEVEN-MINUTE FROSTING:

2 egg whites
1 ½ c. sugar, sifted
5 tbsp. cold water
½ tsp. cream of tartar or 2 tsp. light corn syrup
Few grains of salt
1 tsp. vanilla flavoring

Combine all ingredients except flavoring in top of double boiler; stir until sugar dissolves. Place over briskly boiling water. Beat for 6 to 10 minutes or until peaks form. Add flavoring; beat until thick enough to spread. Frost top and sides of Devil's Food Cake.

Mrs. Dwight D. Eisenhower

HEAVENLY HASH CAKE

1 c. shortening
2 ½ c. sugar
2 eggs
2 tbsp. cocoa
3 ½ c. flour
¼ tsp. salt
2 tsp. soda
2 c. buttermilk
1 tsp. vanilla flavoring

Blend shortening, sugar and eggs by hand or with mixer at medium speed for 2 minutes. Mix cocoa, flour, salt and soda; add to sugar mixture alternately with milk and vanilla. Beat until smooth. Pour into well greased and floured pans. Bake at 375 degrees for 30 minutes. Cool.

FROSTING:

2 c. sugar
2 eggs, slightly beaten
1 c. half and half

(Continued on next page)

1 box coconut
1 c. pecans
1 tsp. vanilla flavoring

Cook sugar, eggs and cream over low heat for 5 minutes or until thickened. Remove from heat; add coconut, pecans and vanilla. Put between layers of cake; pour over top and allow to run down sides.

Mrs. Nell Reagon
Clay City, Ind.

HIGH ALTITUDE CHOCOLATE CAKE

2 ½ squares bitter chocolate, chipped
2 c. milk
2 c. (heaping) flour
1 tsp. salt
¼ lb. butter
1 ½ c. sugar
3 eggs, separated
1 tsp. vanilla flavoring

Put chocolate and 1 cup milk in double boiler over medium heat; cook until thick. Remove from heat; cool. Sift flour and salt four times. Cream butter; gradually add sugar and egg yolks. Stir in flour alternately with remaining 1 cup milk; add chocolate mixture and vanilla. Fold in beaten egg whites. Pour into greased and floured tube pan. Bake at 350 degrees until cake springs back when touched. Cool in pan for 10 minutes. Remove from pan; frost. NOTE: This recipe is adapted for altitudes of 6500 to 7500 feet.

Mrs. Lucy Bushnell
Santa Fe, N.M.

INSTANT CHOCOLATE CAKE

1 ½ c. sifted flour
1 ½ tsp. baking powder
½ tsp. soda
1 tsp. salt
1 ½ c. sugar
¾ c. instant cocoa
½ c. shortening, softened
1 c. milk
1 tsp. vanilla flavoring
3 eggs

Sift dry ingredients together; cut in shortening. Add 3/4 cup milk and vanilla. Mix until all flour is dampened; beat for 2 minutes at low speed with electric mixer. Add eggs and remaining milk; beat for 1 minute. Pour into 8-inch layer pans lined with waxed paper. Bake at 350 degrees for 35 minutes.

Myrtle Rosenberger
Fowler, Ind.

ICE WATER CAKE

¾ c. shortening
2 ¼ c. sugar
1 tsp. vanilla flavoring
3 eggs
2 squares chocolate, melted
3 c. cake flour
1 ½ tsp. soda
¾ tsp. salt
1 ½ c. ice water

Cream shortening, sugar and vanilla until light and fluffy. Add eggs, one at a time, beating after each addition until light. Add chocolate; add flour sifted with soda and salt. Stir in ice water. Pour into three greased 8-inch pans. Bake at 350 degrees for 25 to 30 minutes. Yield: 10 servings.

Mrs. Vada J. DeMoss
Moro, Oreg.

MIDNIGHT CAKE

½ c. butter or shortening
1 ¼ c. sugar
2 eggs
½ c. cocoa
1 c. hot water
1 ½ c. sifted flour
1 tsp. baking powder
1 tsp. soda
½ tsp. salt
1 tsp. vanilla flavoring

Cream butter; blend in sugar. Beat until fluffy. Beat in an egg at a time. Place cocoa in small bowl; gradually stir in hot water, mixing until smooth. Sift flour with baking powder, soda and salt. Add dry ingredients to creamed mixture alternately with cocoa. Add vanilla. Pour into greased and floured 9 x 9 x 2-inch pan. Bake at 350 degrees for 55 minutes or until cake tester inserted comes out clean. Cake may be cooled in the pan or turned out on a rack. Yield: 1 cake.

Mrs. Cleo M. Howery
Speonk, Long Island, N.Y.

MOIST CHOCOLATE CAKE

¼ c. shortening
¼ c. bacon fat
4 tbsp. cocoa
1 c. sugar
2 egg yolks
2 tbsp. cornstarch
2 c. sifted flour
1 ¾ tsp. soda
½ tsp. salt
1 ½ c. milk

Mix shortening, bacon fat, cocoa, sugar and egg yolks. Sift cornstarch with flour, soda and salt. Add alternately with milk to cocoa mixture. Pour into two greased 8-inch layer pans. Bake at 375 degrees for 30 to 35 minutes.

(Continued on next page)

FROSTING:
1 c. sugar
⅓ c. water
2 egg whites
¼ tsp. salt

Mix sugar and water; boil to crack stage. Beat egg whites and salt until peaks form. Combine mixtures. Spread on cake.

Geraldine B. Farley
Kendall Park, N.J.

NEVER-FAIL CAKE AND FROSTING

2 eggs
¾ c. cocoa
1 c. shortening
2 c. flour
1 c. sour milk or buttermilk
2 tsp. vanilla flavoring
2 tsp. soda
2 c. sugar
1 c. hot water
½ tsp. salt

Place ingredients in large mixing bowl; do not mix until all are in bowl. Mix for 2 minutes at low speed. Place in two 8 or 9-inch layer pans. Bake at 375 degrees for 35 minutes.

FROSTING:
1 c. sugar
4 tbsp. cocoa
4 tbsp. evaporated milk
1 egg
1 tsp. vanilla flavoring

Put all ingredients except vanilla in heavy skillet over low heat; stir until melted. Boil for 1 minute. Remove from heat; add vanilla. Stir; spread on cake.

Mrs. B. W. White
Holyroad, Kans.

QUICK AND EASY CAKE

2 c. flour
2 c. sugar
½ c. shortening
1 tsp. salt
3 eggs
2 tsp. vanilla flavoring
1 ¼ tsp. soda
2 squares chocolate
¾ tsp. baking powder

Combine all ingredients in mixer bowl. Beat at medium speed for 2 minutes. Pour into three buttered layer pans. Bake at 350 degrees for 30 to 35 minutes.

Ora Crager
Barstow, Calif.

RED VELVET CAKE

½ c. butter
1 ½ c. sugar
2 eggs
2 tbsp. cocoa
2 oz. red food coloring
2 ½ c. flour
1 tsp. salt
1 c. buttermilk
1 tsp. vanilla flavoring
2 oz. water
1 tsp. soda
1 tsp. vinegar

Cream butter and sugar until fluffy. Add eggs; beat well. Make a paste of cocoa and food coloring; add to sugar mixture. Sift flour and salt; add to batter alternately with buttermilk, vanilla and water. Add soda; blend well. Stir in vinegar gently; do not beat. Pour into two round cake pans. Bake at 350 degrees for 30 minutes. Cool; split layers. Frost.

FLUFFY BUTTER FROSTING:
6 tbsp. flour
1 ½ c. milk
1 ½ c. butter, softened
1 ½ c. sugar
1 ½ tsp. vanilla flavoring

Mix flour and milk; cook until thick, stirring constantly. Cool. Cream butter, sugar and vanilla until fluffy. Add milk mixture; mix for 10 minutes. Spread on cake layers. NOTE: Do not substitute margarine for butter. Yield: 16-20 servings.

Mrs. Grace Halter
Valdosta, Ga.

WALDORF ASTORIA RED CAKE

½ c. shortening or butter
1 ½ c. sugar
2 eggs
½ to 2 oz. red food coloring
2 to 3 tbsp. cocoa
2 ¼ c. flour
¾ to 1 tsp. salt or to taste
1 c. buttermilk
1 tsp. vanilla flavoring (opt.)
1 to 3 tsp. vinegar
1 tsp. soda

Cream shortening, sugar and eggs. Make a paste of food coloring and cocoa; add to creamed mixture. Sift flour and salt; add alternately with buttermilk and vanilla. Stir in vinegar and soda; do not beat. Pour into two or three 8 or 9-inch greased and floured layer cake pans. Bake at 325 to 350 degrees for 20 to 35 minutes. Frost with desired icing.

ICING NO. 1:
½ c. milk
5 tbsp. flour
½ lb. butter

(Continued on next page)

1 box powdered sugar
2 tsp. vanilla flavoring

Heat milk and flour, stirring constantly. Add remaining ingredients; beat until light in texture. Spread on cake.

CREAM FROSTING:
1 c. milk
3 tbsp. flour
Pinch of salt (opt.)
1 c. butter
1 c. sugar
1 tsp. vanilla flavoring

Combine milk, flour and salt. Cook until thickened, stirring constantly; cool thoroughly. Cream butter and sugar with mixer for 7 minutes. Gradually add milk mixture, beating constantly. Continue beating for 5 minutes or until fluffy. Stir in vanilla. Use for icing cake.

Mrs. Ruth Stanley
Milton, W. Va.

SWISS CHOCOLATE CAKE
1 ½ c. sugar
½ c. shortening
3 eggs
1 tsp. vanilla flavoring
2 c. flour
2 ½ tsp. baking powder
¼ tsp. salt
1 c. milk
1 square chocolate, melted

Cream sugar and shortening. Add an egg at a time, beating well after each addition. Add vanilla. Sift flour, baking powder and salt. Add milk and flour alternately. Add chocolate. Pour into three layer pans. Bake at 400 degrees until done.

ICING:
1 pkg. cream cheese
4 tbsp. half and half
Dash of salt
2 c. sifted powdered sugar
1 square chocolate, melted
½ tsp. vanilla flavoring

Soften cream cheese with half and half. Add salt and sugar gradually, beating well after each addition. Add chocolate; beat until smooth. Add vanilla. Spread on cake.

Alyne A. Joplin
Lubbock, Tex.

SOUR CREAM-CHOCOLATE CAKE
2 oz. chocolate
½ c. boiling water

1 tsp. soda
½ c. butter
2 c. brown sugar
3 eggs, separated
½ c. sour cream
2 ½ c. sifted flour

Melt chocolate in water in double boiler. Add soda; cool. Cream butter; add sugar gradually. Blend in well beaten egg yolks; add chocolate mixture and sour cream. Stir in flour; fold in beaten egg whites. Pour into tube pan. Bake at 350 degrees for 45 minutes. Frost with a white butter icing flavored with vanilla. Yield: 10 servings.

Meralda Isabel Brennan
Pottsville, Pa.

SOUR CREAM-CHOCOLATE CAKE
1 ½ c. sugar
2 eggs
1 c. sour cream
1 tsp. vanilla flavoring
2 c. sifted flour
1 tsp. soda
½ c. cocoa or 2 squares chocolate
½ c. boiling water

Combine sugar, eggs, sour cream and flavoring; mix well. Add flour sifted with soda; mix well. Add chocolate; mix in boiling water. Pour into greased and floured cake pan. Bake at 350 degrees for 30 minutes. NOTE: If cocoa is used, add 2 to 3 tablespoons butter to sugar.

Mrs. H. C. Schwab
Mandan, N.D.

TWENTY-FIVE MINUTE MAGIC CHOCOLATE-BUTTER CAKE
2 c. sugar
2 c. flour
1 stick butter or margarine
1 c. shortening
4 tbsp. cocoa
1 c. water
½ c. buttermilk
2 eggs, beaten
1 tsp. soda
1 tsp. vanilla flavoring

Sift sugar with flour into large mixing bowl. Combine butter, shortening, cocoa and water in saucepan; bring to a rapid boil. Pour over flour mixture; stir well. Mix buttermilk, eggs, soda and vanilla; add to flour mixture. Pour into one greased 9 x 13-inch pan and one 9-inch square pan. Bake at 400 degrees for 20 to 25 minutes.

ICING:
1 stick butter
4 tbsp. cocoa
6 tbsp. milk

(Continued on next page)

CHOCOLATE CAKES

1 box sifted powdered sugar
1 tsp. vanilla flavoring
1 c. chopped pecans

Melt butter with cocoa and milk; bring to a boil. Remove from heat; add all remaining ingredients. Beat well. Spread on hot cake in pans. Yield: 12-14 servings.

Nellie M. Vickers
El Paso, Tex.

CRAZY CHOCOLATE CAKE

1 ½ c. flour
1 c. sugar
⅓ c. cocoa
1 tsp. soda
1 tsp. salt
1 tbsp. vinegar
1 tsp. vanilla flavoring
⅓ c. oil
1 c. water

Sift all dry ingredients into ungreased 9 x 12-inch pan; make three holes in dry ingredients. Pour vinegar into first hole, vanilla into second hole and oil into third hole. Pour water over all; stir. Bake at 350 degrees until done. Yield: 9 servings.

Mrs. Dennis Woolley
Kodiak, Alaska

CHOCOLATE-WHIPPED CREAM CAKE

2 eggs
1 c. sugar
1 c. sour cream, whipped
1 tsp. vanilla flavoring
1 ½ c. cake flour
½ tsp. salt
2 squares chocolate, melted
1 tsp. soda
½ c. boiling water

Add eggs and sugar to sour cream. Stir in vanilla, flour, salt, chocolate and soda dissolved in water. Pour into one 9-inch square pan. Bake at 350 degrees for 30 minutes. Yield: 16 servings.

Mrs. Leonard Bock
Sterling, Colo.

BLACK DEVIL'S FOOD CAKE

⅔ c. shortening
1 ½ c. sugar
3 eggs
⅔ c. cocoa
½ c. hot water
1 c. thick sour milk
½ tsp. soda
1 tsp. vanilla flavoring
2 c. flour
1 tsp. salt
2 tsp. baking powder

Blend shortening, sugar and eggs thoroughly. Beat cocoa in hot water until smooth; add to sugar mixture. Add milk mixed with soda and vanilla. Stir in sifted dry ingredients. Pour into three 8-inch layer cake pans. Bake at 350 degrees for 20 minutes.

ICING:
1 ¾ c. sugar
⅛ tsp. salt
½ c. water
2 egg whites, beaten
12 marshmallows, finely cut

Combine sugar, salt and water; cook to soft ball stage or to 238 degrees. Pour slowly into egg whites, beating constantly. Fold in marshmallows; beat until of spreading consistency. Frost cake.

Mrs. William Grant
Tuscumbia, Ala.

BOSTON DEVIL'S FOOD CAKE

4 squares baking chocolate
2 c. sugar
1 c. milk
2 egg yolks, beaten
½ c. butter or margarine
2 eggs
½ c. sour milk or buttermilk
2 ¼ c. sifted cake flour
1 tsp. soda
1 tsp. vanilla flavoring

Melt chocolate over hot water; add 1 cup sugar. Gradually add milk, stirring until smooth. Add egg yolks; cook until mixture thickens. Set aside to cool. Cream butter and 1 cup sugar; beat in whole eggs. Add alternately the sour milk and flour mixed with soda. Beat well; add chocolate custard mixture and vanilla. Pour into two well greased and floured 9-inch round or 8-inch square layer pans. Bake at 350 degrees for 30 to 40 minutes or until top of cake springs back when touched lightly with fingertip. Frost with Seven-Minute frosting. NOTE: If sour milk or buttermilk is not available, use milk to which 2 teaspoons of vinegar have been added.

Elizabeth Carnes
Tampa, Fla.

DEVIL'S FOOD CAKE

½ c. grated sweet chocolate
1 tsp. soda
½ c. boiling water
2 c. brown sugar
¾ c. butter
½ c. sour cream

(Continued on next page)

34

2 eggs, well beaten
2 ½ c. sifted flour
2 tsp. ground cinnamon
2 tsp. (scant) cloves
1 tsp. nutmeg

Melt chocolate, soda and boiling water. Cream brown sugar and butter; add all remaining ingredients. Mix well. Pour into pans lined with greased paper. Bake at 350 degrees for 30 minutes.

Mrs. Marguerite Johnston
Barboursville, W. Va.

1 egg, beaten
Pinch of salt
1 tsp. lemon juice
1 c. finely chopped nuts

Combine butter, chocolate, sugar, egg and salt; beat well. Add lemon juice and nuts. Spread on cake.

Ethelyne Gavin
Jacksonville, Fla.

RED DEVIL'S FOOD CAKE

1 ¾ c. sugar
¾ c. cocoa
1 c. milk
3 eggs
½ c. butter or shortening
1 tsp. vanilla
½ tsp. salt
1 tsp. soda
1 tbsp. hot water
2 c. sifted cake flour

Sift together 3/4 cup sugar and cocoa. Add 1/2 cup milk and 1 egg yolk; mix well. Cook over hot water until thick and smooth, stirring constantly; cool. Cream butter. Add 1 cup sugar, 2 eggs and 1 egg white; beat vigorously. Add 1/2 cup milk, vanilla, salt, soda dissolved in hot water and flour. Add cocoa mixture; mix well. Pour into two buttered and floured layer pans. Bake at 350 degrees until done.

Mrs. Sally Davis
Cookeville, Tenn.

FROSTED CHOCOLATE FUDGE CAKE

½ lb. butter
2 c. sugar
4 squares bitter chocolate, melted
2 eggs, beaten
2 c. cake flour
2 tsp. baking powder
1 ½ c. sweet milk
2 tsp. vanilla flavoring

Cream butter and sugar; add chocolate and eggs. Add sifted dry ingredients alternately with milk and vanilla. Pour into a lightly greased and floured 8 x 10-inch pan. Bake at 350 degrees for 45 minutes or until toothpick inserted comes out clean. Cool in pan.

ICING:
¼ c. butter
2 squares chocolate, melted
1 ⅓ c. powdered sugar

FUDGE RIBBON CAKE

CHEESE MIXTURE:
2 tbsp. butter
¼ c. sugar
1 tbsp. cornstarch
1 8-oz. pkg. cream cheese, softened
1 egg
2 tbsp. milk
½ tsp. vanilla

Cream butter, sugar and cornstarch. Add cream cheese; beat until fluffy. Add remaining ingredients; beat well.

BATTER:
2 c. sifted flour
2 c. sugar
1 tsp. salt
1 tsp. baking powder
1 tsp. soda
½ c. soft shortening
1 ½ c. milk
2 eggs
4 oz. unsweetened chocolate, melted
1 tsp. vanilla

Combine dry ingredients; cut in shortening. Add 1 cup milk; beat for 1 minute and 30 seconds. Add remaining milk and other ingredients; beat for 1 minute and 30 seconds. Put one-half of the batter in well floured 13 x 9 x 2-inch pan. Spoon on cheese mixture; top with remaining batter. Bake at 350 degrees for 50 to 55 minutes. Cool.

FROSTING:
⅓ c. milk
½ c. butter
6 oz. semi-sweet chocolate pieces
1 tsp. vanilla flavoring
2 ¼ c. powdered sugar

Combine milk and butter; bring to a boil. Blend in remaining ingredients; beat well. Frost cakes. Yield: 24 servings.

Mrs. Emily Quigley
Uxbridge, Mass.

RAISIN-FUDGE CAKE

½ c. butter
2 c. light brown sugar
2 eggs, separated
Juice and grated rind of 1 orange
½ c. thick buttermilk
½ c. water
2 ½ c. flour
5 tbsp. cocoa
1 tsp. baking powder
½ tsp. soda
½ tsp. cinnamon
¼ tsp. cloves
1 c. chopped raisins
1 c. chopped almonds

Cream butter and sugar; add beaten egg yolks, orange juice and rind. Mix buttermilk and water; add alternately with sifted dry ingredients. Add raisins and nuts. Fold in stiffly beaten egg whites. Pour into two layer cake pans which have been lined with greased paper. Bake at 350 degrees for 40 to 50 minutes or until done.

FILLING:

8 egg yolks, beaten
2 c. powdered sugar
¾ c. melted butter
2 c. chopped pecans
2 c. chopped raisins
1 sm. box coconut

Combine egg yolks, sugar and butter; cook in top of double boiler until thick, stirring constantly. Remove from heat; add remaining ingredients. Cool; spread between layers.

Mrs. Chesney T. Yarbrough
Corpus Christi, Tex.

COCONUT MIST CAKE

2 tsp. baking powder
¼ tsp. salt
3 c. sifted cake flour
1 c. butter or margarine
1 lb. or 3 ½ c. powdered sugar
5 eggs, separated
1 c. milk
1 tsp. vanilla flavoring
1 c. or 1 can moist coconut

Add baking powder and salt to flour; sift together. Cream butter thoroughly; add sugar gradually. Cream until light and fluffy. Add well beaten egg yolks; beat well. Add flour alternately with milk, a small amount at a time, beating after each addition until smooth. Add vanilla and coconut. Fold in stiffly beaten egg whites quickly and thoroughly. Pour into three 9-inch greased layer cake pans. Bake at 350 degrees for 25 to 30 minutes. Cool.

TINTED FLUFFY FROSTING:

3 egg whites
2 ¼ c. sugar
½ c. water
2 tsp. light corn syrup
Red or green food coloring (opt.)
1 ½ tsp. vanilla flavoring
Coconut

Combine egg whites, sugar, water and corn syrup in top of double boiler, beating with an electric mixer until thoroughly mixed. Place over rapidly boiling water. Beat constantly with mixer and cook for 10 minutes or until frosting stands in peaks. Add a few drops of food coloring. Remove from boiling water. Add vanilla; beat until thick enough to spread. Spread on cooled cake; sprinkle with coconut. Yield: 15 servings.

Mrs. William P. Tatum
New Castle, Va.

FRESH COCONUT CAKE

1 c. shortening
1 tsp. salt
2 c. sugar
3 c. sifted cake flour
2 tsp. baking powder
½ c. milk
½ c. water
1 tsp. vanilla flavoring
8 egg whites, stiffly beaten

Cream shortening, salt and sugar. Mix flour with baking powder. Add alternately with milk and water. Add vanilla; fold in egg whites. Pour into two well greased 8-inch cake pans. Bake at 375 degrees for 25 to 35 minutes. Remove from pans; cool. Yield: 12-14 servings.

FILLING AND FROSTING:

2 lge. or 3 sm. coconuts
Coconut milk
Milk
2 ½ c. sugar
3 egg whites, stiffly beaten

Grind coconut meat; moisten with coconut milk and milk. Add sugar. Cook until coconut is tender. Fold in egg whites. Cook for 3 to 5 minutes. Spread on cake.

Colena D. Wilhoit
Daytona Beach, Fla.

FRESH COCONUT CAKE

1 c. sugar
½ c. butter
1 c. coconut milk
2 c. cake flour
3 tsp. baking powder

(Continued on next page)

Pinch of salt
3 egg whites, stiffly beaten
1 tsp. vanilla flavoring

Cream sugar and butter well. Add coconut milk alternately with dry ingredients. Fold in egg whites. Add vanilla. Bake at 375 degrees for 20 minutes or until cake begins to come away from pan. Cool.

ICING:
1 c. (scant) sugar
1 lge. or 2 sm. egg whites
2 tbsp. corn syrup
3 tbsp. water

Combine all ingredients in top of double boiler. Beat over hot water for 7 minutes; spread on cake.

Mrs. J. W. Little
Vance AFB, Okla.

OLD-FASHIONED COCONUT CAKE

CAKE:
2 ¼ c. sifted flour
⅓ c. cornstarch
1 tsp. baking powder
½ c. butter or margarine
2 c. sugar
¾ c. milk
1 tbsp. vanilla flavoring
6 egg whites, stiffly beaten

Sift flour with cornstarch and baking powder three times. Work butter until soft. Add sugar gradually; continue working until very creamy. Mix milk and vanilla. Stir flour mixture and milk alternately into creamed butter and sugar, beginning and ending with flour. Fold in egg whites. Pour into three greased and floured 8-inch round cake pans. Bake at 375 degrees for 25 minutes or until cakes pull away slightly from sides of pans. Cool for 5 minutes; remove from pans. Cool completely.

FROSTING:
2 egg whites
¾ c. sugar
2 ½ tbsp. cold water
½ tsp. cream of tartar
Pinch of salt
1 c. heavy cream, whipped
1 tbsp. vanilla flavoring
2 3 ½-oz. cans flaked coconut or 2 c. grated fresh coconut

Mix egg whites, sugar, water, cream of tartar and salt in top of double boiler. Beat with rotary or electric beater until well mixed. Set over rapidly boiling water. Cook, beating vigorously and constantly, for 7 minutes.

Frosting should hold definite peaks. Remove from heat; cool. Fold in whipped cream, vanilla and 1 can coconut. Spread frosting between cake layers; frost sides and top of cake. Sprinkle remaining coconut flakes over entire cake.

Mrs. Roland McCabe
Loring AFB, Me.

YELLOW COCONUT CAKE

⅔ c. soft butter
1 ½ c. sugar
3 eggs, separated
2 ½ c. sifted cake flour
2 ½ tsp. baking powder
1 tsp. salt
1 c. milk
1 ½ tsp. vanilla flavoring

Cream butter and sugar until fluffy. Blend in beaten egg yolks. Sift all dry ingredients; stir in alternately with milk and vanilla. Fold in beaten egg whites. Pour into two 9-inch waxed paper-lined and greased pans. Bake at 350 degrees for 25 to 30 minutes or until done. Cool.

SEVEN-MINUTE COCONUT FROSTING:
2 egg whites
1 ½ c. sugar
¼ tsp. cream of tartar
⅓ c. water
1 ½ tsp. vanilla flavoring
1 can coconut

Combine egg whites, sugar, cream of tartar and water in top of double boiler. Place over boiling water; beat until mixture holds its shape. Remove from heat; add vanilla. Spread between layers and on top and sides of cake. Sprinkle with coconut.

Winona Davidson
Louisville, Ky.

VANILLA WAFER-COCONUT CAKE

½ c. butter or margarine
1 c. sugar
1 ½ c. vanilla wafer crumbs
½ tsp. baking powder
3 eggs
1 c. chopped pecans
1 3 ½-oz. can flaked coconut

Cream butter and sugar until fluffy. Blend in crumbs and baking powder. Beat in an egg at a time. Stir in pecans and coconut. Pour into greased and floured 9 x 1 1/2-inch round

(Continued on next page)

baking pan. Bake at 325 degrees for 40 minutes; cool. Cut into six to eight wedges. Yield: 6-8 servings.

Zora Guy Smith
Clanton, Ala.

WHITE COCONUT CAKE

2 c. sifted cake flour
2 tsp. baking powder
½ c. butter or shortening
1 c. sifted sugar
⅔ c. milk
1 tsp. vanilla flavoring
3 egg whites, stiffly beaten

Sift flour with baking powder three times. Cream butter thoroughly; add sugar gradually, creaming until light and fluffy. Add flour alternately with milk, beating until smooth after each addition. Add vanilla; fold in egg whites. Pour into two greased and floured 9-inch layer pans. Bake at 375 degrees for 25 to 30 minutes.

ICING:
1 c. light corn syrup
2 egg whites
8 marshmallows, cut up
½ tsp. vanilla flavoring
1 sm. coconut, grated

Combine syrup and egg whites; cook, beating constantly, until mixture stands in peaks. Add marshmallows; beat until melted. Beat in vanilla. Spread between layers and on top and sides of cake. Sprinkle generously with coconut. NOTE: If desired, cake may be baked in 8 x 8 x 2-inch pan at 350 degrees for 1 hour.

Mrs. Margaret O. Nichols
Asheville, N.C.

CRANBERRY CAKE

2 c. sifted flour
1 c. sugar
1 tsp. salt
½ tsp. soda
1 ½ tsp. baking powder
¼ c. shortening
1 egg, beaten
¾ c. orange juice
1 c. coarsely chopped cranberries
½ c. chopped nuts

Sift all dry ingredients; cut in shortening until blended. Add egg and orange juice; stir until mixed. Fold in cranberries and nuts. Bake at 350 degrees for 50 minutes.

Mrs. R. R. Schaefer
Woodbury, Conn.

COFFEE-CREAM CAKE

½ c. shortening
1 c. sugar
2 eggs, separated
½ c. strong coffee
1 ½ tsp. baking powder
1 ½ c. flour

Cream shortening and sugar; add egg yolks. Beat well. Add coffee. Combine dry ingredients; add to cream mixture. Fold in beaten egg whites. Pour into two greased 9-inch layer pans. Bake at 350 degrees for 25 minutes.

FILLING:
1 c. heavy cream, sweetened
2 tbsp. black coffee
Apple jelly
Powdered sugar

Blend cream and coffee; whip until very thick. Split each layer of cake. Spread cream between layers; top cream with dots of jelly. Sprinkle top with powdered sugar. Yield: 6 servings.

Mrs. J. Irving Wood
Cranston, R. I.

CURRANT CAKE

2 sticks butter
1 ½ c. sugar
4 c. flour
1 tsp. cream of tartar
¼ tsp. nutmeg
½ tsp. soda
3 eggs, separated
1 c. milk
4 to 6 oz. brandy
½ box currants

Cream butter and sugar. Sift flour with cream of tartar, nutmeg and soda. Add beaten yolks to sugar mixture. Add flour alternately with milk. Add brandy and currants. Fold in beaten egg whites. Pour into large tube pan. Bake at 325 degrees for 1 hour and 15 minutes.

Louise Champey
Brunswick, Ga.

DATE CAKE

1 c. boiling water
½ lb. chopped dates
1 tsp. soda
1 c. sugar
½ c. butter
1 egg
1 ½ c. flour
¼ tsp. salt
1 tsp. vanilla flavoring

Pour boiling water over dates; cool. Add soda; mix. Cream sugar and butter; add egg. Add

(Continued on next page)

date mixture to c r e a m e d ingredients. Add flour, salt and vanilla. Pour into greased and floured 8-inch square pan. Bake at 350 degrees for 35 to 40 minutes.

TOPPING:
4 tbsp. butter
2 tbsp. milk
1 c. brown sugar
1 can flaked coconut

Mix all ingredients well. Spread on cake. Broil for 1 to 2 minutes. Yield: 16 servings.

Mrs. Helen K. Miller
York, Pa.

DATE CAKE

1 c. chopped dates
1 tsp. soda
1 c. boiling water
½ c. butter
1 c. sugar
1 egg, beaten
1 ½ c. flour
Dash of salt
1 tsp. vanilla flavoring

Combine dates and soda; soak in b o i l i n g water until cool. Cream butter and sugar; add egg. Mix well; add to dates. Stir in flour, salt and vanilla; blend thoroughly. Bake at 350 degrees for 40 minutes or until cake tests done.

Helene Williams
Concord, N.H.

DATE PUDDING CAKE

1 c. chopped dates
1 c. boiling water
1 tsp. soda
1 c. sugar
1 tbsp. butter
1 egg
1 ½ c. sifted flour
½ tsp. baking powder
½ c. chopped nuts
1 tsp. vanilla

Soak dates in boiling water with soda until cool. Mix in sugar, butter and egg. Add remaining ingredients. Pour into 10 x 14-inch pan. Bake at 350 degrees for 25 minutes.

SAUCE:
1 c. chopped dates
½ c. white sugar
⅔ c. boiling water
½ c. chopped nuts

Combine dates, sugar and water; cook until creamy. Add nuts. Spread over hot cake. Serve with whipped cream. Yield: 12 servings.

Mrs. Clyde Mattingly
Renfrow, Okla.

DATE TORTE CAKE

2 c. flour
1 tsp. soda
½ tsp. salt
1 ½ c. brown sugar
2 c. quick cooking oats
1 c. shortening

Combine all ingredients; mix well. Spread one-half of the mixture on bottom of large cake tin.

FILLING:
1 pkg. dates, chopped
½ c. sugar
1 ½ c. water
Lemon flavoring

Combine all ingredients. Spread filling evenly over batter. Top with remaining batter. Bake at 325 to 350 degrees until brown. Cut into squares; top with whipped cream. Yield: 12 servings.

Rose Chiles
Grand Ledge, Mich.

EGGNOG CAKE

1 c. butter
2 c. sifted sugar
5 egg yolks
¼ c. brandy
1 c. slivered toasted almonds
1 angel food cake
½ pt. heavy cream, whipped

Cream butter and sugar; mix in an egg yolk at a time, blending well. Stir in brandy and 3/4 cup nuts. Slice cake into thirds; fill with mixture. Chill for 24 hours. Just before serving, frost with whipped cream. Sprinkle with remaining 1/4 cup nuts. Yield: 16 servings.

Mrs. L. D. Haldeman
Hawthorne, Nev.

BUTTERLESS FRUIT CAKE

1 c. flour
1 c. sugar
2 tsp. baking powder
Dash of salt
Dash of nutmeg
Dash of allspice
Dash of cloves
1 lb. shelled pecans
1 lb. dates
½ lb. candied cherries
½ lb. candied pineapple
4 eggs
⅓ c. brandy or grape juice

(Continued on next page)

Sift all dry ingredients; mix with nuts and fruits. Beat eggs; add liquid. Blend thoroughly. Pour over fruits and nuts; mix well. Grease loaf pan or 8-inch tube pan; line with brown paper. Grease again. Pour batter into pan. Bake at 250 degrees for 1 hour and 30 minutes to 2 hours.

Robbie Ladd
Atlanta, Ga.

CHRISTMAS FRUIT CAKE

1 ¾ c. Brazil nuts
2 ¼ c. English walnuts
1 lb. whole pitted dates
1 4-oz. bottle whole green Maraschino cherries with liquid
1 4-oz. bottle whole red Maraschino cherries with liquid
1 tsp. baking powder
1 ½ c. sugar
1 ½ c. flour
Dash of salt
4 eggs, separated

Place whole nuts, walnuts, dates and cherries with liquid in a bowl. Pour sifted dry ingredients over mixture. Stir well until all nuts and fruit are coated with flour mixture. Add egg yolks; fold in beaten egg whites. Pour into greased loaf pans, coffee or nut cans. Bake at 350 degrees for 1 hour and 15 minutes. Remove cake while hot; slice thinly to serve. Yield: 32 slices.

Eleanor Murphy
Tampa, Kans.

DARK AND DELICIOUS FRUIT CAKE

1 c. raisins
1 c. currants
1 c. dates
2 lb. mixed diced fruit
1 c. coarsely chopped pecans
1 c. coarsely chopped almonds
1 c. coarsely chopped walnuts
1 tsp. cinnamon
1 tsp. nutmeg
1 tsp. allspice
½ tsp. cloves
½ c. molasses
½ c. brandy
½ c. butter
1 c. dark brown sugar
3 lge. eggs
2 c. flour
½ tsp. salt
½ tsp. soda

Rinse and drain fruits. Combine fruits, nuts, spices, molasses and brandy; mix well. Cream butter and sugar until fluffy. Beat in an egg at a time. Stir in sifted dry ingredients.

Fold in fruit mixture. Pack firmly into 10-inch tube pan lined with heavily greased white paper. Bake at 300 degrees for 2 hours. Cool and store. Yield: One 8-pound cake.

Mrs. Mary V. Brunk
Sault Sainte Marie, Mich.

FIVE-POUND FRUIT CAKE

1 lb. candied pineapple
1 lb. candied cherries
1 lb. candied dates, cut into halves
2 lb. pecans
2 c. flour
4 eggs
1 c. sugar
½ tsp. salt
2 tsp. baking powder

Dredge chopped fruits and nuts with 1 cup flour. Beat eggs; add sugar and salt. Sift remaining 1 cup flour with baking powder. Pour over fruits and nuts; mix thoroughly. Line pan with greased brown paper. Bake at 275 degrees for 2 hours.

Gwen Ellis
Henderson, Tex.

FRUIT WREATH CAKE

1 pkg. yellow cake mix
1 pkg. white cake mix
½ pkg. chocolate cake mix
1 tsp. orange flavoring
¼ tsp. grated orange rind
3 drops yellow food coloring
½ tsp. cinnamon
½ tsp. allspice
½ tsp. nutmeg
1 tsp. almond flavoring
5 drops red food coloring
1 tsp. lemon flavoring
¼ tsp. grated lemon rind

Prepare each cake mix batter separately, according to package directions. Divide yellow mix batter in half. Add orange flavoring, orange rind and yellow food coloring to one half; add spices to other half. Pour each batter into 9-inch layer pan. Bake according to package directions. Divide white batter in half. Blend almond flavoring and red food coloring into one half; blend lemon flavoring and lemon rind into other half. Pour each half into layer pans. Bake according to package directions. Bake chocolate batter in 9-inch layer pan. Cool cakes. Combine cakes using favorite filling, alternating golden, chocolate, rose, white and spice layers. Frost with a fluffy white frosting. Garnish with candied fruits to make a wreath. Yield: 12-16 servings.

Mrs. C. Schneider
Onamia, Minn.

HOLIDAY CANDY CAKE

1 lb. dates, coarsely chopped
1 lb. candied fruit mix
3 c. coarsely chopped mixed nuts
1 lb. seedless raisins
1 lb. currants
1 sm. jar citron
1 box graham cracker crumbs
1 lb. lge. marshmallows, cut
6 tbsp. evaporated milk

Mix all fruits and nuts with cracker crumbs until well coated. Put marshmallows and milk in top of double boiler; melt to form a smooth paste. Pour over fruit mixture; mix well with hands. Put in waxed paper-lined pans; cover with waxed paper. Refrigerate for approximately three weeks. NOTE: Do not wrap in foil. Yield: 12 servings.

Ruth Sisk
McCloud, Calif.

ICEBOX FRUIT CAKE

1 lb. vanilla wafers, crumbled
1 can sweetened condensed milk
½ lb. candied cherries
1 lb. white raisins
1 lb. candied pineapple
1 lb. pecans

Mix vanilla wafers and milk; batter will be very thick. Add fruits and nuts. Knead until well blended. Pack firmly into deep waxed paper-lined dish. Refrigerate for 4 to 5 hours or overnight.

Mrs. T. M. Jablonski
Schenectady, N.Y.

LEMON-FRUIT CAKE

1 lb. margarine
1 box light brown sugar
6 eggs, separated
1 2-oz. bottle lemon flavoring
4 c. flour
1 tsp. baking powder
1 lb. pecans
1 lb. candied pineapple
1 lb. candied cherries

Cream margarine and sugar. Add egg yolks; beat well. Add lemon flavoring; beat well. Add 2 cups flour sifted with baking powder; mix well. Add pecans, pineapple, cherries and remaining 2 cups flour; mix well. Fold in beaten egg whites; refrigerate overnight. Pour into two tube pans. Bake at 250 degrees for 2 hours to 2 hours and 30 minutes. Yield: 35 servings.

Sally R. Johnston
Griffin, Ga.

MAGIC FRUIT CAKE

1 pkg. dates, chopped
½ lb. coconut
1 c. chopped nuts
1 can sweetened condensed milk

Mix all ingredients. Pour into greased 9 x 9-inch pan. Bake at 350 degrees for 40 minutes. Cut into squares while warm. Yield: 15 servings.

Reine D. O'Rear
Commerce, Ga.

MIRACLE FRUIT CAKE

1 lb. candied pineapple
1 lb. candied cherries
1 lb. dates
1 lb. pecans
1 4-oz. pkg. coconut
1 can sweetened condensed milk

Combine all ingredients. Pour into two loaf pans lined with waxed paper or foil. Bake at 300 degrees for 1 hour. Remove paper immediately. NOTE: For individual cakes, line cup cake pans and bake for 45 minutes.

Ouida Moore
Kilgore, Tex.

ORANGE-FRUIT CAKE

1 lb. pecans, chopped
1 lb. pitted dates, chopped
3⅓ c. self-rising flour
2 c. sugar
1 c. soft margarine
6 eggs
1 c. milk
1 tbsp. vanilla flavoring
1 tbsp. lemon flavoring

Dredge nuts and dates in 1/2 cup flour. Cream sugar and margarine; add eggs, one at a time. Add remaining flour alternately with milk; add flavorings. Add nuts and dates; pour into 10-inch tube pan lined with greased waxed paper. Bake at 325 degrees for 1 hour or until done.

ORANGE SYRUP:

2 c. fresh orange juice
1 box confectioners sugar

Mix together and pour over hot cake. Let cool in pan for 30 minutes; turn out. Let stand upside down overnight.

Doris Joe Campbell
Great Falls, S.C.

FRUIT CAKES

FESTIVE NO-BAKE FRUIT CAKE

1 c. evaporated milk
4 c. miniature marshmallows
6 tbsp. rum flavoring
8 c. fine graham cracker crumbs
½ tsp. cinnamon
½ tsp. nutmeg
¼ tsp. cloves
2 c. seedless raisins
1 c. finely cut dates
1 ½ c. broken nuts
1 ½ c. cut up candied fruit

Combine milk, marshmallows and rum flavoring. Combine remaining ingredients; work in milk mixture until all crumbs are moist. Pack into mold; chill for two days before serving. Yield: 12 servings.

Mrs. Charlotte Wright
Ft. Riley, Kans.

PORK CAKE

Flour
½ lb. lean fresh pork
½ lb. pork fat or unseasoned sausage
1 pt. boiling water
2 c. sugar
1 lb. raisins, chopped
1 lb. English walnuts, chopped
1 lb. dates, chopped
1 tsp. salt
1 tsp. cinnamon
1 tsp. nutmeg
½ tsp. cloves
1 tsp. baking powder
1 tsp. soda

Sift flour three times; measure 5 cups. Combine meats and water; stir and partially cool. Add all remaining ingredients, mixing well. Pour into three loaf pans. Bake at 350 degrees until cake is done.

Mrs. Janie Coker
Macon, Ga.

SAUSAGE CAKE

1 lb. pork sausage
3 c. brown sugar
Flour
1 tsp. nutmeg
1 tsp. cinnamon
1 tsp. cloves
1 tsp. soda
1 c. hot black coffee
2 c. raisins
1 c. English or black walnuts

Combine sausage and brown sugar. Add 2 cups flour and spices. Add soda dissolved in coffee. Dredge raisins and nuts in flour; add to batter, mixing well. Pour into layer or loaf pans. Bake at 325 degrees for 2 hours and 30 minutes. Increase heat to 350 degrees; bake for 30 minutes longer.

Catherine Hammerle
Batesville, Ind.

TOMATO SOUP-FRUIT CAKE

½ c. shortening
1 c. sugar
1 tsp. soda
1 can tomato soup
2 c. flour
2 tsp. baking powder
1 tsp. cinnamon
½ tsp. ground cloves
1 tsp. nutmeg
1 c. raisins
1 lb. mixed fruits
1 c. chopped nuts

Cream shortening and sugar; stir in all remaining ingredients. Bake at 350 degrees for 50 to 60 minutes.

Mrs. Martha Hays
Montgomery, Ala.

WHITE FRUIT CAKE

1 lb. candied pineapple, chopped
2 lb. whole dates
1 lb. candied cherries
1 lb. walnuts
1 lb. Brazil nuts
1 ½ c. sugar
1 ½ c. flour
1 tsp. baking powder
Pinch of salt
4 lge. eggs, beaten

Mix fruits, nuts and dry ingredients; pour over eggs. Mix with hands. Put in tins; pat down well. Bake at 300 degrees for 1 hour. Yield: 3 loaves.

Eilene Ponzio
Niagara, Wisc.

FRUIT COCKTAIL CAKE

1 c. sugar
2 c. flour
2 eggs
2 tsp. soda
1 No. 2 can fruit cocktail and juice
½ c. brown sugar
½ c. coconut

Mix all ingredients except brown sugar and coconut; pour into well greased and floured long loaf pan. Sprinkle brown sugar and coconut over cake batter.

(Continued on next page)

TOPPING:
½ c. brown sugar
½ c. white sugar
¾ c. evaporated milk
1 stick margarine
½ c. pecans
½ c. coconut

Mix all ingredients except pecans and coconut; boil for 5 minutes. Add pecans and coconut. Spread over hot cake.

Pat Prosser
Childress, Tex.

FRUIT COCKTAIL CAKE

1 c. sugar
1 c. flour
1 tsp. soda
¼ to ½ tsp. salt
1 or 2 eggs, beaten
1 tsp. vanilla flavoring (opt.)
2 c. fruit cocktail, drained
½ c. brown sugar
½ to 1 c. nuts

Sift sugar, flour, soda and salt into bowl. Add eggs and vanilla; mix well. Add fruit cocktail. Pour into greased 8 x 12-inch pan. Sprinkle brown sugar and nuts over batter. Bake at 300 degrees for 1 hour and 20 minutes or bake at 350 degrees for 30 to 45 minutes. Cut into squares; serve with whipped cream. Yield: 12 servings.

Marian J. Johnson
Escondido, Calif.

FRUIT COCKTAIL PUDDING CAKE

1 egg
1 No. 303 can fruit cocktail and juice
1 c. sugar
1 c. flour
1 tsp. soda
½ tsp. salt
½ c. brown sugar
½ c. walnuts

Mix all ingredients except brown sugar and nuts; spread in greased layer cake pan. Mix brown sugar and nuts; sprinkle over batter. Bake at 325 degrees for 1 hour. Yield: 10 servings.

Mrs. John F. Weber
Sacramento, Calif.

GINGERBREAD

2 c. sifted flour
1 ¼ c. sugar
1 tbsp. cinnamon
1 tsp. baking powder
1 ½ tsp. ginger
¼ tsp. salt
½ c. shortening
1 egg
2 tbsp. molasses
1 tsp. soda
1 c. buttermilk
1 tbsp. butter

Sift all dry ingredients. Cut in shortening with pastry fork or blender until mixture resembles fine meal. Reserve 1/2 cup of the mixture. Add egg, molasses and soda dissolved in buttermilk to remaining dry mixture; beat for 2 minutes. Pour batter into well greased 12 x 9-inch pan. Combine reserved dry mixture with butter; sprinkle over batter. Bake at 350 degrees for 30 minutes. Yield: 12 servings.

Mrs. Curtis LeFever
Seattle, Wash.

GINGERBREAD WITH STREUSEL TOPPING

½ c. butter or margarine
½ c. sugar
1 egg, beaten
1 c. molasses
2 ½ c. flour
1 ½ tsp. soda
1 tsp. cinnamon
1 tsp. ginger
½ tsp. cloves
½ tsp. salt
1 c. hot water

Cream butter and sugar. Add egg and molasses. Sift all dry ingredients; add to sugar mixture. Add hot water; beat until smooth. Pour into greased oblong pan.

TOPPING:
1 c. (firmly packed) brown sugar
1 c. sugar
¼ lb. butter or margarine
1 c. chopped pecans

Combine all ingredients. Work with hands until mixture crumbles. Sprinkle over cake batter. Bake at 350 degrees for 30 minutes. Cut into squares. Yield: 24 servings.

Mrs. Dainty Guilliams
Fort Wolters, Tex.

JAM CAKE

2 c. sugar
1 c. butter
4 eggs
2 ½ c. flour
1 tsp. soda
1 tsp. salt

(Continued on next page)

1 tsp. nutmeg
1 tsp. cinnamon
1 tsp. cloves
1 c. buttermilk
1 tsp. vanilla flavoring
1 c. chopped pecans
1 c. raisins
1 c. blackberry jam

Cream sugar and butter. Beat in an egg at a time. Reserve 1/2 cup flour. Sift all remaining dry ingredients. Alternately add dry ingredients and buttermilk. Add vanilla. Dredge nuts and raisins in remaining 1/2 cup flour; add to batter. Add jam. Pour into three 8-inch paper-lined pans. Bake at 350 degrees for 25 minutes.

ICING:
1 stick margarine
1 box powdered sugar, sifted
7 tbsp. milk
1 tsp. vanilla flavoring

Brown margarine. Add sugar, milk and vanilla; mix until smooth. Spread on cake.

Juanita M. Triplett
Anniston, Ala.

JAM CAKE
3 c. sifted flour
1 tsp. salt
1 tbsp. cocoa
½ tsp. cloves
1 tsp. cinnamon
1 tsp. nutmeg
1 tsp. allspice
1 tsp. soda
1 ½ c. sugar
¾ c. shortening
1 c. buttermilk
3 eggs
1 c. jam

Sift all dry ingredients into large bowl. Cut in shortening; add buttermilk. Beat at medium speed for 2 minutes. Add eggs; beat for 2 minutes. Fold in jam. Pour batter into two greased and floured 9-inch layer pans. Bake at 350 degrees for 45 minutes. Cool in pans for 10 minutes. Remove and ice. Yield: 20 servings.

Mrs. Charles H. McGovney
West Union, O.

LADY BALTIMORE CAKE
3 c. sifted flour
3 tsp. baking powder
½ lb. butter or margarine
1 ½ c. sugar
1 egg
4 egg yolks

1 tsp. vanilla flavoring
1 c. milk

Sift flour with baking powder. Cream butter and sugar; add egg, beating well. Add one yolk at a time, beating after each additions. Add vanilla; add flour and milk alternately, beginning and ending with flour. Bake at 375 degrees for 18 to 20 minutes.

FILLING:
¾ pkg. seeded raisins, cut into fourths
2 oz. whiskey
2 c. sugar
½ c. water
4 egg whites, stiffly beaten
1 lb. nuts
Cherries

Soak raisins in whiskey overnight. Boil sugar and water to soft ball stage. Pour over egg whites. Beat until of spreading consistency. Add raisins and nuts. Spread between layers and on top and sides of cake. Decorate with cherries.

Marion Donahoe
Charleston, S.C.

LANE CAKE
3 ¼ c. flour
3 tsp. baking powder
¼ tsp. salt
1 c. butter
2 c. sugar
1 tsp. vanilla flavoring
1 c. milk
8 egg whites, stiffly beaten

Grease and line bottoms of three 9-inch layer pans. Sift flour with baking powder and salt. Cream butter and sugar until very light. Add vanilla. Alternately beat in flour mixture in fourths and milk in thirds until smooth. Fold in egg whites. Bake at 375 degrees for 20 minutes or until cake tester comes out clean. Cool for 5 minutes; remove from pans. Place on cake racks; remove paper.

FILLING:
8 egg yolks, slightly beaten
1 c. sugar
½ c. butter
1 c. chopped raisins
1 c. cut up candied cherries
1 lb. pecans, chopped
1 fresh coconut, shredded
1 tsp. vanilla flavoring
½ c. brandy

Combine egg yolks, sugar and butter. Cook over low heat or in top of double boiler until thickened, stirring constantly. Remove from heat; cool slightly. Add all remaining ingredients, reserving some coconut for top.

(Continued on next page)

Spread between and on top of layers. Sprinkle reserved coconut over top. Allow to stand for two or three days before slicing. Yield: 16 servings.

Mrs. Rodney K. Lowery
Fort Wainwright, Alaska

LANE CAKE

1 c. butter
2 c. sugar
3 c. sifted flour
⅛ tsp. salt
1 c. milk
1 tsp. vanilla flavoring
7 egg whites, stiffly beaten

Cream butter; add sugar gradually. Cream until fluffy. Add sifted dry ingredients alternately with milk. Add vanilla. Fold in egg whites. Pour into layer pans. Bake at 350 degrees for 25 minutes.

FILLING:
7 egg yolks, well beaten
1 c. sugar
½ c. butter or margarine
1 box seedless raisins
1 c. chopped nuts
1 c. (or more) coconut
1 tsp. vanilla flavoring
½ c. wine (opt.)

Cook egg yolks, sugar and butter until thick over low heat or in double boiler, stirring constantly. Add raisins, nuts, coconut, vanilla and wine. Spread thickly between layers and on top and sides.

Mildred Mason
Cherokee, Ala.

LEMON-CHEESE CAKE

1 c. butter
2 c. sugar
8 egg whites
4 c. flour
3 ½ tsp. baking powder
1 c. cold water
1 tsp. vanilla flavoring

Cream butter; add sugar gradually. Cream until light and fluffy. Add unbeaten egg whites; beat well. Sift all dry ingredients. Add water and flour alternately. Add vanilla. Pour into three layers. Bake at 425 degrees for 25 minutes.

FILLING:
1 c. sugar
1 apple, grated
1 tbsp. butter
Juice of 2 lemons

Grated rind of 2 lemons
8 egg yolks

Combine all ingredients; cook over hot water. Cool; spread between layers.

WHITE ICING:
2 c. sugar
1 c. water
2 egg whites
¼ tsp. cream of tartar

Cook sugar and water until it spins a thread. Beat egg whites with cream of tartar until stiff. Slowly pour syrup over egg whites; beat until thick enough to spread. Frost top and sides of cake.

Ann Fowler
West Point, Ga.

LEMON PARFAIT CAKE

1 pkg. yellow cake mix
4 eggs
1 pkg. all fruit flavored or lemon gelatin
¾ c. oil
¾ c. water
2 c. powdered sugar
Grated rind of 2 lemons
Juice of 2 lemons

Combine cake mix with eggs, gelatin, oil and water; beat for 2 to 4 minutes. Pour into 9 x 13-inch pan. Bake at 350 degrees for 30 to 45 minutes. Remove from oven; punch holes in top with fork. Pour mixture of powdered sugar, lemon rind and juice over hot cake. Return to oven for 1 minute, if desired. Yield: 15-20 servings.

Mrs. Henry A. Claflin
Millbury, Mass.

LEMON WONDER CAKE

½ c. butter or margarine
½ c. (packed) brown sugar
½ c. sugar
2 eggs, slightly beaten
Pulp of 1 med. lemon
Rind of 1 med. lemon
1 c. dates
2 ¼ c. flour
½ tsp. soda
2 tsp. baking powder
1 c. buttermilk or sour milk

Cream butter and sugars. Add eggs; beat for 1 minute. Grind lemon pulp and rind with dates; mix with 1/4 cup flour. Add to egg mixture. Add dry ingredients alternately with buttermilk. Pour into two greased 8-inch pans. Bake at 350 degrees for 30 to 35 minutes.

(Continued on next page)

BUTTER FROSTING:
3 c. sifted confectioners sugar
3 tbsp. cream
½ tsp. grated lemon rind
⅓ c. soft butter
1 tsp. lemon juice

Combine all ingredients; stir until smooth.
Yield: 12 servings.

Dorothy C. Haire
Phoenix, Ariz.

MARBLE CAKE
WHITE BATTER:
½ c. butter
1½ c. sugar
1 c. milk
2 c. flour
2 tsp. baking powder
1 tsp. vanilla flavoring
4 egg whites

Cream butter; add sugar and milk. Sift flour
and baking powder; add gradually to sugar
mixture. Add vanilla; fold in stiffly beaten
egg whites.

DARK BATTER:
½ c. butter
1 c. brown sugar
4 egg yolks, beaten
½ c. molasses
1 tsp. soda
1 c. milk
2½ c. flour
1 tsp. nutmeg
½ tsp. cloves
1 tsp. cinnamon

Cream butter; add sugar, egg yolks and molasses. Dissolve soda in milk; add to mixture.
Add sifted flour and spices. Pour batters alternately into greased tube pan. Bake at 350
degrees for 1 hour to 1 hour and 15 minutes.
Yield: 20 servings.

A. Miriam Wood
Hammonton, N.J.

MARBLE CAKE
1 c. sugar
½ c. shortening
2 eggs
⅔ c. milk
2 c. sifted flour
2 tsp. baking powder
½ tsp. salt
2 tbsp. molasses
1 tsp. cinnamon
½ tsp. nutmeg
¼ tsp. cloves

Cream sugar and shortening; add eggs, one at
a time, beating well. Add milk alternately with
flour sifted with baking powder and salt. Divide batter in half. Add molasses and spices
to one portion of batter. Alternate layers of
plain batter and spice batter in greased 9 x
9 x 2-inch pan. Bake at 350 degrees for 35 to
40 minutes.

LEMON CREAM FROSTING:
2 tbsp. butter
½ tsp. lemon rind
2 c. powdered sugar
3 to 4 tsp. hot cream
1 tsp. lemon juice

Mix all ingredients; spread on cake.

Mrs. Mary O'Shea
Woonsocket, R.I.

MARBLE CAKE
½ lb. butter or margarine
2 c. sugar
4 eggs, separated
2 tsp. vanilla flavoring
3 c. sifted cake flour
3¼ tsp. baking powder
½ tsp. salt
1 c. milk
1 c. chocolate syrup

Cream butter and sugar. Add egg yolks one at
a time; beat well. Add flavoring. Alternately
add sifted dry ingredients and milk. Fold in
stiffly beaten egg whites. Pour one-half batter
into a greased angel food pan. Add chocolate
syrup to remaining batter; mix well. Pour
over batter in pan. Bake at 350 degrees for 1
hour. Yield: 12-14 servings.

Mrs. H. R. Greene
Fairchild AFB, Wash.

MAYONNAISE CAKE
2 c. flour
1 c. sugar
4 tbsp. cocoa
½ tsp. salt
2 tsp. soda
1 c. cold water
1 c. mayonnaise
1 tsp. vanilla or walnut flavoring (opt.)
1 c. chopped walnuts (opt.)

Sift flour with sugar, cocoa, salt and soda. Mix
water and mayonnaise. Stir in dry ingredients.
Add flavoring; stir in nuts. Pour into two well
greased and floured 8-inch cake pans. Bake at
350 degrees for 30 minutes or until tests
done. Cool; frost with your favorite frosting.

Mrs. Helen Scott
Bedford, Va.

MINCEMEAT CAKE

1 c. mincemeat
1 c. chopped walnuts or pecans
1 tbsp. rum flavoring
1 tsp. vanilla flavoring
1 c. mayonnaise
1 ½ c. buttermilk
3 ¼ c. sifted flour
1 ½ c. sugar
1 tsp. salt
¾ tsp. soda
Grated rind of 1 orange

Combine mincemeat, nuts, rum flavoring and vanilla. Blend mayonnaise with buttermilk. Sift dry ingredients into mayonnaise mixture. Add orange rind; mix well. Stir in mincemeat mixture. Pour into tube cake pan lined with heavy brown paper. Bake at 325 degrees for 2 hours. Cool on wire rack. Frost with butter frosting, using orange juice as the liquid. NOTE: Cake improves upon standing and will keep for weeks wrapped in foil and refrigerated. Yield: 10 servings.

LaVerne Bretvick
Mount Vernon, Wash.

ONE-BOWL MINCEMEAT CAKE

2 c. flour
1 c. sugar
¼ tsp. salt
½ tsp. soda
½ tsp. baking powder
½ c. shortening
1 egg
2 c. prepared mincemeat

Sift all dry ingredients into large bowl; add shortening, egg and mincemeat. Beat at low speed on electric mixer for 3 minutes or until well blended. Pour into well greased and floured large loaf pan. Bake at 350 degrees for 40 to 45 minutes. Cool.

ICING:
2 ¼ c. powdered sugar
3 tbsp. margarine or butter
¼ tsp. maple flavoring
¼ c. evaporated milk

Combine all ingredients; beat until smooth. Spread over cool cake. Yield: 12 servings.

Mrs. Lois Peterson
St. Helens, Oreg.

BANANA-NUT CAKE

½ c. shortening
1 ½ c. sugar
2 eggs, slightly beaten
3 bananas, mashed
½ c. pecans
4 tbsp. sour milk

1 tsp. vanilla flavoring
2 c. flour
1 tsp. soda

Cream shortening and sugar. Add eggs and bananas. Add nuts, milk and vanilla gradually. Add mixture of flour and soda; beat well. Bake at 325 degrees until tests done.

Mrs. Margery S. Moffitt
Farmington, N.M.

BRAZIL NUT SENSATION

¾ c. sifted flour
¾ c. sugar
½ tsp. baking powder
½ tsp. salt
3 c. shelled Brazil nuts
2 pkg. pitted dates
1 c. well drained Maraschino cherries
3 eggs
1 tsp. vanilla flavoring

Sift all dry ingredients into combined nuts, dates and cherries. Mix with hands until nuts and fruits are well coated. Beat eggs until foamy; add vanilla. Stir into nut mixture until well mixed. Spread evenly in greased waxed paper-lined loaf pan. Bake at 300 degrees until done. Cool in pan on wire rack for 15 minutes. Remove from pan; peel off paper. Cool on rack. Wrap in aluminum foil; store in refrigerator. Yield: 14 servings.

Mrs. Mary L. Rumph
Columbia, S.C.

BUTTERNUT CAKE

½ c. butter
1 c. sugar
¼ tsp. salt
1 egg
2 egg yolks
¾ c. milk
2 c. cake flour
2 tsp. baking powder
Vanilla flavoring
1 c. chopped butternuts or walnuts

Cream butter and sugar; add salt, egg and yolks. Beat until creamy. Add milk, flour, baking powder and vanilla; beat for 2 minutes with mixer. Fold in butternuts. Pour into two greased and floured 9-inch layer cake tins. Bake at 350 degrees until tests done. Yield: 12 servings.

FROSTING:
½ c. sugar
½ c. brown sugar
½ c. water
2 egg whites, stiffly beaten
1 tsp. vanilla flavoring

(Continued on next page)

Mix sugars and water; boil until it spins a thread. Pour slowly into egg whites. Add vanilla; beat until cool. Yield: 12 servings.

Mrs. Carman H. Scadden
Sherman, N.Y.

NUT LOAF CAKE

½ c. butter
1 ½ c. sugar
3 eggs, slightly beaten
2 ½ c. flour
2 tsp. baking powder
½ c. milk
1 c. black walnuts

Mix butter and sugar until lightly creamed. Add eggs, flour sifted with baking powder, milk and nuts; mix until batter is firm. Bake in paper lined loaf pan at 325 degrees for 45 to 60 minutes. Do not open oven while baking. Glaze with sugar.

Mrs. Arthur F. Eliason
Charleston, S.C.

ENGLISH DATE-NUT CAKE

1 lb. dates, finely chopped
4 eggs, beaten
1 ½ oz. vanilla flavoring
2 tsp. orange flavoring
1 tsp. lemon flavoring
1 tsp. almond flavoring
2 tbsp. brandy or whiskey
1 c. sugar
1 c. flour
2 tsp. baking powder
½ tsp. salt
1 lb. walnuts or pecans

Combine dates, eggs, flavorings, brandy and sugar; beat well. Add flour sifted with baking powder and salt; mix well. Mix in nuts. Pour into loaf pan. Bake at 275 degrees for 2 hours and 30 minutes. Let stand for two weeks. Slice thin to serve. Yield: 30 servings.

Eythel J. Richardson
Jacksonville, Fla.

MILE-A-MINUTE CAKE

1 ¾ c. sifted flour
2 tsp. baking powder
1 tsp. salt
½ tsp. cinnamon
½ tsp. nutmeg
⅓ c. shortening
1 ⅓ c. brown sugar
2 eggs
½ c. milk

½ lb. dates, chopped
½ c. chopped nuts

Sift flour with baking powder, salt and spices. Combine all ingredients. Beat for 5 minutes; pour into 9-inch pan. Bake at 350 degrees for 1 hour. Ice with peanut butter icing.

Rosemary Reid
Old Town, Me.

HICKORY NUT CAKE

1 ½ c. sugar
½ c. butter
2 c. cake flour
2 tsp. baking powder
¾ c. milk
1 c. nuts
1 tsp. vanilla flavoring
4 egg whites
⅛ tsp. salt

Cream sugar and butter until light and fluffy. Sift flour with baking powder; add alternately with milk to sugar mixture. Add nuts and vanilla. Beat egg whites with salt; fold into batter. Pour into well greased and floured cake pans. Bake at 350 degrees for 30 to 35 minutes. Frost with a Seven-Minute frosting.

Marilynn J. Pilgrim
Muscatine, Iowa

LEMON-PECAN CAKE

1 lb. margarine
1 lb. brown sugar
6 eggs
4 c. flour
2 tsp. baking powder
1 lb. pecans
1 lb. candied cherries
1 lb. candied pineapple
2 oz. lemon flavoring

Cream margarine and brown sugar; add remaining ingredients, mixing thoroughly. Pour into large angel food cake pan. Place over a pan of water. Bake at 275 degrees for 2 hours or until done. Yield: 30 servings.

Dolphia Dawson Dies
Corpus Christi, Tex.

LEMON-PECAN CAKE

4 ½ c. sifted flour
1 tbsp. baking powder
¼ tsp. salt
2 c. margarine
1 box brown sugar
6 eggs, separated
½ c. milk
3 tbsp. lemon flavoring
4 c. chopped pecans

(Continued on next page)

Sift flour with baking powder and salt. Cream margarine and brown sugar. Add well beaten egg yolks. Add sifted dry ingredients alternately with milk and lemon flavoring. Fold in stiffly beaten egg whites and pecans. Pour into greased 10-inch tube pan. Bake at 325 degrees for 1 hour and 30 minutes. Cool in pan on rack.

Alice Edington
Jackson, Miss.

ORANGE-NUT-DATE CAKE

1 c. butter
2 c. sugar
4 eggs
1 tsp. soda
1 ⅓ c. buttermilk
4 c. sifted flour
2 tbsp. grated orange rind
1 lb. dates, chopped
1 c. broken pecans

Cream butter and sugar; beat in eggs, one at a time. Dissolve soda in buttermilk. Add flour alternately with buttermilk to butter mixture. Beat until smooth after each addition. Add orange rind, dates and pecans; pour into stem pan. Bake at 325 degrees for 1 hour and 30 minutes.

SAUCE:
2 c. sugar
1 c. orange juice
2 tbsp. grated orange

Combine all ingredients. Pierce top of cake with toothpick; pour sauce over cake.

Mrs. Julia B. Willey
Lone Grove, La.

NUT-RAISIN CAKE

2 c. sugar
2 sticks margarine or butter
5 eggs
3 c. self-rising flour
1 qt. whole pecans
1 box white seedless raisins

Cream sugar and margarine; beat in an egg at a time. Mix flour with nuts and raisins. Add to sugar mixture; mix until all nuts and raisins are covered. Pour into well greased tube cake pan. Bake at 325 degrees for 1 hour and 30 minutes.

Jean H. Alexander
Bishopville, S.C.

SOUTHERN PECAN CAKE

1 ½ c. butter
2 c. sugar
6 eggs
4 c. flour
1 nutmeg, grated
1 orange rind, grated
2 tbsp. baking powder
1 c. whiskey
1 qt. (or less) coarsely chopped pecans
½ lb. seedless raisins

Cream butter and sugar; beat in an egg at a time. Blend in all remaining ingredients. Pour into tube pan. Bake at 350 degrees for 2 hours.

Mrs. Earl L. Johnson
Orlando, Fla.

TOASTED BUTTER-PECAN CAKE AND FROSTING

1 ⅓ c. chopped pecans
1 ¼ c. butter
3 c. sifted flour
2 tsp. baking powder
½ tsp. salt
2 c. sugar
4 eggs
1 c. milk
2 tsp. vanilla flavoring

Toast pecans in 1/4 cup butter at 350 degrees for 20 to 25 minutes. Sift flour, baking powder and salt. Cream remaining butter; gradually add sugar, creaming well. Blend in eggs; beating after each addition. Add dry ingredients alternately with milk; add vanilla and pecans. Pour into three cake pans. Bake at 350 degrees for 20 to 30 minutes.

FROSTING:
¼ c. butter
1 lb. powdered sugar
1 tsp. vanilla flavoring
4 to 6 tbsp. cream
⅔ c. pecans

Cream butter, sugar and vanilla; add cream. Add pecans; frost cake layers. Yield: 16-18 servings.

Mrs. Mazie M. Rogers
Seminary, Miss.

BANANA-WALNUT CAKE

¼ lb. butter
1 c. sugar
1 c. mashed bananas
1 c. ground walnuts
2 eggs, separated
4 tbsp. sour cream
1 ¾ c. flour
1 tsp. soda
1 tsp. baking powder

(Continued on next page)

Cream butter, sugar and bananas; add walnuts, egg yolks and sour cream. Sift all dry ingredients; add to creamed mixture. Stir in beaten egg whites. Pour into tube pan. Bake at 350 degrees for 1 hour.

Ella Schwartz
Trenton, N.J.

DAINTY WALNUT CAKE

½ c. sugar
½ c. butter
2 eggs, separated
Vanilla flavoring
1 ½ c. flour
1 tsp. baking powder
1 ½ c. brown sugar
Finely chopped walnuts

Cream sugar and butter; beat in egg yolks. Stir in 1 teaspoon vanilla, flour and baking powder. Mix well; pat on bottom of pan. Beat egg whites well; add brown sugar and a small amount of vanilla. Spread over batter. Sprinkle with nuts. Bake at 375 degrees until done.

Sophie Aitken
Ipswich, Mass.

WALNUT CAKE

1 c. shortening
1 ¾ c. sugar
1 tsp. maple flavoring
4 eggs
3 c. cake flour
¾ c. milk
1 c. chopped walnuts

Blend shortening and sugar; beat until light and fluffy. Add maple flavoring. Add an egg at a time, beating well after each addition. Gradually add flour alternately with milk, ending with flour. Mix in walnuts. Bake at 350 degrees for 45 to 50 minutes. Yield: 8-10 servings.

Mrs. Rose Gangi
Newport, R.I.

WALNUT WONDER CAKE

2 c. sifted flour
1 tsp. baking powder
1 tsp. soda
½ tsp. salt
1 c. butter or margarine
1 ¼ c. sugar
2 eggs
1 tsp. vanilla flavoring
1 c. sour cream
⅓ c. (packed) light brown sugar
1 tsp. cinnamon
1 c. chopped walnuts

Sift flour with baking powder, soda and salt. Cream butter with 1 cup sugar until light and fluffy. Add eggs and vanilla; beat thoroughly. Blend in sour cream alternately with dry ingredients. Spread one-half of the batter in greased and floured 9 x 13 x 2-inch pan. Combine brown sugar, remaining 1/4 cup sugar, cinnamon and walnuts. Sprinkle one-half of mixture over batter. Repeat layers of batter and sugar mixture. Bake at 350 degrees for 35 minutes. Cut into squares; serve warm as coffee cake or dessert.

Mrs. Harold J. Hain
Whitehall, Mich.

APPLE-NUT CAKE

2 c. sugar
1 ¼ c. oil
3 eggs
3 c. cake flour
1 tsp. salt
1 tsp. soda
1 tbsp. almond flavoring
1 c. chopped nuts
4 med. apples, diced

Mix sugar, oil and eggs; add flour, salt and soda. Add flavoring, nuts and apples. Stir well; place on greased cookie sheet. Cook at 350 degrees for 45 minutes. Cut into squares. Yield: 24 squares.

Ada Barnes
Waycross, Ga.

DATE-PUMPKIN-NUT CAKE

1 ⅔ c. flour
1 ⅓ c. sugar
¼ tsp. baking powder
1 tsp. cinnamon
½ tsp. ground cloves
1 tsp. soda
½ c. margarine
½ c. water
½ c. chopped nuts
⅔ c. dates
1 c. pumpkin
2 eggs, well beaten

Sift all dry ingredients. Stir in margarine and water. Add nuts, dates and pumpkin. Stir in eggs. Pour into tube pan. Bake at 350 degrees for 40 to 45 minutes. Serve plain or with whipped cream. Yield: 12 servings.

Mrs. Mildred W. Klockau
Rock Island, Ill.

MARASCHINO-NUT CAKE

2 ⅛ c. sifted flour
1 ⅓ c. sugar
3 tsp. baking powder

(Continued on next page)

½ tsp. salt
½ c. shortening
¼ c. Maraschino cherry juice
16 Maraschino cherries, cut into eighths
½ c. milk
4 lge. egg whites
½ c. chopped nuts

Sift dry ingredients into bowl. Cut in shortening; add cherry juice, cherries and milk. Beat for 2 minutes with electric mixer on slow or medium speed or 300 strokes by hand. Add unbeaten egg whites. Beat for 2 minutes longer. Fold in nuts. Pour into two greased and floured 8-inch round layer pans. Bake at 350 degrees for 30 to 35 minutes. Cool; frost with a white icing.

Ilah Wilson
Herington, Kans.

ORANGE SLICE CAKE

1 tsp. baking soda
½ c. buttermilk
1 c. butter
2 c. sugar
4 eggs
1 tsp. salt
3 ½ c. plain flour
2 c. chopped nuts
1 lb. candy orange slices, chopped
1 box dates, finely chopped
1 can coconut

Dissolve soda in buttermilk. Cream butter and sugar; add eggs one at a time, mixing well after each addition. Alternately add one-half of flour-salt mixture with milk. Roll nuts, candy and dates in remaining flour. Add to batter with coconut. Pour into tube pan. Bake at 250 degrees for 2 hours and 30 minutes.

ORANGE SAUCE:
1 c. orange juice
2 c. powdered sugar

Mix well; pour over hot cake. Let stand overnight.

Martha L. Thurman
Newborn, Ga.

ORANGE LOVER'S CAKE

1 lge. orange
1 c. seedless raisins
⅓ c. walnuts
2 c. sifted flour
1 tsp. soda
1 tsp. salt
1 c. sugar
½ c. oil
1 c. milk
2 eggs

Grind orange pulp and rind, raisins and walnuts; reserve orange juice for topping. Sift dry ingredients; add oil and 3/4 cup milk. Mix well. Beat eggs with remaining milk; mix into

batter. Fold in ground mixture. Pour into well greased lightly floured 12 x 8 x 2-inch pan. Bake at 350 degrees for 40 minutes.

TOPPING:
Orange juice
⅓ c. sugar
1 tsp. cinnamon
¼ c. walnuts (opt.)

Pour orange juice over warm cake. Sprinkle with mixture of sugar, cinnamon and nuts. Yield: 12 servings.

Mrs. Frederick Jackson
Charleston, S.C.

OATMEAL CAKE

½ c. margarine
1 c. quick cooking oats
1 ¼ c. boiling water
1 ⅓ c. flour
1 c. sugar
1 c. brown sugar
2 eggs
1 tsp. cinnamon or vanilla flavoring
1 tsp. soda
1 tsp. salt

Place margarine, oats and water in bowl; stir well. Cool. Add all remaining ingredients, stirring well; pour into greased and floured 9 x 13-inch pan. Bake at 325 degrees for 40 minutes. Let cake set out of oven for 5 minutes.

TOPPING:
1 c. brown sugar
1 c. coconut
¼ c. margarine, melted
¼ c. evaporated milk

Blend sugar and coconut into margarine; stir in milk. Spread topping on cake; broil until bubbly. Yield: 12 servings.

Mrs. Helen Fisher
Baltimore, O.

BAKE-AHEAD ORANGE CAKE

½ c. shortening
1 c. sugar
2 eggs
2 c. flour
½ tsp. salt
½ tsp. baking powder
1 tsp. soda
⅔ c. buttermilk
1 c. raisins
Rind of 1 orange
½ c. chopped nuts

Cream shortening and sugar. Add eggs; mix well. Sift flour with salt and baking powder. Dissolve soda in buttermilk; add to sugar mixture alternately with dry ingredients. Grind raisins with orange rind. Add to batter with nuts. Pour into greased tube pan. Bake at 350 degrees for 45 minutes or until toothpick inserted in cake comes out clean.

(Continued on next page)

FROSTING:
Juice of 1 orange
½ c. sugar

Combine juice and sugar; pour over hot cake. Return to oven for 5 minutes or until topping is sugared. Yield: 18 servings.

Kay Wagner
Pope AFB, N.C.

FRESH ORANGE CAKE

1 c. shortening
1 c. sugar
2 eggs
2 c. flour
1 tsp. soda
½ tsp. salt
1 tsp. vanilla flavoring
1 c. buttermilk
1 c. raisins
Rind of 1 lge. orange

Cream shortening and sugar. Beat in an egg at a time. Add sifted dry ingredients alternately with vanilla and buttermilk. Grind raisins and orange rind; add to batter. Bake at 350 degrees for 45 to 60 minutes.

TOPPING:
1 c. sugar
Juice of 1 orange

Dissolve sugar in orange juice; pour over hot cake.

Mrs. W. C. Cathren
Natchez, Miss.

FROSTED ORANGE CAKE

1 c. butter
1 ¾ c. sugar
1 ½ tbsp. grated orange rind
4 eggs, separated
3 ½ c. flour
3 ½ tsp. baking powder
1 tsp. salt
1 c. minus 2 tbsp. water
2 tsp. orange flavoring

Cream butter and sugar; add orange rind. Add beaten egg yolks. Sift flour with baking powder and salt four times; add to creamed mixture alternately with water. Add orange flavoring. Fold in stiffly beaten egg whites. Pour into 9 x 13-inch cake loaf pan. Bake at 350 degrees for 40 minutes. Cool cake in pan.

ORANGE FROSTING:
2 c. powdered sugar
3 tbsp. butter, melted
Grated rind of 1 lge. orange
Orange juice

Combine all ingredients, adding enough orange juice to make a thick paste. Spread over cake in pan. Yield: 12 servings.

Mable Altoonjian
St. Augustine, Fla.

ORANGE-AMBROSIA CAKE

2 ½ c. cake flour
2 ½ tsp. baking powder
1 tsp. salt
1 ½ tsp. grated lemon rind
¾ c. shortening
¾ c. milk
3 eggs

Sift dry ingredients into bowl. Add lemon rind, shortening, 1/2 cup milk and 1 egg. Beat for 2 minutes with electric mixer at low speed or 200 strokes by hand. Add remaining milk and 2 eggs; beat for 2 minutes. Pour into two greased deep 9-inch round layer pans. Bake at 375 degrees for 25 to 30 minutes.

ORANGE FILLING:
¾ c. sugar
4 tbsp. cornstarch
Pinch of salt
1 c. fresh orange juice
¼ c. water
2 egg yolks, slightly beaten
2 tbsp. butter or margarine
2 tsp. lemon juice
¾ tsp. grated orange rind
¼ tsp. grated lemon rind

Mix sugar, cornstarch and salt; blend in orange juice, water and egg yolks. Cook over hot water for 10 minutes or until smooth and thick, stirring constantly. Add remaining ingredients, mixing well. Spread between layers of hot cake.

SEVEN-MINUTE FROSTING:
1 unbeaten egg white
¾ c. sugar
2 ½ tbsp. water
½ tsp. light corn syrup
Dash of salt
½ tsp. vanilla flavoring
1 marshmallow, cut up
1 c. coconut
1 tbsp. grated orange rind

Combine egg white, sugar, water, corn syrup and salt in top of double boiler; mix thoroughly. Place over rapidly boiling water; beat constantly with rotary beater for 5 minutes or until mixture holds a peak. Remove from heat; add vanilla and marshmallow. Beat until cool and thick enough to spread. Frost top and sides

(Continued on next page)

of cake. Combine coconut with orange rind; sprinkle over cake.

Elsie Whitmire
Milton, Fla.

ORANGE DRIBBLE CAKE

4 eggs, well beaten
1 box yellow cake mix
1 pkg. instant lemon pudding mix
¾ c. cold water
½ to ¾ c. oil
¼ tsp. salt (opt.)

Mix all ingredients; beat until smooth with an electric mixer at medium speed. Pour into a greased 9-inch square pan or ungreased 10-inch tube pan with removable bottom. Bake at 350 degrees for 35 minutes for square pan or 50 minutes for tube pan. If square pan is used, leave cake in pan. Cool for 5 minutes; prick holes in cake. Pour warm sauce over cake in pan. If tube pan is used, remove hot cake from sides of pan, leaving cake on bottom of pan. Prick holes in top of cake; pour glaze over cake.

ORANGE SAUCE:
2 c. confectioners sugar
⅓ c. orange juice
2 tbsp. water or additional orange juice
2 tbsp. butter

Combine all ingredients in double boiler over hot water; mix until blended. Pour over cake in square pan.

LEMON GLAZE:
2 c. sifted confectioners sugar
⅓ c. lemon juice

Combine sugar and juice; heat to boiling. Pour over warm cake. Garnish with thin lemon slices. Yield: 8 servings.

Mrs. George Powers
Pensacola, Fla.

ORANGE KISS-ME CAKE

Pulp and rind of 1 large orange
1 c. raisins
⅓ to ½ c. walnuts
2 c. flour
1 tsp. soda
1 tsp. baking powder (opt.)
1 tsp. salt (opt.)
1 c. sugar
½ c. shortening
1 c. milk
2 eggs

Grind orange pulp and rind with raisins and nuts. Sift dry ingredients. Cut in shortening; add 3/4 cup milk. Beat for 2 minutes until batter is well blended. Add eggs and remaining milk; beat for 2 minutes. Fold in orange mixture. Pour into greased and floured pan. Bake at 350 degrees for 30 to 45 minutes.

TOPPING:
⅓ c. orange juice
⅓ to ½ c. sugar
1 tsp. cinnamon
¼ c. chopped nuts

Drizzle orange juice over hot cake. Combine remaining ingredients; sprinkle over cake. NOTE: If desired, orange juice may be mixed with remaining ingredients and poured over cake.

Mrs. Harold Mackle
Amers, Okla.

ORANGE-RUM CAKE

1 c. butter or margarine
1 c. sugar
Grated rind of 2 oranges
Grated rind of 1 lemon
2 eggs
2 ½ c. sifted flour
2 tsp. baking powder
1 tsp. soda
½ tsp. salt
1 c. buttermilk
1 c. finely chopped walnuts or pecans

Cream butter; add sugar gradually, beating until light and fluffy. Add orange and lemon rind. Add eggs; beat until very light. Sift flour with baking powder, soda and salt. Add to creamed mixture alternately with milk. Fold in nuts. Pour into greased tube pan. Bake at 350 degrees for 1 hour.

RUM SAUCE:
Juice of 2 oranges
Juice of 1 lemon
1 c. sugar
2 tbsp. rum

Strain juices; mix with remaining ingredients. Bring to a boil. Pour over cake in pan. Store for one or two days before serving. Yield: 12-14 servings.

Mrs. Ruth H. Wall
Columbus, Ga.

SUNSHINE CAKE

¾ c. butter or margarine
1 c. sugar
1 tbsp. grated orange rind
1 tsp. vanilla flavoring
3 eggs
1 c. orange marmalade
½ c. raisins
3 c. sifted flour
1 ½ tsp. soda
1 tsp. salt
1 c. buttermilk

Cream butter with sugar, orange rind and vanilla until fluffy. Add an egg at a time, beating well after each addition. Stir in marmalade and raisins. Sift flour, soda and salt. Add to creamed mixture alternately with buttermilk. Turn batter into greased and lined 9-inch tube pan. Bake at 350 degrees for 1 hour. Cool in pan for 10 minutes; remove from pan. Yield: 12 servings.

AMBROSIA FROSTING:

1 ½ c. sugar
2 egg whites
5 tbsp. orange juice
⅛ tsp. salt
2 tsp. grated orange rind

Mix sugar, egg whites, orange juice and salt in top of double boiler. Beat with rotary beater until sugar is dissolved. Place over boiling water; cook, beating constantly, for 7 minutes or until frosting stands in peaks. Remove from heat; add orange rind. Beat until thick enough to spread. Frost cake; garnish with shredded coconut and orange sections. Yield: Frosting for two 8 or 9-inch layers.

Photograph for this recipe above.

WILLIAMSBURG ORANGE-WINE CAKE

Rind of 1 medium orange
1 c. raisins
½ c. butter or shortening
1 c. sugar
2 eggs, beaten
1 tsp. vanilla flavoring (opt.)
½ c. chopped nuts (opt.)
2 c. flour
1 tsp. soda
¼ to ½ tsp. salt
1 c. milk or sour milk

Grind orange rind and raisins. Cream butter and sugar until light. Add eggs, vanilla, nuts, raisins and rind. Sift flour with soda and salt; add alternately with milk. Pour into greased 9 x 13-inch pan or 8-inch square pan. Bake at 350 degrees for 30 to 40 minutes or until done. Frost or glaze.

(Continued on next page)

WINE ICING:
⅓ c. butter
2 c. powdered sugar
1 tbsp. grated orange rind (opt.)
Sherry

Mix all ingredients, adding enough Sherry to make of spreading consistency. Spread on cooled cake.

ALTERNATE GLAZE:
Juice of 1 orange
½ c. sugar

Combine juice and sugar; bring to a boil. Pour over warm cake. Yield: 16 servings.

Mrs. William J. Wheeler
Norfolk, Va.

MASHED POTATO CAKE

2 ½ c. flour
¾ c. cocoa
2 tsp. baking powder
1 tsp. cinnamon
1 tsp. nutmeg
1 c. butter
2 c. sugar
4 eggs, beaten
1 c. mashed potatoes
½ c. milk
1 tsp. vanilla flavoring
1 c. broken nuts

Sift flour several times; add cocoa, baking powder and spices. Cream butter and sugar; add eggs and potatoes. Add dry ingredients alternately with milk and vanilla. Add nuts. Pour into greased and floured tins. Bake at 350 degrees until tests done.

Mrs. Lillian Harvey
Las Cruces, N.M.

PEANUT BUTTER CAKE

½ c. shortening
1 c. peanut butter
1 c. sugar
2 eggs, well beaten
1 ½ c. flour
½ tsp. salt
3 tsp. baking powder
1 c. milk

Cream shortening, gradually adding peanut butter and sugar. Beat well; add eggs. Sift all dry ingredients; add alternately with milk. Pour into two layer pans. Bake at 375 degrees for 25 minutes. Ice with chocolate frosting when cool.

Louise Stanford
Honeoye Falls, N.Y.

BROWN SUGAR

1 c. butter
½ c. shortening
1 c. sugar
1 lb. light brown sugar
5 lge. eggs
3 c. flour
½ tsp. baking powder
1 c. milk
1 tsp. vanilla flavoring
1 c. chopped nuts

Cream butter and shortening. Add sugars; cream again. Add eggs. Sift all dry ingredients; add alternately with milk. Add vanilla and nuts. Pour into greased and floured pan. Bake at 325 degrees for 1 hour. Cool in pan.

Mrs. DeLanie Winchester
Morganton, N.C.

BUTTERMILK POUND CAKE

1 c. soft butter or margarine
3 c. sugar
5 eggs, at room temperature
¼ tsp. soda
1 tbsp. water
1 c. buttermilk
4 c. sifted flour
2 tsp. vanilla flavoring

Beat butter until fluffy with electric mixer. Add sugar gradually, beating constantly. Beat until well blended. Add an egg at a time, beating well after each addition. Dissolve soda in water; add to 1/2 cup buttermilk. Add 1 cup flour alternately with milk-soda mixture; beat well. Add remaining 3 cups flour and milk alternately, blending well. Add vanilla. Grease bottom of 10-inch tube pan; pour in batter. Stick a spatula every 1/2 inch vertically in batter to prevent air bubbles. Bake at 325 degrees for 1 hour and 30 minutes. Cool in pan on rack. Yield: 20 servings.

Sarah Miller
Moorhead, Miss.

CARAMEL POUND CAKE

1 box brown sugar
1 c. sugar
2 sticks margarine
½ c. shortening
5 eggs
3 c. flour
1 tbsp. baking powder
¼ tsp. salt
1 c. milk
1 tsp. vanilla flavoring
1 c. finely chopped pecans

Cream sugars, margarine and shortening thoroughly; add an egg at a time, beating after each addition. Sift all dry ingredients; add to

(Continued on next page)

creamed mixture alternately with milk. Add vanilla; fold in pecans. Pour into well greased and floured tube pan. Bake at 350 degrees for 1 hour and 30 minutes. Yield: 16-20 servings.

Mrs. Mamie G. Braun
Danville, Va.

CARROT POUND CAKE

1 ½ c. oil
3 c. self-rising flour
⅛ tsp. salt
2 c. sugar
1 tsp. cinnamon
4 eggs
1 c. chopped nuts
2 c. grated carrots
1 c. coconut

Pour oil in bowl; add sifted dry ingredients alternately with eggs. Add nuts, carrots and coconut; mix well. Pour into tube pan. Bake at 325 degrees for 1 hour.

Mrs. Lucy Gandy
Walhalla, S.C.

CHERRY POUND CAKE

1 c. shortening
1 c. sugar
1 tsp. grated lemon rind
1 tbsp. lemon juice
5 eggs
1 c. glace cherries
½ c. mixed peel
2 ½ c. sifted flour
½ tsp. salt
1 tsp. baking powder

Cream shortening, sugar, lemon rind and juice. Add an egg at a time, beating well after each addition. Combine cherries and peel with 1/2 cup flour. Sift remaining 2 cups flour with salt and baking powder; add to batter in three additions. Add fruit. Bake at 315 degrees for 1 hour and 45 minutes to 2 hours or until well done. Cool; wrap in waxed paper. Let stand for a week before using.

Mrs. R. D. Parkhurst
Cape May, N.J.

CHOCOLATE POUND CAKE

½ lb. butter
½ c. shortening
3 c. sugar
5 eggs
3 c. flour
½ tsp. soda
1 tsp. salt
4 tbsp. cocoa

1 c. milk
1 tbsp. vanilla flavoring

Cream butter, shortening and sugar. Add an egg at a time, beating after each addition. Sift all dry ingredients; add alternately with milk to sugar mixture. Add vanilla. Pour into greased tube pan. Bake at 325 degrees for 1 hour and 20 minutes. Yield: 20 servings.

Mrs. Phyllis Huskey
Belleville, Ill.

COCONUT POUND CAKE

2 c. sugar
1 c. shortening
5 eggs
1 pkg. flaked coconut
1 c. milk
2 c. flour
1 ½ tsp. baking powder
½ tsp. salt
1 tsp. coconut flavoring
1 tsp. butter flavoring
1 tsp. almond flavoring

Cream sugar and shortening. Add an egg at a time. Add coconut and milk. Add flour sifted with baking powder and salt. Add flavorings; mix well. Pour into well greased and floured tube cake pan or Bundt pan. Bake at 350 degrees for 1 hour.

TOPPING:
1 c. sugar
½ c. water
1 tsp. coconut flavoring

Combine sugar and water in a saucepan. Bring to boil; add flavoring. Drizzle on warm cake with a pastry brush. Yield: 24 servings.

Charlotte E. Kenell
Victoria, Tex.

CHOCOLATE-WALNUT POUND CAKE

1 pkg. German's chocolate
½ c. shortening
2 sticks butter
3 c. sugar
5 eggs
1 tsp. baking powder
1 tsp. lemon flavoring
1 tsp. vanilla flavoring
3 c. flour
½ tsp. salt
1 c. milk
1 c. black walnuts

Blend all ingredients. Bake at 350 degrees for 1 hour and 15 minutes.

(Continued on next page)

ICING:
1 box powdered sugar
2 tbsp. lemon juice
1 egg
½ c. cocoa
1 stick margarine
1 tbsp. black walnut flavoring
Milk

Beat all ingredients together, adding enough milk to make of smooth spreading consistency. Yield: 10 servings.

Mabel B. Mayes
Gastonia, N.C.

EASY AND DELICIOUS POUND CAKE

1 ½ c. shortening
3 c. sugar
3 ½ c. flour
1 tsp. baking powder
1 tsp. salt
1 c. milk
2 tsp. vanilla flavoring
1 tsp. lemon flavoring
6 eggs

Cream shortening and sugar well. Sift all dry ingredients; add alternately with milk. Add flavorings and eggs; mix well. Bake at 325 degrees for 1 hour and 15 minutes. Yield: 23 servings.

Mrs. A. O. Funderburk, Jr.
Greensboro, N.C.

EASY POUND CAKE

6 eggs, beaten
1 box powdered sugar
1 ½ c. soft butter
1 sugar box flour
½ c. pineapple juice
1 tsp. vanilla flavoring

Combine eggs and sugar; beat in butter. Add flour to mixture; beat well. Add pineapple juice; mix well. Stir in flavoring. Place in cold oven; turn heat to 325 degrees. Bake for 1 hour and 15 minutes.

Mrs. Harry A. Blount
Salisbury, N.C.

FROSTED CHOCOLATE POUND CAKE

1 ½ c. shortening
3 c. sugar
3 c. cake flour
6 eggs
1 c. milk
4 tbsp. cocoa

1 tbsp. vanilla flavoring
1 tbsp. almond flavoring
Dash of salt

Cream shortening and sugar; add flour, eggs and milk alternately. Beat thoroughly. Add all remaining ingredients; mix well. Pour into greased tube cake pan. Bake at 250 degrees for 1 hour and 30 minutes. Remove from pan; cool.

FROSTING:
1 box powdered sugar
1 egg white
½ stick margarine
3 tbsp. cold water

Blend sugar, egg white and butter; add cold water. Beat until smooth; spread on cake. Yield: 30 servings.

Mattie Lou Cato
LaFayette, Ala.

GERMAN'S CHOCOLATE POUND CAKE

½ lb. butter
½ c. shortening
3 c. sugar
1 pkg. German's chocolate, melted
5 eggs
3 c. flour
1 tsp. baking powder
1 c. milk
1 tsp. vanilla flavoring
¼ tsp. almond flavoring
1 tsp. lemon flavoring
1 c. black walnuts

Cream butter and shortening; add sugar, blending well. Mix in chocolate. Add an egg at a time, beating well after each addition. Add sifted dry ingredients alternately with milk and flavorings. Add nuts. Pour into large tube pan. Bake at 325 degrees for 1 hour and 15 minutes.

C.J. Truesdale
Tampa, Fla.

JIFFY POUND CAKE

2 c. flour
½ lb. butter or margarine
5 eggs
2 c. sugar
½ c. milk
2 tsp. baking powder
1 tsp. vanilla flavoring

Combine all ingredients; mix for 10 minutes. Pour into greased tube pan. Bake at 350 degrees for 50 to 60 minutes.

Mrs. S. Zimmelman
Camden, N.J.

LEMON POUND CAKE

1 ⅓ c. shortening
2 c. sugar
8 eggs
2 ⅔ c. flour
½ tsp. salt
1 tsp. baking powder
3 to 5 tbsp. milk
2 ½ tbsp. lemon flavoring
1 tsp. vanilla flavoring

Cream shortening and sugar until very creamy; add an egg at a time, mixing well. Blend in flour, salt, baking powder and enough milk to moisten. Add flavorings. Pour into well greased tube pan. Bake at 350 degrees for 1 hour or until done. Yield: 15 servings.

Mrs. George P. Graeser
Bartlesville, Okla.

LEMON POUND CAKE

1 stick corn oil margarine
1 c. shortening
2 ⅔ c. sugar
3 c. flour
¼ tsp. salt
1 c. milk
2 ½ tbsp. lemon flavoring
1 tsp. baking powder
5 eggs

Mix margarine, shortening and sugar until creamy. Add sifted flour and salt alternately with milk; beat with mixer at medium speed. Add flavoring and baking powder. Add eggs, one at a time, beating after each only until blended. Pour into greased and floured tube pan. Bake at 325 degrees for 1 hour. Immediately run knife around sides and tube; cool on rack for 5 minutes. Yield: 15 servings.

Mrs. Mary G. Aldridge
Elkin, N.C.

MAPLE-PECAN POUND CAKE

3 c. flour
¼ to ½ tsp. soda
1 c. butter
3 c. sugar
6 eggs, separated
1 c. sour cream
2 tsp. maple flavoring
1 c. chopped pecans

Sift flour and soda three times. Cream butter and sugar well. Add an egg yolk at a time; beat well. Add flour mixture and sour cream alternately beginning and ending with flour. Add flavoring and nuts. Fold in stiffly beaten egg whites. Pour into greased tube pan lined with greased waxed paper. Bake at 300 degrees for 1 hour and 30 minutes or bake at 325 degrees for 1 hour to 1 hour and 15 minutes. NOTE: For a lemon flavored cake, substitute lemon flavoring for maple; omit pecans.

Clara Nelle Nix
Conyers, Ga.

MILLION-DOLLAR POUND CAKE

1 lb. margarine, softened
3 c. sugar
6 eggs
4 c. flour
¾ c. milk
½ tsp. vanilla flavoring
½ tsp. almond flavoring

Cream margarine and sugar. Add eggs; beat well. Add flour alternately with milk and flavorings. Beat for 1 minute at high speed. Pour batter into greased and floured angel food pan. Bake at 300 degrees for 2 hours. Cool in pan; do not invert. Yield: 20 servings.

Mrs. Thelma Cooper
Tecumseh, Okla.

MOCK POUND CAKE

3 c. sifted cake flour
3 ½ tsp. baking powder
½ tsp. salt
½ c. margarine
1 8-oz. pkg. cream cheese
1 ½ c. sugar
3 eggs, beaten
⅓ c. milk
1 tsp. vanilla flavoring

Sift cake flour, baking powder and salt; set aside. Cream margarine and cream cheese. Gradually add sugar; beat until fluffy. Blend in beaten eggs. Add sifted dry ingredients alternately with milk, blending well after each addition. Stir in vanilla. Pour into greased and floured 10 x 4-inch tube pan. Bake at 350 degrees for 1 hour or until cake tests done.

Photograph for this recipe on page 11 .

ORANGE POUND CAKE

1 ⅔ c. sugar
1 c. shortening
5 eggs
5 tbsp. orange juice
2 c. cake flour

Cream sugar and shortening. Add an egg at a time, beating well after each addition. Add

(Continued on next page)

orange juice; beat well. Add flour. Pour into greased and floured tube pan. Bake at 325 degrees for 1 hour or until done. Yield: 15 servings.

Myra H. Patrick
Clermont, Fla.

POUND CAKE

½ lb. butter
2 c. sugar
6 eggs
1 tsp. vanilla flavoring
2 c. sifted flour

Cream butter well; gradually add sugar, beating after each addition. Add an egg at a time, beating well after each addition. Add vanilla. Fold flour into mixture, a small amount at a time. Pour into greased and floured 10-inch tube pan. Bake at 350 degrees for 45 minutes. Cool before removing from pan. No icing is needed. Yield: 16 servings.

Mary W. DeMyer
Fulton, Ky.

POWDERED SUGAR POUND CAKE

1 box powdered sugar
3 sticks margarine
6 eggs
3 ½ c. flour
1 tsp. orange flavoring
1 tsp. almond flavoring
1 tsp. vanilla flavoring
1 to 4 tbsp. milk (opt.)

Cream sugar and margarine. Add an egg at a time, mixing well after each addition. Mix in flour gradually. Stir in flavorings. If batter is too thick, add milk. Pour into greased and floured tube pan. Bake at 225 degrees for 2 hours. Yield: 25 servings.

Julia E. Miniard
Atmore, Ala.

RUM POUND CAKE

1 lb. soft margarine
1 1-lb. box confectioners sugar
1 sugar box flour
6 eggs
1 tsp. rum flavoring
½ tsp. nutmeg

Cream margarine and sugar. Add flour and eggs alternately, beating well after each addition. Add flavoring and nutmeg; beat well. Pour into greased and floured tube pan. Bake at 325 degrees for 1 hour and 15 minutes. Cool for 5 minutes; remove from pan. Yield: 20 servings.

Ouida Jones
New Albany, Miss.

SMALL POUND CAKE

1 1-lb. box confectioners sugar
¾ lb. butter
6 eggs
1 sugar box plain flour
3 tbsp. milk

Cream sugar and butter; add an egg at a time. Add flour slowly; add milk. Pour into greased tube cake pan. Bake in preheated 325 degree oven for 1 hour and 15 minutes.

Mrs. Louise B. Cobb
Hartsville, S.C.

VELVET POUND CAKE

2 sticks butter
½ c. shortening
3 c. sugar
6 eggs
3 c. flour
1 tsp. baking powder
¼ tsp. salt
1 c. milk
1 tsp. lemon flavoring
1 tsp. vanilla flavoring

Cream butter, shortening and sugar well. Add an egg at a time, beating well. Sift flour, baking powder and salt. Add flour mixture and milk alternately to sugar mixture. Add flavorings. Pour into greased and floured cake pan. Bake at 325 degrees for 1 hour and 30 minutes.

Mrs. Hoyt Watson
Florence, S.C.

SOUR CREAM POUND CAKE

2 ½ c. sugar
½ lb. margarine
6 eggs, separated
3 c. self-rising flour
¼ tsp. soda
½ pt. sour cream
½ tsp. vanilla flavoring
½ tsp. lemon flavoring

Cream sugar and margarine; beat in egg yolks. Mix in flour, soda, sour cream and flavorings; beat until fluffy. Beat egg whites until peaks form; fold into mixture. Pour into well greased angel cake pan. Bake at 325 degrees for 1 hour.

Mrs. T. L. Terrell
Cross City, Fla.

PRUNE CAKE

1 c. oil
2 ½ c. sugar
2 eggs

(Continued on next page)

59

1 tsp. vanilla flavoring
2 c. flour
1 tsp. soda
½ tsp. salt
1 tsp. cinnamon
1 tsp. nutmeg
1 tsp. allspice
1 c. buttermilk
1 c. cooked prunes, pitted
1 c. chopped nuts

Cream oil, sugar and eggs; add vanilla. Add sifted dry ingredients alternately with buttermilk. Stir in prunes and nuts. Pour into 9 x 12-inch pan. Bake at 325 degrees for 1 hour.

ICING:
1 c. sugar
½ c. buttermilk
½ tsp. soda
½ c. butter
1 tbsp. white corn syrup
Chopped nuts

Combine all ingredients except nuts; boil over low heat for 30 minutes or until soft ball stage. Do not beat. Pour over hot cake in pan; sprinkle with nuts. Yield: 8 servings.

Mrs. A. A. Lipscomb
Fairbanks, Alaska

PUMPKIN CAKE

2 c. sugar
1 c. shortening
3 c. mashed cooked pumpkin
2 eggs
3 ½ c. sifted flour
2 tsp. soda
2 tsp. baking powder
2 tsp. salt
2 tsp. cinnamon
1 tsp. cloves
2 c. seedless raisins
2 c. broken pecans

Cream sugar, shortening and pumpkin. Add eggs; beat until light and fluffy. Add dry ingredients. Lightly fold in raisins and nuts. Pour into 10-inch tube pan. Bake at 325 degrees for 1 hour and 30 minutes to 2 hours.

Mrs. William C. Harrelson
Asheboro, N.C.

RHUBARB CAKE

1 c. sugar
1 c. sour cream
1 egg
1 ½ c. flour
1 tsp. soda
½ tsp. salt
2 c. chopped rhubarb
½ c. brown sugar
½ c. chopped nuts

Mix sugar, sour cream and egg. Sift dry ingredients; add to sugar mixture. Add rhubarb. Put in greased 13 x 9 x 2-inch pan. Sprinkle with mixture of brown sugar and nuts. Bake at 350 degrees for 30 to 35 minutes. NOTE: Frozen rhubarb may be used, but cake must bake for 20 minutes longer. Yield: 20-30 servings.

Mrs. Kenneth Nielsen
New England, N.D.

ARABIAN SPICE CAKE

½ c. shortening
½ tsp. salt
¾ tsp. ginger
½ tsp. cloves
½ tsp. allspice
1 tsp. vanilla flavoring
1 c. (firmly packed) brown sugar
1 egg
½ tsp. soda
2 tsp. baking powder
2 ½ c. sifted flour
1 c. thick sour milk

Blend shortening, salt, spices and vanilla. Add sugar gradually; cream well. Add egg; beat well. Sift soda and baking powder with flour three times; add to creamed mixture alternately with milk, mixing after each addition until smooth. Pour into greased 9-inch square pan. Bake at 350 degrees for 50 minutes. Cool.

BROWN SUGAR FUDGE FROSTING:
¾ c. (firmly packed) brown sugar
¼ c. sugar
½ c. milk
1 tbsp. butter

Boil sugars and milk until syrup reaches 232 degrees or forms soft ball in cold water. Add butter. Cool to lukewarm, 110 degrees. Beat until thick and creamy. Spread over cake. Yield: 8 servings.

Mrs. Ruth M. Miles
Pittsburgh, Pa.

BACON GREASE CAKE

2 c. sugar
1 c. bacon grease
1 lb. raisins
1 tsp. cloves or allspice
1 tsp. cinnamon
2 c. hot water
⅛ tsp. salt
2 tsp. soda
3 ½ c. flour
1 tsp. vanilla flavoring
¼ c. chopped nuts

Mix sugar, grease, raisins, spices, water and salt; boil for 3 minutes. Add soda; beat well.

(Continued on next page)

Cool; add flour, flavoring and nuts. Pour into greased and floured 13 x 9-inch pan. Bake at 325 degrees for 1 hour.

Mrs. Gretta Anderson
Sutherland, Nebr.

COCOA-SPICE CAKE

1 c. shortening
1 tsp. vanilla flavoring
2 c. sugar
2 eggs
3 c. flour
3 tbsp. cocoa
½ tsp. cloves
1 tsp. cinnamon
¼ tsp. salt
2 tsp. (scant) soda
2 c. buttermilk

Cream shortening, vanilla and sugar. Add eggs; beat until smooth. Sift flour with cocoa, cloves, cinnamon and salt. Stir soda into buttermilk; add to creamed mixture. Before stirring, add sifted dry ingredients. Pour into large flat cake pan or tube cake pan. Bake at 350 degrees for 45 minutes or until cake springs back at touch. Yield: 24 servings.

Dorothy O'Neal
Carlsbad, N.M.

CRANBERRY-SPICE LOAVES

½ c. shortening
1 c. sugar
1 egg, beaten
1 c. raisins
½ c. chopped nuts
1 ¾ c. sifted flour
¼ tsp. salt
1 tsp. soda
1 tsp. baking powder
1 tsp. cinnamon
½ tsp. cloves
1 1-lb. can cranberry sauce, drained

Cream shortening and sugar; beat in egg. Stir in raisins and nuts. Sift dry ingredients; add to creamed mixture. Stir in cranberry sauce. Spoon into two greased and floured loaf pans. Bake at 350 degrees for 40 to 50 minutes. Cool. Yield: 8-16 servings.

Betty V. Addy
Toccoa, Ga.

EGGLESS-BUTTERLESS-MILKLESS CAKE

1 c. sugar
1 c. brown sugar
2 c. boiling water
1 c. shortening
1 c. chopped dates
1 c. dark and white raisins
1 tsp. cinnamon
1 tsp. nutmeg

4 tbsp. cocoa
2 tsp. soda
3 ½ c. flour
1 tsp. baking powder
½ tsp. salt
½ c. chopped nuts

Combine sugars, water, shortening, dates, raisins, spices and cocoa in saucepan. Simmer over low heat for 10 minutes. Cool to lukewarm. Add soda dissolved in a small amount of hot water. Stir in sifted dry ingredients; blend well. Add nuts. Pour into 9 x 12-inch pan. Bake at 325 degrees for 1 hour. Serve with whipped cream or ice with a caramel icing. Yield: 12 servings.

Mrs. Ruth Proctor
Jones, Okla.

FEATHER SPICE CAKE

2 ½ c. sifted cake flour
2 ½ tsp. baking powder
¼ tsp. salt
1 tsp. cinnamon
½ tsp. mace
¼ tsp. cloves
½ c. butter or other shortening
1 c. sugar
2 eggs
⅓ c. molasses
¾ c. milk

Sift all dry ingredients three times. Cream butter thoroughly. Gradually add sugar, creaming until light and fluffy. Add an egg at a time, beating well after each. Blend in molasses. Add dry ingredients alternately with milk, beating after each addition until smooth. Pour into two greased 9-inch layer pans. Bake at 375 degrees for 25 minutes or until done.

RAISIN NUT FILLING:

¾ c. (firmly packed) brown sugar
2 tbsp. butter
¼ c. water
¾ c. broken walnuts, toasted
¾ c. seeded raisins
2 tbsp. cream or rich milk

Heat sugar, butter and water in skillet; cook until it reaches 236 degrees or until a small amount of mixture forms a soft ball in cold water. Remove from heat; add nuts and raisins. Add cream until of right consistency to spread. Makes enough filling to spread between two 9-inch layers or on top of an 8-inch square cake. Spread between layers. Frost top and sides with Seafoam Icing.

Mary Agnes Crockett
Roanoke, Va.

MILKLESS, EGGLESS, BUTTERLESS CAKE

2 c. brown sugar
2 c. hot water
1 lb. raisins
⅔ c. lard
2 tsp. cinnamon
1 tsp. cloves
½ tsp. nutmeg
¼ tsp. salt
1 tsp. soda
4 c. flour
2 tsp. baking powder
Nuts (opt.)

Combine sugar, water, raisins, lard and spices; boil for 3 minutes. Add soda, flour, baking powder and nuts. Pour into mold pan. Bake at 350 degrees until cake tester comes out clean.

Mrs. Harry R. Puster
Charles Town, W. Va.

OLD SOUTH SPICE CAKE

2 c. sugar
1 c. butter or ½ c. shortening plus ½ c. butter
2 c. flour
½ c. cocoa
1 tbsp. allspice
1 tbsp. cinnamon
1 tbsp. cloves
½ tsp. salt
5 eggs
1 c. buttermilk
1 tsp. soda

Cream sugar and butter. Sift flour with cocoa, spices and salt. Mix 1/2 cup of dry ingredients with creamed mixture. Add an egg at a time, beating for 1 minute after each addition. Alternately add remaining dry ingredients and buttermilk mixed with soda. Pour into three greased and floured 9-inch cake pans. Bake at 375 degrees for 25 minutes. Cool on rack.

NUT-FRUIT FILLING:
¾ c. sweetened condensed milk
1 ½ c. sifted confectioners sugar
1 tsp. allspice
1 tsp. cinnamon
1 tsp. cloves
1 ½ c. ground raisins
1 c. chopped pecans

Blend all ingredients; do not cook. Spread between cake layers.

CARAMEL FROSTING:
½ tsp. soda
1 c. buttermilk
2 c. sugar
½ c. light brown sugar
1 stick butter
2 tbsp. white corn syrup

Dissolve soda in buttermilk; combine all ingredients. Cook over low heat until mixture forms a soft ball when tested in cold water. Remove from heat; beat to desired spreading consistency. If mixture hardens too much for spreading, add a little milk or cream. Frost top and sides of cake. Cool; wrap cake in foil or store in airtight container. Store at least two days before serving.

Ola Newberry
Gadsden, Ala.

ORANGE-SPICE CAKE

¼ c. shortening
1 c. sugar
1 egg, beaten
½ tsp. vanilla flavoring
2 c. flour
½ tsp. salt
1 tsp. soda
1 tsp. baking powder
2 tsp. mixed nutmeg, cinnamon and allspice
1 c. sour milk
2 oranges
1 c. nuts
1 c. golden raisins
Powdered sugar

Cream shortening and sugar; add egg and vanilla. Add sifted dry ingredients alternately with sour milk. Grind whole oranges, removing seed; grind nuts and raisins. Mix with oranges. Reserve 3/4 cup of the mixture; add remaining mixture to cake batter. Pour into greased flat baking pan. Bake at 350 degrees for 35 minutes. Blend reserved orange mixture with powdered sugar. Top hot cake with mixture. NOTE: Can be put under broiler for a few minutes to toast or lightly brown. Yield: 10-15 servings.

Mildred J. Lockwood
Horicon, Wisc.

SUGARPLUM CAKE

1 ½ c. prunes, cooked
2 c. sifted flour
1 ½ c. sugar
2 ½ tsp. baking powder
1 ¼ tsp. soda
1 tsp. salt
1 tsp. cinnamon
1 tsp. nutmeg
1 tsp. allspice
1 c. buttermilk
¾ c. cooking oil
3 eggs
1 c. chopped walnuts

Drain, pit and cut cooked prunes into small pieces. Sift flour with sugar, baking powder, soda and spices. Add buttermilk, oil and prunes, beating well for 1 minute and 30

(Continued on next page)

seconds with electric mixer or 225 strokes with spoon. Add eggs; beat for 1 minute and 30 seconds more. Stir in walnuts. Pour into well greased and lightly floured 13 x 9-inch pan. Bake at 325 degrees for 40 to 45 minutes. Serve warm with butter sauce.

BUTTER SAUCE:
1 c. sugar
2 tbsp. cornstarch
½ c. buttermilk
½ c. butter
1 tsp. vanilla flavoring

Combine sugar and cornstarch in saucepan. Add buttermilk, butter and vanilla. Bring to a boil; boil for 1 minute, stirring constantly. Serve warm over cake. If too thick, thin with a few drops of water. Yield: 12-16 servings.

Mrs. Helen S. Bader
Cincinnati, O.

MOLASSES SPONGE CAKE
½ c. shortening
½ c. sugar
2 eggs
1 c. molasses
2 ½ c. flour
1 tsp. (scant) soda
1 tsp. salt
1 tsp. cloves
1 tsp. nutmeg
1 tsp. cinnamon
1 c. hot water
1 c. semi-sweet chocolate pieces

Cream shortening and sugar; add an egg at a time, beating well after each addition. Add molasses. Beat until thoroughly creamed and fluffy. Add sifted dry ingredients; mix. Blend in hot water. Pour into greased and floured 13 x 9-inch pan. Lightly coat chocolate pieces with flour; add to batter. Tap chocolates lightly with fork to press into batter. Bake at 350 degrees for 30 minutes. Cool before serving. Yield: 12 servings.

Mrs. Margaret A. Tonyes
Carle Place, N.Y.

ANGEL SPONGE CAKE
4 eggs, separated
7 tbsp. water
1 ½ c. sugar
1 ½ c. sifted cake flour
½ tsp. salt
½ tsp. vanilla or almond flavoring
½ tsp. cream of tartar

Beat egg yolks and water for 10 minutes at high speed. Gradually add sugar; beat for at least 5 minutes. Sift flour again; add salt. Fold flour mixture gradually into egg mixture. Add flavoring. Beat egg whites and cream of tartar until peaks are formed.

Pour into sponge cake pan. Bake at 350 degrees for 1 hour. Yield: 12 servings.

Mrs. Edward M. Simon, Jr.
Metuchen, N.J.

ORANGE SPONGE CAKE
6 eggs, separated
1 tbsp. grated orange peel
½ c. orange juice
1 ½ c. sugar
¼ tsp. salt
1 ⅓ c. sifted cake flour
1 tsp. cream of tartar

Beat egg yolks until thick and lemon colored; add orange peel and orange juice. Beat until very thick. Gradually beat in 1 cup sugar and salt. Fold in flour, a little at a time. Beat egg whites with cream of tartar until soft peaks form. Gradually add remaining 1/2 cup sugar, beating until stiff peaks form. Thoroughly fold into yolk mixture. Pour into ungreased 10-inch tube pan. Bake at 325 degrees for 55 minutes or until done. Invert pan to cool. Glaze.

ORANGE GLAZE:
1 ½ c. powdered sugar
2 tbsp. orange juice

Combine sugar and juice. Spoon over cake. Garnish with orange slices. Yield: 16 servings.

Mrs. Roy W. Snead
Boron, Calif.

QUICK SPONGE CAKE
2 eggs, well beaten
1 c. sugar
1 tsp. vanilla flavoring
1 tsp. baking powder
1 c. flour
⅛ tsp. salt
½ c. milk
1 tbsp. butter

Mix eggs, sugar and vanilla; beat well. Combine all dry ingredients; fold into egg mixture. Heat milk with butter to boiling point; add to egg mixture. Beat well. Batter will be thin. Pour into 9-inch square pan. Bake at 350 degrees for 30 minutes.

ICING:
5 tbsp. butter
5 tbsp. brown sugar
2 tbsp. thin cream
⅔ c. coconut
½ c. chopped nuts

Mix all ingredients; boil for 1 minute. Pour over hot cake; place under broiler for a few

(Continued on next page)

seconds or until coconut browns. Yield: 6 servings.

Mrs. C. E. Jones
Leitchfield, Ky.

SPONGE CAKE

6 eggs, separated
1 c. sugar
1 tbsp. lemon juice
1 ½ tsp. grated lemon rind
½ tsp. salt
1 c. sifted cake flour

Beat egg yolks until thick; gradually add sugar. Add lemon juice and rind. Beat salt with egg whites until stiff but not dry. Fold one-half of the mixture into sugar mixture. Gradually fold in flour. Fold in remaining egg whites. Pour into ungreased shallow pan or tube pan. Bake at 300 degrees for 30 to 60 minutes, depending on size of pan. Invert pan on cake cooler; remove when cold. Sprinkle top with powdered sugar. Yield: 12 servings.

Mrs. Charlotte Whalley
River Edge, N.J.

VELVET SPONGE CAKE

1 ½ c. cake flour
3 tsp. baking powder
¼ tsp. salt
6 egg yolks, beaten
2 c. sugar
4 egg whites, beaten
1 c. boiling milk
Powdered sugar frosting
Ground peanuts

Sift flour, baking powder and salt three times. Combine egg yolks and sugar; beat for 15 minutes. Gradually mix in egg whites, milk and flour mixture alternately, beating until smooth. Pour into ungreased 9 x 13 1/2-inch pan. Bake at 325 degrees for 1 hour. Cool; cut into squares. Frost with a thin butter and powdered sugar frosting. Sprinkle with ground peanuts. Place on waxed paper to set before storing. Yield: 24 servings.

Mrs. William G. Cherry
Hermiston, Oreg.

SWEET POTATO CAKE

1 c. butter or margarine
2 c. sugar
4 eggs
2 ½ c. reconstituted yam flakes or mashed
    sweet potatoes
1 tsp. vanilla flavoring
1 tsp. cinnamon
½ tsp. nutmeg
3 c. flour
½ tsp. salt
2 tsp. baking powder
1 tsp. soda
½ c. chopped nuts
½ c. coconut

Cream butter thoroughly. Pour in sugar gradually, beating and creaming well. Beat in an egg at a time, beating well after each addition. Add mashed potatoes, vanilla and spices. Add sifted flour, salt, baking powder and soda. Fold in nuts and coconut. Pour into large loaf pan. Bake at 325 degrees for 1 hour and 15 minutes. Yield: 25 servings.

Mrs. Suzanne H. Peery
Chatham, Va.

STRAWBERRY JAM CAKE

¾ c. butter or margarine
1 c. sugar
3 eggs
2 c. flour
1 tsp. soda
1 tsp. cinnamon
¾ tsp. allspice
¾ tsp. cloves
¾ tsp. nutmeg
6 tbsp. buttermilk
1 c. strawberry jam, beaten

Cream butter and sugar. Add an egg at a time, beating after each addition. Add flour sifted with soda and spices alternately with buttermilk. Add jam. Pour into two layer pans. Bake at 350 degrees for 40 to 45 minutes.

ICING:
2 c. sugar
2 tbsp. light corn syrup
1 c. buttermilk
1 tsp. soda
1 stick margarine
1 tsp. vanilla flavoring
1 c. pecans

Boil sugar, syrup, buttermilk and soda in large saucepan; stir occasionally until it forms soft ball in cool water. Stir in margarine and vanilla. Beat while it cools. Spread on cake. Sprinkle with nuts. Yield: 10-12 servings.

Frankie Spicer
Magnolia, Ark.

CHOCOLATE UPSIDE-DOWN CAKE

1 square chocolate
2 tbsp. butter
1 c. sifted flour
½ tsp. salt
¾ c. sugar

(Continued on next page)

Make a batch of homemade candy and your children will think you're the best Mom in the world. Give a gift of candy and your neighbors will think you're the best friend in the world.

FONDANT-STUFFED FRUITS

⅓ c. each margarine and light corn syrup
1 tsp. vanilla
½ tsp. salt
1 lb. sifted confectioners sugar
Food coloring
Dried, pitted apricots, prunes and dates

Cream margarine slightly; blend in syrup, vanilla and salt. Add sugar and mix in with spoon. Knead mixture. Turn onto board; knead again until mixture is blended and smooth. Knead in food coloring as desired. Store in cool place. Shape fondant into small rolls; stuff into fruits. Yield: 1⅓ lb. fondant.

PEANUT BRITTLE

1 c. light or dark corn syrup
⅛ tsp. salt
1 c. sugar
¼ c. water
2 tbsp. margarine
1½ c. shelled peanuts
2 tsp. hot water
1 tsp. baking soda

Combine first five ingredients. Cook to soft crack stage (280 degrees) or until small amount separates into hard, but not brittle threads when dropped into cold water. Gradually stir in peanuts so mixture continues to boil. Cook, stirring, to hard crack stage (300 degrees) or until small amount seperates into hard, brittle threads when tested in cold water. Remove from heat. Stir hot water into soda; beat thoroughly into brittle. Turn onto heavily buttered baking sheet; spread very thin with a spatula. Cool 5 minutes. Turn warm brittle upside down; stretch to desired thickness. Cool and break into irregular pieces. Yield: 1¼ lb. brittle.

NO-COOK PEANUT BUTTER ROLL

¼ c. creamy peanut butter
¼ c. dark corn syrup
2 tsp. water
2 c. sifted confectioners sugar
¼ c. instant nonfat dry milk
¼ tsp. salt
1 c. flaked coconut

Blend peanut butter and syrup; stir in water. Sift sugar with dry milk and salt; mix into peanut butter. Add coconut. Knead until well blended. Shape into roll; wrap in waxed paper. Chill until firm. Cut into ¼-inch slices. Yield: ¾ lb. candy.

See photograph on reverse page.

2 tsp. baking powder
½ c. nuts
½ c. milk
1 tsp. vanilla flavoring

Melt chocolate with butter. Sift all dry ingredients; add nuts. Add to chocolate alternately with milk. Stir in vanilla. Pour into baking pan.

TOPPING:
½ c. sugar
½ c. brown sugar
4 tsp. (rounded) cocoa
1 c. boiling water

Combine sugars and cocoa; sprinkle over batter. Pour water over all. Bake at 325 degrees for 20 to 25 minutes. Yield: 12 servings.

Marcia Traer
Davenport, Iowa

CHOCOLATE UPSIDE-DOWN CAKE
¾ c. sugar
3 tbsp. cocoa
½ c. nuts
1 tsp. vanilla flavoring
½ c. milk
2 tsp. butter, melted
1 c. flour
2 tsp. baking powder

Combine all ingredients; mix thoroughly. Pour into 9-inch square pan.

TOPPING:
½ c. brown sugar
1 tbsp. cocoa
Dash of salt
1 ½ c. hot water

Mix sugar, cocoa and salt; sprinkle over batter. Pour hot water over batter. Bake at 375 degrees for 20 minutes. Serve with whipped cream. Yield: 4 servings.

Mrs. Elva Hauser
Hayden, N.M.

EASY UPSIDE-DOWN CAKE
1 c. (packed) brown sugar
¼ c. butter, melted
1 No. 2 can sliced pineapple
7 Maraschino cherries, halved
1 egg
½ c. milk
½ tsp. vanilla flavoring
1 9½-oz. pkg. yellow cake mix
Whipped cream

Sprinkle brown sugar into 9 x 9 x 2-inch pan. Pour butter over sugar. Arrange pineapple

slices and cherries on top of sugar. Combine egg, milk and flavoring; add cake mix. Beat for 2 minutes at a medium speed. Spread batter over pineapple. Bake at 350 degrees for 50 minutes. Cool in pan for 5 minutes. Invert on serving plate. Serve with whipped cream. Yield: 8 servings.

Mrs. Chesley Platner
Burlington, Wisc.

PEACH UPSIDE-DOWN CAKE
BATTER:
1 c. flour
½ c. sugar
2 tsp. baking powder
¼ stick butter
½ c. milk

Combine all ingredients, mixing well. Put batter in baking dish.

FRUIT MIXTURE:
Peaches
1 c. sugar
Nutmeg to taste
1 c. water

Combine all ingredients. Pour over batter. Bake at 375 to 400 degrees for 50 minutes. Cake will rise to top and fruit will be on bottom. NOTE: Canned or frozen fruit or berries may be used. Yield: 6 servings.

Mrs. Naomi Burrows
Columbus, O.

PEAR UPSIDE-DOWN CAKE
TOPPING:
2 tbsp. butter or margarine
¼ c. corn syrup
¼ c. brown sugar
6 pear halves, cooked or canned
½ c. walnut halves

Melt butter in 9-inch square cake pan. Add syrup and brown sugar; blend. Place pears and walnuts over mixture.

BATTER:
⅓ c. shortening
½ c. sugar
1 egg, beaten
⅔ c. molasses
2 c. flour
½ tsp. salt
2 tsp. soda
1 tsp. cinnamon
2 tsp. ginger
¾ c. sour milk

Thoroughly cream shortening and sugar. Add egg; beat thoroughly. Add molasses; beat. Add sifted dry ingredients alternately with milk. Pour batter over pears. Bake at 350 degrees

(Continued on next page)

for 1 hour to 1 hour and 10 minutes. Serve with whipped cream cheese.

Mrs. Freda B. Muir
El Centro, Calif.

PINEAPPLE UPSIDE-DOWN CAKE

TOPPING:
Light brown sugar
Butter
Drained pineapple slices

Cover bottom of heavy baking pan with brown sugar. Dot generously with butter. Place pineapple slices in pan.

BATTER:
3 eggs
1 ½ c. sugar
½ c. water
1 ½ c. pastry flour
1 ½ tsp. baking powder
1 tsp. vanilla flavoring

Beat eggs until very light; gradually beat in sugar. Add water and sifted dry ingredients alternately; stir in vanilla. Pour over topping. Bake at 350 degrees for 1 hour to 1 hour and 15 minutes. Invert on platter. Garnish with cherries and nuts. Serve with whipped cream.

Mrs. John H. Ballinger
Bridgeton, N.J.

PINEAPPLE UPSIDE-DOWN CAKE

½ c. (firmly packed) brown sugar
Butter
9 canned pineapple slices
9 Maraschino cherries
1 10-oz. pkg. white cake mix

Spread sugar in greased 9-inch square pan. Dot with butter; put pineapple in pan with a cherry in center of each slice. Prepare cake mix as directed on package. Pour over fruit. Bake as directed on package for a square cake. Remove from oven; invert at once onto plate. Yield: 9 servings.

Mrs. Clyde Green
Remlik, Va.

CRUNCH CAKE

2 c. sugar
2 c. sifted cake flour
1 c. shortening
6 eggs
1 tsp. vanilla flavoring
1 tsp. lemon flavoring

Mix sugar, flour, shortening and eggs in mixing bowl until creamy and smooth. Beat

for 8 to 10 minutes with electric mixer or by hand mix for 12 minutes. Add vanilla and lemon flavorings. Mix well for 1 minute. Pour into slightly greased tube pan. Bake at 350 degrees for 1 hour or until firm and brown. NOTE: In warm weather, be sure shortening and eggs are cold. Yield: 20 servings.

Mrs. R. D. Dyson
Cairo, Ga.

FLUFFY YELLOW PINEAPPLE-
MARSHMALLOW CAKE

1 c. shortening or margarine
2 c. sugar
4 eggs, separated
1 tsp. vanilla flavoring
3 c. cake flour
¼ tsp. salt
3 tsp. baking powder
1 c. milk

Cream shortening and sugar. Add egg yolks and vanilla; beat well. Add sifted dry ingredients alternately with milk. Fold in egg whites. Pour into three waxed paper-lined 8-inch cake pans. Bake at 350 degrees for 30 minutes.

FILLING:
3 c. sugar
1 ½ c. water
¾ pkg. marshmallows
3 egg whites, stiffly beaten
1 No. 2 ½ can crushed pineapple
Grated coconut (opt.)

Boil sugar and water until it spins a thread. Add marshmallows. Pour over egg whites. Spread slightly drained pineapple between layers. Cover with filling. Sprinkle coconut over filling.

Quay Michael
Booneville, Miss.

FOUNDATION CAKE

¾ c. butter
2 c. sugar
4 eggs
3 c. plain flour
3 tsp. baking powder
1 tsp. salt
1 tsp. vanilla flavoring
1 c. sweet milk

Cream butter until soft. Add sugar gradually while beating. Add an egg at a time, beating well after each. Sift flour, baking powder and salt three times. Add vanilla to milk. Add dry ingredients alternately with milk to creamed mixture, beating well after each addition. Place in three 9-inch cake pans which have been lined with waxed paper and

(Continued on next page)

greased. Bake at 375 degrees for 25 minutes.
Yield: 30 cup cakes or one 3-layer cake.

Doris Gunter
Pelion, S.C.

OLD-FASHIONED YELLOW LAYER CAKE

¾ c. butter
1 ¾ c. sugar
4 eggs, separated
2 ½ c. cake flour
2 ½ tsp. baking powder
¾ c. milk
Vanilla flavoring

Cream butter and sugar until light and
fluffy. Add beaten egg yolks; mix well. Sift
flour and baking powder three times. Add
flour mixture and milk alternately to cream
mixture. Add vanilla. Fold in stiffly beaten
egg whites; do not beat. Bake at 350 degrees
until cake springs back when touched. Cool;
add frosting. Yield: 24 servings.

Mrs. Estella Leary
Winston-Salem, N.C.

1-2-3-4 CAKE

1 c. butter
2 c. sugar
3 eggs
4 c. flour
4 tsp. baking powder
1 c. milk

Cream butter and sugar. Add eggs; beat
well. Sift dry ingredients; add alternately
with milk to batter. Pour into greased and
floured 15 x 10-inch sheet pan. Bake at 350
degrees for 35 minutes. Yield: 30 servings.

Alberta Burton
Carlsbad, N.M.

CARAWAY LUNCHEON CAKE

¼ c. margarine or butter
⅔ c. plus 1 tbsp. sugar
1 egg, beaten
1 ⅔ c. sifted flour
2 tsp. baking powder
¼ tsp. salt
¾ c. milk
½ tsp. vanilla flavoring
1 tbsp. caraway seed

Cream margarine and 2/3 cup sugar; add egg.
Beat until mixture is fluffy. Sift all dry ingredients; combine milk and vanilla. Add dry
mixture and liquid alternately to creamed
mixture. Stir in caraway seed. Pour into
greased pan; sprinkle with 1 tablespoon sugar.

Bake at 375 degrees for 25 minutes. Yield: 8
servings.

Eunice Hager
Chelsea, Mass.

GRAHAM CRACKER CAKE

½ lb. butter
2 c. sugar
4 eggs
1 1-lb. bag graham cracker crumbs
1 tsp. baking powder
1 tsp. soda
1 c. milk
1 tsp. vanilla flavoring
1 c. chopped nuts
1 c. grated coconut

Cream butter and sugar. Add eggs, one at a
time, beating well after each addition. Mix
graham cracker crumbs, baking powder and
soda. Add to sugar mixture alternately with
milk; blend well. Add vanilla. Stir in nuts and
coconut. Pour into greased cake pans. Bake at
350 degrees for 20 to 30 minutes.

FILLING:
1 box powdered sugar
1 stick butter
1 can crushed pineapple, drained
¼ to ½ c. fresh coconut

Combine sugar, butter and pineapple. Cook
over medium heat until thick. Add coconut;
spread between layers of cake. Yield: 10 servings.

Mrs. Ethel S. Helms
Waxha, N.C.

GUM DROP CAKE

1 c. chopped gum drops
1 c. chopped nuts or dates
2 c. flour
1 tsp. baking powder
½ tsp. salt
½ c. butter
½ c. sugar
2 eggs
1 tsp. vanilla flavoring
½ c. milk

Dredge gum drops and nuts with 1/2 cup
flour. Sift remaining flour with baking powder
and salt. Cream butter and sugar; add eggs
and vanilla, beating until fluffy. Alternately
add dry ingredients and milk. Beat for 2
minutes at medium speed of electric mixer.
Fold in gum drops and nuts. Pour into
greased loaf pan. Bake at 325 degrees for 30
minutes. Increase heat to 350 degrees; bake
for 30 minutes longer or until done. Frost
with a thin icing. Yield: 12-16 servings.

Frieda B. Cooley
Windsor, Vt.

MISCELLANEOUS CAKES

MAPLE SUGAR CAKE

1 c. maple sugar
½ c. shortening
1 egg
2 c. flour
½ tsp. soda
2 tsp. baking powder
1 tsp. salt
1 ½ tsp. cinnamon
½ tsp. cloves
1 c. buttermilk or sour milk
½ c. raisins (opt.)

Cream sugar and shortening. Add egg; beat well. Combine all dry ingredients; add alternately with milk to creamed mixture. Fold in raisins. Pour into greased loaf pan. Bake at 350 degrees for 30 minutes. Yield: 12 servings.

Mrs. Clyde A. Dunlap
Arlington, Vt.

PEACH DESSERT CAKE

½ c. butter
½ c. plus ⅓ c. sugar
2 eggs
1 c. sifted flour
1 tsp. baking powder
¼ tsp. salt
2 c. sliced peaches, drained
1 ½ tsp. cinnamon

Cream butter; gradually add 1/2 cup sugar, beating until light and fluffy. Add eggs, one at a time, beating vigorously after each addition. Add mixed and sifted dry ingredients. Spread in greased and floured 13 x 9 x 2-inch pan; top with peaches. Sprinkle with mixture of remaining 1/3 cup sugar and cinnamon. Bake at 350 degrees for 35 to 40 minutes. Yield: 8 servings.

Isabella Walters
Rosedale, N.Y.

PEPPER CAKE

1 c. sugar
1 c. brown sugar
1 c. oil
3 eggs
2 ½ c. flour
1 tsp. nutmeg
1 tsp. cinnamon
1 tsp. salt
1 tsp. soda
1 tsp. baking powder
1 ⅓ c. buttermilk
1 tsp. vanilla flavoring
1 c. nuts
1 c. dates

Cream sugars and oil; beat in eggs. Add sifted dry ingredients alternately with buttermilk. Stir in vanilla flavoring, nuts and dates. Pour into large greased and floured

pan. Bake at 350 degrees for 1 hour and 15 minutes or until done. Remove from oven; block off into squares, but do not remove from pan.

TOPPING:
2 c. white sugar
¾ c. water
¼ tsp. black pepper

Cook sugar and water for 2 minutes; add black pepper. Pour over cake. Return to oven for 2 minutes. Serve from pan. Yield: 15 servings.

Leeoline Warf
Corona, N.M.

RUM CAKE

½ c. butter
½ c. shortening
2 c. sugar
4 eggs
3 c. flour
⅓ tsp. salt
½ tsp. soda
½ tsp. baking powder
1 c. buttermilk
2 tsp. vanilla flavoring
2 tsp. rum flavoring

Cream butter, shortening and sugar; add eggs, one at a time, beating well after each addition. Sift all dry ingredients; add alternately with buttermilk. Add flavorings; pour into a greased and floured tube pan. Bake at 325 degrees for 1 hour.

GLAZE:
1 c. sugar
½ c. water
1 tsp. vanilla flavoring
1 tsp. rum flavoring

Bring sugar and water to boil; cool slightly. Add flavorings; brush on warm cake. Yield: 10-12 servings.

Mrs. Louise Wright
Baxter Springs, Kans.

SALAD DRESSING CAKE

1 c. hot water
1 c. salad dressing
1 tsp. vanilla flavoring
2 c. flour
1 tsp. baking powder
1 tsp. soda
1 tsp. salt
5 tbsp. cocoa
1 ¼ c. sugar

Pour water, salad dressing and vanilla in jar; shake well. Sift all dry ingredients three times. Add salad dressing mixture to dry

(Continued on next page)

ingredients; beat well. Pour into greased and floured 10 x 14-inch pan. Bake at 350 degrees until sides pull away from edges of pan. Yield: 18 servings.

Mrs. Ed Lutz
Westphalia, Kans.

SCRIPTURE CAKE
4 ½ c. 1 Kings 4:22 (flour)
1 c. Judges 5:25 (butter)
2 c. Jeremiah 6:20 (sugar)
2 c. 1 Samuel 30:12 (raisins)
2 c. Nahum 3:12 (figs)
2 c. Numbers 17:8 (almonds)
2 tbsp. Samuel 14:25 (honey)
Pinch of Leviticus 2:13 (salt)
6 Jeremiah 17:11 (eggs)
1 ¼ c. Judges 4:19 (milk)
2 tsp. Amos 4:5 (soda)
II Chronicles to taste 9:9 (spices)

Mix ingredients as for a fruit cake. Bake at 375 degrees for 1 hour. Frost as desired, or sprinkle with powdered sugar.

Elizabeth M. Willis
Chase City, Va.

SILVER SEAFOAM LOAF
½ c. shortening
1 c. sugar
⅔ c. milk
1 tsp. almond or vanilla flavoring
2 c. pastry flour
3 tsp. baking powder
½ tsp. salt
3 egg whites, well beaten

Cream shortening until light and creamy; gradually add sugar, beating well. Add milk and flavoring, beating constantly. Stir in sifted dry ingredients. Fold in egg whites. Pour into round greased and floured loaf pan. Bake at 350 degrees for 35 minutes. Cool; cover with sea foam icing. Yield: 1 loaf.

Mrs. Gelena Hubert
San Antonio, Tex.

THANKSGIVING CAKE
1 c. sugar
½ c. salad oil
2 eggs
1 tsp. soda
1 tsp. baking powder
1 tsp. cinnamon
½ tsp. cloves
½ tsp. nutmeg
1 ½ c. flour
1 c. canned pumpkin
1 c. raisins
¼ c. chopped walnuts

Combine sugar and oil; mix well. Add eggs; beat well. Sift all dry ingredients. Add one-fourth at a time; beat well. With the last addition, add pumpkin, raisins and nuts. Pour into 9 x 9 x 3-inch pan. Bake at 350 degrees for 45 minutes. Cool.

ICING:
1 ½ c. powdered sugar
1 tbsp. butter
Orange juice

Mix sugar and butter with enough orange juice to make a spreading consistency. Spread on cake. Yield: 9 servings.

Maybelle Willson
Hoodsport, Wash.

TOFFEE BAR DESSERT CAKE
2 c. light brown sugar
2 c. flour
½ c. margarine or butter
1 egg
1 c. buttermilk or sweet milk
1 tsp. soda
½ tsp. salt (opt.)
½ to 1 tsp. vanilla flavoring
½ c. chopped nuts (opt.)
6 Heath bars, crushed

Combine sugar and flour; cut in margarine. Reserve 2/3 to 1 cup of mixture. Add egg, buttermilk, soda, salt and vanilla to remaining sugar mixture. Pour into greased 9 x 13-inch pan. Top with reserved sugar mixture, nuts and Heath bars. Bake at 350 degrees for 25 to 30 minutes. Serve with whipped cream. Yield: 12 servings.

Mrs. Thelma K. Brubaker
Eureka, Ill.

VANILLA WAFER CAKE
2 sticks butter
1 ½ to 2 c. sugar
6 eggs
1 12-oz. pkg. vanilla wafers, crushed
1 7-oz. pkg. or 2 cans flaked coconut
1 c. chopped pecans
½ to ¾ c. milk

Cream butter; add sugar. Beat until smooth. Add an egg at a time, beating well after each addition. Add remaining ingredients; mix thoroughly. Pour batter into well greased and floured tube pan. Bake at 275 degrees for 1 hour and 15 minutes to 1 hour and 30 minutes. Cool for 5 minutes in pan.

Mrs. Marie D. Garner
Newport, N.C.

APRICOT CAKE

1 box yellow cake mix
¾ c. oil
¾ c. apricot nectar
3 tsp. vanilla or orange flavoring
4 eggs, separated

Mix all ingredients except egg whites in
mixer for 5 minutes at high speed. Fold in
stiffly beaten egg whites. Pour into tube
pan. Bake at 350 degrees for 45 to 60 minutes. Remove from pan.

TOPPING:
2 c. sifted powdered sugar
Grated rind and juice of 2 oranges

Combine all ingredients; pour over warm
cake.

Mrs. Irene Burlison
Leesville, La.

CHERRY DRIZZLE CAKE

1 pkg. white cake mix
Cherry juice
1 No. 2 can pitted sour red cherries
1 tsp. red food coloring
1 c. sugar
Sweetened whipped cream

Prepare cake batter as directed on package.
Pour batter evenly into 9 x 13-inch pan. Measure juice from cherries; add enough water
to make 3/4 cup. Combine cherries, juice,
red coloring and sugar. Heat just to boiling
point; pour over batter. Bake at 350 degrees
for 40 to 45 minutes. Let stand in pan for 3
minutes on cooling rack. Loosen cake from
sides of pan with knife. Invert onto tray or
large platter. Garnish with whipped cream.
Serve warm or cold. Yield: 15-18 servings.

Clara Giger
Toledo, Iowa

QUICK CHERRY CAKE

1 can cherry pie filling
1 sm. pkg. cake mix
½ c. chopped nuts
¼ c. butter, melted

Place pie filling in pan; sprinkle with dry
cake mix. Place nuts over mix; dribble
butter over nuts. Bake at 350 degrees for 30
minutes or until set. Yield: 6 servings.

Mrs. Miriam Meazell
Athens, Tex.

FIESTA PEACH SHORTCAKE

1 honey spice cake mix
1 pkg. vanilla pudding mix
1 can sliced peaches, drained

Bake cake mix in two layers according to
directions on package; cool. Prepare vanilla
pudding mix; cool. Fill and top cake with pudding mix and peach slices. Yield: 8 servings.

Mrs. Lorraine Malinowski
Rochester, N.Y.

PINEAPPLE CAKE

BATTER:
½ c. crushed pineapple, drained
1 c. water
2 egg whites
1 pkg. white cake mix

Add pineapple, water and egg whites to cake
mix; beat with electric mixer according to
package directions. Bake at 350 degrees
until tests done.

FILLING:
¾ c. sugar
1 tbsp. flour
3 tbsp. lemon juice (opt.)
2 egg yolks
1 c. crushed pineapple
1 c. grated coconut

Combine all ingredients. Cook over low heat,
stirring often. Put between layers and on top
of cake.

FROSTING:
2 c. powdered sugar
2 tbsp. butter
Milk

Combine sugar and butter; add enough milk
for easy spreading consistency. Cover entire
cake with frosting. Yield: 15 servings.

Irma Tyhurst
Annapolis, Ill.

STRAWBERRY CAKE

1 pkg. white cake mix
1 pkg. strawberry gelatin
½ 10-oz. pkg. frozen strawberries, thawed
⅓ c. cooking oil
½ c. cold water
4 egg whites

Mix ingredients. Beat for 5 minutes at low
speed. Bake at 350 degrees for 30 minutes.
Cool.

ICING:
1 lb. powdered sugar
½ c. butter or margarine
½ 10-oz. pkg. frozen strawberries

Mix all ingredients; beat well until thick and
creamy. Spread on cooled cake.

Mrs. Alice Ridgway
McLouth, Kans.

Frostings, Fillings, Toppings

RECIPE FOR CREAMY SEMI-SWEET FROSTING ON PAGE 80

The Frosting on a Cake . . .

. . . is like a jewel in a crown. It makes something beautiful even more lovely.

A frosting is a thicker sugar-liquid mixture used for cakes. All frostings may be used to cover a cake, but special ones are used for decorating it.

An icing is a mixture of confectioners sugar and a liquid. An icing is thin enough to be brushed on with a pastry brush or spread. It is usually used on pastries, rolls and coffee cakes. An icing is sometimes used on simple cakes.

A glaze is a mixture of sugar and a liquid that is thin enough to be poured. A glaze is about the consistency of thin corn syrup. It is used to coat cupcakes, fruit cakes and pieces of cake which are to be used as petit fours and tea cakes.

A filling is a thick mixture which is used to hold the layers of a cake together. A filling may be a frosting to which fruits, marshmallows or nuts are added. Whipped cream and custard mixtures are sometimes used for fillings.

HINTS FOR MAKING FROSTINGS

Some frostings call for brown sugar. To measure brown sugar, pack into a dry measuring cup firmly enough so that it holds the shape of the cup when turned out. Crush the lumps from brown sugar with a rolling pin, then press it through a coarse sieve. Store any left-over brown sugar in a tightly covered container to prevent it from becoming lumpy.

Sift confectioners sugar by pressing it through a wire strainer onto a piece of waxed paper. Then simply spoon the sifted sugar into a dry measuring cup and level off with a spatula.

If frosting is too thin, add a little confectioners sugar at a time until the desired consistency is obtained. Variations in the weather, temperature or the size or freshness of eggs can cause variations in the consistency of frosting.

If frosting becomes too thick, add more liquid, just a drop at a time, until the desired consistency is reached.

Place a small amount of frosting in a cup if you plan to tint it. Add enough pure food coloring to give it a rather bright color. Blend this frosting into the rest of the mixture, a little at a time, until you get the desired color. Tint frosting delicately . . . too much color may give it a cheap, unappetizing appearance.

To keep frosting from crusting over, keep the bowl of frosting covered with a damp cloth when not in use.

THE ART OF CAKE DECORATING

Cake decorating is an art, and practice makes perfect. Inexpensive cake decorator sets may be purchased at variety or department stores. Many of these give excellent results, and if given proper care, last for years.

Directions for using the decorator come with the set. Decorating becomes easier if you practice on a piece of waxed paper or the bottom of an enameled pan or cake pan. The frosting can be scraped back into the decorator and used over and over until you have mastered the design you want.

Test the consistency of the frosting by placing a little in the decorator with the tube or tip to be used. It should be thin enough to force easily but should be thick enough to hold its shape.

Most decorator sets come with four tips—plain, rosette, leaf and shell or star.

THE PLAIN TIP . . .

. . . has a small, round opening. This tip is used for fine writing and lines. To use, first trace the letters or design on the frosted cake with a toothpick. Place the plain tip in the decorator and fill decorator two-thirds full of frosting. Hold tip so it barely touches the cake. Squeeze the bag or force gun so frosting flows with steady, even pressure. Follow the toothpick tracing. Once you have started a line of work, continue until it is finished. Stopping leaves a ragged line.

Many simple designs may be made with this tip. For flower stems, make curved lines. For flowers, make dots by forcing a bit of frosting on the cake, releasing the pressure, then lifting the tip.

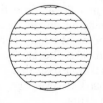

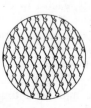

Use the plain tip to pipe diagonal lines across the cake to form diamonds. Place a flower dot on the crossed line. For a beautiful web effect, pipe circles 1 inch apart on cake, extending from center to edge of cake. While frosting is still soft, draw a toothpick through the lines, starting first in the center, then from the edge to the center.

For a marbled effect, pipe lines of contrasting color straight across the cake, making them about ¾ inch apart. Before the lines harden, draw a toothpick through them, first from the bottom to the top, then from top to bottom.

For borders, use piped lines of loops and curves around the cake.

THE LEAF TIP . . .

. . . has a narrow opening, formed by long, narrow notches. Frosting forced through this tip forms a wide, flat ribbon with lines or veins. Use it for leaves, borders and decorating sides of the cake. For leaves, hold up at an angle, press (increasing pressure widens leaf), release pressure then lift tip. This tip may also be used to make flower petals.

THE ROSETTE TIP . . .

. . . has a much larger opening than the plain tip. The opening consists of several slots or notches that are cut into the metal. Frosting forced through this tube forms a rigid, rope-like ribbon. It is used to write large letters or greetings or it may be used to make borders.

THE SHELL OR STAR TIP . . .

. . . has a smaller opening than a rosette tip. It may be used for borders and decorations in much the same way as the rosette tip.

FLOWER NAILS . . .

. . . have sharp points, much like a common nail. The heads are of various sizes, depending on the size of the flower to be made. Flower nails may be purchased from bakery supply houses. A flower nail helps you do a better job of shaping petals because you can rotate the nail while piping.

Roses and other large flower shapes may look flat if piped directly onto the cake. To avoid this flat look, you can do as the baker does—make the flower on a flower nail, let stand overnight, then place on the cake.

To use a flower nail, first pipe a little mound of frosting in the center of the greased nail head. Stick nail in cardboard box and let stand until the frosting is set. Then, with leaf tip, pipe petals around the frosting mound, turning the nail in your hand as you pipe the petals. Let stand until set. For best results, each row of petals should be allowed to set before another row is added. Stick the nail with the finished flower into the cardboard box and let stand for several hours before placing on the cake.

If you have no flower nail, get a dozen or so six or eight-penny common nails from a hardware store. Cut pieces of cardboard the size you want your flowers to be. Thrust the nails through the cardboard so that the underneath side of the nail head touches the cardboard. Brush tops of nails and cardboard with melted paraffin. Let dry before using.

DECORATING SPECIAL OCCASION CAKES

White, chocolate, spice or sponge—they're all delicious, but most need a little help to make them glamorous for special occasions. You don't have to be an artist to decorate cakes that will give delight and pleasure to your family and friends. Here are suggestions for decorating your cakes for special occasions with special consideration for the days when you have little time.

A suggestion to follow is to design your pattern on paper, then transfer to cardboard and cut out. Trace the letters or design on the frosted cake with a toothpick. Take your time and have fun.

New Year's Eve Cake

Christmas Cake

Valentine Cake

Halloween Cake

St. Patrick's Day Cake

Wedding or Anniversary Cake

Patriotic Cake

Mother's Day Cake

Easter Cake

FILLING AND ICING FOR ANGEL FOOD CAKE

3 tbsp. cocoa
¼ c. sugar
1 c. heavy cream
Pinch of salt

Mix all ingredients; chill for 2 hours. Whip mixture until stiff. Split cake crosswise; fill and frost cake.

Mary Lou Wooten
Orlando, Fla.

APRICOT FILLING

½ lb. dried apricots
½ c. sugar
½ c. drained crushed pineapple
1 c. chopped nuts

Wash apricots; barely cover with water. Add sugar. Cover and simmer slowly for 30 minutes; strain. Add pineapple and nuts. Cool; spread between layers.

Mrs. Neil B. Arbo
Brownville, Me.

BEVILLE FILLING

1 c. sugar
1 tbsp. cornstarch
Milk from 1 coconut
1 tbsp. lemon juice
1 fresh coconut, grated
1 c. chopped nuts

Mix sugar and cornstarch; add gradually to coconut milk. Cook over low heat until thick, stirring constantly. Add lemon juice, coconut and nuts; cool. Spread between cake layers. Yield: One 3 layer cake.

Mrs. Harry W. Burns
Mobile, Ala.

FROSTING AND FILLING

1 c. milk
6 tsp. flour
1 c. sugar
2 tbsp. marshmallow creme
1 c. shortening
1 tsp. vanilla flavoring

Combine milk and flour; cook until thickened. Cool. Combine remaining ingredients; add cooled mixture. Beat until light and fluffy.

Doris Wood
Sabattus, Me.

COCONUT FILLING

2 c. sugar
1 ½ c. water
4 egg whites, stiffly beaten
1 tsp. vanilla flavoring
1 can coconut

Mix sugar and water; cook until it spins a thread. Pour over beaten egg whites; beat until creamy. Add vanilla and coconut; beat until well mixed. Spread on cake. Yield: Filling for a 3-4 layer cake.

Mrs. C. P. Daugherty
Carthage, Miss.

CRANBERRY-ORANGE FILLING

2 c. cranberries
½ c. water
1 c. sugar
4 tbsp. cornstarch
2 tsp. grated orange rind

Cook cranberries in water until skins burst. Mix sugar and cornstarch. Add to cranberries; cook until thickened, stirring constantly. Remove from heat; add orange rind. Mix thoroughly; cool. Yield: 1 1/2 cups.

Annie L. Thomas
Marshall, Tex.

CRANBERRY-PINEAPPLE FILLING

1 pkg. dessert topping mix
½ c. cold milk
2 tbsp. sugar
¼ can cranberry sauce
¼ c. crushed pineapple, drained
1 lge. angel food cake

Mix topping mix and milk; beat with electric mixer until stiff. Add sugar and cranberry sauce, beating until well mixed. Stir in pineapple. Cut cake into three layers; spread generously with filling. Spread remainder evenly over top and sides of cake. Yield: 12-15 servings.

Mrs. Edith DeHart
Laton, Calif.

MOCHA CAKE FILLING

1 box powdered sugar
2 tbsp. cocoa
1 stick butter
1 tsp. vanilla flavoring
⅓ c. boiling coffee

(Continued on next page)

Put sugar and cocoa in a 2-quart bowl. Cut butter into thin slices; add butter and flavoring to sugar mixture. Add boiling coffee; beat for 1 minute. Yield: Frosting for a 2 layer cake.

Hazel Philips
Pittsburg, Kans.

PINEAPPLE FILLING

Pinch of salt
2 c. crushed pineapple, drained
1 c. sugar
3 tbsp. flour
2 egg yolks, beaten
½ stick butter

Mix salt, pineapple, sugar and flour; beat until thoroughly mixed. Pour slowly over beaten egg yolks. Cook over low heat until thickened. Add butter; cool. Spread between layers of cake. Frost cake with white icing. Yield: 12-16 servings.

Emily Paul
Marion, S.C.

PINEAPPLE FILLING AND FROSTING

1 lge. can crushed pineapple, drained
1 pkg. instant vanilla pudding mix
1 pt. heavy cream, whipped
½ c. chopped pecans (opt.)

Stir pineapple into pudding mix. Fold in whipped cream and pecans. Chill. This is especially good used as a filling and topping for an orange chiffon cake, plain sponge or angel food cake. NOTE: Frosting keeps well in refrigerator for three to four days. Yield: 10-12 servings.

Mrs. Sherwin W. Boswell
Blytheville, Ark.

PINEAPPLE FILLING

½ c. sugar
2 tbsp. cornstarch
1 egg
Grated rind of 1 lemon
1 lge. can crushed pineapple

Mix sugar and cornstarch in top of double boiler. Add egg; beat until smooth. Stir in lemon rind and pineapple. Cook over hot water, stirring constantly, until mixture is thick. Remove from heat; cover and cool.

Mrs. Fred C. Holt
Norfolk, Va.

CARAMEL FILLING

4 c. sugar
1 c. milk
1 stick butter
1 tsp. vanilla flavoring

Melt 1 cup sugar in skillet. Mix remaining sugar and milk; bring to a boil. Add melted sugar, stirring constantly. Add butter and flavoring. Cook until dissolved, stirring constantly. Remove from heat; beat until thickened. Spread on and between cake layers.

Mrs. Hammond Dooley
Forrest City, Ark.

CARAMEL FROSTING

½ c. butter
1 c. brown sugar
¼ c. milk
1 ¾ to 2 c. powdered sugar

Melt butter in pan; add brown sugar. Boil over low heat for 2 minutes, stirring constantly. Add milk; continue stirring until mixture comes to a boil. Remove from heat; cool. Add powdered sugar; beat until thick enough to spread. Yield: Frosting for a 2 layer cake.

Delores Porter
Ashland, Me.

QUICK CARAMEL FROSTING

⅔ c. butter
1 c. brown sugar
⅓ c. milk
3 c. powdered sugar

Melt butter; add brown sugar. Cook over low heat for 2 minutes, stirring constantly. Add milk. Bring to a boil, stirring constantly. Cool for 10 minutes. Add powdered sugar until of spreading consistency, beating well after each addition. Yield: Frosting for a 2 layer cake.

Mrs. Arthur F. Hrabak
Maynard, O.

SPEEDY CARAMEL FROSTING

½ c. margarine
1 c. brown sugar
¼ tsp. salt
¼ c. milk
2 c. powdered sugar
½ tsp. vanilla flavoring

Melt margarine in large saucepan. Blend in brown sugar and salt. Cook over low heat for 2 minutes, stirring. Add milk; continue

77

(Continued on next page)

stirring until mixture comes to a boil. Remove from heat. Blend in powdered sugar gradually. Add vanilla; mix well. Thin with small amount of milk or thicken with powdered sugar if necessary.

Mrs. Graphet E. Johnson
Waynesboro, Va.

BEAT AND EAT FROSTING

1 egg white
¾ c. sugar
¼ tsp. cream of tartar
1 tsp. vanilla flavoring
¼ c. boiling water
1 c. coconut

Place egg white, sugar, cream of tartar and flavoring in deep mixing bowl. Add boiling water; beat to stiff peaks. Spread on cake; sprinkle with coconut.

Mrs. Joe Bryant
Tuskahoma, Okla.

BROILER COCONUT FROSTING

6 tbsp. melted butter
½ c. brown sugar
¼ c. cream
½ tsp. vanilla flavoring
1 c. shredded coconut
¾ c. broken pecans

Combine all ingredients; spread over warm cake. Brown under broiler. Yield: Frosting for a 9 x 12-inch cake.

Mrs. Baker W. Herbert
Traverse City, Mich.

COCONUT-PECAN FROSTING

1 c. evaporated milk
1 c. sugar
3 egg yolks
1 stick butter or margarine
1 tsp. vanilla flavoring
1 ⅓ c. flaked coconut
1 c. chopped pecans

Combine all ingredients except coconut and pecans. Cook over medium heat for 10 to 12 minutes, stirring until thickened. Remove from heat; add coconut and pecans. Beat until cool and of spreading consistency.

Emily B. Rice
La Plata, Md.

BELGIAN BUTTER CREAM FROSTING

1 c. sugar
1 c. strong coffee
1 c. unsalted butter

Boil sugar and coffee for several minutes; cool. Cream butter; slowly beat in cooled syrup. Split layers of white or yellow cake in half; frost all layers, sides and top of cake. Refrigerate until frosting is firm. NOTE: Cake and frosting freeze well.

Mrs. Mac P. Kesler
Fort McPherson, Ga.

BUTTERMILK ICING

3 c. powdered sugar
1 stick butter
2 tbsp. buttermilk
3 tbsp. cold coffee
½ tsp. vanilla flavoring
1 egg yolk

Combine all ingredients; beat with electric mixer until fluffy and of spreading consistency. NOTE: For chocolate icing, add cocoa to taste.

Ruth Downing
Rolla, Mo.

COFFEE FROSTING

½ c. shortening
½ c. cocoa
1 egg
¼ tsp. salt
2 tsp. instant coffee
1 tsp. vanilla flavoring
4 c. sifted powdered sugar
7 or 8 tbsp. hot milk

Beat all ingredients except powdered sugar and milk. Alternately add powdered sugar and milk to mixture; beat until smooth. Yield: Frosting for 2 layers or 1 loaf.

Joan Dabson
Pecatonica, Ill.

COFFEE FROSTING

¼ c. butter
1 ½ c. powdered sugar
½ tsp. vanilla flavoring
1 tsp. instant coffee
Cream or evaporated milk

(Continued on next page)

Cream butter and sugar; add vanilla, coffee and enough cream to make of spreading consistency.

Mrs. Victoria Ponce
Chicago, Ill.

TRIPLE-SIX FROSTING

6 tbsp. hot strong coffee
6 tbsp. butter
6 tbsp. cocoa
1 tsp. rum flavoring
1 box powdered sugar, sifted

Blend coffee, butter and cocoa; cool for 20 minutes. Add rum flavoring. Gradually add sugar, blending after each addition; beat well. Spread on cake. Yield: Frosting for a 2 layer cake.

Mrs. George Lake
Honolulu, Hawaii

CHOCOLATE FORTUNE FROSTING

2 ½ oz. chocolate
2 c. sifted powdered sugar
3 tbsp. hot water
1 egg
⅓ c. soft butter or margarine
1 tsp. vanilla flavoring

Melt chocolate in mixing bowl over hot water. Remove from heat. With electric mixer blend in sugar and water. Beat in egg; add butter and flavoring. Beat until of spreading consistency. Yield: Frosting for a 2 layer cake.

Mrs. Mildred Pingrey
Strykersville, N.Y.

CHOCOLATE FROSTING

2 c. sugar
½ stick margarine
½ c. milk
¼ c. corn syrup
Pinch of salt
2 squares unsweetened chocolate
1 tsp. vanilla flavoring

Combine sugar, margarine, milk, syrup, salt and chocolate in saucepan. Stir and cook until boiling. Cook for 1 minute; remove from heat. Beat until of spreading consistency. Add vanilla. Yield: Frosting for two 9-inch layers.

Mrs. R. G. Kidd
Stony Creek, Va.

CHOCOLATE FROSTING

1 c. brown sugar
½ tsp. salt
⅓ c. light cream
1 square chocolate, melted
2 tbsp. butter
1 ½ c. sifted powdered sugar
Vanilla flavoring

Blend brown sugar, salt and cream with chocolate; add butter. Cook, covered, until boiling; boil for 1 minute. When cool, stir in powdered sugar and flavoring.

Mrs. Robert W. Berres
Racine, Wisc.

CHOCOLATE FROSTING

½ c. shortening, melted
2 c. sugar
2 tsp. cocoa
2 tsp. vanilla flavoring
⅔ c. milk

Mix shortening, sugar and cocoa. Bring to a boil; cook, without stirring, until mixture reaches soft ball stage. Add flavoring and milk. Place in pan of ice cubes; stir until creamy.

Mrs. Rose Roering
Waubun, Minn.

CHOCOLATE FUDGE FROSTING

1 square bitter chocolate
3 tbsp. butter
¼ c. hot water
½ tsp. vanilla flavoring
Powdered sugar

Place all ingredients except sugar in a saucepan; bring to a boil. Add enough powdered sugar to make of spreading consistency. If frosting thickens before spreading, add a small amount of hot water.

Bernice Lemanczyk
Milwaukee, Wisc.

CHOCOLATE ICING

2 squares unsweetened chocolate
½ c. sugar
½ tsp. baking powder
¼ c. milk
3 tsp. butter
1 tsp. vanilla flavoring
½ tsp. lemon flavoring

79

(Continued on next page)

Melt chocolate; add sugar, baking powder, milk and butter. Cook until soft ball forms or 200 degrees on candy thermometer. Add flavorings; spread frosting on cake.

Mrs. Rose Farrington
Colorado Springs, Colo.

CHOC-O-NUT FROSTING

2 squares chocolate
¼ c. butter
2 c. miniature marshmallows
¼ c. water
2 c. powdered sugar
½ c. nuts
1 tsp. vanilla flavoring

Melt chocolate, butter and 1 cup marshmallows in water. Cool. Add sugar, remaining 1 cup marshmallows, nuts and vanilla. Beat well; spread over cake. Yield: Frosting for a 9 x 12-inch cake.

Mrs. Dale Lindholm
Sidney, Nebr.

CREAM CHEESE-CHOCOLATE FROSTING

2 squares unsweetened chocolate
1 3-oz. pkg. cream cheese
2 to 3 tbsp. top milk
⅛ tsp. salt
2 c. sifted powdered sugar

Melt chocolate over hot water. Combine cheese, milk and salt, working with back of spoon until smooth. Add sugar gradually, creaming and beating. Add melted chocolate; beat until smooth. NOTE: If desired, grated orange rind may be added to cream cheese; orange juice may be used instead of milk.

Mrs. Franklin Hazlett
Quaker Hill, Conn.

FUDGE FROSTING

1 ½ c. sugar
2 tbsp. (heaping) cocoa
½ stick butter
1 tbsp. dark corn syrup
Pinch of salt
½ c. minus 1 tbsp. milk
Vanilla flavoring to taste

Combine all ingredients except flavoring in saucepan; boil for 1 minute or until it forms a soft ball in cold water. Add vanilla flavoring; whip until glossy and of spreading consistency.

Caroline V. Waters
St. Francis, Kans.

CREAMY SEMI-SWEET FROSTING

1 6-oz. pkg. semi-sweet chocolate pieces
¼ c. butter or margarine
½ c. evaporated milk
1 7 ½-oz. jar marshmallow creme

Melt chocolate pieces and butter over hot, but not boiling, water; blend well. Remove from heat. Gradually add milk, stirring until smooth. Let cool to room temperature. Add marshmallow creme; beat until smooth. Garnish with nuts or coconut if desired. NOTE: Frosting freezes well. Let frosting stand at room temperature for 1 hour or until soft enough to spread. Yield: Frosting for two 8 or 9-inch cake layers or 24 medium cupcakes.

Photograph for this recipe on page 71 .

FUDGE FROSTING

¼ c. butter
1 c. sugar
¼ c. milk
½ c. chocolate pieces
1 tsp. vanilla flavoring

Combine butter, sugar and milk. Bring to a rolling boil. Remove from heat; add chocolate pieces and vanilla. Beat until of spreading consistency.

Mrs. Paul Ramsell
Huron, S.D.

MINUTE FUDGE FROSTING

2 squares chocolate
2 c. sugar
4 tbsp. light syrup
½ c. salad oil
⅔ c. milk

Melt chocolate over hot water; remove from heat. Add sugar, syrup, salad oil and milk. Bring to rolling boil; boil for 1 minute, stirring constantly. Remove from heat; beat and cool until of spreading consistency. NOTE: May be cooled in pan of cold water. Yield: Frosting for 1 large cake.

Daisymae Eckman
Pawnee City, Nebr.

GLOSSY CHOCOLATE FROSTING

6 tbsp. hot milk
4 tbsp. soft butter
3 ½ c. sifted confectioners sugar
2 tsp. vanilla flavoring
4 squares baking chocolate, melted

80

(Continued on next page)

Combine hot milk and butter; add sifted sugar and vanilla. Beat until smooth. Add melted chocolate; mix thoroughly. If frosting is too thick, add more milk. If too thin add more sugar. Yield: Frosting for 1 layer cake or a 9-inch cake.

Dorothy Abbate
Chicago, Ill.

HURRY-UP FROSTING

1 c. sugar
1 tbsp. cocoa
¼ c. butter
¼ c. milk

Combine all ingredients. Bring to a boil; cook for 2 minutes. Beat until thick enough to spread. Yield: Frosting for 1 layer cake.

Janet W. Pickett
Greensburg, Ky.

LAST-MINUTE CHOCOLATE ICING

1 c. semi-sweet chocolate pieces
¼ c. butter
1 ½ c. sifted powdered sugar
⅓ c. evaporated milk

Melt chocolate and butter in small saucepan; cool thoroughly. Blend in sugar alternately with milk. Beat until of spreading consistency. Spread on cooled cake.

Mrs. James McNally
Chokio, Minn.

MAGIC CHOCOLATE FROSTING

1 15-oz. can sweetened condensed milk
1 tbsp. water
⅛ tsp. salt
2 squares unsweetened chocolate
½ tsp. vanilla flavoring

Combine all ingredients except vanilla in top of double boiler. Cook over rapidly boiling water until thick, stirring often. Cool. Stir in vanilla. Spread on cake. Yield: Frosting for two 8-inch cake layers.

Mrs. Elaine D. Landis
York, Pa.

MINUTE FROSTING

1 c. sugar
¼ c. milk

¼ c. cocoa
¼ c. shortening
Vanilla flavoring (opt.)

Mix all ingredients except vanilla in small saucepan. Bring to a boil; boil for 1 minute. Add vanilla; stir until cool. Yield: Frosting for 1 layer cake.

Beatrice Tuttle
Groveton, N.H.

NEVER-FAIL CHOCOLATE FROSTING

1 ½ c. sugar
2 tbsp. shortening
1 tbsp. light corn syrup
2 squares unsweetened chocolate
2 tbsp. butter
7 tbsp. milk
1 tsp. vanilla flavoring

Combine all ingredients except vanilla. Stir until dissolved. Boil for 1 minute; cool. Add vanilla; beat until thick.

Mrs. Allan Tharalson
Hoople, N.D.

NEVER-FAIL CHOCOLATE FROSTING

1 ½ squares bitter chocolate
⅔ c. milk
2 c. sugar
¼ tsp. salt
2 tbsp. corn syrup
1 tbsp. butter
1 tsp. vanilla flavoring

Melt chocolate in milk over low heat, stirring constantly. Add sugar, salt and corn syrup; stir until sugar is dissolved and mixture boils. Continue cooking without stirring until it forms a soft ball. Add butter and flavoring; cool. Beat until of spreading consistency. Add a small amount of cream if frosting gets hard. Yield: Frosting for a 3 layer cake.

Mrs. James Enstad
Pekin, N.D.

ONE-MINUTE CHOCOLATE FROSTING

2 c. sugar
¼ c. cocoa
1 stick butter
½ c. milk
½ tsp. vanilla flavoring

81

(Continued on next page)

Combine sugar, cocoa, butter and milk; slowly bring to a boil, stirring constantly, over medium heat. Boil for exactly 1 minute. Remove from heat; add vanilla. Cool; beat until of spreading consistency. Yield: Frosting for two 9-inch layers.

Mrs. R. J. Gaudet
Charlotte, N.C.

ONE-MINUTE FUDGE ICING

¼ c. butter
1 c. sugar
¼ c. cocoa
¼ c. cream
¼ tsp. salt

Combine all ingredients in saucepan. Stir until mixture comes to a rolling boil; boil for 1 minute without stirring. Cool slightly; beat until creamy. Spread on cake. Yield: Icing for one 2 layer cake.

Marietta Rapp
Greenville, O.

RICHMOND CHOCOLATE FROSTING

1 c. sugar
3 tbsp. cornstarch
2 1-oz. squares unsweetened chocolate
Dash of salt
1 c. boiling water
3 tbsp. butter
1 tsp. vanilla flavoring

Mix sugar and cornstarch; add chocolate and salt. Add water; cook until mixture thickens. Remove from heat; add butter and vanilla. Spread on cake while hot. Yield: Frosting for an 8 or 9-inch cake.

Mrs. W. J. Baugh
Rapid City, S.D.

WHIPPED CHOCOLATE FROSTING

6 tbsp. butter
4 squares bitter chocolate
2 c. powdered sugar
½ tsp. salt
½ c. milk
2 eggs
1 tsp. vanilla flavoring

Melt butter and chocolate over low heat. Combine powdered sugar, salt, milk, eggs and flavoring in large bowl; blend with electric mixer. Add butter and chocolate. Place bowl in pan of ice water. Beat until light and fluffy

and of spreading consistency. Yield: Frosting for 1 layer cake.

Mrs. Robert W. Hansen
Milwaukee, Wisc.

BEAT 'N' EAT FROSTING

1 egg white
1 c. sugar
¼ tsp. cream of tartar
1 tsp. vanilla flavoring
¼ c. boiling water

Combine egg white, sugar, cream of tartar and vanilla with electric mixer. Add boiling water; beat at high speed until stiff.

Mrs. Shirley Force
Danville, Ill.

BEST IN THE WEST FROSTING

1 box powdered sugar
½ tsp. salt
6 tbsp. milk
6 tbsp. shortening
1 tsp. vanilla flavoring

Combine all ingredients. Beat at high speed until fluffy. Spread on cake.

Mrs. Bruce Crabb
Independence, Iowa

BIRTHDAY CAKE FROSTING

2 ½ c. sugar
3 tbsp. corn syrup
½ c. water
4 egg whites
Pinch of cream of tartar
⅓ to ½ c. powdered sugar

Boil sugar, corn syrup and water until it reaches 240 degrees on candy thermometer, keeping sides of pan clean with a damp cloth wrapped around a fork. In large bowl of mixer beat egg whites with cream of tartar until very stiff. Add syrup in a slow steady stream, beating at high speed until firm peaks form; stir in p o w d e r e d sugar. NOTE: If weather is very humid cook syrup to 242 degrees.

Gwyneth Harrison
Livingston, Tex.

CREAM FROSTING

2 tbsp. (heaping) flour
2 tbsp. sugar

(Continued on next page)

1 egg
1 c. milk
½ c. shortening
½ c. butter or margarine
9 tbsp. (heaping) powdered sugar
1 tsp. vanilla flavoring

Combine flour, sugar, egg and milk. Cook until thick; cool thoroughly. Cream shortening and butter; add powdered sugar and vanilla. Add egg mixture; beat well.

Mrs. William Schott
Buffalo, N.Y.

DECORATOR'S FROSTING

1 lge. egg white
½ c. shortening
1 lb. powdered sugar
⅓ c. evaporated milk
½ tsp. vanilla flavoring
½ tsp. almond flavoring

Beat egg white and shortening with electric mixer. Add sugar alternately with milk. Add flavorings; beat well. Refrigerate until used. NOTE: Food coloring may be used. Yield: Frosting for 2 cakes.

Mildred Ekard
Rockford, Ill.

DAWSON CREAM FROSTING

3 Tbsp. cornstarch
½ tsp. salt
1 c. milk
¾ c. butter
1 c. sugar
1 tsp. vanilla

Mix cornstarch, salt and milk in a saucepan. Cook over low heat, stirring constantly. Remove from heat when thick; beat until white. Cream butter and sugar with an electric mixer. Gradually add cornstarch paste. Add vanilla. Beat until light and fluffy. Yield: Frosting for a 2 layer cake.

Mrs. Jacqueline Parr
Port Angeles, Wash.

DIVINE DIVINITY FROSTING

3 tbsp. light corn syrup
1 ½ c. sugar
½ c. water
3 egg whites
1 tsp. baking powder
¼ tsp. salt

Combine syrup, sugar and water; bring to a rolling boil. Beat egg whites, baking powder and salt. Add 1 tablespoon syrup at a time to egg whites until 5 tablespoons of hot mixture have been added, beating constantly. Cook remaining syrup until it spins an 8-inch thread. Pour slowly over egg whites, beating constantly. Continue beating until frosting is stiff enough to spread. Yield: Frosting for a 2 or 3 layer cake.

Mrs. Edward L. Parham
Fort McClellan, Ala.

DIVINITY ICING

2 ½ c. sugar
½ c. corn syrup
½ c. hot water
¼ tsp. salt
2 egg whites, stiffly beaten
½ tsp. lemon flavoring

Combine sugar, syrup, water and salt; cook to soft ball stage. Pour one-half of the syrup over egg whites, beating constantly. Cook remaining syrup to hard ball stage; pour over egg whites. Add flavoring. Beat until of spreading consistency.

Alta L. Johnson
Lubbock, Tex.

FLUFFY ICING

1 pkg. powdered sugar
4 tbsp. flour
4 tbsp. milk
1 c. shortening, melted
1 egg white
1 tsp. vanilla flavoring

Beat sugar, flour, milk and shortening for 5 minutes. Beat egg white and flavoring for 5 minutes. Combine mixtures; beat for 5 minutes.

Mrs. Mary Lou Aikins
Elderton, Pa.

FLUFFY WHITE FROSTING

1 c. light corn syrup
2 egg whites
2 tbsp. sugar

Bring corn syrup to a boil over medium heat. Remove from heat; cool for 1 minute. Beat egg whites until frothy; gradually add sugar. Beat until stiff peaks form. Pour hot corn syrup gradually into egg whites. Beat until stiff enough to spread.

Mamie H. Winder
Richmond, Va.

MOLASSES TAFFY FROSTING

1 egg white, unbeaten
¼ c. water
1 c. sugar
2 tbsp. unsulphured molasses
⅛ tsp. salt
½ tsp. vanilla flavoring

Combine egg white, water, sugar, unsulphured molasses and salt in top of double boiler. Beat over rapidly boiling water with rotary or electric beater until frosting stands in peaks. Remove from heat; add flavoring. Beat until of spreading consistency. Frost cake; garnish with nuts if desired.

Photograph for this recipe above.

MOCK WHIPPED CREAM FROSTING

1 stick margarine
½ c. shortening
1 c. sugar
1 c. warm milk

Blend margarine and shortening; alternately add sugar and milk. Beat until mixture forms a peak. Spread between layers and on top of cake.

Mrs. Ruff
Buchanan, Mich.

NEVER-FAIL, NEVER-HARDEN FROSTING

1 ½ c. powdered sugar
1 egg
2 tbsp. cold water
2 tbsp. flour
1 tsp. vanilla flavoring
½ c. butter or margarine, softened

Combine all ingredients; beat until thoroughly mixed. Spread on cake.

Mrs. Clyde H. Kratochvil
Holloman AFB, N.M.

NEVER-FAIL WHITE FLUFFY FROSTING

1 c. sugar
1 tbsp. vinegar
5 tbsp. water
2 egg whites, stiffly beaten
Flavoring

Boil sugar, vinegar and water for 3 minutes. Slowly add to beaten egg whites. Add flavoring.

Mrs. Ralph L. Cavalli
Requa, Calif.

NO-COOK MARSHMALLOW FROSTING

¼ tsp. salt
2 egg whites
¼ c. sugar
¾ c. light corn syrup
1 ¼ tsp. vanilla flavoring

Add salt to egg whites; beat until foamy. Gradually add sugar; beat until dissolved. Slowly add corn syrup; beat until firm and stands in peaks. Fold in vanilla.

Mrs. Nat D. King
McGuire AFB, N.J.

NONE-STICKY FROSTING

3 ½ c. sifted powdered sugar
½ c. shortening
2 egg whites, stiffly beaten
½ tsp. salt
Flavoring

Cream 1/2 cup sugar and shortening until light. Add remaining ingredients; mix well.

Mrs. Merena Cassel
Long Island, Kans.

1-2-3 WHITE FROSTING

1 c. sugar
2 egg whites
3 tbsp. cold water
Pinch of salt
Cream of tartar

Combine all ingredients in top of double boiler. Beat for 4 minutes over boiling water until fluffy. Yield: Frosting for a 9-inch layer cake.

Mary E. Clark
Jackson, Mich.

PERFECT FROSTING

½ c. boiling water
1 c. sugar
1 egg white
¼ tsp. cream of tartar
1 tsp. vanilla flavoring

Pour boiling water over sugar, egg white and cream of tartar. Beat with electric beater at high speed for several minutes. When frosting peaks, add vanilla. Frost cake. Yield: Frosting for 2 layers.

Mrs. Carl Noell
Burns, Kans.

SEVEN-MINUTE FROSTING

2 egg whites, unbeaten
1 ½ c. sugar
¼ tsp. cream of tartar
⅓ c. cold water
Dash of salt
1 ½ tsp. vanilla flavoring

Combine all ingredients except vanilla in top of double boiler. Beat, without cooking, for 1 minute. Place over boiling water; cook until stiff peaks form, beating constantly. Remove from boiling water. Add vanilla; beat until of spreading consistency.

Valborg Birkeness
St. Paul, Minn.

SOFT CREAMY FROSTING

1 c. milk
5 tbsp. flour
⅛ tsp. salt
1 c. sugar
½ c. shortening
½ c. butter or margarine
1 tsp. vanilla or other flavoring

Cook milk, flour and salt in pan over direct heat until mixture is thick. Set aside to cool. Cream sugar, shortening, butter and vanilla in large bowl until fluffy. Add flour paste mixture to creamed ingredients; beat until fluffy. Yield: Frosting to cover two 9-inch layers.

Mrs. Fred J. Ackerson
Middleport, N.Y.

SPECIAL CAKE ICING

1 pkg. powdered sugar
½ c. cooking oil
2 egg whites

Cream one-half of sugar with oil. Beat egg whites until stiff; whip in remaining sugar. Combine mixtures; whip.

Mrs. Emmett Moss
Gower, Mo.

VELVET CAKE FROSTING

5 tbsp. flour
1 c. milk
1 c. margarine
1 c. sugar
1 tsp. vanilla or almond flavoring

(Continued on next page)

Mix flour and milk carefully to avoid lumps. Cook slowly, stirring constantly, until thick. Cream margarine and sugar; add to cooled flour mixture. Add flavoring. Beat until light and fluffy. Spread on cooled cake or pastry.

Mrs. Robert L. Eychaner
Whidbey Island, Wash.

WHIPPED CREAM ICING

5 tbsp. flour
1 c. milk
½ c. margarine
½ c. shortening
1 c. sugar
¼ tsp. salt
1 tsp. vanilla flavoring

Beat flour with milk until smooth. Heat in saucepan, stirring constantly until thickened; cool. Combine all remaining ingredients; beat until fluffy. Add flour mixture; beat until fluffy and stiff. Spread on cake.

Mrs. Marge Edwards
Albany, Ga.

WHIPPED ICING

3 tbsp. cornstarch
1 ½ c. milk
Dash of salt
¾ c. shortening
1 c. sugar
1 tsp. vanilla flavoring

Combine cornstarch, milk and salt; boil until thickened. Cool. Combine all remaining ingredients; beat until creamy and thick. Combine mixtures; beat until smooth. Yield: Icing for a 2 layer cake.

LaVerne Sedlock
Glassport, Pa.

WHITE FROSTING

1 egg white
3 tbsp. water
1 c. sugar
1 tsp. baking powder
1 tsp. cornstarch
1 tsp. vanilla flavoring

Combine egg white, water and sugar; cook over hot water for 7 minutes, beating with an electric mixer. Add all remaining ingredients; mix until of spreading consistency.

Mrs. Florence Wesely
Mt. Pleasant, Iowa

WHITE MOUNTAIN FROSTING

1 c. sugar
½ c. water
2 egg whites
Pinch of salt
1 tsp. light syrup
1 tsp. vanilla flavoring

Put sugar and water in pan; heat until sugar dissolves. Cook until mixture spins a thread. Beat egg whites until stiff; add salt. Pour boiled mixture over egg whites, beating as you pour. Add syrup; beat until mixture stands in peaks. Add vanilla. Yield: Frosting for 1 large cake.

Mrs. Lola Stone
Benton, Ill.

ALL 'ROUND ICING

2 ½ c. sugar
½ c. light corn syrup
½ c. water
2 egg whites
1 ½ tsp. vanilla flavoring

Combine sugar, syrup and water; cook to soft ball stage. Pour over stiffly beaten egg whites, beating constantly until mixture is stiff enough to hold shape. Add vanilla; beat until well mixed. Icing may be stored in refrigerator and softened over warm water when ready to use. Yield: Frosting for one 9-inch layer cake.

Mrs. Eugene Leonard
South Elgin, Ill.

BUTTER CREAM FROSTING

½ c. butter
4 c. sifted powdered sugar
1 tsp. vanilla flavoring
Dash of salt
6 tbsp. cream

Cream butter until soft. Gradually stir in 1 cup sugar. Add vanilla and salt. Add remaining sugar alternately with cream. Beat until smooth. Add additional cream until icing has proper consistency for spreading. Yield: Frosting for a 3 layer cake.

Mrs. Lloyd R. Armstrong
Klamath Falls, Oreg.

BUTTER FROSTING

1 c. milk
4 tbsp. flour
1 c. sugar
1 ½ c. butter
1 tsp. rum flavoring

(Continued on next page)

Combine milk and flour. Cook until thick; cool. Beat sugar and butter with electric mixer for 4 minutes. Add cooled mixture; beat for 4 minutes longer. Add rum flavoring; mix well.

Mrs. Helen Deters
Sigel, Ill.

BUTTERSCOTCH CREAM FROSTING

1 c. brown sugar
⅓ c. butter or margarine
¼ c. sweet or sour cream or evaporated milk
2 c. sifted powdered sugar

Combine sugar and butter; cook over medium-high heat for 2 minutes, stirring constantly. Add cream; bring to a full boil, stirring. Remove from heat; add powdered sugar gradually, beating until smooth. Spread on cake.

Mrs. Geroma R. Gallow
Calumet, Mich.

CARROT CAKE FROSTING

1 lge. pkg. cream cheese, softened
½ stick butter, softened
1 box powdered sugar
2 tsp. vanilla flavoring
Milk

Cream cheese and butter. Add powdered sugar; mix until smooth. Stir in vanilla. Add enough milk for spreading consistency. Spread between layers and on top and sides of cake. Garnish with black walnuts.

Hester Sheridan
Springfield, Mo.

CREAMY NUT ICING

½ c. mixed shortening and butter
2 ½ tbsp. flour
¼ tsp. salt
½ c. milk
½ c. brown sugar
2 c. sifted powdered sugar
½ tsp. vanilla flavoring
½ c. chopped nuts

Melt shortening in saucepan; blend in flour and salt. Gradually add milk, stirring constantly. Bring to a boil; boil for 1 minute. Stir in brown sugar; remove from heat. Add sifted powdered sugar, vanilla and nuts.

Mrs. Howard Keener
Chicago, Ill.

CHEESE FROSTING

1 sm. pkg. cream cheese
2 tbsp. margarine
½ box powdered sugar
1 tsp. vanilla flavoring

Beat cheese and margarine; add sugar and vanilla. Beat until smooth and of spreading consistency. If too thick, add a small amount of milk.

Mrs. John Pilant, Jr.
Switz City, Ind.

FIFTY-DOLLAR FROSTING

3 tbsp. butter
3 tbsp. milk
3 tbsp. brown sugar
1 ½ c. sifted powdered sugar
1 tsp. vanilla flavoring

Mix butter, milk and brown sugar; bring to a boil. Add sugar; mix well. Stir in flavoring.

Mrs. Ethel E. Endlich
Moline, Ill.

LEMON-BUTTER CREAM FROSTING

½ c. butter or margarine
1 tsp. grated lemon rind
⅛ tsp. salt
4 c. sifted powdered sugar
2 egg yolks
2 tbsp. milk

Cream butter and lemon rind. Add salt, part of sugar and egg yolks. Beat in remaining sugar alternately with milk until creamy.

Violet P. Edgecomb
Central City, Colo.

MARASCHINO CHERRY FROSTING

1 ½ c. sugar
¼ c. cherry juice
1 tbsp. lemon juice
1 tbsp. light corn syrup
2 egg whites
Maraschino cherries

Place all ingredients except cherries in top of double boiler; mix well. Place over boiling water; beat constantly with rotary beater until stiff enough to stand in peaks. Remove from heat; beat until cool. Spread on cake; decorate with cherries.

Mrs. Marge Hubbard
Waterloo, Iowa

LORD BALTIMORE FROSTING

1 ½ c. sugar
½ c. water
1 ½ tsp. vinegar
3 egg whites
Dash of salt
1 tsp. vanilla flavoring
½ c. toasted coconut
½ c. candied cherries
¼ c. chopped pecans

Boil sugar, water and vinegar to 238 degrees or until syrup spins long thread. Beat egg whites stiff; gradually add syrup, beating constantly, until frosting holds shape. Add salt and flavoring. Fold in coconut, cherries and pecans. Spread between layers and on top and sides of cake.

Carolyn Strumsky
Baltimore, Md.

NUTTY CREAM CHEESE ICING

1 stick butter
8 oz. cream cheese
½ to 1 tsp. vanilla flavoring
1 box powdered sugar
1 c. nuts

Cream butter and cheese; add vanilla and sugar. Beat; add nuts.

Mrs. John Noall
Akron, O.

ORANGE-LEMON FROSTING

2 tsp. grated orange rind
½ tsp. grated lemon rind
3 tbsp. butter
1 egg
Dash of salt
3 ½ c. sifted powdered sugar
2 tbsp. orange juice
1 tbsp. lemon juice

Blend rinds and butter. Add egg and salt; blend well. Add sugars alternately with fruit juices; beat until smooth and of spreading consistency. Yield: Frosting for a layer cake.

Mrs. Polly Speriky
Nederland, Tex.

PENUCHE FROSTING

1 ½ c. (lightly packed) brown sugar
1 ½ c. sugar
2 tbsp. light corn syrup
¾ c. milk
¼ c. shortening
¼ c. butter

¼ tsp. salt
1 tsp. orange flavoring
1 c. chopped nuts

Combine sugars, syrup, milk, shortening, butter and salt; bring slowly to rolling boil, stirring constantly. Boil briskly for 2 minutes. Cool to lukewarm. Add flavoring; beat until thick enough to spread. Add nuts; mix. Yield: Frosting for a 2 layer cake.

Mrs. Ronald Warner
Tripoli, Iowa

PENUCHE ICING

½ c. butter
1 c. brown sugar
¼ c. milk
1 ¾ to 2 c. sifted powdered sugar

Melt butter; add brown sugar. Bring to a boil; boil over low heat for 2 minutes, stirring constantly. Stir in milk; bring to a boil again, stirring constantly. Cool to lukewarm. Gradually add powdered sugar; beat until thick enough to spread. If icing becomes too stiff, add a small amount of hot water. Yield: Frosting for a 2 layer cake.

Mrs. John P. Schlatter
Condon, Oreg.

PEANUT BUTTER ICING

3 c. powdered sugar
¼ c. peanut butter
¼ to ⅓ c. milk

Blend sugar and peanut butter. Slowly stir in milk until of spreading consistency.

Mrs. Frank Dagustime
Johnsonburg, Pa.

SEAFOAM FROSTING

1 c. (firmly packed) brown sugar
⅓ c. light corn syrup
2 egg whites
2 tbsp. water
⅛ tsp. salt
1 tsp. vanilla flavoring
½ c. chopped walnuts (opt.)

Combine all ingredients except flavoring and walnuts in top of double boiler over rapidly boiling water; beat with an electric mixer until mixture stands in peaks. Remove from heat; add flavoring. Beat until thick enough to spread. Add walnuts.

Mrs. Wade A. Schaffter
Rittman, O.

VANILLA BUTTER FROSTING

1 ½ c. milk
6 tbsp. flour
1 ½ c. butter
3 c. sifted confectioners sugar
1 tbsp. vanilla flavoring

Blend milk and flour. Cook over low heat, stirring constantly, until smooth and thick. Cool. Cream butter and confectioners sugar until light and fluffy. Stir in milk mixture and vanilla. Beat until smooth and fluffy.

Photograph for this recipe above.

STRAWBERRY WHIP

1 egg white
1 c. sugar
1 c. fresh strawberries

Whip all ingredients until stiff enough to spread on cake layers. Yield: Whip for one 2 layer cake.

Mrs. Albert O. Ness
Bayport, N.Y.

SOUR CREAM ICING

1 c. sugar
1 c. sour cream
1 c. chopped nuts
1 tsp. vanilla flavoring

Combine sugar, cream and nuts. Cook to soft ball stage. Remove from heat; add vanilla. Stir until slightly cooled. Spread over layers of cake.

Mrs. Shirley McManus
Glen Aubrey, N.Y.

AMBROSIA SAUCE FOR CREAM PUFFS

1 c. crushed pineapple
½ c. sugar
2 tbsp. chopped blanched almonds
2 tbsp. chopped Maraschino cherries
1 banana, sliced

Cook pineapple and sugar for 7 minutes or until syrupy. Add almonds and cherries; cool. Add banana; refrigerate. Spoon over ice cream or whipped cream-filled cream puffs. Yield: 10-12 servings.

Mrs. Ben F. Kirkpatrick
York, Nebr.

BUTTERSCOTCH SAUCE

2 c. sugar
2 c. brown sugar
2 c. light corn syrup
2 c. water
¾ c. plus 2 tbsp. sweetened condensed milk
¼ c. butter
1 14½-oz. can evaporated milk
1 tsp. vanilla flavoring

Combine sugars, syrup and water in saucepan. Cook to a rolling boil over low heat; boil for 10 minutes. Add condensed milk. Add butter only if sauce is to be used immediately. Cool; add evaporated milk and vanilla. NOTE: This sauce keeps indefinitely in the refrigerator. It is good as a topping for ice cream. Yield: 2 quarts.

Mrs. Robert F. Haskins
Port Clinton, O.

CREAMY CHOCOLATE SAUCE

1 10-oz. pkg. marshmallows
1 6-oz. pkg. chocolate pieces
½ c. light cream
1 tsp. vanilla flavoring

Melt marshmallows and chocolate pieces in cream over hot water. Remove from heat. Beat until smooth; stir in vanilla. NOTE: Very good served hot over ice cream. Yield: 2 1/2 cups.

Mrs. Walter Schlichting
Lake Park, Iowa

FUDGE SAUCE

¼ lb. butter
3 squares chocolate
3 c. sugar
1 can evaporated milk

Melt butter and chocolate slowly; add sugar. Add milk; mix over low heat until sugar is melted. Refrigerate. Serve over ice cream. Yield: 20-30 servings.

Mrs. Orville Thorman
Lake Mills, Wisc.

HEAVENLY HOT FUDGE SAUCE

½ c. butter
4 squares unsweetened chocolate
3 c. sugar
½ tsp. salt
1 can evaporated milk

Melt butter in double boiler. Add chocolate; melt. Slowly add sugar and salt; stir in

evaporated milk. Cook until sugar is dissolved.

Mrs. E. C. Walter
Harrisville, Pa.

HOT FUDGE SAUCE

½ c. powdered sugar
½ c. light cream
1 square chocolate
1 tsp. vanilla flavoring
½ stick butter

Combine all ingredients; simmer until sauce begins to thicken. Remove from heat; stir, mixing well. Serve on ice cream. Yield: 5 servings.

Mrs. Helen Parker
Amherst, Wisc.

ICE CREAM SAUCE

1 egg yolk, beaten
¼ c. butter
¼ c. water
⅔ c. brown sugar
⅓ c. corn syrup

Blend all ingredients. Cook until done.

Mrs. Harold Greenlee
South English, Iowa

LEMON-BUTTER SAUCE

½ c. butter
2 c. sugar
3 eggs, well beaten
½ c. water
Juice of 3 lemons
Grated rind of 3 lemons

Cream butter and sugar until light and fluffy; add an egg at a time, mixing well after each addition. Gradually add water and lemon juice, stirring constantly. Blend in lemon rind. Cook in top of double boiler over simmering water for 10 minutes or until thickened, stirring occasionally.

Mrs. William M. Lloyd
Seaford, Del.

LEMON SAUCE

1 tbsp. (heaping) cornstarch
½ c. sugar
¼ tsp. salt

(Continued on next page)

1 c. water
1 tsp. grated lemon rind
3 tbsp. lemon juice
2 tsp. butter

Mix cornstarch, sugar and salt; blend in water. Cook until mixture boils. Remove from heat; add rind, juice and butter. Use as topping for cakes and puddings.

Mrs. George Rusteberg
Maeystown, Ill.

MOCK HARD SAUCE

1 stick butter
1 lge. pkg. cream cheese
1 egg
1 lb. powdered sugar
3 tbsp. rum or whiskey

Bring butter and cream cheese to room temperature. Combine all ingredients with electric mixer; beat until smooth. Store in refrigerator in tightly covered container. NOTE: Sauce keeps well up to one month. Yield: 1 quart.

Mrs. H. B. Turner, Jr.
Savanna, Ill.

ORANGE TOPPING

3 or 4 egg yolks
1 c. sugar
Juice of 2 oranges
Grated rind of 2 oranges
2 c. whipped cream

Place egg yolks in top of double boiler; beat until foamy. Add sugar, juice and rind; mix well. Cook until thick. Fold in whipped cream.

Mrs. Duane Morgan
Hatton, N.D.

PEAR-ORANGE TOPPING

4 pears
1 c. sugar
½ c. orange juice
½ c. water
3 tsp. grated orange rind

Pare, halve and core pears. Heat sugar, orange juice and water to boiling; add pears. Simmer, covered, until tender. Remove

pears; add orange rind. Simmer for 5 to 10 minutes or until of desired consistency. Chill. Serve as a topping for vanilla ice cream. Yield: 8 servings.

Mrs. Arthur J. Connelson
New Orleans, La.

PRALINE CRUNCH TOPPING

½ c. butter
1 c. brown sugar
½ c. broken pecans
2 ½ c. corn flakes

Boil butter and sugar for 2 minutes. Remove from heat. Add pecans and flakes; toss with fork to coat. Spread on foil to cool. Break up; store in a jar. Serve over vanilla ice cream. Yield: 10 servings.

Mrs. John G. Long
Honolulu, Hawaii

QUICK CAKE TOPPING

Butter
2 c. brown sugar
5 tbsp. milk
1 tsp. vanilla flavoring
⅓ c. coconut

Spread butter over hot cake. Combine sugar, milk and flavoring; spread mixture on cake. Sprinkle coconut on top. Broil for a few minutes to brown. Yield: Frosting for 1 large loaf cake.

Luella Babrock
South Boardman, Mich.

RHUM BLANC MANGE

6 tbsp. cornstarch
Pinch of salt
1 qt. light cream
Sugar
1 c. light rum
Fruit

Mix cornstarch, salt and cream until smooth. Add sugar to taste. Heat in heavy saucepan until cream boils. Cook for a few minutes, stirring constantly. Remove from heat; add rum. Chill. Serve with sweetened sliced peaches or other fruit. Yield: 8 servings.

Mrs. John E. Goldom
Ft. Irwin, Calif.

SAUCES

SAUCE FOR ANGEL FOOD CAKE

½ c. sugar
¼ c. cornstarch
1 c. cherry juice
1 c. pineapple juice
4 egg yolks, beaten
1 pt. heavy cream, whipped
1 c. seeded and halved Royal Anne cherries
1 c. pineapple chunks
¼ c. Maraschino cherry halves
½ c. chopped nuts
1 angel food cake

Mix sugar and cornstarch with fruit juices. Cook in top of double boiler until thickened. Add egg yolks; cook for 5 minutes. Cool. Add whipped cream, fruit and nuts. Slice cake; serve with sauce. Yield: 12 servings.

Mrs. Lewis Teeple
Sparta, Tenn.

SAUCE FOR ANGEL FOOD OR POUND CAKE

Juice of 2 oranges
Juice of 1 lemon
1 banana, mashed
1 c. sugar

Mix all ingredients; refrigerate for 1 hour. Spoon over ice cream and cake. Yield: 6-8 servings.

Mrs. Walter Folger
Portland, Me.

SAUCE FOR ICE CREAM

½ c. butter
2 squares bitter chocolate
2 c. sifted powdered sugar
¾ c. evaporated milk

Melt butter and chocolate; add all remaining ingredients. Cook over low heat for 10 minutes.

Mrs. Alden Hanes
Amherst Junction, Wisc.

SHERRIED MINCEMEAT SAUCE

2 ½ c. mincemeat
½ c. walnuts
½ c. Sherry

Combine mincemeat and walnuts in saucepan; heat to boiling, stirring. Remove from heat; stir in Sherry. Serve warm over vanilla ice cream in sherbet dishes. Yield: 8 servings.

Mrs. C. J. Mair
Norfolk, Va.

TOPPING FOR FRUIT

1 c. sugar
2 eggs, separated
1 c. Sherry
1 c. heavy cream, whipped

Add 2/3 cup sugar to beaten yolks; add remaining sugar to beaten egg whites. Add yolks and Sherry to whipped cream; fold in egg whites. Serve on fruit. Yield: 6 servings.

Mrs. James E. Henderson
Fort Ord, Calif.

TOPPING FOR GINGERBREAD

¼ c. butter, softened
½ c. sugar
1 egg
Flavoring

Combine all ingredients; beat until smooth and sugar is dissolved. Add any flavoring desired.

Mrs. William Evans
Medicine Bow, Wyo.

WARM LEMON SAUCE

½ c. sugar
1 tbsp. cornstarch
1 c. boiling water
2 tbsp. butter
2 tbsp. lemon juice
Pinch of salt
Nutmeg to taste (opt.)

Mix sugar and cornstarch in heavy saucepan. Gradually add boiling water, stirring constantly. Boil for 5 minutes. Remove from heat. Add butter, lemon juice, salt and nutmeg. Serve warm. This is especially good served over hot gingerbread or hot spice cake. Yield: 4-6 servings.

Mrs. G. K. Robinson, Jr.
Colts Neck, N.J.

YUMMY HOT FUDGE SAUCE

2 c. sugar
1 tbsp. (heaping) flour
1 ⅔ c. evaporated milk
4 squares semi-sweet chocolate
1 tsp. vanilla flavoring
¼ c. butter
½ tsp. salt

Boil sugar, flour, milk and chocolate for 1 minute, stirring constantly. When chocolate is melted, beat well with spoon. Remove from heat; stir in vanilla, butter and salt. Store in refrigerator; heat before serving over ice cream. Yield: 1 pint.

Mrs. Donald McKee
Montezuma, Iowa

RECIPE FOR QUICK PEANUT FUDGE ON PAGE 98

Candies
and Confections

Candy Making Time . . .

. . . is fun time for most folks. But candy doesn't always turn out right. To help you have successful candy making sessions, try these suggestions.

The secret to successful candy making lies in following the recipe closely, using correct equipment, measuring carefully and accurately and making accurate tests for the "doneness" of the candy.

A. EQUIPMENT:

Always use standard measuring spoons and cups. A cooking pan four times the volume of the ingredients or a 3-quart capacity for each 1½ pounds of candy is necessary. This lets the candy boil up without overflowing the pan.

A long handled wooden spoon, spatula, sturdy wire egg beater and a candy thermometer are the other essentials. Large, shallow cooling pans are handy, but platters, bowls or utility pans will serve the purpose.

B. MEASURING:

Always measure carefully. Sift granulated sugar into a standard dry measuring cup and level off with a spatula. Sift confectioners sugar and dip into cup with a spoon; level off. Pack brown sugar firmly into a cup and level off.

C. MAKE ACCURATE TESTS:

The temperature at which candy is considered done is known as the "finish point."

1. Cold Water Test—This test is fairly accurate for experienced candy makers, but is best used in combination with the candy thermometer. Fill a cup with cold water and drop about ½ teaspoon of the boiling candy syrup into the water. Form into a ball with your fingers, keeping the candy under the water. Pick up the ball to judge its consistency as to the stage of cooking.

2. Candy Thermometer—The candy thermometer gives the most accurate results. Under normal conditions water boils at 212° F. The altitude and atmospheric pressure affects candy making. Use the following chart as a guide to success in making candy.

D. CRYSTAL CONTROL:

The proper control of the crystals affects the quality of candy. There should be small crystals in fondants and fudges and none in caramels.

For fondants, mix ingredients thoroughly. Cover and bring slowly to a boil, stirring as needed. Remove the cover and increase the heat to cook more rapidly to the finish point. For fondant, wipe the crystals from the edges of the pan.

Place pan of candy in cold water or pour into pans to cool quickly. Let cool to room temperature before stirring. When the bottom of the pan can be held comfortably in the hand, stir vigorously until creamy.

Fudge may be poured into a buttered pan to harden, or like fondant, poured onto a buttered surface and kneaded. It may be kneaded immediately or covered with a damp cloth and left for 20 minutes.

Candy is kneaded to make it creamier, however, it must not be over-kneaded. Press the candy into a buttered pan or dish; cover with waxed paper and let stand until firm.

Avoid tough, hard or chewy caramels by increasing the amount of fat in cream or butter and by not overcooking. Crystallization may be controlled by increasing the amount of corn syrup and by stirring the cooking mixture only enough to thoroughly mix the ingredients.

HIGH ALTITUDE ADJUSTMENTS

To adjust sugar recipes for altitude, reduce the finish temperature. If you use a candy thermometer, first test the temperature at which water boils. While there will be minor changes from day to day due to weather conditions, the range is usually slight. At 5,000 feet altitude, water boils at approximately 202° F., or 10° less than at sea level. Therefore, correct the finish temperature for the candy by subtracting the 10°. For example, if a sea-level recipe for creamy fudge gives a finish temperature for syrup at 238° F., at 5,000 feet the thermometer reading would be 228° F.

TEMPERATURE TESTS FOR CANDY MAKING AT VARIOUS ALTITUDES

CANDY	TEST IN COLD WATER	DEGREES F. ON CANDY THERMOMETER			
		SEA LEVEL	2,000 ft.	5,000 ft.	7,500 ft.
FUDGE, FONDANT	SOFT BALL (can be picked up but flattens)	234-240	230-236	224-230	219-225
CARAMELS	FIRM BALL (holds shape unless pressed)	242-248	238-244	232-238	227-233
DIVINITY, TAFFY, CARAMEL CORN	HARD BALL (holds shape though pliable)	250-268	246-264	240-258	235-253
BUTTERSCOTCH, ENGLISH TOFFEE	SOFT CRACK (separates into hard threads but not brittle)	270-290	266-286	260-280	255-275
BRITTLES	HARD CRACK (separates into hard, brittle threads)	300-310	296-306	290-300	285-295

CARAMELS

4 c. sugar
1 c. milk
1 tsp. salt
2 c. nuts
2 tbsp. butter

Caramelize 1 cup sugar in heavy saucepan or skillet. Place remaining sugar and milk in saucepan; cook over low heat. Add caramelized sugar to mixture in saucepan slowly, stirring constantly. Continue cooking to soft ball stage. Remove from heat; add salt, nuts and butter. Beat until creamy. Pour into well greased pan; cool. Cut into squares. Yield: 4 pounds.

Mary Ella Porter
Como, Tex.

COCONUT SQUARES

2 c. sugar
2 tbsp. butter
½ c. milk
1 c. shredded coconut
1 tsp. vanilla flavoring

Mix sugar, butter and milk until sugar dissolves. Cook slowly, stirring constantly, to 280 degrees or to soft ball stage. Remove from heat; stir in coconut and vanilla. Beat until creamy. Place in buttered 8 or 9-inch pan. Let set for 30 minutes. Yield: 6 servings.

Mrs. W. T. Sode
Seattle, Wash.

CREAM CANDY

1 pt. heavy cream
2 c. sugar
½ c. light corn syrup
½ c. walnuts
½ tsp. vanilla flavoring

Combine 1/2 pint cream, sugar and syrup; cook until light brown and creamy. Add remaining cream, a small amount at a time; keep boiling. Cook until candy forms a firm ball in water. Remove from heat; beat. Add nuts and vanilla. Pour into buttered pan.

Mrs. Luolo Walch
Coeur d'Alene, Idaho

BEST EVER CARAMEL FUDGE

1 c. milk
4 c. sugar
2 tbsp. light corn syrup
½ stick butter
1 c. (or more) pecans

Put milk and 3 cups sugar into 6-quart pan. Simmer gently. Put remaining sugar into a separate pan; stir well until sugar is thoroughly liquified and brown. Pour into milk mixture; stir well. When thoroughly blended, add corn syrup. Cook to soft ball stage. Turn off heat; stir in butter. When partially cool, beat well. Add nuts. Pour onto buttered platter; cut when cool.

Virginia Tidball
Fayetteville, Ark.

BEST CHOCOLATE FUDGE

2 squares unsweetened chocolate, cut into
    pieces
⅔ c. cold milk
2 c. sugar
Dash of salt
2 tbsp. butter
1 tsp. vanilla flavoring

Add chocolate to milk; place over low heat. Cook until mixture is smooth and blended, stirring constantly. Add sugar and salt; stir until sugar is dissolved and mixture boils. Continue cooking, without stirring, until mixture reaches 232 degrees or until a small amount forms a very soft ball in cold water. Remove from heat. Add butter and vanilla. Cool to lukewarm or 110 degrees. Beat until mixture begins to thicken and loses its gloss. Pour at once into greased pan. Cool; cut into squares. Yield: 18 pieces.

Mrs. Clyde H. Webb
Parkersburg, W. Va.

BUTTERMILK FUDGE

2 c. sugar
2 tbsp. corn syrup
1 c. buttermilk
2 tbsp. butter
1 tsp. soda
1 tsp. vanilla flavoring
1 c. nuts
Pinch of salt

Combine all ingredients except flavoring, in deep heavy boiler. Cook, stirring constantly, until mixture forms a soft ball in cold water. Remove from heat; beat until creamy. Add flavoring, nuts and salt. Yield: 24 servings.

Mrs. Lovic Langheld
Minden, La.

CREAMY CHOCOLATE FUDGE

3 c. sugar
1 tbsp. unflavored gelatin
3 squares chocolate

(Continued on next page)

½ c. (scant) corn syrup
1 c. milk
1 ¼ c. margarine
2 tsp. vanilla flavoring
1 c. chopped nuts

Mix sugar and gelatin; add all remaining ingredients except vanilla and nuts. Cook over medium heat to soft ball stage. Add vanilla; cool for 15 minutes. Beat for 7 minutes or until firm. Add nuts; pour into greased pan. Cool; cut into squares.

Lera Nette Sturdivant
Flomaton, Ala.

CREAMY FUDGE

4 ½ c. sugar
1 can evaporated milk
½ lb. butter
4 pkg. chocolate pieces
1 jar marshmallow creme
1 tsp. vanilla flavoring
Nuts (opt.)

Boil sugar, milk and butter for 8 minutes. Remove from heat; stir in chocolate pieces, marshmallow creme and vanilla. Add nuts; stir quickly. Turn into large greased pan. Yield: 5 pounds.

Mrs. Margaret Koran
Homewood, Ill.

HAWAIIAN FUDGE

2 c. sugar
½ c. drained crushed pineapple
½ c. thin cream
1 tbsp. butter
½ c. pecans
Green food coloring (opt.)

Mix all ingredients except pecans. Cook to soft ball stage; cool. Beat until creamy, adding nuts. Tint light green.

Mrs. Alice E. Daggett
Camp Point, Ill.

NEVER-FAIL FUDGE

10 marshmallows
¼ lb. butter
¾ c. evaporated milk
2 c. sugar
1 ½ c. chocolate pieces
½ c. nuts (opt.)

Melt marshmallows with butter. Boil milk with sugar for 6 minutes. Pour over marshmallows and chocolate pieces; stir until creamy and thick. Add nuts. Pour into buttered pan; cool.

Mrs. Billy G. Miller
Dam Neck, Va.

NEVER-FAIL PEANUT BUTTER FUDGE

2 c. sugar
1 c. milk
Dash of salt
2 tbsp. butter
1 tsp. vanilla flavoring
¾ c. crunchy peanut butter

Boil sugar, milk and salt for 10 minutes; add butter. Continue boiling until mixture forms a soft ball in cold water. Remove from heat; add vanilla and peanut butter. Beat until mixture starts to set. Pour quickly into buttered pan. Cut into squares.

Frances G. Young
Lowville, N.Y.

PEANUT BUTTER FUDGE

1 c. butter or margarine
1 ⅔ c. evaporated milk
4 c. sugar
1 pt. marshmallow creme
1 c. peanut butter

Combine butter, milk and sugar. Boil until it reaches 240 degrees or soft ball stage. Remove from heat; add marshmallow creme and peanut butter. Beat well; pour into 10 x 14-inch pan. Let set for several hours; cut when cooled. Keeps well in a closed container. Yield: 3 1/2 pounds.

Hanna Rees
St. Charles, Ill.

PEANUT BUTTER-MARSHMALLOW FUDGE

3 c. sugar
1 ½ c. milk
1 tbsp. corn syrup
Pinch of salt
1 c. peanut butter
1 c. marshmallow creme

Combine sugar, milk, corn syrup and salt; cook to soft ball stage. Remove from heat; add peanut butter and marshmallow creme. Beat well; pour onto buttered platter or shallow pan. Cut into squares before it completely hardens. Yield: 24 large squares.

Mrs. H. H. Guy
Waiteville, W. Va.

CANDIES, CONFECTIONS

QUICK PEANUT FUDGE

2 c. sugar
3 tbsp. butter
1 c. evaporated milk
1 c. miniature marshmallows
1 12-oz. jar chunk-style peanut butter
1 tsp. vanilla extract

Combine sugar, butter and evaporated milk in an electric skillet. Set thermostat at 280 degrees. Bring mixture to a boil; boil for 5 minutes, stirring constantly. Turn off skillet. Add marshmallows, peanut butter and vanilla. Stir until marshmallows and peanut butter are melted and blended. Pour into buttered 8-inch square pan. Cool; cut into squares. Yield: 2 pounds candy.

Photograph for this recipe on page 93 .

VANILLA FUDGE

1 ½ lb. sugar
½ c. light syrup
1 ¼ c. evaporated milk
¼ lb. margarine or butter
1 tsp. vanilla flavoring

Combine sugar, syrup, milk and margarine. Cook over medium heat to hard ball stage. Remove from heat. Add vanilla; beat until it loses its glossy appearance. Pour onto greased plates; cool. Cut into squares. Yield: 2 pounds.

Elizabeth Triplett
Strange Creek, W. Va.

GELATIN CANDY

3 c. sugar
¾ c. water
¾ c. light corn syrup
2 egg whites
1 pkg. gelatin
Nuts or coconut (opt.)

Cook sugar, water and syrup to soft ball stage. Beat egg whites until stiff, gradually adding gelatin. Continue beating with electric mixer, slowly adding one-half of the cooked syrup. Cook remaining syrup to hard ball stage; add to mixture. Add nuts. Continue beating until it has a dull appearance and will hold its shape. Drop by teaspoonfuls onto waxed paper. Yield: 100 pieces.

Mrs. Neil Fisher
Bellefontaine, O.

HOLIDAY DELIGHT

3 c. sugar
1 c. light syrup

1 ½ c. light cream
1 ½ tsp. vanilla flavoring
½ lb. Brazil nuts, halved
½ lb. whole pecans
½ lb. English walnuts, broken
½ lb. candied cherries, halved
½ lb. candied pineapple, chopped

Cook sugar, syrup and cream to soft ball stage. Remove from heat; begin beating without cooling. Mixture will thicken and change colors. Beat in vanilla. Gradually add all remaining ingredients. Pack into well buttered, paper-lined pan. Press into corners with wet spoon. Chill for 24 hours; slice. Candy will keep for months in refrigerator. Yield: 5 pounds.

Isabel Kelly
Rice Lake, Wisc.

PECAN CANDY

2 c. sugar
1 ½ c. water
8 tbsp. light syrup
2 c. chopped pecans
2 tbsp. butter
2 tsp. vanilla flavoring

Combine sugar, water, syrup and nuts; cook to soft ball stage. Remove from heat; add butter and vanilla. Beat until smooth and creamy. Pour into buttered 5 x 8-inch pan.

Mrs. James D. Higgins
Springfield, Mo.

PENUCHE CANDY

2 lb. dark brown sugar
1 lb. sugar
1 ⅔ c. evaporated milk
1 c. milk
½ lb. butter
2 sm. pkg. caramel pieces
1 c. chopped pecans
1 jar marshmallow creme

Combine sugars, milks and butter; boil for 10 minutes, stirring constantly. Remove from heat; add all remaining ingredients, stirring until set. Pour onto buttered cookie sheet. Let harden; cut into squares. Yield: 5 pounds candy.

Rose L. Rohde
Elmira, N.Y.

BUTTERMILK CANDY

2 c. sugar
1 c. buttermilk
2 tbsp. light corn syrup

(Continued on next page)

98

1 tsp. soda
1 stick butter or margarine
1 tsp. vanilla flavoring
Pinch of salt
1 c. chopped pecans

Combine sugar, buttermilk, syrup, soda and butter in large pan. Cook to soft ball stage; remove from heat. Add vanilla and salt; beat well. Add pecans; drop from teaspoon.

Mrs. Roe Sowards
Pine Bluff, Ark.

COCOA-OATMEAL CANDY

2 c. sugar
3 tbsp. cocoa
½ tsp. salt
1 stick margarine
½ c. milk
½ c. peanut butter
4 ½ c. uncooked oats
1 tsp. vanilla flavoring

Mix sugar, cocoa, salt, margarine and milk in saucepan. Boil for 2 minutes. Remove from heat; add peanut butter, oats and vanilla. Mix thoroughly; drop onto waxed paper. Yield: 4 dozen.

Amelia Terrebonne
Loranger, La.

CREAM FONDANT

3 c. sugar
1 ⅓ c. water
½ tsp. cream of tartar
½ tsp. salt
¼ c. orange juice
3 c. pecan halves

Combine all ingredients except juice and nuts. Cook over medium heat until it forms a soft ball. Do not stir. Cool; add juice and nuts. Beat until creamy and holds shape; drop by spoonfuls onto waxed paper.

Mrs. M. W. Patrick
White Oak, S.C.

CAN'T FAIL DIVINITY

2 c. sugar
½ c. water
Pinch of salt
1 pt. marshmallow creme
½ c. nuts or fruit
1 tsp. vanilla flavoring

Boil sugar, water and salt until mixture forms a hard ball in cold water. Place marshmallow creme in mixing bowl; stir in hot syrup. Continue stirring until slightly stiff. Fold in nuts

and vanilla. Drop from spoon onto waxed paper. Yield: 24 servings.

Mrs. E. G. Roberson, Jr.
DeWitt, Ark.

CARAMEL DIVINITY

1 c. sugar
1 c. brown sugar
⅓ c. light corn syrup
½ c. water
2 egg whites, stiffly beaten
1 tbsp. vanilla flavoring
1 ½ c. chopped pecans

Combine sugars, syrup and water in pan; boil to soft ball stage. Pour one-third of mixture over egg whites; beat or mix at slow speed. Boil remaining mixture for 5 minutes. Add one-half of mixture to egg white mixture. Cook remaining mixture for 2 minutes. Add egg white mixture. Add vanilla; fold in pecans by hand until mixture loses its gloss. Drop by teaspoonfuls onto oiled paper. Yield: 20 servings.

Mrs. Zelma Null
San Angelo, Tex.

DIVINITY

5 c. sugar
1 c. light corn syrup
1 c. water
3 egg whites, stiffly beaten
1 tbsp. vanilla flavoring
1 c. chopped English walnuts or pecans
½ c. chopped black walnuts

Cook sugar, syrup and water to soft ball stage. Add one-half of the hot mixture to egg whites; beat until cool. Let remaining syrup cool until it forms hard ball in cold water. Add to egg white mixture; beat until smooth. Add vanilla and nuts. Pour into buttered pan; spread 1-inch thick. Cut into squares.

Mrs. E. C. Beeson
Norman, Okla.

DIVINITY

2 ½ c. sugar
¼ c. light corn syrup
½ c. water
2 egg whites, stiffly beaten
1 tsp. vanilla flavoring

Mix sugar, syrup and water. Cook over moderate heat until mixture forms a soft ball in cold water. Pour hot syrup mixture slowly into beaten egg whites, beating constantly.

(Continued on next page)

Beat until mixture begins to hold its shape. Add vanilla; mix thoroughly. Spoon lightly into soft mounds on waxed paper. Let set; serve. Yield: 36 pieces.

Mary Louise Sexton
Warsaw, O.

GELATIN DIVINITY

3 c. sugar
¾ c. light corn syrup
¾ c. water
2 egg whites, stiffly beaten
1 pkg. flavored gelatin
1 c. chopped pecans

Combine sugar, corn syrup and water; bring to a boil, stirring constantly. Reduce heat and cook until hard ball stage is reached, stirring occasionally. Combine egg whites and gelatin; beat until mixture forms peaks. Pour hot syrup into egg whites in a thin stream, beating until candy loses gloss and holds shape. Fold in nuts; pour into greased pan. Cut into squares.

Mrs. W. W. Ziegler
Waterboro, S.C.

MARBLE DIVINITY

½ c. light corn syrup
1 c. water
3 c. sugar
¼ tsp. salt
2 egg whites
1 tsp. vanilla flavoring
1 6-oz. pkg. semi-sweet chocolate pieces

Bring syrup and water to a boil; remove from heat. Add sugar; return mixture to heat, stirring constantly, until sugar is dissolved. Cover and boil for 3 minutes. Remove cover; insert candy thermometer. Boil to 266 degrees or to hard ball stage. Beat salt and egg whites almost stiff; pour in hot syrup slowly, beating continuously. Add vanilla; continue beating until mixture begins to get waxy, so the path of the beater is well defined and remains. Quickly fold in chocolate pieces; spread in buttered 9-inch pan. Cut while warm; cool in pan. Yield: 2 pounds.

Altha Bisaillon
Aroma Park, Ill.

NEVER-FAIL DIVINITY FUDGE

4 c. sugar
1 ¾ c. water
3 egg whites
1 c. light corn syrup
2 tsp. vanilla flavoring
1 c. broken nuts

Cook 1 cup sugar and 3/4 cup water until it spins a thread. Slowly add to stiffly beaten egg whites, beating with electric mixer on medium speed. Cook remaining sugar, water and corn syrup until brittle when tested in cold water. Add slowly to egg white mixture, beating constantly until stiff. Add vanilla and nuts. Pour into 9 x 13-inch pan. When cool, cut into 1-inch squares. Store in a tight container.

Mrs. F. J. Statts
Cape May, N.J.

PASTEL DIVINITY

3 c. sugar
¾ c. light corn syrup
¾ c. water
2 egg whites
1 3-oz. pkg. flavored gelatin
1 c. chopped nuts
½ c. grated coconut
1 tsp. vanilla flavoring

Mix sugar, syrup and water; stir until sugar is dissolved. Cook to hard ball stage. Beat egg whites until fluffy. Gradually add gelatin powder, beating until mixture holds peak. Pour syrup into egg white mixture, beating constantly until candy holds shape and loses gloss. Fold in nuts and coconut. Add vanilla. Drop from spoon onto waxed paper or quickly pour into 8-inch square pan. Let stand until set. Cut into pieces with a knife which has been dipped into hot water.

Beth N. Crosland
Fillmore, Utah

RASPBERRY DIVINITY

3 c. sugar
¾ c. light syrup
½ c. hot water
2 egg whites
1 pkg. raspberry gelatin
1 c. chopped nuts

Cook sugar, syrup and water to hard ball stage or 252 degrees, stirring often. Beat egg whites until foamy; add gelatin. Continue beating until egg whites form a peak. Slowly beat in hot syrup mixture. Continue beating until mixture will hold shape. Add nuts; drop quickly onto waxed paper or pour into greased pan.

Maude Dixon
Bentonville, Ark.

HAWAIIAN CANDY

1 c. sugar
½ c. brown sugar

(Continued on next page)

1 c. cream
1 tsp. butter
1 tsp. ginger
1 tsp. vanilla flavoring
2 c. crushed pineapple, well drained
½ c. chopped nuts

Combine sugars, cream, butter and ginger; boil to soft ball stage, stirring constantly. Cool to lukewarm; add vanilla. Beat until creamy; add pineapple and nuts. Spread on oiled surface to harden.

Mrs. George H. Beaulieu
Pawhuska, Okla.

ORANGE CANDY

2 c. sugar
½ c. light corn syrup
½ c. evaporated milk
2 tbsp. margarine
Grated rind of 1 large orange
1 c. chopped nuts

Combine all ingredients except nuts; blend well. Cook until it forms a soft ball in cold water, stirring just enough to prevent sticking. Cool; beat until creamy. Add nuts just before candy is ready to drop or pour. Drop by teaspoonfuls onto waxed paper or pour into buttered container. Cut into squares. Yield: 20 to 30 pieces.

Mrs. H. M. Thomas
Breckenridge, Tex.

MASHED POTATO MINTS

1 med. potato, peeled and quartered
2 tbsp. milk
1 tsp. salt
1 tsp. vanilla flavoring
2 boxes powdered sugar, sifted
Flavoring
Food coloring

Boil potato in small amount of water. When tender, remove cover; boil away all water. Beat until fluffy with electric mixer. Add milk, salt and vanilla. Slowly add powdered sugar until mixture is thick. Divide mixture into thirds or quarters; add favorite flavoring and coloring as desired. Drop by teaspoonfuls onto waxed paper or push through cookie press. Let stand until firm. Store in airtight container. NOTE: Suggested combinations are pink with wintergreen, green with peppermint, yellow with lemon flavoring and red with cinnamon.

Mrs. J. P. Vollmer
Albuquerque, N.M.

MEXICAN PECAN CANDY

1 c. milk
2 c. sugar
3 tbsp. light corn syrup
2 c. nut halves
2 tbsp. butter
1 tsp. vanilla flavoring

Cook milk, sugar, corn syrup and nuts to 240 degrees or soft ball stage. Remove from heat; add butter and vanilla. Cool to lukewarm. Beat until candy begins to thicken; drop from teaspoon onto buttered waxed paper.

Charlotte Becker
Slaton, Tex.

MEXICAN PECAN CANDY

4 c. brown sugar
4 c. pecans
1 c. milk
3 tbsp. butter

Cook all ingredients to soft ball stage as indicated on candy thermometer. Beat until candy begins to thicken and is creamy. Drop by teaspoonfuls onto greased baking tin. Yield: 48 servings.

Mrs. Richard A. Steele
Lubbock, Tex.

OATMEAL CANDY

3 c. quick cooking oats
6 tbsp. cocoa
1 c. coconut
½ c. nuts
2 c. sugar
1 stick margarine
¾ c. milk

Combine oats, cocoa, coconut and nuts; mix well. Combine remaining ingredients. Bring to a boil; cook for 3 minutes. Pour over oat mixture; mix well. Cool. Drop by teaspoonfuls onto waxed paper.

Mrs. W. H. Graham
New River, N.C.

SEAFOAM NUT KISSES

1 egg white
¼ c. instant dry milk
1 tbsp. water
¾ c. brown sugar
⅛ tsp. salt
1 tbsp. flour
1 c. chopped nuts

(Continued on next page)

Beat egg white, dry milk and water in small bowl with electric mixer at high speed until stiff. Beat in 1 tablespoon brown sugar at a time until glossy and thick. Scrape sides of bowl often. Fold in mixture of salt, flour and nuts. Drop by teaspoonfuls onto greased and floured cookie sheet. Bake at 325 degrees for 15 minutes or until light brown. Remove from sheet; cool on wire rack.

Mrs. Ann Rushing
Fayette, Miss.

ALMOND BRITTLE

1 c. almonds
½ c. sugar
2 tbsp. butter
Salt

Mix all ingredients except salt. Cook over low heat for 10 to 12 minutes or until color changes, stirring constantly. Spread on foil. Salt lightly; break into pieces.

Mrs. O. S. Dews
Ogden, Utah

ALMOND-BUTTER CRUNCH

1 lb. butter
1 lb. sugar
1 c. coarsely chopped almonds
1 lge. or 2 sm. pkg. chocolate pieces

Combine butter, sugar and 1/2 cup almonds in heavy 3-quart saucepan. Heat slowly to boiling point; boil gently until mixture reaches 305 degrees or hard crack stage, stirring constantly. Pour onto large buttered jelly roll sheet. Sprinkle with one-half of the chocolate pieces; spread with spatula. Sprinkle with 1/4 cup almonds; cool. Turn sheet over; sprinkle with remaining chocolate pieces. Place under broiler to melt chocolate; spread with spatula. Sprinkle with remaining almonds. When cool, break into pieces. Store in airtight can. Yield: 80 pieces.

Mrs. William C. Ryan
Charleston, S.C.

ENGLISH ALMOND TOFFEE

⅔ c. butter
½ c. sugar
⅓ c. water
¾ tsp. salt
⅔ c. blanched almonds
½ c. semi-sweet chocolate pieces
½ c. chopped pecans

Combine butter, sugar, water and 1/2 teaspoon salt; bring to a boil over low heat, stirring constantly. Cook without stirring to 236 degrees or until it forms soft ball. Add almonds and continue cooking to 290 degrees or to soft crack stage, stirring constantly. Remove from heat. Mixture will change to a deep caramel color. Stir in remaining salt; turn out onto greased baking sheet. Spread to 1/4-inch thickness. Sprinkle chocolate over top; spread as it melts. Sprinkle with pecans; cool. Break into pieces.

Mrs. E. S. Stacy
Whiteman AFB, Mo.

BUTTER CRUNCH

1 ¼ c. butter
1 ⅔ c. sugar
4 tsp. light corn syrup
¼ c. water
1 tsp. salt
½ c. coarsely ground nuts
½ lb. milk chocolate, melted
1 c. finely chopped nuts

Combine all ingredients except chocolate and chopped nuts in heavy saucepan. Cook to 300 degrees. Pour onto cookie sheet. Spread melted chocolate over candy when cool. Sprinkle chopped nuts over top.

Mrs. G. D. Brewster
Condon, Oreg.

MOLASSES-BUTTERSCOTCH CANDY

1 c. sugar
¼ c. molasses
½ c. butter
1 tbsp. vinegar
3 tbsp. hot water
Pinch of salt
½ tsp. lemon flavoring

Combine all ingredients except lemon flavoring. Cook over low heat, stirring constantly. When mixture reaches hard ball stage or 260 degrees, add lemon flavoring. Pour into greased 8-inch square tin; cool. Break into bite-sized pieces.

Martha Jane Lightfoote
Geneva, N.Y.

MOLASSES-PEANUT BRITTLE

2 c. sugar
1 c. light corn syrup
½ c. water
¼ c. dark molasses
2 tbsp. butter
2 c. salted peanuts
1 tbsp. soda

(Continued on next page)

102

Combine sugar, syrup and water in 3-quart saucepan. Bring to a boil, stirring until sugar is dissolved. Cook to hard crack stage or to 290 degrees. Stir in molasses and butter; continue to cook for 30 seconds. Remove from heat; quickly stir in peanuts and soda. Mix thoroughly; pour immediately onto large buttered cookie sheet. When cool, break into pieces. Yield: 2 pounds.

Mrs. Glenn Harris
Jennings, La.

PEANUT BRITTLE

3 c. sugar
1 c. corn syrup
½ c. water
2 c. raw Spanish peanuts
½ tsp. salt
1 tbsp. butter
1 tsp. vanilla flavoring
2 tsp. soda

Put sugar, syrup and water into large heavy saucepan. Boil to 250 degrees, being sure to stir until sugar is dissolved. Add peanuts, salt and butter all at once. Cook to 300 degrees. Peanuts will begin to brown, skins will pop and syrup will turn a yellow-brown. Remove from heat. Immediately stir in vanilla and soda. Pour quickly in a ribbon down center of four buttered cookie sheets; candy will foam. Do not spread out in pans with spoon, but as soon as you can, slip a knife under edges and carefully pull candy out thin toward edges of pans. One must work quickly in pulling this candy thin before it sets up and hardens.

Mrs. Don Majeres
Garrison, N.D.

PEANUT BRITTLE CANDY

1 c. sugar
½ c. light syrup
½ c. water
1 c. raw peanuts
1 tbsp. butter
1 tsp. vanilla flavoring
2 tsp. soda

Boil sugar, syrup and water until mixture spins a thread. Add peanuts; cook until mixture becomes amber-colored. Remove from heat; add butter, vanilla and soda. Mix well; pour onto buttered cookie sheet. Do not try to spread. Candy will be ready to break in about 10 minutes.

Mrs. Clara Hudson
Chandlerville, Ill.

CHINESE NEW YEAR'S CANDY

1 pkg. semi-sweet chocolate pieces
1 pkg. butterscotch or caramel pieces

1 sm. can salted peanuts
1 can Chinese noodles

Melt chocolate and butterscotch pieces in top of double boiler. Add peanuts and noodles; mix with fork. Spread in buttered pan or plate. Cool; cut into pieces. Store in refrigerator. Yield: 20-25 pieces.

Mrs. James E. McKenna
Norfolk, Va.

CANDY TREATS

1 pkg. butterscotch pieces
1 can chow mein noodles
1 can cocktail peanuts or pecans

Melt butterscotch; add noodles and peanuts. Drop onto waxed paper; chill.

Mrs. W. K. Sargent
Montgomery, Ala.

CHOCOLATE ANGELETTES

½ 7-oz. pkg. semi-sweet chocolate pieces
½ c. butter
½ c. sifted powdered sugar
3 tbsp. milk, cream or evaporated milk
24 1-in. cubes angel or sponge cake
½ c. chopped pecans
½ c. shredded coconut

Melt chocolate and butter in pan over hot water. Stir in powdered sugar and milk. Keep over hot, not boiling, water. Dip cubes of cake with fork into chocolate mixture; roll one-half of the cubes in chopped nuts. Roll remaining half in coconut. Place on waxed paper. Yield: 24 servings.

Mrs. Edith M. Luttman
Wakefield, Kans.

CHOCOLATE-COVERED CANDY

1 pkg. powdered sugar
1 stick butter or margarine, melted
1 can sweetened condensed milk
1 qt. chopped pecans
½ pkg. paraffin
1 pkg. semi-sweet chocolate pieces

Mix sugar, butter, milk and nuts. Shape into balls. Set in refrigerator for 15 to 20 minutes. Melt paraffin and chocolate in double boiler; dip candy balls into mixture. Place on waxed paper until chocolate coating is hard.

Mildred DeBlieux
Bastrop, La.

CHOCOLATE-COCONUT BALLS

1 stick butter
3 c. chopped nuts
2 cans flaked coconut
1 ½ boxes powdered sugar
1 can sweetened condensed milk
2 tsp. vanilla flavoring
½ lb. paraffin
2 12-oz. pkg. semi-sweet chocolate pieces

Mix melted butter and nuts. Add coconut, sugar, condensed milk and vanilla; mix well. Shape into balls the size of quarters; chill for 15 minutes. Melt paraffin and chocolate pieces in top of double boiler. Dip balls into melted mixture using toothpicks or tongs. Place on waxed paper to dry. Keeps well in covered container. Yield: 60 pieces.

Mrs. R. B. Stuart
Washington, D.C.

COCONUT BALLS

2 ¾ c. crushed vanilla wafers
1 stick margarine, melted
½ c. chopped pecans
Powdered sugar
Orange juice
Coconut

Combine wafer crumbs, margarine and pecans; shape into small balls. Roll balls in powdered sugar; dip into orange juice. Roll in coconut. Chill. NOTE: Slightly diluted frozen orange juice may be used. Yield: 50 balls.

Pat James
Hermleigh, Tex.

PECAN-COCONUT CREAM

1 stick butter
3 c. pecan halves or pieces
1 can sweetened condensed milk
2 cans flaked coconut
1 ½ boxes powdered sugar
1 c. chopped dates (opt.)
3 6-oz. pkg. chocolate pieces

Melt butter; add pecans. Mix well. Add condensed milk, coconut and powdered sugar; mix thoroughly with hands. Refrigerate for 4 hours. Roll into balls the size of walnuts. Divide candy into two portions; add dates to one-half of the mixture. Melt chocolate pieces in double boiler; dip balls into mixture. Place on waxed paper until chocolate sets. Store in refrigerator in warm climates. Yield: 48 servings.

Mrs. Earl Seay
Rapid City, S.D.

FRENCH VANILLA CREAMS

2 egg whites, beaten
Water
Powdered sugar
1 tsp. flavoring

Measure egg whites; add equal amount of water. Add enough powdered sugar to make mixture stiff enough to mold. Knead well. Add flavoring. If mixture is too stiff, soften with cream. Shape into desired forms. Roll in pecans or dip into desired coating. Mixture may be tinted.

Marjorie H. Hardman
Cross City, Fla.

JELLIED MARSHMALLOW SQUARES

1 sm. pkg. gelatin
⅔ c. hot water
1 c. sugar
¼ c. light corn syrup
Powdered sugar

Dissolve gelatin in hot water over low heat. Add sugar; stir until dissolved. Mix in corn syrup. Chill until slightly thickened. Beat for 5 minutes or until stiff. Pour into 8 x 8 x 2-inch waxed paper-lined pan. Chill overnight. Turn mixture with waxed paper onto board heavily dusted with powdered sugar. Moisten paper with damp sponge; let stand for a few minutes. Peel off paper. Dust top with powdered sugar. Cut into squares; roll edges in sugar. Yield: 5 dozen.

Mrs. William C. Boyd
Atlanta, Ga.

PARAFFIN CANDY

1 can sweetened condensed milk
1 can shredded coconut
1 c. chopped nuts
1 stick margarine
2 boxes powdered sugar
1 lge. pkg. chocolate pieces
1 paraffin brick

Combine all ingredients except chocolate pieces and paraffin; chill well. After chilling, roll into small balls. Melt paraffin with chocolate pieces. Dip candy balls into chocolate mixture. Yield: 3 1/2 pounds.

Grace Trogdon
Anadarko, Okla.

PEANUT CLUSTERS

1 6-oz. pkg. chocolate pieces
⅔ c. sweetened condensed milk

(Continued on next page)

1 tsp. vanilla flavoring
1 ½ c. salted Spanish peanuts

Melt chocolate pieces in double boiler; remove from heat. Add condensed milk, vanilla and peanuts; mix. Drop by teaspoonfuls onto a buttered cookie sheet or waxed paper. Yield: 18 pieces.

Mary Lou Meyer
Aviston, Ill.

MASHED POTATO CANDY

¾ c. cold mashed potatoes
4 c. powdered sugar
4 c. shredded coconut
1 ½ tsp. vanilla flavoring
½ tsp. salt
8 squares chocolate

Mix potatoes and sugar. Stir in coconut, vanilla and salt; blend well. Press into large pan to 1/2-inch thickness. Melt chocolate over hot water; do not allow water to boil. Pour chocolate on top of candy. Cool; cut into squares. Yield: 32 pieces.

Mary Nicholella
Canonsburg, Pa.

POTATO CHRISTMAS CANDY

1 med. baked potato
1 lb. powdered sugar
1 tbsp. flavoring
2 tbsp. butter or shortening
2 squares bitter chocolate
2 tbsp. paraffin

Peel and mash potato. Add powdered sugar, flavoring and butter; knead to a stiff dough. Make round balls; place on cookie sheet to dry. Melt chocolate and paraffin; drop candy into mixture. Place on cookie sheet to dry.

Mrs. Gertrude Coushman
Chippewa Falls, Wisc.

CINNAMON NUTS

3 c. nuts
1 c. sugar
1 tsp. cinnamon
5 tbsp. water
1 tbsp. vanilla flavoring

Combine all ingredients except vanilla. Cook over low heat until mixture spins a thread. Add vanilla. Turn onto buttered cookie sheet. Yield: 12 servings.

Mrs. Helen Duckett
Columbia, La.

CANDIED NUTS

1 ½ c. sugar
½ c. sour cream
2 tbsp. butter
1 tsp. vanilla flavoring
1 tsp. cinnamon
2 ½ c. walnuts

In heavy saucepan, bring sugar, sour cream and butter to a boil. Cook gently to 238 degrees or to soft ball stage, stirring often. Cool; add vanilla and cinnamon. Stir in walnuts. Spoon onto buttered foil.

Mrs. Robert E. Weidner
Moffett Field, Calif.

ICED ALMONDS

1 c. whole almonds, blanched
½ c. sugar
2 tbsp. butter or margarine
½ tsp. vanilla flavoring
¾ tsp. salt

Heat almonds, sugar and butter in heavy skillet over medium heat. Stir constantly for 15 minutes or until almonds are toasted and sugar is golden brown. Stir in vanilla. Spread nuts on sheet of aluminum foil; sprinkle with salt. Cool; break into two or three nut clusters.

Mrs. John Danhof
Ripon, Calif.

SOUR CREAM-SUGARED NUTS

½ c. sour cream
1 ½ c. sugar
1 ½ tsp. vanilla flavoring
13 oz. walnuts

Mix cream and sugar. Heat to 223 degrees, stirring constantly. Add vanilla and walnuts. Stir rapidly until mixture has sugared and coated nuts. Spread on tray; separate nuts. Cool thoroughly. Store in an airtight container. NOTE: Nuts will keep for three or four months.

Mrs. Mary Esther Rowe
Swartz Creek, Mich.

SUGARED PECANS

1 egg white
1 tbsp. water
1 c. sugar
1 tsp. salt
1 tsp. cinnamon
1 lb. pecan halves

(Continued on next page)

Beat egg white and water until frothy. Mix sugar, salt and cinnamon. Dip pecan halves into egg white mixture; roll in sugar mixture. Place in shallow pan. Bake at 300 degrees for 30 to 45 minutes, stirring every 15 minutes.

Mrs. James M. Edwards
Battle Creek, Mich.

CREAMY CREOLE PRALINES

¾ c. brown sugar
¾ c. sugar
½ c. evaporated milk
1 c. pecan halves
¼ tsp. vanilla flavoring
1 tbsp. butter

Combine sugars and milk in saucepan; bring to a boil. Lower heat; continue cooking to soft ball stage. Remove from heat, beating until creamy; add pecans and vanilla. Drop by spoonfuls onto buttered dish.

Mrs. Rene J. Broussard
New Iberia, La.

CREAMY PRALINES

3 c. sugar
1 c. evaporated milk
Pinch of salt
⅛ stick butter or margarine
Pecans

Dissolve 1 cup sugar in skillet. Boil 2 cups sugar, milk and salt in heavy kettle; add butter. Add dissolved sugar. Cook to soft ball stage. Remove from heat; beat well. Add pecans; drop onto waxed paper. Pralines may be flattened or left in mounds.

Mrs. C. L. Frisbie
Mobile, Ala.

EASY PRALINES

1 pkg. instant Butterscotch Pudding
1 c. sugar
½ c. brown sugar
½ c. evaporated milk
1 tbsp. butter
15 lge. pecans or 1 ½ c. chopped pecans

Mix all ingredients except pecans in heavy 1 1/2-quart saucepan; cook and stir to a full boil. Boil slowly for 3 to 5 minutes, stirring often, until candy reaches soft ball stage. Remove from heat; beat until candy begins to thicken but still is shiny. Drop mixture quickly onto waxed paper to form 2-inch patties. Place a whole pecan on top of each pattie. NOTE: If chopped pecans are used,

add to mixture after removing from heat. Yield: 15 servings.

Mrs. William S. Harmon
Dugway, Utah

ORANGE PRALINES

3 c. sugar
1 c. heavy cream
2 tbsp. corn syrup
1 orange rind, finely chopped
2 c. pecans

Cook sugar, cream and syrup until a soft ball is formed when tested in cold water. Remove from heat; add rind. Cool; add pecans. Drop onto waxed paper.

Mrs. Martha Thompson
Nocona, Tex.

PRALINES

3 c. sugar
1 c. milk
1 tbsp. corn syrup
1 tbsp. (heaping) butter
2 c. pecans
1 tsp. vanilla flavoring
½ tsp. mapeline

Put 2 cups sugar and milk in 2 to 3-quart pan; stir until sugar is well dissolved. Add corn syrup; bring to a full boil. In iron skillet, caramelize remaining sugar, being careful not to burn; remove from heat. Add syrup mixture; place over heat. Cook until soft ball stage or 238 degrees. Remove from heat; add butter and pecans. Cook for 1 minute. Add flavorings; beat until light brown or firm enough to drop.

Frances C. Allen
Kenbridge, Va.

PRALINES

3 c. sugar
1 c. buttermilk
2 c. chopped pecans
¼ tsp. salt
1 tsp. soda
⅓ stick butter
1 tsp. vanilla flavoring

Combine all ingredients except butter and vanilla. Cook to hard ball stage. Add butter and vanilla. Beat until mixture begins to thicken. Drop onto waxed paper.

Mrs. Henry Hale
Perryton, Tex.

LOUISIANA CREAM PRALINES

1 1-lb. box brown sugar
⅛ tsp. salt
¾ c. evaporated milk
1 tbsp. butter
2 c. pecan halves

Mix brown sugar, salt, evaporated milk and butter in 2-quart saucepan. Cook and stir over low heat until sugar is dissolved. Add pecans. Cook over medium heat to 234 degrees or soft ball stage, stirring constantly. Remove from heat; cool for 5 minutes. Stir rapidly until mixture begins to thicken and coat pecans lightly. Drop rapidly from tablespoon onto aluminum foil or lightly buttered baking sheet to form patties. Stir in a few drops of hot water if candy becomes too stiff to handle easily toward the last. Let patties stand until cool and set. Yield: 20 large pralines.

Photograph for this recipe above.

SHERRY PRALINES

2 ½ c. sugar
⅛ tsp. soda
¼ c. light corn syrup
½ c. milk
2 tbsp. Sherry

2 c. pecans
1 tbsp. butter

Combine sugar, soda, syrup and milk; cook over medium heat, stirring, until sugar is completely dissolved. Continue cooking to 236 degrees or until a small amount of mixture forms a soft ball in cold water. Do not stir while cooking. Add Sherry, pecans and butter; stir lightly until mixture becomes creamy. Drop by spoonfuls onto waxed paper. Yield: 24 patties.

Mrs. Louis A. Raeke
Westover AFB, Mass.

SOUTHERN PECAN PRALINES

2 c. sugar
1 c. light brown sugar
¼ c. light corn syrup
1 tsp. vinegar
½ tsp. salt
½ c. water
3 c. pecans
1 6-oz. pkg. butterscotch pieces
1 tsp. vanilla flavoring

Combine sugars, syrup, vinegar, salt and water; mix well. Bring to a boil, stirring constantly. Lower heat; cook for 3 minutes.

(Continued on next page)

Do not stir until 3 minutes are up. Add nuts, butterscotch pieces and vanilla. Stir until butterscotch pieces are completely dissolved. Drop onto waxed paper by spoonfuls, working rapidly.

Mrs. Irene Wilson
Jacksonville, Ark.

BEST-EVER CARAMELS

2 c. sugar
1 c. brown sugar
1 c. light syrup
1 c. heavy cream
1 c. milk
1 c. butter or margarine
1 ½ tbsp. vanilla flavoring

Combine all ingredients except vanilla. Cook slowly to hard ball stage, stirring occasionally. Remove from heat; add vanilla. Pour into greased 8 x 8 x 12-inch pan. Cool. When firm, turn out onto board. Cut into pieces; wrap in waxed paper.

Edna McDonald
Brook, Ind.

CARAMELS

2 ½ c. sugar
¾ c. corn syrup
⅛ tsp. cream of tartar
2 ½ c. cream
1 tsp. vanilla flavoring
½ c. butter

Combine sugar, corn syrup, cream of tartar and cream. Boil to hard ball stage, stirring constantly. Add vanilla and butter. Pour into buttered pan; cool. Cut into squares. Wrap in waxed paper or dip into melted chocolate. Yield: 50 squares.

Ruth Volhard
Marathon, Wisc.

FOOL-PROOF FUDGE

32 lge. marshmallows
¼ c. water
2 ½ c. sugar
1 6-oz. can evaporated milk
Dash of salt
½ c. margarine
1 ½ pkg. chocolate pieces
½ tsp. vanilla flavoring

Melt marshmallows in water in double boiler. Combine sugar, milk, salt and margarine. Boil for 8 minutes. Add melted marshmallows and chocolate pieces to syrup; mix well. Add

vanilla. Pour into buttered 13 x 9 x 2-inch pan. Cool; cut into squares.

Barbara Worton
Somerset, Mass.

FRUIT CANDY

2 c. brown sugar
2 c. sugar
½ c. butter
1 c. cream
1 c. figs
1 c. chopped dates
1 c. flaked coconut
1 c. chopped English walnuts
1 tsp. vanilla flavoring

Mix sugars, butter and cream. Boil to soft ball stage. Stir all remaining ingredients into candy. Cook for 1 minute.

Mrs. Ludovic Hill
Westfield, Ind.

FRENCH CHOCOLATES

3 12-oz. pkg. semi-sweet chocolate pieces
1 can condensed milk
¼ tsp. salt
2 tsp. vanilla flavoring
Powdered sugar
Ground walnuts
Flaked coconut
Decorative candies

Melt chocolate and milk in double boiler over hot water. Remove from heat; add salt and vanilla. Chill thoroughly; shape into small balls. Roll in sugar, nuts, coconut and candies. Yield: 5 pounds.

Mrs. John A. Kitko
Columbus, O.

GOURMET FUDGE

3 pkg. chocolate pieces
1 8-oz. jar marshmallow creme
1 c. butter
3 c. coarsely chopped nuts
2 tbsp. vanilla flavoring
4 ½ c. sugar
1 ⅔ c. evaporated milk

Combine chocolate pieces, marshmallow creme, butter, nuts and vanilla. Mix sugar and milk; heat to boiling. Boil for 9 minutes. Pour over chocolate mixture; stir until chocolate pieces are melted and well blended. Pour into buttered tins; store in refrigerator.

Mathilde Ruggles
Eureka, Nev.

QUICK CHOCO-NUT FUDGE

2 c. sugar
3 tbsp. butter
½ tsp. salt
1 c. evaporated milk
½ c. miniature marshmallows
1 ½ c. semi-sweet chocolate pieces
⅔ c. chopped pecans
½ tsp. peppermint flavoring

Combine sugar, butter, salt and evaporated milk in large saucepan. Bring mixture to a rolling boil over medium heat, stirring constantly. Continue boiling and stirring for 5 minutes. Remove from heat. Add marshmallows, chocolate, pecans and peppermint flavoring. Stir until marshmallows and chocolate are melted and smoothly blended. Pour into buttered 8-inch square pan. Cool; cut into squares. Yield: 2 pounds candy.

Photograph for this recipe above.

MARVELOUS FUDGE

4 c. sugar
1 ⅔ c. evaporated milk
1 c. butter or margarine
1 12-oz. pkg. semi-sweet chocolate pieces
1 pt. marshmallow creme

1 tsp. vanilla flavoring
1 c. broken walnuts
Walnut halves

Butter sides of heavy 3-quart saucepan. Add sugar, milk and butter. Cook over medium heat to 236 degrees or to soft ball stage, stirring frequently. Do not scorch. Remove from heat; add chocolate, marshmallow creme, vanilla and nuts. Beat until chocolate is melted and blended. Pour into buttered 9 x 9 x 2-inch pan. Score into squares while warm; top each with a walnut half. Cut when firm. NOTE: Pour candy into 13 x 9 x 2-inch pan for thinner pieces. Yield: 36 pieces.

Mrs. Alice I. Gardner
Parowan, Utah

MILLION-DOLLAR FUDGE

2 lge. chocolate candy bars, broken
2 pkg. chocolate pieces
1 pt. marshmallow creme
4 ½ c. sugar
1 ⅔ c. evaporated milk
½ c. margarine
½ c. nuts
1 tsp. vanilla flavoring

(Continued on next page)

Mix chocolate bars, pieces and marshmallow creme in large mixing bowl. Mix sugar, milk and margarine; bring to a boil over low heat, stirring constantly. Boil for 7 minutes. Remove from heat. Pour over chocolate mixture; stir until chocolate is melted and smooth. Add nuts and vanilla. Pour into 8 x 12 x 2-inch buttered dish; cool. Yield: 96 squares.

Mrs. Charles Whitbeck
Keyport, Wash.

MILLION-DOLLAR FUDGE

4 ½ c. sugar
1 ⅓ sticks butter
1 ⅔ c. evaporated milk
1 12-oz. jar marshmallow creme
2 6-oz. pkg. chocolate pieces
6 5-cent chocolate almond bars
1 qt. pecans

Boil sugar, butter and milk for 8 to 10 minutes. Add marshmallow creme, chocolate pieces and chocolate bars to mixture; beat until creamy. Add pecans; cool slightly for 20 minutes. Stir mixture; pour into greased pan. Cool; cut. Yield: 4 pounds.

Betty Pasternak
Oklahoma City, Okla.

QUICK NUT FUDGE

1 box powdered sugar
½ c. cocoa
¼ tsp. salt
6 tbsp. butter
4 tbsp. milk
1 tbsp. vanilla flavoring
1 c. chopped pecans

Combine all ingredients except nuts in top of double boiler. Stir and cook over medium heat until smooth. Remove from heat; add nuts. Spread in buttered pan. Cool. Cut into 12 squares. Yield: 12 servings.

Mrs. James M. Hough
Moorehead City, N.C.

RAINBOW CANDIES

1 ¾ c. plus 2 tbsp. sugar
¾ c. plus 2 tbsp. light syrup
½ c. water
Assorted food colorings
Oil of cloves
Oil of anise
Oil of sassafras
Oil of wintergreen
Oil of peppermint

Boil sugar, syrup and water to 300 degrees; divide mixture into five portions. Add 1/2 teaspoon yellow coloring and 1/2 teaspoon oil of cloves to one portion. Using same measurements, add one combination to each of three portions: Pink or red coloring and anise, green coloring and sassafras and blue coloring and wintergreen. To the last portion, add only peppermint flavoring; do not use any coloring. Pour immediately onto buttered cookie sheet; mark into squares. Usually some break, but these add variety. Put into jars or boxes.

Mrs. B. L. Marceil
Wisconsin Rapids, Wisc.

BON BONS

¼ c. fresh lemon juice
¼ c. fresh orange juice
1 tbsp. grated lemon or orange rind
3 c. finely crushed vanilla wafers
2 tbsp. cocoa
1 c. powdered sugar
1 c. finely chopped nuts

Combine all ingredients; blend well. Shape into balls; roll in sugar, if desired.

Mrs. Wilda Jean Davis
Dahlonega, Ga.

BOLOGNA CANDY

2 c. sugar
1 c. milk
1 lb. dates
1 c. shredded coconut
½ c. chopped nuts

Combine sugar and milk in heavy saucepan. Cook over medium heat to 234 degrees or to soft ball stage, stirring occasionally. Add dates; cook, stirring constantly, until mixture is thick and leaves side of pan when stirred. Remove from heat. Stir in coconut and nuts. Cool slightly; turn out onto wet towel. Make a roll 2 inches in diameter and 18 inches long when cool enough to handle and hold shape; chill. Slice with sharp knife into thin rounds.

Mrs. Arnold I. Cousins
South Portland, Me.

CARAMEL-NUT ROLL

1 pkg. caramel pieces
¼ c. butter
Dash of salt
2 c. powdered sugar

(Continued on next page)

¼ c. evaporated milk
1 tsp. vanilla flavoring
¾ c. chopped pecans or walnuts

Melt caramel pieces with butter in saucepan over low heat, stirring constantly. Remove from heat; add salt. Add powdered sugar alternately with milk, blending well after each addition. Add vanilla; mix well. Chill for 20 to 30 minutes. Form into a cylinder; roll in chopped nuts. Refrigerate until ready to slice and serve. Yield: 2 dozen slices.

Mrs. Kenneth B. Lindner
Fort Devens, Mass.

CARAMEL CORN

2 c. light brown sugar
½ c. light corn syrup
2 sticks butter
½ tsp. soda
Pinch of cream of tartar
Dash of salt
8 qt. popped corn

Mix sugar, syrup and butter in heavy saucepan. Bring to a boil; cook for 5 minutes. Remove from heat; add soda, cream of tartar and salt. Immediately pour mixture over popped corn. Mix lightly but thoroughly; place in large roaster. Bake at 200 degrees for 1 hour. Pour onto waxed paper; separate grains. Yield: 20 servings.

Mrs. Marjorie Evans
Princeton, Ind.

CHOCOLATE POPCORN

2 c. sugar
2 oz. chocolate or 3 tbsp. cocoa
⅓ c. milk
1 tsp. vanilla flavoring
1 tbsp. butter
⅓ c. popcorn, popped

Cook sugar, chocolate and milk until soft ball forms in cold water. Add vanilla and butter. Pour over popped corn; stir until evenly coated. Yield: 4-6 servings.

Mrs. Richard E. Tracey
Enid, Okla.

CRACKER JACKS

2 c. sugar
⅔ c. light corn syrup
½ c. water
2 tsp. soda
2 tsp. vanilla flavoring
Butter
20 c. popped corn

Cook sugar, syrup and water until it cracks when dropped into cold water. Add soda,

vanilla and a large lump of butter. Stir over heat until golden brown. Pour over corn; stir thoroughly. Spread in thin layer on table. Work swiftly.

Mrs. Noah E. Yoder
Auburn, Ind.

POPCORN BALLS

1 c. corn syrup or molasses
¼ tsp. salt
1 c. sugar
½ c. water
5 qt. unseasoned popcorn

Boil syrup, salt, sugar and water until mixture spins a thread. Pour over popcorn. Shape into balls with buttered hands; place on waxed paper to cool.

Mrs. Arlene R. Hewey
Emery Mills, Me.

SKILLET CANDY

½ stick butter or margarine
1 8-oz. pkg. pitted dates
1 c. sugar
1 egg, slightly beaten
½ tsp. vanilla flavoring
2 c. Rice Krispies
1 c. pecans
Powdered sugar or coconut

Melt butter in double boiler; add dates, sugar and egg. Cook until dates are soft. Remove from heat; cool. Add vanilla. Pour over Rice Krispies and pecans. Form small bite-sized balls; roll in powdered sugar or coconut. Yield: 3 dozen.

Mrs. Abe Daigle
Lafayette, La.

CREAMY-ROLLED FUDGE

2 tbsp. butter
1 ½ squares chocolate
2 c. sugar
1 c. milk
½ tsp. vanilla flavoring
Pinch of salt
Nuts (opt.)

Melt butter and chocolate slowly. Add sugar; mix thoroughly. Add milk; bring to a boil, stirring slowly. Reduce heat; boil slowly to soft ball stage. Remove from heat; pour into buttered platter. Cool until bottom of dish is just warm. Add vanilla, salt and nuts; beat until mixture loses its gloss. Shape mixture into rolls with buttered hands.

Mrs. Bruce O. McGuire
Bedford, Mass.

DANDY BRANDY BALLS

1 sm. can evaporated milk
1 6-oz. pkg. semi-sweet chocolate pieces
2 ½ c. crushed vanilla wafers
½ c. sifted powdered sugar
2 c. chopped pecans
⅓ c. apricot brandy

Combine evaporated milk and chocolate pieces in heavy 2-quart saucepan. Cook over medium heat, stirring constantly, until chocolate melts and mixture is smooth and thickened. Remove from heat. Add crushed wafers, sugar, 1/2 cup pecans and brandy, mixing well. Let stand at room temperature for 30 minutes. Shape into balls 1 inch in diameter. Roll in remaining pecans. Refrigerate for 1 hour or until firm. Yield: 4 dozen.

Mrs. Billy R. Wesson
Corpus Christi, Tex.

DATE BALLS

1 c. butter or margarine
1 ½ c. sugar
2 c. cut up dates
2 eggs, beaten
1 sm. pkg. or 5 c. Rice Krispies
1 can flaked coconut

Melt butter; add sugar. Bring to a boil, stirring constantly. Add dates; cook for 5 minutes or until dates are tender and mashed. Remove from heat; cool for a few minutes. Add a spoonful of hot mixture at a time to eggs, stirring rapidly. Boil for 2 minutes longer; remove from heat. Pour over Rice Krispies. Cool; shape into balls. Roll in coconut. Chill.

Mrs. Elmer Warnick
Hartselle, Ala.

DATE ROLL CANDY

2 ½ c. sugar
1 tbsp. butter
1 c. milk
1 c. chopped dates
1 c. chopped nuts

Boil sugar, butter and milk to soft ball stage. Add dates and nuts. Shape into a roll; chill. Slice when cold.

Mrs. James Williams
Galt, Mo.

DROP CHOCOLATES

1 stick butter or margarine
2 boxes powdered sugar

1 can condensed milk
1 box shredded coconut or 1 c. nuts or both
2 tsp. vanilla flavoring
3 bars German's chocolate
1 bar paraffin wax

Blend butter, sugar, milk, coconut and vanilla; shape into small balls. Refrigerate on waxed paper for 10 minutes or until firm. Melt chocolate and paraffin in double boiler. Dip balls into chocolate with toothpick. Place on waxed paper. Refrigerate until hard.

Carrie Robinson
Port Richey, Fla.

EASTER EGG

2 c. sugar
½ c. light corn syrup
½ c. warm water
2 egg whites
1 sm. jar candied cherries
1 c. chopped nuts
¾ c. coconut
Powdered sugar
Melted semi-sweet chocolate

Boil sugar, syrup and water to crack stage. Add slowly to stiffly beaten egg whites; beat until mixture begins to thicken. Add cherries, nuts and coconut. Cool slightly; form into shape, using powdered sugar to prevent sticking to hands. Cool. Spread with chocolate when cool. Yield: 2 pounds.

Dorothy Kitko
Union City, Pa.

MARTHA WASHINGTON'S CREAMS

¼ lb. butter, softened
1 lb. powdered sugar, sifted
1 tsp. vanilla flavoring
Pinch of salt
4 squares unsweetened baking chocolate
1 tbsp. shaved paraffin

Cream butter; add sifted sugar. Beat until light and foamy. Add vanilla and salt. Refrigerate for 12 hours. Make into desired forms. Melt chocolate and paraffin over boiling water. Dip molded creams into mixture. Set on greased platter or waxed paper to harden. NOTE: Creams may be molded around Maraschino cherries, nuts or other fruit. They may be shaped like Easter eggs. Yield: 1 1/2 pounds.

Mrs. Hugh C. Mason
Key West, Fla.

Cookies,
Bars and
Squares

RECIPE FOR OATMEAL DROP COOKIES ON PAGE 142

Nothing is More Fun . . .

. . . than whipping up a batch of cookies. Perfect cookies are easy to make if you follow simple suggestions such as reading and following the recipe, measuring exactly, using the correct pans and baking at the correct temperature.

A perfect cookie has a good flavor and a tender crumb—unless the kind you're making is a hard cookie. The perfect cookie is crisp or soft, depending again on the kind you're making, with a uniform color and shape.

There are several types of cookies. Cookies are classified by the texture of the baked cookies—soft or crisp, the consistency of the batter or dough soft or stiff—or by the method used in shaping the cookie.

ROLLED COOKIES	The dough is rolled out to the desired thickness on a lightly floured board and cut into shapes with a cookie cutter.
MOLDED OR SHAPED COOKIES	The dough is shaped by hand before baking.
DROP COOKIES	The dough is dropped from a teaspoon onto a lightly greased baking sheet.
PRESSED COOKIES	The dough is soft enough to hold a shape.
REFRIGERATOR COOKIES	The dough is pressed into a cookie mold or shaped into a thick roll or bar, chilled in the refrigerator until ready to be sliced and baked.
BAR COOKIES	The dough is baked in a four-sided pan and cut into bars or squares after baking.

SELECTING COOKIE PANS

Bake cookies in pans that are the proper size and kind. Always use cookie sheets or pans that are bright and shiny. Use pans that will leave at least 1 to 2 inches between the sides of the pan and the sides of the oven. This will let the heat circulate between the oven walls and pan and will keep cookies from burning on the bottom.

Another way to prevent cookies from browning too much on the bottom is to use two pans of the same size placed one on top of the other. If pans with sides are used, turn upside down and bake cookies on the bottom of the pan.

If you're baking one sheet of cookies at a time, adjust the oven rack so the cookies will be in the center of the oven. If you are baking two sheets or pans of cookies at a time, adjust the racks to divide the oven into thirds.

PREPARING SHEETS OR PANS

Don't grease the cookie sheets or pans if your cookies contain a considerable amount of shortening. For all other cookies, grease the sheets with a bland fat that contains no salt.

If cookie bars are to be made, grease the baking pan and line it with waxed paper. Grease the waxed paper. Bake macaroons on heavy plain paper.

COOKIE CHATTER

Below are some hints for turning out perfect cookies every time you bake!

1. Here's a neat trick—for extra cookie sheets, cut pieces of foil the same size as your cookie sheet. Drop dough onto foil and slip onto the cookie sheet as soon as it comes from the oven. A real timesaver!

2. Don't let your lack of a cookie sheet stop you from baking cookies. Just turn a baking pan over and use the bottom. Presto—your problem is solved!

3. If the cookie sheet is to be greased, always grease it lightly. Avoid brown spots by greasing only the spots where the dough is to be dropped.

4. Have all ingredients at room temperature for glamorous, perfect cookies.

5. A tidy bowl is important. Use a rubber scraper often, so the ingredients are well blended. Do leave a few drops for "bowl lickin' " fun though.

6. Check cookies when the minimum baking time is up. Use a handy clock or timer to check the baking time.

7. Bars and squares are done when the sides shrink from the pan, or the top springs back when lightly touched with the finger. Soft cookies will also spring back when touched. Crisp cookies are done when they are fairly firm and lightly browned around the edges.

8. Unless otherwise directed, remove cookies from sheets or pans right after taking from the oven and place on a wire rack to cool. Never overlap, stack, pile or store warm cookies.

9. Use a wide spatula to remove cookies from sheets and pans.

10. Store cookies, bars and squares in a tightly covered container or right in the baking pan, covered with foil. If cookies begin to dry out, add a piece of bread, apple or orange to supply the needed moisture.

11. Crisp cookies should be stored in a container with a loose fitting cover. If cookies soften and become limp, freshen them in a 300 degree oven for about 5 minutes before serving.

12. Never store soft and crisp cookies in the same container.

ALMOND SQUARES

1 c. margarine, softened
1 c. powdered sugar
¼ c. brown sugar
1 egg
1 tsp. vanilla flavoring
2 c. flour
½ tsp. soda
½ tsp. salt

Mix all ingredients. Spread one-half of the mixture in bottom of 9 x 13-inch pan.

FILLING:
¾ lb. or ¾ c. almond paste
3 eggs
1 c. sugar

Combine all ingredients; spread over dough. Dot filling with remaining dough. Bake at 325 degrees for 45 minutes. Cut while warm. Yield: 20 servings.

Mrs. J. Houseward
Terre Haute, Ind.

ALMOND STICKS

1 lb. butter
4 c. flour
1 c. water
1 lb. almond paste
2 c. sugar
4 eggs, beaten
Beaten egg whites or evaporated milk

Blend butter, flour and water; let stand overnight. Combine almond paste, sugar and eggs; let stand overnight. Divide dough into eight parts; roll out to a circle. Spread paste on each circle; roll up like a jelly roll. Brush with egg whites or milk. Place on greased cookie sheet. Bake at 400 degrees for 30 minutes.

Audrey Katt
Grand Haven, Mich.

DUTCH ALMOND PASTE COOKIES

½ c. butter
½ c. sugar
¼ tsp. salt
1 egg plus 1 yolk
1 c. flour

Cream butter and sugar; add all remaining ingredients. Press onto 14 x 10-inch cookie sheet. Bake at 400 degrees for 10 minutes.

TOPPING:
1 c. plus 2 tsp. sugar
1 c. grated almond paste

2 egg yolks
Juice of ½ lemon
3 egg whites
1 tsp. vanilla flavoring
Coconut or chopped nuts

Combine 1 cup sugar, almond paste, egg yolks and lemon juice. Beat egg whites until stiff; add 2 teaspoons sugar and vanilla. Fold almond paste mixture into egg whites. Spread over partially baked crust. Sprinkle with coconut. Yield: 2 dozen.

Mrs. Ann K. Boyd
Holland, Mich.

APPLE BARS

1 ¼ c. sugar
1 ½ c. flour
1 tsp. cinnamon
1 tsp. baking powder
½ tsp. salt
½ tsp. nutmeg
Pinch of ginger
Pinch of allspice
½ c. oil or butter
2 eggs
2 c. grated apples
1 tsp. vanilla flavoring
1 c. chopped nuts

Mix all dry ingredients; add remaining ingredients. Bake at 350 degrees for 1 hour. Yield: 3 dozen.

Mrs. Homer E. Land
Alamogordo, N.M.

SPICY APPLE BARS

½ c. shortening
1 c. sugar
2 eggs
1 c. sifted flour
1 tsp. baking powder
½ tsp. soda
½ tsp. salt
1 tbsp. cocoa
1 tsp. cinnamon
½ tsp. nutmeg
¼ tsp. cloves
1 c. oats
1 ½ c. diced pared apples
Powdered sugar

Cream shortening and sugar until light and fluffy. Beat in an egg at a time. Sift all dry ingredients except powdered sugar; add to creamed mixture. Stir in oats and apples. Spread in large greased pan. Bake at 375 degrees for 25 minutes. Cool slightly; cut into bars or squares. Sprinkle with powdered sugar. NOTE: If desired, bake in small pan and serve warm as pudding. Yield: 36 servings.

Mrs. Barton Lewis
Norris City, Ill.

APRICOT BARS

BASE:
½ c. soft shortening
¼ c. sugar
1 c. flour

Cream shortening; mix in sugar and flour. Pat into 8 x 12-inch pan. Bake at 350 degrees for 10 minutes or until light brown.

TOPPING:
⅔ c. dried apricots
2 eggs, beaten
1 c. brown sugar
⅓ c. flour
½ c. chopped nuts
1 tsp. vanilla flavoring
½ tsp. baking powder
¼ tsp. salt

Soak apricots; cut into pieces. Cook until tender. Combine all remaining ingredients; mix in apricots. Spread over base. Bake at 350 degrees for 20 to 30 minutes. Cut into bars. Yield: 2 dozen.

Mrs. Spencer Lundquist
Wheaton, Minn.

BANANA-NUT BARS

⅔ c. shortening
1 ½ c. sugar
2 eggs, separated
½ c. mashed banana
1 ½ c. flour
1 tsp. soda
½ tsp. salt
4 tbsp. sour cream or milk
1 tsp. vanilla flavoring
½ c. nuts

Cream shortening and sugar; beat in egg yolks. Add banana. Sift all dry ingredients; add alternately with sour cream to banana mixture. Stir in flavoring; fold in beaten egg whites and nuts. Pour into flat pans. Bake at 350 degrees until done. Cut into bars while warm; ice with a powdered sugar or other thin icing. Yield: 3 dozen.

Mrs. Robert K. Pethtel
Cambridge, O.

APPLESAUCE BROWNIES

1 c. sugar
½ c. margarine
1 egg, well beaten
1 c. applesauce
1 ¼ c. sifted flour
½ tsp. baking powder
½ tsp. soda
¼ tsp. salt
½ tsp. cinnamon

Cream sugar and margarine; beat in egg. Add applesauce. Sift all dry ingredients; add. Pour into 7 x 11-inch buttered pan. Bake at 350 degrees for 35 minutes. Cut into small squares.

Mrs. Ralph S. Ingraham
Augusta, Me.

BLONDE BROWNIES

¼ c. butter or margarine
1 c. light brown sugar
1 egg
¾ c. sifted flour
1 tsp. baking powder
½ tsp. salt
1 tsp. vanilla flavoring
½ c. chopped nuts
Slivered dates (opt.)

Melt butter; remove from heat. Stir in brown sugar; cool. Beat in egg. Sift all dry ingredients; stir into brown sugar mixture. Add vanilla and nuts; mix well. Spread in well greased 8 x 8 x 2-inch pan. Bake at 350 degrees for 30 to 35 minutes. Cut in diamonds or squares. Decorate with slivers of dates. Yield: 1 1/2 dozen.

Mrs. Wayne Jenkins
New Castle, Ky.

BROWNIES

1 ½ c. sugar
¾ c. shortening
3 eggs, beaten
1 ½ c. flour
1 tsp. salt
½ c. milk
3 squares chocolate, melted
1 tsp. vanilla flavoring
½ c. nuts

Cream sugar and shortening; add eggs. Add all dry ingredients alternately with milk, beating after each addition. Add chocolate, vanilla and nuts. Bake at 350 degrees for 35 minutes. Yield: 12 servings.

Mrs. Velma Malone
Stead AFB, Nev.

BROWNIES WITH DATES

1 c. chopped dates
1 tsp. soda
1 c. boiling water
1 c. margarine
1 c. sugar
2 eggs
2 c. flour
3 tbsp. cocoa
½ c. chocolate pieces
½ c. nuts (opt.)
1 tsp. vanilla flavoring

(Continued on next page)

Soak dates in soda and water. Cream margarine and sugar; add an egg at a time. Sift flour and cocoa; add to creamed mixture. Add dates and chocolate pieces. Fold in nuts and vanilla. Spread in a greased and floured 15 x 10-inch pan. Bake at 350 degrees for 45 minutes. Yield: 20-24 servings.

Mrs. E. A. Ricci
Portsmouth, N.H.

CANDY BAR BROWNIES

2 c. brown sugar
2 c. flour
1 stick margarine or butter
Dash of salt
1 egg
1 c. buttermilk
1 tsp. soda
1 tsp. vanilla flavoring
½ c. nuts
6 Heath bars, chopped

Blend sugar, flour and margarine as for pie dough. Reserve 1 cup mixture for topping. To remaining crumbs, add salt, egg, buttermilk and soda mixed and vanilla. Mix well; pour into well greased 9 x 13-inch pan. Add nuts and chopped Heath bars to reserved 1 cup topping mixture. Spread on top of batter. Bake at 350 degrees for 30 to 40 minutes. Serve warm. Yield: 1 dozen.

Mrs. Gary Unsworth
Berne, Ind.

CARAMEL BROWNIES

1 1-lb. box brown sugar
1 ½ sticks butter or margarine
3 eggs
2 ⅔ c. flour
1 tsp. baking powder
1 tsp. salt
1 pkg. chocolate pieces
½ c. chopped pecans
1 tsp. vanilla flavoring

Combine sugar and butter; melt over low heat. Cool. Add an egg at a time; beat well. Combine flour, baking powder and salt; add. Add chocolate pieces, nuts and vanilla; mix well. Pour into 9 x 12-inch pan. Bake at 350 degrees for 25 to 30 minutes. Cut into squares. Yield: 2-3 dozen.

Mrs. Floyd West, Jr.
Waverly, Va.

CHEWY FUDGE BROWNIES

4 squares unsweetened chocolate
⅔ c. cooking oil

4 eggs
2 c. sugar
1 ½ c. flour
1 tsp. salt
1 tsp. baking powder
1 c. chopped walnuts

Combine chocolate and oil; melt over low heat. Beat eggs; add sugar, mixing well. Sift flour with salt and baking powder; add to egg mixture. Mix until smooth. Add chocolate mixture; blend well. Add nuts. Spread in a well greased 9 x 13-inch pan. Bake in preheated 350 degree oven for 30 minutes. Cool slightly; cut into squares. Yield: 2 dozen.

Mrs. Albert Miller
Hampton, N.H.

CHRISTMAS BROWNIES

19 graham crackers
1 sm. pkg. chocolate pieces
1 c. walnuts
1 sm. can sweetened condensed milk

Break crackers into small pieces. Add all remaining ingredients; mix well. Grease an 8-inch square baking pan; line with waxed paper. Grease again. Pour mixture into pan. Bake at 350 degrees for 30 minutes. Five minutes after removing from oven, take out of pan; remove waxed paper. Yield: 20 pieces.

Mrs. Gwin L. Walker
El Centro, Calif.

COCONUT BROWNIES

1 c. butter
1 ½ c. sugar
3 eggs, well beaten
1 c. flour
¼ tsp. salt
½ tsp. vanilla flavoring
4 ½ tbsp. cocoa
¼ lb. walnuts
1 can condensed milk
½ lb. flaked coconut
Chocolate frosting or melted chocolate
   pieces

Cream butter and sugar; beat in eggs. Mix in flour, salt, flavoring, cocoa and walnuts. Spread in large pan. Bake at 375 degrees for 20 minutes. Mix condensed milk and coconut; spread on cookies in pan. Broil until brown; frost with chocolate frosting.

Mrs. Clarence Ost
Alfred, N.D.

DATE BROWNIES

2 eggs
¾ c. brown sugar
½ c. sifted flour
1 ⅔ c. graham cracker crumbs
1 7 ½-oz. pkg. chopped dates
½ c. chopped walnuts
½ tsp. vanilla flavoring

Beat eggs until light. Combine sugar, flour and cracker crumbs. Fold in eggs. Stir in dates, walnuts and vanilla. Spread mixture in a greased 8-inch square pan. Bake at 325 degrees for 20 minutes or until done. Cool; cut into small pieces. Yield: 15 servings.

Mrs. Ruth Byer
Cattaraugus, N. Y.

FILLED BROWNIES

⅓ c. shortening
1 c. sugar
¼ tsp. salt
2 eggs
½ tsp. vanilla flavoring
2 squares chocolate, melted
⅔ c. sifted flour
½ c. chopped nuts

Cream shortening, sugar, salt, eggs and vanilla. Stir in remaining ingredients. Mix well. Line baking pan with greased waxed paper. Pour batter into pan. Bake at 350 degrees for 15 minutes. Remove from pan; peel off waxed paper. Cut in half.

FILLING:
1 tbsp. hot milk
1 tsp. shortening
¼ tsp. almond flavoring
1 c. powdered sugar

Cream all ingredients. Spread filling on half of brownie; put other half on top. Cut into small squares. Yield: 15 squares.

Mrs. William Peirce
Smithtown, N.Y.

FROSTED BROWNIES

3 squares baking chocolate
⅓ c. shortening
1 c. sugar
2 eggs, well beaten
½ c. flour
½ tsp. baking powder
½ tsp. salt
1 c. chopped walnuts
1 tsp. vanilla flavoring

Melt chocolate and shortening. Add sugar to eggs; add chocolate mixture. Sift all dry

ingredients; add to mixture. Beat well. Fold in nuts and flavoring. Pour into a greased 8-inch square pan. Bake at 350 degrees for 20 to 30 minutes.

FROSTING:
1 square chocolate
1 tbsp. butter
¾ c. powdered sugar
1 to 2 tbsp. warm water

Melt chocolate and butter; blend in sugar. Add water until mixture is of spreading consistency. Frost cool brownies. Yield: 8 servings.

Mrs. Bruce E. Losty
Waterbury, Conn.

FROSTED BROWNIE-MALLOW BARS

BASE:
⅓ c. margarine
1 square unsweetened chocolate
1 c. sugar
¾ c. flour
½ tsp. salt
½ tsp. baking powder
2 eggs
1 c. chopped nuts
1 tsp. vanilla flavoring
3 c. miniature marshmallows

Melt margarine with chocolate; remove from heat. Add sugar; mix well. Add flour, salt and baking powder, blending well. Add eggs; beat well. Mix in nuts and flavoring. Pour into a greased and floured pan. Bake at 350 degrees for 35 minutes. Top with marshmallows; return to oven for 2 to 3 minutes or until marshmallows are soft. Cool.

FROSTING:
1 oz. chocolate
½ c. brown sugar
¼ c. water
3 tbsp. margarine
1 tsp. vanilla flavoring
½ tsp. salt
1 ⅔ c. sifted powdered sugar

Combine chocolate, brown sugar and water. Boil for 4 minutes. Add margarine, flavoring and salt; cool. Add powdered sugar. Spread on base; cut into bars.

Mrs. Roy Zilko
Carthage, S.D.

FUDGE-FROSTED BROWNIES

½ c. shortening
1 c. sugar
2 eggs
2 1-oz. squares unsweetened chocolate, melted
1 tsp. vanilla flavoring
½ c. flour
½ c. chopped nuts

(Continued on next page)

Thoroughly cream shortening and sugar. Add eggs; beat thoroughly. Blend in chocolate; add vanilla. Stir in flour and nuts. Pour batter into an 8 x 8 x 2-inch pan. Bake at 325 degrees for 35 minutes. Cool.

FUDGE FROSTING:
1 c. sifted powdered sugar
1 tbsp. cocoa
2 tbsp. cream
1 tbsp. butter

Combine all ingredients; cook until mixture boils. Remove from heat; beat until of spreading consistency. Spread on brownies. Cut into squares while warm. Yield: 16 servings.

Mrs. Lee Simpson
Groveport, O.

THREE-LAYER BROWNIES
½ c. butter
2 eggs
1 c. sugar
1 c. flour
½ tsp. salt
6 tbsp. cocoa
1 c. nuts (opt.)
1 pkg. miniature marshmallows
1 pkg. chocolate fudge mix

Melt butter over low heat. Beat eggs and sugar; add butter. Stir in flour, salt and cocoa. Mix in nuts. Pour into an ungreased 8-inch square cake pan. Bake at 300 degrees for 30 minutes. Top with marshmallows when done; leave in warm oven, with the heat off, until marshmallows melt. When cool, top with fudge icing. Yield: 12-16 brownies.

Grace M. Sheppard
Williamston, S.C.

TWO-TONE BROWNIES
OATMEAL LAYER:
1 c. quick cooking oats
⅓ c. sifted flour
¼ tsp. soda
⅛ tsp. salt
½ c. brown sugar
⅓ c. melted margarine or butter

Add oats to dry ingredients. Pour melted margarine over mixture. Press into 9 x 11-inch pan. Bake at 350 degrees for 10 minutes.

CHOCOLATE LAYER:
1 oz. unsweetened baking chocolate
¼ c. margarine or butter
⅔ c. sifted flour
¼ tsp. baking powder
¼ tsp. salt
¾ c. sugar
1 egg

¼ c. milk
1 tsp. vanilla flavoring

Melt chocolate and margarine over low heat. Combine flour, baking powder and salt. Add sugar and egg to chocolate mixture in pan. Stir well. Add to flour mixture; stir again. Add milk and vanilla, mixing well. Pour over oatmeal layer. Bake at 350 degrees for 25 to 30 minutes.

Mrs. George Piar
Cleveland, O.

BUTTER SQUARES
1 lb. soft butter
1 ½ c. sugar
2 tsp. vanilla flavoring
6 eggs
1 lb. vanilla wafers, finely crumbled

Cream butter and sugar for 10 minutes. Add vanilla; beat well. Beat eggs until very light; add slowly to creamed mixture. Put one-half of the crumbs in bottom of a 10-inch square pan. Spread butter mixture evenly on crumbs. Cover with remaining crumbs. Chill. Cut into squares; top with whipped cream, if desired. Yield: 8 squares.

Mrs. Jack Silmser
Massena, N. Y.

BUTTERSCOTCH-PECAN BARS
1 c. flour
2 tsp. baking powder
½ tsp. salt
½ c. butter
2 c. brown sugar
2 eggs, unbeaten
2 tsp. vanilla flavoring
1 c. chopped pecans

Mix flour, baking powder and salt. Melt butter; remove from heat. Add brown sugar and eggs. Add dry ingredients; mix thoroughly. Add vanilla and nuts; mix. Put into a greased 7 x 9-inch pan which has been lined with waxed paper. Bake at 375 degrees for 30 minutes. Cut into squares when cold. Yield: 16 squares.

Mrs. A. H. Wood
Hunter AFB, Ga.

BUTTERSCOTCH SQUARES
1 lb. light brown sugar
⅔ c. melted margarine
3 eggs
2 ¾ c. flour
2 ½ tsp. baking powder
½ tsp. salt

(Continued on next page)

1 c. chopped walnuts
1 c. chocolate pieces
1 tsp. vanilla flavoring

Mix sugar with margarine; cool. Add an egg at a time, beating after each addition. Sift flour with baking powder and salt. Add small amounts at a time to sugar mixture, beating well. Mix in remaining ingredients. Press mixture into a 13 x 9-inch pan. Bake at 350 degrees for 30 minutes. Do not overbake. Cut into squares when cool. Yield: 2 dozen squares.

Mrs. H. B. Thorsen
San Diego, Calif.

CARAMEL-COCONUT BARS

2 eggs
1 c. sugar
1 c. flour
1 tsp. baking powder
½ c. milk
2 tbsp. butter
1 tsp. vanilla flavoring

Beat eggs and sugar; add flour and baking powder. Heat milk and butter until butter melts. Add to egg mixture. Add vanilla. Bake at 375 degrees for 25 minutes.

ICING:
7 tbsp. brown sugar
3 tbsp. butter
2 tbsp. milk
1 pkg. coconut

Heat brown sugar, butter and milk until melted. Add coconut; bring to a boil. Spread over warm cake. Brown under broiler. Cut into bars. Yield: 1 dozen.

Mrs. Roy W. Paxton
Tenaha, Tex.

CHERRY-COCONUT BARS

PASTRY:
1 c. flour
½ c. butter or margarine
3 tbsp. powdered sugar

Mix all ingredients with hands until smooth. Spread in an 8-inch square pan. Bake at 350 degrees for 25 minutes.

FILLING:
2 eggs, slightly beaten
1 c. sugar
¼ c. flour
1 tsp. vanilla flavoring
¼ tsp. baking powder
¼ tsp. salt

¾ c. chopped nuts
½ c. coconut
¼ c. quartered Maraschino cherries

Combine all ingredients. Spread over top of baked pastry. Bake for 30 minutes longer. Cool; cut into bars. Yield: 18 servings.

Mrs. George Witham
Janesville, Minn.

CHERRY-CREAM CHEESE DELIGHT

26 graham crackers, finely rolled
⅔ c. light brown sugar
1 tsp. cinnamon
⅔ c. butter
2 8-oz. pkg. cream cheese, softened
2 c. powdered sugar
2 cans cherry pie mix
2 c. whipped cream
Sugar
Vanilla flavoring

Mix crackers, brown sugar, cinnamon and butter; place in a 2-quart flat baking dish. Chill well. Mix cream cheese with powdered sugar; whip until smooth. Spread mixture on top of crust. Spread cherry pie mix over top. Whip cream with sugar and vanilla to taste; spread over cherry mix. Cut into squares. NOTE: Cherry pie mix and cream may be reversed if desired. Yield: 12-14 servings.

Mrs. Reiman K. Williams
Petaluma, Calif.

CHEWY NOELS

1 c. brown sugar
5 tbsp. flour
⅛ tsp. soda
1 tsp. vanilla flavoring
2 eggs, beaten
1 c. chopped pecans
5 tbsp. butter
Powdered sugar

Combine sugar, flour, soda, vanilla, eggs and nuts. Melt butter in large shallow baking pan; immediately spread batter over butter. Bake at 350 degrees for 20 minutes. Turn out immediately on waxed paper sprinkled with powdered sugar. Cut into small squares; turn to coat with powdered sugar. Yield: 2-3 dozen.

Mrs. Rosemarie Glaser
Ft. Sill, Okla.

CHINESE CHEWS

1 c. flour
½ c. butter
1 ½ c. plus 2 tbsp. brown sugar
2 eggs, well beaten
1 c. coconut
1 c. chopped nuts

(Continued on next page)

Combine flour, butter and 2 tablespoons brown sugar; press into an 8-inch square pan. Bake at 325 degrees for 20 minutes. Mix eggs, coconut, nuts and 1 1/2 cups brown sugar. Spread over first mixture; return to oven. Bake at 325 degrees for 30 minutes. Cut into squares. Yield: 8 servings.

Mrs. S. P. Quint
Bunker Hill, Kans.

CHINESE CHEWS
BOTTOM MIXTURE:
1 c. butter
4 tbsp. brown sugar
2 c. flour
2 dashes of salt

Blend butter, sugar, flour and salt with a pastry blender. Pat into a 9 x 12-inch baking pan. Bake at 350 degrees for 20 minutes. Remove from oven.

TOP MIXTURE:
3 c. brown sugar
4 tsp. vanilla flavoring
1 ½ c. chopped nuts
4 eggs, beaten
1 ½ c. coconut

Combine brown sugar, vanilla, nuts, eggs and coconut. Spread over bottom mixture; return to oven. Bake at 350 degrees for 30 minutes. Cool; cut into squares. Yield: 48 pieces.

Mrs. V. J. Tielke
Atkinson, Nebr.

CHOCOLATE-CREAM COOKIES
2 c. sugar
½ c. shortening
2 eggs
4 c. flour
2 tsp. soda
½ tsp. baking powder
½ tsp. salt
½ c. cocoa
1 c. sour milk
1 tsp. vanilla flavoring
1 c. boiling water

Cream sugar and shortening; add eggs. Add sifted dry ingredients alternately with milk. Add vanilla and boiling water. Refrigerate for 4 to 5 hours. Drop onto an ungreased cookie sheet. Bake at 450 degrees for 5 minutes. Cool. NOTE: Do not use milk made sour by adding vinegar.

FILLING:
1 c. milk
5 tbsp. flour

1 c. powdered sugar
½ c. shortening
½ c. margarine
¼ tsp. salt
1 tsp. vanilla flavoring

Cook milk and flour until thick; cool. Cream sugar, shortenings, salt and vanilla. Stir in flour mixture; beat with mixer until fluffy. Spread between cookies.

Mrs. Margaret Burkholder
Chambersburg, Pa.

CHOCOLATE-MALT BAR
¾ c. butter
⅔ c. plus ½ c. sugar
1 ¾ c. flour
3 eggs
¼ c. flour
1 tsp. baking powder
¼ tsp. salt
¾ c. chocolate malted milk powder
2 tsp. vanilla flavoring
1 c. coconut
Nuts

Blend butter, 2/3 cup sugar and flour. Place in a greased 9 x 13-inch dish. Bake at 350 degrees for 10 minutes. Beat eggs until fluffy; add 1/2 cup sugar and remaining ingredients except nuts. Place on top of baked mixture; sprinkle with nuts. Bake at 350 degrees for 25 to 30 minutes. Cool; cut into bars.

Alice M. Lewin
Thurston, Nebr.

CHOCOLATE-PECAN BARS
2 c. brown sugar
⅓ c. shortening
⅓ c. butter
3 eggs
2 ¾ c. flour
3 tsp. baking powder
½ tsp. salt
1 tsp. vanilla flavoring
1 6-oz. pkg. chocolate pieces
½ c. chopped pecans
Powdered sugar icing

Cream sugar with shortening and butter. Add eggs; beat until fluffy. Add sifted dry ingredients; beat well. Add vanilla, chocolate pieces and pecans. Stir in well. Pour batter into a 10 x 15-inch pan. Bake at 350 degrees for 25 to 30 minutes. Do not overbake. Frost with powdered sugar frosting; sprinkle top with chocolate pieces.

Betty Krenik
Goodhue, Minn.

SPICY CHOCOLATE BARS

1 ½ c. shortening
1 ½ c. sugar
1 ½ c. (packed) brown sugar
4 eggs
2 tsp. vanilla flavoring
4 c. unsifted flour
2 tsp. soda
2 tsp. salt
4 tsp. cinnamon
1 tsp. ground cloves
1 tsp. nutmeg
2 c. cocoa

Cream shortening and sugars until fluffy. Beat in eggs; add flavoring. Blend in dry ingredients. Spread in two ungreased pans. Bake at 375 degrees for 20 minutes. Cut into 80 bars; cool. NOTE: Can be frosted if desired. Yield: 80 servings.

Mrs. Ross M. King
Jesup, Iowa

LEBKUCHEN CHRISTMAS COOKIES

1 12-oz. pkg. pitted dates
2 ¼ c. flour
1 c. nuts
¼ tsp. salt
1 tsp. cinnamon
1 lb. brown sugar
4 eggs, well beaten
Milk
Powdered sugar

Roll dates in 1/4 cup flour; grind nuts with dates. Sift remaining 2 cups flour, salt and cinnamon; add date mixture. Beat brown sugar into eggs. Add flour mixture, mixing well. Spread mixture 1/2-inch thick in a shallow pan. Bake at 325 degrees for 15 minutes. Cool. Spread with a thin glaze made of milk and powdered sugar. Cut into bars. Yield: 36 bars.

Carol Easter
Mason, O.

NOEL CHRISTMAS COOKIES

2 eggs, beaten
1 c. dark brown sugar
⅛ tsp. soda
5 tbsp. unsifted flour
½ c. chopped nuts
1 tsp. vanilla flavoring
2 tbsp. butter
Powdered sugar

Combine eggs, sugar and soda; blend in flour. Stir in nuts and flavoring. Pour over butter melted in an 8-inch square pan. Bake at 350 degrees for 25 minutes. Turn cake onto waxed paper sprinkled with powdered sugar. Cool; cut into small squares.

Mrs. Edna Dodds
Casey, Ill.

CINNAMON CRISPIES

2 c. flour
1 tsp. baking powder
½ tsp. salt
1 ½ c. plus 1 tbsp. sugar
2 sticks butter or margarine
1 egg, beaten
Milk
1 tbsp. cinnamon

Sift dry ingredients using 1 tablespoon sugar. Cut in 1 stick margarine until mixture resembles coarse meal. Mix egg and enough milk to make 3/4 cup liquid. Add, stirring, only until dough forms a ball. Place on floured board; fold over and knead 25 times. Roll into a rectangle about 1/4-inch thick. Melt remaining butter; spread 3 tablespoonfuls on rectangle. Mix remaining sugar and cinnamon; sprinkle 1/4 cup of the mixture over butter. Roll dough as for jelly roll; cut into 1/2-inch slices. Put 1/4 cup sugar mixture on waxed paper. Dip rolls into melted butter; place cut-side down on sugar. Cover with more sugar mixture. Put layer of waxed paper on top. Roll or pat to 1/4-inch thickness. Remove paper; place on lightly greased cookie sheet. Bake at 425 degrees for 7 to 10 minutes. Serve warm. Yield: 2 dozen.

Mrs. Ruth M. Wachtler
Chowchilla, Calif.

CINNAMON-NUT COOKIES

½ c. plus 2 tbsp. shortening
½ c. sugar
2 c. (heaping) flour
1 ½ tsp. baking powder
Pinch of salt
3 eggs
1 tsp. vanilla flavoring
Jam
½ c. chopped nuts
Cinnamon and sugar mixture

Mix 1/2 cup shortening, sugar, flour, baking powder and salt; add eggs and vanilla. Mix well. Wrap in waxed paper; refrigerate for 2 hours. Knead; roll out thin. Combine remaining shortening, jam, nuts and cinnamon-sugar mixture; spread over dough. Roll as for a jelly roll. Wet tops with cold water; sprinkle with cinnamon-sugar mixture. Bake at 400 degrees for 20 to 30 minutes.

Mrs. Shirley Kushin
Indio, Calif.

COCONUT BARS

2 c. graham cracker crumbs
½ c. butter, melted
2 tbsp. powdered sugar
2 c. coconut
1 can condensed milk
6 chocolate bars

(Continued on next page)

Combine crumbs, butter and sugar; press into pan. Bake at 350 degrees for 10 minutes. Mix coconut with condensed milk; pour over baked crust. Top with chocolate; return to oven until melted.

Mrs. Leo W. Treinen
Lodi, Wisc.

COCONUT BARS

½ c. butter
1 c. flour
2 eggs
1 ½ c. brown sugar
1 c. nuts
1 c. coconut
2 tbsp. flour
½ tsp. salt
¼ tsp. baking powder
1 tsp. vanilla flavoring

Blend butter and flour. Bake at 325 degrees for 15 minutes. Combine all remaining ingredients; spread on top of baked mixture. Bake for 30 minutes longer.

ICING:
1 ½ c. powdered sugar
2 tbsp. butter
2 tbsp. orange juice
1 tbsp. lemon juice

Combine all ingredients; spread over mixture.

Mrs. E. G. F. Pollard
Norfolk, Va.

COCONUT-CHOCOLATE MERINGUE BITS

¾ c. butter
1 ½ c. (packed) brown sugar
½ c. sugar
3 eggs, separated
1 tsp. vanilla flavoring
2 c. flour
1 tsp. baking powder
¼ tsp. soda
¼ tsp. salt
1 6-oz. pkg. chocolate pieces
1 c. grated coconut
¾ c. chopped nuts

Combine butter, 1/2 cup brown sugar, sugar, egg yolks and flavoring; beat for 2 minutes at medium speed. Add sifted dry ingredients. Pat dough into greased pan. Sprinkle with chocolate pieces, coconut and nuts. Beat egg whites until frothy. Add remaining brown sugar gradually; beat until stiff. Spread over top. Bake at 350 degrees for 35 to 40 minutes. Cool; cut into bars. Yield: 50 servings.

Mrs. Franklin Bernhard
Shelton, Nebr.

COCONUT DREAM SQUARES

1 ¼ c. sifted cake flour
1 ¼ c. (firmly packed) brown sugar
⅓ c. butter or margarine
2 eggs
½ tsp. baking powder
1 tsp. vanilla flavoring
1 ⅓ c. flaked coconut
1 c. chopped walnuts

Combine 1 cup flour and 1/4 cup sugar. Add butter; mix until thoroughly blended and smooth. Press into ungreased 9 x 9 x 2-inch pan. Bake at 350 degrees for 15 minutes. Beat eggs until light; add remaining sugar gradually, beating constantly until mixture is light and fluffy. Sift remaining flour with baking powder; fold into egg mixture. Add flavoring, coconut and nuts; mix thoroughly. Spread on top of baked mixture in pan. Bake for 20 to 25 minutes longer or until lightly browned. Cut into squares while warm. Yield: 24 servings.

Mrs. Henry F. Newth
Venango, Nebr.

COCONUT-PINEAPPLE SQUARES

1 ¼ c. drained crushed pineapple
1 c. coconut
½ c. shortening
¾ c. sugar
2 eggs
2 c. flour
¼ tsp. salt
½ tsp. soda
¼ tsp. ginger
2 to 3 tbsp. pineapple juice
1 6-oz. pkg. chocolate pieces

Mix 1/2 cup pineapple and coconut. Cream shortening, sugar and eggs. Sift together dry ingredients; add to creamed mixture with 3/4 cup crushed pineapple and pineapple juice. Add chocolate pieces. Spread in greased 8 x 13-inch pan. Top with coconut-pineapple mixture. Bake at 350 degrees for 30 minutes. Cut into squares when cool. Yield: 24 servings.

Mrs. Betty Tutko
Dravosburg, Pa.

HONEY-COCONUT BARS

½ c. shortening
½ c. sugar
½ c. honey
1 egg, well beaten
⅔ c. sifted flour
½ tsp. soda
½ tsp. baking powder
½ tsp. salt
1 c. quick cooking oats
1 c. shredded coconut

(Continued on next page)

½ c. chopped nuts
1 tsp. vanilla flavoring

Cream shortening, sugar and honey until light and fluffy. Add egg; blend in flour sifted with soda, baking powder and salt. Mix well. Stir in remaining ingredients. Spread in well greased 9 x 15-inch baking pan. Bake at 350 degrees for 12 to 15 minutes. Cut into bars. Yield: 20 bars.

> Mrs. Mary M. Anderson
> Orion, Ill.

CONGO SQUARES

⅔ c. shortening or butter
1 box light brown sugar
3 eggs
2 ¾ c. sifted flour
1 tsp. vanilla flavoring
2 tbsp. water
1 c. nuts
1 pkg. chocolate pieces

Melt shortening; add brown sugar. Stir until well mixed. Add an egg at a time; beat well. Add remaining ingredients; mix well. Pour into greased pans. Bake at 300 degrees for 25 to 30 minutes. Cool; cut into squares. Yield: 50 servings.

> Mrs. Verna Gibbs
> Engelhard, N.C.

CRYSTAL BARS

CRUST:
½ c. butter
½ c. brown sugar
1 c. flour

Mix butter, sugar and flour to crumb stage; pat into 8 x 10-inch pan. Bake at 375 degrees for 10 minutes. Cool.

BATTER:
2 eggs
1 tsp. vanilla flavoring
1 c. brown sugar
2 tbsp. flour
1 tsp. baking powder
½ tsp. salt
½ c. coconut
½ c. nuts

Combine all ingredients; mix well. Spread over crust. Bake at 375 degrees for 25 minutes. Cut into bars while warm. Yield: 24 servings.

> Mrs. Viola Tegethoff
> Beattie, Kans.

DATE-CHEESE DREAMS

2 c. grated Cheddar cheese
½ lb. butter, softened
10 dashes of paprika
1 ½ c. flour
1 egg
Dates
Pecans

Combine all ingredients except dates and pecans as for pastry. Refrigerate for 2 hours or overnight. Roll pastry thin; cut the size of small biscuits. Place a date and a pecan on each; roll. Bake at 300 degrees on cookie sheet for 10 minutes or until light brown. Delicious for coffee or tea. Serve hot or cold. Yield: 3 dozen.

> Mrs. Edgar Green
> Lewisburg, Tenn.

DATE MARGUERITES

2 egg whites
½ c. sugar
½ c. coarse graham cracker crumbs
1 tsp. baking powder
¼ tsp. salt
1 c. chopped pitted dates
½ c. chopped walnuts
½ tsp. vanilla flavoring

Beat egg whites until stiff; gradually add sugar, beating constantly. Mix crumbs, baking powder and salt; fold into egg white mixture with dates, nuts and flavoring. Spread in greased 8 x 8 x 2-inch pan. Bake at 350 degrees for 35 minutes. Cool; cut into squares. Yield: 16 servings.

> Mrs. George Hornbach
> Guilford, Ind.

DATE-NUT-CHOCOLATE SQUARES

½ c. lard
1 square chocolate
¾ c. sugar
2 eggs, beaten
1 c. sifted flour
¼ tsp. salt
1 tsp. vanilla flavoring
½ c. chopped dates
1 c. chopped pecans

Melt lard with chocolate. Add sugar; mix well. Add eggs; stir thoroughly. Add remaining ingredients. Pour batter into cake pan. Bake at 350 degrees for 30 minutes. NOTE: If glass square cake dish is used, reduce oven temperature to 325 degrees. Yield: 16 squares.

> Mrs. Paul Cunningham
> Hartwell, Ga.

COFFEE-DATE BARS

1 ½ c. sifted flour
2 tbsp. plus 1 tsp. instant coffee
½ c. butter, melted
2 tbsp. water
½ c. sugar
2 eggs, slightly beaten
2 c. pitted and finely cut dates

Sift flour and 2 tablespoons instant coffee into a bowl. Pour butter and water over flour mixture; stir until mixture forms a ball. Press one-half of the mixture evenly against bottom of ungreased 8-inch square baking pan. Combine sugar and remaining instant coffee. Stir into eggs. Pour over dates; mix until dates are separated and coated with egg mixture. Spread over pastry in pan. Roll remaining pastry between two sheets of waxed paper to an 8-inch square. Peel off top sheet of waxed paper. Place pastry over date mixture; carefully peel off waxed paper. Seal edges of pastry; prick pattern in center. Bake at 425 degrees for 35 to 40 minutes or until pastry is completely dry. Cool; cut into 1 x 2 1/2-inch bars. Yield: 24 bars.

Photograph for this recipe above.

DATE-NUT FILLED COOKIES

1 lb. margarine

1 lb. cream cheese
3 c. flour

Mix all ingredients; chill overnight. Roll out thin; cut with round cutter. Fill with filling; press ends closed. Bake at 375 degrees for 20 to 25 minutes. When cool, frost; decorate with a chopped cherry.

FILLING:
1 lb. chopped dates
1 c. chopped nuts
½ c. sugar
½ c. water

Mix all ingredients. Boil until thick. Cool. Yield: 10 dozen.

Mrs. Janie Ingavo
Dunkirk, N.Y.

DATE AND NUT SQUARES

2 eggs
½ c. sugar
½ tsp. vanilla flavoring
½ c. sifted flour
½ tsp. baking powder
½ tsp. salt
1 c. chopped walnuts
2 c. finely chopped dates
Powdered sugar (opt.)

(Continued on next page)

Beat eggs until foamy; beat in sugar and flavoring. Add sifted dry ingredients. Stir in nuts and dates. Spread in well greased 8-inch square pan. Bake at 325 degrees for 25 to 30 minutes or until top has dull crust. Cut into squares while warm. Cool; remove from pan. Dip into powdered sugar. Yield: 16 servings.

Dorothea Carey
Brookfield, N.Y.

DATE STICKS
½ c. shortening
½ c. sugar
1 ½ c. sifted flour
1 tsp. baking powder
1 tsp. salt
2 tbsp. milk
2 eggs, beaten
1 c. chopped nuts
1 pkg. chopped dates
1 tsp. vanilla flavoring
Powdered sugar

Cream shortening and sugar; mix in flour, baking powder and salt. Add milk and eggs; mix well. Add nuts, dates and flavoring; mix thoroughly. Bake at 325 degrees for 30 minutes. Brush with powdered sugar; cut into sticks.

Elaine Lessen
Emden, Ill.

EASY FILLED DATE COOKIES
1 c. soft shortening
2 c. brown sugar
2 eggs
½ c. water, buttermilk or sour milk
1 tsp. vanilla flavoring
3 ½ c. sifted flour
1 tsp. salt
1 tsp. soda
⅛ tsp. cinnamon

Cream shortening and sugar; add eggs. Stir in all remaining ingredients. Drop from teaspoon onto ungreased sheet. Fill with date filling.

FILLING:
2 c. cut up dates
¾ c. sugar
¾ c. water
½ c. chopped nuts

Cook dates, sugar and water, stirring constantly until thickened. Add nuts; cool. Put 1/2 teaspoon filling on each unbaked cookie; cover with 1/2 teaspoon cookie dough. Bake at 400 degrees for 10 to 12 minutes or until lightly browned. Yield: 5 dozen.

Alice M. Erkerle
Hart, Mich.

FROSTED CREAMS
⅓ c. hot coffee
½ c. shortening
¾ c. molasses
1 egg
2 egg yolks
2 ½ c. sifted flour
1 c. sugar
1 ½ tsp. baking powder
½ tsp. soda
1 tsp. salt
½ tsp. cinnamon
½ tsp. cloves

Pour coffee over shortening; add molasses, egg and egg yolks. Mix well. Sift dry ingredients into mixing bowl. Add molasses mixture; beat for 2 minutes at low speed on electric mixer. Spread batter in greased and floured shallow pan. Bake at 350 degrees for 35 minutes or until cake springs back when touched gently with finger.

FROSTING:
¼ c. soft butter
½ c. sifted powdered sugar
2 tbsp. cream
1 tsp. vanilla flavoring

Mix all ingredients; beat until fluffy. Spread over warm cookies. Yield: 36-40 cookies.

Mrs. Willard Schelbitzki
Strang, Nebr.

CHEROKEE FRUIT BARS
2 eggs
1 c. (packed) brown sugar
2 tsp. vanilla flavoring
1 c. minus 2 tbsp. flour
1 tsp. baking powder
½ tsp. salt
1 c. chopped figs
1 c. currants
1 c. chopped nuts
1 c. mixed fruits and peels

Beat eggs until thick and lemon colored; blend in brown sugar and vanilla. Sift all dry ingredients; fold into mixture. Fold in fruits and nuts. Place in waxed paper-lined pan. Bake at 350 degrees for 35 minutes or until golden. Remove from pan while warm; cut into squares.

Mrs. Eliot B. MacLean
Seneca, S.C.

FRUIT SQUARES

½ lb. butter
½ box light brown sugar
2 eggs
1 ¼ c. flour
½ tsp. baking powder
2 c. chopped nuts
¾ lb. cherries, chopped
¾ lb. pineapple, chopped

Cream butter and sugar; add an egg at a time. Add flour sifted with baking powder. Spread nuts evenly over bottom of greased 13 x 9 x 2-inch pan. Pour batter over nuts; top with cherries and pineapple. Bake at 300 degrees until done. Cool; cut into squares. Yield: 20 servings.

Mrs. Gussie Chatmon
Cairo, Ga.

FUDGE SQUARES

½ lb. margarine
4 squares bitter chocolate
4 eggs, well beaten
2 c. sugar
1 ¼ c. flour
2 c. pecans
2 tsp. vanilla flavoring

Melt margarine with chocolate in double boiler. Combine eggs and sugar; mix in flour and pecans. Add chocolate mixture; stir in vanilla. Bake at 350 degrees until done.

ICING:
1 square chocolate
1 stick margarine
¾ box powdered sugar
¼ to ½ c. coffee

Melt chocolate with margarine; add sugar and coffee, beating well. Spread over warm cookies; cut into squares.

Mrs. Beulah Rushing
Sabinal, Tex.

SOFT GINGER COOKIES

1 c. sugar
⅓ c. shortening
1 egg
½ c. molasses
2 tsp. soda
4 tbsp. hot water
1 tsp. cinnamon
1 tsp. ginger
1 tsp. salt
3 ¼ c. flour

Cream sugar and shortening. Thoroughly mix in egg and molasses. Dissolve soda in hot water. Sift all dry ingredients; add alternately with soda and hot water to creamed mixture. Spread on greased cookie sheet.

Bake in 350 degree oven for 15 to 20 minutes. Cool. Frost with a powdered sugar icing. Cut into squares or bars.

Mrs. Kenny Handel
Freeman, S.D.

GRAHAM CRACKER SQUARES

22 graham crackers, finely crushed
1 can condensed milk
¼ tsp. salt
1 pkg. chocolate pieces
1 c. chopped nuts
1 tsp. vanilla flavoring

Mix crumbs and condensed milk. Add all remaining ingredients; mix well. Put in well greased 8 x 8-inch pan. Bake at 350 degrees for 25 to 30 minutes. Yield: 16 servings.

Edrie H. Burrows
Center Sandwich, N.H.

LEMON FROSTED PECAN BARS

½ c. butter or margarine
1 ½ c. light brown sugar
1 ¼ c. flour
2 eggs
1 tsp. vanilla flavoring
1 tsp. baking powder
½ tsp. salt
1 c. flaked coconut
¾ c. chopped pecans or almonds

Cream butter and 1/2 cup brown sugar until light and fluffy. Add 1 cup flour; mix well. Press mixture evenly in 13 x 9 x 2-inch baking pan. Bake at 350 degrees for 10 minutes. Beat eggs, flavoring and remaining brown sugar until frothy. Sift remaining flour with baking powder and salt; fold into egg mixture. Add coconut and pecans; mix well. Spread evenly over mixture in pan. Bake at 350 degrees for 20 minutes or until done.

LEMON FROSTING:
1 c. sifted powdered sugar
2 ½ tbsp. lemon juice
1 tsp. grated lemon rind

Combine all ingredients; spread on warm cookies. When cold, cut into bars. Yield: 24 bars.

Maud B. Rice
Sulphur, La.

MARBLEIZED CHOCOLATE SQUARES

½ c. butter
6 tbsp. sugar
6 tbsp. brown sugar

(Continued on next page)

Plump, juicy, red strawberries—who doesn't love them? Here are strawberry recipes which will draw raves and requests for second helpings from guests and family.

STRAWBERRY-RICE CREAM

3 c. water
2 c. milk
¾ c. uncooked rice
¾ tsp. salt
Dash of cinnamon
3 envelopes unflavored gelatin
¾ c. sugar
2 tsp. vanilla
1 c. heavy cream, whipped

Combine first five ingredients in double boiler. Cover and cook over simmering water for 40 minutes or until rice is tender. Stir occasionally. Mix gelatin and sugar; stir into rice until gelatin dissolves. Pour into large bowl; cool. Add vanilla. Chill until slightly thickened. Fold in whipped cream. Turn into 8-cup ring mold. Chill until firm. Unmold.

STRAWBERRY SAUCE

1 10-oz. pkg. frozen sliced California strawberries, thawed but not drained
2 tsp. cornstarch
3 tbsp. sugar
¼ c. water
2 tbsp. orange juice, Strega or orange Curacao
2 tbsp. lemon juice

Puree stawberries. Gradually blend into cornstarch and sugar in saucepan. Add water. Cook, stirring, until sauce boils for 30 seconds. Stir in juices. Chill. Pour over rice cream. Yield: 8-10 servings.

STRAWBERRY WAFFLES

3 10-oz. pkg. frozen sliced California strawberries, thawed and drained
1½ c. (about) milk
3 eggs
⅓ c. salad oil
3 c. buttermilk pancake and waffle mix

Puree strawberries. Combine with milk to measure 3 cups. Add remaining ingredients and beat until batter is smooth. Bake on preheated waffle iron until steaming stops. Yield: 6 large waffles.

See photograph on reverse page.

1 egg
1 c. plus 2 tbsp. flour
½ tsp. salt
½ tsp. soda
¼ tsp. water
½ tsp. vanilla flavoring
½ c. nuts
1 c. chocolate

Cream butter and sugars thoroughly; beat in egg. Blend in remaining ingredients except chocolate pieces. Spread evenly in 13 x 9-inch pan. Sprinkle chocolate pieces over top. Put in 375 degree oven for 2 minutes. Remove from oven; blend in chocolate pieces to marbleize. Return to oven. Bake for 15 minutes longer.

Mrs. Walter H. Peterson
Amherst, Wisc.

MATRIMONIAL COOKIES

FILLING:
½ lb. dates
½ c. sugar
½ c. nuts
½ c. water

Mix all ingredients; bring just to a boil. Cool before spreading between crumbs.

COOKIES:
1 c. (packed) brown sugar
1 ¼ c. uncooked oats
1 ½ c. flour
1 tsp. soda
¼ tsp. salt
¾ c. butter

Combine all ingredients; mix with fingers into fine crumbs. Put one-half of the mixture in loaf pan; gently pat down. Spread on cooled date mixture. Top with remaining crumbs; pat gently. Bake at 350 degrees for 20 to 25 minutes. Cut into squares.

Loramay S. Couch
Monticello, N.Y.

CHOCOLATE-MINCEMEAT BARS

2 c. sifted flour
2 tsp. soda
1 c. sugar
½ c. soft shortening
3 eggs
1 lge. or 2 sm. pkg. semi-sweet chocolate pieces
1 ¾ c. mincemeat

Sift flour with soda. Combine sugar and shortening; beat until creamy. Beat in an egg at a time; continue beating until light. Stir in flour mixture and chocolate pieces.

Add mincemeat. Spread in greased and lightly floured jelly roll pan. Bake at 375 degrees for 30 minutes. Cool; cut into bars. Yield: 5 dozen.

Mrs. Ruth B. Jensen
Milton, Del.

MINCE MIX-UP BARS

¼ c. shortening
¾ c. sugar
2 eggs
¾ c. mincemeat
½ c crushed pineapple
½ c. chopped nuts
1 ½ c. sifted flour
½ tsp. salt
½ tsp. cinnamon
¼ tsp. soda

Cream shortening and sugar; add eggs, mincemeat, pineapple and nuts. Add sifted dry ingredients. Pour into 15 x 10-inch pan. Bake at 350 degrees for 25 minutes. Cool slightly; frost if desired.

FROSTING:
1 ½ c. powdered sugar
1 ½ tbsp. hot pineapple juice

Mix sugar and juice; spread on warm cookies. Yield: 2 dozen.

Muriel Vaughan
Dansville, N.Y.

MINCEMEAT MIX-UP BARS

1 ½ c. flour
½ tsp. salt
½ tsp. cinnamon
¼ tsp. soda
¾ c. sugar
¼ c. shortening
2 eggs
¾ c. mincemeat
½ c. crushed pineapple
½ c. nuts
2 c. powdered sugar
2 to 3 tbsp. pineapple juice

Sift flour, salt, cinnamon and soda. Cream sugar and shortening; add eggs, beating well after each addition. Stir in mincemeat, pineapple and nuts; mix well. Add dry ingredients. Spread mixture in 15 1/2 x 10 1/2 x 1-inch pan. Bake at 350 degrees for 20 to 30 minutes. While still hot, cover with a glaze made from powdered sugar and pineapple juice. Cut into bars. Yield: 4 dozen.

Mrs. Dan Fitzgerald
Battle Creek, Mich.

COOKIES, BARS, SQUARES

MOUNDS BAR COOKIES

½ c. butter, melted
2 c. graham cracker crumbs
1 can condensed milk
6 oz. flaked coconut
½ tsp. vanilla flavoring
¼ lb. shredded German's chocolate

Pour butter over graham crackers; pat into 9 x 13-inch loaf pan. Bake at 375 degrees for 10 minutes. Mix condensed milk, coconut and vanilla; spread on crumb mixture. Bake at 350 degrees for 10 minutes. Sprinkle chocolate on top while hot; spread evenly. Cool; cut into bars. Yield: 18 servings.

Mrs. Robert O. Brown
Brooklyn Center, Minn.

OATMEAL-PECAN BAR

1 c. sugar
2 sticks soft margarine
1 egg
1 tsp. vanilla flavoring
½ tsp. salt
3 c. oats
½ c. pecans

Cream sugar, margarine and egg. Add flavoring and salt. Mix in 1 cup oats at a time; mixture will be extremely dry. Add pecans. Spread in well greased 9 x 15-inch pan. Bake at 350 degrees for 15 minutes. Cut into bars while warm. Yield: 12 servings.

Mrs. Wilton Allen
Marietta, Okla.

OATMEAL-TOFFEE SQUARES

1 c. butter, melted
1 c. brown sugar
1 egg
¼ tsp. salt
1 c. flour
1 c. quick cooking oats
1 tsp. vanilla flavoring

Mix all ingredients; spread in 9 x 12-inch pan. Bake at 350 degrees for 15 to 20 minutes.

TOPPING:
3 oz. semi-sweet chocolate
1 tbsp. butter
Nuts

Melt chocolate with butter; spread on warm cookies. Sprinkle with nuts; cut into squares. Yield: 20 servings.

Mrs. H. B. Bickel
Herreid, S.D.

ORANGE SLICE COOKIES

2 ½ c. brown sugar
4 eggs
½ tsp. salt
2 c. sifted flour
1 c. chopped nuts
1 tsp. vanilla flavoring
18 candy orange slices

Mix brown sugar, eggs and salt. Combine remaining ingredients; add to sugar mixture. Pour into shallow cake pan or cookie sheet. Bake at 275 to 300 degrees for 45 to 60 minutes. Cool; cut into squares. Frost with a thin powdered sugar icing. Yield: 20 servings.

Katherine Daude
Killeen, Tex.

OUT-OF-THIS-WORLD BARS

2 c. graham cracker crumbs
½ c. butter or margarine, melted
1 lge. can condensed milk
2 c. flaked coconut

Mix crumbs and butter; press into 9 x 13-inch pan. Bake at 350 degrees for 10 minutes. Mix condensed milk and coconut; spread over crumb mixture. Bake for 15 minutes longer.

FROSTING:
1 ½ c. brown sugar
6 tbsp. cream
¼ c. butter
¾ c. chocolate pieces

Combine all ingredients except chocolate pieces; boil for 1 minute. Cool for 1 minute. Add chocolate pieces. Spread over coconut mixture. Cool; cut into bars. Yield: 25 servings.

Mrs. Dean Godtland
Gonvick, Minn.

PEANUT BUTTER FINGERS

½ c. butter
½ c. sugar
½ c. brown sugar
1 egg
⅓ c. peanut butter
½ tsp. soda
¼ tsp. salt
½ tsp. vanilla flavoring
1 c. flour
1 c. oats
1 6-oz. pkg. chocolate pieces

Cream butter, sugars, egg and peanut butter; stir in soda, salt, flavoring, flour and oats. Spread in greased and floured 9 x 13-inch pan. Bake at 350 degrees for 20 to 25 minutes.

(Continued on next page)

Sprinkle chocolate pieces over hot cake, spreading as they melt.

FROSTING:
½ c. sifted powdered sugar
¼ c. peanut butter
2 to 4 tbsp. milk

Combine all ingredients; beat until smooth. Spread over chocolate on cookies. Cool; cut into bars. Yield: 24 servings.

Mrs. James H. Andrews
Erie, Pa.

PECAN TASSIES

1 3-oz. pkg. cream cheese
½ c. butter
1 c. sifted flour
1 egg
¾ c. brown sugar
1 tbsp. soft butter
1 tsp. vanilla flavoring
Dash of salt
⅔ c. nuts

Cook cream cheese and butter at a low temperature until soft; stir in flour. Chill; shape into two dozen 1-inch balls. Place in ungreased 1 1/2-inch muffin tins. Shape into shells. Combine egg, sugar, butter, vanilla and salt. Place one-half of the nuts in shells; add egg mixture. Top with remaining nuts. Bake at 325 degrees for 25 minutes.

Lois Joyner
Columbia, S.C.

PINEAPPLE FINGERS

1 pkg. yellow cake mix
2 eggs, separated
3 tbsp. butter, melted
1 tsp. vanilla flavoring
⅔ c. sugar
½ c. coconut
1 sm. can crushed pineapple, well drained

Mix cake mix, egg yolks, butter and flavoring. Press into 9 x 13-inch pan. Beat egg whites until stiff; gradually beat in sugar. Fold in coconut and pineapple. Pour over cake mixture. Bake at 325 degrees for 30 minutes. Cool thoroughly. Cut into finger strips.

Katherine Hirth
Fernandina, Fla.

PRALINE STRIPS

24 graham crackers
1 c. butter
1 c. (packed) brown sugar
1 c. chopped pecans

Arrange crackers in ungreased 10 x 15 x 1-inch pan. Heat butter and sugar to boiling point; boil for 2 minutes. Remove from heat; stir in nuts. Spread over crackers. Bake at 350 degrees for 10 minutes. Cut while warm along cracker grooves. Yield: 4 dozen.

June M. Schallock
Menomonee Falls. Wisc.

RAISIN BARS

1 c. raisins
2 c. water
1 c. sugar
½ c. shortening
2 eggs
2 c. flour
1 tsp. cinnamon
1 tsp. soda
½ tsp. cloves
½ tsp. allspice
½ tsp. salt
⅓ c. nuts
Powdered sugar
Cream

Boil raisins in water until 3/4 cup liquid remains; cool. Cream sugar and shortening; beat in eggs. Mix all ingredients except powdered sugar and cream. Spread on greased cookie sheet. Bake at 375 degrees for 20 minutes. Cover with a thin icing made with powdered sugar and cream. Cut into bars.

Mrs. Ollie Key
Glasco, Kans.

SUGARLESS RAISIN COOKIES

1 c. raisins
1 c. water
½ c. margarine
1 ½ c. flour
1 tsp. soda
2 tbsp. liquid sugar substitute
1 tsp. nutmeg
1 tsp. cinnamon
1 c. nuts

Cook raisins in water until 1/2 cup water remains. Add margarine; cool. Add flour, soda mixed with sugar substitute, spices and nuts. Spread in pan. Bake at 350 degrees for 15 to 20 minutes.

Grace Thornberry
Medicine Lodge, Kans.

SCOTCH SQUARES

½ c. butter
1 c. (packed) brown sugar
1 egg
1 c. flour

(Continued on next page)

1 tsp. baking powder
½ c. walnuts or pecans

Cream butter and sugar; beat in egg. Mix in flour, baking powder and nuts. Spread in greased 8 x 8-inch pan. Bake at 350 degrees for 30 minutes. Cut into squares when cool.

Pauline M. Treadway
Frewsburg, N.Y.

SCOTCH-TOFFEE BARS

⅓ c. butter, melted
2 c. oats
½ c. brown sugar
¼ c. dark syrup
½ tsp. salt
1 ½ tsp. vanilla flavoring
1 6-oz. pkg. chocolate pieces, melted
¼ c. chopped nuts

Pour butter over oats; mix well. Add brown sugar, syrup, salt and flavoring; mix well. Pack into well greased oblong pan. Bake at 450 degrees for 12 minutes. Cool; sprinkle chocolate on top. Sprinkle with nuts.

Mrs. Melba Schaefer
Marblehead, O.

SCRUMPTIOUS SCOTCHIES

1 6-oz. pkg. butterscotch pieces
¼ c. butter or shortening
1 c. (firmly packed) light brown sugar
2 eggs
½ tsp. vanilla flavoring
¾ c. sifted flour
1 tsp. baking powder
¾ tsp. salt
½ c. chopped nuts

Melt butterscotch and butter over hot but not boiling water; remove from heat. Stir in sugar; cool for 5 minutes. Beat in eggs and flavoring. Stir in sifted dry ingredients; stir in nuts. Spread in greased 13 x 9 x 2-inch pan. Bake at 350 degrees for 25 minutes. Cut into squares while warm. Yield: 2 dozen squares.

Mrs. Albert J. Bateson
Rolla, N.D.

SHERRIED FUDGE BARS

½ c. flour
½ tsp. baking powder
½ tsp. soda
¼ tsp. salt
2 eggs
1 c. (firmly packed) brown sugar
⅓ c. melted butter or margarine

2 1-oz. squares chocolate, melted
¼ c. med. or sweet Sherry
1 c. chopped walnuts or pecans
Powdered sugar (opt.)

Sift flour with baking powder, soda and salt. Beat eggs until light; add sugar gradually, beating well. Stir in butter and chocolate. Add dry ingredients; add Sherry and nuts. Blend well. Pour into greased and floured 8-inch square pan. Bake in 325 degree oven for 45 minutes or until toothpick inserted in center comes out clean. Cool slightly; cut into squares. Roll in powdered sugar if desired. Yield: 12-14 squares.

Mrs. R. H. Baker
Randolph AFB, Tex.

ORANGE-BROWN SUGAR COOKIES

1 ½ c. brown sugar
1 c. shortening
2 eggs
4 c. flour
2 tsp. baking powder
1 tsp. soda
¼ tsp. salt
1 c. sour milk
Grated rind of 2 oranges
1 c. nuts (opt.)

Cream sugar and shortening. Add eggs; beat. Sift all dry ingredients; add alternately with sour milk to creamed mixture, beating after each addition. Add orange rind and nuts. Spread in pan. Bake at 375 degrees for 8 to 10 minutes. Frost with orange juice thickened with granulated or powdered sugar.

Mrs. Harold W. Mount
Norfolk, Va.

TOFFEE-NUT BARS

BOTTOM LAYER:
¾ c. mixed soft butter and shortening
¾ c. brown sugar
1 ½ c. sifted flour

Thoroughly mix all ingredients. Press into ungreased 13 x 9-inch pan. Bake at 350 degrees for 15 minutes.

COCONUT TOPPING:
1 ½ c. brown sugar
1 ½ tsp. vanilla flavoring
2 eggs, well beaten
3 tbsp. flour
1 ½ tsp. baking powder
¾ tsp. salt
1 ½ c. moist shredded coconut
1 ½ c. chopped pecans or almonds

Stir sugar and vanilla into eggs. Mix flour, baking powder and salt; stir into egg mixture.

(Continued on next page)

Mix in coconut and nuts. Spread topping over baked layer; return to oven. Bake at 350 degrees for 30 minutes or until topping is brown. Cool slightly; cut into bars.

Mrs. A. G. Kouts
Montgomery, Ala.

WHEAT FLAKE SQUARES

FILLING:
1 c. chopped dates
1 c. water
½ c. brown sugar
Juice of 1 lemon

Combine all ingredients; mix well. Simmer gently until smooth; cool.

CRUMB MIXTURE:
1 c. brown sugar
1 ¼ c. wheat flakes
1 ½ c. sifted flour
½ tsp. salt
½ tsp. cinnamon
¾ c. shortening
1 egg yolk
1 tbsp. water

Combine all ingredients except egg yolk and water; mix until crumbly. Spread one-half of the mixture in 8 x 12-inch shallow pan. Spread with date filling; top with remaining crumb mixture. Press flat with spoon. Brush with mixture of egg yolk and water. Bake at 350 degrees for 20 to 25 minutes. When cool, cut into squares. Yield: 16-20 squares.

Mrs. Charles S. Stone
Cleveland, O.

ALMOND DROP COOKIES

2 ½ c. shortening
3 ½ c. sugar
5 eggs
Juice of 1 orange
Grated rind of 1 orange
1 sm. bottle almond flavoring
10 c. flour
16 tsp. baking powder
2 c. milk
Powdered sugar

Cream shortening and sugar; add an egg at a time. Add orange juice, rind and almond flavoring. Add all dry ingredients and milk; mix well. Drop by teaspoonfuls into powdered sugar; place on greased cookie sheet. Bake at 350 degrees for 10 to 12 minutes. Remove immediately from cookie sheet. Yield: 8 dozen.

Marie Sartini
Niagara Falls, N. Y.

APPLE COOKIES

½ c. shortening
1 ⅓ c. brown sugar
1 egg
2 c. flour
1 tsp. soda
½ tsp. salt
½ c. milk
1 c. chopped nuts
1 c. raisins
1 c. finely chopped unpared apples

Cream shortening, sugar and egg. Add one-half the dry ingredients. Blend in milk and remaining dry ingredients. Add nuts, raisins and apples; mix. Drop onto greased cookie sheet. Bake at 400 degrees for 10 to 12 minutes. Spread with vanilla glaze.

VANILLA GLAZE:
1 ½ c. powdered sugar
2 ½ tsp. milk
⅛ tsp. salt
¼ tsp. vanilla flavoring
1 tsp. butter, melted

Mix all ingredients until creamy.

Harriet Summerville
Rimersburg, Pa.

FRESH APPLE COOKIES

½ c. shortening
½ tsp. salt
1 ⅓ c. brown sugar
1 tsp. nutmeg
1 tsp. cinnamon
½ tsp. cloves
1 tsp. soda
1 egg
⅓ c. sweet or sour milk
1 c. raisins
1 c. finely chopped unpeeled apples
2 c. flour
½ c. nuts

Mix all ingredients; drop by heaping teaspoonfuls onto baking sheet. Bake at 400 degrees for 11 to 14 minutes.

FROSTING:
1 ½ c. powdered sugar
½ tsp. vanilla flavoring
Pinch of salt
Cream

Combine all ingredients, adding enough cream to make of spreading consistency. Spread on warm cookies. Yield: 2-3 dozen.

Mrs. Margarita Brodie
Norway, Oreg.

APPLESAUCE COOKIES

½ c. shortening
¾ c. sugar
1 egg, beaten
1 c. applesauce
2 c. flour
1 tsp. salt
1 tsp. cinnamon
½ tsp. cloves
1 tsp. soda
1 c. raisins
1 c. walnuts

Cream shortening and sugar. Add egg and applesauce. Mix in dry ingredients, raisins and walnuts. Drop by spoonfuls onto greased cookie sheet. Bake at 375 degrees for 12 to 15 minutes.

Mrs. Lottie Blanchette
Eagle Lake, Me.

BACHELOR BUTTONS

¾ c. shortening
1 c. (firmly packed) brown sugar
1 egg, beaten
1 tsp. vanilla flavoring
½ c. chopped nuts (opt.)
2 c. sifted flour
¾ tsp. salt
1 tsp. soda

Cream shortening and sugar; add egg, vanilla and nuts. Blend with rubber spatula. Stir in sifted dry ingredients. Drop from a teaspoon onto a greased cookie sheet or shape into crescents with floured fingertips. Bake at 375 degrees for 12 minutes. NOTE: One-half cup of any of the following may be substituted for the nuts: c o c o n u t, candied cherries, Maraschino cherries, chocolate pieces or raisins. Yield: 5-6 dozen.

Mrs. Joyce Mauldin Redstone
Weir, Miss.

BANANA-DATE CIRCLES

¾ c. soft butter
1 c. sugar
1 egg
1 ¼ c. flour
¾ tsp. salt
½ tsp. baking powder
½ tsp. nutmeg
1 c. mashed bananas
1 ½ c. quick cooking oats
1 c. cut up dates
½ c. chopped nuts
1 6-oz. pkg. butterscotch pieces

Cream butter and sugar; add egg. Sift dry ingredients; add to mixture. Add remaining ingredients. Drop from spoon onto greased

cookie sheet. Bake at 400 degrees for 10 to 12 minutes. Yield: 6 dozen.

Mabel Brown
Miami, Fla.

BOILED COOKIES

2 c. sugar
½ c. milk
¼ c. butter or margarine
3 tbsp. cocoa
3 c. quick cooking oats
½ c. peanut butter
1 tsp. vanilla flavoring
½ to 1 c. nuts (opt.)

Combine sugar, milk, butter and cocoa in a pan. Bring to a boil; cook for 1 minute. Remove from heat; quickly add remaining ingredients. Stir well. Drop by teaspoonfuls onto waxed paper. Let stand for 30 minutes or until dry. Yield: 40 cookies.

Mrs. Leonard Bell
Higginsville, Md.

BUTTER-CREAM DROPS

1 ½ c. brown sugar
½ c. mixed shortening and butter
2 eggs
2 ⅓ c. flour
1 tsp. soda
½ tsp. baking powder
½ tsp. salt
1 c. sour cream
1 tsp. vanilla flavoring
⅔ c. chopped walnuts

Cream s u g a r and shortening mixture thoroughly. Add eggs; mix well. Add blended dry ingredients alternately with sour cream. Add vanilla and nuts. Drop by teaspoonfuls onto greased baking sheet. Bake at 350 degrees for 10 to 12 minutes.

ICING:
6 tbsp. butter
1 ½ c. powdered sugar
1 tsp. vanilla flavoring
4 tsp. hot water

Melt and brown butter. Stir in powdered sugar, vanilla and hot water. Spread on warm cookies. Yield: 5 dozen.

Mrs. Adrien Zimmerman
Cleveland, O.

EASY BUTTERSCOTCH COOKIES

2 6-oz. pkg. butterscotch pieces

(Continued on next page)

1 No. 2 can chow mein noodles
½ c. chopped nuts

Melt butterscotch pieces over low heat; stir constantly until smooth. Remove from heat; mix in noodles and nuts until well coated. Drop by teaspoonfuls onto greased cookie sheet. Cool. Yield: 36 servings.

Mrs. William Slattery
Girard, Kans.

CARROT DROP COOKIES

1 c. shortening or margarine
¾ c. sugar
1 c. mashed cooked carrots, drained
1 egg, slightly beaten
½ tsp. lemon juice
1 tsp. vanilla flavoring
2 c. flour
2 tsp. baking powder
½ tsp. salt
Juice of 1 orange
Grated rind of 1 orange
Powdered sugar

Cream shortening and sugar. Add carrots, egg, lemon juice and vanilla. Sift flour with baking powder and salt; add to creamed mixture. Drop by spoonfuls onto greased cookie sheets. Bake at 350 degrees until light brown. Combine orange juice and rind with enough powdered sugar to make of spreading consistency. Spread on hot cookies.

Emma M. Snyder
Jensen Beach, Fla.

CHERRY-ALMOND DROPS

1 c. brown sugar
1 c. sugar
1 c. butter or shortening
2 eggs
2 ½ c. flour
1 tsp. soda
1 tsp. salt
1 10-oz. bottle Maraschino cherries, chopped and drained
1 ½ c. flaked or shredded coconut
¾ tsp. almond flavoring

Cream sugars and butter; mix eggs in thoroughly. Add blended dry ingredients; mix well. Stir in cherries, coconut and flavoring; mix well. Drop by teaspoonfuls onto greased baking sheet. Bake at 325 degrees for 15 to 20 minutes. NOTE: For variation, substitute 1 1/2 cups chopped dates and 1 1/2 cups chopped nuts for cherries, coconut and flavoring. Or, substitute 1 1/4 cups chocolate pieces and 1 1/2 cups powdered sugar for the cherries, coconut and flavoring. If this variation

is used, melt chocolate and add to the dough. Shape dough into 1-inch balls; roll in sugar. Bake as directed above. Yield: 6-7 dozen.

Mrs. Gordon Schultz
Balaton, Minn.

CHOCOLATE DROP COOKIES

1 c. shortening
½ c. sugar
½ c. (packed) brown sugar
3 tsp. (heaping) cocoa
1 egg, beaten
1 tsp. salt
½ tsp. soda
½ tsp. baking powder
2 c. flour
1 c. milk
1 tsp. vanilla flavoring

Cream shortening and sugars; add cocoa and egg. Add dry ingredients alternately with milk. Add vanilla; drop onto cookie sheet. Bake at 350 degrees for 10 to 15 minutes. Cool and frost.

ICING:
1 tbsp. butter
1 tbsp. cocoa
5 tbsp. hot coffee
1 tsp. vanilla flavoring
2 c. powdered sugar

Combine all ingredients. Yield: 2-3 dozen.

Emma Kuhn
S. New Berlin, N. Y.

CHOCOLATE-PECAN COOKIES

½ c. shortening
½ tsp. salt
1 tsp. vanilla flavoring
1 c. sugar
2 eggs, well beaten
3 oz. chocolate, melted
¾ c. sifted flour
¾ c. chopped pecans

Combine shortening, salt and vanilla. Add sugar gradually; cream well. Add eggs; mix thoroughly. Blend in chocolate. Add flour and nuts; mix well. Drop from a teaspoon onto greased baking sheets. Let stand a few minutes. Flatten cookies by stamping them with a glass that has been covered with a damp cloth. Bake at 325 degrees for 12 to 15 minutes. Yield: 30 cookies.

Mrs. Paul L. Smith
Richland, N. Y.

CHOCO-NUT DROPS

½ c. butter or margarine
1 c. (firmly packed) brown sugar
½ c. sugar
1 egg
3 squares unsweetened chocolate, melted and cooled
2 c. sifted flour
½ tsp. soda
½ tsp. salt
½ c. sour cream
¼ c. milk
⅓ c. chopped nuts
1 c. oats
Walnut halves

Beat butter and sugars until creamy. Add egg and cooled chocolate; beat thoroughly. Sift flour, soda and salt; stir in one-half flour mixture. Add sour cream and milk, mixing well. Add remaining flour mixture, blending thoroughly. Stir in nuts and oats. Drop by teaspoonfuls onto greased cookie sheets; top with a walnut half. Bake in preheated 350 degree oven for 12 to 15 minutes. Yield: 4 dozen cookies.

Photograph for this recipe above.

CHOCOLATE SURPRISES

½ c. shortening
1 c. sugar
1 egg
1 tsp. vanilla flavoring
¼ c. milk
1 ¼ c. flour
½ tsp. salt
½ tsp. soda
½ c. cocoa
Marshmallow halves

Cream shortening and sugar; add egg and vanilla. Beat well. Add all remaining ingredients except marshmallows. Drop from a teaspoon onto lightly greased cookie sheet. Bake at 350 degrees for 8 minutes. Remove from oven; press marshmallow halves, cut-side down, into center of each cookie. Return to oven for 2 minutes. Cool.

FROSTING:

⅛ tsp. salt
3 tbsp. butter or shortening
5 tbsp. cocoa
5 tbsp. cream or milk

Combine all ingredients. Spread over cooled cookies. Yield: 3 dozen cookies.

Mrs. Ruth Rorick
Sharon Springs, N.Y.

FROSTED CHOCOLATE DROP COOKIES

3 squares chocolate
2 c. brown sugar
1 c. shortening
2 eggs
½ c. milk
1 tsp. vanilla flavoring
3 to 3 ½ c. flour
2 tsp. baking powder
½ tsp. soda
1 c. walnuts

Melt chocolate over hot water; cool slightly. Cream sugar and shortening; add eggs, milk and chocolate. Stir in vanilla. Add sifted dry ingredients to sugar mixture to make a smooth batter. Fold in walnuts. Drop by teaspoonfuls onto an ungreased cookie sheet. Bake at 350 degrees for 12 to 15 minutes. Cool and frost.

FROSTING:
3 c. sifted powdered sugar
2 tbsp. melted butter
2 squares chocolate, melted
2 tbsp. cream or milk

Combine all ingredients; mix well. Yield: 7 dozen.

Mrs. Kathleen Roseberry
Chula Vista, Calif.

CHRISTMAS COOKIES

1 c. margarine
1 ½ c. sugar
¼ tsp. nutmeg
1 tsp. vanilla flavoring
3 eggs
1 tsp. soda
2 ½ c. flour
1 ½ c. raisins
1 ½ c. walnuts
2 c. pecans
2 c. dates
2 c. candied pineapple
1 c. candied cherries

Cream margarine and sugar. Add nutmeg, vanilla, eggs, soda and flour; mix well. Mix nuts with fruit; add to batter. Mix with large spoon. Drop by teaspoonfuls onto greased cookie sheet. Bake at 350 degrees until done. Yield: 75-100 cookies.

Mrs. Billie Roeder
Yorktown, Tex.

CINNAMON JUMBOS

2 c. sugar
1 c. shortening
2 eggs
4 c. flour
1 tsp. soda
1 tsp. salt
1 ½ c. sour milk

2 tsp. vanilla flavoring
1 tsp. cinnamon
2 tbsp. sugar

Mix sugar with shortening and eggs. Gradually add dry ingredients along with milk. Add flavoring; drop by spoonfuls onto cookie sheet. Mix cinnamon and sugar; sprinkle on each cookie. Bake at 350 degrees for 10 to 15 minutes. Yield: 4 dozen.

Mrs. Arthur Erford
Oakwood, O.

COCONUT PUFFS

1 lb. powdered sugar
3 egg whites, stiffly beaten
½ lb. coconut
2 tsp. baking powder

Thoroughly mix sugar and egg whites. Add coconut and baking powder. Drop onto buttered pans. Bake at 300 degrees for 18 minutes or until lightly browned. NOTE: Crushed nuts may be used instead of coconut. Cookies may be frozen for an indefinite period of time. Yield: 3 dozen.

Mrs. Earl Kordell
Pickerington, O.

COFFEE DROPS

3 ½ c. sifted flour
1 tsp. baking powder
1 tsp. soda
1 tsp. cinnamon
1 tsp. nutmeg
½ tsp. salt
1 c. shortening
2 c. brown sugar
2 eggs
¾ c. cold coffee
1 c. raisins
½ c. chopped nuts

Sift all dry ingredients. Cream shortening and brown sugar. Add eggs; beat well. Add flour mixture and coffee alternately. Add raisins and nuts. Drop by teaspoonfuls 2 inches apart onto greased baking sheet. Bake at 400 degrees for 10 minutes. Yield: 5 dozen.

Ruth E. Sundstrom
Roslyn, S.D.

COFFEE DROPS

2 c. sugar
6 tbsp. shortening
2 eggs
1 c. molasses
2 tsp. soda
1 c. hot coffee
1 tsp. allspice
1 tsp. cinnamon
5 c. flour

(Continued on next page)

1 c. raisins
½ c. chopped walnuts

Cream sugar and shortening; add eggs, molasses, soda, coffee and spices. Mix well. Stir in flour, raisins and nuts; blend well. Drop from teaspoon onto well greased cookie sheet. Bake at 375 degrees for 10 to 12 minutes or until firm. Yield: 6-7 dozen cookies.

Mrs. Vivian Dexter
Elma, N.Y.

DATE-FILLED DROP COOKIES

2 c. brown sugar
1 c. shortening
2 eggs
4 c. flour
½ c. water
1 ½ tsp. soda
1 tsp. vanilla flavoring
½ tsp. salt
Chopped dates

Mix all ingredients except dates. Drop by teaspoonfuls onto cookie sheet; flatten slightly. Place 1/2 teaspoon dates in center of each cookie; top with a small amount of cookie dough. Bake at 350 degrees for 12 to 15 minutes. Yield: 5 dozen.

Mrs. Martin Sitar
Lakota, N.D.

SOUR CREAM-DATE DELIGHTS

1 ¼ c. sifted flour
½ tsp. soda
¼ tsp. baking powder
¼ tsp. salt
¼ tsp. cinnamon
⅛ tsp. nutmeg
¼ c. butter
¾ c. (firmly packed) brown sugar
1 egg
½ tsp. vanilla flavoring
½ c. sour cream
⅔ c. chopped pitted dates
½ c. chopped nuts

Sift flour with soda, baking powder, salt, cinnamon and nutmeg. Cream butter and sugar; add egg and vanilla. Mix well. Add dry ingredients alternately with sour cream. Fold in dates and nuts. Drop by teaspoonfuls onto a greased cookie sheet. Bake at 400 degrees for 10 to 12 minutes. Yield: 5 dozen cookies.

Mrs. Don Gaither
Crane, Ind.

DIET COOKIES

1 c. shortening
2 eggs
½ c. diet syrup

1 c. ground raisins
1 c. walnuts
1 c. oats
1 tsp. soda
2 c. all purpose, gluten or rye flour
1 tsp. sweetener
1 tsp. vanilla flavoring

Mix all ingredients. Drop by teaspoonfuls onto a greased pan. Bake at 350 to 375 degrees until done.

Mrs. Orin Johnson
Belleville, Kans.

ELEPHANT EARS

½ c. shortening
1 c. (scant) sugar
2 eggs
Salt to taste
1 tsp. cinnamon
1 tsp. cloves
1 c. molasses
4 c. flour
2 tsp. soda
½ c. sour milk
1 c. raisins

Cream shortening and sugar; add eggs and seasonings. Add molasses and flour. Dissolve soda in milk; add to mixture. Fold in raisins. Drop onto a greased cookie sheet. Bake at 400 degrees for 12 to 15 minutes. Yield: 4 dozen.

Myra French
Skowhegan, Me.

FRUIT CAKE COOKIES

1 lb. butter or margarine
1 lb. brown sugar
3 eggs
1 lb. white raisins, steamed
1 lb. candied pineapple, diced
1 lb. candied cherries
1 lb. nuts
1 can flaked coconut
4 c. sifted flour
1 tsp. soda
3 tbsp. milk

Cream butter; gradually add sugar. Cream until light and fluffy. Add an egg at a time, beating thoroughly after each. Dredge fruit, nuts and coconut in 1 cup flour; add to egg mixture, mixing well. Sift remaining 3 cups flour with soda; add to batter alternately with milk. Drop from teaspoon onto lightly greased baking sheet. Bake at 375 degrees for 10 minutes. Cool before removing from sheet. Yield: 15 dozen.

Lois Brewer
Chester, W. Va.

FRUIT COOKIES

1 c. butter or margarine
1 ½ c. (packed) brown sugar
3 eggs, separated
1 tsp. soda
2 tbsp. boiling water
3 ¾ c. sifted flour
1 tsp. nutmeg
1 tsp. cinnamon
Grated rind of 1 orange
2 c. washed and ground raisins
2 c. washed and ground currants
1 c. chopped nuts
Juice of 1 orange
1 tsp. vanilla flavoring
1 tsp. lemon flavoring

Cream butter and sugar. Add egg yolks; mix well. Add soda dissolved in water. Combine flour, nutmeg and cinnamon; add to egg yolk mixture. Add orange rind, raisins, currants and nuts. Stir in orange juice and flavorings. Mix well. Fold in beaten egg whites. Drop from teaspoon onto greased cookie sheets. Bake at 350 degrees for 10 minutes. Yield: 6-7 dozen cookies.

Mrs. John Billings
Flora, Ind.

GINGERSNAPS

½ c. shortening
1 c. sugar
½ c. molasses
3 c. flour
1 tsp. salt
1 tbsp. ginger
1 ½ tsp. soda
½ c. plus 1 tbsp. cold water

Cream shortening, sugar and molasses. Sift all dry ingredients; add alternately with water to mixture. Drop by spoonfuls onto a greased cookie sheet. Bake at 475 degrees for 6 minutes. Yield: 9 dozen cookies.

Mrs. Bernice Devendorf
Oswego, N.Y.

GOLDEN NUGGETS

½ c. butter
½ c. lard or shortening
1 ½ c. sugar
½ c. brown sugar
2 eggs, beaten
1 c. crushed pineapple, drained
4 c. sifted flour
1 tsp. baking powder
1 tsp. soda
1 tsp. vanilla
1 c. chopped nuts

Combine butter, lard and sugars. Add all remaining ingredients; beat well. Drop onto greased cookie sheets. Bake at 350 degrees

for 15 minutes or until golden brown. Remove at once onto cooling rack. Yield: 50 servings.

Mildred McDougal
Safford, Ariz.

GUM DROP COOKIES

1 c. sifted flour
½ tsp. baking powder
½ tsp. soda
½ tsp. salt
½ c. shortening
½ c. (packed) brown sugar
½ c. sugar
1 egg
1 tbsp. water
1 tsp. vanilla flavoring
1 ½ c. oats
¾ c. chopped gumdrops

Sift all dry ingredients into bowl. Add shortening, sugars, egg, water and vanilla. Beat until smooth. Fold in oats and gumdrops. Drop batter onto ungreased cookie sheets. Bake at 350 degrees for 10 minutes. Yield: 48 cookies.

Mrs. Herbert O. Root
Coral Gables, Fla.

LACE COOKIES

¼ c. butter
¼ c. margarine
¼ c. shortening
1 c. brown sugar
½ c. white sugar
1 egg
¼ c. flour
¼ tsp. salt
½ tsp. soda
½ tsp. baking powder
2 c. uncooked oatmeal

Preheat oven to 375 degrees. Cream butter, margarine, shortening, sugars and egg. Make a well in center of creamed mixture; place flour in well. Put salt, soda and baking powder in center of flour; mix. Add oatmeal and 1 or 2 teaspoons of water if dough is too thick. If dough is too thin add more oatmeal. Drop from a teaspoon onto cookie sheet. Reduce oven temperature to 350 degrees. Bake for 8 minutes or until golden brown.

Mrs. Gordon T. Gould
Scott AFB, Ill.

KISSES

3 egg whites
⅓ tsp. cream of tartar
Pinch of salt
2 c. powdered sugar
1 c. chopped nuts
1 c. chocolate pieces or chopped dates

Beat egg whites until foamy. Add cream of tartar and salt; continue beating until stiff.

(Continued on next page)

Add sugar; beat until batter is stiff enough to stand in high peaks. More sugar may be added if necessary. Stir in nuts and chocolate pieces. Drop from a teaspoon onto a heavily greased and floured cookie sheet. Bake at 275 to 300 degrees for 10 to 20 minutes or until delicately brown. Immediately remove from cookie sheet. Yield: 40 cookies.

Mrs. Paul Huber
Kenney, Ill.

LEMON ICED COOKIES

1 c. shortening
2 c. sugar
2 eggs
3 ½ c. flour
1 tsp. soda
1 tsp. baking powder
1 c. buttermilk
Juice of 1 orange
Grated rind of 1 orange

Cream shortening and sugar; add eggs. Add sifted dry ingredients to creamed mixture alternately with buttermilk. Add juice and rind. Drop from a teaspoon onto a greased cookie sheet. Bake at 400 degrees for 12 minutes. Ice while hot.

ICING:
2 c. powdered sugar
Juice of 2 lemons
Grated rind of 2 lemons

Mix all ingredients with electric mixer at high speed until thick and smooth. Yield: 5 dozen.

Mary Helen Bennett
Minford, O.

TART LEMON DROPS

2 c. sifted flour
3 tsp. baking powder
¾ tsp. salt
1 tbsp. grated lemon rind
½ c. shortening
1 c. sugar
1 egg
¼ c. lemon juice
¼ c. cold water

Sift flour with baking powder and salt. Blend rind and shortening; add sugar gradually, creaming well. Add egg, lemon juice and water; beat well. Add dry ingredients; mix thoroughly. Drop by level tablespoonfuls onto a greased cookie sheet. Bake at 400 degrees for 8 minutes. Do not stack or store until cold. Yield: 5 dozen cookies.

Mrs. Michael Vrabel
Colts Neck, N.J.

COCONUT MACAROONS

1 ⅓ c. sweetened condensed milk
6 c. shredded coconut
2 tsp. vanilla flavoring

Blend all ingredients. Drop by teaspoonfuls, 1 inch apart, onto well greased baking sheet. Bake at 350 degrees for 8 to 10 minutes or until a delicate brown. Remove from pan at once. NOTE: A candied cherry may be placed in the center of each cookie before baking. Yield: 5 dozen.

Mrs. Iva W. Ammon
Brownsville, Pa.

COCONUT MACAROONS

2 egg whites
1 c. sugar
1 c. shredded coconut
2 c. corn flakes
½ tsp. salt
1 tsp. vanilla flavoring

Beat egg whites; gradually beat in sugar. Fold in remaining ingredients. Drop 3 inches apart onto well greased cookie sheet. Bake at 325 degrees for 12 minutes or until light brown. Yield: 2 1/2 dozen.

Mrs. Rollande Henry
Heuvelton, N.Y.

CORN FLAKE MACAROONS

2 egg whites
1 c. sugar
2 c. corn flakes
1 c. shredded coconut
⅛ tsp. salt
½ tsp. almond flavoring

Beat egg whites until stiff but not dry. Add sugar slowly, continuing to beat. Fold in all remaining ingredients. Drop by spoonfuls onto a greased baking sheet. Bake at 350 degrees for 10 to 12 minutes. Yield: 2 dozen.

Florence M. Grine
Tiffin, O.

CORN FLAKE MACAROONS

3 egg whites
1 c. sugar
1 tsp. vanilla flavoring
2 c. corn flakes
1 c. shredded coconut

Beat egg whites until stiff; gradually add sugar and vanilla. Gently fold in corn flakes and coconut. Drop by teaspoonfuls onto buttered cookie sheet. Bake at 300 degrees for 20

(Continued on next page)

minutes or until light brown. Yield: 36 cookies.

Mrs. Bob Hutchison
Dubois, Wyo.

MACAROONS

2 eggs
⅛ tsp. salt
¾ c. sugar
½ c. flour
1 tbsp. butter, melted
2 c. flaked coconut
1 6-oz. pkg. semi-sweet chocolate pieces
1 tsp. grated lemon rind
1 tsp. vanilla flavoring

Beat eggs and salt until foamy. Gradually add sugar; continue beating for 5 to 7 minutes or until thick and ivory colored. Fold in flour and butter. Stir in coconut, chocolate pieces lemon rind and vanilla. Drop dough by rounded teaspoonfuls onto lightly greased and floured cookie sheets. Bake at 325 degrees for 12 to 15 minutes or until delicately browned. Cool for 1 minute; remove from cookie sheet. Yield: 3 dozen cookies.

Mrs. Grant W. Johnson
Hastings, Minn.

MINCEMEAT DROP COOKIES

¾ c. shortening
1 ½ c. sugar
3 eggs, well beaten
3 c. sifted enriched flour
1 tsp. soda
¾ tsp. salt
1 9-oz. pkg. mincemeat
3 tbsp. water
1 c. broken California walnuts

Thoroughly cream shortening and sugar. Add eggs; beat well. Sift all dry ingredients. Add one-half of the dry ingredients to creamed mixture. Add finely crumbled mincemeat and water; stir until blended. Add nuts and remaining flour mixture; mix well. Drop from teaspoon onto a greased cookie sheet. Bake in 350 degree oven for 10 to 15 minutes. NOTE: One cup canned mincemeat may be used and water omitted. Yield: 4 dozen cookies.

Mrs. Esther Iaquinto
Morgantown, W. Va.

PEANUT BUTTER COOKIES

½ c. butter
½ c. peanut butter
1 c. brown sugar
1 egg
½ tsp. salt
½ tsp. soda
1 ¼ c. flour

Cream butter, peanut butter and sugar. Add egg, salt, soda and flour; mix well. Drop by teaspoonfuls onto greased cookie sheet; press down with a fork. Bake at 350 degrees for 8 minutes or until brown. Yield: 4 dozen.

Mrs. Theresa Sampson
Hamburg, N.Y.

PEANUT BUTTER BON BONS

1 6-oz. pkg. butterscotch pieces
½ c. peanut butter
2 c. chow mein noodles
½ c. chopped nuts

Melt butterscotch and peanut butter in a double boiler or over low heat. Add noodles and nuts. Drop by spoonfuls onto waxed paper. NOTE: Candied cherries may be added if desired.

Mrs. James Barton
Mellette, S.D.

SALTED PEANUT COOKIES

1 c. sugar
1 c. brown sugar
1 ½ c. shortening
2 eggs, well beaten
1 tsp. soda
4 tbsp. hot water
1 tsp. baking powder
4 ½ c. flour
1 c. salted peanuts

Cream sugars and shortening; stir in remaining ingredients. Drop by spoonfuls onto cookie sheet. Bake at 350 degrees until done.

Mrs. Ben Glass
Bellingham, Wash.

PECAN CRISPIES

1 c. shortening
1 c. brown sugar
1 c. sugar
2 eggs
2 c. flour
2 c. oats
1 c. chopped nuts
1 tsp. soda
1 c. crushed corn flakes

Mix all ingredients. Drop by teaspoonfuls onto cookie sheet. Flatten with fork dipped in powdered sugar. Bake at 400 degrees for 10 minutes. Yield: 6-7 dozen.

Maxine Lamberson
Mitchell, Nebr.

PECAN COOKIES

½ c. butter or margarine
½ c. powdered sugar
1 tsp. salt
2 c. flour
2 tbsp. vanilla flavoring
1 c. ground pecans

Cream butter and sugar. Add salt and flour; mix well. Stir in vanilla and pecans. Drop from a teaspoon onto an ungreased cookie sheet. Bake at 350 degrees for 20 minutes. Cool.

ICING:
1 egg, beaten
1 tbsp. butter
½ tsp. vanilla flavoring
Powdered sugar

Combine all ingredients, adding enough powdered sugar to thicken mixture to spreading consistency. Spread over cooled cookies. NOTE: If icing is too dry, add cream. Yield: 3 dozen cookies.

Mrs. Max Schrougham
Trafalgar, Ind.

PECAN DROP COOKIES

1 egg white
1 c. brown or granulated sugar
2 c. chopped nuts

Beat egg white until stiff; gradually beat in sugar. Add nuts. Drop from a teaspoon onto cookie sheet, 2 inches apart. Bake at 350 degrees until brown. Yield: 2 dozen.

Mrs. Blanche W. Welsh
Columbia, S.C.

PECAN DROPS

½ c. butter or margarine
½ c. plus 2 tbsp. shortening
1 ½ c. powdered sugar
2 ½ c. sifted cake flour
1 c. coarsely chopped pecans
2 tsp. vanilla flavoring

Cream butter and shortening until smooth. Beat in powdered sugar gradually. Stir in flour; add pecans and vanilla. Mix well; drop from teaspoon onto an ungreased baking sheet. Bake at 325 degrees for 15 to 20 minutes or until cookies are a delicate brown. Yield: 4 dozen.

Mrs. James B. Roberts
Fairfax, Va.

BLACK WALNUT COOKIES

⅔ c. shortening
1 c. sugar
1 tsp. vanilla flavoring
1 egg
3 sm. bananas, mashed
2 ¼ c. flour
½ tsp. salt
2 tsp. baking powder
1 c. chopped black walnuts

Cream shortening, sugar and vanilla. Beat egg and bananas; add to creamed ingredients. Add dry ingredients and nuts. Drop from teaspoon onto a greased cookie sheet. Bake at 375 degrees for 15 minutes.

Helen J. Eddy
Parkersburg, W. Va.

BLACK WALNUT-MERINGUE COOKIES

2 egg whites
4 dashes of salt
½ c. sugar
2 tsp. cinnamon
¼ tsp. cloves
¼ tsp. nutmeg
1 c. chopped black walnuts
Whole pecans

Beat egg whites, adding salt and sugar, until stiff. Add spices; fold in walnuts. Drop onto greased baking sheet. Place a pecan on top of each cookie. Bake at 250 degrees for 35 to 40 minutes. Yield: 4 dozen.

Mrs. George A. Zirkle, Jr.
Knoxville, Tenn.

OATMEAL DROP COOKIES

2 c. sifted flour
1 tsp. baking powder
1 tsp. salt
1 tsp. cinnamon
½ tsp. soda
½ tsp. soda
3 c. quick cooking oats
1 c. raisins
1 ¼ c. margarine
1 ¼ c. sugar
2 eggs, slightly beaten
¼ c. milk

Sift flour, baking powder, salt, cinnamon and soda into bowl. Mix in oats and raisins. Cream margarine and sugar in mixing bowl. Add eggs; beat until fluffy. Stir in one-half of the dry ingredients; add milk. Add remaining dry ingredients. Drop batter by teaspoonfuls 2 inches apart onto an ungreased cookie sheet. Bake at 400 degrees for 10 to 12 minutes or until edges are lightly browned. Remove from cookie sheet immediately. Yield: 6 dozen.

Photograph for this recipe on page 113 .

GLAZED OATMEAL COOKIES

1 c. oats
1 c. brown sugar
1 tbsp. flour
Dash of soda
1 tbsp. lemon juice
⅓ c. melted butter

Mix oats, brown sugar, flour and soda. Add lemon juice and melted butter; mix well. Drop from a teaspoon onto an ungreased pan. Bake in 350 degree oven until brown. Remove from pan while still warm. Yield: 2 dozen cookies.

Mrs. John B. Colwell
Coronado, Calif.

ORANGE DROP COOKIES

½ c. shortening
¾ c. sugar
1 egg
1 ¼ c. sifted flour
¼ tsp. salt
½ tsp. baking powder
½ tsp. soda
2 tbsp. orange juice
1 ½ tsp. grated orange rind

Cream shortening and sugar. Add egg; blend well. Sift all dry ingredients; add to creamed mixture. Add orange juice and rind; mix well. Drop by teaspoonfuls 2 inches apart onto ungreased cookie sheet. With small measuring spoon, indent center of each cookie.

FILLING:
¼ c. sugar
2 tsp. orange juice

Mix sugar and orange juice; put in each cookie. Bake at 400 degrees for 8 to 10 minutes. Yield: 6 dozen.

Eva Correll
Tryon, Nebr.

ORANGE DROP COOKIES

1 ½ c. light brown sugar
2 eggs, beaten
1 c. butter
1 c. sour milk
3 c. flour
1 tsp. soda
3 tsp. baking powder
Grated rind of 1 orange
1 c. chopped nuts

Cream sugar, eggs and butter; add milk. Mix in flour, soda and baking powder, blending well. Add orange rind and nuts. Bake at 350 degrees until no thumb print remains when pressed lightly in center. If desired, frost with confectioners sugar combined with grated orange rind.

Nancy J. Dart
Churchville, N.Y.

PORCUPINES

1 c. crushed walnuts
1 ¼ c. flaked coconut
2 c. quartered dates
2 eggs
¼ tsp. vanilla flavoring
1 tbsp. melted butter
1 c. brown sugar

Mix walnuts, 1 cup coconut and dates. Mix in an egg. Beat remaining egg with vanilla; add to first mixture. Mix in butter and brown sugar. Roll 1 teaspoonful of dough at a time in remaining 1/4 cup coconut; drop onto a well greased cookie sheet. Bake at 300 degrees for 10 minutes or until brown. NOTE: Will keep well in covered container for one week. Yield: 4 1/2 dozen cookies.

Mrs. H. I. Katz
Key West, Fla.

PRUNE-OAT DROPS

1 ½ c. dried pitted prunes
1 ½ c. sugar
⅔ c. shortening
2 eggs, beaten
⅓ c. milk
2 c. sifted flour
2 tsp. baking powder
1 tsp. salt
1 ½ tsp. cinnamon
2 c. oats
1 tsp. vanilla flavoring

Cover prunes with water. Boil for 10 minutes; drain. Cream sugar and shortening thoroughly. Add eggs and milk. Sift flour with baking powder, salt and cinnamon; blend into creamed mixture. Stir in oats, prunes and vanilla. Drop by teaspoonfuls onto greased cookie sheet. Bake at 375 degrees for 15 minutes. Yield: 6 dozen cookies.

Mattie Courtney
Yacolt, Wash.

RAISIN COOKIES

1 c. seedless raisins
½ c. water
1 ½ c. sugar
⅔ c. shortening
1 tsp. vanilla flavoring
2 eggs, beaten
1 tsp. salt
3 c. flour
1 tsp. soda
2 tbsp. cream or evaporated milk

Combine raisins and water. Cover and cook until water is absorbed. Cream sugar with shortening and vanilla; add eggs. Sift all dry ingredients; add to creamed mixture. Add cream and cooled raisins. Drop onto greased

(Continued on next page)

cookie sheet. Bake at 350 degrees for 12 minutes.

Mrs. A. Scott Hamilton
Wyckoff, N.J.

RAISIN-SPICE COOKIES

1 ½ c. brown sugar
1 c. shortening
3 eggs, well beaten
1 tsp. cinnamon
1 tsp. nutmeg
¼ tsp. cloves
2 c. flour
1 tsp. baking powder
1 tsp. soda
1 c. liquid from raisins
1 lb. raisins, cooked
1 c. broken walnuts

Cream brown sugar and shortening. Add eggs; stir until blended. Add spices. Sift dry ingredients; add alternately with raisin water. Sprinkle a small amount of flour on raisins and walnuts; add to mixture. Drop from a teaspoon onto a greased cookie sheet. Bake at 350 degrees for 10 to 15 minutes. Yield: 3-4 dozen.

Harriett L. Truax
New Kensington, Pa.

SKILLET COOKIES

1 stick margarine, melted
1 c. sugar
1 c. chopped dates
1 egg, well beaten
1 c. chopped nuts
2 c. Rice Krispies
1 tsp. vanilla flavoring
Flaked coconut

Cook margarine, sugar, dates and egg for 5 minutes. Remove from heat; add nuts, Rice Krispies and vanilla. Mix; drop by teaspoonfuls. Roll in coconut.

Mrs. Kate Hughes
Lexington, Miss.

OLD-FASHIONED SUGAR COOKIES

1 c. butter
1 ¼ c. sugar
2 eggs
3 c. flour
½ tsp. soda
1 tsp. salt
2 tsp. baking powder
3 tbsp. milk

Cream butter and sugar. Add eggs; beat for 2 minutes. Sift flour with soda, salt and baking powder; add to creamed mixture alternately

with milk. May be dropped from teaspoon or rolled. If rolled out, chill dough before rolling and cutting. Place on greased cookie sheet. Bake at 375 degrees for 12 minutes or until golden brown. NOTE: Dough may be sprinkled with white or colored sugar before cutting. Yield: 4 dozen.

Mrs. Joe Wyass
Dixon, Mo.

SUGAR DROP COOKIES

1 stick soft margarine
1 c. sugar
1 egg
2 c. sifted flour
2 tsp. baking powder
½ tsp. salt
½ c. milk
1 tsp. vanilla flavoring

Cream margarine and sugar until fluffy. Beat in egg. Add sifted dry ingredients alternately with milk; blend thoroughly. Add vanilla. Drop by teaspoonfuls onto lightly greased cookie sheet. Flatten with bottom of buttered glass dipped in sugar. Bake at 375 degrees for 10 to 12 minutes. NOTE: For variation, omit vanilla and add 1/2 teaspoon almond flavoring. Yield: 4 dozen.

Esther J. Webb
Deland, Ill.

SUGARLESS DROP COOKIES

½ c. butter
1 egg
2 tbsp. condensed orange juice
1 tbsp. orange rind
4 tsp. dietetic liquid sweetener
½ tsp. vanilla flavoring
1 ¼ c. flour
¼ tsp. salt
1 tsp. baking powder
½ tsp. soda
½ c. buttermilk or sour cream
Finely chopped nuts
Finely chopped raisins

Cream butter well. Beat egg with orange juice, rind, sweetener and vanilla; add to butter. Reserve 1 tablespoon flour; sift remaining flour with salt, baking powder and soda. Add to egg mixture alternately with buttermilk. Mix reserved flour with nuts and raisins; stir into batter. Drop by tablespoonfuls onto greased cookie sheet. Bake at 375 degrees for 15 minutes.

Vivian Blackburn
Story City, Iowa

VANILLA COOKIES

1 c. butter
1 ½ c. powdered sugar

(Continued on next page)

1 egg
1 tsp. vanilla flavoring
2 ½ c. sifted flour
1 tsp. soda
1 tsp. cream of tartar
¼ tsp. salt

Cream butter and sugar until smooth. Add egg and vanilla. Sift all dry ingredients; blend into creamed mixture. Drop from level teaspoon onto ungreased cookie sheet. Bake at 350 degrees for 10 minutes. Do not brown. Yield: 6 dozen.

Mrs. Jack A. Holz
Wayne, Ill.

VANILLA WAFER COOKIES

1 stick margarine
2 c. sugar
1 sm. can evaporated milk
2 c. vanilla wafer crumbs
1 c. coconut
1 c. nuts

Combine margarine, sugar and milk; cook to soft ball stage. Remove from heat; immediately add all remaining ingredients. Drop at once onto cookie sheet. Yield: 2 dozen.

Mrs. Ruth Moon
Nashville, Tenn.

EASY FILLED COOKIES

1 c. shortening
2 c. (packed) brown sugar
2 eggs
½ c. sour milk
1 tsp. vanilla flavoring
3 ½ c. sifted flour
1 tsp. salt
1 tsp. soda
⅛ tsp. cinnamon

Thoroughly mix shortening, brown sugar, eggs, milk and vanilla. Sift all dry ingredients; combine with first mixture. Drop from a teaspoon onto ungreased cookie sheet.

FILLING:
2 c. finely cut dates
¾ c. sugar
¾ c. water
½ c. chopped nuts

Combine all ingredients. Cook until thickened. Drop 1/4 teaspoon filling onto each cookie; cover with 1/2 teaspoon dough. Bake at 375 to 400 degrees for 10 to 12 minutes. Yield: 6 dozen cookies.

Mrs. George M. Smith
Brunswick, Me.

FILLED RAISIN COOKIES

⅔ c. shortening
1 c. sugar
2 eggs
⅓ c. milk
1 tsp. vanilla flavoring
3 c. flour
3 tsp. baking powder
½ tsp. salt

Cream shortening and sugar; stir in eggs, milk and vanilla. Sift all dry ingredients; gradually add to creamed mixture. Roll thin; cut into rounds. Put on greased cookie sheet.

RAISIN FILLING:
½ c. sugar
1 tbsp. flour
½ c. water
1 c. raisins

Combine sugar and flour; add to water and raisins. Cook until thick, stirring constantly. Place 1 teaspoon of filling on each cookie. Place another cookie on top. Press edges together. Bake at 400 degrees for 10 to 15 minutes. Yield: 2 dozen.

Bernice M. Coleman
Dayton, Pa.

JELLY-FILLED COOKIES

1 c. butter or margarine
1 8-oz. pkg. cream cheese, at room temperature
1 egg yolk, beaten
1 tbsp. sugar
1 tbsp. milk
½ tsp. baking powder
1 ½ c. flour
Jelly or jam

Mix butter and cream cheese. Add egg yolk, sugar and milk; beat well. Mix baking powder and flour; add to cheese mixture. Drop by teaspoonfuls onto cookie sheet; pat into circles 1/2 to 1/3-inch high. Press thumbprint in center; fill with jellies or jams. Bake at 400 degrees for 10 minutes. Yield: 3-3 1/2 dozen cookies.

Mrs. R. W. Cornell
Ft. Monroe, Va.

OLD-FASHIONED PRESERVE BARS

1 c. shortening
2 c. flour
½ tsp. salt
⅓ c. water
Preserves or lemon filling
Milk

Cut shortening into flour and salt. Stir in water. Roll out one-half of dough to fit a square cookie sheet. Spread with preserves.

(Continued on next page)

Cover with remaining dough. Pinch edges to seal; pierce top with fork. Brush top with milk. Bake at 350 degrees until golden brown. NOTE: Any desired preserves may be used. Yield: 24 cookies.

Mrs. Dorothy Duracher
Mendon, Mass.

ANGEL DELIGHTS

¼ c. butter
1 c. sugar
1 8-oz. pkg. dates, chopped
Dash of salt
1 tsp. vanilla flavoring
2 c. crisp rice cereal
1 3 ½-oz. can flaked coconut
Confectioners sugar

Mix butter, sugar and dates in heavy saucepan. Cook, stirring constantly, over low heat until blended. Add salt, vanilla, cereal and coconut; mix well. Form into balls, 1 inch in diameter. Roll each ball in confectioners sugar. Cool on waxed paper. Yield: 5 dozen cookies.

Mrs. Ruth S. Capps
Wheaton, Ill.

BRANDY-RUM BALLS

2 7¼-oz. pkg. vanilla wafers, finely rolled
½ c. honey
⅓ c. brandy
⅓ c. white rum
1 lb. shelled California walnuts, finely ground
Sugar

Mix vanilla wafer crumbs, honey, brandy, rum and walnuts. Shape into bite-sized balls; roll in sugar. Wrap each in plastic wrap. Store for at least one week before serving. The flavor improves with age. Yield: 5 dozen balls.

Mrs. W. H. Helden, Jr.
Bainbridge, Md.

NO-BAKE BROWNIES

2 6-oz. pkg. chocolate pieces
1 c. evaporated milk
3 c. fine vanilla wafer crumbs
2 c. miniature marshmallows
1 c. chopped nuts
1 c. powdered sugar
½ tsp. salt
2 tsp. milk

Stir chocolate pieces and evaporated milk over low heat until chocolate melts. Combine remaining ingredients except 2 teaspoons milk. Stir one-half of the chocolate mixture into crumb mixture; mix well. Press into well greased 9-inch pan. Add milk to

remaining chocolate; spread on top of crumb mixture. Chill; cut into squares. Yield: 24 squares.

Mrs. Thomas E. Frazee
Delavan, Ill.

CANDIED COOKIES

2 c. sugar
½ c. milk
1 stick butter or margarine
4 tbsp. cocoa
2 ½ c. quick cooking oats
¼ c. chopped nuts
2 tsp. vanilla flavoring
½ c. peanut butter

Cook sugar, milk, butter and cocoa for 1 minute and 30 seconds; start counting time when mixture has reached a full rolling boil. Remove from heat; add remaining ingredients. Beat until mixture is well blended. Drop by teaspoonfuls onto waxed paper. Cool; serve. Yield: 50 cookies.

Faye Quinley
Corsicana, Tex.

CHOCOLATE MACAROONS

½ c. margarine
½ c. milk
2 c. sugar
Few grains of salt
3 c. quick cooking oats
1 c. coconut
7 tsp. (heaping) cocoa

Melt margarine with milk and sugar in saucepan; add all remaining ingredients. Bring to boil, stirring constantly. Boil for 2 minutes. Drop from teaspoon onto lightly greased cookie sheet or waxed paper. Refrigerate until firm. Store in covered container in a cool place. NOTE: Add nuts if desired. Yield: 50-60 servings.

Nancy McCormack
Bancroft, Idaho

CHOCOLATE-NUT COOKIES

1 pkg. chocolate pieces
3 tbsp. white corn syrup
3 ½ c. sifted powdered sugar
1 c. chopped nuts
2 tbsp. instant coffee
⅓ c. hot water
1 ¾ c. finely crushed vanilla wafers

Melt chocolate pieces over hot water; remove from heat. Add all ingredients except 1/2 cup powdered sugar. Form into 1-inch balls;

(Continued on next page)

dredge in reserved 1/2 cup sugar. Yield: 2 dozen.

Melissa Loy
Billings, Mont.

NO-BAKE CHOC-OATS

2 c. sugar
¼ lb. margarine
½ c. cocoa
½ c. milk
½ c. peanut butter
1 tsp. vanilla flavoring
3 c. quick cooking or old-fashioned oats

Combine all ingredients except vanilla and oats in saucepan; boil for 2 minutes. Remove from heat; add vanilla. Pour hot mixture over oats; mix well. Pour into buttered pan. Cool; cut into squares. NOTE: One-half cup coconut or 1/4 cup chopped nuts or both may be added if desired. Yield: 3 dozen squares.

Mrs. J. E. Leatherman
Glasgow AFB, Mont.

CHOW MEIN NOODLE COOKIES

1 6-oz. pkg. chocolate pieces
1 6-oz. pkg. butterscotch pieces
1 3-oz. can chow mein noodles
1 12-oz. pkg. cashew nuts

Mix chocolate and butterscotch pieces in double boiler; melt. Add noodles and nuts. Drop from teaspoon onto waxed paper. Yield: 3 dozen.

Mrs. Earl Holmbeck
Wymore, Nebr.

COCONUT-PECAN- CHOCOLATE DROPS

1 stick margarine
3 boxes powdered sugar
1 can sweetened condensed milk
1 can angel flake coconut
3 c. chopped pecans
1 paraffin wax
2 pkg. chocolate pieces

Combine margarine, sugar, milk, coconut and nuts. Melt paraffin and chocolate in top of double boiler. Roll coconut mixture into small ball; dip into chocolate mixture with a toothpick. Lay on waxed paper.

Mary E. Roddam
Jasper, Ala.

DATE BALLS

1 pkg. dates
1 c. nuts
18 marshmallows

1 tsp. vanilla flavoring
½ c. cream or canned milk
2 c. graham cracker crumbs

Chop dates, nuts and marshmallows. Add vanilla to milk; mix all ingredients except crumbs. Form into small balls; roll in cracker crumbs. Yield: 30-50 small balls.

Mrs. Newton V. Colston
Martinsville, Va.

FIFTEEN-MINUTE COOKIES

2 c. sugar
¼ c. butter
4 tbsp. cocoa
½ c. milk
2 c. oats
½ c. peanut butter
1 tsp. vanilla flavoring

Combine sugar, butter, cocoa and milk; boil for 1 minute. Stir in oats, peanut butter and vanilla. Drop from spoon onto waxed paper. NOTE: One cup chopped nuts may be substituted for 1 cup oats. Yield: 20 servings.

Martha O'Neal
Cookville, Tex.

FUDGE COOKIES

2 c. sugar
2 c. brown sugar
1 c. butter
1 c. milk
2 c. chocolate pieces
4 c. quick cooking oats
1 c. nuts
1 c. coconut

Bring sugars, butter and milk to a boil; boil for 2 minutes. Place remaining ingredients in a large bowl; pour hot mixture over oat mixture. Mix well. Drop from teaspoon onto waxed paper. Yield: 8 dozen.

Charlene Montgomery
Woodstock, Ill.

GRAHAM CRACKER LOG

½ lb. marshmallows, diced
1 pkg. dates, chopped
2 c. chopped walnuts
30 graham crackers, finely crushed
1 c. heavy cream

Combine marshmallows, dates and walnuts; mix thoroughly with 1 3/4 cups cracker crumbs. Add unwhipped cream; mix well. Shape into roll; coat in remaining crumbs. Wrap well in waxed paper; refrigerate for at least 6 hours. Slice; serve with whipped cream. Yield: 8-10 servings.

Lydia E. Griffin
Gatesville, N.C.

MARSHMALLOW NO-BAKE SQUARES

½ pkg. graham crackers, crushed
1 c. sugar
½ c. butter
2 eggs, well beaten
72 miniature marshmallows
3 tbsp. grated coconut
½ c. chopped nuts
1 tsp. vanilla flavoring
Pinch of salt
1 pkg. chocolate pieces

Place cracker crumbs in 9-inch square pan. Cook sugar, butter and eggs in double boiler for 10 minutes; cool. Remove from heat; add marshmallows, coconut, nuts, vanilla and salt. Pour over crumbs. Melt chocolate; spread over filling. Yield: 2 dozen.

Mrs. Charles E. Ketchum
Wakefield, Mass.

MOCHA PEANUT CLUSTERS

⅓ c. butter
1 c. chocolate pieces
16 lge. marshmallows
1 tbsp. instant coffee
2 c. chopped salted peanuts

Melt butter, chocolate pieces and marshmallows in double boiler; stir occasionally. When creamy, add instant coffee. Remove from heat; stir in peanuts. Drop by teaspoonfuls onto waxed paper or cookie sheet. Cool. Yield: 48 clusters.

Mrs. Carl Weidenheim
Princeton, Ill.

QUICKIE COOKIES

1 c. light corn syrup
1 c. sugar
1 c. peanut butter
4 c. Special K cereal

Cook syrup and sugar until clear; add peanut butter. Stir until dissolved; pour over cereal. Drop from spoon onto waxed paper; cool. Yield: 4 dozen.

Mrs. Ray Segler
Electra, Tex.

REFRIGERATOR FRUIT COOKIES

1 10¼-oz. pkg. short bread cookies
1 3½-oz. can flaked coconut
1 ½ c. coarsely chopped pecans
1 9-oz. can crushed pineapple

Crush cookies; add remaining ingredients. Shape into 2-inch rolls. Wrap in waxed paper; chill. Cut into 1/2-inch slices just before serving. Yield: 3 dozen.

Mrs. James Risinger
Cooper, Tex.

SNOWBALLS

½ c. soft margarine or butter
1 c. powdered sugar
2 eggs, separated
1 c. drained crushed pineapple
¾ c. chopped nuts
1 box vanilla wafers

Cream margarine and sugar; add beaten egg yolks. Fold in stiffly beaten egg whites, pineapple and nuts. Spread mixture on a vanilla wafer; add another wafer. Repeat until four wafers have been stacked. Do not add mixture to fourth wafer. Set in refrigerator for 3 to 4 hours.

TOPPING:

1 pt. heavy cream
1 tsp. vanilla flavoring
¼ c. powdered sugar
1 c. flaked coconut

Whip cream until stiff; add vanilla and powdered sugar. Spread topping on all sides of wafers. Sprinkle with coconut. Refrigerate until ready to serve. Yield: 14 servings.

Mrs. Joseph Pospichal
Pontiac, Mich.

BUTTER THINS

1 c. butter
1 ½ c. sifted powdered sugar
1 egg
1 tsp. vanilla flavoring
2 ½ c. flour
1 tsp. baking soda
1 tsp. cream of tartar
¼ tsp. salt
Nuts or coconut

Cream butter and sugar; add egg and vanilla. Cream until fluffy. Add sifted dry ingredients; mix well. Divide dough into 2-inch rolls. Wrap in waxed paper; chill until firm. Slice 1/8-inch thick. Sprinkle with nuts or coconut. Place on ungreased cookie sheet. Bake at 375 degrees for 6 minutes. Yield: 6 dozen.

Mrs. S. B. Fields
Briarcliff Manor, N.Y.

CRISP BUTTER COOKIES

1 c. shortening
2 c. sugar
2 eggs
2 tsp. vanilla flavoring
4 c. sifted cake flour
4 tsp. baking powder
½ tsp. salt
¼ c. milk

Cream shortening and sugar; add eggs and vanilla. Sift all dry ingredients; add with

(Continued on next page)

milk to creamed mixture. Blend well. Roll dough in waxed paper; chill thoroughly. Cut into thin slices. Bake at 375 to 400 degrees for 10 minutes or until golden. NOTE: Dough may also be rolled out on floured board and cut into desired shapes.

Mrs. Jane C. Arndt
Morganton, N.C.

BUTTERSCOTCH COOKIES
4 c. flour
1 tsp. soda
1 tsp. cream of tartar
½ tsp. salt
1 c. butter
2 c. brown sugar
2 eggs
1 tsp. vanilla flavoring
1 c. chopped nuts

Sift all dry ingredients. Cream butter and sugar until fluffy. Add eggs and vanilla. Beat well. Add dry ingredients to creamed mixture. Add nuts; mix well. Shape into rolls; wrap in waxed paper. Chill until firm; slice thin. Place on ungreased baking sheet. Bake at 400 degrees for 8 to 10 minutes. Yield: 6 dozen cookies.

Dorothy Rose
Linton, Ind.

CARAMEL REFRIGERATOR COOKIES
½ c. shortening, softened
1 c. (packed) brown sugar
1 egg
½ tsp. vanilla flavoring
1 ¾ c. sifted self-rising flour
1 c. chopped pecans (opt.)

Thoroughly mix shortening, sugar, egg and vanilla. Stir in flour; add nuts. Shape into a roll, 2 1/2 inches in diameter. Wrap in waxed paper; chill until firm. Slice 1/8-inch thick; place on ungreased baking sheet. Bake at 400 degrees for 8 to 10 minutes. Yield: 5 dozen.

Mrs. W. E. Clements
Tifton, Ga.

CHOCOLATE-ALMOND HERMITS
1 ¾ c. sifted flour
½ c. chocolate drink mix
⅓ c. cocoa
½ tsp. salt
1 tsp. baking powder
¾ c. butter
1 c. sugar
1 egg
1 tsp. cold water
4 tbsp. chopped almonds

Sift flour, drink mix, cocoa, salt and baking powder. Cream butter and 3/4 cup sugar thoroughly. Add egg, reserving 1 tablespoon of egg white. Chill dough for 1 hour. Shape dough into three rolls on baking sheets. Flatten rolls with fork. Brush with mixture of 1 tablespoon egg white and cold water. Sprinkle with mixture of almonds and remaining sugar. Bake at 400 degrees for 10 minutes. Cut into 2-inch bars; cool. Yield: 2 dozen bars.

Elizabeth K. Stewart
New Boston, N.H.

COCONUT SHORTBREAD
1 lb. butter
1 c. sugar
4 c. flour
2 tsp. vanilla flavoring
16 oz. shredded coconut, chopped

Cream butter and sugar. Add flour, vanilla and coconut. Press dough into pan; chill overnight. Slice. Bake at 325 degrees for 20 to 25 minutes or until light brown. NOTE: If cookies are sliced too thin, they burn easily. Yield: 3-5 dozen cookies.

Mrs. Robert J. Everett
Norfolk, Va.

COCONUT TEA COOKIES
1 c. butter or margarine
1 c. sugar
1 egg
3 c. grated coconut
1 ½ c. sifted flour
½ tsp. soda
1 egg yolk, beaten
1 tbsp. milk
Cherries, almonds or pecans

Cream butter well. Add sugar; beat. Add egg, coconut, flour and soda. Knead dough until mixture holds together. Separate into six portions; form into rolls about 1-inch wide. Roll in coconut. Wrap in waxed paper; roll gently to make rolls round. Place in refrigerator until firm. Slice into 1/2-inch thick slices. Brush each slice with egg yolk and combine with milk. Place cherry or nut on each cookie. Place on inverted cookie sheet. Bake at 325 degrees for 25 to 30 minutes or until golden brown. Yield: 6 dozen.

Mrs. R. A. Dougherty
Whiting, Ind.

COFFEE NUGGETS
½ c. butter
Powdered sugar
1 tsp. vanilla flavoring
1 tbsp. instant coffee
1 c. sifted flour
½ c. finely chopped pecans

(Continued on next page)

Cream butter, 3 tablespoons sugar, vanilla and coffee until light and fluffy. Add flour and nuts; mix thoroughly. Chill dough for 1 hour. Use 1 teaspoon dough per cookie; shape into balls. Place on ungreased cookie sheets. Bake at 350 degrees for 12 to 15 minutes. Roll in powdered sugar while warm and again when cool. Yield: 2 dozen.

Ann Szydlowski
Freesoil, Mich.

CHRISTMAS FRUIT COOKIES

1 c. butter
2 c. brown sugar
2 eggs
1 tsp. vanilla flavoring
1 c. chopped dates
½ c. candied cherries
½ c. broken pecans
4 c. flour
1 tsp. salt
1 tsp. soda
1 tsp. cream of tartar

Cream butter and sugar. Add eggs; beat well. Add vanilla, dates, cherries and nuts. Sift all dry ingredients; gradually add until a stiff dough is formed. Shape with hands into three rolls; wrap in waxed paper. Chill for at least 8 hours. Slice. Bake at 425 degrees for 9 minutes. Yield: 4 dozen cookies.

Mrs. Paul C. Graff
Fowler, Mich.

ORIGINAL GIRL SCOUT COOKIES

1 c. butter
1 c. sugar
2 eggs, well beaten
2 tbsp. milk
1 tsp. vanilla flavoring
2 c. bread flour
½ tsp. salt
2 tsp. baking powder

Cream butter and sugar. Add eggs, milk, vanilla and flour which has been sifted with salt and baking powder; mix well. Chill for 1 hour. Roll thin; cut out about the size of a baking powder can cover. Bake at 425 degrees for 8 to 10 minutes. Sprinkle baked cookie with sugar. Yield: 6-7 dozen.

Natalie MacKay
Holden, Mass.

ICEBOX COOKIES

1 c. shortening
2 c. light brown sugar
2 eggs, beaten
3 tsp. baking powder
3 ¾ c. flour
1 tsp. cinnamon
1 tsp. vanilla flavoring

Cream shortening and sugar; add eggs. Add sifted dry ingredients; mix well. Add vanilla. Mold into loaf; refrigerate for 24 hours. Slice. Bake at 375 degrees until done.

Winnie Harris
Tracy City, Tenn.

ICEBOX COOKIES

1 c. shortening
2 c. brown sugar
2 eggs
1 tsp. vanilla or almond flavoring
3 c. flour
1 tsp. cream of tartar
1 ½ tsp. salt
1 tbsp. water
1 tsp. soda
1 c. chopped walnuts
Dates (opt.)

Cream shortening and sugar; add eggs and flavoring. Add sifted dry ingredients, soda dissolved in water, nuts and dates. Form into a roll, 1 1/2-inches in diameter. Wrap in waxed paper; refrigerate for several hours. Slice 1/8 to 1/4-inch thick. Place on ungreased cookie sheet. Bake at 375 degrees for 10 minutes or until done.

Mrs. Eugene Leonard
South Elgin, Ill.

CHEWY OATMEAL COOKIES

¾ c. butter
½ c. sugar
1 ½ c. brown sugar
2 eggs
1 tsp. vanilla flavoring
1 ¼ c. flour
1 tsp. baking powder
½ tsp. soda
1 tsp. salt
2 ½ c. quick cooking oats
⅔ c. chopped nuts
½ c. finely shredded coconut

Cream butter and sugars; beat in eggs and vanilla. Add sifted dry ingredients. Stir in remaining ingredients; mix well. Refrigerate for 2 hours. Roll into small balls. Bake at 350 degrees for 12 minutes. Remove from pan while hot. Yield: 4 dozen.

Mrs. L. E. Weston
Olympia, Wash.

CHOCOLATE-OATMEAL CHEWS

1 12-oz. pkg. chocolate pieces
½ c. shortening
½ tsp. salt
3 eggs
¾ c. sugar
1 c. oats
1 tsp. vanilla flavoring

(Continued on next page)

Melt chocolate pieces over hot water; remove from heat. Stir in shortening and salt; set aside. Beat eggs until thick; gradually add sugar until mixture is thick. Add oats, vanilla and chocolate mixture. Chill dough for at least 30 minutes. Drop by teaspoonfuls onto greased cookie sheet. Bake at 375 degrees for 6 to 8 minutes. Let cool a minute before removing from cookie sheet. Yield: 6 dozen.

Laura Fruin
Springfield, Ill.

OATMEAL CRISPS

1 c. shortening
1 c. brown sugar
1 c. sugar
2 eggs
1 tsp. vanilla flavoring
1 ½ c. sifted flour
1 tsp. salt
1 tsp. soda
3 c. quick cooking oats
½ c. chopped pecans

Cream shortening and sugars; add eggs and vanilla. Beat well. Sift flour with salt and soda; add to creamed mixture. Stir in oats and nuts; mix well. Form dough into long rolls, 1 1/2 inches in diameter. Wrap in waxed paper; chill thoroughly. Slice 1/2-inch thick. Bake at 350 degrees for 10 minutes or until lightly browned. Yield: 5 dozen.

Mrs. Katie Wagoner
High Point, N.C.

RICH OATMEAL COOKIES

¾ c. shortening, softened
¼ c. butter or margarine, softened
1 c. sifted powdered sugar
2 tsp. vanilla flavoring
1 ¼ c. sifted flour
½ tsp. salt
1 c. quick cooking oats

Mix shortenings, sugar and vanilla thoroughly until creamy. Add flour, salt and oats; mix well. Divide dough in half; roll each half in waxed paper. Chill for 1 hour or more in refrigerator. Slice about 1/4-inch thick; place on ungreased cookie sheet. Bake at 350 degrees for 12 to 15 minutes or until lightly browned. Yield: 4 dozen.

Mrs. Edna Hornburg
Angola, N.Y.

PEANUT BUTTER SURPRISE COOKIES

½ c. peanut butter
½ c. shortening
2 c. (firmly packed) brown sugar
1 tsp. vanilla flavoring
2 eggs

2 ¼ c. sifted flour
2 tsp. soda
1 tsp. salt
1 c. finely cut raisins
2 c. oats
½ c. chopped nuts

Cream peanut butter and shortening until well combined. Add sugar and vanilla; continue to cream until fluffy. Add eggs; beat well. Add sifted dry ingredients, raisins, oats and nuts. Shape into rolls; wrap each roll in waxed paper. Chill. Slice into 1/8-inch slices. Place on cookie sheet. Bake at 350 degrees for 15 minutes. Store in loosely covered container to keep crisp. Yield: 7-8 dozen.

Patsy Springer
Somerville, Tenn.

PECAN COOKIES

¾ c. shortening
1 ½ c. brown sugar
1 egg
2 c. sifted flour
½ tsp. salt
⅛ tsp. soda
¼ c. chopped pecans
¼ c. whole pecans

Cream shortening. Add sugar; blend well. Thoroughly blend in egg. Sift flour with salt and soda three times; add to shortening mixture. Mix in chopped nuts. Shape into rolls; refrigerate until ready to bake. Slice into thin wafers; top with whole pecans. Bake at 350 degrees for 6 to 10 minutes. Yield: 5 dozen cookies.

Mrs. C. F. Perry
Norfolk, Va.

PECAN COOKIES

¾ c. butter
1 ½ c. brown sugar
1 egg
2 c. flour
½ tsp. soda
½ tsp. salt
1 c. pecan halves

Cream butter; add sugar. Blend well. Add egg; mix thoroughly. Sift flour, soda and salt; add to creamed mixture gradually. Add nuts; chill. Form into tiny balls; put pecan half on top of each. Bake at 350 degrees until done. Yield: 3 dozen.

Mrs. Margaret Klugh
Vicksburg, Miss.

PECAN CRUNCHES

2 c. melted butter or margarine
1 c. brown sugar
1 c. sugar

(Continued on next page)

3 eggs, beaten
½ tsp. almond flavoring or vanilla flavoring
4 ¼ c. sifted flour
1 tsp. baking powder
½ tsp. salt
1 tsp. cinnamon
1 c. chopped pecans

Combine butter, sugars, eggs and flavoring; beat with electric mixer at medium speed for 3 minutes. Sift all dry ingredients; add to creamed mixture. Add pecans; mix at slow speed only enough to mix thoroughly. Shape into long rolls the size of desired cookie. Chill for several hours. Slice thin; place on ungreased tin. Bake at 400 degrees for 10 minutes. NOTE: Dough may be kept for several weeks in refrigerator. Yield: 6 dozen.

Mrs. Albertine P. McKellar
Rowland, N.C.

PLAIN OR FANCY COOKIES

1 c. shortening
1 ½ c. sugar
1 ¼ tsp. salt
2 tsp. vanilla flavoring
½ tsp. almond or rum flavoring
3 eggs
4 ½ c. sifted flour

Cream shortening, sugar and salt; add flavorings and eggs. Mix well. Add flour. Shape into oval roll. Wrap in waxed paper; chill. Roll dough 1/8-inch thick; cut. Place on greased cookie sheet. Bake at 350 degrees for 12 to 15 minutes.

Mrs. Helen Kaiser
East St. Louis, Ill.

PRIZE WINNER ICE BOX COOKIES

½ c. butter or margarine
1 c. sugar
2 tsp. vanilla flavoring
1 egg
1 ¾ c. sifted flour
½ tsp. baking powder
½ tsp. salt
1 c. chopped nuts

Cream butter and sugar; add vanilla and egg. Beat until blended. Sift dry ingredients; add nuts. Gradually add to sugar mixture, stirring well after each addition. Shape into long roll, 2 inches in diameter, on waxed paper. Chill overnight. Slice 1/8 to 1/4-inch thick. Bake at 400 degrees for 7 minutes. Yield: 4-5 dozen.

Mrs. Cliff Winstead
Union, Miss.

SPICE ICE BOX COOKIES

1 ½ c. melted shortening
1 c. brown sugar
1 c. sugar
3 eggs, well beaten
4 ½ c. sifted flour
¼ tsp. salt
2 tsp. soda
1 tsp. cinnamon
1 tsp. cloves
1 tsp. allspice
1 tsp. vanilla flavoring
1 c. chopped nuts

Cream shortening and sugars; add eggs. Mix well. Sift all dry ingredients twice; add to creamed mixture. Add vanilla and nuts. Make into four rolls; chill for several hours or overnight. Slice; place on ungreased cookie sheet at least 1 inch apart. Bake at 375 degrees for 10 minutes or until lightly browned. Yield: 12 dozen.

Mrs. Ruby Maynard
Angleton, Tex.

EASY SUGAR COOKIES

1 c. butter
1 ½ c. sugar
3 eggs
½ tsp. salt
1 tsp. soda
1 tbsp. warm water
½ tsp. vanilla flavoring
3 c. flour

Cream butter; add sugar gradually. Cream. Beat eggs; stir into butter-sugar mixture. Add salt and soda dissolved in water. Add vanilla. Sift flour; add gradually until dough is stiff enough to roll out. Chill; roll thin. Bake at 350 degrees for 10 minutes. Yield: 150 cookies.

Mrs. Carl Rusch
Chicago, Ill.

TEA COOKIES

1 c. butter
2 c. light brown sugar
2 eggs
1 tsp. vanilla flavoring
1 c. chopped pecans
3 ½ c. flour
1 tsp. soda
½ tsp. salt

Cream butter and sugar thoroughly. Add unbeaten eggs; mix well. Add vanilla and nuts. Sift dry ingredients three times; add to mixture. Mix well. Form into rolls about 1 1/2-inches thick. Place in refrigerator for several hours. Slice 1/4-inch thick. Place on ungreased cookie sheet. Bake at 400 degrees for 10 to 12 minutes. Yield: 10 dozen.

Mildred H. Christman
York Springs, Pa.

GREEK ALMOND COOKIES

2 c. blanched almonds
1 ½ c. margarine
¾ c. sugar
½ tsp. nutmeg
4 ½ c. sifted flour
Powdered sugar

Put almonds through food chopper, using a coarse blade. Soften margarine; gradually blend in sugar and nutmeg. Stir in almonds and flour. Roll dough to 1/2-inch thickness on a lightly floured board. Shape with crescent-shaped cookie cutter. Place on ungreased baking sheet. Bake at 350 degrees for 15 minutes. Roll in powdered sugar while hot. Cool; roll in sugar again. Yield: 8 dozen cookies.

Mrs. Eugene T. Brown
San Antonio, Tex.

BUTTER COOKIES

½ lb. butter
1 3-oz. pkg. cream cheese
4 ½ tbsp. sugar
¾ tsp. vanilla flavoring
2 c. sifted flour

Cream butter, cheese and sugar; add vanilla. Blend. Add flour in two additions, beating thoroughly. Roll thinly on floured pastry board or floured pastry cloth. Cut into fancy shapes. Place on ungreased cookie sheet. Bake at 325 degrees for 5 to 7 minutes or until delicately browned. Yield: 5 dozen.

Barbara M. Shaw
Homlock, Mich.

CHRISTMAS COOKIES

3 c. flour
1 tsp. baking powder
¼ tsp. salt
1 ¼ c. sugar
1 c. shortening
3 eggs
1 tsp. vanilla flavoring

Sift all dry ingredients. Add shortening; mix with fork. Add eggs and vanilla; mix. Roll out thin; cut into desired shapes. Bake at 375 degrees for 8 minutes. Yield: 4 dozen.

Patricia Lee
Wapkoneta, O.

REALLY CRISP COOKIES

1 c. butter or ½ c. margarine and ½ c.
   shortening
2 c. sugar
3 eggs, beaten
1 tsp. vanilla flavoring
1 tsp. baking powder
4 c. sifted flour

Cream butter; gradually add sugar, eggs and vanilla. Add combined baking powder and flour to creamed mixture. Blend thoroughly. Roll on lightly floured board. Cut with biscuit cutter. Bake at 375 degrees until light brown. Yield: 5 dozen.

Mrs. John Daniel
Iuka, Miss.

DATE COOKIES

1 ½ c. sugar
1 c. shortening
2 eggs, beaten
2 tbsp. cream
1 tsp. vanilla flavoring
3 ½ c. flour
1 tsp. baking powder
1 c. finely cut dates

Cream sugar and shortening; add eggs, cream and vanilla. Add sifted flour and baking powder; mix well and stir in dates. Roll out thin; cut into desired shapes. Bake at 350 degrees for 8 to 10 minutes. Yield: 4 dozen.

Mrs. Viola Y. Grubbs
Mt. Sterling, Ky.

DATE-CREAM CHEESE ROLL-UPS

1 c. butter
½ lb. cream cheese
2 c. flour
¼ tsp. salt
Powdered sugar
Pitted dates

Cream butter and cheese. Sift flour and salt; beat into creamed mixture. Chill for several hours. Roll to 1/8-inch thickness on board sprinkled with powdered sugar. Cut into 1 x 3-inch strips. Place date on each strip; roll up. Place, folded-side down, on greased cookie sheets. Bake at 375 degrees for 15 minutes. Sprinkle with powdered sugar.

Mrs. W. F. Lester
Great Lakes Naval Trng Ctr, Ill.

SOFT GINGER COOKIES

1 ½ c. molasses
1 c. lard
1 egg
1 c. sugar
1 c. boiling water
1 tbsp. ginger
1 tbsp. soda
¾ tsp. salt
6 to 8 c. flour

Combine all ingredients, adding enough flour to make a thick dough. Mix well. Refrigerate

(Continued on next page)

for several hours. Roll on floured board. Bake at 350 degrees until browned. Yield: 6 dozen cookies.

Mrs. William Rowe
Ravenswood, W. Va.

HICKORY NUT COOKIES

2 c. sugar
⅓ c. mixed butter and lard
½ tsp. salt
4 tsp. baking powder
2 tsp. vanilla flavoring
2 eggs
2 tsp. soda
1 c. sour milk
1 c. hickory nuts
Flour

Cream sugar and butter mixture; add salt, baking powder and vanilla. Mix well. Beat in an egg at a time. Mix soda in sour milk; add slowly. Add nuts and enough flour to make dough stiff enough to roll; press out. Cut into desired shapes. Bake at 375 degrees until brown. Yield: 5 dozen.

Mrs. Ruth Ream
Junction City, O.

SOFT LEMON COOKIES

1 ¼ c. sugar
1 c. shortening
½ tsp. salt
Yellow food coloring
1 egg
1 c. sour milk or buttermilk
1 tsp. soda
2 tsp. lemon flavoring
3 to 4 c. flour

Combine sugar, shortening, salt and food coloring; blend thoroughly. Add remaining ingredients; mix well. Roll out small portion of dough at a time; cut with a biscuit cutter. Place on cookie sheet; if desired, sprinkle sugar over top of cookies. Bake at 375 degrees for 10 minutes. Yield: 24 servings.

Mrs. Everett L. Thomson
DeKalb Junction, N.Y.

PECAN CRESCENT COOKIES

½ lb. margarine
½ c. powdered sugar
2 c. flour
½ c. chopped nuts
1 tsp. vanilla flavoring
2 tbsp. evaporated milk or cream

Cream margarine and powdered sugar. Sift flour; add to mixture with nuts. Add vanilla and milk. Roll into small pieces; shape as

crescents. Place on ungreased pans. Bake at 350 degrees for 12 to 15 minutes. While warm, roll in powdered sugar. Yield: 3-4 dozen.

Mildred Krejcir
Pebble Beach, Calif.

SAND TARTS

1 c. shortening
1 ¼ c. sugar
3 eggs
1 tbsp. water
1 tsp. vanilla flavoring
3 ½ c. flour
1 tsp. salt
Sugar-cinnamon mixture
½ lb. peanut halves

Cream shortening with sugar; add 2 whole eggs, 1 egg yolk, water and vanilla. Sift flour and salt; add. Roll one-fourth of dough at a time on floured board. Roll dough square and thin. Brush lightly with egg white; sprinkle with sugar-cinnamon mixture. Cut into small squares; place 2 peanut halves on each cookie. Bake at 350 degrees until golden brown. Cool; store in airtight container. Yield: 200-250 cookies.

Mrs. Clifford E. Horton
Normal, Ill.

SHORTBREAD COOKIES

2 sticks margarine, softened
1 c. powdered sugar
2 c. flour
1 tsp. baking powder
1 tsp. vanilla flavoring

Cream margarine and sugar; add flour, baking powder and vanilla. Blend together until it forms a ball. Roll out on floured board about 1/4-inch thick; cut into desired shape or size. Place on ungreased sheet. Bake at 325 degrees for 10 to 15 minutes.

Mrs. Orville Angell
Athens, Mich.

OLD-FASHIONED SUGAR COOKIES

4 ½ c. sifted flour
1 tsp. salt
1 tsp. soda
1 tsp. baking powder
½ tsp. nutmeg
1 c. butter
1 ½ c. sugar
2 eggs
1 c. sour cream
1 ½ tsp. vanilla flavoring

Sift all dry ingredients. Cream butter and sugar until fluffy; add an egg at a time,

(Continued on next page)

beating well after each addition. Add dry ingredients alternately with sour cream, mixing until smooth after each addition. Blend in vanilla. Wrap in waxed paper; chill until firm enough to roll. Roll on floured board to about 1/4-inch thick; cut with large cookie cutter. Place on ungreased baking sheet; sprinkle with additional sugar. Bake at 375 degrees for 12 minutes or until browned. Yield: 5 dozen.

Billie F. Hamilton
Supply, N.C.

OLD-FASHIONED SUGAR COOKIES

1 c. butter or margarine
2 c. brown sugar
3 eggs
2 tsp. vanilla flavoring
1 tsp. soda
1 tsp. baking powder
½ tsp. mace
Flour
1 tsp. salt
1 c. sour milk

Cream butter and sugar; add an egg at a time. Stir in vanilla and sifted dry ingredients, including 2 cups flour. Add milk and enough flour so that dough will roll easily. Roll dough to desired thickness. Cut into desired shapes. Bake at 350 degrees for 10 minutes. Yield: 5 dozen.

Mrs. Martin Houston
Richmond, Mich.

SUGAR COOKIES

1 ½ c. sugar
1 c. shortening
2 eggs
4 ½ c. flour
¼ tsp. salt
1 ¼ tsp. soda
4 tsp. baking powder
1 c. milk
1 tsp. vanilla flavoring

Cream sugar and shortening. Add eggs; mix well. Add sifted dry ingredients alternately with milk and vanilla; mix well. Using one-half of the dough at a time, roll out on floured pastry cloth to 1/4-inch thickness. Cut with cookie cutter. Place on ungreased cookie sheet. Bake at 350 degrees for 10 minutes or less. Yield: 5 dozen.

Mrs. Charlie Gilbreath
Harrod, O.

ALMOND CHRISTMAS BALLS

1 c. butter
¼ c. powdered sugar
2 c. flour
½ tsp. salt
1 c. ground almonds
1 tsp. vanilla flavoring
Candied cherries

Cream butter; add sugar. Add all remaining ingredients except cherries. Mix well. Shape into small balls using 1 teaspoon of dough. Place cherry in the center; roll into a ball. Place on greased cookie sheet. Bake at 325 degrees for 30 minutes. Remove from oven; roll in powdered sugar. Yield: 4 dozen cookies.

Mrs. Raymond Willms
Oakdale, Calif.

ALMOND COOKIES

1 c. blanched almonds
1 c. sifted flour
½ c. butter or margarine
½ c. sugar

Finely chop 2/3 cup almonds. Toast remaining almonds for garnish. Mix flour and chopped almonds. Cream butter and sugar until fluffy; add flour mixture slowly. Shape dough into 1-inch balls. Place on cookie sheet 2 inches apart; flatten to 1/2-inch thickness. Press a toasted almond into top. Bake at 350 degrees for 15 minutes or until light golden brown. Yield: 2 1/2 dozen cookies.

Mrs. Henry H. Wishart
Dover, N.J.

ALMOND-TEA COOKIES

1 c. margarine
1 c. sugar
2 egg yolks
1 tsp. almond flavoring
2 c. flour
1 c. chopped almonds

Cream margarine. Add sugar; beat until light and fluffy. Add egg yolks and almond flavoring. Blend well. Add sifted flour and chopped almonds. Mix thoroughly. Form into 1-inch balls. Place on ungreased baking sheet. Press balls to 1/4-inch thick. Bake at 325 degrees for 15 minutes. Cool.

FROSTING:
4 tbsp. instant tea
2 tbsp. milk
½ c. margarine
2 ½ c. sifted powdered sugar
Almond halves

Dissolve tea in milk. Cream margarine until light and fluffy. Add powdered sugar and tea mixture, beating until smooth. Frost

(Continued on next page)

cool cakes; top with almond halves. Yield: 4 dozen.

Mrs. Eva A. Beasley
Portland, Ind.

CINNAMON BALLS

1 stick soft butter
3 tbsp. powdered sugar
1 c. sifted flour
1 c. chopped pecans
Cinnamon and sugar mixture

Cream butter; add all remaining ingredients except cinnamon-sugar mixture. Roll into small balls. Bake at 375 degrees for about 10 minutes. Roll in cinnamon-sugar mixture. Yield: 30 cookies.

Sandra Cranmer
Oregonia, O.

COCONUT FINGERS

1 c. brown sugar
2 eggs
1 tsp. vanilla flavoring
2 c. chopped dates
1 c. chopped nuts
2 c. coconut

Mix all ingredients except coconut; mix well. Drop dough by heaping teaspoonfuls into coconut; roll like fingers. Place on ungreased cookie sheet. Bake at 350 degrees for 10 to 12 minutes or until golden brown. NOTE: Cookies may be frozen for future use. Yield: 2 dozen.

Mrs. Ethel M. Miller
Boston, Pa.

GINGER SNAPS

1 c. sugar
¾ c. shortening
1 egg, beaten
¼ c. molasses
2 c. sifted flour
½ tsp. salt
2 tsp. soda
1 tsp. cinnamon
1 tsp. ginger
1 tsp. cloves

Cream sugar and shortening. Add egg and molasses. Sift all dry ingredients; add to sugar mixture. Chill dough. Roll small pieces of dough in hands; flatten. Dip into sugar. Bake at 375 degrees for 10 to 12 minutes. Yield: 5 dozen.

Mrs. Clarence Prosise
Mauston, Wisc.

LADY FINGERS

⅔ c. margarine
6 tbsp. powdered sugar
1 tsp. vanilla flavoring
2 c. sifted flour
¼ tsp. salt
1 c. chopped nuts

Cream margarine. Add remaining ingredients; mix well. Press into eighteen 2-inch long fingers. Put on ungreased baking sheet. Bake at 325 degrees for 30 minutes. Roll in powdered sugar. Yield: 18 cookies.

Mrs. Audrey S. Bowers
Duncan, S.C.

PEANUT BUTTER COOKIE CRISPS

½ c. butter
½ c. margarine
1 c. sugar
1 c. brown sugar
2 eggs, slightly beaten
1 c. peanut butter
1 tsp. vanilla flavoring
2 ½ c. sifted flour
1 tsp. soda
1 tsp. salt

Cream butter, margarine and sugars. Add eggs; blend. Add peanut butter and vanilla; mix well. Add all dry ingredients; stir until well blended. Chill dough if too soft to handle. Roll into balls the size of large walnuts. Place 3 inches apart on lightly greased baking sheet. Flatten with fork, making crisscross design. Bake at 375 degrees until set but not hard. Store in covered container when cool. Yield: 6 dozen.

Mrs. Milton T. Kuntz, Jr.
Houston, Tex.

WINE COOKIES

1 lb. shortening
1 ½ c. sugar
4 egg yolks
½ tsp. salt
5 c. flour
6 tbsp. sweet red wine
2 egg whites, beaten
1 c. chopped nuts
Colored jelly

Cream shortening, sugar and yolks; add dry ingredients alternately with wine. Form walnut-sized balls; dip into egg whites. Roll in nuts. Place on greased cookie sheet; dent middle with thumb. Bake at 350 degrees for 15 minutes or until light brown. Remove from cookie sheet; fill dent with jelly. Yield: 10 dozen.

Mrs. Dorothy Morrison
Corry, Pa.

RECIPE FOR FRESH PEACH ANGEL PIE ON PAGE 165

ALMOND-MERINGUE CANADIAN

6 egg whites
2 c. fruit sugar
2 tsp. baking powder
Pinch of salt
1 tbsp. vinegar
1 ½ tsp. almond flavoring
1 tsp. vanilla flavoring
Whipped cream
Toasted almonds

Beat egg whites until stiff. Mix remaining ingredients except whipped cream and almonds. Add 1 tablespoon mixture at a time to egg whites. Pour into two foil-lined 9-inch layer cake pans. Bake at 275 degrees for 1 hour. Cool; frost and fill with whipped cream that has been flavored with additional 1 teaspoon almond flavoring and sugar. Garnish with toasted almonds. Chill for several hours. Yield: 12 servings.

Mrs. Foster McClellan
Truax Field, Wisc.

ANGEL'S DESSERT

5 egg whites
¼ tsp. salt
½ tsp. cream of tartar
1 ½ c. sugar
1 tsp. vanilla flavoring
½ pt. heavy cream, whipped
1 can cherry pie filling or 1 box frozen
    strawberries

Beat egg whites and salt until foamy. Add cream of tartar; continue beating until eggs stand in peaks. Add sugar and vanilla slowly. Place in a greased 7 1/2 x 12 x 2-inch pan. Place in 450 degree oven. Turn off oven; leave meringue in oven overnight. Do not open oven door. Top with whipped cream flavored with additional vanilla and sugar. Refrigerate for 6 hours. Top with cherry pie filling or strawberries just before serving. Cut into squares. Yield: 10 servings.

Mrs. Jack S. French
Fort Riley, Kans.

ANGEL PIE

8 eggs, separated
½ tsp. cream of tartar
10 drops of vinegar
3 c. sugar
Juice of 2 lemons
Grated rind of 2 lemons
2 c. heavy cream

Beat egg whites until stiff and dry. Add cream of tartar, vinegar and 2 cups sugar. Spread meringue in two buttered 9-inch pans, hollowing center. Bake in 300 degrees oven for 1 hour. Cool. Combine egg yolks, remaining 1

cup sugar, lemon juice and rind; cook in double boiler until thick. Pour into meringue shell. Chill. Top with whipped cream. Yield: 15 servings.

Mrs. John C. Milner
K. I. Sawyer AFB, Mich.

ANGEL MERINGUE

4 egg whites
½ c. sugar
½ c. powdered sugar
Pinch of salt
½ tsp. vanilla flavoring
½ pt. heavy cream, whipped
1 sm. bar semi-sweet chocolate, grated

Beat egg whites until stiff but not dry; add sugars, salt and vanilla. Pour into an oiled 9-inch pie pan. Bake at 250 degrees for 1 hour. Cool; pour whipped cream into meringue. Sprinkle with chocolate. Refrigerate overnight. Yield: 6-9 servings.

Mrs. Robert Vonderheid
Cincinnati, O.

CHOCOLATE ANGEL PIE

MERINGUE SHELL:
3 egg whites
⅛ tsp. cream of tartar
Pinch of salt
¾ c. sugar
1 c. chopped pecans
1 tsp. vanilla flavoring

Beat egg whites until foamy. Add cream of tartar and salt; beat until soft peaks form. Gradually add sugar, beating until stiff. Fold in pecans and vanilla. Turn into a buttered 9-inch pie plate; make a nest-like shell, building up sides of meringue 1/2-inch above edge of plate. Bake at 300 degrees for 50 to 55 minutes. Cool thoroughly.

FILLING:
1 ½ pt. heavy cream
Sugar
2 tsp. vanilla flavoring
1 bar German's sweet chocolate
2 tbsp. creme de cacao (opt.)

Whip 1/2 pint cream; sweeten to taste and flavor with 1/2 teaspoon vanilla. Spread over cool meringue. Melt chocolate in double boiler. Cool; stir in 1 teaspoon vanilla and creme de cacao. Whip 1/2 pint cream; fold in chocolate mixture. Spread over first layer of whipped cream. Whip remaining 1/2 pint cream; sweeten and flavor with remaining 1/2 teaspoon vanilla. Spread over chocolate layer. Garnish with shaved chocolate. NOTE: Dessert topping mix may be substituted for

(Continued on next page)

whipped cream in the chocolate layer. Yield: 6-8 servings.

Mrs. Lawrence R. Hawkins
Marietta, Ga.

CHOCOLATE MERINGUE

8 egg whites
¼ tsp. cream of tartar
1 ½ c. sugar
1 pkg. chocolate pieces
3 egg yolks, beaten
2 tsp. vanilla flavoring
½ pt. heavy cream, whipped

Beat 6 egg whites until foamy; add cream of tartar. Slowly add sugar; beat until stiff. Spread in a buttered loaf cake pan. Bake at 275 degrees for 1 hour. Melt chocolate pieces; add egg yolks and vanilla. Beat remaining 2 egg whites until stiff. Fold whipped cream into egg whites. Fold mixture into cooled chocolate mixture. Spread over meringue. May be covered with whipped cream and nuts if desired. Yield: 16 servings.

Mrs. Roy Hanson
Hills, Minn.

CHOCOLATE-NUT ANGEL PIE

MERINGUE SHELL:
½ c. sugar
⅛ tsp. cream of tartar
2 egg whites

Sift sugar with cream of tartar. Beat egg whites until stiff but not dry. Slowly add sifted ingredients, beating constantly. Line bottom and sides of a well greased 9-inch pie plate. Bake at 275 degrees for 1 hour or until lightly browned and crisp to touch. Cool.

FILLING:
1 c. chopped pecans or filberts
2 pkg. semi-sweet chocolate pieces
6 tbsp. hot water
2 tsp. vanilla flavoring
2 c. heavy cream, whipped

Sprinkle one-half of nuts over meringue shell. Melt chocolate in double boiler. Stir in water; cook until thickened. Cool slightly; add vanilla. Fold in whipped cream. Pour into pie shell. Chill for 2 to 3 hours or until set. Sprinkle remaining nuts on top. Yield: 6-8 servings.

Mrs. Vernon R. Porter
Atlanta Army Depot, Ga.

CHOCOLATE-TOFFEE MERINGUE

MERINGUE:
6 egg whites
Dash of salt

1 ¾ c. sugar
1 tsp. vanilla flavoring

Beat egg whites with salt until stiff. Gradually add sugar, beating until all sugar is added. Add vanilla. Spread on large cookie sheet lined with brown paper. Bake at 300 degrees for 40 to 45 minutes. Remove from paper; cut in half.

FILLING:
2 c. heavy cream
1 tsp. vanilla flavoring
12 chocolate toffee bars, ground

Whip cream; add vanilla. Spread a meringue with one-half of whipped cream; sprinkle with one-half of ground toffee bars. Top with remaining meringue; spread with remaining whipped cream and toffee candy. Refrigerate for 12 hours or overnight. Yield: 12 servings.

Mrs. Wallace L. Russell
Sanford NAS, Fla.

GERMAN'S CHOCOLATE ANGEL PIE

MERINGUE SHELL:
2 egg whites
⅛ tsp. salt
⅛ tsp. cream of tartar
½ c. sugar
½ c. chopped pecans
1 tsp. vanilla flavoring

Beat egg whites with salt and cream of tartar until foamy. Add 2 tablespoons sugar at a time; beat until mixture forms stiff peaks. Fold in pecans and vanilla. Spoon into pie plate. Shape into a nest, building up sides above edge of pan. Bake at 300 degrees for 50 to 55 minutes. Cool.

FILLING:
1 pkg. German's chocolate
3 tbsp. water
1 tsp. vanilla flavoring
1 c. heavy cream, whipped

Melt chocolate in water over low heat; stir well. Cool until thickened; add vanilla. Fold chocolate mixture into whipped cream. Pour into meringue shell; chill for at least 2 hours. Yield: 6-8 servings.

Mrs. Paul Graham
Northampton, Mass.

SWEET CHOCOLATE MERINGUE

7 eggs, separated
⅓ c. sugar
⅓ c. ground almonds or pecans
¼ lb. sweet chocolate, grated

159

(Continued on next page)

Beat egg yolks until thick; gradually add sugar while beating. Beat egg whites until stiff but not dry. Fold egg yolk mixture, nuts and chocolate into egg whites. Pour into three greased and waxed paper-lined 8-inch pans. Bake at 350 degrees for 45 minutes. Turn out of pans at once; cool. Frost with chocolate frosting or serve with whipped cream. Yield: 8-10 servings.

Mrs. Andrew J. Toman
Riverside, Ill.

VIENNESE CHOCOLATE MERINGUE

3 egg whites, at room temperature
¼ tsp. cream of tartar
Dash of salt
¾ c. sugar

Beat egg whites until soft peaks form. Sprinkle with cream of tartar and salt. Add sugar gradually, beating until precise points form. Spread two-thirds of the meringue on bottom of greased 8-inch pie pan. Use remaining meringue to cover sides; mound around rim of pan. Bake in preheated 275 degree oven for 1 hour or until shell is a delicate brown. Cool.

FILLING:
2 6-oz. pkg. or 2 c. semi-sweet chocolate
  pieces
1 tbsp. instant coffee
1 c. heavy cream
1 tsp. vanilla flavoring

Melt chocolate pieces over hot, not boiling, water. Stir in coffee and 1/4 cup boiling water; beat until creamy. Cool. Beat cream until stiff; fold into chocolate mixture. Add vanilla. Pour into meringue shell. Chill. Yield: 6-8 servings.

Mrs. Kenneth B. Hobson
Wright-Patterson AFB, O.

COCOA MERINGUES

3 egg whites
½ tsp. cream of tartar
¼ tsp. salt
1 c. sugar
¼ c. sifted cocoa

Beat egg whites, cream of tartar and salt until frothy. Sift sugar with cocoa. Add gradually to egg whites, beating until stiff peaks form. Draw six 3 1/2-inch circles on ungreased waxed paper; place on baking sheet. Spread meringue over circles; shape into cups with spoon. Bake in 275 degree oven for 1

hour. Turn off heat; cool in oven for 1 hour with door closed. At serving time, place a scoop of vanilla ice cream in each cup and top with chocolate sauce and nuts if desired.

Mrs. Lenna Stottlemyer
Anderson, Ind.

COFFEE MERINGUES GLACE

2 egg whites
½ tsp. lemon juice
⅔ c. sugar

Combine egg whites and lemon juice; beat until egg whites hold a peak. Gradually add sugar, beating well after each addition. Continue beating until very stiff and glossy. Shape meringue into six circles on a lightly buttered baking sheet. Build up edge to 1/2 inch with back of spoon, leaving a 1/4-inch base. Bake at 275 degrees for 25 minutes. Turn off heat; leave meringue shells in oven until completely cooled.

BITTERSWEET CHOCOLATE SAUCE:
1 12-oz. pkg. semi-sweet chocolate pieces
1 ⅔ c. evaporated milk
1 qt. coffee ice cream

Melt chocolate in evaporated milk over low heat, stirring until well blended. Cool; chill. Mound coffee ice cream into meringue shell. Pour sauce over ice cream; serve immediately. Yield: 6 servings.

Mrs. E. T. Raspberry
Nellis AFB, Nev.

DATE MERINGUE

½ c. sugar
4 egg whites, beaten
1 tsp. vanilla flavoring
¼ tsp. salt
1 c. chopped nuts
1 c. chopped dates

Fold sugar into egg whites; beat until smooth. Add vanilla and salt. Fold in nuts and dates. Pour into oiled and crumb-lined spring pan. Bake at 350 degrees until firm. Yield: 8 servings.

Mrs. John Lorance
Holyoke, Colo.

DATE MERINGUE

½ c. sugar
1 pkg. pitted dates, finely chopped
1 tbsp. flour
1 tsp. baking powder

(Continued on next page)

½ c. chopped nuts
2 egg whites, stiffly beaten
⅔ c. heavy cream, whipped

Fold sugar, dates, flour, baking powder and nuts into egg whites. Spread in greased 9-inch square baking pan. Bake at 350 degrees for 25 minutes. Top with whipped cream. Yield: 6 servings.

Gladys Waggett
Highland Park, Ill.

DATE-NUT MERINGUES

4 egg whites
¼ tsp. salt
1 ½ c. sugar
1 tsp. vanilla flavoring
1 c. chopped dates
1 c. chopped pecans

Beat egg whites until frothy; add salt. Gradually add sugar, beating continuously until egg whites stand in stiff peaks. Fold in flavoring, dates and nuts. Drop from teaspoon onto lightly greased cookie sheet. Bake at 325 degrees for 20 minutes. Remove from pan immediately. Yield: 4 dozen.

Mrs. Sarah B. Estes
Lincoln, Nebr.

DATE-PECAN MERINGUE

3 egg whites
1 c. sugar
12 dates, finely chopped
24 pecan halves, finely chopped
12 saltine crackers, crushed

Whip egg whites until stiff but not dry while slowly adding sugar. Mix dates, pecans and crumbs. Fold into egg white mixture. Press into greased 9-inch pie pan. Bake at 350 degrees for 35 minutes. Slice into wedges; serve topped with buttered pecan ice cream. Yield: 6-8 servings.

Mrs. John D. Sapp
Fort Bragg, N.C.

EGGS A LA NEIGE

4 c. milk
6 eggs, separated
1 ¼ c. sugar
Salt
1 ¼ c. heavy cream
¾ tsp. vanilla
1 ½ tbsp. flour
2 pt. fresh strawberries
1 square unsweetened chocolate

Scald milk in large skillet. Beat egg whites until frothy. Gradually add 3/4 cup sugar and 1/4 teaspoon salt, beating until stiff. Drop three large mounds of meringue, 1 inch apart into hot milk. Cook for 5 minutes, turning once with slotted spoon. Drain on paper towels. Repeat until all meringue is used. Refrigerate meringues. Scald cream with vanilla and 1 1/2 cups milk used for meringues in double boiler. Beat egg yolks until light. Beat in 1/2 cup sugar, pinch of salt, flour and a small amount of cream-milk mixture. Stir into remaining cream-milk mixture. Cook, stirring over hot, not boiling, water until sauce coats a metal spoon. Cool; refrigerate. Hull, wash and slice strawberries into deep serving dish 20 minutes before serving time. Heap chilled meringues over strawberries. Pour custard sauce over meringues. Shave chocolate with vegetable parer over all. NOTE: Meringues and custard may be made the day before or at the latest, early on the day to be served. Yield: 8 servings.

Mrs. G. M. Durham
Oakland, Calif.

FABULOUS MERINGUE

6 egg whites, at room temperature
¼ tsp. salt
½ tsp. cream of tartar
1 ½ c. sugar
¼ tsp. vanilla flavoring
Ice cream
Thawed frozen strawberries

Beat egg whites until soft peaks form; add salt and cream of tartar, beating until stiff. Gradually add sugar and vanilla, beating until smooth. Spread mixture in a heavily buttered 8 x 12-inch glass baking dish. Place in oven preheated to 425 degrees; immediately turn off heat. Leave in oven overnight; do not open oven door. Serve with ice cream topped with strawberries. Yield: 6-8 servings.

Mrs. Robert M. Hansen
K. I. Sawyer AFB, Mich.

SCHAUM TORTE

6 egg whites
2 c. sugar
1 ½ tsp. lemon juice or vinegar

Beat egg whites until stiff; gradually beat in 1 cup sugar. Continue beating alternately, adding remaining 1 cup sugar and lemon juice; beat until stiff and glossy. Drop by spoonfuls onto brown paper on cookie sheet. Bake at 275 degrees for 40 to 60 minutes or until delicately browned and crusty. Remove from paper while

(Continued on next page)

still warm. Serve with strawberries, ice cream or any desired fruit. Yield: 12 servings.

Mrs. Jessie Harris
Scotland, S.D.

FORGOTTEN DESSERT

5 eggs, separated
¼ tsp. cream of tartar
2 c. sugar
Juice or grated rind of 1 lemon
1 pt. heavy cream, whipped

Beat egg whites and cream of tartar until foamy. Gradually add 1 1/2 cups sugar, beating until stiff. Spread into a 13 x 9-inch baking pan. Put into a 450 degree oven. Turn off heat; leave overnight or until cold without opening oven door. Beat egg yolks until smooth; add remaining 1/2 cup sugar, lemon juice or rind. Cook in double boiler until thick enough to spread easily. Spread one-half of whipped cream over baked meringue. Spread lemon mixture on top; spread with remaining whipped cream. NOTE: Both lemon rind and juice may be used. This keeps well in refrigerator up to 24 hours. Yield: 8-10 servings.

Mrs. K. W. Strebel
Yorktown, Va.

FRUIT MERINGUES

MERINGUE:
3 egg whites
1 c. sugar
1 tsp. vinegar
1 tsp. vanilla flavoring

Beat egg whites until they stand in peaks. Add sugar gradually, beating well after each addition. Put heaping tablespoons of meringue on a greased cookie sheet. Make a well in each. Bake at 275 degrees for 50 minutes; cool.

CUSTARD:
3 egg yolks
¾ c. sugar
1 tsp. vanilla flavoring
1 tbsp. flour
2 c. hot milk
Drained fruit
Whipped cream
Nuts
Maraschino cherries

Combine egg yolks, sugar, vanilla, flour and milk. Cook until thick; cool. Fill meringues with custard; add desired fruit. Top with whipped cream, nuts and cherries.

Mrs. E. A. Keyser
Covington, Va.

GRAHAM CRACKER AND WALNUT MERINGUE

1 c. sugar
3 eggs, separated
1 c. graham cracker crumbs
½ c. chopped walnuts
1 tbsp. almond flavoring

Gradually add 1/2 cup sugar to egg whites; beat until stiff. Set aside. Gradually add remaining 1/2 cup sugar to egg yolks; beat until thick. Stir in crumbs, nuts and flavoring; fold in egg whites. Pour into 9-inch greased pie plate. Bake at 350 degrees for 30 minutes. Yield: 6 servings.

Mrs. Beatrice D. Hawkins
Winthrop, Me.

HEAVENLY PIE

1 ½ c. sugar
¼ tsp. cream of tartar
4 eggs, separated
3 tbsp. lemon juice
1 tbsp. finely grated lemon rind
⅛ tsp. salt (opt.)
1 pt. heavy cream, whipped

Sift 1 cup sugar and cream of tartar. Beat egg whites until stiff but not dry; gradually add sugar mixture, beating until thoroughly blended. Line bottom and sides of a 9 or 10-inch well greased pie plate with mixture, hollowing out the center and being careful not to spread the meringue too close to the rim. Bake at 275 to 300 degrees for 1 hour; cool. Beat egg yolks slightly; stir in remaining 1/2 cup sugar, lemon juice, rind and salt. Cook in top of double boiler over boiling water. Combine one-half of the whipped cream with lemon mixture. Fill meringue shell; cover top of pie with remaining whipped cream. Chill for 24 hours. NOTE: Meringue crust may be sprinkled with flaked coconut before baking if desired. Top of chilled pie may be garnished with strawberry halves, coconut or chocolate curls. Yield: 6 servings.

Mrs. Jack M. Park
Oakland, Calif.

EGG KISSES

6 egg whites
¼ tsp. salt
1 tsp. baking powder
2 c. sugar
1 tsp. vinegar
1 tbsp. flour
1 tsp. vanilla flavoring
¼ tsp. almond flavoring

Combine egg whites and salt; beat until frothy. Sprinkle with baking powder; beat until stiff. Add sugar slowly by spoonfuls, beating well after each addition. When most of the sugar

(Continued on next page)

is used, add vinegar and flour. Add remaining sugar; beat until thick and glossy. Fold in flavorings. Divide into 16 portions in pan lined with greased brown paper. Bake in preheated 300 degree oven for 5 minutes. Turn heat off; leave in oven for 1 hour. Do not open oven door until time is up. NOTE: Be sure to use a brown paper sack to line pan. Yield: 16 servings.

Mrs. Pat Ruh, Jr.
Knoxville, Tenn.

MERINGUE KISSES

4 egg whites
1 c. sugar
1 c. coarsely chopped nuts
1 tsp. flavoring

Beat egg whites and sugar with electric mixer for 20 minutes. Fold in nuts and flavoring. Drop from spoon onto greased cookie sheet or white paper. Bake at 200 to 225 degrees for 1 hour. Fill as desired. NOTE: Mixture may be shaped into 1 large nest meringue. Yield: 4-6 servings.

Mrs. C. B. Duff
Colorado Springs, Colo.

LEMON-MERINGUE SURPRISE

5 eggs, separated
½ tsp. cream of tartar
¼ tsp. salt
1 ½ c. sugar
1 tsp. vanilla flavoring
2 tbsp. grated lemon rind
⅓ c. lemon juice
1 c. heavy cream, whipped
4 tbsp. powdered sugar
⅔ c. shredded coconut

Beat egg whites until frothy; add cream of tartar and salt. Beat until very stiff; gradually add 1 cup sugar and 1/2 teaspoon vanilla. Spoon meringue into buttered 9-inch glass pie pan. Bake at 275 degrees for 1 hour. Cool in plate. Blend egg yolks, lemon rind, juice and remaining 1/2 cup sugar in double boiler. Cook over hot water until thick; cool. Spread over meringue crust. Combine whipped cream, powdered sugar, remaining 1/2 teaspoon vanilla and coconut. Spread over filling. Yield: 6 servings.

Helen L. Curley
Denver, Colo.

MERINGUES

2 eggs whites
1 c. powdered sugar
1 c. chopped nuts
1 c. dates or raisins

Beat egg whites until stiff; add sugar. Fold in nuts and dates. Bake on waxed paper on cookie sheet at 300 degrees until dry. Yield: 12 servings.

Mrs. William R. Hall
Crane, Ind.

MERINGUE DESSERT

6 egg whites
⅓ tsp. cream of tartar
2 c. sugar
1 tbsp. vinegar
1 tsp. vanilla flavoring

Beat egg whites until stiff; add cream of tartar, sugar, vinegar and vanilla. Draw an 8-inch circle on cookie sheet. Place meringue inside circle or place in torte pan. Bake at 325 degrees for 1 hour. Cool; fill with ice cream and favorite fruit. Yield: 8 servings.

Mrs. Opal Hill
Indianapolis, Ind.

MERINGUE DESSERT

25 graham crackers, crushed
½ c. melted butter
4 egg whites
1 c. sugar
1 can cherry, blueberry or raspberry pie
  filling
1 ½ c. heavy cream, whipped
Chopped nuts

Mix cracker crumbs and butter; press into a 9 x 13-inch pan. Beat egg whites until stiff; gradually add sugar. Spread over crumb mixture. Bake at 400 degrees for 10 to 15 minutes or until meringue is done. Cool. Cover meringue with pie filling. Spread whipped cream over filling. Sprinkle with nuts. Yield: 12-15 servings.

Mrs. William Maier
Hartford, S.D.

MERINGUE NESTS WITH LEMON CREAM
MERINGUE NESTS:

½ c. egg whites
Dash of salt
¾ c. sugar
4 drops lemon flavoring

Beat egg whites with salt until stiff. Add a spoonful of sugar at a time, beating well after each addition. Add flavoring. Place by spoonfuls on a cookie sheet which has been lined

(Continued on next page)

with two layers of heavy brown paper. Shape into nests. Bake at 300 degrees for 10 to 15 minutes or until a delicate brown. Lower heat to 250 degrees; bake for 30 to 40 minutes or until dry. Cool slightly; remove from paper. Shells may be frozen before or after filling them, if desired. Unfilled shells may be kept in a tightly covered container for several days.

FILLING:
3 egg yolks
Grated rind of 1 lemon
¼ c. lemon juice
⅔ c. sugar
2 c. whipped cream

Combine yolks, lemon rind and juice. Stir in sugar. Cook in double boiler until thick. Cool; fold in whipped cream. Fill nests with mixture. Refrigerate for at least 2 hours before serving. Top with additional whipped cream. Yield: 12 servings.

Mrs. Doyal Keller
Loring AFB, Me.

MERINGUE SHELLS

3 egg whites, at room temperature
1 tsp. baking powder
1 c. sugar
1 tsp. vanilla flavoring

Beat egg whites until foamy; add baking powder. Beat until stiff; slowly add sugar. Continue beating until sugar is well blended. Add vanilla; mix well. Put rounded teaspoonfuls of meringue on greased cookie sheet. Spread out in round shape until size of half dollar or larger. Build sides on base with spoon and knife until 1 1/2 inches high. Bake at 250 degrees for 30 minutes. Do not let brown. Yield: 12 shells.

Mrs. S. C. Bramlett
Louisville, Ky.

SURPRISE MERINGUES

2 egg whites
⅛ tsp. salt
⅛ tsp. cream of tartar
1 tsp. vanilla flavoring
¾ c. sugar
1 6-oz. pkg. semi-sweet chocolate pieces
¼ c. chopped nuts

Beat egg whites, salt, cream of tartar and vanilla until soft peaks form; add sugar gradually, beating until stiff. Fold in chocolate pieces and nuts. Cover cookie sheet with paper; drop mixture from a teaspoon onto

cookie sheet. Bake at 300 degrees for 25 minutes. Yield: 2 dozen.

Wren Hewitt
Santa Fe, N.M.

MIRACLE PIE

3 egg whites
¾ c. sugar
20 Ritz crackers, crushed
Chopped pecans
½ tsp. baking powder
½ tsp. vanilla flavoring
½ pt. heavy cream, whipped

Beat egg whites; gradually add sugar. Mix crumbs, 3/4 cup pecans, baking powder and vanilla. Fold into egg white mixture. Pour into well greased pie pan. Bake at 325 degrees for 30 minutes. Cool. Cover with whipped cream; sprinkle with chopped pecans. Yield: 8 servings.

Mrs. William Creech
Rogers, Ark.

MYSTERY PIE

3 egg whites
Pinch of salt
½ tsp. baking powder
1 c. sugar
16 Ritz crackers, finely crushed
½ c. chopped nuts
1 tsp. vanilla flavoring
½ pt. heavy cream, whipped
Grated chocolate

Beat egg whites with salt and baking powder until stiff; gradually beat in sugar. Fold in cracker crumbs, nuts and vanilla. Pour into greased 9-inch layer cake pan. Bake at 325 degrees for 30 minutes. Chill; spread with whipped cream. Sprinkle with chocolate. Chill for several hours or overnight. Yield: 6 servings.

Anna Marie Walters
Huntingdon, Tenn.

CRUSTLESS NUT PIE

3 egg whites
1 c. sugar
½ tsp. baking powder
1 tsp. vanilla flavoring
14 Ritz crackers, broken
⅔ c. pecans
½ pt. heavy cream, whipped

Beat egg whites until light. Add sugar, continue beating. Add baking powder and vanilla,

(Continued on next page)

beating until of meringue consistency. Stir in crackers and nuts. Line 9-inch pie pan with mixture. Bake at 325 degrees for 30 minutes. Cool; top with whipped cream. Yield: 6 servings.

Mrs. Velma Siefers
Dorrance, Kans.

FRESH PEACH ANGEL PIE

MERINGUE PIE SHELL:
2 lge. egg whites
⅛ tsp. salt
Pinch of cream of tartar
½ c. sugar
Pinch of almond flavoring

Place egg whites and salt in a mixing bowl; beat until foamy. Add cream of tartar; beat until egg whites stand in stiff peaks. Gradually beat in sugar and almond flavoring. Continue beating until egg whites stand in sharp peaks. Spread mixture around bottom and sides of a lightly buttered 9-inch pie plate. Decorate edge of pie plate with some of the meringue put through a cake decorator tube. Bake in a preheated 275 degree oven for 1 hour. The crust will shrink slightly.

FILLING:
1 envelope unflavored gelatin
¼ c. cold water
1 c. crushed fresh peaches
2 tsp. fresh lemon juice
¾ c. sugar
2 lge. egg yolks
1 lge. egg
¼ tsp. salt
¾ c. milk
1 tsp. vanilla flavoring
1 c. heavy cream, whipped

Soften gelatin in cold water; set aside. Combine peaches, lemon juice and 1/4 cup sugar; set aside. Beat egg yolks and whole egg slightly. Mix with salt, 1/2 cup sugar and milk in a saucepan or top of a double boiler. Cook over hot water or low heat until custard coats a metal spoon, stirring frequently. Remove from heat; stir in softened gelatin until dissolved. Chill until mixture is about as thick as fresh egg whites. Fold in vanilla, whipped cream and peach mixture. Turn into prepared meringue shell. Chill until firm and ready to serve. Garnish with additional whipped cream and sliced fresh peaches. Yield: One 9-inch pie.

Photograph for this recipe on page 157.

PEPPERMINT RING

6 egg whites
Dash of salt
1 ½ c. sugar

1 tsp. vanilla flavoring
1 tsp. almond flavoring
1 ½ c. fine chocolate wafer crumbs
1 c. chopped walnuts
2 c. heavy cream
½ c. crushed peppermint stick candy

Beat egg whites and salt until soft peaks form. Add 1 tablespoon sugar at a time; beat until glossy. Add flavorings. Fold in wafer crumbs and nuts. Put in greased large ring mold. Bake at 325 degrees for at least 1 hour; cool. Three hours before serving, whip cream until stiff; fold in sugar to taste and crushed peppermint candy. Put in center of ring mold and around cake. Chill until serving time. Garnish with curls of shaved chocolate if desired. Yield: 8-9 servings.

Mrs. R. E. Vermette
Key West Naval Base, Fla.

RED RASPBERRY-MERINGUE PIE

3 egg whites
1 c. sugar
1 tsp. vanilla flavoring
½ tsp. baking powder
14 Ritz crackers, crushed
¾ c. chopped nuts
1 carton frozen red raspberries, drained
½ pt. heavy cream

Beat egg whites until stiff. Gradually add sugar and vanilla. Mix baking powder, cracker crumbs and nuts. Fold into egg white mixture. Pour into a well greased 9-inch pie pan. Bake at 325 degrees for 45 minutes. Cool thoroughly. Whip cream; fold in raspberries. Fill meringue shell with whipped cream mixture. Chill for 1 hour before serving. Yield: 8 servings.

Mrs. Jean H. Teale
Ellsworth, Pa.

RHUBARB MERINGUE

1 ½ c. cake flour
5 tbsp. powdered sugar
½ c. butter
3 eggs
2 c. sugar
1 tsp. baking powder
3 c. chopped rhubarb

Beat 1 cup flour, powdered sugar and butter. Put in 9 x 13-inch pan. Bake at 350 degrees for 15 minutes. Beat eggs, sugar, remaining 1/2 cup flour, baking powder and rhubarb. Spread on top of first mixture. Bake at 350 degrees for 45 minutes. Top with whipped cream. Yield: 15 servings.

Mrs. Lois Lovas
Mayville, N.D.

STRAWBERRY MERINGUE

4 egg whites
½ tsp. cream of tartar
¼ tsp. salt
1 ½ tsp. vanilla flavoring
1 ¼ c. sugar
1 box frozen strawberries
3 tbsp. cornstarch
1 tbsp. butter
1 tbsp. lemon juice
1 c. heavy cream, whipped
2 tbsp. powdered sugar

Beat egg whites until stiff; add cream of tartar, salt and 1/2 teaspoon vanilla. Gradually add 1 cup sugar, beating constantly. Pour into greased pie plate; push with spoon to sides and over bottom, arranging mixture into little peaks. Bake at 325 degrees for 1 hour. Cool. Drain strawberries, reserving juice. Combine cornstarch and remaining 1/4 cup sugar; mix with juice drained from strawberries. Cook over low heat, stirring constantly, until thick and clear. Add butter and lemon juice; cool slightly. Fold in strawberries; pile in meringue crust. Combine whipped cream, powdered sugar and remaining 1 teaspoon vanilla; spread over strawberries. Chill for 24 hours. Yield: 6 servings.

Mrs. James P. Neville
North Platte, Nebr.

WALNUT-MERINGUE PIE

1 ⅓ c. finely crushed butter crackers
2 tsp. baking powder
1 c. chopped walnuts
3 egg whites
1 c. sugar

Combine crackers, baking powder and walnuts. Beat egg whites to soft peaks; gradually add sugar. Beat until stiff. Fold into cracker mixture. Pour into ungreased 9-inch pie pan. Bake at 350 degrees for 25 minutes. Cool. Serve with ice cream, whipped cream or fruit. Yield: 6 servings.

Mrs. Jon P. Didlo
Bellefontaine AFB, O.

APPLE TORTE

1 c. oats
½ c. sugar
½ c. brown sugar
¾ c. flour
½ c. butter
1 tsp. cinnamon
6 c. sliced apples

Combine all ingredients except apples; mix well. Press one-half of mixture into 9 x 9 x 2-inch pan. Top with apples. If apples are tart, sprinkle with additional sugar. Put remaining crumb mixture on top of apples. Bake at 375 degrees for 50 minutes. Serve with whipped cream. Yield: 9 servings.

Mrs. Arthur Willer
New Lisbon, Wisc.

APPLESAUCE TORTE

18 graham crackers, crushed
⅓ c. sugar
⅓ c. melted butter
2 c. applesauce
2 egg yolks
1 can sweetened condensed milk
Juice of 1 lemon
2 egg whites

Combine cracker crumbs, sugar and melted butter; mix well. Place one-half of mixture in bottom of 8-inch square pan. Combine applesauce, egg yolks, condensed milk and lemon juice. Fold in beaten egg whites; pour over graham crackers. Sprinkle remaining crumbs on top. Bake at 350 degrees for 30 to 40 minutes or until nicely browned. Serve with whipped cream. Yield: 8 servings.

Mrs. Louise Onsgard
De Forest, Wisc.

APRICOT-CREAM TORTE

¼ c. butter
1 ½ c. sifted sugar
4 eggs, separated
1 ½ tsp. vanilla flavoring
1 c. sifted cake flour
1 tsp. baking powder
Salt
5 tbsp. cream
½ c. chopped blanched almonds
1 c. heavy cream
¾ c. sweetened apricot pulp

Beat butter until soft. Add 1/2 cup sugar gradually; blend until light and creamy. Beat in an egg yolk at a time. Add 1/2 teaspoon vanilla. Sift flour with baking powder and 1/4 teaspoon salt; add to butter mixture alternately with cream. Beat until smooth. Spread in two greased 9-inch layer pans. Whip egg whites with 1/8 teaspoon salt until stiff. Slowly add remaining 1 cup sugar, 1/2 teaspoonful at a time; beat constantly. When all sugar has been added, continue beating for several minutes. Fold in remaining 1 teaspoon vanilla. Spread meringue lightly over cake batter in both pans; stud one meringue with chopped almonds. Bake at 325 degrees for 25 minutes. Increase heat to 350 degrees; bake for 30 minutes longer. Remove from oven; cool in pans.

(Continued on next page)

Shortly before serving, place plain layer, meringue-side down, on a cake plate. Whip cream until stiff; fold in apricot pulp. Spread over plain layer; place almond studded layer, meringue-side up, on top. NOTE: Another cream or custard filling may be used if desired. Yield: 8-10 servings.

Mrs. John H. Hoye
Fort Carson, Colo.

BANANA-CRUMB TORTE

2 c. vanilla wafers, crushed
⅓ c. melted butter
½ c. minus 1 tbsp. butter
1 ½ c. sifted powdered sugar
2 eggs
¼ c. sugar
2 tbsp. cocoa
½ pt. heavy cream
1 c. chopped walnuts
1 c. mashed bananas
¼ c. Maraschino cherries, sliced

Mix crumbs and butter. Press into 8-inch square pan, reserving 2 tablespoons of mixture. Cream butter and powdered sugar. Add an egg at a time; beat well after each addition. Chill; spread mixture over crumbs. Refrigerate. Combine sugar, cocoa and cream; whip until stiff. Fold in nuts and fruits; pour over filling. Top with remaining crumbs; chill overnight.

Mrs. Ella Kleinschmidt
North Freedom, Wisc.

BLUEBERRY TORTE

24 graham crackers, crushed
1 ¼ c. sugar
⅓ c. melted butter
12 oz. cream cheese
3 eggs
1 can blueberry pie filling
½ pt. heavy cream, whipped

Mix cracker crumbs, 1/2 cup sugar and butter. Pat into 9 x 13-inch pan. Cream the cheese and remaining 3/4 cup sugar; add an egg at a time, beating well after each. Spread over crust. Bake at 350 degrees for 30 minutes. Cool. Spread with pie filling; chill overnight. Before serving, spread with whipped cream. Cut into desired shapes; serve. NOTE: Cherries, peaches, pineapple or strawberries may be substituted for blueberries. Yield: 8 servings.

Mrs. Clyde M. Powell
Mt. Olive, Miss.

BUTTER-CREAM TORTE

2 c. vanilla wafer crumbs
½ lb. butter, softened
2 c. sifted powdered sugar
4 eggs
½ c. chopped almonds
¼ c. chopped green Maraschino cherries
¼ c. chopped red Maraschino cherries
1 c. heavy cream, whipped

Spread one-half of crumbs in 9-inch cake pan. Cream butter and powdered sugar. Add an egg at a time; beat until well blended. Slight separation of mixture is normal. Stir in almonds; spoon mixture over crumbs. Sprinkle with 3/4 cup crumbs. Fold cherries into whipped cream; spread over crumbs. Sprinkle with remaining crumbs; garnish with cherries. Chill for 12 hours. Yield: 9-12 servings.

Mrs. Charles E. Roesser
St. Pairs, O.

BUTTERSCOTCH-NUT TORTE

1 ½ c. sugar
1 tsp. baking powder
6 eggs, separated
1 tsp. almond flavoring
2 tsp. vanilla flavoring
2 c. graham cracker crumbs
1 c. chopped nuts

Combine sugar and baking powder; add to beaten egg yolks. Add flavorings. Beat egg whites until stiff. Fold in egg yolk mixture. Fold in crumbs and nuts. Pour into greased 9 x 12-inch pan. Bake at 350 degrees for 30 to 35 minutes.

SAUCE:
1 c. brown sugar
¼ c. water
1 tsp. flour
1 egg, beaten
¼ c. butter
¼ c. orange juice
1 tsp. vanilla flavoring

Combine all ingredients except vanilla. Cook over low heat until thickened. Add vanilla; cool. Spread over cake; top with whipped cream. Yield: 9-12 servings.

Mrs. Ted Damm
Valders, Wisc.

CHERRY TORTE

¼ c. butter
⅓ c. sugar
20 graham crackers, crushed
Pinch of salt
1 10 ½-oz. pkg. miniature marshmallows
1 pt. heavy cream, whipped
1 can cherry pie filling

(Continued on next page)

Melt butter; stir in sugar while butter is hot. Add cracker crumbs. Press into 9 x 12-inch pan. Add salt and marshmallows to whipped cream. Pour mixture into crust. Top with pie filling. Refrigerate overnight. Yield: 18 servings.

Mrs. Vivian Kramer
Abbotsford, Wisc.

FRENCH CHERRY TORTE

1 c. flour
½ c. sugar
1 c. graham cracker crumbs
¾ c. nuts
⅔ c. butter or margarine

Combine all ingredients; mix well. Put in 13 x 9-inch pan. Bake at 375 degrees for 10 to 15 minutes. Let cool.

FILLING:
1 lge. pkg. dessert topping mix
1 c. cold milk
1 8-oz. pkg. cream cheese
1 c. powdered sugar
1 tsp. vanilla flavoring
1 can cherry pie filling

Beat dessert topping mix with milk. Beat cheese, powdered sugar and vanilla. Fold cheese mixture into dessert topping mixture. Pour filling into cool crust; let stand. Spread cherry pie filling on top. Yield: 15 servings.

Patricia Kreifels
Springfield, Nebr.

FROZEN CHERRY OR PINEAPPLE TORTE

1 No. 2 can sour pitted cherries or crushed
    pineapple
2 ½ c. sugar
3 eggs, separated
2 tsp. lemon juice
1 c. heavy cream, whipped
⅔ c. rolled graham cracker crumbs

Drain juice from cherries or pineapple; pour juice into top of double boiler. Add 1/2 cup sugar and slightly beaten egg yolks. Cook until slightly thickened. Remove from heat; add fruit and lemon juice. Cook until thick but not firm. Fold in whipped cream. Beat eggs with remaining 2 cups sugar; fold into mixture. Pour into 9 x 12-inch cake pan coated with cracker crumbs. Sprinkle a few crumbs on top of cake. Freeze until firm.

Mrs. John Morse
Belleview, Fla.

CHEESE TORTE

2 c. graham cracker crumbs
2 c. sugar
1 tsp. cinnamon
½ c. melted butter
4 eggs
Dash of salt
Juice and rind of ½ lemon
1 c. cream
1 ½ lb. cottage cheese
¼ c. flour

Combine crumbs, 1 cup sugar, cinnamon and butter. Reserve 3/4 cup mixture for topping. Press remainder into oiled spring form pan. Beat eggs and remaining 1 cup sugar until light; add salt, lemon juice and rind. Add cream, cheese and flour; mix well. Strain through sieve; pour over crumbs. Sprinkle with remaining crumbs. Bake at 325 degrees for 1 hour. Yield: 25 servings.

Eileen Heiden
Milwaukee, Wisc.

CREAM CHEESE TORTE

CRUST:
20 graham crackers, crushed
½ c. melted butter
½ c. (scant) sugar

Combine all ingredients; press into 9 x 12-inch pan. Chill for 15 minutes.

FILLING:
1 3-oz. pkg. cream cheese, softened
1 c. heavy cream, whipped
1 pkg. lemon gelatin
2 ¼ c. hot water
2 ¼ c. cold water
1 sm. can crushed pineapple, drained
1 lge. pkg. cherry gelatin

Fold cream cheese into whipped cream; whip until soft and creamy. Dissolve lemon gelatin in 3/4 cup hot water; add 3/4 cup cold water. Refrigerate until partially set. Add pineapple and cheese mixture. Pour over crumbs. Chill until partially set. Dissolve cherry gelatin in 1 1/2 cups hot water and 1 1/2 cups cold water; pour over cheese mixture. Chill. Yield: 12-15 servings.

Mrs. Bernice Simon
St. Cloud, Wisc.

CHOCOLATE-NUT TORTE

5 eggs
2 ½ c. sugar
1 tbsp. butter
1 ¼ c. milk, scalded
2 ½ c. sifted cake flour

(Continued on next page)

⅛ tsp. salt
2 ½ tsp. baking powder
1 tsp. vanilla flavoring

Beat eggs until light. Gradually add 1 cup sugar; continue beating. Add remaining 1 1/2 cups sugar; beat until light colored and fluffy. Combine butter and hot milk; gradually add to egg mixture. Add sifted dry ingredients and vanilla; mix well. Pour into two waxed paper-lined 9-inch layer pans. Bake at 350 degrees for 30 minutes. Cool; cut layers into halves.

TORTE FROSTING:
2 ⅓ c. milk or cream
½ c. sugar
½ c. flour
½ c. cocoa
1 c. butter or margarine
1 c. powdered sugar
2 tsp. vanilla flavoring
1 ½ c. chopped English walnuts

Heat 2 cups milk in double boiler. Combine sugar, flour, cocoa and remaining 1/3 cup cold milk. Add to hot milk; cook over hot water for 20 minutes or until thickened, stirring constantly. Remove from heat; cover and cool to room temperature. Thoroughly cream butter and powdered sugar. Add to cooled mixture. Add vanilla; beat until smooth. Spread between layers and on top and sides of torte. Decorate with chopped walnuts.

Beaulah Mullins
Pound, Va.

CHOCOLATE TORTE

1 tsp. vanilla flavoring
5 eggs, separated
2 4-oz. bars German's chocolate, melted
12 ladyfingers, halved

Add vanilla and well beaten egg yolks to chocolate; beat well. Fold into stiffly beaten egg whites. Pour small amount of chocolate mixture into waxed paper-lined mold. Line sides with ladyfingers. Add a layer of ladyfingers; add remaining filling. Top with ladyfingers. Refrigerate for 12 to 24 hours. Unmold on serving dish. Serve with whipped cream and grated chocolate. Yield: 8 servings.

Mrs. Dorothy M. Springer
Bradley, S.D.

COCONUT-CRUNCH TORTE

1 c. graham cracker crumbs
½ c. chopped shredded coconut
½ c. chopped walnuts
4 egg whites
¼ tsp. salt

1 tsp. vanilla flavoring
1 c. sugar
Ice cream

Combine crumbs, coconut and nuts. Beat egg whites with salt and vanilla until foamy. Gradually add sugar; continue beating until egg whites form stiff peaks. Fold crumb mixture into egg white mixture. Spread in well greased 9-inch pie plate or 10 x 6-inch baking pan. Bake in 350 degree oven for 30 minutes. Cool. Cut into wedges; top with scoops of ice cream. Yield: 6-8 servings.

Mrs. Cecil Hutchings
Dallas, Tex.

CRUMB TORTE

6 eggs, beaten
½ lb. sugar
½ lb. dates, chopped
5 tbsp. white bread crumbs
½ lb. walnuts, chopped
1 tsp. baking powder
½ pt. heavy cream, whipped

Combine all ingredients except cream. Pour into two pans. Bake at 350 degrees for 20 minutes. Cool; crumble cake. Fold in whipped cream. Yield: 10 servings.

Mrs. Hilda Abraham
Freemont, Wisc.

CRUMBLED TORTE

1 c. sugar
2 eggs, separated
1 c. chopped dates
1 c. chopped nuts
1 tbsp. flour
1 tsp. baking powder
Whipped cream
Cherries

Gradually add sugar to beaten egg yolks. Add dates, nuts, flour and baking powder. Stir until moistened. Fold in stiffly beaten egg whites. Spread in greased 9-inch square pan. Bake at 425 degrees for 15 minutes. Cool. Crumble into dessert glasses. Top with whipped cream and a cherry. Yield: 4-6 servings.

Mrs. Tommy Crossland
Seymour, Iowa

CRUNCH TORTE

3 egg whites
½ tsp. cream of tartar
½ tsp. vanilla flavoring
17 salted crackers
1 c. sugar
½ c. chopped pecans or walnuts

(Continued on next page)

Beat egg whites until fairly frothy. Add cream of tartar; beat until stiff. Beat in vanilla. Crush crackers with rolling pin, but do not roll them too fine. Mix crumbs with sugar; fold into egg whites. Add nuts. Pour into a greased 9-inch pie pan. Bake at 325 degrees for 30 minutes. Yield: 6-8 servings.

Mrs. Robley Earl West
Parris Island, S.C.

DANISH TORTE

CRUST:
⅔ pkg. Holland Rusk
⅛ lb. butter or margarine
1 tsp. cinnamon
½ c. sugar or 1 tbsp. liquid sugar substitute
Pinch of salt

Mix all ingredients; press in pie tin, reserving 1 cup for topping.

FILLING:
2 c. milk
1 tbsp. cornstarch
5 tbsp. sugar or 2 ½ tsp. liquid sugar substitute
3 eggs, separated
1 tsp. vanilla flavoring

Combine milk, c o r n s t a r c h, 2 tablespoons sugar, 3 egg yolks and vanilla. Cook in double boiler until thick. Cool; place on crumb crust. Beat egg whites; gradually add remaining 3 tablespoons sugar. Pile on filling. Cover with remaining 1 cup crumbs. Bake at 350 degrees for 30 minutes or until brown.

Mrs. W. A. Gesner
Jensen Beach, Fla.

FRUIT COCKTAIL TORTE

1 ½ c. flour
1 c. sugar
1 tsp. soda
1 tsp. salt
1 No. 303 can fruit cocktail
1 egg
1 c. brown sugar
½ c. finely chopped nuts

Sift all dry ingredients. Drain fruit cocktail, reserving liquid. Add liquid and egg to dry ingredients; mix well. Add fruit cocktail; mix well. Place in greased 9 x 9-inch pan. Mix brown sugar and nuts; spread over batter. Bake at 350 degrees for 50 to 55 minutes.

Serve with whipped cream. Yield: 9 servings.

Martha Beritela
Rochester, N.Y.

LEMON SCHAUM TORTE

MERINGUE:
4 egg whites
¼ tsp. cream of tartar
1 c. sugar

Beat egg whites until frothy; add cream of tartar. Continue beating until whites are stiff. Slowly add sugar; continue beating until stiff and shiny peaks form. Pour into a large greased and floured pie tin. Bake at 275 degrees for 20 minutes; increase heat to 300 degrees. Bake for 40 minutes longer. Remove immediately from pie tin, using a spatula to loosen edges. Cool. NOTE: If meringue is not removed immediately, it will become spongy and soggy and will stick to pan.

FILLING:
1 c. sugar
4 egg yolks, well beaten
Juice of 2 or 3 lemons
1 tsp. grated lemon rind (opt.)
Sweetened whipped cream

Gradually beat sugar into yolks. Add lemon juice and rind. Cook in double boiler, stirring constantly, until thick. Cool; spread on meringue. Top with sweetened whipped cream; chill.

Mrs. Gordon L. Fears
Orlando, Fla.

LEMON TORTE

1 pkg. lemon gelatin
1 c. hot water
8 eggs, separated
2 c. sugar
Juice of 1 lemon
Grated rind of ½ lemon
20 graham crackers, crushed
2 tbsp. melted butter

Dissolve gelatin in hot water; cool. Beat egg yolks and 1 cup sugar until light. Add lemon juice and rind. Cook in double boiler until thickened; cool. Add gelatin. Beat egg whites; gradually beat in remaining 1 cup sugar. Beat until stiff. Fold in lemon mixture. Combine crumbs and butter. Line a pan; reserve small amount. Pour in lemon mixture. Sprinkle with remaining crumbs; top with whipped cream. Yield: 12 servings.

Mrs. F. L. Schipper
Rock Rapids, Iowa

HOLIDAY TORTE

4 eggs, separated
¾ c. sugar
¾ c. sifted cake flour
¾ tsp. baking powder
¼ tsp. salt
1 tsp. vanilla flavoring
¼ tsp. green food coloring
½ gal. strawberry ice cream
1 tbsp. red colored decorating sugar
1 ½ c. heavy cream, whipped

Beat egg yolks until light. Gradually add sugar; continue beating until thick and fluffy. Gradually add sifted dry ingredients; beat until smooth. Beat egg whites until stiff but not dry. Fold lightly into batter. Fold in vanilla and green food coloring. Pour into a waxed paper-lined 15 1/2 x 10 x 1-inch jelly roll pan. Bake at 350 degrees for 15 to 17 minutes. Cool for 5 minutes. Loosen sides; turn onto waxed paper sprinkled with sifted confectioners sugar. Peel off waxed paper; trim crust. Cool. Cut into three equal portions crosswise. Spread ice cream between layers; freeze. Fold red decorating sugar into whipped cream. Frost sides and top of torte with whipped cream. Freeze. Yield: 10-12 servings.

Photograph for this recipe above.

MARSHMALLOW TORTE

30 marshmallow
½ c. milk
1 ½ to 2 c. heavy cream, whipped or dessert
    topping mix
1 tsp. vanilla flavoring
1 pkg. caramel pieces or ½ box bittersweet
    chocolate
2 tbsp. brown sugar
⅓ c. melted butter
20 graham crackers, crushed
Chopped nuts

Dissolve marshmallows in milk in double boiler. Cool; add whipped cream. Whip until stiff; add vanilla and caramel pieces. Combine brown sugar, butter and cracker crumbs. Press three-fourths of the crumbs into 13 x 9 x 2-inch pan. Pour in marshmallow mixture. Sprinkle with remaining crumbs and nuts. Yield: 12-15 servings.

Mrs. Frank Kline
Loyal, Wisc.

MOCHA TORTE

5 eggs
1 c. sugar
1 c. sifted cake flour
1 tsp. baking powder

(Continued on next page)

TORTES

Pinch of salt
¾ c. grated chocolate
¼ tsp. vanilla flavoring

Beat eggs and sugar for 10 minutes. Sift flour with baking powder and salt; fold into egg mixture. Gently fold in chocolate; add vanilla. Pour into three greased and floured pans. Bake at 350 degrees for 15 to 20 minutes. Put custard between layers; frost with a chocolate icing. Yield: 20 servings.

Mrs. Bert Allen
Port Washington, Wisc.

ADA'S ORANGE-CREAM TORTE

TORTE:
6 egg yolks
1 c. sifted sugar
1 c. sifted flour
3 tbsp. orange juice
½ tsp. lemon flavoring
4 egg whites
½ tsp. salt
1 tsp. baking powder

Beat egg yolks until thick. Gradually beat in 1/2 cup sugar. Fold in flour alternately with juice and flavoring. Beat egg whites with salt and baking powder until stiff. Gradually add remaining 1/2 cup sugar. Fold into egg yolk mixture. Pour into two ungreased 9-inch layer cake pans. Bake at 325 degrees for 35 minutes. Cool.

FILLING:
¾ c. sugar
2 tbsp. grated orange rind
¾ c. orange juice
2 egg whites
½ pt. heavy cream, whipped

Combine sugar, orange rind and juice. Beat egg whites until stiff; fold into orange mixture. Spread each cake layer with filling mixture. Refrigerate overnight. Spread one layer with sweetened whipped cream. Top with second layer; frost top and sides with whipped cream. Sprinkle with additional shredded orange rind. Serve cold. Yield: 8-10 servings.

Mrs. A. D. Chambers
Sidney, Nebr.

PINEAPPLE BLITZ TORTE

½ c. butter or margarine
½ c. sugar
4 egg yolks, well beaten
⅔ c. cake flour
¼ tsp. salt
1 tsp. baking powder
¼ c. milk

Thoroughly cream butter and sugar. Add egg yolks; beat well. Add sifted dry ingredients alternately with the milk. Pour into two waxed paper-lined 8-inch round layer cake pans. Bake at 350 degrees for 15 minutes.

MERINGUE TOPPING:
4 egg whites
¾ c. sugar
1 tsp. vanilla flavoring
¾ c. chopped walnuts

Beat egg whites to stiff foam. Add a tablespoon of sugar at a time, beating until moist peaks form. Add vanilla. Spread meringue on top of layers immediately upon removing from oven. Sprinkle chopped nuts over meringue. Return cake to oven. Bake at 350 degrees for 15 minutes longer. Cool; remove from pans.

PINEAPPLE FILLING:
1 ½ tbsp. confectioners sugar
1 c. crushed pineapple, well drained
¼ tsp. vanilla flavoring
1 c. heavy cream, whipped

Fold sugar, pineapple and vanilla into whipped cream. Place a layer of cake, meringue-side down, on cake plate. Spread with filling. Place remaining cake layer, meringue-side up, on top of filling. Yield: 8 servings.

Mrs. Albert L. Buehler
Philadelphia, Pa.

RHUBARB TORTE

CRUST:
2 c. flour
½ tsp. salt
4 tbsp. sugar
1 c. soft butter

Combine all ingredients; pat into an 8 x 12-inch pan. Bake at 325 degrees for 25 minutes.

FILLING:
2 ¾ c. sugar
4 tbsp. flour
1 c. cream
6 eggs, separated
4 ½ c. cut rhubarb

Combine 2 1/2 cups sugar, flour, cream, egg yolks and rhubarb in top of double boiler; cook until thick and clear. Beat egg whites until stiff, gradually adding remaining 1/4 cup sugar. Pour filling into crust; top with meringue. Brown under broiler; cool. Cut into squares. Yield: 12-15 servings.

Mrs. Walter W. Johnson
Frankfort, S.D.

Pies and Pastries

RECIPE FOR ORANGE MERINGUE PIE ON PAGE 196

Pies Are Probably . . .

. . . the favorite dessert of most Americans. And anyone who can make a tender, flaky pie crust has something to boast about. For no matter if the filling is delicious, if the crust is tough and chewy, the entire pie is ruined.

Perfect pastry is tender, flaky, delicate and evenly browned. It is crumbly, but when broken shows even layers of flat flakes piled one above another with air spaces in between.

Pastry . . .

. . . can be used as the base for a main dish—such as a meat pie or turnovers, or for a dessert pie. The right proportion of shortening and flour is very important in making tender, good pastry. Use at least ⅓ cup of shortening for each cup of sifted flour. Measure ingredients—don't guess—when you want a good pie crust.

BASIC PASTRY RECIPE:
(Will make pastry for one 9-inch pie)

1 cup sifted all-purpose flour
½ teaspoon salt
⅓ cup shortening
3 tablespoons cold water

Be sure ingredients are chilled. A cold, solid fat and ice water are absolutely necessary.

1. Sift the measured flour and salt together. Cut in the shortening with a pastry blender or two knives until the mixture is the size of small peas. Sprinkle water, a tablespoon at a time, over the mixture while tossing quickly with a fork, until the particles stick together. Usually no definite amount of water can be specified since this varies with the dryness of the flour and the amount of shortening used. Usually 2 to 4 tablespoons of water are required for 1 cup of flour.

2. Form pastry into a smooth ball. Wrap dough in waxed paper and chill in the refrigerator. Sprinkle flour lightly on the board and rolling pin and rub into the wood. A coarse linen kitchen towel or canvas cloth to cover the board and a "stocking" for the rolling pin will help in rolling the dough and prevent sticking without using too much flour.

Lightly roll the pastry into a circle 1-inch larger than the pie plate. Lift loosely into the pie plate. Pat out air. Fold edges under and crimp.

3. Prick the entire crust throughly before baking. This prevents bubbles and excess shrinkage. Bake in a 450° F. oven for about 12 minutes or until golden brown. Cool and fill.

PASTRY TIPS

IF THIS HAPPENS	IT MAY BE CAUSED BY THIS	TRY THIS
DRY DOUGH HARD TO WORK WITH	1. Incomplete mixing	1. Don't worry about overmixing. Final mixing or shaping of dough may be done with the hands.
	2. Not enough water	2. Use level measures of water.
TOUGH PASTRY	1. Not enough shortening or too much flour	1. Use at least ⅛ cup of shortening for each cup of sifted all-purpose flour. Use very little flour on board for rolling.
SHRINKING OR BUCKLING OF PASTRY	1. Pastry stretched during fitting into pie pan	1. Use large enough recipe to fit pan without stretching. Don't stretch dough when fitting to pie plate.
	2. Pastry shell not adequately pricked on sides and bottom before baking	2. Prick pastry generously over bottom and sides of pie plate.

Pastry for one single 8-inch crust will make:
      Six or seven 4-inch tart shells
      Topping for a deep dish pie
      Four to six 4-inch turnovers

Pastry for one double 8-inch crust will make:
      Eight or nine 4-inch tart shells
      Two single 8-inch crusts
      Latticed pie
      Ten or twelve 4-inch turnovers

APPLE-WALNUT COBBLER

1 ½ c. sugar
½ tsp. cinnamon
¾ c. coarsely chopped English walnuts
4 c. thinly sliced pared tart apples
1 c. sifted flour
1 tsp. baking powder
¼ tsp. salt
1 egg, well beaten
½ c. evaporated milk
⅓ c. butter, melted

Mix 1/2 cup sugar with cinnamon and 1/2 cup walnuts. Place apples in a greased 8 1/4 x 1 3/4-inch round baking dish. Sprinkle with cinnamon mixture. Sift remaining 1 cup sugar with dry ingredients. Combine egg, milk and butter. Add dry ingredients all at once; mix until smooth. Pour over apples; sprinkle with remaining 1/4 cup walnuts. Bake at 325 degrees for 55 minutes or until done. Spoon warm cobbler onto dessert plates; serve topped with cinnamon, whipped cream or ice cream. Yield: 8 servings.

Mrs. Maude Stypa
Cape Charles AS, Va.

APRICOT COBBLER

½ c. butter
1 c. sifted flour
1 ½ c. sugar
1 ½ tsp. baking powder
¾ c. milk
1 can apricots

Melt butter in baking dish. Combine flour, 3/4 cup sugar, baking powder and milk. Pour batter over melted butter. Place apricots over batter. Do not stir. Sprinkle remaining 3/4 cup sugar over mixture. Bake at 350 degrees for 45 minutes.

Hazel Williams
Cameron, Tex.

CHERRY COBBLER

1 No. 2 can red sour cherries
1 ½ c. sugar
¼ c. water
1 stick margarine
1 tbsp. baking powder
½ tsp. salt
1 c. flour
1 c. milk

Heat cherries with 3/4 cup sugar and water until mixture boils. Cream margarine and remaining 3/4 cup sugar in a cobbler pan. Sift all dry ingredients; add alternately with milk to creamed mixture. Pour cherries into center of batter; do not stir. Bake at 350 degrees for 45 minutes. Serve warm. Yield: 6-8 servings.

Mrs. H. L. Houston, Jr.
Lewisville, Tex.

PEACH COBBLER

1 stick butter
1 c. sugar
¾ c. flour
2 tsp. baking powder
Pinch of salt
¾ c. milk
1 can sliced peaches

Melt butter in deep baking dish. Combine sugar, flour, baking powder, salt and milk. Pour over butter; do not stir. Put peaches on top of batter; do not stir. Bake at 350 degrees for 1 hour.

Mrs. W. F. Givens
Waterloo, S.C.

RAISIN-APPLE COBBLER

3 apples, peeled and cored
½ c. raisins
Sugar
3 tbsp. butter
1 egg
1 c. flour
1 tsp. baking powder
¼ c. milk
½ tsp. vanilla flavoring

Slice apples; put in a buttered baking dish. Add raisins and 1/3 cup sugar. Dot with 1 tablespoon butter. Beat egg until light; add 1/2 cup sugar. Mix thoroughly. Sift flour and baking powder; add to mixture alternately with milk. Beat until smooth; add remaining 2 tablespoons melted butter and vanilla. Pour over fruit. Bake at 350 degrees for 35 minutes. Yield: 8 servings.

Mrs. Claude Grainger
Centerview, Mo.

QUICK FRUIT COBBLER

¾ stick butter
1 c. flour
1 tsp. baking powder
½ tsp. salt
1 c. milk
Fruit

Melt butter in a deep 1 1/2-quart casserole. Mix flour, baking powder, salt and milk. Pour into pan with butter; spoon fruit on top. Cook at 350 degrees for 45 to 60 minutes. Yield: 6 servings.

Mrs. Martin J. Burke
Denver, Colo.

ANGEL PIE

4 ½ tbsp. cornstarch
¾ c. plus 3 tbsp. sugar
1 ½ c. boiling water
½ tsp. (scant) salt
3 egg whites
1 ½ tsp. vanilla flavoring

(Continued on next page)

1 graham cracker pie shell
½ c. heavy cream, whipped
Graham cracker crumbs

Mix cornstarch and 3/4 cup sugar in double boiler; add water. Cook until clear. Add salt to egg whites; beat until stiff. Add remaining 3 tablespoons sugar and vanilla. Pour hot mixture over egg whites, beating continuously. Cool slightly; fill pastry shell. Cover with whipped cream; sprinkle a few crumbs over top. Yield: 6 servings.

Mrs. Archie Neely
Franklin, Pa.

BUTTERSCOTCH PIE

2 c. brown sugar
4 tbsp. butter
4 eggs, separated
6 tbsp. flour
2 c. milk
1 baked pie shell
4 tbsp. sugar

Mix brown sugar and butter; bring to a boil. Beat egg yolks slightly. Make a paste of flour and milk; stir into egg yolks. Add to butter mixture; cook until thick, stirring constantly. Pour into pie shell. Beat egg whites; add sugar. Pile on top of pie. Bake at 325 degrees for 20 to 25 minutes or until lightly browned. Yield: 6 servings.

Mrs. T. E. Van Sant, Sr.
Piedmont, Ala.

CHOCOLATE-ALMOND PIE

3 milk chocolate-almond bars
12 marshmallows
½ c. milk
1 c. heavy cream, whipped
1 graham cracker pie crust, chilled
Slivered chocolate
Slivered almonds

Melt chocolate and marshmallows in milk; cool. Add whipped cream to cooled mixture. Pour into pie crust. Garnish with slivered chocolate and almonds.

Mrs. Dale Madsen
Arlington, S.D.

CHOCOLATE-MERINGUE PIE

3 squares unsweetened chocolate
2 ½ c. milk
1 c. sugar
3 tbsp. flour
½ tsp. salt
2 egg yolks, slightly beaten
2 tbsp. butter
1 tsp. vanilla flavoring
1 9-in. pie shell

Add chocolate to milk; heat in double boiler. When chocolate is melted, beat with rotary egg beater until blended. Combine sugar, flour and salt; add gradually to chocolate mixture. Cook until thick, stirring constantly; continue cooking for 10 minutes, stirring. Add egg yolks gradually, stirring vigorously. Cook for 2 minutes longer. Add butter and vanilla; cool. Pour into a 9-inch pie shell.

MERINGUE:
2 egg whites
4 tbsp. sugar

Beat egg whites until foamy. Add sugar, 1 tablespoon at a time. Top pie. Bake at 350 degrees for 15 minutes.

Mrs. Charles Samuel Mason
Virginia Beach, Va.

EASY CHOCOLATE PIE

½ c. milk
2 ½ c. miniature marshmallows
5 chocolate-almond candy bars, shaved
1 c. whipped cream
1 baked 8 or 9-in. pie shell

Melt milk and marshmallows in double boiler. Add shaved chocolate bars. Cool; fold in whipped cream. Pour into baked pie shell. Yield: 8 servings.

Mrs. Myrna Smith
Des Moines, Iowa

SUPREME MARSHMALLOW PIE

30 marshmallows
½ c. milk
½ pt. heavy cream, whipped
1 ½ squares bitter chocolate
1 9-in. graham cracker crust

Heat marshmallows and milk over low heat until marshmallows dissolve. Cool to room temperature. Fold in whipped cream. Grate 1 square chocolate into marshmallow mixture. Pour into crust. Shave remaining chocolate; sprinkle pie with chocolate curls. NOTE: Best if made a day before. Yield: 8 servings.

Mrs. D. F. Ancona
Lathrop, Calif.

VINEGAR PIE

1 c. plus 2 tbsp. sugar
2 eggs, separated
¼ tsp. salt
2 tbsp. butter or margarine
3 tbsp. flour
1 c. cold water
4 tbsp. vinegar
1 baked pie shell
Lemon juice
Meringue

(Continued on next page)

Mix 1 cup sugar, egg yolks, salt, butter with flour dissolved in small amount of water. Add remaining water and vinegar. Cook over hot water for 25 minutes. Pour into pie shell. Beat egg whites until stiff; add remaining 2 tablespoons sugar and small amount of lemon juice. Spread meringue over pie. Brown at 350 degrees.

Mrs. Maribel Lee
White Mills, Ky.

CANDY PIE

½ pkg. pie crust mix
½ c. sugar
3 eggs, beaten
1 c. light corn syrup
1 tsp. vanilla flavoring
¼ tsp. salt
½ c. smooth peanut butter
½ c. semi-sweet chocolate pieces
¼ c. flaked coconut

Make one 9-inch pastry shell according to package directions. Gradually beat sugar into eggs. Mix in remaining ingredients except chocolate pieces and coconut in order given, blending thoroughly. Pour into pastry shell. Bake at 300 degrees for 45 minutes. Place chocolate pieces in circle in center of hot pie; sprinkle remaining chocolate pieces around edge of pie. Fill remainder of top with coconut. Yield: 6 servings.

Esther Sprinkle
Young America, Ind.

CHESS PIE

1 qt. milk
¼ lb. American cheese, shredded
1 ½ c. egg yolks
½ tsp. vanilla flavoring
½ c. cake flour
6 tbsp. cocoa
4 c. sugar
½ tsp. salt
½ lb. minus 4 tbsp. margarine
2 unbaked pie shells

Heat milk; add cheese. Heat until cheese is melted. Beat all remaining ingredients. Combine milk and egg mixtures. Pour into pie shells. Bake at 300 degrees for 1 hour. Yield: Two 9-inch pies.

Mrs. Lucious Tyce
Spencer, Okla.

OLD-STYLE EGG CUSTARD PIE

3 eggs, well beaten
½ c. sugar
¼ tsp. salt
¼ tsp. nutmeg
2 c. evaporated milk
1 unbaked pie shell

Combine all ingredients, beating well after each addition. Pour into pie shell. Bake at 425 degrees for 10 minutes. Reduce heat to 350 degrees; bake for 25 to 30 minutes or until custard is set. Yield: 6 servings.

Mrs. Cloe Culwell
Hector, Ark.

FUDGE PIE

1 ¾ squares baking chocolate
¼ lb. butter or margarine
2 eggs, beaten
1 c. sugar
¼ c. flour
1 tsp. vanilla flavoring

Melt chocolate and butter in top of double boiler. Beat eggs; add sugar, flour, chocolate mixture and vanilla. Pour into a buttered pie pan. Bake at 350 degrees for 25 minutes. Serve with ice cream or whipped cream. Yield: 6 servings.

Mrs. W. V. Millman
Moline, Ill.

HEAVENLY PIE

1 c. sugar
2 egg whites
Pinch of cream of tartar
Pinch of salt
3 bananas, mashed
½ c. chopped nuts
1 unbaked pie shell

Beat sugar, egg whites, cream of tartar and salt until it stands in peaks. Fold in bananas; add nuts. Pour into an unbaked pie shell. Bake at 350 degrees for 25 to 30 minutes. Let cool. Serve topped with whipped cream; sprinkle with chopped nuts. Yield: 6 servings.

Mrs. August V. Fischer
Pease AFB, N.H.

MACAROON PIE

4 egg whites
1 c. sugar
30 Ritz crackers, crushed
1 tsp. baking powder
1 tsp. vanilla flavoring
Pinch of salt
½ c. chopped nuts

Beat egg whites until fairly stiff; add sugar gradually. Mix all remaining ingredients; fold into egg mixture. Spread into a greased 8-inch pie pan. Bake at 350 degrees for 15 minutes. Reduce heat to 325 degrees; bake for 15 minutes longer. Serve cold, topped with whipped cream or ice cream. Yield: 6 servings.

Mrs. John Canan
Pompano Beach, Fla.

OATMEAL PIE

½ c. sugar
½ c. brown sugar
½ c. butter or margarine, melted
¾ c. quick cooking oats
1 c. milk
¾ c. light corn syrup
2 eggs
1 tsp. vanilla flavoring
1 c. coconut
1 unbaked pie shell
Chopped nuts

Thoroughly mix all ingredients except pie shell and nuts. Pour into pie shell; sprinkle with nuts. Bake at 425 degrees for 10 minutes. Reduce heat to 375 degrees; bake for 25 minutes longer. Do not overbake. Yield: 6-8 servings.

Mrs. C. B. Burns
Amanda, O.

BEST-EVER OSGOOD PIE

2 eggs, separated
1 c. sugar
1 tsp. cinnamon
½ tsp. nutmeg
½ c. pecan halves
½ c. raisins
1 tbsp. butter, melted
1 tbsp. vinegar
Unbaked pie shell
Unsweetened whipped cream

Beat egg yolks until light. Gradually add sugar which has been sifted with cinnamon and nutmeg. Add pecans, raisins and butter. Beat egg whites until stiff, but not dry; fold into sugar mixture with vinegar. Pour into pie shell. Bake at 400 degrees for 10 minutes. Reduce heat to 350 degrees; bake for 25 minutes longer. Cover with whipped cream when cool; chill. Yield: 1 pie.

Mrs. R. C. Lasswell
Bronte, Tex.

PENNSYLVANIA DUTCH SHOO-FLY PIE

4 c. flour
½ tsp. baking powder
½ tsp. salt
Shortening
1 c. boiling water
1 c. molasses
1 tsp. soda
1 c. sugar

Blend 3 cups flour, baking powder and salt; cut in 1/3 cup shortening. Add 3 to 4 tablespoons water to make a soft dough. Roll out to fit pie plate. Pour boiling water over molasses and soda; stir briskly. Pour mixture into pie shell. Combine remaining 1 cup flour, sugar and 1/2 cup shortening; rub together to make crumbs. Sprinkle over pie. Bake at 400

degrees for 10 minutes. Reduce heat to 325 degrees; bake for 30 minutes. Yield: 6 servings.

Mrs. John S. Simmons
Annville, Pa.

SHOO-FLY PIE

¾ c. flour
½ c. brown sugar
⅛ tsp. nutmeg
⅛ tsp. ginger
⅛ tsp. cloves
½ tsp. cinnamon
¼ tsp. salt
2 tbsp. shortening
½ c. molasses
1 egg yolk, well beaten
½ tbsp. soda
¾ c. boiling water
1 unbaked 9-in. pastry

Combine flour, sugar, spices and salt; work in shortening until crumbly. Combine molasses, egg yolk and soda dissolved in boiling water. Alternate layers of crumb mixture and egg mixture in pastry shell; top with crumb mixture. Bake at 450 degrees until crust edges start to brown. Reduce heat to 350 degrees; bake for 20 minutes or until firm. Yield: 8 servings.

Mrs. W. D. Pratt
Texarkana, Tex.

SOUTHERN BUTTERMILK PIE

½ c. margarine or butter
1 ¼ c. sugar
⅛ tsp. salt
1 tsp. vanilla flavoring
3 lge. or 4 sm. eggs, separated
1 pt. buttermilk
5 tbsp. flour
1 9-in. pie crust, unbaked

Let margarine reach room temperature; cream with sugar, salt and vanilla. Add yolks; mix well. Add milk and flour; beat until blended. Fold in stiffly beaten, but not dry, egg whites. Pour into unbaked pie shell. Bake at 375 degrees for 15 minutes. Reduce heat to 300 degrees; bake for 25 minutes longer. Cool quickly away from draft. Yield: 6-8 servings.

Mrs. Dean L. Heitman
O'Fallon, Ill.

TRANSPARENT PIE

CRUST:
2 c. flour
¾ tsp. salt
⅔ c. shortening
⅓ c. ice water

Combine flour and salt; cut in shortening. Add water. Roll out to fit a 9-inch pie pan.

(Continued on next page)

FILLING:
2 tbsp. butter, softened
1 c. sugar
3 egg yolks, beaten
5 tbsp. cream
¼ tsp. nutmeg or 1 tsp. vanilla flavoring

Cream butter and sugar; add eggs and cream. Stir in flavoring. Pour into pie shell. Bake at 350 degrees for 30 minutes or until firm and light brown.

MERINGUE:
3 egg whites
6 tbsp. sugar
¼ tsp. cream of tartar
1 tsp. vanilla flavoring

Beat egg whites until stiff; beat in all remaining ingredients. Spoon onto pie. Bake at 325 degrees for 15 to 20 minutes or until brown. Yield: 6 servings.

Mrs. Eli Roberts
Sharpsburg, Ky.

BROWN BAG APPLE PIE

4 or 5 lge. tart apples
½ c. plus 2 tbsp. flour
1 c. sugar
½ tsp. nutmeg
2 tbsp. lemon juice
1 9-in. uncooked pie crust
1 stick margarine

Pare apples; cut into eighths. Work into 2 tablespoons flour, 1/2 cup sugar, nutmeg and lemon juice. Arrange in 9-inch pastry-lined pie pan. Sprinkle with mixture of 1/2 cup sugar, 1/2 cup flour and margarine. Place pie in brown paper bag, tucking the open end under. Bake at 425 degrees for 10 minutes. Reduce heat to 350 degrees; bake for 40 minutes. Yield: 6 servings.

Mrs. R. S. Siefken
Williams AFB, Ariz.

MOCK APPLE PIE

1 ½ c. water
1 ¼ c. sugar
1 tsp. cinnamon
1 ½ tsp. cream of tartar
2 tbsp. butter
18 crackers
1 recipe double pastry

Heat water; add sugar, cinnamon, cream of tartar and butter, stirring well. Break crackers coarsely into mixture. Pour mixture into a 9-inch pastry-lined pie pan; adjust top crust. Bake at 400 degrees for 50 minutes.

Mrs. Olan D. Crowl
Morse, Tex.

AVOCADO PIE

1 c. (heaping) avocado pulp
1 c. sugar
1 can evaporated milk
2 eggs
½ tsp. salt
½ tsp. cloves
½ tsp. ginger
1 tsp. cinnamon
2 tbsp. (heaping) cornstarch

Mix all ingredients. Pour into a 9-inch pie dish. Bake at 450 degrees for 20 minutes. Reduce heat to 350 degrees; bake until knife inserted in center comes out clean.

Grace Stevens
Perrine, Fla.

BANANA-CREAM PIE

3 tbsp. flour
3 tbsp. cornstarch
¾ c. sugar
¼ tsp. salt
2 ½ c. milk
3 eggs
1 tsp. vanilla flavoring
1 9-in. pie shell, baked
2 or 3 bananas, sliced
1 c. heavy cream
¼ c. powdered sugar

Sift all dry ingredients. Beat 1 cup milk with eggs; add dry ingredients. Mix well. Blend in remaining milk. Cook over low heat, stirring constantly, until mixture comes to a boil. Remove from heat; add vanilla. Cool. Pour a layer of custard into pie shell; add a layer of bananas. Repeat layers, ending with custard. Whip cream with powdered sugar; spread on pie. Garnish with bananas; chill. Yield: 6 servings.

Patricia Truscott
Adams, Nebr.

BANANA ICE BOX PIE

1 cracker crumb pie crust
3 med. bananas
1 8-oz. pkg. cream cheese, softened
1 ⅓ c. sweetened condensed milk
⅓ c. lemon juice
1 tsp. vanilla flavoring

Line pie crust with 2 sliced bananas. Whip cream cheese until light and fluffy; gradually beat in milk. Add lemon juice and vanilla; blend well. Pour over bananas. Chill for 2 hours or until firm. Slice remaining banana; arrange on pie. Yield: 6 servings.

Mrs. Betty Sue Tiner
McCrory, Ark.

BLACKBERRY PIE WITH SWEET DOUGH PIE CRUST

CRUST:
½ c. sugar
¼ c. cooking oil
1 egg
¼ c. milk
2 c. sifted flour
1 ½ tsp. baking powder

Mix sugar, oil and egg well; add milk, flour and baking powder. Roll one-half of dough to form one pie crust. If dough breaks up when rolling, knead more flour into dough. Put in pie plate. Roll remaining dough.

FILLING:
1 qt. fresh or frozen blackberries, cleaned
1 c. sugar
1 tsp. vanilla flavoring
1 tsp. butter

Combine berries, sugar, vanilla and butter. Pour over crust; top with remaining crust. Bake at 350 degrees for 1 hour or until crust is golden brown. Yield: 8 servings.

Mrs. Donald Campbell
Oberlin, La.

BLUEBERRY-CREAM CHEESE PIE

24 graham crackers, finely crushed
½ c. brown sugar
½ c. melted butter
1 8-oz. pkg. cream cheese, melted
½ c. sugar
2 eggs, well beaten
1 can blueberry filling

Combine cracker crumbs, brown sugar and butter; press mixture into a 9 x 13-inch pan. Combine cream cheese, sugar and eggs thoroughly; pour over crust. Bake at 350 degrees for 20 minutes. Cool; add blueberry filling. Serve topped with whipped cream or ice cream. Yield: 6 servings.

Mrs. Velda Felton
Indianola, Iowa

BOYSENBERRY PIE

¾ c. sugar
3 tbsp. flour
2 c. frozen or canned boysenberries, thawed and drained
1 double crust pie shell
2 tbsp. butter

Combine sugar, flour and boysenberries. Pour into pastry-lined pan. Dot with butter. Place top crust over filling. Fold edge under bottom crust, pressing to seal; flute edge. Bake at 450 degrees for 10 minutes. Reduce heat to 375 degrees; bake for 20 to 25 minutes. Yield: 1 pie.

Jacquelyn F. Dalton
Oak Harbor, Wash.

CANTALOUPE PIE

1 sm. cantaloupe
1 c. plus 3 tbsp. sugar
2 tbsp. cornstarch or flour
4 tbsp. cold water
3 eggs, separated
¼ tsp. salt
Lemon flavoring

Scoop out pulp of cantaloupe; place in top of double boiler with sugar. Cook until sugar is dissolved. Mix flour and cold water; add to cantaloupe. When thick, add beaten egg yolks; cook for a few minutes. Add salt; cool. Pour into a 9-inch pastry shell. Beat egg whites until stiff; add lemon flavoring and remaining 3 tablespoons sugar. Top with meringue; brown. Yield: 6 servings.

Gwen Nesbit
Shreveport, La.

CRANBERRY CHIFFON PIE

1 envelope unflavored gelatin
½ c. cold water
1 can cranberry sauce
⅓ tsp. salt
1 tsp. grated lemon rind
2 tsp. lemon juice
2 egg whites
2 tsp. sugar
1 8-in. baked pastry shell
Whipped cream (opt.)

Soak gelatin in cold water for 2 minutes; dissolve over boiling water. Add to cranberry sauce; add salt, lemon rind and lemon juice. Chill until mixture begins to set. Beat egg whites until stiff; beat in sugar. Fold into cranberry mixture. Pour filling into pastry shell; chill until firm. Top with whipped cream. Yield: 6 servings.

Mrs. Harry E. Knuffman
Baltimore, Md.

CRANBERRY-RAISIN PIE

2 ½ c. cranberries
½ c. raisins
1 c. sugar
2 tbsp. flour
1 recipe double crust
½ c. hot water

Combine cranberries, raisins, sugar and flour; pour into an unbaked pie crust. Crisscross strips of dough over top. Pour water over top and through holes. Bake at 375 degrees for 45 to 60 minutes. Yield: 6 servings.

Eva K. Sheen
Union Grove, Wisc.

WILD ELDERBERRY PIE

2 c. well-ripened elderberries
1 c. sugar
2 tbsp. instant tapioca
1 tsp. grated lemon rind or 1 tsp. lemon
  flavoring
¼ tsp. salt
1 c. thick sour cream
1 recipe double pastry crust

Wash, dry and remove stems from berries. Combine berries, sugar, tapioca, lemon rind and salt. Fold berries into sour cream. Pour into pastry-lined dish; cover with top crust. Cut air vents in top crust. Bake in a preheated 425 degree oven for 10 minutes. Lower temperature to 350 degrees; continue baking until fruit bubbles through air vents and crust is a delicate brown. Serve warm. Yield: 6-8 servings.

Alice Latson
Howell, Mich.

ENGLISH PIE

1 c. sugar
½ c. butter
2 eggs, separated
1 c. raisins
1 c. chopped pecans
1 tsp. vanilla flavoring
1 pastry shell

Combine sugar and butter; add egg yolks, raisins and pecans. Beat egg whites until stiff; fold into filling. Fold in vanilla. Pour into pastry shell. Bake at 350 degrees until done. Yield: 6 servings.

Annie Abbott
Pleasant Hill, Miss.

CONCORD GRAPE PIE

2 lb. Concord grapes
¾ c. sugar
1 ½ tbsp. flour
1 double crust pie shell

Wash grapes under warm water; slip skins off, placing pulp in one bowl and skins in another. Cook pulp in covered saucepan until soft and seed begin to separate from pulp. Place colander in pulp; pour in pulp using a wooden spoon to stir until all pulp is pressed through. Use 2 cups of this mixture. Add sugar and flour; mix well. Pour mixture into pastry-lined pan; cover with lattice top. Bake at 500 degrees for 10 minutes. Reduce heat to 350 degrees; bake for 25 to 30 minutes longer. Yield: 6 servings.

Doris Richardson
Milwaukie, Oreg.

SPICED GRAPE PIE

4 eggs, separated
1 c. sugar

1 c. coconut
1 c. milk
5 tbsp. butter, melted
2 tbsp. flour
1 tsp. vanilla flavoring
Spiced grapes
1 9-in. unbaked pie shell

Blend egg yolks with all ingredients except grapes and pie shell. Spread a thin layer of grapes in pie shell; cover with mixture. Bake at 350 degrees for 15 minutes. Reduce heat to 325 degrees; bake until done. Beat egg whites until stiff; spread over pie. Brown lightly. Yield: 6 servings.

Mrs. Harold Jarman
Morven, N.C.

HUCKLEBERRY COBBLER

½ stick margarine or butter
1 ¼ c. sugar
1 pt. huckleberries or blueberries
¼ tsp. lemon juice
⅛ tsp. nutmeg
¾ c. milk
¾ c. flour

Melt margarine; add 1/2 cup sugar, huckleberries, lemon juice and nutmeg. Mix lightly; pour into greased casserole. Mix remaining 3/4 cup sugar, milk and flour; pour over casserole. Bake at 350 degrees for 45 minutes. Yield: 4-6 servings.

Annie C. Rhodes
Kenansville, N.C.

FAMOUS LEMON PIE

3 eggs, separated
3 tbsp. water
Juice of 1 lemon
Grated rind of 1 lemon
1 c. sugar
1 baked pie shell

Thoroughly mix egg yolks, water, lemon juice, rind and 1/2 cup sugar. Cook until thickened. Beat egg whites until stiff; gradually add remaining 1/2 cup sugar, beating constantly. Fold hot mixture into egg whites. Pour mixture into crust. Bake at 425 to 450 degrees until brown. Yield: 6 servings.

Mrs. George M. Koch
Dayton, Wash.

ICE BOX LEMON PIE

16 marshmallows
Juice of 1 ½ lemons
3 eggs, separated
½ pt. heavy cream, whipped
Vanilla wafer crumbs

(Continued on next page)

Combine marshmallows, lemon juice and egg yolks in double boiler; cook until melted, stirring constantly. Cool. Fold in stiffly beaten egg whites; fold in whipped cream. Line pie pan with vanilla wafer crumbs. Pour mixture on top. Sprinkle more crumbs over mixture. Refrigerate for 4 to 6 hours. Serve cold. Yield: 6 servings.

Mrs. I. M. Kovar
Columbus, O.

LEMON-MERINGUE PIE

1 c. sugar
1 ¼ c. water
1 tbsp. butter
4 tbsp. cornstarch
3 tbsp. cold water
6 tbsp. lemon juice
1 tsp. grated lemon rind
3 egg yolks
2 tbsp. milk
1 8-in. baked pie shell

Combine sugar, water and butter; heat until sugar dissolves. Add cornstarch blended with cold water. Cook slowly for 8 minutes or until clear. Add lemon juice and rind. Cook for 2 minutes. Add egg yolks beaten with milk. Bring to boiling point. Pour into an 8-inch pie shell; cool.

MERINGUE:
3 egg whites
6 tbsp. sugar
1 tbsp. lemon juice or flavoring

Beat egg whites stiff but not dry. Add 2 tablespoons sugar; beat thoroughly. Continue until all sugar has been added. Beat in lemon juice. Pile on pie. Bake at 350 degrees for 15 minutes. Yield: 6 servings.

Mrs. Paul K. Yates
Ronceverte, W. Va.

LEMON-WALNUT PIE

1 c. sugar
2 tbsp. flour
¼ c. melted butter or margarine
3 eggs, separated
¼ c. lemon juice
1 c. milk
1 tsp. grated lemon rind
1 baked 9-in. pastry shell
½ c. walnut halves

Combine sugar, flour, butter, beaten egg yolks and lemon juice. Mix with electric mixer at medium speed until light and fluffy. Add milk; beat at low speed until blended. Fold in lemon rind and stiffly beaten egg whites. Pour mixture into pastry shell; arrange walnut halves in spoke-wheel pattern on top. Bake at 350 degrees for 35 minutes or until filling is set.

Cool pie on rack; refrigerate. Yield: 6-8 servings.

Mrs. James L. Knox
Akron, O.

MILE HIGH LEMON CHIFFON PIE

1 envelope unflavored gelatin
1 c. sugar
⅛ tsp. salt
5 eggs, separated
½ c. lemon juice
¼ c. water
2 tsp. grated lemon rind
1 9-in. baked pie shell

Mix gelatin, 1/2 cup sugar and salt thoroughly in top of double boiler. Beat egg yolks with juice and water; add to gelatin mixture. Cook over boiling water, stirring constantly, for 5 minutes or until gelatin is dissolved. Remove from heat; add rind. Chill, stirring occasionally, for 40 minutes or until mixture mounds slightly when dropped from a spoon. Beat egg whites until stiff; beat in remaining 1/2 cup sugar. Fold gelatin mixture into egg whites. Pour into baked shell. Chill until firm. Yield: 8 servings.

Mrs. Albert W. Newhall
Glenview, Ill.

OLD-FASHIONED LEMON-MERINGUE PIE

5 tbsp. flour
⅛ tsp. salt
¾ c. plus 4 tbsp. sugar
1 c. boiling water
Grated rind of 1 lemon
¼ c. lemon juice
2 eggs, separated
1 tsp. melted butter
1 baked pie shell

Mix flour, salt and 3/4 cup sugar; stir in small amount of hot water. Mix well; add remaining water. Cook over low heat, stirring constantly, until mixture thickens. Cover pan; cook slowly for 5 minutes, stirring occasionally. Add lemon rind and juice. Add small amount of thickened mixture to beaten egg yolks, stirring well. Add egg yolks to remaining thickened mixture. Cook for 1 minutes. Remove from heat; stir in butter. Cool slightly. Pour into pie shell. Beat egg whites until stiff; gradually add remaining sugar. Pile lightly on top of pie. Bake at 350 degrees for 15 minutes or until lightly browned. Yield: 6-7 servings.

Mary B. Hardy
Caliente, Nev.

KEY LIME PIE

4 eggs, separated
1 can sweetened condensed milk
½ c. lime juice
8 tbsp. sugar
Baked pastry or graham cracker crust

(Continued on next page)

183

Beat egg yolks; alternately add milk and lime juice, beating constantly. Beat egg whites until stiff; add sugar. Fold into mixture. Pour into pie shell; chill until ready to serve. Yield: 8-9 servings.

Mrs. Albert H. Gross
Islamorada, Fla.

MANGO PIE

4 or 5 ripe mangoes, sliced
1 10-in. unbaked pie shell
1 c. sugar
3 tbsp. cornstarch
⅛ tsp. salt
½ tsp. cinnamon
¼ tsp. nutmeg
1 egg, slightly beaten
1 c. heavy cream
1 ¼ tsp. vanilla flavoring
4 tsp. butter
½ c. coarsely chopped walnuts

Place sliced mangoes in pie shell. Mix sugar, cornstarch, salt and spices. Blend egg, cream and vanilla. Add sugar mixture gradually, mixing well. Pour over mangoes. Dot with butter; sprinkle with nuts. Bake at 450 degrees for 10 minutes. Reduce heat to 350 degrees; bake for 55 minutes longer. Serve warm or cool with ice cream. Yield: 6-8 servings.

Mrs. G. M. Reeves
Honolulu, Hawaii

ORANGE-BAVARIAN CREAM PIE

1 pkg. orange gelatin
1 c. hot water
½ c. sugar
¼ tsp. salt
1 tbsp. lemon juice
½ c. orange juice
1 c. heavy cream, whipped
1 or 2 11-oz. cans Mandarin oranges,
    drained
1 8-in. graham cracker crust, chilled

Dissolve gelatin in hot water; stir in sugar, salt and juices. Chill until thickened. Slowly fold into whipped cream. Add oranges. Pour into pie shell. Chill for 2 to 3 hours. Yield: 6-8 servings.

Mrs. Norman E. Muller
Middletown, Pa.

ORANGE-NUT PIE

1 c. dark syrup
4 tbsp. melted butter
4 tbsp. sugar
1 tbsp. orange juice
1 tbsp. grated orange rind
1 c. broken nuts
½ tsp. salt
3 eggs, slightly beaten
1 unbaked pie shell

Combine all ingredients except pie shell; mix thoroughly. Pour into pie shell. Bake at 450 degrees for 10 minutes. Reduce heat to 350 degrees and bake for 40 minutes. Yield: 6 servings.

Edna L. Flom
Wesley, Iowa

ORANGE PIE

1 ½ c. orange juice
1 ¼ c. sugar
2 tbsp. butter
3 eggs, separated
1 ½ tbsp. cornstarch
Pinch of salt
1 baked pie shell
Pinch of cream of tartar

Place orange juice and sugar in top of double boiler; heat to boiling. Add butter. Mix beaten egg yolks with cornstarch which has been blended with a small amount of water. Slowly pour hot juice over eggs and cornstarch. Add salt. Return to double boiler; cook until thick and clear. Pour into pie shell. Beat egg whites until stiff; add cream of tartar. Beat until peaks form. Cover pie with meringue. Bake at 350 degrees until golden brown. Yield: 8 servings.

Mrs. L. V. Minear
Jupiter, Fla.

FRESH PEACH PIE

8 to 10 ripe peach halves
1 9-in. unbaked pie shell
2 eggs
1 c. sugar
1 tbsp. melted butter
½ tsp. almond flavoring

Place peach halves, cavity-side up, in pie shell. Beat eggs with sugar, butter and flavoring; pour over peaches. Bake at 325 degrees for 25 minutes or until custard is set and peaches are tender. Yield: 6 servings.

Mrs. C. C. Ely
Hastings, Okla.

FRESH PEACH PIE

PASTRY:
1 ½ c. flour
1 tsp. salt
½ c. shortening
3 tbsp. water

Cut flour and salt into shortening; blend in water. Roll to make a 9-inch pie crust.

FILLING:
1 c. sugar
⅔ c. flour
¼ c. butter
4 or 5 peaches, sliced

184

(Continued on next page)

Mix sugar, flour and butter; sprinkle one-half of the mixture over bottom of crust. Place peaches over mixture; sprinkle with remaining mixture. Bake at 425 degrees until crust is golden brown. Reduce heat to 350 degrees; bake until peaches are tender. Serve with whipped cream. Yield: 8 servings.

Mrs. Vilas D. Balk
Alameda, Calif.

FRESH PEACH-PECAN PIE

¼ c. butter, softened
¼ c. sugar
2 tbsp. flour
½ c. light corn syrup
¼ tsp. salt
3 eggs
1 ½ c. diced fresh peaches
1 9-in. unbaked pie shell

Cream butter with sugar and flour. Stir in syrup and salt; mix well. Beat in eggs until just blended. Add peaches; pour into unbaked pie shell. Sprinkle with topping. Bake at 400 degrees for 35 minutes. Cool.

NUT-CRUMB TOPPING:

¼ c. flour
¼ c. brown sugar
2 tbsp. butter, softened
½ c. coarsely chopped pecans

Combine flour and brown sugar; work in butter until crumbly. Add pecans. Yield: 6 servings.

Esther Springman
Gordon, Nebr.

LUSCIOUS PEACHES 'N' CREAM PIE

1 No. 2 ½ can sliced peaches or halves
1 3-oz. pkg. lemon gelatin
½ c. cold water
1 pt. vanilla ice cream
⅛ tsp. almond flavoring
1 9-in. baked pie shell
1 c. heavy cream, whipped

Drain peaches; reserve syrup. Heat 1 cup peach syrup to boiling. Add gelatin; stir until dissolved. Add cold water. Cut ice cream into six pieces. Add to hot liquid; stir until melted. Add almond flavoring. Chill until mixture begins to thicken or mound. Reserve a few peach slices or halves for decorating. Fold in the remaining peaches. Pour mixture into baked pie shell. Chill for 4 hours or until firm. Cover pie almost to edge with whipped cream. Top with reserved peaches to form a blossom as decoration. Yield: 8 servings.

Mrs. Henry E. Davidson
Warren, Mich.

PEACH CHIFFON PIE

1 c. sugar
2 tbsp. cornstarch

1 ½ c. crushed canned peaches
½ c. orange juice
3 eggs, separated
2 baked pie shells
Nuts (opt.)

Mix 1/2 cup sugar and cornstarch. Add peaches and orange juice; cook until thick. Beat egg yolks; slowly add to cooked mixture, beating constantly. Remove from heat. Beat egg whites until stiff; add remaining 1/2 cup sugar. Fold into peach mixture. Place in baked pie crusts. Nuts may be sprinkled over top. NOTE: Pie keeps indefinitely in freezer. Yield: 2 pies.

Mrs. O. D. Noller
Mankato, Kans.

PEAR CRUMBLE PIE

6 med. pears, pared and cored
1 c. sugar
1 tsp. grated lemon rind
3 tbsp. lemon juice
1 9-in. unbaked pie shell
½ c. flour
½ tsp. ginger
½ tsp. cinnamon
¼ tsp. mace
⅓ c. butter
½ pt. heavy cream, whipped

Cut pears into strips. Mix with 1/2 cup sugar, lemon rind and juice. Arrange in pastry shell. Combine flour, 1/2 cup sugar and spices; cut in butter until crumbly. Sprinkle over pears. Bake at 400 degrees for 45 minutes or until done. Serve warm with whipped cream. Yield: 6 servings.

Clara Hunter
Highland Mills, N.Y.

CHILLED PINEAPPLE PIE

4 eggs, separated
¾ c. sugar
¼ tsp. salt
¼ c. crushed pineapple
1 tbsp. lemon juice
1 tsp. lemon rind
1 tbsp. lemon gelatin
½ c. boiling pineapple juice
¼ tsp. cream of tartar
1 baked pie shell
Whipped cream (opt.)

Beat egg yolks until thick; add 1/2 cup sugar, salt, pineapple, lemon juice and lemon rind. Cook in top of double boiler until thick; cool. Mix gelatin in hot pineapple juice; add to custard. Cool. Combine beaten egg whites, remaining 1/4 cup sugar and cream of tartar; fold into cooled mixture. Pile into baked pie shell. Top with pineapple. Chill for 1 hour. Top with whipped cream. Yield: 6 servings.

Mrs. Marjorie Moe
Milan, Minn.

PEAR-PINEAPPLE-CHEESE PIE

1 1-lb. 13-oz. can pear halves
1 1-lb. can pineapple chunks
¼ c. cornstarch
¼ c. sugar
⅛ tsp. salt
Dash of nutmeg
¼ tsp. vanilla flavoring
1 tbsp. butter
1 ½ c. shredded Cheddar cheese
Egg white

Drain and reserve pear and pineapple juices. Line a 9-inch plate with a pastry shell. Arrange pear halves, cut-side up, with narrow ends toward center in pie shell. Arrange pineapple chunks around pear halves; set aside. Combine 1/2 cup pear juice with 1/2 cup pineapple juice; set aside remaining juice for topping. Mix a small amount of combined pear and pineapple juice with cornstarch; add remaining juice. Cook until clear and thickened. Reduce heat; stir in sugar, salt, nutmeg, vanilla, butter and cheese. Spread cheese-fruit sauce over fruit. Roll out remaining pastry; cut into 3/8-inch strips. Make a lattice top on pie. Bake in preheated 450 degree oven for 12 minutes. Reduce heat to 375 degrees; bake for 35 minutes longer. Brush lattice top with egg white for last 10 minutes of baking to give a golden glaze.

SOUR CREAM TOPPING:

1 pt. sour cream
2 tbsp. combined pear and pineapple juice, reserved
2 tbsp. confectioners sugar

Blend sour cream, juice and sugar. Refrigerate topping until needed.

Photograph for this recipe above.

PINEAPPLE PIE

1 c. sugar
1 egg
1 tbsp. cornstarch
1 sm. can crushed pineapple
½ stick butter

Mix all ingredients; pour into an unbaked pie shell. Bake at 350 degrees for 25 minutes. Yield: 6 servings.

Nettie Burnett
McCamey, Tex.

PINEAPPLE-COCONUT PIE

3 eggs
1 c. sugar
¼ c. drained crushed pineapple
½ c. light corn syrup
¼ c. melted butter

(Continued on next page)

Juice of ½ lemon
¼ c. shredded coconut
1 9-in. pie shell, unbaked

Beat eggs slightly. Add all remaining ingredients except pie shell; blend well. Pour into pie shell. Bake at 350 degrees for 45 to 50 minutes. Yield: 6-8 servings.

Lura Hester
Brownwood, Tex.

SOUR CREAM-RAISIN PIE

1 c. raisins
1 c. brown sugar
1 c. sweet or sour cream
2 egg yolks
2 tbsp. water
3 tbsp. flour
1 tsp. vanilla flavoring
1 baked pie shell
Meringue

Heat raisins, sugar and cream to boiling. Beat egg yolks with water; add flour. Mix until smooth. Gradually add to raisin mixture; cook until mixture comes to a boil, stirring constantly. Remove from heat; add vanilla. Cool. Pour into pie shell; cover with meringue. Brown at 350 degrees. Yield: 6 servings.

Mrs. Elsie Stagers
Douds, Iowa

SOUR CREAM-RAISIN PIE

2 tbsp. cornstarch
¾ c. sugar
¼ tsp. salt
1 tsp. cinnamon
½ tsp. nutmeg
¼ tsp. cloves
2 egg yolks, well beaten
1 c. sour cream
1 c. raisins
1 ½ tsp. lemon juice
½ c. chopped walnuts or pecans
1 9-in. pie shell, baked

Mix cornstarch, sugar, salt and spices in top of double boiler. Add egg yolks; mix well. Add sour cream, raisins and lemon juice; cook over hot water until thick. Cool slightly. Add nuts; blend well. Pour into pie shell.

MERINGUE:
2 egg whites
¼ tsp. cream of tartar
4 tsp. sugar

Beat egg whites until frothy; add cream of tartar. Beat until stiff enough to hold a peak. Gradually add sugar; continue beating until mixture becomes stiff and glossy. Top pie

with meringue. Bake at 300 degrees for 15 to 20 minutes. Yield: 8 servings.

Beatrice Alford
Yarba Linda, Calif.

SWISS SOUR CREAM-RAISIN PIE

¾ c. raisins
1 9-in. pie crust
1 c. sour cream
1 ½ c. sugar
4 egg yolks, beaten

Wash raisins; drain well. Put in pie crust. Beat sour cream until smooth; add sugar gradually, beating after each addition. Add egg yolks. Beat for 30 seconds longer. Pour over raisins in pie crust. Bake at 375 degrees for 10 minutes. Reduce heat to 350 degrees; bake for 30 minutes. Yield: 5 servings.

Mrs. Paul A. Dodge
Potosi, Wisc.

PASTEL PARTY PIE

2 pkg. frozen raspberries or strawberries, sliced
1 lge. pkg. gelatin
1 qt. vanilla ice cream
2 baked pie shells

Drain fruit; add enough water to juice to measure 2 1/2 cups. Heat to boiling. Dissolve gelatin in hot liquid. Add ice cream by spoonfuls, stirring until melted. Chill until thickened; fold in berries. Pour into pie shells; chill until firm. Yield: 2 pies.

Audrey Pantle
Clearfield, Utah

RASPBERRY ANGEL PIE

Sugar
⅓ c. plus 2 tbsp. water
2 egg whites, stiffly beaten
2 tsp. gelatin
⅛ tsp. salt
1 tbsp. lemon juice
½ pt. heavy cream, whipped
1 9-in. baked pie shell
1 c. sieved fresh or frozen raspberries
1 tbsp. cornstarch

Boil 1/2 cup sugar and 1/3 cup water to soft ball stage or 235 degrees. Pour syrup in fine stream over stiffly beaten egg whites, beating constantly. Soften gelatin in 2 tablespoons cold water; dissolve over hot water. Combine with egg white mixture. Beat for 1 minute. Add salt and lemon juice; cool. Fold whipped cream into egg white mixture. Pour into cooled pie shell; chill until set. For topping,

(Continued on next page)

press raspberries through sieve; add enough water to make 1 cup. Gradually blend with 1/3 cup sugar and cornstarch. Stir constantly over medium heat until thick and clear. Cook over low heat for 10 minutes. Cool; spread over top of pie. Yield: 6-8 servings.

Mrs. C. S. Campbell
Anniston, Ala.

RASPBERRY PIE

1 can sweetened condensed milk
¼ c. lemon juice
1 c. raspberries
1 baked 9-in. pie shell
½ c. heavy cream, whipped
2 tbsp. sugar

Blend condensed milk and lemon juice. Stir until mixture thickens. Fold in raspberries, being careful not to break them up too much. Pour into pie shell; chill. Cover with whipped cream sweetened with sugar. NOTE: Sliced strawberries, sliced peaches or apricots or 2 medium bananas cut into small pieces may be substituted for raspberries. If using frozen fruit, drain well before using.

Mrs. W. J. Mellinger
Fortuna AFS, Mont.

DIFFERENT RHUBARB PIE

2 c. flour
1 c. brown sugar
⅔ c. margarine or shortening
1 ½ c. sugar
2 tbsp. (heaping) cornstarch
1 c. cold water
Cinnamon
1 ½ qt. chopped rhubarb

Combine flour, brown sugar and margarine; mix until crumbly. Reserve 1 cup of the mixture. Spread remaining mixture in baking dish. Combine sugar, cornstarch, water and cinnamon. Boil until thickened, stirring constantly. Stir in rhubarb. Spread over flour mixture in dish. Sprinkle reserved flour mixture over top. Bake at 375 degrees for 30 minutes or until done.

Julia K. Miller
Luray, Va.

FRESH RHUBARB PIE

3 c. chopped rhubarb
2 c. sugar
2 tbsp. corn syrup
2 tbsp. tapioca
1 recipe double pastry

Combine 2 cups rhubarb, 1 cup sugar and syrup; bring to a boil. Remove from heat;

stir in mixture of remaining 1 cup rhubarb, 1 cup sugar and tapioca. Mix well; pour into a 9-inch pie shell. Crisscross top with strips of dough. Bake at 425 degrees for 30 minutes. Yield: 6 servings.

Mrs. Lavera McConnell
Independence, Kans.

RHUBARB CUSTARD PIE

1 recipe for double crust
3 eggs
2 ⅔ tbsp. milk
4 tbsp. flour
1 c. sugar
1 c. brown sugar
¼ tsp. salt
¾ tsp. nutmeg
1 tbsp. lemon juice
½ tsp. grated lemon rind
4 c. chopped pink rhubarb
1 tbsp. butter

Line pie pan with pastry. Beat eggs slightly; add milk. Mix in flour, sugars, salt and nutmeg. Add juice, rind and rhubarb. Pour into pie pan; dot with butter. Cover with lattice top. Bake at 400 degrees for 50 to 60 minutes or until browned. Serve slightly warm. Yield: One 9-inch pie.

Mrs. Robert A. Wilson
Ketchikan, Alaska

RHUBARB CUSTARD PIE

Pastry
2 to 2 ½ c. fresh rhubarb, sliced ¼-in. thick
3 eggs
1 ½ c. sugar
1 tbsp. flour
Juice of ½ lemon
Nutmeg to taste

Line a large pie plate with pastry. Add rhubarb. Beat eggs well; add sugar mixed with flour. Add lemon juice and nutmeg; mix well. Pour over rhubarb. Bake at 425 degrees until lightly browned. Reduce heat to 375 degrees; bake until rhubarb is tender. Yield: 6-8 servings.

Vivian Bloomgarden
Florence, Oreg.

STRAWBERRY CHIFFON PIE

3 eggs, separated
¾ c. sugar
¼ tsp. salt
2 tsp. lemon juice
1 c. crushed strawberries
2 tbsp. hot strawberry juice
4 tbsp. strawberry gelatin
⅓ c. heavy cream, whipped
¼ tsp. cream of tartar
1 baked pie crust or graham cracker crust

(Continued on next page)

Combine egg yolks, one-half of the sugar, salt, lemon juice and strawberries. Cook over low heat, stirring, until mixture boils. Remove from heat. Add strawberry juice and gelatin. Chill until partially set; beat with rotary beater. Fold in whipped cream. Beat egg whites with cream of tartar and remaining sugar until stiff. Fold into mixture. Chill in pie shell until set. Yield: 6 servings.

Jetret S. Petersen
Kenai, Alaska

STRAWBERRY GLAZE PIE

1 ½ qt. fresh strawberries
1 9-in. pie shell, baked
½ c. water
1 c. sugar
3 tbsp. cornstarch
2 tbsp. butter
Red food coloring

Wash, drain and hull strawberries. Place 1 quart of berries in pastry shell. Crush remaining berries; combine with water, sugar and cornstarch in a saucepan. Boil for 2 minutes or until clear. Add butter and enough red coloring to give a bright red color. Spoon glaze over whole berries, making sure that all berries are covered. Cool; cover with whipped cream before serving. Yield: 8 servings.

Mrs. Henry Lustgarten
Wilmette, Ill.

STRAWBERRY-RHUBARB PIE

1 pt. sliced strawberries
2 c. chopped rhubarb
1 c. sugar
3 tbsp. cornstarch
½ tsp. salt
1 recipe double crust

Combine strawberries, rhubarb and sugar; let stand for 1 hour. Drain juice from fruit into cornstarch and salt in saucepan. Cook over medium heat, stirring constantly until mixture thickens. Remove from heat; carefully stir in strawberries and rhubarb. Pour cooled mixture into pie shell. Crisscross pastry strips over filling. Bake at 400 degrees for 30 minutes. Yield: 6 servings.

Mrs. Ann M. Loetz
Moran, Mich.

STRAWBERRY SHORTCAKE PIE

1 ½ c. powdered sugar
1 stick margarine or butter
2 eggs
1 baked pie crust
1 qt. strawberries
Whipped cream

Cream sugar and butter; add an egg at a time. Spread custard on crust; chill. Slice berries; spread over custard. Cover with whipped cream. Refrigerate for several hours before serving. NOTE: Fresh peaches may be used instead of strawberries. Yield: 6 servings.

Margret Mayo
Caruthersville, Mo.

COCONUT-CREAM PIE

¾ c. toasted coconut
4 eggs
2 tbsp. sugar
1 ¾ tsp. liquid sugar substitute
¼ tsp. salt
1 tsp. vanilla flavoring
2 ½ c. skim milk, scalded
Nutmeg

Press coconut against bottom and sides of 8-inch buttered pie plate. Beat eggs, sugar, sugar substitute, salt and vanilla; gradually add milk, stirring constantly to prevent curdling. Pour into prepared pie plate. Bake at 375 degrees for 35 minutes or until a knife inserted in the center comes out clean. Sprinkle with nutmeg. NOTE: Ninety calories per serving. Yield: 8 servings.

Mrs. Robert D. Klein
Kingsville, Tex.

COCONUT-CREAM PIE

2 eggs, separated
1 c. plus 2 to 3 tbsp. sugar
2 tbsp. flour
1 ½ c. milk
2 tsp. butter
1 tsp. vanilla flavoring
1 baked pastry shell
Coconut

Beat egg yolks. Add 1 cup sugar and flour; mix well. Add milk, a small amount at a time; stir well. Cook until thick in double boiler, adding butter. Remove from heat; add vanilla. Pour into pie crust. Beat egg whites until foamy. Add 2 to 3 tablespoons sugar; beat until stiff. Pile lightly on pie. Sprinkle with coconut. Brown at 400 degrees. NOTE: For chocolate pie, melt chocolate and add to mixture before adding milk. Yield: 6 servings.

Mrs. Vincent J. Wolf
Brooklyn, N.Y.

COCONUT CUSTARD PIE

2 eggs, beaten
1 c. milk
½ c. butter
1 tbsp. flour

(Continued on next page)

1 c. sugar
1 tsp. vanilla flavoring
1 c. coconut
1 unbaked pie shell

Combine eggs, milk and butter. Blend flour and sugar; add to milk mixture. Stir in vanilla and coconut; pour into pie shell. Bake at 400 degrees for 10 minutes. Reduce heat to 350 degrees; bake for 30 minutes. Yield: 6 servings.

Mrs. Ann Hill
Juniata, Nebr.

COCONUT PIE

½ c. butter, softened
2 c. sugar
3 ½ tbsp. flour
1 ½ c. milk
2 eggs
1 tsp. vanilla flavoring
1 can coconut
2 unbaked pie shells

Cream butter, sugar and flour. Add milk, eggs, flavoring and coconut; blend thoroughly. Pour into two pastries. Bake at 350 degrees for 30 minutes. Yield: 12 servings.

Myrtle O. Roach
Green Bay, Va.

FRENCH COCONUT PIE

CRUST:
1 c. flour
½ tsp. salt
⅓ c. shortening
2 ½ tbsp. ice water

Sift flour and salt; cut in shortening until particles are the size of small peas. Sprinkle ice water over mixture, stirring with fork. Form into a ball; roll out into a circle 1 1/2-inches larger than pie pan. Fit into pan. Fold edge to form rim; flute.

FILLING:
3 eggs, beaten
1 ½ c. sugar
1 can flaked coconut
1 tbsp. vinegar
1 tsp. vanilla flavoring
1 stick butter, melted

Combine all ingredients; mix thoroughly. Put in baked crust. Bake at 350 degrees for 1 hour. Yield: 6 servings.

Mrs. C. H. Tatom
Norfolk Naval Sta., Va.

HOLIDAY NUT PIE

1 tbsp. (heaping) flour
¾ c. sugar
¼ tsp. allspice
¼ tsp. cinnamon
2 egg yolks, beaten

¼ c. milk
¾ c. pecans
½ c. raisins
2 tbsp. melted butter
1 baked pie shell
Meringue

Mix flour, sugar, allspice and cinnamon. Add egg yolks and milk; blend well. Stir in nuts and raisins. Add butter; cook over medium heat until mixture thickens, stirring constantly. Pour into pie shell. Top with meringue. Bake at 325 degrees for 12 to 15 minutes. Yield: 6 servings.

Marilyn Parsons
Alice, Tex.

PEANUT BRITTLE PIE

1 lb. peanut brittle, finely ground
1 lb. marshmallows, chopped
1 pt. heavy cream, whipped
1 graham cracker crumb crust
Maraschino cherries

Fold peanut brittle and marshmallows into whipped cream. Pour into pie shell. Garnish with cherries. Chill until ready to serve. Yield: 6 servings.

LaVeta Lyons
Hopkins, Mo.

PEANUT BUTTER PIE IN GRAHAM CRACKER CRUST

CRUST:
1 ¼ c. crushed graham crackers
1 tbsp. molasses
¼ c. butter or margarine, softened
1 tbsp. sugar

Combine graham crackers, molasses, butter and sugar; mix well. Press into greased 9-inch pie pan. Bake at 375 degrees for 10 minutes. Cool thoroughly.

FILLING:
1 ¼ c. evaporated milk
¼ c. water
½ c. sugar
¼ c. cornstarch
¼ tsp. salt
2 egg yolks, slightly beaten
3 tbsp. (heaping) peanut butter
1 tbsp. butter
1 tsp. vanilla flavoring

Combine evaporated milk and water; scald in top of double boiler. Combine sugar, cornstarch and salt; stir into milk. Cook over boiling water for about 15 minutes or until thick, stirring occasionally. Add a small amount of mixture gradually to egg yolks. Return to double boiler; cook for 2 minutes. Remove from heat; add peanut butter and butter. Beat until smooth. Cool; add vanilla. Blend well. Pour into pie shell. Top with graham cracker crumbs or meringue. Yield: 6 servings.

Mrs. Norma Rowe
New Tazewell, Tenn.

PEANUT BUTTER-CANDY PIE

3 eggs
½ c. sugar
1 c. light corn syrup
1 tsp. vanilla flavoring
¼ tsp. salt
½ c. smooth peanut butter
1 9-in. unbaked pie shell
½ c. semi-sweet chocolate pieces
¼ c. flaked coconut

Beat eggs; gradually beat in sugar, mixing well. Mix in syrup, vanilla, salt and peanut butter, blending thoroughly. Pour into pie shell. Bake at 300 degrees for 40 to 45 minutes. While pie is still hot, put a circle of chocolate pieces in center of pie; sprinkle remaining chocolate pieces around outside edge. Fill in remainder of top with coconut. Cool to serve.

Photograph for this recipe above.

COCONUT-PECAN PIE

2 tbsp. butter
1 c. brown sugar
¾ c. light or dark corn syrup
3 eggs, well beaten
1 tsp. vanilla flavoring
¼ tsp. salt
1 c. coconut
1 c. pecans
1 pie shell

Cream butter; add sugar and syrup. Add eggs, vanilla and salt; blend well. Add coconut and pecans. Pour into pie shell. Bake at 250 degrees for 1 hour and 30 minutes.

Mrs. Bertice Roberts
Swainsboro, Ga.

DELUXE PECAN PIE

3 eggs
1 c. dark corn syrup
1 c. sugar
2 tbsp. margarine, melted
1 tsp. vanilla flavoring
⅛ tsp. salt
1 c. pecans
1 9-in. pastry shell, unbaked

Beat eggs slightly. Mix in corn syrup, sugar, margarine, vanilla and salt. Mix in nuts last. Pour into unbaked shell. Bake in 400 degree oven for 15 minutes. Reduce oven temperature to 350 degrees and continue baking for 30 to 35 minutes. When pie is done filling should be slightly less set in center than around edge. Yield: 6-8 servings.

Photograph for this recipe on front cover.

OLD-FASHIONED PECAN PIE

¼ c. butter
1 ¼ c. sugar
½ c. corn syrup
3 eggs, beaten
1 c. pecan halves
1 unbaked pie crust

Combine butter, sugar and corn syrup; bring to a boil over medium heat. Remove from heat; add eggs slowly. Add pecans. Pour mixture into pie crust. Bake at 350 degrees for 30 minutes. Yield: 6 servings.

Mrs. A. W. Watkins
Roanoke, Va.

PECAN PIE

3 eggs, beaten
½ c. sugar
1 c. corn syrup
⅛ tsp. salt
1 tsp. vanilla flavoring
¼ c. butter or fat, melted
1 c. pecans
Unbaked pie pastry

Combine eggs, sugar, syrup, salt, vanilla and butter. Arrange pecans in pastry-lined pie pan; add mixture. Bake at 350 degrees for 50 to 60 minutes. Yield: 6 servings.

Mrs. Ross Guffey
Unionville, Mo.

PECAN PIE IMPERIAL

¼ c. pecans
1 10-in. pie shell
1 ¼ sticks butter or margarine
1 1-lb. box brown sugar
4 eggs
½ c. light cream
1 ½ tsp. vanilla flavoring

Distribute pecans evenly in pie shell. Cream butter and add sugar; blend well. Add an egg at a time, blending thoroughly. Add cream and vanilla; blend well. Pour into pie shell over pecans. Bake at 350 degrees for 1 hour. Cool thoroughly before cutting. Yield: 6 servings.

Bethel Leonard
Olustee, Okla.

SOUR CREAM-PECAN PIE

2 eggs, well beaten
1 c. sugar
1 c. sour cream
1 tsp. vanilla flavoring
Pinch of salt
1 pie shell, unbaked
Pecans
Raisins

Make custard of eggs, sugar, sour cream, vanilla and salt. Pour into unbaked pie shell in which pecans and raisins have been sprinkled. Bake at 350 degrees for 45 minutes or until lightly browned and firm.

Mrs. L. A. Eveland
Mendota, Ill.

SOUTHERN PECAN PIE

1 c. chopped pecans
1 9-in. pie crust
1 stick butter
1 c. sugar
Pinch of salt
¾ c. light corn syrup
3 eggs, slightly beaten
1 tsp. vanilla flavoring

Sprinkle nuts in pie shell. Cream butter, sugar and salt; add corn syrup, eggs and vanilla. Pour over nuts. Bake at 375 degrees for 40 to 45 minutes. Yield: 5 servings.

Mrs. Jess O. Park, Jr.
Fairmont, W. Va.

TEXAS PECAN PIE

2 eggs, beaten
1 c. dark corn syrup
⅛ tsp. salt
1 tsp. vanilla flavoring
1 c. sugar
2 tbsp. butter, melted
1 c. pecans
1 9-in. unbaked pastry shell

Mix all ingredients except pastry shell, adding pecans last. Pour into pastry shell. Bake at 400 degrees for 15 minutes. Reduce heat to 350 degrees; bake for 30 to 35 minutes longer or until inserted knife comes out clean. Yield: 6 servings.

Mrs. Dorothy Wilson
Lackland AFB, Tex.

V.I.P. PECAN PIE

1 c. corn syrup
3 eggs, slightly beaten
⅛ tsp. salt
1 tsp. vanilla flavoring
1 c. sugar
2 tbsp. margarine, melted
1 c. broken pecans
1 unbaked 9-in. pastry shell

Combine all ingredients for filling, adding pecans last. Pour into pastry shell. Bake at 400 degrees for 15 minutes. Reduce heat to 350 degrees; bake for 30 to 35 minutes.

Mrs. B. W. Caldwell
Newell, N.C.

WALNUT-CREAM PIE

1 ½ c. sugar
¾ c. flour
½ tsp. salt
4 c. milk
4 eggs, separated
4 tsp. butter or margarine
1 tsp. vanilla flavoring
¾ c. finely chopped walnuts
1 baked pie shell

Mix sugar, flour and salt; add milk. Cook over low heat until thickened, stirring constantly. Beat egg yolks; combine with cooked mixture. Cook for 2 to 3 minutes. Add butter, flavoring and 1/2 cup walnuts. Pour into pastry shell; spread with sweetened stiffly beaten egg whites. Sprinkle with remaining walnuts. Bake at 350 degrees until brown. Yield: 6 servings.

Mrs. Clem Scheulen
Rye, Colo.

ANGEL FOOD PIE

4 tbsp. cornstarch
¾ c. plus 3 tbsp. sugar
1 ½ c. boiling water
½ tsp. (scant) salt
3 egg whites
1 ½ tsp. vanilla flavoring
Baked pastry shell
½ c. heavy cream, whipped
1 square chocolate, grated

Mix cornstarch and 3/4 cup sugar; add boiling water, stirring constantly. Cook until clear. Add salt to egg whites; beat until stiff. Add 3 tablespoons sugar and vanilla; beat until creamy. Pour hot cornstarch syrup over egg whites, beating continuously. Cool slightly; fill shell. Refrigerate for 8 to 24 hours. Before serving, cover with whipped cream; sprinkle with grated chocolate. Yield: 6-8 servings.

Velma C. Ames
Canaan, Vt.

BAKED ALASKA PIE

CRUST:
1 ¼ c. flour
½ tsp. salt
½ c. shortening
2 to 3 tbsp. cold water

Sift flour and salt into bowl. Cut in shortening until crumbly. Sprinkle in water, 1 tablespoon at a time; mix lightly. Roll out; fit into 10-inch pie plate. Prick all over with fork. Bake at 425 degrees for 15 minutes. Cool.

FILLING:
1 10-oz. pkg. red raspberries
⅔ c. sugar
Dash of cream of tartar
½ gal. vanilla ice cream, softened

Press berries through a sieve into saucepan. Stir in sugar and cream of tartar. Heat quickly to boiling, stirring constantly. Cook for 3 minutes, stirring constantly. Pour into small bowl; chill. Spread ice cream in pie shell; drizzle with raspberry sauce. Repeat layers, mounding top. Freeze overnight.

MERINGUE:
4 egg whites
Dash of tartar
1 tsp. vanilla flavoring
½ c. sugar

Beat egg whites with cream of tartar and vanilla until foamy. Gradually sprinkle in sugar, beating until meringue stands in firm peaks. Spread over ice cream, working quickly. Freeze until ready to bake. Bake at 425 degrees for 5 minutes. Serve immediately. Yield: 8-12 servings.

Mrs. M. L. Smith
Valdosta, Ga.

BLACK BOTTOM PIE

25 to 30 gingersnaps, finely crushed
6 tbsp. margarine, melted
2 c. milk
4 eggs, separated
Sugar
3 tbsp. cornstarch
1 ½ squares unsweetened chocolate
1 envelope gelatin
4 tbsp. water
1 tsp. vanilla flavoring
1 c. whipped cream

Mix gingersnaps and margarine. Line 10 or 11-inch pie pan. Bake at 300 degrees for 10 minutes. Scald milk in double boiler; add egg yolks, beaten with 1/3 cup sugar and cornstarch. Cook until it coats spoon. Add 1 square chocolate to 1 cup custard, stirring until melted. Pour into pie shell; cool. Add gelatin softened in water to remaining custard. Cool mixture; fold in stiffly beaten egg whites that have been beaten with 1/2 cup sugar. Add vanilla. Pour over chocolate mixture in pie shell. Chill. Top with whipped cream. Cover top with remaining grated chocolate. Yield: 8 servings.

Mrs. Robert L. Henry
Little Rock, Ark.

BLACK BOTTOM PIE

1 c. sugar
1 tbsp. cornstarch
2 c. milk, scalded
4 eggs, separated
1 6-oz. pkg. semi-sweet chocolate pieces
1 tsp. vanilla flavoring
1 baked 9-in. pie shell
1 envelope unflavored gelatin
¼ c. cold water
1 c. heavy cream, whipped
Chocolate decorettes

(Continued on next page)

193

Combine 1/2 cup sugar and cornstarch. Slowly add scalded milk to beaten egg yolks; stir into sugar mixture. Cook over medium to low heat or in top of double boiler until custard coats a spoon. Add 1 cup custard mixture to the chocolate pieces; stir until chocolate melts. Add vanilla. Pour into cooled pie shell. Chill. Soften gelatin in cold water; add to remaining hot custard. Chill until slightly thick. Beat egg whites, adding remaining sugar gradually until mixture stands in stiff peaks; fold in custard mixture. Pour over chocolate layer; chill until set. Garnish with whipped cream and decorettes. Yield: 8-10 servings.

Mrs. Ernest H. Rickard
Charleston AFB, S.C.

BROKEN GLASS PIE

3 pkg. gelatin, different colors
Hot water
1 envelope unflavored gelatin
¼ c. cold water
1 c. hot pineapple juice
1 pt. heavy cream
½ c. sugar
1 tsp. vanilla flavoring
2 9-in. crumb or pastry crusts

Dissolve each flavored gelatin, separately, in 1 1/2 cups hot water; chill until firm. Soften unflavored gelatin in cold water; add to hot pineapple juice. Cool. Whip cream in large bowl; add sugar and vanilla. Cut colored gelatins into cubes; fold into whipped cream with pineapple mixture. Pour into pie crusts; chill until firm. Yield: 12 servings.

Mrs. E. W. Guy
Dover AFB, Del.

CHOCOLATE CHIFFON PIE

2 squares baking chocolate
½ c. black coffee
1 tbsp. unflavored gelatin
¼ c. cold water
3 eggs, separated
1 c. sugar
Pinch of salt
1 tsp. vanilla flavoring
1 baked 9-in. pie shell

Melt chocolate in coffee. Dissolve gelatin in water; add to chocolate mixture. Cool. Beat egg yolks with 1/2 cup sugar until thick and very light. Add salt and vanilla; blend in chocolate mixture. Beat egg whites until stiff; add remaining sugar gradually. Fold egg yolk-chocolate mixture into egg whites; pour into pie shell. Chill until firm. Gar-

nish with whipped cream and shaved chocolate. Yield: 8 servings.

Mrs. Margery S. Golin
Metuchen, N.J.

CHOCOLATE-PEPPERMINT-CREAM PIE

⅔ c. soft butter or margarine
1 c. sugar
2 oz. unsweetened chocolate
2 oz. semi-sweet chocolate
3 eggs, lightly beaten
¼ tsp. peppermint flavoring
1 9-in. graham cracker crust
1 c. heavy cream, whipped
2 tbsp. powdered sugar

Cream butter and sugar in mixer at high speed for 10 minutes or until very fluffy. Melt chocolate; cool until lukewarm. Add to butter mixture. Add eggs and flavoring. Pour into shell; chill for 8 hours or overnight. Top with cream whipped with powdered sugar. Yield: 8 servings.

Mrs. B. E. Carr
Fort Wainwright, Alaska

FRENCH MINT PIE

CRUST:
⅔ sm. box vanilla wafers, crushed
⅓ c. butter

Combine wafer crumbs and butter; press into pie plate to form crust. Bake at 350 degrees for 10 minutes.

FILLING:
¼ lb. butter
1 c. powdered sugar or ⅔ c. sugar
2 eggs, beaten
2 squares chocolate, melted
4 drops oil of peppermint

Cream butter and sugar. Add eggs; beat for 5 minutes or until fluffy. Add chocolate and peppermint. Pour into crust; chill for 24 hours. Top with whipped cream and grated chocolate. Yield: 6 servings.

Mrs. W. H. Ketchum
San Diego, Calif.

COFFEE-ICE CREAM PIE

2 1-oz. squares unsweetened chocolate
2 tbsp. butter
2 tbsp. hot milk
⅔ c. sifted powdered sugar
1 ½ c. shredded coconut
1 qt. ice cream, softened
2 tsp. instant coffee
¼ c. chopped nuts

(Continued on next page)

Melt chocolate and butter over hot water. Mix milk and sugar; add to chocolate mixture. Stir in coconut; mix well. Press into a buttered 9-inch pie pan; chill. Combine ice cream, coffee and nuts; mix well. Spread in pie shell; swirl top. Chill. Yield: 6 servings.

Mrs. Carl Portwood
East Alton, Ill.

EGGNOG PIE

1 c. vanilla wafer crumbs
¼ c. butter
½ c. finely chopped pecans
1 c. top milk
3 eggs, separated
½ c. sugar
¼ tsp. nutmeg
¼ tsp. salt
1 tbsp. unflavored gelatin
¼ c. cold water
1 tsp. vanilla flavoring

Combine crumbs, butter and pecans. Press into a pie plate; chill. Combine milk, beaten egg yolks, 1/4 cup sugar, nutmeg and salt. Heat in a double boiler until mixture coats a spoon. Dissolve gelatin in water; add to mixture. Cool; add vanilla. Beat egg whites until firm; add remaining 1/4 cup sugar. Beat until very stiff; fold into cooled mixture. Pour into crust; chill. Garnish with pecans. Yield: 6 servings.

Lizzie Cummings
Ely, Nev.

EGGNOG PIE

4 tbsp. cake flour
½ c. sugar
1 c. milk
4 egg yolks, beaten
1 tbsp. gelatin
¼ c. water
4 tbsp. butter
1 c. heavy cream, whipped
3 tbsp. rum
1 baked pie crust
Nutmeg

Mix flour and sugar; add milk. Cook in double boiler until thick. Add a small amount of custard to egg yolks; return to mixture. Cook for a few minutes longer, stirring constantly. Remove from heat; add gelatin softened in water and butter. Cool; fold in whipped cream. Add rum. Pour into baked pie crust; sprinkle with nutmeg. Chill. NOTE: This pie freezes well. Yield: 6-8 servings.

Mrs. J. A. Wallace, Jr.
Ft. Carson, Colo.

EGGNOG PIE

CRUST:
1 ½ c. quick cooking oats

⅓ c. melted butter or margarine
½ c. brown sugar

Toast oats in 350 degree oven for 15 minutes or until edges are curled. Remove from oven; add butter and sugar. Mix well. Line bottom of pie pan with mixture.

FILLING:
1 c. sugar
1 c. milk
¼ tsp. salt
3 eggs, separated
1 tbsp. unflavored gelatin
¼ c. cold water
¼ tsp. cream of tartar
½ c. heavy cream
2 tsp. rum flavoring

Combine 1/2 cup sugar, milk and salt; scald. Beat egg yolks; gradually stir in part of milk mixture at a time, stirring until mixture coats a spoon. Soak gelatin in cold water; dissolve in custard mixture. Cool until congealed. Add beaten egg whites to which cream of tartar has been added. Whip cream; add remaining 1/2 cup sugar and rum flavoring. Combine with congealed custard; beat with rotary beater until smooth. Pour into cooled crust; chill for 3 to 4 hours.

Jeanne Perisho
Paris, Ill.

ESKIMO PIE

24 graham crackers, crumbled
3 tbsp. melted butter
32 marshmallows
½ c. milk
1 lge. can fruit cocktail, drained
½ pt. heavy cream, whipped

Combine crumbs and butter; press one-half of the mixture into pie pan. Melt marshmallows in milk over hot water; cool. Stir in fruit cocktail and whipped cream. Mix well. Pour into pie shell; sprinkle with remaining crumbs. Refrigerate for 2 to 3 hours. Yield: 6 servings.

Mrs. Darlene Vander Bloemen
Crivitz, Wisc.

GALA GRASSHOPPER PIE

CHOCOLATE CRUMB SHELL:
1 ¼ c. chocolate wafer crumbs
¼ c. sugar
⅓ c. butter or margarine, melted

Mix chocolate crumbs, sugar and butter. Press against bottom and up sides of 9-inch pie plate. Bake at 400 degrees for 5 minutes. Cool.

FILLING:
1 envelope unflavored gelatin
½ c. sugar

(Continued on next page)

⅛ tsp. salt
½ c. cold water
3 eggs, separated
¼ c. green creme de menthe
¼ c. white creme de cacao
1 c. heavy cream, whipped

Combine gelatin, 1/4 cup sugar and salt in top of double boiler. Add water and an egg yolk at a time, stirring to blend well. Place over boiling water, stirring for 5 minutes or until gelatin is dissolved and mixture thickens slightly. Remove from water. Stir in creme de menthe and creme de cacao. Chill, stirring occasionally, until mixture is consistency of unbeaten egg white. Beat egg whites stiff but not dry. Gradually add remaining 1/4 cup sugar, beating until very stiff. Fold in gelatin mixture. Fold in whipped cream. Pour into shell. Chill for 2 hours or overnight. If desired, garnish with additional whipped cream and chocolate crumbs. Yield: One 9-inch pie.

Mrs. W. J. Burk
Ft. Chaffee, Ark.

GRASSHOPPER PIE

14 chocolate sandwich cookies, crushed
2 tbsp. melted butter or margarine
24 lge. marshmallows
½ c. milk
4 tbsp. creme de menthe
3 tbsp. creme de cacao
½ pt. heavy cream, whipped

Combine cookie crumbs and butter; line pie pan with mixture. Melt marshmallows in milk over low heat; cool slightly. Add creme de menthe, creme de cacao and whipped cream. Pour into crust; chill. Yield: 6-8 servings.

Mrs. Milda D. Dethlefs
Hastings, Nebr.

ORANGE-MERINGUE PIE

1¼ c. sugar
7 tbsp. cornstarch
½ tsp. salt
1½ c. warm water
3 egg yolks
1 tbsp. grated orange rind
½ c. orange juice
2 tbsp. butter
1 9-in. baked pie shell

Mix sugar, cornstarch and salt in a heavy saucepan. Stir in warm water. Gradually bring to a boil over low heat, stirring constantly. Continue to cook for 8 to 10 minutes, stirring constantly, until mixture is smooth, clear and thick. Remove from heat. Stir several spoonfuls of hot mixture into beaten egg yolks; mix well. Pour yolks into saucepan. Bring to a boil, stirring constantly. Add rind; cook over low heat for 4 to 5 minutes. Remove from heat; gradually add orange juice and butter. Cool filling; pour into baked pie shell.

Chill filling while making meringue or chill until ready to serve, then top with meringue. Filling will be cold and meringue warm.

MERINGUE:
3 egg whites
¼ tsp. salt
6 tbsp. sugar

Place egg whites and salt in medium bowl. Beat until soft peaks form. Slowly add 1 tablespoon sugar at a time, beating well after each addition until stiff peaks form. Spread meringue over cool filling; seal edges. Bake at 425 degrees for 4 minutes or until golden brown.

Photograph for this recipe on page 173.

PEPPERMINT PIE

12 marshmallows, quartered
½ c. crushed peppermint candy
¼ c. chopped walnuts
½ pt. heavy cream, whipped
Red food coloring
1 graham cracker pie shell

Fold marshmallows, candy and walnuts into whipped cream; tint with food coloring. Pour into pie shell; sprinkle with crumbs. Chill until firm. Serve with whipped cream an Maraschino cherries if desired. Yield: 8 servings.

Violet F. Higgins
Bremerton, Wash.

SNOW PIE

1½ c. milk
2 tsp. butter
1 c. sugar
4 tbsp. flour
1 tsp. vanilla flavoring
2 egg whites, stiffly beaten
1 graham cracker crumb crust

Heat milk in double boiler; add butter, sugar and flour. Cook until thickened, stirring constantly. Remove from heat. Blend in vanilla and egg whites. Pour into pie crust. Chill. Yield: 6 servings.

Mrs. Ora Parman
Sheridan, Mo.

CARROT PIE

1½ c. mashed cooked carrots
1 c. brown sugar
½ tsp. salt
1 tsp. ginger
1 tsp. cinnamon
⅛ tsp. allspice
2 tbsp. molasses
3 eggs, beaten
1 c. evaporated milk
1 pie shell

(Continued on next page)

Combine all ingredients in order given except pie shell. Pour mixture into pie shell. Bake at 400 degrees for 40 to 45 minutes. Yield: 6 servings.

Mrs. Faeth V. Eaton
Wendell, Idaho

DIETETIC PUMPKIN PIE

½ tsp. nutmeg
½ tsp. cinnamon
¼ tsp. ginger
¼ tsp. mapeline flavoring (opt.)
½ tsp. salt
1 tbsp. artificial sweetener
1 ¾ c. pumpkin
2 eggs, beaten
1 ½ c. milk
1 9-in. pastry shell, slightly baked

Stir spices, flavoring, salt and sweetener into pumpkin. Add eggs and milk; mix well. Place mixture in a 9-inch pastry shell. Bake at 425 degrees for 15 minutes. Reduce heat to 350 degrees; bake for 30 minutes. NOTE: Filling may be baked at 400 degrees for 35 minutes in custard cups as pumpkin pudding. Yield: 5 servings.

Mrs. Frederic Westmaas
Marion, Mich.

LOW-CALORIE PUMPKIN PIE

¾ c. crushed corn flakes
1 tsp. butter
4 tbsp. powdered skim milk
¾ c. water
¼ tsp. salt
½ tsp. cinnamon (opt.)
1 c. pumpkin
8 sweetener tablets
¼ tsp. ginger
¼ tsp. nutmeg
Grated orange rind
1 egg, separated

Combine corn flakes and butter; spread on bottom and sides of pie pan. Dissolve skim milk in water. Add remaining ingredients except egg white. Beat egg white; fold into mixture. Bake at 350 degrees for 40 minutes. Yield: 6 servings.

Mrs. Chester Bacon
Excelsior Springs, Mo.

PUMPKIN CHIFFON PIE

3 eggs, separated
1 c. sugar
1 ¼ c. canned pumpkin
½ c. milk
½ tsp. salt
½ tsp. ginger

½ tsp. cinnamon
½ tsp. nutmeg
1 envelope unflavored gelatin
¼ c. cold water
1 baked pie shell
Sweetened whipped cream

Beat egg yolks and 1/2 cup sugar until thick. Add pumpkin, milk, salt and spices; cook in double boiler until thick. Add gelatin softened in cold water; stir until gelatin dissolves. Beat egg whites with remaining 1/2 cup sugar until stiff. Add to mixture. Pour into baked shell; chill. Top with sweetened whipped cream. Yield: 8 servings.

Margaret Pruitt
Tonasket, Wash.

PUMPKIN PIE

1 pt. milk
1 lge. can pumpkin
4 eggs, separated
1 ½ c. sugar
¼ tsp. salt
2 tsp. vanilla flavoring
1 can moistened coconut
1 recipe pastry
Cinnamon

Combine all ingredients except egg whites, pastry and cinnamon. Fold in stiffly beaten egg whites; pour into unbaked pie shell. Sprinkle with cinnamon. Bake at 425 degrees for 10 minutes. Reduce heat to 350 degrees; bake for 40 minutes or until firm.

Dorothea Harris
Pennsville, N.J.

FAVORITE SQUASH OR PUMPKIN PIE

1 c. sieved winter squash or pumpkin
1 tsp. (scant) nutmeg
1 tsp. (scant) cinnamon
½ c. sugar
2 eggs, well beaten
1 c. sweetened condensed milk or sweetened cream
1 9-in. unbaked pie shell

Mix squash, nutmeg, cinnamon and sugar; mix thoroughly. Add eggs and milk; mix thoroughly. Pour into pie shell. Bake at 350 degrees for 30 to 40 minutes or until done. Yield: 6 servings.

Lucy M. Lofton
Dayton, Oreg.

SWEET POTATO PIE

½ c. sugar
¼ tsp. salt
1 tsp. cinnamon

(Continued on next page)

1 tsp. nutmeg
½ tsp. ginger
2 c. strained steamed sweet potatoes
1 c. milk
2 eggs, slightly beaten
Unbaked pie pastry

Combine all dry ingredients; add to sweet potatoes. Mix milk and eggs; add. Line pie pan with pastry; pour in filling. Bake at 450 degrees for 10 minutes. Reduce heat to 350 degrees; bake for 35 minutes. Yield: One 9-inch pie.

Mrs. Linda S. Varnum
Supply, N.C.

SWEET POTATO PIE WITH COCONUT

1 c. sugar
½ tsp. salt
1 tbsp. vanilla flavoring
1 ½ c. mashed cooked sweet potatoes
½ c. coconut
1 ⅔ c. evaporated milk
2 eggs
1 9-in. unbaked crust

Combine all ingredients except pie crust; pour into crust. Bake at 425 degrees for 15 minutes. Reduce heat to 350 degrees; bake for 35 minutes or until firm. Yield: 6 servings.

Mrs. John Sease
West Columbia, S.C.

GREEN TOMATO PIE

3 or 4 green tomatoes, peeled and chopped
2 tbsp. vinegar
2 tbsp. water
1 c. sugar
Pinch of salt
2 tbsp. flour
1 tsp. cinnamon
¾ tsp. allspice
½ tsp. ground cloves
1 pie shell
Butter

Squeeze liquid from tomatoes; discard juice. Add vinegar and water to tomatoes. Sift sugar with salt, flour and spices; mix in tomatoes. Pour into pie shell; dot with butter. Bake at 450 degrees for 15 minutes. Reduce heat to 350 degrees; bake for 30 minutes. Yield: 6-8 servings.

Marjory Phillips
Rochester, Ind.

BROWNIE PIE

3 egg whites
Dash of salt

¾ c. sugar
¾ c. finely crushed chocolate wafers
½ c. chopped pecans
½ tsp. vanilla flavoring
1 c. heavy cream, whipped and sweetened

Beat egg whites with salt; add sugar. Fold in crushed wafers, nuts and vanilla. Pour into a buttered 9-inch pie plate. Bake at 325 degrees for 30 minutes. Cool thoroughly; spread with whipped cream.

Mrs. Vetta H. Burrows
Ashboro, N.C.

CRACKER PIE

11 crackers, finely rolled
Pinch of salt
¾ c. sugar
1 c. chopped nuts
1 tsp. vanilla flavoring
3 egg whites, stiffly beaten

Combine all ingredients except egg whites; fold in egg whites. Pour into a greased 8-inch pie pan. Bake at 350 degrees for 30 minutes. Yield: 5-6 servings.

Mrs. Albert Easingwood
Gainesville, Fla.

DUTCH FUNNY CAKE

SAUCE:
1 square chocolate
½ c. water
⅔ c. sugar
¼ c. butter
1 tsp. vanilla flavoring

Melt chocolate in water over low heat; add sugar. Boil; remove from heat. Add butter and flavoring.

BATTER:
¼ c. shortening
1 ¼ c. flour
1 tsp. baking powder
½ tsp. salt
¾ c. sugar
½ c. milk
1 tsp. vanilla flavoring
1 egg
Unbaked pie shell
Nuts

Cream shortening; add sifted dry ingredients. Add milk and flavoring; beat well. Add egg; beat again. Pour into pie shell; pour sauce over batter. Sprinkle with nuts. Bake at 350 degrees for 50 minutes. Serve warm or cool, plain or with whipped cream or ice cream. Yield: 8 servings.

Mrs. John M. Van Toll
Kimberly, Wisc.

QUICK CHERRY TART

1 No. 303 can pitted cherries
1 c. sugar
4 drops red food coloring
1 tbsp. cornstarch
1 tbsp. cold water
6 to 8 vanilla cookies
1 pt. ice cream or whipped topping

Heat cherries, sugar and food coloring to boiling point. Mix cornstarch and water; add to mixture. Boil for 2 minutes; cool. Place cherry mixture in dessert dishes; place 1 cookie on cherries. Top with ice cream or whipped topping or both. Yield: 6-8 servings.

Mrs. June Shell
Immokalee, Fla.

CHESS TARTS

1 c. brown sugar
½ c. butter
2 eggs, well beaten
1 tbsp. vanilla flavoring
6 tbsp. evaporated milk
1 c. chopped dates
1 c. chopped walnuts
Baked tart shells

Cream sugar and butter; add eggs and vanilla. Add milk; blend thoroughly. Fold in dates and walnuts. Pour into tart shells. Bake at 350 degrees until set and golden brown. Yield: 1 1/2 dozen.

Mrs. M. J. McArtor
Asheville, N.C.

LEMON TARTS

TART SHELLS:
3 c. sifted flour
1 ½ tsp. salt
1 c. shortening
6 tbsp. cold water

Combine flour and salt; cut in shortening. Add water; mix well. Press into shells. Bake at 450 degrees for 10 to 20 minutes.

FILLING:
Grated rind of 2 lemons
½ c. lemon juice
2 c. sugar
1 c. butter
4 eggs, well beaten

Combine lemon rind, lemon juice and sugar in top of double boiler; add butter. Heat over boiling water, stirring until butter is melted. Stir in eggs. Continue cooking and stirring for 15 minutes or until mixture thickens. Place lemon filling in tart shells; top with whipped cream. Yield: 4 dozen.

Mrs. C. A. Ashley
Ocilla, Ga.

PINEAPPLE TART

2 c. sugar
1 sm. can crushed pineapple
2 eggs
½ c. butter
1 c. milk
½ tsp. baking powder
½ tsp. salt
½ tsp. vanilla flavoring
½ c. walnuts
½ c. raisins (opt.)
1 1-lb. box graham crackers

Boil 1 cup sugar and pineapple for 10 minutes; cool. Cream eggs, remaining 1 cup sugar and butter; add all remaining ingredients. Fold in pineapple mixture. Pour into a loaf pan. Bake at 375 degrees for 30 minutes. Yield: 15 servings.

Mrs. William Gregory
Webb City, Mo.

EMPANADAS-MINCEMEAT TURNOVERS

DOUGH:
2 c. flour
1 tsp. baking soda
1 tbsp. sugar
1 tsp. salt
1 tbsp. (heaping) shortening
1 c. buttermilk

Sift all dry ingredients; cut in shortening. Add buttermilk; blend. Roll out to 1/8-inch thick; cut with biscuit cutter.

FILLING:
1 lb. boiling meat
1 ½ c. raisins
2 c. applesauce
1 c. sugar
1 tsp. coriander
½ tsp. cloves
1 tsp. cinnamon
1 tsp. salt
½ c. chopped nuts

Cook meat; grind. Add remaining ingredients. Blend thoroughly, using hands if necessary. Place 1 1/2 teaspoons filling on each piece of pastry. Fold; seal edges. Fry in deep fat until browned. Yield: 6 dozen.

Mrs. Mike Anaya
Moriarty, N.M.

EGG YOLK PASTRY

5 c. sifted flour
4 tsp. sugar
½ tsp. salt
½ tsp. baking powder
1 ½ c. lard
2 egg yolks
Cold water

(Continued on next page)

Combine all dry ingredients; cut in lard. Place egg yolks in measuring cup; stir with fork until smooth. Blend in enough water to make a scant cupful. Sprinkle over dry ingredients; toss with fork to make a soft dough. Roll out to a 9-inch crust. Keeps in refrigerator for two weeks. Fill with favorite pie filling. Yield: Three 9-inch pies.

Mrs. Alvin Kozlovsky
Coleman, Wisc.

EVERLASTING PIE CRUST

6 c. flour
2 tsp. salt
1 lb. shortening
1 egg
2 tsp. vinegar
Cold water

Mix flour and salt well; cut in shortening. Break egg into 1 cup measuring cup; beat lightly with fork. Add vinegar and enough water to fill cup. Mix well. Add to flour mixture. Wrap dough in waxed paper; place in tight cellophane bag. Refrigerate. Break off dough and use as needed.

Mrs. Donna Williams
Mooreland, Ind.

HOT WATER PIE CRUST

1 c. lard
½ c. boiling water
1 tbsp. sugar
1 tsp. salt
½ tsp. baking powder
3 c. flour

Melt lard in water; cool. Stir in all remaining ingredients. Cool before using. Yield: 5 single crusts.

Florence C. Packer
Irvington, N.J.

IOWA PIE CRUST

3 c. sifted flour
1 tsp. salt
1 ⅓ c. shortening
1 lge. egg, beaten
1 tbsp. vinegar
5 tbsp. cold water

Thoroughly mix flour, salt and shortening; mixture will be coarse. Combine egg, vinegar and water; mix well. Add to flour mixture all at once. Mix and shape into a ball. Divide into four equal parts. Refrigerate until needed. Dough will keep for three weeks in refrig-

erator or for three months in freezer. Yield: 4 pie crusts.

Mrs. Gifford W. Thrasher
Santa Monica, Calif.

NEVER-FAIL PIE CRUST

3 c. flour
1 tsp. baking powder
1 tsp. salt
1 ⅓ c. shortening
1 egg
5 tbsp. water
1 tbsp. vinegar

Blend dry ingredients with shortening; add egg and liquids. Form into roll; wrap in waxed paper. Store in refrigerator. Take off as much as needed; bring to room temperature. Roll on heavily floured board. Bake as usual for pie crust. Yield: Crust for at least 3 pies.

Mrs. Marjorie Bilden
Northwood, N.D.

PASTRY

5 ½ to 6 c. flour
1 lb. shortening
1 tsp. salt
1 egg
2 tbsp. vinegar
Water

Mix flour, shortening and salt. Beat egg in measuring cup; add vinegar and finish filling with water to measure 1 cup. Mix with flour mixture. Put in plastic bag; close securely. Store in refrigerator. This may be rolled out for use immediately or will keep three to four weeks in refrigerator. This is very easy to handle and can be handled or rolled as much as necessary. Yield: Pastry for 6 one-crust pies.

Mrs. T. J. R. Preston, Jr.
Webb AFB, Tex.

PASTRY

2 c. flour
1 tsp. salt
½ c. salad or cooking
5 tbsp. ice water

Sift flour and salt. Combine oil and ice water. Beat with fork until thickened and creamy. Pour immediately, all at once, over surface of flour. Toss and mix with a fork; form into a ball. Roll between two squares of waxed paper or on an unfloured board. Handle dough as little as possible for more flaky and tender crust. Roll out to fit pan. Yield: Pastry for one 8 or 9-inch two-crust pie.

Mrs. Kenneth Thomson
Kure Beach, N.C.

Puddings
and Custards

RECIPE FOR HONEY RICE PUDDING ON PAGE 221

Puddings and Custards . . .

. . . are delicious and really aren't hard to make at all, if you'll follow these simple suggestions.

PUDDINGS

The nature of a pudding depends largely upon the temperature at which it is served. Certain puddings, such as the steamed ones and baked batters and doughs, become soggy when cold. Souffles must be served hot because they begin to fall as soon as they are removed from the oven.

Some puddings may be chilled almost to the point of freezing before being served. To keep your puddings from developing a tough surface while in the refrigerator, simply put waxed paper or clear plastic wrap directly on the surface of the hot pudding. Secure the paper or plastic wrap with a rubber band.

Pudding molds may be as fancy as you like . . . or as practical as a clean coffee can. Generously grease the molds and tops. Fill the molds one-half to two-thirds full of the pudding mixture. Secure a piece of waxed paper with a rubber band over the top of the mold to prevent the water from condensing and dropping onto the pudding.

Have rapidly boiling water that will reach halfway up the sides of the mold ready in a steamer or deep covered kettle with a rack. Place the molds in the water and steam for the designated length of time given in the recipe. If you like, place the pudding in the oven for five minutes to dry the top after steaming.

CUSTARDS

There are two common causes of custard failure: 1) cooking too long; or 2) cooking at too high a temperature.

A baked custard should be poured into cups and the cups set in a pan of water. Bake in a moderate oven only until the mixture is set. To test for doneness, insert a knife near the edge of the custard. If the blade comes out clean, the custard will be solid all the way through when it is cool. There will be enough heat stored in the cups to finish cooking the custard when it is removed from the oven. Cool the custard in cups set on a rack.

If, when tested, the custard is as well done in the center as on the edges, place the cups in ice water immediately to stop further cooking.

For custards that are cooked on the top of the stove, use a double boiler. Do not cook over high heat because the heat will toughen and shrink the albumen in the eggs and it will not hold the liquid in suspension as it should. Beat the eggs well. Add about ¼ cup of the hot liquid to the eggs. Slowly add the rest of the hot liquid, stirring constantly. Cook over hot water until the custard is thick enough to coat a metal spoon.

Remove from heat and strain the mixture. Continue stirring to release the steam. If the steam is allowed to condense, it may make the custard "watery." If the custard gets too hot while cooking, turn it into a chilled dish and whisk quickly or blend at high speed in blender to cool rapidly.

BAKED CUSTARD

3 eggs
4 tbsp. sugar
¼ tsp. salt
2 c. milk, scalded
½ tsp. vanilla flavoring
Nutmeg

Beat eggs slightly; add sugar and salt. Slowly add hot milk and vanilla. Pour into buttered custard cups; sprinkle with nutmeg. Set in pan of hot water. Bake at 325 degrees until firm. Yield: 6 servings.

Mrs. Gerda Heisterkamp
Granger, Minn.

BOILED CUSTARD

1 qt. milk
5 eggs, well beaten
6 tbsp. sugar
1 tsp. salt
1 tsp. vanilla flavoring

Bring milk to scalding point without boiling. Combine eggs with sugar and salt; mix thoroughly. Add to hot milk slowly, stirring constantly. Cook over low heat until custard coats a spoon, stirring constantly. Add vanilla; cool. Serve plain or with whipped cream topped with a cherry or nut. Yield: 8-10 servings.

Mrs. Charles I. Allen
Wadesboro, N.C.

BOILED CUSTARD

1 qt. plus 1 c. milk
3 eggs, separated
1 c. sugar
2 tsp. vanilla flavoring

Scald 1 quart milk. Combine egg yolks with 1 cup cold milk. Add slowly to hot milk. Bring to a boil; do not scorch. Add sugar to stiffly beaten egg whites; fold into egg yolk mixture. Cook for 1 minute, beating with wire beater. Cool; add flavoring.

Mrs. Sara Helen McPeake
Camden, Tenn.

BAKED FRUIT WHIP

2 egg whites
6 tbsp. sugar
⅛ tsp. salt
1 tbsp. lemon juice
1 ½ c. cooked pureed apricots or prunes

Beat egg whites until stiff but not dry. Gradually beat in sugar. Combine salt, lemon juice and pureed fruit. Fold, a small amount at a time, into egg whites. Pile lightly into pudding pan. Set pan in shallow pan of hot water. Bake at 300 degrees for 45 minutes. Serve warm or chilled with whipped cream and chopped nuts. Garnish with a Maraschino cherry. NOTE: Both apricots and prunes may be used. Yield: 6 servings.

Frances Dahl
Isobel, S.D.

CARAMEL CUSTARD

½ to 1 c. brown sugar, sifted
3 eggs
¼ c. sugar
⅛ tsp. salt
2 c. milk, scalded
½ tsp. vanilla flavoring or 1 tsp. rum flavoring

Spread brown sugar over bottom of baking dish or mold. Beat eggs until light; add sugar and salt. Slowly stir in milk; add vanilla. Pour over brown sugar. Place in pan of hot water. Bake at 350 degrees until firm. Invert onto platter. Yield: 5 servings.

Mrs. K. L. Anderson
San Diego, Calif.

COCONUT CUSTARD

3 eggs, slightly beaten
¼ c. sugar
¼ tsp. salt
2 c. milk, scalded
½ tsp. vanilla flavoring
Nutmeg to taste
1 c. flaked coconut

Combine eggs, sugar and salt; slowly add scalded milk, vanilla, nutmeg and coconut. Pour into custard dishes or a small casserole dish. Place in a pan of hot water. Bake at 325 degrees for 30 to 40 minutes or until mixture does not stick to an inserted knife. Serve warm or cooled. Yield: 6 servings.

Mrs. Betty Kirschten
Rosebud, Montana

EGG CUSTARD

3 or 4 eggs, beaten
½ to ¾ c. sugar
1 can evaporated milk
1 c. water (opt.)
Pinch of salt
½ to 1 tsp. vanilla
Nutmeg

Combine all ingredients except nutmeg; mix well. Pour mixture into baking dish. Sprinkle with nutmeg. Set baking dish in pan of water. Bake at 300 degrees for 40 to 60 minutes. NOTE: Two cups milk may be substituted for evaporated milk and water. Yield: 6 servings.

Geneva Keen
Immokolee, Fla.

CRUNCHY FRENCH CUSTARD

2 c. light cream
4 egg yolks
2 ½ tbsp. sugar
Few grains of salt
1 tsp. vanilla flavoring
2 tbsp. brown sugar

Heat cream until film puckers over top. Beat egg yolks until thick; gradually add sugar and salt. Stir scalded cream into egg mixture very, very slowly. Add vanilla. Pour into a 1-quart dish; place dish in pan of water. Bake at 350 degrees for 1 hour. Sift brown sugar over top; place under broiler until sugar melts. Refrigerate for 1 to 2 hours.

Mrs. George S. Conkin
New Castle, Ind.

LEMON CUP CUSTARD

1 c. sugar
4 tbsp. flour, sifted
Pinch of salt
2 tbsp. butter, melted
3 eggs, separated
1 ½ c. milk
5 tbsp. lemon juice
Grated rind of 1 lemon

Mix sugar, flour and salt; add butter. Beat egg yolks; add milk. Pour egg mixture over dry ingredients; mix well. Add lemon juice and rind. Fold in beaten egg whites. Place in baking dishes over pan of water. Bake at 350 degrees for 45 minutes. Yield: 6-8 servings.

Mrs. Louis Lashley
Barnesville, Ga.

NEVER-FAIL CUSTARD

1 c. sugar
1 tbsp. butter
3 tbsp. water
6 eggs
2 cans sweetened condensed milk
2 milk cans water
1 tsp. vanilla flavoring

Caramelize sugar; add butter and water. Line ring mold with mixture. Beat all remaining ingredients well. Pour into ring mold. Put mold in a pan of water. Bake at 300 degrees for 1 hour and 30 minutes or until firm. Cool; refrigerate. Unmold to serve. Yield: 8 servings.

Mrs. R. E. Foster
Norfolk Naval Shipyard, Va.

LOW CALORIE CUSTARD

2 tsp. liquid sugar substitute
2 c. skim milk
3 eggs, beaten
1 tsp. vanilla flavoring
Dash of nutmeg

Combine all ingredients. Place over pan of hot water. Bake at 300 degrees for 1 hour. Yield: 6 servings.

Doris Noellsch
Rock Port, Mo.

PRINCESS CUSTARD

2 lge. bananas, diced
1 ½ tsp. grated orange rind
6 tbsp. orange juice
5 tbsp. sugar
2 tbsp. cornstarch
¼ tsp. salt
1 ½ c. milk
2 eggs, separated
2 eggs, separated
3 graham crackers, finely crushed

Combine bananas, orange rind and orange juice. Combine 3 tablespoons sugar, cornstarch and salt in double boiler. Add milk gradually; cook until thickened. Slowly stir into slightly beaten egg yolks. Cook for 2 to 3 minutes or until thick. Remove from heat; fold in banana mixture. Chill. Gradually add remaining sugar to stiffly beaten egg whites; fold into custard. Place in sherbet glasses; sprinkle with cracker crumbs. Yield: 6 servings.

Mrs. Patrick Cullen
Platteville, Wisc.

SMOOTH SOFT CUSTARD

1 ¾ c. milk
3 tbsp. flour
¼ c. sugar
½ tsp. salt
2 egg yolks, slightly beaten
½ tsp. vanilla flavoring

Heat 1 1/4 cup milk until a skim forms on top. Blend remaining 1/2 cup milk with flour; stir into hot milk. Cook almost to the boiling point. Gradually add sugar and salt to egg yolks; beat until smooth. Slowly add hot milk mixture to egg yolk mixture, stirring constantly. This step must be done slowly or custard will curdle. Cook over gently boiling water, stirring frequently, until custard is smooth and thick enough to coat a spoon. Add vanilla; cool. Yield: 4 servings.

Mrs. W. Porter Murray
Knob Noster, Mo.

BAKED BLUEBERRY CUSTARD

1 c. fresh blueberries
1 qt. milk
5 eggs
5 tbsp. sugar
½ tsp. salt
¼ tsp. nutmeg
1 ½ tsp. vanilla flavoring

Wash and drain blueberries, being careful not to crush or break berries. Dry on paper towel. Scald milk. Break eggs into a bowl; beat well. Add sugar, salt, nutmeg and vanilla. Pour in scalded milk; stir well. Pour milk mixture into custard cups. Carefully arrange blueberries on top of custard; some will sink. Sprinkle additional nutmeg on top if desired. Place cups in a pan of hot water. Bake at 350 degrees for 15 to 20 minutes or until an inserted silver knife comes out clean. Do not overcook, as custard will turn watery. Remove cups from water; cool. Chill in refrigerator; serve icy cold. Yield: 8 servings.

Photograph for this recipe above.

ALABAMA PUDDIN'

¼ lb. margarine
1 No. 2 can applesauce
1 tsp. cinnamon
1 pkg. gingerbread mix

Melt margarine in kettle. Pour in applesauce seasoned with cinnamon. Mix gingerbread according to directions on package. Pour gently over applesauce. Cover tightly. Cook for 30 minutes. This can be cooked over low heat on the top of the stove or baked in oven. Serve plain or with whipped cream.

Mrs. Anne M. Parnham
Seymour Johnson AFB, N.C.

ANGEL PUDDING

1 envelope unflavored gelatin
1 c. sugar
1 c. cold milk
2 eggs, separated
Pinch of salt
1 c. heavy cream, whipped
1 tsp. vanilla flavoring
16 graham crackers, crumbled
1 tbsp. butter, melted

Combine gelatin, 1/2 cup sugar and milk in a double boiler; let soak for 1 hour. Add well beaten egg yolks, 1/2 cup sugar and salt; cook for 15 minutes. Cool. Beat whites until stiff. Fold whipped cream and stiffly beaten egg whites into the cooked mixture; add vanilla. Mix cracker crumbs and melted butter. Place one-half of the crumbs in a dish; pour pudding

(Continued on next page)

over crumbs. Sprinkle remaining crumbs on
top. Yield: 10-12 servings.

Mrs. Delbert Young
Ossian, Ind.

APPLE PUDDING

½ c. shortening
1 c. sugar
1 egg
¼ tsp. soda
¼ tsp. salt
1 tsp. cinnamon
1 c. sifted flour
2 ½ c. chopped raw apples

Cream shortening and sugar. Add unbeaten
egg, soda, salt, cinnamon and flour; mix well.
Add apples; mix. Pour into a greased pan.
Bake at 350 degrees for 35 to 45 minutes.
Yield: 6 servings.

Mrs. W. A. Robinson
Marion, Ill.

APPLE PUDDING DELIGHT

⅓ c. tapioca
¼ tsp. salt
¼ c. dark corn syrup
2 ½ c. hot water
3 tart apples, thinly sliced
1 c. raisins
½ c. sugar
¼ tsp. nutmeg
¼ tsp. cinnamon
2 tbsp. butter

Combine tapioca, salt, syrup and water. Cook
in double boiler until tapioca is clear, stirring
frequently. Place apples in buttered baking
dish. Add raisins; place sugar and spices on
top. Pour tapioca mixture over all; dot with
butter. Bake at 350 degrees for 50 to 60 minutes or until apples are tender. Serve with
cream or lemon sauce. Yield: 6 servings.

Mrs. Alfred Williams
Vero Beach, Fla.

APRICOT PUDDING

1 large can apricot halves
Juice from apricots
1 c. flour
1 c. sugar
1 tsp. baking powder
1 egg

Pour apricots and one-half of the juice into a
buttered 6 x 11-inch baking dish. Mix all remaining ingredients; spread over apricots.
Bake at 350 degrees for 25 to 30 minutes.
Yield: 6 servings.

Mrs. Marlin Haag
Cullom, Ill.

BANANA PUDDING

2 ½ c. scalded milk
⅓ c. cornstarch
¾ c. sugar
Pinch of salt
2 eggs, beaten
1 tsp. vanilla flavoring
Sliced bananas
Crushed vanilla wafers or graham crackers

Combine milk, cornstarch, sugar and salt,
stirring constantly. Add eggs; cook until thick.
Remove from heat; add vanilla. Cool. Alternate layers of bananas, custard and wafers in
pan. Yield: 6 servings.

Mrs. Joy Christiansen
Milnor, N.D.

BLACKBERRY PUDDING

1 tbsp. butter
Sugar
1 egg, well beaten
1 c. flour
1 tsp. baking powder
½ tsp. salt
¼ c. milk
¾ c. blackberries

Cream butter and 1/2 cup sugar. Add egg; beat
well. Sift flour with baking powder and salt;
add to egg mixture alternately with milk.
Place 2 tablespoons berries and 1 tablespoon
sugar in each well greased pudding mold.
Place batter on top of berries, filling molds
two-thirds full. Steam for 30 minutes. Serve
with whipped cream or berry sauce.

SAUCE:
4 tbsp. flour
1 c. sugar
1 ½ c. boiling water
⅛ tsp. salt
½ c. crushed blackberries
3 tsp. lemon juice
4 tbsp. butter

Combine all ingredients; cook until thick.
Serve over pudding. NOTE: Canned or fresh
blueberries, raspberries, huckleberries and
loganberries may be substituted for blackberries. Yield: 8 servings.

Mrs. William P. Maloney
North Creek, N.Y.

BUTTERSCOTCH FLUFF

3 tbsp. melted butter
1 c. brown sugar
1 qt. scalded milk
3 c. soft bread crumbs
3 eggs, slightly beaten
½ tsp. salt

(Continued on next page)

206

1 tsp. vanilla flavoring
2 c. marshmallows

Combine butter, sugar and scalded milk. Add bread crumbs; cool. Mix eggs, salt and vanilla; add to milk mixture. Place marshmallows in buttered casserole; cover with pudding. Bake at 350 degrees for 1 hour and 30 minutes. Yield: 9 servings.

Mrs. Karen Locke
Chillicothe, Ill.

FRESH BLACKBERRY PUDDING

1 ½ sticks butter, softened
1 ¼ c. sugar
1 egg, at room temperature
2 tsp. vanilla flavoring
2 c. flour, sifted
¾ tsp. soda
1 qt. fresh blackberries
1 1-lb. box powdered sugar, sifted

Cream 1/2 stick butter and sugar. Add egg and 1 teaspoon vanilla. Combine and sift all dry ingredients except powdered sugar; add to creamed mixture. Fold berries into flour mixture. Pour into greased 9 x 10 x 3-inch pan. Bake at 350 degrees for 1 hour. Blend remaining butter with powdered sugar and remaining vanilla. Serve hot pudding with sauce. Yield: 8 servings.

Eurylee Yost Covington
Dade City, Fla.

BLUEBERRY PUDDING

1 c. sugar
1 c. flour
2 tsp. baking powder
¼ tsp. salt
½ c. milk
½ tsp. vanilla flavoring
1 tbsp. butter, melted
1 c. blueberries
¾ c. boiling water

Sift 1/2 cup sugar with flour, baking powder and salt into mixing bowl. Stir in milk, vanilla and butter. Spread batter in buttered 10 x 6 x 2-inch baking dish. Scatter blueberries over batter. Sprinkle remaining sugar over berries. Pour boiling water over all. Bake at 375 degrees for 25 to 30 minutes or until well browned and done. Serve with light cream or ice cream. Yield: 6 servings.

Mrs. Freeman J. Singer
Adak, Alaska

CARROT AND SWEET POTATO PUDDING

1 c. flour
1 c. grated raw carrots
1 c. grated raw sweet potatoes
½ c. chopped dates
½ c. chopped dried apricots
1 c. seedless raisins
1 c. sugar
½ c. vegetable oil or melted fat
¼ tsp. salt
2 tsp. cinnamon
1 tsp. nutmeg
½ tsp. soda

Combine all ingredients; stir until blended. Pour into well greased casserole. Cover and bake at 250 degrees for 2 hours and 30 minutes. Remove from oven; cool while still covered. Serve with favorite pudding sauce.

Mrs. Walter E. Broadbent
Lansing, Mich.

BLUEBERRY PUDDING

White bread slices
Cooked sweetened blueberries
Whipped cream

Trim crusts from bread. Layer in casserole or bowl with blueberries. Chill for several hours. Serve plain or with whipped cream.

Mrs. Franklin D. Roosevelt

OLD-FASHIONED BREAD PUDDING

4 c. soft bread crumbs
2 c. milk
¼ c. butter
½ c. sugar
2 eggs, slightly beaten
¼ tsp. salt
1 tsp. cinnamon
½ c. seedless raisins
2 apples, peeled and cut

Place bread crumbs in 1 1/2-quart baking dish. Scald milk with butter; pour over crumbs. Add sugar, eggs, salt and cinnamon; blend well. Top with raisins and apples.

(Continued on next page)

Bake in 350 degree oven for 40 minutes. Serve warm with or without cream. Yield: 6 servings.

Mrs. Ivan Kirkhus
DeKalb, Ill.

BRIDE'S PUDDING

2 envelopes unflavored gelatin
½ c. cold water
6 egg whites
¼ tsp. salt
¾ c. sugar
1 pt. heavy cream
3 tbsp. powdered sugar
1 tsp. vanilla flavoring
1 can flaked coconut
Raspberries

Dissolve gelatin in cold water; soften over boiling water. Beat egg whites with salt until frothy. Gradually beat in sugar; continue beating until mixture holds peaks. Slowly beat in gelatin. Whip cream, powdered sugar and vanilla until stiff; fold into gelatin mixture. Sprinkle one-half of the coconut in bottom of buttered dish. Pour in mixture. Top with raspberries; sprinkle top with remaining coconut. Yield: 15 servings.

Mrs. Ruby Anderson
Wilcox, Nebr.

BUTTERSCOTCH PUDDING

1 c. dark brown sugar
2 tbsp. flour
¼ tsp. salt
2 tbsp. butter
1 egg yolk
3 tbsp. water
1 c. milk

Mix all ingredients. Cook over medium heat until mixture boils, stirring constantly. Cool; pour into serving dishes. Chill; serve. Yield: 4 servings.

Mrs. Jimmy A. Jones
Bluefield, W. Va.

CARAMEL PUDDING

2 pkg. unflavored gelatin
½ c. cold water
1 qt. milk
6 eggs
2 c. sugar
¼ tsp. salt
½ c. hot water
1 tsp. vanilla flavoring

Soak gelatin in cold water. Make a custard of milk, eggs and 1/2 cup sugar; add salt. Remove from heat. Caramelize remaining sugar until brown; add to egg mixture. Dissolve gelatin mixture in hot water. Add gelatin to brown sugar mixture with vanilla. Pour

into flat pan. Refrigerate until firm. Cut into squares and serve with whipped cream. Yield: 12 servings.

Mrs. Margaret Waldo
Forest Lake, Minn.

CARAMEL PUDDING

1 c. sugar
1 c. flour
2 tsp. baking powder
¼ tsp. mace
1 c. seedless raisins
½ c. milk
⅔ c. brown sugar
1 ¾ c. boiling water
1 tbsp. butter

Sift sugar, flour, baking powder and mace; add raisins and milk. Pour into greased 2-quart casserole. Mix brown sugar, boiling water and butter. Pour over mixture in casserole. Bake at 375 degrees for 40 minutes. Yield: 6 servings.

Mrs. Joseph Rivett
Old Forge, N.Y.

CARAMEL PUDDING

2 c. (packed) brown sugar
2 tbsp. butter
2 c. hot water
1 egg
1 c. flour
2 tbsp. baking powder
1 tsp. cinnamon
½ c. milk
1 c. raisins

Combine 1 cup brown sugar, 1 tablespoon butter and hot water in 11 x 7 x 1-inch pan. Bring to a boil; cool. Cream remaining butter and brown sugar with egg. Sift all dry ingredients; add to creamed mixture alternately with milk. Fold in raisins. Drop by spoonfuls over top of syrup mixture. Bake at 350 degrees for 35 minutes. Serve with whipped cream. Yield: 8 servings.

Patricia Hovis
Keyser, W. Va.

CARROT PLUM PUDDING

½ tsp. salt
1 tsp. cinnamon
½ tsp. cloves
¼ tsp. nutmeg
1 c. flour
1 tsp. soda
2 tbsp. hot water
1 c. sugar
1 c. grated raw carrots
1 c. grated raw potatoes
1 c. raisins
1 lge. apple, grated
¼ c. shortening, melted

(Continued on next page)

Mix salt and spices with flour. Add soda to hot water. Mix all ingredients. Place in greased mold. Steam for 3 hours over boiling water. Serve with sauce, whipped cream or ice cream. NOTE: This pudding freezes well. Yield: 10 servings.

Mrs. Lester Byrd
Oroville, Wash.

CARROT PUDDING

1 c. grated carrots
1 c. grated potatoes
1 c. sugar
1 c. flour
1 tsp. cloves
1 tsp. nutmeg
1 tsp. cinnamon
1 tsp. soda
½ tsp. salt
¼ c. melted butter
1 c. chopped raisins
1 c. chopped nuts
3 tbsp. coffee, strained

Mix carrots, potatoes and sugar. Sift flour, spices, soda and salt. Add to carrot mixture. Add remaining ingredients. Steam for 3 hours to 3 hours and 30 minutes, depending on size of mold. Serve with pudding sauce. Yield: 6 servings.

Corinne Gunderson
Auburn, Wash.

CARROT AND SWEET POTATO PUDDING

1 c. flour
1 c. grated raw carrots
1 c. grated raw sweet potatoes
½ c. chopped dates
½ c. chopped dried apricots
1 c. seeded raisins
1 c. sugar
½ c. vegetable oil or melted fat
¼ tsp. salt
2 tsp. cinnamon
1 tsp. nutmeg
½ tsp. soda

Combine all ingredients; stir until blended. Pour into well greased casserole. Cover and bake at 250 degrees for 2 hours and 30 minutes. Cool while covered. Serve with favorite pudding sauce.

Mrs. Walter E. Broadbent
Lansing, Mich.

CHERRY-NUT PUDDING

2 c. crushed corn flakes or ½ c. corn
    flake crumbs
1 pkg. white cake mix
1 can cherry pie filling
½ c. finely chopped nuts
¼ c. butter or margarine, melted

Combine corn flake crumbs with cake mix. Spread pie filling in greased 8-inch square baking pan. Sprinkle cake mix mixture evenly over filling. Top with nuts. Drizzle with butter. Bake at 350 degrees for 1 hour or until brown. Serve warm or cold with ice cream or whipped cream, if desired. Yield: 8 servings.

Mrs. C. W. Daniel
Fort Worth, Tex.

CHERRY PUDDING

¼ lb. butter or margarine
1 c. flour
1 ½ c. sugar
¾ c. milk
1 ½ tsp. baking powder
1 ¼ tsp. salt
1 can cherries and juice

Melt butter in 2-quart glass baking dish. Combine flour, 1 cup sugar, milk, baking powder and salt; pour over butter. Do not stir. Pour cherries and liquid and remaining sugar into center of batter. Do not stir. Bake at 350 degrees for 1 hour. Serve warm. Yield: 6 servings.

Mrs. H. G. O'Neill
Dallas, Tex.

CHERRY PUDDING

2 c. sour cherries
2 tbsp. shortening
2 c. sugar
1 egg
1 c. milk
2 c. flour
2 tsp. baking powder

Drain cherries, reserving 1 cup juice. Cream shortening with 1 cup sugar; beat in egg. Add milk alternately with flour sifted with baking powder. Beat until smooth. Pour into greased cake pan. Mix cherries with remaining sugar and reserved cherry juice; heat and pour over batter. Bake at 370 degrees for 20 to 25 minutes.

Mrs. Shirley Skinner
Payson, Utah

CHERRY PUDDING

1 stick margarine or butter, melted
1 ¾ c. sugar
1 c. flour
¾ c. milk
1 can pie cherries
1 tbsp. cinnamon

Melt margarine in 12 x 9 x 2-inch baking dish. Mix 1 cup sugar, flour and milk. Pour over margarine; do not stir. Cover with cherries; sprinkle remaining sugar over top. Sprinkle

(Continued on next page)

with cinnamon. Bake at 350 degrees for 45 minutes. Yield: 8 servings.

Mrs. Sylvia Buckner
Hoyt, Okla.

UPSIDE-DOWN CHERRY PUDDING

1 ½ c. sifted flour
1 ½ tsp. baking powder
¼ tsp. salt
1 c. sugar
½ c. butter or shortening
1 egg
1 tsp. vanilla flavoring
1 c. milk

Sift flour with baking powder and salt. Cream sugar and butter gradually until light and fluffy. Beat in egg; stir in vanilla. Add dry ingredients alternately with milk, beginning and ending with milk. Pour into buttered 9-inch square pan.

SAUCE:
1 c. sugar
1 No. 2 can sour red pitted cherries and juice
½ c. boiling water

Heat sugar, cherries with juice and boiling water; pour over batter. Bake at 325 degrees for 35 to 40 minutes or until pudding begins to shrink from pan and top and sides are golden brown. Sauce will be on bottom. Serve warm with whipped cream. Yield: 8 servings.

Mrs. R. R. Johnson
Atlantic City, N.J.

CHOCOLATE SOUFFLE

1 c. milk
1 oz. chocolate
2 tbsp. butter
1 tbsp. flour
⅓ c. sugar
3 eggs, separated
1 tsp. vanilla flavoring
⅛ tsp. salt

Heat milk and chocolate over low heat until chocolate is melted; do not boil. Melt butter in separate saucepan; stir in flour. Gradually add hot milk; cook until thickened, stirring constantly. Stir in sugar. Beat egg yolks until light; stir in small amount of hot custard. Return to remaining hot mixture. Cook until thickened; cool. Stir in flavoring. Beat egg whites with salt until stiff. Fold into chocolate mixture; pour into 7-inch baking dish. Set in pan of hot water. Bake at 350 degrees for about 30 minutes. Serve at once with Lemon Sauce.

LEMON SAUCE:
½ c. sugar
1 tsp. cornstarch
¼ tsp. salt
1 tsp. grated lemon rind
3 tbsp. lemon juice
2 tbsp. butter

Blend sugar, cornstarch and salt; stir in 1 cup boiling water. Cook for 15 minutes or until thickened, stirring constantly. Stir in lemon rind, juice and butter. Serve over Chocolate Souffle.

Mrs. Lyndon B. Johnson

GERMAN'S CHOCOLATE PUDDING

1 bar German's chocolate
¼ lb. butter
3 eggs, separated
1 c. powdered sugar
1 tsp. vanilla flavoring
1 pt. whipped cream
10 oz. vanilla wafers, crumbled

Melt chocolate and butter; pour over beaten egg yolks. Add 2/3 cup powdered sugar and vanilla; beat until smooth. Cool in refrigerator. Fold whipped cream into chocolate mixture. Beat egg whites until stiff; add remaining sugar. Fold into chocolate mixture. Put one-half of the crumbs into dish; pour in chocolate mixture. Top with remaining crumbs. Yield: 8 servings.

Thelma L. Greathouse
Marion, Ill.

LOUISBURG CHOCOLATE PUDDING

3 oz. chocolate
1 tbsp. water
1 ¼ tbsp. flour
½ c. sugar
½ c. melted butter
4 eggs, separated
2 tsp. vanilla flavoring

Melt chocolate in water. Add flour, sugar, melted butter, well beaten egg yolks and vanilla. Fold in well beaten egg whites. Pour into buttered mold or individual molds. Bake at 350 degrees for 30 to 45 minutes. Serve cold with mocha sauce.

(Continued on next page)

MOCHA SAUCE:
2 eggs, separated
¼ c. sugar
½ c. strong coffee
1 c. heavy cream, whipped

Beat egg yolks and sugar; add coffee. Cook in double boiler until thickened. Fold in well beaten egg whites and whipped cream. Serve with pudding.

Mrs. H. Turner Hodgdon
Brookline, Mass.

CHRISTMAS PUDDING

1 tsp. soda
3 tbsp. hot water
1 c. sugar
1 c. grated carrots
1 c. raisins
1 tsp. salt
1 ½ c. flour
1 c. grated potatoes
1 c. currants
1 pkg. candied fruit

Dissolve soda in hot water; add all remaining ingredients. Steam for 3 hours. Serve with favorite sauce. NOTE: To steam puddings, generously grease molds and covers. Use steamer or deep covered kettle with rack. Have water to half the depth of the mold boiling rapidly. Keep water boiling constantly, adding more as needed. Place in oven for 5 minutes to dry top. Yield: 8 servings.

Mrs. A. S. Patrick
Mancelona, Mich.

CINNAMON PUDDING

2 c. brown sugar
1 ½ c. water
4 tbsp. butter
1 c. sugar
2 c. flour
2 tsp. baking powder
2 tsp. cinnamon
1 c. milk

Combine brown sugar, water and 2 tablespoons butter to make a syrup. Cream sugar and remaining butter. Sift all dry ingredients. Add with milk to creamed mixture. Pour into 9-inch baking pan; cover with syrup. Bake at 350 degrees for 40 minutes.

Mrs. Kenneth Mears
Chalmers, Ind.

DELUXE CHOCOLATE PUDDING

1 6-oz. pkg. semi-sweet chocolate
    pieces
2 tbsp. sugar
Pinch of salt

1 egg
1 tsp. vanilla flavoring
¾ c. milk

Place all ingredients except milk in an electric blender. Heat milk just to boiling; pour over ingredients. Cover; blend for 1 minute. Pour immediately into 6 serving dishes. Chill if desired. Top with whipped cream if desired. Yield: 6 servings.

Mrs. Burton E. Slesinger
Arlington Hall Sta., Va.

COFFEE PUDDING

1 c. strong coffee
¾ c. sugar
2 tbsp. cornstarch
Pinch of salt
1 tsp. vanilla flavoring
½ pt. heavy cream, whipped

Blend all ingredients except cream in saucepan. Cook until clear and thick; cool. Before serving, add whipped cream; blend in well. Serve with ladyfingers. Yield: 4-6 servings.

Mrs. F. J. Kroesen
Carlisle Barracks, Pa.

CORN FLAKE PUDDING

¼ c. butter, melted
2 squares baking chocolate, melted
2 c. milk, scalded
1 c. (scant) sugar
1 egg, slightly beaten
3 c. corn flakes
1 tsp. vanilla flavoring

Combine all ingredients; turn into buttered baking dish. Bake at 400 degrees for 1 hour. Serve hot with hard sauce or cold with whipped cream. Yield: 6-8 servings.

Mrs. Robert G. Record, Jr.
Hemet, Calif.

CORN FLAKE PUDDING

4 eggs, beaten
1 ½ c. sugar
1 c. milk
1 c. cream
6 c. corn flakes
1 c. raisins

Combine eggs, sugar, milk and cream; mix well. Stir in corn flakes and raisins. Pour into buttered casserole. Bake at 325 degrees for 30 minutes or until done. Serve warm with cream, whipped cream or ice cream. Yield: 6 servings.

Mrs. Ross M. Becker
Cumberland, Iowa

CRACKER PUDDING

12 white crackers, finely crushed
1 c. sugar
1 c. nuts
1 tsp. vanilla flavoring
3 egg whites, stiffly beaten
1 pt. heavy cream, whipped

Mix crackers, sugar, nuts and vanilla with egg whites. Spread thinly on greased flat pan. Bake at 350 degrees for 30 minutes. Cool; break into small pieces. Mix with sweetened, flavored whipped cream. Serve at once. Yield: 12 servings.

Mrs. Beulah Campbell
Forsyth, Mo.

CRANBERRY PUDDING

3 tbsp. butter
1 c. sugar
2 c. flour
1 tbsp. baking powder
½ tsp. salt
1 c. milk
2 c. whole cranberries, washed and dried

Cream butter and sugar; add dry ingredients alternately with milk. Add cranberries. Pour into greased 9 x 13-inch pan. Bake at 350 degrees for 30 minutes.

SAUCE:

1 c. sugar
½ c. butter
½ c. light cream
1 tsp. vanilla flavoring

Combine all ingredients. Heat and stir to combine flavors. Serve over hot pudding. Yield: 8-10 servings.

Mrs. Donald R. Caughey
Portsmouth Naval Shipy'd and Hosp., N.H.

CREME BRULEE

3 c. heavy cream
1 1-in. piece vanilla bean
6 egg yolks
6 tbsp. white sugar
½ c. brown sugar

Heat cream and vanilla bean in top of double boiler. Beat egg yolks with white sugar until light and creamy. Remove vanilla bean; carefully and slowly stir warm cream into egg yolks. Return mixture to double boiler over boiling water. Stir constantly until mixture coats spoon. Pour into glass serving dish; chill until firm. Cover top of custard with brown sugar. Place serving dish in a tray of crushed ice and melt and caramelize sugar under broiler. Watch carefully to prevent burning. Serve immediately. Yield: 6 servings.

Mrs. John F. Kennedy

DATE PUDDING

1 c. corn syrup
1 tsp. baking powder
2 tbsp. flour
2 eggs
1 c. chopped dates
1 c. chopped pecans

Mix all ingredients. Bake in buttered biscuit pan at 300 to 350 degrees for 20 minutes. Yield: 8 servings.

Mrs. Robert N. Denniston
Fort Hamilton, N.Y.

FIG PUDDING

2 c. bread crumbs
2 c. suet
1 lb. figs
1 c. sugar
3 eggs
¾ c. flour
1 tbsp. baking powder
1 c. milk

Coarsely grind bread crumbs and suet. Finely grind figs. Mix all ingredients; pack into 1-pound cans. Steam for 1 hour. Serve hot with whipped cream or pudding sauce. NOTE: Can be stored indefinitely in freezer. Yield: 12 servings.

Margaret Osburn
Big Rapids, Mich.

FLAPPER PUDDING

1 c. fine vanilla wafer crumbs
¾ c. soft butter or margarine
2 c. sifted powdered sugar
2 egg yolks
2 egg whites, stiffly beaten
1 9-oz. can crushed pineapple, drained
½ c. chopped walnuts

Spread one-half of the crumbs on bottom of 10 x 6 x 1 1/2-inch baking dish. Cream butter; gradually add powdered sugar, beating until light and fluffy. Add an egg yolk at a time, beating well after each addition. Beat for 1 minute. Fold in egg whites; beat until smooth. Fold in pineapple and nuts. Carefully spread over crumbs; top with remaining crumbs. Chill for 5 hours, overnight or until firm. Cut into squares; garnish with cherries. Yield: 10 servings.

Mrs. Lillian Richardson
Nevada, Mo.

FRUIT COCKTAIL PUDDING

1 med. can fruit cocktail
2 c. flour

(Continued on next page)

2 tsp. soda
¼ tsp. salt
1 ½ c. sugar
2 eggs, unbeaten
½ c. chopped nuts
¼ c. brown sugar

Drain fruit cocktail, reserving juice. Sift flour, soda and salt three times. Mix in sugar and eggs; add reserved fruit juice. Beat well. Fold in fruit. Put mixture into 9 x 12-inch greased pan. Sprinkle nuts and sugar over top. Bake at 350 degrees for 40 minutes.

TOPPING:
½ c. Milnot milk
¾ c. sugar
1 stick butter or margarine
1 tsp vanilla flavoring

Combine all ingredients. Boil for 3 minutes; cool. Spread topping on cool cake. Yield: 12 servings.

Mrs. Arthur Temme
Evansville, Ind.

FRUIT COCKTAIL PUDDING

1 c. sifted flour
1 c. sugar
1 tsp. soda
¼ tsp. salt
1 egg, beaten
1 c. fruit cocktail, drained
1 tsp. vanilla flavoring
¼ c. brown sugar
¼ c. chopped nuts

Sift flour with sugar, soda and salt. Combine egg and fruit cocktail; add flour mixture and vanilla. Mix well; place in 8-inch square greased pan. Sprinkle top with brown sugar and nuts. Bake at 350 degrees for 45 to 50 minutes. Cool; cut into squares. Yield: 6 servings.

Mrs. Logan J. Jordan
Titusville, Pa.

FRUIT MYSTERY PUDDING

1 c. flour
1 c. sugar
1 tsp. soda
½ tsp. salt
2 c. canned fruit cocktail
1 egg
1 tsp. vanilla flavoring

Sift all dry ingredients; add to remaining ingredients. Mix well. Pour into greased and floured 8 x 13-inch pan.

TOPPING:
¾ c. brown sugar
½ c. chopped walnuts

Mix sugar and nuts; sprinkle over batter. Bake at 325 degrees for 50 to 60 minutes. Yield: 10 servings.

Mrs. R. M. Wright
Dinuba, Calif.

GRAHAM CRACKER PUDDING

5 eggs, separated
2 c. sugar
1 c. chopped walnuts
½ tsp. baking powder
½ tsp. salt
1 ¼ c. graham cracker crumbs

Cream egg yolks and sugar; add nuts, baking powder, salt and crumbs. Add stiffly beaten egg whites. Pour into greased pan. Bake at 325 degrees until done. Yield: 6-8 servings.

Mrs. Glenn H. Parry
Carson, Iowa

HASTY PUDDING

1 c. flour
1 ½ tsp. baking powder
½ tsp. salt
¼ c. (firmly packed) brown sugar
½ c. milk
1 tsp. vanilla flavoring
¼ c. melted butter
¼ c. seedless raisins or chopped nuts
¾ c. maple syrup
⅓ c. water

Sift flour, baking powder and salt; add brown sugar. Blend in milk, flavoring and butter; pour mixture into 1-quart casserole. Sprinkle with raisins. Combine syrup and water in saucepan; bring to a boil. Pour over batter. Bake at 350 degrees for 35 minutes. Yield: 6 servings.

Juna M. White
Jericho, Vt.

HOLIDAY PUDDING

2 eggs
½ c. melted shortening
1 c. brown sugar
2 c. drained cherries
½ tsp. salt
1 c. flour
1 tsp. soda
1 tbsp. milk
1 c. chopped nuts

Beat eggs; add shortening and sugar. Add cherries. Add salt and flour. Dissolve soda in milk; add to mixture. Add nuts. Pour into custard cups. Steam bake at 350 degrees for 1 hour.

(Continued on next page)

213

SAUCE:
1 egg
5 tbsp. melted butter
1 ½ c. powdered sugar
1 c. heavy cream, whipped

Beat egg; slowly add butter. Add powdered sugar; beat until smooth. Fold in whipped cream. Serve over pudding. Yield: 12 servings.

Mrs. Ernest Sterna
Beloit, Wisc.

HAUPIA

2 c. coconut milk
Pinch of salt
4 to 6 tbsp. sugar
5 tbsp. cornstarch

Combine all ingredients in cold saucepan. Cook over medium heat, stirring constantly, until thickened. Pour into pans; chill. Cut into squares to serve.

Mrs. Francisca P. Santon
Makule U.E. Koloa, Kauai, Hawaii

HOLIDAY PUDDING

1 c. milk
½ c. molasses
2 eggs, beaten
½ c. finely chopped suet
3 c. flour
2 tsp. baking powder
1 tsp. salt
1 tsp. cinnamon
¼ tsp. cloves
½ c. finely chopped citron
1 c. raisins

Combine milk, molasses and eggs; add suet. Sift dry ingredients; add to egg mixture with citron and raisins. Mix thoroughly. Pour into well greased 1-quart mold. Steam for 2 hours. Serve hot with pudding sauce. Yield: 6 servings.

Mrs. John R. Hall
Oakville, Wash.

JAM PUDDING

¾ c. (scant) butter
1 ½ c. sugar
3 eggs, separated
1 ½ c. pastry flour
3 tbsp. sour milk or buttermilk
1 c. raspberry jam
1 tsp. soda

Cream butter and sugar; add egg yolks, flour, milk, jam and soda. Fold in egg whites. Steam for 3 hours. Serve hot.

SAUCE:
1 egg
1 c. sugar
½ pt. heavy cream, whipped
3 tbsp. Sherry or vanilla flavoring

Cream egg and sugar; add whipped cream and Sherry. Serve over pudding. NOTE: Pudding may be reheated. Yield: 10 servings.

Mrs. C. H. Garbutt
Cincinnati, O.

LEMON-BREAD PUDDING

2 c. soft bread crumbs
Juice of 2 lemons
½ c. water
2 eggs, separated
1 c. sugar
¼ c. shortening or margarine
Few grains of salt
Meringue

Combine crumbs, juice, water and egg yolks with 3/4 cup sugar and shortening. Mix well; pour mixture into buttered baking dish. Bake at 350 degrees for 25 minutes. Add salt to stiffly beaten egg whites and remaining sugar. Cover lemon-batter mixture with meringue. Bake at 350 degrees for 15 to 20 minutes or until meringue is brown. Yield: 6-8 servings.

Mable M. Johnston
Arcadia, Fla.

LEMON CAKE PUDDING

3 eggs, separated
6 tbsp. sugar
1 ½ c. milk
¼ c. sugar
⅓ c. flour
⅛ tsp. salt
2 tbsp. melted butter
4 tbsp. lemon juice
1 tsp. grated lemon rind

Whip egg whites, gradually adding sugar; beat until peaks are formed. Combine all remaining ingredients; fold into egg whites. Pour into 1 1/2-quart casserole; place casserole in pan with 1 inch of water. Bake at 325 degrees for 45 minutes. Yield: 4-6 servings.

De Anna Henderson
Honolulu, Hawaii

LEMON PUDDING

¼ c. flour
1 c. sugar
¼ tsp. salt
1 ½ tsp. grated lemon rind
¼ c. lemon juice
2 eggs, separated
1 c. milk

Sift flour, sugar and salt into mixing bowl. Add lemon rind, lemon juice, well beaten egg yolks and milk. Fold in stiffly beaten egg whites. Pour into six custard cups. Set in pan of hot water. Bake at 350 degrees for 50 minutes. Yield: 6 servings.

Mrs. Thomas Kurtz
Waco, Tex.

INDIAN PUDDING

¼ c. corn meal
3 c. milk
½ tsp. salt
⅛ tsp. soda
¼ tsp. nutmeg
¼ tsp. ginger
¼ tsp. cinnamon
1 tbsp. sugar
1 tbsp. butter or margarine
½ c. unsulphured molasses

Mix corn meal and 2 cups milk. Cook, stirring constantly, for 5 minutes or until thickened. Remove from heat; stir in remaining ingredients. Turn into 1-quart casserole. Bake at 275 degrees for 2 hours. Serve warm with cream or ice cream. Yield: 6 servings.

Photograph for this recipe above.

BAKED INDIAN PUDDING

2 qt. milk
1 ⅓ c. dry corn meal crumbs
Raisins (opt.)
1 ½ c. sugar
2 eggs, beaten
¾ tsp. ginger
1 ½ tsp. cinnamon
½ tsp. salt
Butter

Combine milk, crumbs and raisins; cook over boiling water for 45 minutes, stirring occasionally. Add sugar, eggs, ginger, cinnamon and salt. Pour into buttered 2-quart baking dish. Bake at 350 degrees for 1 hour and 30 minutes. When nearly done, push a large piece of butter into center of pudding; add more milk if necessary. Do not boil. NOTE: Dried Johnnycake or corn muffin crumbs may be used. Yield: 8-10 servings.

Ora B. Maxwell
Uxbridge, Mass.

MOCHA-PECAN PUDDING

1 pkg. orange gelatin
3 tsp. (slightly heaped) instant coffee
½ c. hot water
⅔ c. dark corn syrup
1 c. chopped pecans
½ pt. heavy cream, whipped

Dissolve gelatin and coffee in hot water; stir in syrup. Refrigerate for 1 hour or until syrupy. Whip gelatin; fold in nuts and whipped cream. Chill overnight in fancy mold or in 6 x 10-inch dish. Yield: 6-8 servings.

Mrs. J. P. Patterson
North Hollywood, Calif.

MAPLE PUDDING

1 c. flour
2 tsp. baking powder
¼ tsp. salt
¼ c. sugar
2 tbsp. butter
1 egg
½ c. milk
1 c. maple syrup
Whipped cream (opt.)

Combine all ingredients except syrup and cream; beat until well blended. Heat maple syrup to boiling point; pour into greased 8-inch square baking dish. Blend batter and hot syrup. Bake at 350 degrees for 30 to 35 minutes. Serve hot; garnish with whipped cream. Yield: 5-6 servings.

Mrs. Janice Karakas
Baldwinsville, N.Y.

ORANGE-PINEAPPLE-TAPIOCA PUDDING

¼ c. tapioca
½ c. sugar
1 tsp. grated orange rind
⅛ tsp. salt
1 ½ c. pineapple juice
1 ½ c. orange juice
1 tbsp. lemon juice
¼ c. orange pulp or crushed pineapple

Combine tapioca, sugar, orange rind, salt and fruit juices. Cook in double boiler for 15 to 20 minutes or until tapioca is clear. Remove from heat; add orange pulp. Serve cold with whipped cream. Yield: 6 servings.

Mrs. Robert G. Walker
Middletown, N.Y.

ORANGE PUDDING

2 eggs, separated
½ c. sugar
5 tbsp. cornstarch
1 pt. milk
3 oranges, sectioned

Beat egg yolks in double boiler. Add sugar and cornstarch; blend well. Slowly add milk, stirring constantly. Cook until mixture begins to thicken. Remove from heat; cool thoroughly. Pour over orange sections; cover with beaten egg whites.

Mrs. Arthur E. Gerken
Sault Sainte Marie, Mich.

ORANGE PUDDING

¾ c. sugar
3 oranges, peeled and diced
2 tbsp. cornstarch

2 c. scalded milk
2 eggs, separated

Sprinkle 1/2 cup sugar over oranges; mix well. Let stand for 1 hour. Combine 1/4 cup sugar and cornstarch; add to milk. Cook until mixture coats a spoon. Add beaten egg yolks; cook for 3 minutes. Remove from heat; fold in stiffly beaten egg whites. Pour mixture over oranges; cool. Yield: 6 servings.

Mrs. Ernest Kohn
Westboro, Wisc.

BAKED PEACH PUDDING

2 c. sliced fresh peaches
4 tbsp. butter
¾ c. sugar
½ tsp. salt
1 tsp. baking powder
1 c. flour
½ c. milk

Spread peaches in 8 x 8 x 2-inch pan. Cream butter and sugar. Add all remaining dry ingredients alternately with milk. Spread over fruit.

TOPPING:
1 c. sugar
1 tbsp. cornstarch
¼ tsp. salt
1 c. boiling water

Combine sugar, cornstarch and salt; sift over batter in pan. Pour water over all. Bake at 325 degrees for 50 minutes. Serve plain or with cream. Yield: 8-10 servings.

Mrs. P. B. Gooch
Hinton, W. Va.

BAKED PERSIMMON-DATE PUDDING

3 c. flour
3 tsp. soda
3 tsp. baking powder
1 tsp. salt
2 c. sugar
2 c. chopped nuts
1 c. buttermilk
2 tsp. vanilla flavoring
3 tbsp. butter, melted
2 c. persimmon pulp
2 c. chopped dates

Combine all dry ingredients. Combine all remaining ingredients; sift flour mixture over it. Mix well. Fill two large or three small greased loaf pans three-fourths full. Bake at 325 degrees for 1 hour and 30 minutes. NOTE: May be wrapped in foil and frozen.

Hazel Wilson
Okmulgee, Okla.

216

PERSIMMON PUDDING

1 ½ c. sugar
½ c. butter
3 eggs, beaten lightly
1 pt. persimmon pulp
3 c. sifted flour
1 tsp. cinnamon
½ tsp. soda
½ tsp. salt
1 pt. water
1 pt. milk

Cream sugar and butter. Add eggs and persimmon pulp. Sift flour with cinnamon, soda and salt. Mix water and milk. Alternately add dry ingredients and liquids to creamed mixture. Batter will be very thin, but do not add more flour. Bake at 325 degrees for 1 hour and 30 minutes. Yield: 8-10 servings.

Mrs. E. B. Paine
Longview, Ill.

PERSIMMON PUDDING WITH SAUCE

1 c. persimmon pulp
1 c. sugar
1 c. milk
1 tsp. cinnamon (opt.)
1 c. flour
2 eggs
2 tsp. baking powder
1 tbsp. butter, melted

Thoroughly mix all ingredients except butter. Add butter. Mix thoroughly again. Bake at 350 degrees for 1 hour.

WHITE SAUCE:
½ c. sugar
1 tbsp. butter
⅓ c. water
1 tbsp. flour
1 tsp. vanilla flavoring

Combine all ingredients. Boil until thickened. Serve over pudding. Yield: 8-10 servings.

Mrs. Harold S. Fisher
Corydon, Ind.

WALNUT-PERSIMMON PUDDING

2 tbsp. butter
1 c. sugar
1 c. persimmon pulp
1 ½ c. flour
1 tsp. soda
½ tsp. salt
1 tsp. cinnamon
½ tsp. nutmeg
½ c. milk
1 c. raisins
1 c. English walnuts

Cream butter and sugar; add persimmon pulp. Sift all dry ingredients. Alternately add dry ingredients and milk to pulp mixture. Mix in raisins and walnuts. Pour into buttered casserole. Bake at 350 degrees for 1 hour. Serve warm or cold with hot lemon sauce. Yield: 6 servings.

Mrs. Lester Reed
Stillwater, Okla.

PINEAPPLE-CHEESE PUDDING

1 No. 2 can crushed pineapple
2 tbsp. cornstarch
¼ c. water
1 c. cottage cheese
1 c. sugar
¼ c. softened butter
½ c. unsifted flour
2 eggs
1 tsp. vanilla flavoring
¾ c. milk

Put pineapple in saucepan; add cornstarch dissolved in water. Simmer until clear. Spread in a 10-inch ovenproof baking dish; cool. Have remaining ingredients at room temperature. Mix cottage cheese with sugar. Add butter, flour and an egg at a time. Mix in vanilla and milk. Pour batter over pineapple. The batter might look separated, but it does not affect the results. Bake at 450 degrees for 10 minutes. Reduce heat to 350 degrees; bake for 30 minutes. Serve cold. Yield: 10-12 servings.

Mrs. W. J. Faucher
Suffolk County AFB, N.Y.

PINEAPPLE PUDDING

4 tbsp. butter
¾ c. sugar
2 eggs
1 c. finely chopped nuts
1 lge. can crushed pineapple, drained
1 pt. heavy cream, whipped
½ lb. graham crackers, ground

Cream butter and sugar. Add eggs; beat until very light. Add nuts and pineapple. Fold in whipped cream. Line a 2 1/2-quart pan with one-half of the cracker crumbs. Add pineapple mixture. Top with remaining cracker crumbs. Chill until ready to serve. Yield: 12 servings.

Mrs. Hugh M. Morgan
Bossier City, La.

PINE-SCOTCH PUDDING

2 eggs
1 c. sugar
1 c. pineapple
1 c. nuts
¾ c. flour
1 tsp. baking powder
¼ tsp. salt

(Continued on next page)

Beat eggs until fluffy. Add sugar; beat until thick and ivory-colored. Fold in pineapple and nuts. Sift flour, baking powder and salt; fold in. Pour into 12 x 8 x 2-inch pan. Bake in 325 degree oven for 30 to 35 minutes.

BUTTERSCOTCH SAUCE:
¼ c. butter
1 tbsp. flour
1 c. (firmly packed) brown sugar
¼ c. pineapple juice
¼ c. water
1 egg
½ tsp. vanilla flavoring

Melt butter; blend in flour. Add brown sugar, pineapple juice and water. Boil for 3 minutes, stirring constantly. Gradually add hot sauce to beaten egg. Cook for 1 minute. Add vanilla; chill.

Mrs. Marybelle Faur
Oak Lawn, Ill.

JELLIED PLUM PUDDING
1 pkg. orange flavored gelatin
2 c. boiling water
1 c. pineapple juice
1 c. chopped dates
½ c. broken nuts
½ c. chopped candied fruit peel
½ c. chopped citron
1 tsp. cinnamon
½ tsp. cloves
¼ tsp. grated lemon rind
⅛ tsp. salt
1 pkg. raspberry gelatin
1 c. orange juice

Dissolve orange gelatin in 1 cup water. Add pineapple juice; chill. Fold in all remaining ingredients except raspberry gelatin, orange juice and remaining water. Pour into a large mold; chill until firm. Cover with raspberry gelatin dissolved in remaining 1 cup boiling water and orange juice. Chill until firm. Unmold carefully; surround with whipped cream. NOTE: This dessert should be made a day prior to serving. Yield: 12 servings.

Evelyn Stoneberger
Miami, Fla.

PLUM PUDDING
2 tsp. soda
⅔ c. sugar
1 c. ground suet
½ c. molasses
1 c. milk
1 box raisins, ground
1 tsp. cinnamon
1 tsp. salt
½ tsp. nutmeg
2 boxes dates, ground
3 eggs
1 c. chopped nuts
4 c. flour

Dissolve soda in hot water. Mix all ingredients. Steam for 3 hours covered with a cloth or tin foil in an angel food cake pan. Freeze until needed. Serve with lemon sauce. Yield: 12 servings.

Mrs. H. L. Marshall
Jackson, Mich.

PLUM PUDDING
1 lb. raisins
1 lb. currants
1 pt. chopped suet
½ c. citron, finely chopped
1 c. sugar
½ tsp. nutmeg
½ tsp. salt
1 ½ pt. bread crumbs
5 eggs, lightly beaten
4 tbsp. flour
2 tbsp. milk
½ lb. cooked prunes, finely chopped
2 glasses or 1 jar orange marmalade
1 lb. almonds, blanched and chopped
½ c. brandy flavoring (opt.)

Flour raisins, currants, suet and citron. Combine remaining ingredients; blend well. Add fruit mixture. Tie pudding in cheesecloth bags; steam for 3 hours. When serving, warm in double boiler without bag; serve with hard sauce or brandy sauce. Yield: 8-10 servings.

Jean I. Law
Nutley, N.J.

SUGARPLUM PUDDING
2 c. sifted flour
½ tsp. salt
1 ½ c. sugar
1 ¼ tsp. soda
1 tsp. nutmeg
1 tsp. cinnamon
2 ½ tsp. baking powder
3 eggs
1 c. buttermilk
1 c. cooked prunes
1 c. chopped nuts
¾ c. salad oil

Sift all dry ingredients; stir in remaining ingredients. Pour into two greased and floured 9-inch pans or one rectangular pan. Bake in preheated 325 degree oven for 40 minutes.

ICING:
1 c. sugar
1 stick margarine
½ c. buttermilk
1 tsp. light corn syrup
1 tsp. vanilla flavoring

Combine all ingredients in a saucepan; bring to a boil. Pour over pudding while hot. Yield: 6-8 servings.

Mrs. Betty A. Cox
Dover, N.J.

VEGETABLE-PLUM PUDDING

2 c. flour
1 c. sugar
1 tsp. salt
1 c. ground beef suet
1 c. nuts, chopped
1 tsp. cinnamon
1 tsp. soda
1 tsp. cloves
1 c. grated raw carrots
1 c. grated potatoes
1 c. seeded raisins
2 eggs, beaten

Mix flour, sugar, salt, suet, nuts, cinnamon, soda and cloves. Add vegetables, raisins and eggs. Place mixture in a greased tin can; put waxed paper under lid. Boil for 4 hours.

SAUCE:

8 tbsp. sugar
4 tbsp. butter, melted
2 tbsp. flour
1 egg
1 c. water
1 tsp. vanilla flavoring

Combine all ingredients. Serve with plum pudding.

Mrs. Bernice Broscius
Hollywood, Fla.

NORWEGIAN PRUNE PUDDING

½ lb. prunes
1 c. sugar
⅛ tsp. salt
1 2-in. stick cinnamon
1 ½ c. boiling water
¼ c. cornstarch
1 tbsp. lemon juice

Cook prunes in 2 cups water; remove stones. Add sugar, salt, cinnamon and boiling water. Simmer for 10 minutes. Dilute cornstarch with enough cold water to pour easily; add to prune mixture. Stir and cook for 10 minutes. Remove cinnamon; add lemon juice. Pour into mold; chill and serve. Yield: 4 servings.

Mrs. Harole Kebler
Six Lakes, Mich.

DATE-NUT-PUMPKIN PUDDING

½ c. chopped dates
½ c. chopped walnuts
½ c. plus 2 tbsp. flour
½ tsp. baking powder
¼ tsp. soda
½ tsp. salt
½ tsp. cinnamon
½ tsp. nutmeg
½ tsp. ginger
¼ c. butter or margarine
1 c. brown sugar
⅔ c. pumpkin
½ tsp. vanilla flavoring
2 eggs

Combine dates and nuts with 2 tablespoons flour. Sift 1/2 cup flour. with baking powder, soda, salt and spices. Melt butter; add brown sugar. Stir until blended. Remove from heat. Blend in pumpkin and vanilla. Add an egg at a time, beating well after each addition. Blend in dry ingredients; stir in date mixture. Pour into greased 9 x 9 x 2-inch pan. Bake at 350 degrees for 30 to 35 minutes. Serve topped with whipped cream or warm lemon sauce. Yield: 9 servings.

Mrs. Marie A. Scheatzle
Akron, O.

HOLIDAY PUMPKIN PUDDING

¼ c. flour
¼ tsp. salt
½ tsp. soda
1 tsp. cinnamon
½ c. chopped nuts
1 No. 303 can pumpkin
1 c. gingersnap crumbs
½ c. shredded coconut
¼ c. melted margarine
½ c. molasses
1 c. evaporated milk

Sift all dry ingredients. Add nuts; mix well. Combine with all remaining ingredients. Mix until smooth. Pour into greased 1 1/2-quart mold; cover. Set in pan of hot water. Bake at 350 degrees for 1 hour and 30 minutes. Serve hot or cold with ice cream, whipped cream or hard sauce. Yield: 8-10 servings.

Mrs. Minnie Kelley
Cameron, Mo.

RAISIN PUDDING

2 c. raisins
4 egg yolks, beaten
4 c. buttermilk
1 tbsp. vinegar
1 tbsp. butter
1 tsp. cinnamon
1 tsp. allspice
2 c. sugar
3 tbsp. cornstarch
1 tsp. nutmeg
1 tsp. salt

Soak raisins in boiling water for a few minutes; drain well. Mix egg yolks, buttermilk, vinegar and butter in a saucepan. Combine remaining ingredients; add to egg mixture. Cook until thickened; pour into a baking dish.

MERINGUE:

4 egg whites, stiffly beaten
½ c. sugar
½ tsp. vanilla or lemon flavoring

Beat egg whites until frothy. Gradually beat in sugar, a small amount at a time. Continue beating until stiff and glossy; beat in flavoring.

(Continued on next page)

Swirl meringue over pudding. Bake in a 400 degree oven for 8 to 10 minutes or until golden. Yield: 8 servings.

Mrs. Fern Whittaker
Madera, Calif.

RASPBERRY PUDDING

1 qt. raspberries
1 ½ c. plus 2 tbsp. sugar
2 c. milk
1 c. bread crumbs
2 tbsp. butter
3 eggs, separated

Cook raspberries with 3/4 cup sugar. Heat milk; pour over bread crumbs. Add 1/2 cup sugar and butter. Cool slightly; stir in beaten egg yolks. Pour into a buttered 9-inch tubed pan. Bake at 350 degrees for 20 to 25 minutes or until firm when tested. Pour cooked raspberries over custard. Top with beaten egg whites mixed with 6 remaining tablespoons sugar. Bake at 200 to 250 degrees for 5 to 10 minutes or until brown. Yield: 6 servings.

Mrs. Wayne W. Cupp
Texarkana, Tex.

RHUBARB PUDDING

3 c. chopped rhubarb
1 c. sugar
⅓ tsp. cinnamon
1 tbsp. butter
½ c. sugar
½ c. milk
1 egg, beaten
1 c. flour
1 tsp. baking powder

Mix rhubarb, sugar and cinnamon; pour into buttered 8 x 10-inch baking dish. Mix remaining ingredients; pour over rhubarb mixture. Bake at 350 degrees for 30 minutes. Yield: 10 servings.

Mrs. Lawrence E. Olson
Calumet AFS, Mich.

BUTTERSCOTCH-RICE PUDDING

½ c. rice
4 c. milk
½ tsp. salt
1 tsp. vanilla flavoring
½ tsp. nutmeg
½ c. sugar
½ tsp. cinnamon
3 tbsp. butterscotch pudding mix

Place all ingredients except pudding mix in 1 1/2-quart greased baking dish; stir well. Bake at 325 degrees for 1 hour and 45 minutes, stirring every 20 minutes during the first hour. Add pudding mix; continue cooking until thickened to desired consistency. Yield: 6 servings.

Mrs. April Primerano
Ferndale, Mich.

CENTURY OLD LEMON-RICE PUDDING

1 c. cold cooked rice
1 pt. cold milk
3 eggs, separated
Grated rind of 1 lemon
1 ½ to 2 tbsp. butter
2 c. sugar
Juice of 1 lemon

Combine rice and milk; add egg yolks, lemon rind and butter. Mix well. Bake at 350 degrees for 2 hours. Beat egg whites until stiff; add sugar and lemon juice. Cover cool pudding with meringue. Bake at 350 degrees until brown. Yield: 6 servings.

Vivian L. Smith
Wendell, N.H.

GINGER-RICE PUDDING

½ c. rice
5 c. cold milk
½ c. sugar
½ tsp. salt
1 tsp. vanilla flavoring
½ c. preserved ginger and syrup
1 c. heavy cream, whipped

Soak rice for 30 minutes; drain. Add cold milk. Bake at 350 degrees for 1 hour, stirring several times. Add sugar, salt and vanilla. Bake for 1 to 2 hours without stirring. Chill. Fold in chopped ginger, syrup and whipped cream. Serve cold. Garnish with whipped cream. Yield: 8 servings.

Mrs. George C. Dewey
Fort George G. Meade, Md.

GLORIFIED RICE PUDDING

⅓ c. rice, cooked
2 c. milk
2 tbsp. butter or margarine
½ c. brown sugar
¼ c. dry powdered milk
½ tsp. vanilla flavoring
2 eggs, beaten

Combine all ingredients; blend thoroughly. Pour into a buttered baking dish; place in a pan of water. Bake at 320 degrees for 30 minutes. Yield: 6 servings.

Rubie Morse Berger
Prospect, Conn.

HONEY-RICE PUDDING

½ c. uncooked rice
4 c. milk
¼ c. honey
½ tsp. salt
½ c. seeded raisins
¼ tsp. ground nutmeg
1 tsp. grated lemon rind

Combine all ingredients in a greased 1 1/2-quart baking dish. Bake at 300 degrees for 2 hours or until pudding is of creamy consistency. Serve with honey or cream. Yield: 6 servings.

Photograph for this recipe on page 201 .

OLD-FASHIONED CREAMY RICE PUDDING

⅓ c. rice
⅓ c. brown sugar
1 qt. milk
½ tsp. salt
½ tsp. nutmeg
¼ tsp. cinnamon

Wash rice; add all remaining ingredients. Pour into a greased baking dish. Bake at 300 degrees for 2 hours or until thick and creamy, stirring occasionally. This mixture should not boil. NOTE: Baking time may be shortened by scalding milk. Yield: 6 servings.

Mrs. Alberta Hawkins
Battle Creek, Mich.

PINEAPPLE-MERINGUE-RICE PUDDING

¼ c. plus 5 tbsp. sugar
⅓ c. flour
⅓ tsp. salt
2 c. milk, scalded
3 eggs, separated
1 ¼ tsp. vanilla flavoring
2 c. cooked rice
1 sm. can crushed pineapple, drained

Combine 1/4 cup sugar, flour and salt; add scalded milk gradually. Add beaten egg yolks. Cook in a double boiler until thickened; cool. Add 1 teaspoon vanilla. Blend rice and pineapple; add custard. Place in a square baking dish. Beat egg whites with remaining 5 tablespoons sugar and 1/4 teaspoon vanilla; spread over custard. Bake at 450 degrees for 5 minutes or until browned. Yield: 12 servings.

Mrs. David Kopel
Brookline, Mass.

POOR MAN'S PUDDING

½ c. rice
½ c. sugar
⅛ tsp. salt
⅛ tsp. nutmeg
4 c. milk

Sprinkle washed rice into baking dish; add sugar, salt, nutmeg and milk. Bake at 350 degrees for 1 hour and 30 minutes. Serve with milk or cream. Yield: 6 servings.

Mrs. Arnold Watermeier
Burr, Mo.

RICE AND RAISIN PUDDING

1 c. rice
½ c. raisins
¾ tsp. salt
4 c. water
3 eggs, well beaten
1 c. milk
½ tsp. vanilla flavoring
½ tsp. lemon flavoring
1 c. sugar
⅛ tsp. cinnamon
3 slices white bread, cubed
Butter

Cook rice and raisins in salted water until rice is tender. Combine eggs, milk and flavorings. Stir in sugar and cinnamon. Add bread cubes to egg mixture; combine with rice and raisins. Pour into buttered baking dish; dot butter over top. Bake at 325 degrees about 1 hour. Yield: 6-8 servings.

Mrs. John Doremire
Chalmers, Ind.

RUM PUDDING

2 tbsp. unflavored gelatin
2 tbsp. cold water
6 tbsp. boiling water
1 c. sugar
⅓ c. rum
4 tbsp. bourbon
2 egg whites, stiffly beaten
1 ½ pt. heavy cream, whipped
½ c. slivered toasted almonds

Soak gelatin in cold water; add boiling water. Set aside in warm place so it does not harden. Fold sugar, rum and bourbon into egg whites. Add gelatin mixture; fold in 1 pint whipped cream. Pour into mold or square pan; refrigerate until firm. Unmold; cover with remaining 1/2 pint whipped cream and slivered toasted almonds. Yield: 8 servings.

Mrs. J. G. Osborn
USNS Mayport, Fla.

SUMMER PUDDING

1 No. 303 can fruit cocktail
1 c. flour
1 c. sugar
¾ tsp. soda
1 egg

Drain fruit cocktail, reserving liquid. Mix flour, sugar, soda, egg and liquid from fruit; fold in fruit. Pour into greased and floured pan.

(Continued on next page)

TOPPING:
½ c. brown sugar
¼ c. chopped raisins
¼ c. chopped nuts

Combine all ingredients; sprinkle over pudding. Bake at 350 degrees for 40 to 50 minutes. Yield: 4 servings.

Mrs. Frances Lauderdale
Anderson, Mo.

SWING PUDDING

2 c. cooked rice, chilled
1 c. drained crushed pineapple
1 c. chopped apples
½ c. sugar
24 marshmallows, cut up
1 c. chopped pecans (opt.)
1 pt. heavy cream, whipped

Combine all ingredients except whipped cream. Fold in cream. Chill. NOTE: One family-size package dessert topping may be used in place of cream. Yield: 10 servings.

Mrs. Floyd Branson
Manilla, Ind.

APRICOT SOUFFLE WITH BRANDY SAUCE

1 ¼ c. dried apricots
¾ c. water
¼ tsp. almond flavoring
4 egg whites
⅛ tsp. cream of tartar
Dash of salt
¼ c. sugar
1 c. cold heavy cream
1 tbsp. confectioners sugar

Cover and simmer apricots in water for 30 minutes or until very tender. Press apricots with cooking liquid through sieve or food mill, or mix in blender to make puree. To 1 cup apricot puree, add 1/8 teaspoon almond flavoring; refrigerate for several hours or overnight. Let apricot puree and egg whites set out at room temperature. Beat egg whites until foamy; add cream of tartar and salt, continuing to beat until soft peaks are formed. Gradually add sugar, 1 tablespoon at a time, beating after each addition until whites form stiff peaks. Gently fold puree into whites; pour into buttered and lightly sugared casserole. Set in pan of hot water. Bake at 325 degrees for 40 minutes. Whip cream until stiff; add confectioners sugar and 1/8 teaspoon almond flavoring. Serve souffle at once with whipped cream and hot brandy sauce.

BRANDY SAUCE:
½ c. soft butter
1 c. sifted confectioners sugar
1 egg, beaten
2 to 3 tbsp. brandy

Beat butter until creamy; add sugar gradually, beating until light and fluffy. Beat in egg; refrigerate for several hours or overnight. About 15 minutes before serving, pour sauce into double boiler. Add brandy; heat, stirring occasionally until hot. Serve at once. Yield: 8 servings.

Mrs. Albert C. Petersen
Duluth AFB, Minn.

FOOD-OF-THE-GODS

2 eggs
Pinch of salt
1 c. sugar
1 tsp. (heaping) flour
1 tsp. baking powder
1 c. chopped English walnuts
1 pkg. dates
Milk
Whipped cream

Stir, do not beat, eggs; add salt. Add sugar, flour and baking powder; mix by hand. Add nuts and dates; mix. Cover with milk. Bake at 350 degrees for 40 minutes. Serve with whipped cream. Yield: 8-10 servings.

Edythe F. Geer
Pataskala, O.

MAGIC ORANGE CUPS

¾ c. sugar
1 ½ tbsp. shortening
1 tbsp. grated orange rind
2 eggs, separated
3 tbsp. sifted flour
1 c. (scant) milk
⅓ c. orange juice

Cream sugar and shortening; add orange rind and egg yolks. Beat well. Add flour alternately with milk and juice; fold in beaten egg whites. Put into greased custard cups or a 4 x 8-inch pan. Set in pan containing 1-inch hot water. Bake at 350 degrees for 20 minutes. Yield: 5 servings.

Mrs. Willa Dailey
Gibbon, Nebraska

PEACH-TAPIOCA DESSERT

1 c. pearl tapioca
3 c. water
Pinch of salt
¾ c. sugar
1 c. whipped cream or dessert topping mix
1 lge. can sliced peaches, drained
1 tsp. vanilla flavoring

Soak tapioca overnight in water. Cook over low heat until transparent. Add salt and sugar. Set in cool place. Add whipped cream, peaches and vanilla when ready to serve. Yield: 6-8 servings.

Mrs. George Lee
Soldier, Iowa

Fruit Desserts

RECIPE FOR ORANGE BLOSSOM BOWL ON PAGE 229

APPLE BETTY

3 lb. apples, sliced
1 c. graham cracker crumbs
½ c. sugar
¼ lb. butter

Place layer of apples in 11 x 7 x 2-inch buttered dish. Sprinkle with crumbs and sugar. Dot with butter. Make three layers of each. Cover with foil. Bake at 350 degrees for 1 hour; remove foil after 50 minutes. Serve warm with ice cream. Yield: 8 servings.

Mrs. Dorothy Brady
Arlington, Vt.

APPLE-BRAN SCALLOP

6 tart apples, sliced
¾ tsp. cinnamon
1 c. sugar
Juice of 1 lemon
4 tbsp. butter
1 ½ c. bran flakes

Combine apple slices, cinnamon and 3/4 cup sugar. Add lemon juice; place in baking dish. Cover and bake at 400 degrees for 45 minutes. Cream butter; add remaining 1/4 cup sugar. Cream until blended; work in bran evenly. Sprinkle over apples. Bake, uncovered, at 400 degrees for 15 minutes longer or until topping is crusty. Yield: 6 servings.

Marie L. Andorf
Finley, N.D.

APPLE-BUTTER ROLL

½ pt. heavy cream
½ c. apple butter
30 vanilla wafers
1 c. chopped nuts

Whip cream; fold in apple butter. Spread each wafer with mixture, placing one on top of another until all wafers are used. Cover outside of roll with remaining cream mixture; sprinkle with nuts. Refrigerate for 3 hours. Cut into diagonal slices; serve with whipped cream.

Mrs. Harvey W. Eddy
Bedford, Mass.

APPLE-COCONUT CRISP

5 or 6 c. sliced pared apples
1 c. sifted flour
¾ c. sugar
1 tsp. baking powder
¾ tsp. salt
½ c. coconut
1 egg
⅓ c. shortening, melted
½ tsp. cinnamon

Place apples in buttered 8-inch square baking dish. Mix flour with sugar, baking powder, salt, coconut and egg until crumbly; sprinkle over apples. Pour cooled shortening over flour mixture. Sprinkle with cinnamon. Bake at 350 degrees for 30 to 40 minutes. Serve with cream. NOTE: Peaches may be substituted for apples. Yield: 6-8 servings.

Mrs. Walter Zalla
Burlington, Ky.

APPLE CRISP

1 c. chopped apples
1 egg, beaten
1 c. sugar
½ c. shortening
1 c. flour
1 tsp. baking powder
¼ tsp. soda
1 tsp. cinnamon
½ tsp. nutmeg
¼ tsp. salt

Combine apples, egg, sugar and shortening. Sift all dry ingredients; add to apple mixture. Blend well; pour into baking dish. Bake at 350 to 375 degrees for 30 minutes. Serve with whipped cream or ice cream. Yield: 6-8 servings.

Mrs. Clarence M. Curtis
Endicott, N.Y.

APPLE CRUNCH

Peeled and diced apples
½ c. sugar
1 tsp. cinnamon
1 c. brown sugar
½ c. butter or margarine
¾ c. quick cooking oats
¾ c. flour

Fill pie tin one-half full of apples; cover with white sugar and cinnamon. Mix brown sugar, butter, oats and flour; press mixture down on top of apples. Bake at 350 degrees until brown. Serve with cream or ice cream. Yield: 6 servings.

Mrs. Enid Stanley
What Cheer, Iowa

APPLE CRUNCH

4 lge. apples, peeled
1 c. sugar
Cinnamon
¼ lb. butter
1 c. flour
½ c. brown sugar

Slice apples in baking dish; sprinkle sugar and cinnamon over apples. Cream butter; stir in flour and brown sugar. Spread smoothly

(Continued on next page)

224

*There'll be no tricks at your house come Hallo-
ween if you treat the witches and hobgoblins with
this delicious, refreshing punch and cherries. This
combination is so good you'll want to serve it year
'round.*

SWEDISH SPICED HALLOWEEN PUNCH

12 whole cloves
12 whole allspice
1 whole nutmeg, cracked
3 cinnamon sticks
4 oranges, sliced
4 lemons, sliced
$\frac{3}{4}$ c. red Maraschino cherries
$\frac{1}{3}$ c. Maraschino cherry syrup
$\frac{1}{8}$ tsp. salt
6 c. water
2 qt. apple juice
2 6-oz. cans frozen lemonade concentrate
1 c. sugar
$\frac{1}{2}$ c. dairy sour cream
$\frac{1}{4}$ tsp. salt
1 c. heavy cream, whipped

Tie first four ingredients in a cheesecloth bag.
Combine spice bag, oranges, lemons, cherries,
syrup, ⅛ teaspoon salt and water in saucepan.
Simmer 1 hour. Strain through a cheesecloth-lined
sieve. Return to saucepan with apple juice, lemonade concentrate and sugar. Heat, stirring occasionally, to serving temperature. Fold sour cream
and ¼ teaspoon salt into whipped cream; spoon
onto hot punch. Yield: 4 quarts.

GLAZED SWEDISH DUNKING CHERRIES

$\frac{1}{4}$ c. light corn syrup
3 tbsp. currant jelly
1 tbsp. lemon juice
$\frac{1}{4}$ tsp. cinnamon
2 tbsp. Maraschino cherry syrup
1 c. red Maraschino cherries, well drained

Combine first four ingredients in saucepan. Cook
over low heat, stirring occasionally, until mixture
spins a ¼-inch thread. Add cherry syrup and continue cooking over low heat, stirring occasionally,
until mixture again spins a ¼-inch thread. Dip
cherries, one at a time, into hot glaze. Drain on
waxed paper. Yield: 40 cherries.

See photograph on reverse page.

over apples. Bake at 300 degrees for 55 minutes. Serve warm with ice cream or whipped cream. Yield: 4-5 servings.

Mrs. Robert C. Lloyd
Whidbey Island, Wash.

APPLE DAPPLE

¼ c. margarine
1 c. sugar
1 egg
1 c. sifted flour
1 tsp. soda
¼ tsp. salt
1 tsp. cinnamon
¼ tsp. nutmeg
1 tsp. vanilla flavoring
2 c. grated tart apples
½ c. chopped walnuts

Mix all ingredients. Pour into greased 8 x 8 x 2-inch pan. Bake at 350 degrees for 45 minutes. Serve warm with whipped cream or ice cream. Yield: 6 servings.

Mrs. Paul F. Dietzel
West Point, N.Y.

BAKED APPLES WITH FOAMY LEMON DELIGHT

6 med. baking apples, cored
½ c. sugar
¼ c. milk
1 tbsp. grated lemon rind
1 tbsp. lemon juice
¼ tsp. salt
¼ c. melted butter or margarine
1 egg, beaten

Remove 1 inch of peeling from stem end of apples. Place in baking dish. Cover and bake at 350 degrees for 35 to 40 minutes. Add remaining ingredients to egg; blend. Pour over apples. Continue baking for 15 minutes. Yield: 6 servings.

Eleanor Fairchild
Owosso, Mich.

BEST APPLE CRISP

6 lge. tart cooking apples, pared, cored and diced
½ c. orange juice
1 c. sugar
½ tsp. cinnamon
¾ c. flour
¼ tsp. salt
6 tbsp. butter

Arrange apples in a greased 11 x 7 x 2-inch baking dish; pour orange juice over apples. Combine 1/2 cup sugar and cinnamon; sprinkle evenly over apples. Combine flour, remaining 1/2 cup sugar and salt; cut in butter until mixture is crumbly. Spoon over apple slices. Bake at 350 degrees for 45 to 60 minutes or until apples are tender and crust is brown. Serve warm or cold, with cream or milk.

Mrs. Elizabeth Weaver
Allen, Kans.

BLUSH BAKED APPLES

8 baking apples, cored
1 pkg. cinnamon candies
½ c. sugar
1 c. water

Peel one-third of each apple beginning at stem end. Place in deep baking dish; stuff with 7 to 10 cinnamon candies and 1 tablespoon sugar. Finish filling center with water; pour remaining water around apples. Bake at 350 degrees for 45 to 60 minutes or until tender. Baste occasionally. Yield: 8 servings.

Margaret Christensen
San Bernardino, Calif.

CARAMEL APPLES

4 lge. apples, peeled and sliced
1 stick butter
1 c. sugar
1 c. brown sugar
1 c. flour
Juice of ½ lemon

Place apples in baking dish. Cream butter; add remaining ingredients to make a paste. Spread over apples. Bake at 350 degrees for 35 minutes. Yield: 8 servings.

Mrs. J. E. Rylee
Jacksonville, Fla.

DEVILED APPLES

½ c. water
½ c. sugar
¼ c. red cinnamon candies
Cloves
4 tart peeled apples, cored and halved

Boil water, sugar, candies and cloves for 5 minutes. Put apples in syrup. Reduce heat; cover and cook until apples are tender. Garnish with mint leaves if desired.

Mrs. May Puckett
Oak Hill, W. Va.

FLAMING APPLE MELBA

1 baking apple, cored
1 ½ tbsp. orange marmalade
½ c. cranberry juice
1 sugar cube
1 tsp. lemon flavoring

(Continued on next page)

Peel one-half of apple. Fill center with marmalade. Place in shallow baking pan. Pour cranberry juice over apple. Bake at 375 degrees for 30 minutes or until tender, basting with pan juices every 5 minutes. Serve hot or chilled with pan drippings spooned over apple. Place sugar cube in center of apple. Pour lemon flavoring over cube. Ignite; serve immediately.

Mrs. Carmela Castellano
Island Park, N.Y.

FRUIT CRISP

1 c. sifted flour
1 c. brown sugar
⅓ c. butter
6 apples, sliced

Mix flour and sugar; cut in butter. Arrange apples in buttered dish. Spread with sugar mixture. Bake at 350 degrees for 45 minutes or until golden brown. Serve warm. NOTE: Eight peaches, 4 cups cherries or 4 cups rhubarb may be used. Add 1/3 to 1/2 cup sugar if cherries or rhubarb are used. Yield: 6-8 servings.

Mrs. F. D. Sanger
Franklin, Nebr.

GERMAN APPLE KUCHEN

2 ¼ c. flour
½ c. sugar
3 tsp. baking powder
¼ tsp. salt
10 oz. med. cream, whipped
Peeled and quartered apples
3 tbsp. melted butter
½ c. sugar
2 tsp. cinnamon
Chopped nuts (opt.)

Sift flour with sugar, baking powder and salt. Fold in cream. Pat mixture into greased 9 x 13-inch pan. Place sliced apples on top in rows; brush with melted butter. Mix sugar, cinnamon and nuts; sprinkle on top of apples. Bake at 400 degrees for 15 minutes. Reduce heat to 350 degrees; bake until apples are soft.

Mrs. Doris S. Trianovich
Seymour, Conn.

JELLIED APPLES

6 apples, halved
½ lemon, sliced
2 c. water
2 c. sugar

Place apples, skin-side down, in flat pan; add lemon and water. Cover and boil briskly until

apples are tender. Add sugar; continue boiling until syrup thickens. Serve in flat dish; pour syrup over apples. Yield: 6 servings.

Mrs. Fritz Michalke
Schulenburg, Tex.

OLD-FASHIONED APPLE ROLL

PASTRY:
1 ½ c. flour
½ tsp. salt
½ c. lard or shortening
2 ½ tbsp. cold water

Combine flour, salt and lard; work together until fine and evenly mixed. Stir in water. Roll into a sheet.

FILLING:
4 or 5 apples, peeled and chopped
Sugar to taste
Cinnamon or nutmeg to taste

Combine all ingredients. Spread on dough; roll as for jelly roll. Cut into 1 1/2-inch pieces. Place in 9 x 9-inch pan, cut-side up. Pour boiling water almost to top of rolls. Bake at 400 degrees for 1 hour. Yield: 6 servings.

Gladys Piersol
Davisville, W. Va.

ORANGE-FLAVORED APPLES

6 lge. baking apples
⅓ c. flour
⅔ c. sugar
⅓ c. butter or margarine
¼ tsp. cinnamon
¼ c. water
½ c. orange juice

Pare and core apples; arrange in buttered baking dish. Combine flour, sugar, butter and cinnamon; mix until crumbly. Fill cavities of apples with crumb mixture; sprinkle remaining crumbs over top. Add water and orange juice. Bake at 350 degrees for 1 hour to 1 hour and 15 minutes. Yield: 6 servings.

Mrs. Ivan R. Webb
Lathrop, Calif.

APRICOT ROLL

2 c. flour
1 ½ c. plus 2 tbsp. sugar
3 tsp. baking powder
1 tsp. salt
6 tbsp. shortening
⅔ to ¾ c. milk
3 c. chopped apricots
1 tbps. butter
2 c. water

(Continued on next page)

Sift flour with 2 tablespoons sugar, baking powder and salt; cut in shortening. Stir in milk to make soft dough. Knead lightly; roll out to 6 x 12-inch rectangle, 1/3-inch thick. Spread with apricots; dot with butter. Roll up like a jelly roll; pinch edges to seal. Slice 1 1/2-inches thick. Put remaining 1 1/2 cups sugar and water in 9 x 13-inch pan. Cook for 5 minutes. Place slices, cut-side down, in boiling sugar mixture. Bake at 450 degrees for 20 to 25 minutes. Serve warm. Yield: 10 servings.

Mrs. E. E. Sabbe
Wheeler, Tex.

BAKED BANANAS

6 tbsp. sugar
Juice of 3 or 4 lemons
Pinch of salt
4 tbsp. butter, melted
6 ripe bananas, peeled

Blend sugar, lemon juice, salt and butter. Pour sauce over bananas in a shallow baking pan. Broil slowly, turning once; baste frequently. Remove when slightly browned. Serve warm as a meat accompaniment or a dessert sprinkled with cinnamon. Yield: 6 servings.

Mrs. Franklyn W. Oatman
Berkeley, Calif.

BANANAS FLAMBE

3 tbsp. butter or margarine
¾ c. brown sugar
¼ c. dark rum
6 med. bananas, sliced lengthwise
2 tbsp. brandy
Ice cream

Heat butter and sugar in chafing dish. Add rum. Place bananas in pan; simmer for 7 minutes. Heat brandy; ignite. Pour into pan. Stir gently until flame burns out. Serve over vanilla ice cream. Yield: 6 servings.

Mrs. J. H. B. Smith
Sunnyvale, Calif.

BOYSENBERRY DELIGHT

1 ½ c. fine graham cracker crumbs
¼ c. melted butter or margarine
½ c. milk
½ lb. marshmallows
1 c. heavy cream
¼ c. sugar
3 tbsp. cornstarch
1 lge. can sweetened boysenberries
1 tbsp. lemon juice

Mix crumbs with butter; line an 8 x 12-inch pan, reserving 3 tablespoons for topping. Stir milk and marshmallows in top of double boiler; melt and cool. Whip cream; fold in marshmallow mixture. Mix sugar and cornstarch; add to berries. Cook over medium heat until thick. Stir in lemon juice; cool. Pour one-half of the marshmallow mixture into crumb-lined pan; cover with berries. Add remaining marshmallow mixture. Sprinkle with reserved crumbs. Chill for several hours before serving. Yield: 10 servings.

Mrs. William L. Sutterfield
Detroit, Mich.

CHERRIES WITH BRANDY

1 can dark cherries
4 oz. red currant jelly
2 oz. brandy

Mix cherries with currant jelly; refrigerate for several hours. Pour brandy over cherries and jelly just before serving. Yield: 4 servings.

Mrs. Daniel F. Munster
Schenectady, N.Y.

CHERRY DELIGHT

18 graham crackers, crushed
¼ lb. butter
1 8-oz. pkg. cream cheese
1 c. powdered sugar
1 c. finely chopped walnuts
1 pkg. dessert topping mix
1 can cherry pie filling

Mix cracker crumbs with butter; press into a dish. Bake at 350 degrees for 10 minutes. Blend cheese and powdered sugar; spread on crust. Sprinkle with walnuts. Prepare topping mix according to package directions; spread on cheese mixture. Pour cherry pie filling on top; chill. Yield: 8 servings.

Nancy Littler
Rome, N.Y.

CRANBERRY CRISP

1 stick margarine
¾ c. dark brown sugar
1 c. quick oats
⅔ c. flour
⅔ can whole cranberry sauce

Cream margarine and sugar; add oats and flour. Press one-half of mixture in greased 8-inch square pan. Spread with cranberry sauce. Sprinkle remaining mixture on top. Bake at 350 degrees for 40 to 45 minutes. Top with vanilla ice cream. Yield: 9 servings.

Mrs. Paul E. Whittington
Natick Lab., Mass.

CRANBERRY CRUNCH

1 c. oats
½ c. flour
1 c. dark brown sugar
½ c. margarine
½ tsp. vanilla flavoring
1 1-lb. can cranberry jelly, strained

Mix all ingredients except jelly. Put one-half of mixture on bottom of greased 8-inch square pan. Put cranberry jelly over mixture. Spread remaining mixture on top of cranberry layer. Bake at 350 degrees for 45 minutes. Cool in pan. Serve warm or cold with whipped cream or ice cream. Yield: 8 servings.

Mrs. George G. Zimmerman
Lemoore, Calif.

CRANBERRY DESSERT

1 c. oats
1 c. brown sugar
½ c. butter
½ c. flour
1 can whole berry cranberry sauce

Mix oats, sugar, butter and flour. Place one-half of mixture in greased 8-inch square pan or 8-inch round pie plate. Spread with cranberry sauce; cover with remaining mixture. Bake at 350 degrees for 35 to 45 minutes. Serve with whipped cream or ice cream. Yield: 6 servings.

Mrs. James H. Downey
Albany, Ga.

CRIMSON CRANBERRY FLAMBE

1 ½ c. sugar
1 c. water
2 c. fresh cranberries
¼ to ½ c. brandy or 6 to 8 sugar cubes, soaked in lemon flavoring

Bring sugar and water to a boil. When sugar dissolves, add cranberries; simmer gently for 5 minutes or until skins pop open. When ready to serve, heat sauce in chafing dish. Pour brandy over top or place sugar cubes on top; ignite. Ladle sauce over scoops of coconut ice cream or coconut ice cream balls. Yield: 6-8 servings.

Mrs. Arthur J. Walsh
Woods Hole, Mass.

DATE-FILLED PASTRIES

DATE FILLING:
1 6-oz. pkg. chopped pitted dates
½ c. brown sugar
¼ c. water

Combine all ingredients. Cook over medium heat until of jam consistency. Cool.

DOUGH:
½ c. butter
¼ lb. grated sharp cheese
1 ⅓ c. sifted flour
¼ tsp. salt
2 tbsp. water

Cream butter and cheese until light. Sift flour with salt; blend into creamed mixture. Add water; mix well. Chill for 1 hour. Roll dough 1/8-inch thick on well floured surface. Cut circles about 2 3/4-inches. Place 1/2 teaspoon filling on each. Fold in half; seal with fork. Place on ungreased baking sheet. Bake at 375 degrees for 8 to 10 minutes. Cool slightly on sheet. Yield: 2 dozen pastries.

Mrs. Vernon L. Anderson
Norfolk, Va.

CANNED FIGS IN BRANDY

1 can figs
1 can coconut
½ c. chopped walnuts
¼ c. brandy

Pour figs into an ovenproof serving dish. Sprinkle 1/2 cup coconut over figs. Add walnuts and brandy. Cover and bake until heated through. Sprinkle with remaining coconut. Serve hot. Whipped cream may be added. Yield: 6 servings.

Mrs. J. W. Gannon
Moffet Field, Calif.

FIGS AFLAME

1 lge. can Kadota figs
1 tsp. arrowroot or cornstarch
2 thin lemon slices
¼ c. plus 2 tbsp. brandy
½ pt. coffee or heavy cream
Lemon wafers

Pour syrup from figs into a chafing dish. Add arrowroot; stir until thickened. Add figs, lemon slices and 2 tablespoons brandy; heat thoroughly. Heat remaining 1/4 cup brandy. Just before serving, ignite brandy; pour over figs, coating each one. Serve at once with cream and lemon wafers. Yield: 4 servings.

Mrs. Raymond M. Harris
Little Creek, Va.

FRUIT ROLL

FILLING:
1 c. figs
1 c. nuts
¼ c. water
½ c. sugar

Combine all ingredients. Cook until thick; cool.

(Continued on next page)

DOUGH:
½ c. butter
½ c. brown sugar
½ c. sugar
1 egg
2 c. flour
½ tsp. soda
¼ tsp. salt

Cream butter and sugars; add egg. Add sifted dry ingredients. Roll on floured board or cloth. Spread with filling. Roll up like jelly roll; chill. Cut slices. Bake at 400 degrees for 12 minutes.

Mrs. G. R. Gray
Sanford, Fla.

GRAPEFRUIT ALASKA

2 grapefruit
4 tbsp. curacao
1 pt. vanilla ice cream
2 egg whites
¼ tsp. cream of tartar
¼ c. sugar

Cut grapefruit into halves; remove fruit carefully. Peel off white membrane; discard seed. Return fruit to shells; flavor each half with 1 tablespoon curacao. Divide vanilla ice cream among the shells, spreading ice cream to edges. Beat egg whites with cream of tartar, gradually beat in sugar. Continue beating until meringue is stiff. Spread over ice cream; bring meringue over cut edge of shell. Bake in preheated 450 degree oven for 5 minutes or until meringue is brown. Serve at once. Yield: 4 servings.

Mrs. Harold R. Johnston
Letterkenny Army Depot, Pa.

LEMON VELVET

1 13-oz. can evaporated milk
1 pkg. lemon gelatin
1 ¼ c. boiling water
⅓ c. honey
⅛ tsp. salt
3 tbsp. lemon juice
Grated rind of 1 lemon
2 ½ c. vanilla wafer crumbs

Chill canned milk for at least 24 hours. Dissolve lemon gelatin in boiling water; add honey, salt, lemon juice and rind. Chill until slightly congealed. Whip milk until very stiff. Lightly fold in gelatin mixture. Spread one-half of the vanilla wafer crumbs in a 10 x 10 x 2-inch pan; pour lemon mixture over crumbs. Top with remaining crumbs. Chill for at least 3 hours. NOTE: Ninety calories per serving. Yield: 10-12 servings.

Mrs. R. E. Hegdahl
Dugway Proving Ground, Utah

LO-CAL LEMON FROST

1 egg, separated
⅓ c. water
⅓ c. non-fat dry milk
⅓ c. sugar
¼ tsp. grated lemon peel
3 tbsp. lemon juice
Dash of salt
3 tbsp. graham cracker crumbs

Combine egg white, water and dry milk. Beat to stiff peaks. Combine egg yolk, sugar, lemon rind, lemon juice and salt. Fold in egg white. Sprinkle 2 tablespoons crumbs into two trays. Spoon in lemon mixture. Dust with remaining 1 tablespoon crumbs. Yield: 4 servings.

Mrs. Joe Riedl
Thermopolis, Wyo.

MANGO BROWN BETTY

3 lge. mangoes, sliced
1 c. grapenuts
Juice of ½ lemon
Grated rind of ½ lemon
¼ c. brown sugar
1 tbsp. butter
½ c. water

Put layer of mangoes in baking dish; cover with 1/2 cup grapenuts. Pour on lemon juice and grated rind. Add remainder of mangoes; top with remaining 1/2 cup grapenuts. Sprinkle with brown sugar; dot with butter. Add water. Bake at 375 degrees for 30 minutes. Yield: 6 servings.

Mrs. Annie S. Root
West Palm Beach, Fla.

ORANGE BLOSSOM BOWL

1 pt. heavy cream
2 tbsp. honey
6 tbsp. frozen orange juice concentrate, thawed and undiluted
12 double ladyfingers
1 orange, sectioned

Combine heavy cream and honey in a large bowl. Beat until consistency of whipped cream. Fold in orange juice concentrate. Split ladyfingers; line bottom and sides of a glass serving dish. Pour cream mixture into dish. Chill for at least 4 hours before serving. Garnish with orange sections. Yield: 8 servings.

Photograph for this recipe on page 223.

CURRIED PEACH HALVES

1 16-oz. can cling peach halves, drained
2 tbsp. butter or margarine, melted
2 tbsp. brown sugar
¼ tsp. curry powder

(Continued on next page)

Place peach halves, cut-side up, on a rack in open roasting pan. Brush with butter. Mix brown sugar and curry powder; sprinkle on peach halves. Bake at 300 degrees for 30 minutes. Yield: 6-8 servings.

Mrs. Vera D. Jacobs
Subic Bay, Philippines

FROSTED FRUIT DESSERT

4 to 6 peach halves
1 egg white
2 tsp. lemon juice
¼ c. sugar
½ tsp. grated lemon rind
½ c. flaked coconut

Drain peaches, reserving 1 tablespoon syrup. Combine egg white, lemon juice, syrup and sugar in top of double boiler. Beat with electric or rotary beater over boiling water until stiff peaks form. Fold in lemon rind and coconut. Cool. Spoon into peach halves. Yield: 4-6 servings.

Mrs. Gerrit H. Barth
Canton, Minn.

PEACHY CREAM

CRUST:
1 ¼ c. graham cracker crumbs
½ c. sugar
½ c. butter

Mix all ingredients. Press into 9-inch pie pan. Bake at 350 degrees for 8 minutes; chill.

FILLING:
1 pt. heavy cream
1 can peach pie filling

Whip cream in chilled bowl; put into pie shell. Pour peach filling over top; chill. May be served with whipped cream. Yield: 6 servings.

Mrs. Donald Sims
Warrenton, Va.

PEACH DUMPLINGS

3 c. sliced fresh peaches
2 c. water
1 c. sugar
2 tbsp. lemon juice
1 c. pancake mix
¼ c. (firmly packed) brown sugar
¼ tsp. nutmeg
½ c. milk
2 tbsp. melted or liquid shortening

Combine peaches, water, sugar and lemon juice in 3-quart saucepan; bring to a boil. Combine all remaining ingredients, stirring lightly. Drop batter from tablespoon onto hot

peach mixture. Reduce heat; cover tightly. Cook for 15 minutes without lifting cover. Serve warm with cream or peach or vanilla ice cream. Yield: 6-8 servings.

Mrs. Richard W. Mantyla
Seneca, N.Y.

PEACHES SUPREME

¼ c. brown sugar
½ c. corn syrup
⅓ c. Sherry
2 tbsp. butter or margarine
1 No. 2 ½ can cling peach halves, drained
Toasted flaked coconut

Combine sugar, corn syrup, Sherry and butter; simmer for 5 minutes. Pour over peaches; let stand until ready to serve. Fill peaches with coconut. Serve warm. Serve with whipped cream, sour cream, or ice cream. Yield: 5-6 servings.

Mrs. John P. Schmitt
Hoyt Lakes, Minn.

BAKED PEARS IN WHITE WINE

6 pears, peeled
White wine
Sugar

Place pears in baking dish; cover with white wine. Add sugar. Cover and bake at 375 degrees for 45 minutes. Serve with whipped cream. Yield: 4-6 servings.

Mrs. J. T. Crosby
Port Washington, L.I., N.Y.

CREME DE MENTHE PEARS

2 lge. cans pear halves
½ c. white creme de menthe
1 c. whipped cream
1 tbsp. instant coffee

Drain pears, reserving 1/2 cup juice. Place pear halves in large flat dish; cover with reserved pear juice and creme de menthe. Let stand for a few hours or overnight. Serve in sherbet glasses with juice. Top with whipped cream; sprinkle top with instant coffee. Yield: 8 servings.

Mrs. LaMar L. Woodward
Portsmouth, N.H.

GINGER PEAR MOLD WITH CUSTARD
SAUCE

1 pkg. lemon gelatin
1 c. hot water
1 c. ginger ale
1 c. diced fresh or canned pears
¼ tsp. powdered ginger

(Continued on next page)

Dissolve gelatin in hot water. Add ginger ale; cool until slightly thickened. Add pears sprinkled with ginger. Put into six individual molds; when firm, turn into sherbet glass. Add custard sauce.

SAUCE:
⅔ c. non-fat dry milk
¼ c. sugar
2 egg yolks
⅛ tsp. salt
1 ¼ c. water
1 tsp. vanilla flavoring

Mix dry milk, sugar, egg yolks and salt in saucepan. Add water gradually; stir until smooth. Cook over low heat until mixture coats spoon. Remove from heat; add vanilla. Strain; chill. Serve over pear mixture. NOTE: Eighty-nine calories per serving. Yield: 6 servings.

Mrs. J. C. Swearingen
Norfolk, Va.

STUFFED PEARS MILANESE

6 lge. firm pears
3 oz. powdered sugar
4 Maraschino cherries, finely chopped
¼ lb. shelled toasted almonds, finely ground
¼ tsp. almond flavoring
½ c. dry Sherry

Wash pears; cut into halves, lengthwise. Scoop out cores. Blend remaining ingredients except Sherry. Fill pear halves with mixture. Place in baking dish; pour Sherry over pears. Bake at 350 degrees for 15 minutes or until pears are done, but not too soft. Serve hot or cooled. Yield: 6-8 servings.

Mrs. Jack B. Baugh
Fort Irwin, Calif.

CINNAMON-PINEAPPLE RINGS

2 tbsp. red cinnamon candy
½ c. pineapple juice
6 slices pineapple
1 tbsp. fat

Dissolve candy in juice. Pour over pineapple; let stand for 3 to 4 hours. Drain. Brown over medium heat in hot fat. Yield: 6 servings.

Mrs. May Schuler
Wilmington, Ill.

PINEAPPLE DELIGHT

1 No. 1 can pineapple, diced
1 egg, beaten
½ c. sugar
1 tbsp. cornstarch
1 c. miniature marshmallows
½ c. chopped nuts

Drain and reserve pineapple juice. Combine egg, sugar, cornstarch and juice; cook until consistency of salad dressing. Cool. Add pineapple, marshmallows and nuts. Mix well. Serve in sherbet glasses. Top with a cherry. Yield: 4-6 servings.

Mrs. E. Edward Silverman
Milwaukee, Wisc.

PINEAPPLE IN PORT WINE SYRUP

1 pineapple
Rind of 1 orange, finely shredded
Rind of 1 grapefruit, finely shredded
5 tbsp. sugar
½ c. Port wine

Skin, core and slice pineapple, reserving 1/2 cup juice. Combine all remaining ingredients with reserved juice in a saucepan; cook until rinds are clear. Remove from heat; add pineapple. Let cool; serve cold.

Mrs. Henry S. Persons
Pearl Harbor, Hawaii

SCALLOPED PINEAPPLE

8 slices bread, cubed
2 c. sugar
1 c. melted butter
3 eggs, beaten
¾ c. milk
2 sm. or 1 lge. can pineapple chunks, drained

Mix bread, sugar and butter. Add eggs, milk and pineapple; mix well. Pour into greased 13 x 9 1/2-inch baking dish. Bake at 350 degrees for 45 minutes.

Edith L. Schaefer
Pesotum, Ill.

RASPBERRY MOUSSE

1 c. milk
4 eggs, separated
3 tbsp. sugar
1 tbsp. red Maraschino cherry syrup
½ tsp. vanilla flavoring
2 c. fresh red raspberries or frozen raspberries, thawed and drained
2 c. heavy cream, whipped

Combine milk, slightly beaten egg yolks and sugar in top of double boiler. Cook over hot water, stirring constantly, until custard coats a spoon. Remove from heat; blend in cherry syrup and vanilla. Chill thoroughly. Rub raspberries through a wire strainer. Fold in whipped cream and stiffly beaten egg whites. Fold into custard. Pour into serving bowl; chill for at least 4 hours. Garnish with additional whipped cream, red raspberries and a

(Continued on next page)

sauce of crushed, sweetened raspberries. Yield: 10-12 servings.

Mrs. H. G. Goodlad
Langley AFB, Va.

RHUBARB-BUTTER CRUNCH

3 c. diced rhubarb
1 c. sugar
1 c. plus 3 tbsp. flour
1 c. brown sugar
1 ½ c. uncooked oats
½ c. butter

Combine rhubarb, sugar and 3 tablespoons flour. Place in 9-inch square pan. Combine brown sugar, oats, 1 cup flour and butter. Sprinkle over rhubarb. Bake at 375 degrees for 40 minutes. Serve with whipped cream or ice cream if desired. Yield: 6-8 servings.

Phyllis Madsen
Dell Rapids, S.D.

RHUBARB CRISP

6 c. cubed rhubarb
1 c. sugar
1 c. brown sugar
1 ½ c. flour
½ c. softened butter
½ tsp. salt
1 egg

Place rhubarb in greased and floured pan. Mix sugars, flour, butter, salt and egg; pour over rhubarb. Bake at 350 degrees for 40 minutes. Yield: 12-15 servings.

Mrs. Eugene Pence
Frederick, S.D.

STRAWBERRY CROWN

1 envelope unflavored gelatin
½ c. cold water
2 envelopes low calorie strawberry flavored gelatin
2 ½ c. hot water
2 c. strawberries, chilled
1 c. vanilla-flavored yogurt

Soften unflavored gelatin in cold water in a small saucepan; heat, stirring constantly, until dissolved. Remove from heat. Dissolve strawberry flavored gelatin in hot water in a medium bowl; stir in plain gelatin. Pour 1/2 cup mixture into a 6-cup mold. Chill for 15 minutes. Let remaining gelatin in bowl stand at room temperature to cool. Set aside 12 strawberries for garnish. Put 6 strawberries in mold; spoon 2 tablespoons gelatin over berries. Beat yogurt into cooled gelatin mixture in bowl; chill with layer in mold just until syrupy and layer is sticky-firm. Slice remaining whole strawberries. Fold into yogurt mixture. Spoon over sticky-firm layer in mold. Chill for several hours until firm. Remove from mold; garnish with reserved whole strawberries. NOTE: Fifty-three calories per serving. Yield: 6 servings.

Mrs. Wayne Rounsavill
Corvallis, Oreg.

STRAWBERRIES 'N' CREAM

2 pt. boxes fresh strawberries
½ c. brown sugar
¾ c. sour cream

Gently wash and hull berries; slice into large bowl. Add brown sugar and sour cream. Mix gently; pile lightly into six serving dishes.

TOPPING:
6 tbsp. sour cream
6 tsp. brown sugar

Top each dish with 1 tablespoon sour cream and 1 teaspoon brown sugar. Chill for at least 1 hour before serving. Yield: 6 servings.

Mrs. Errol D. Clark
Washington, D.C.

STRAWBERRY DELIGHT

⅓ c. sugar
1 ½ tbsp. flour
1 7-oz. bottle lemon-lime carbonated beverage
1 pt. fresh strawberries, sliced
1 pt. vanilla ice cream
8 meringue shells, baked

Mix sugar and flour. Add beverage; mix well. Cook over low heat, stirring constantly, until slightly thickened. Cool; stir in berries. Chill. Spoon ice cream into meringue shells; top with strawberry mixture. Yield: 8 servings.

· Mrs. Arlene Hansen
Bath, Mich.

STRAWBERRY MOUSSE

1 egg white
⅛ tsp. salt
¾ c. powdered sugar
1 c. heavy cream
1 ¼ c. fresh strawberries

Beat egg white and salt until foamy. Gradually add sugar; beat until stiff. Whip cream until stiff; add to egg white. Wash, hull and mash strawberries; fold into mixture. Pour into refrigerator tray. Freeze, without stirring, until firm. Let stand at room temperature a few minutes before serving. Yield: 4 servings.

Mrs. Robert L. Pfluger
Corvallis, Oreg.

STRAWBERRY FLUFF

1 10-oz. pkg. frozen sweetened strawberry
   slices or halves
⅓ c. sugar
¼ tsp. red food coloring
3 tbsp. lemon juice
1 tbsp. water
1 envelope unflavored gelatin
⅔ c. evaporated milk, chilled

Thaw strawberries; empty into a small bowl.
Add sugar; stir until dissolved. Stir in food
coloring. Place lemon juice and water in a
custard cup; sprinkle gelatin over top. Let
stand for 5 minutes to soften. Place custard
cup in a small saucepan; surround with a
small amount of water. Heat over low heat
until gelatin is dissolved. Blend gelatin into
strawberries. Chill until mixture begins to
thicken. Whip chilled evaporated milk until
stiff and will hold a peak. Fold in gelatin
mixture lightly but thoroughly. Chill, if
necessary, until mixture mounds when
dropped from a spoon. Pile lightly into four
cups, mugs or parfait glasses. Chill for 3 to 4
hours or until set. Yield: 4 servings.

Photograph for this recipe above.

STRAWBERRIES IN SNOW

3 tbsp. unflavored gelatin
½ c. water
4 c. boiling water
2 tbsp. liquid sugar substitute
2 tbsp. lemon juice
Red food coloring
2 3-oz. pkg. cream cheese, softened
2 c. sliced strawberries

Soften gelatin in cold water. Dissolve in boiling water. Add sugar substitute, lemon juice
and a few drops of food coloring. Add one-
half the gelatin mixture very slowly to cream
cheese, blending until smooth. Pour into a 1-
quart mold; chill until set. Add strawberries
to remaining gelatin mixture. Pour over
cream cheese mixture; chill until set. NOTE:
Each serving contains 142 calories. Yield: 6
servings.

Mrs. M. N. Huston
Fort Carson, Colo.

STRAWBERRY BABAS

1 can petits babas in rum
1 pkg. frozen sliced strawberries
1 c. heavy cream
2 tbsp. powdered sugar

(Continued on next page)

Refrigerate babas in can for at least 2 hours. Thaw strawberries in package in refrigerator. Place 2 to 3 babas in each serving dish; spoon strawberries and juice over babas. Beat cream with sugar until almost stiff; spoon over strawberry babas. Serve at once. Yield: 6 servings.

Mrs. Robert L. Phelps
St. Petersburg, Fla.

STRAWBERRY WHIP

1 c. crushed strawberries
1 c. sugar
1 egg white

Combine all ingredients. Whip until stiff peaks are formed. Serve in parfait glasses or over cake. Garnish with whole berries. Yield: 8 servings.

Mrs. Edythe Evert
Bonner Springs, Kans.

STRAWBERRIES IN WINE

1 qt. strawberries
4 to 6 tbsp. sugar
1 ½ c. Rose wine
1 tbsp. cognac
Sour cream (opt.)

Wash and hull strawberries. Place in a bowl; add all remaining ingredients, using only 4 tablespoons sugar; let strawberries stand at room temperature for 30 minutes. Taste for sweetness, adding more sugar if desired. Cover and chill well before serving. Serve with a spoonful of sour cream. Yield: 4 servings.

Mrs. George M. Gans, Jr.
Port Hueneme, Calif.

HOT FRUIT AMBROSIA

1 1-lb. can apricot halves
1 1-lb. can Elberta peach halves
1 1-lb. can purple plums
1 can figs (opt.)
2 tbsp. butter
1 orange, thinly sliced
½ c. orange juice
¼ c. brown sugar
½ tsp. grated lemon rind
2 tbsp. brandy (opt.)
½ c. shredded coconut

Drain canned fruits well; arrange in a shallow 9 x 13-inch casserole. Dot butter over plums.

Place halved orange slices on top. Mix orange juice, sugar, lemon rind and brandy; pour over fruit. Sprinkle coconut over top. Bake at 425 degrees for 15 minutes. Yield: 10 servings.

Mrs. Wilson Freeman
Washington, D.C.

AMBROSIA

1 c. fresh or frozen strawberries
1 c. blueberries, cooked
1 ½ c. pineapple
1 c. applesauce
2 c. diced apples
⅔ c. raisins
2 c. grape juice
1 c. shredded coconut
4 diced bananas
2 c. pineapple juice
1 sm. jar cherries and juice
1 c. chopped pecans

Combine all ingredients; mix well. Refrigerate until served. Yield: 6 servings.

Mrs. Harry T. Howle
Galivants Ferry, S.C.

APPLES IN BALL GOWNS

2 c. sugar
4 c. water
¼ tsp. cinnamon
Few grains of salt
3 Winesap apples, peeled and cored
½ c. crushed pineapple
2 egg whites
¼ c. sugar
½ c. chopped walnuts

Combine sugar, water, cinnamon and salt; heat to boiling. Add apples; cook until tender. Drain; cool slightly. Fill apples with pineapple. Place in greased pan. Beat egg whites until light and moist; gradually add sugar, whipping until stiff. Fold in 1/4 cup walnuts. Cover apples with meringue. Sprinkle with remaining walnuts. Bake at 350 degrees until browned. Yield: 3 servings.

Lois Brown
Montandon, Pa.

APPLE-CHAMPAGNE COMPOTE

3 golden delicious apples
1 ½ c. Champagne
2 c. frozen sliced strawberries
1 c. powdered sugar
Shredded coconut or nuts

Peel, core and slice apples into thin circles. Cover with Champagne and strawberries. Sprinkle with powdered sugar; chill for 3 hours. Sprinkle with shredded coconut or nuts. Yield: 6-8 servings.

Mrs. Edward C. Fritsch, Jr.
Oak Harbor, Wash.

BANANA-PINEAPPLE DESSERT

1 can crushed pineapple
20 lge. marshmallows
1 pkg. lemon gelatin
1 pt. heavy cream, whipped
6 med. bananas, sliced
Crushed vanilla wafers

Heat pineapple, marshmallows and gelatin in top of double boiler until blended; cool. Add whipped cream and sliced bananas. Cover bottom of 9 x 12-inch pan with crushed vanilla wafers. Pour mixture into pan; sprinkle crushed wafers on top. Refrigerate overnight. Yield: 12 servings.

Mrs. Alfred C. Alder
Minneapolis, Minn.

BRANDIED BANANAS WITH GREEN GRAPES

4 ripe bananas
½ lb. seedless grapes
½ c. butter
1 c. sugar
Juice of 2 lemons
¼ to ½ c. brandy
Toasted ladyfingers

Cut bananas and grapes into halves. Melt butter in chafing dish. Arrange banana halves in pan; sprinkle part of sugar over top. Add lemon juice. Turn bananas while cooking, adding sugar until all is used. Toss grapes in sauce gently when bananas are brown. Pour brandy over fruits; ignite. When flame dies down, blow it out. Serve in individual dessert plates with toasted ladyfingers. Yield: 4 servings.

Mrs. Henry W. Fuller
Key West Naval Sta., Fla.

CANTALOUPE ALASKAN

Cantaloupe
Strawberries
Ice cream
Meringue

Cut cantaloupe in half; scoop out seed. Fill cantaloupe halves with ripe strawberries. Just before serving, spread berries with ice cream. Top with meringue, spreading to edges of cantaloupe to seal. Bake at 500 degrees for 3 to 4 minutes or until meringue is brown. Serve immediately.

Mrs. Dorothy McMillan
Guerneville, Calif.

CHERRIED FLAMBE

1 10-oz. jar currant jelly
1 No. 2 ½ can pitted Bing cherries, drained
1 ½ qt. vanilla ice cream
12 slices pound cake
1 c. cognac

Melt jelly in chafing dish over direct heat, stirring gently. Add cherries; mix and heat slowly. Spoon ice cream over a slice of pound cake in 12 dessert dishes. Pour almost all of cognac into center of cherries; do not stir. Pour remaining cognac into large spoon. Ignite; pour flaming cognac into cognac in chafing dish to ignite. Spoon flaming cherries over ice cream in dishes. NOTE: For cherries jubilee, omit the pound cake. Yield: 12 servings.

Mrs. Kermit Vandenbos
Richards-Gebaur AFB, Mo.

CHERRY TOSS-UP

1 can cherry pie filling
1 can pineapple chunks
1 can mandarin oranges
2 or 3 lge. bananas, diced or sliced
2 c. miniature marshmallows

Drain cherries; add remaining ingredients. Mix well. Top with cherry syrup. Yield: 8 servings.

Mrs. Joe Finnegan
Sutton, Nebr.

CRANBERRY FLUFF

2 c. ground cranberries
3 c. miniature marshmallows
1 c. sugar
2 c. diced apples
1 sm. can crushed pineapple, drained
½ c. nuts. (opt.)
1 pkg. dessert topping mix, whipped
¼ tsp. salt

Combine cranberries, marshmallows and sugar; refrigerate for 12 hours. Combine all remaining ingredients; add to cranberry mixture. Refrigerate for several hours. Yield: 10-12 servings.

Mrs. B. K. Artman
Mt. Hope, Kans.

CURRIED FRUIT BAKE

1 No. 1 can pear halves
1 No. 1 can cling peach halves
1 No. 1 can apricot halves
1 No. 2 can pineapple slices or chunks
5 Maraschino cherries
⅓ c. butter or margarine
¾ c. brown sugar
4 tsp. curry powder

Drain fruit well. Melt butter; add sugar and curry. Place fruit in 1 1/2-quart casserole; add butter mixture. Bake at 325 degrees for 1 hour. Refrigerate overnight. Reheat at 350 degrees before serving. Yield: 12 servings.

Mrs. Kenneth B. Austin
Norfolk, Va.

FRUIT COCKTAIL CRUNCH

1 egg
1 c. sugar
1 tsp. vanilla flavoring
1 No. 303 can fruit cocktail
1 c. flour
½ tsp. cinnamon
1 tsp. soda
1 tsp. salt

Beat egg with sugar. Add flavoring, fruit cocktail and sifted dry ingredients. Stir just enough to mix thoroughly. Pour into greased 8 x 12-inch pan.

FRUIT CRUNCH TOPPING:

⅔ c. chopped walnuts
½ c. brown sugar
½ tsp. cinnamon

Mix all ingredients thoroughly; sprinkle evenly over cake batter. Bake at 325 degrees for 45 minutes. Serve with whipped cream or ice cream. Yield: 6 servings.

Birdie Ingham
Tacoma, Wash.

FRUIT COCKTAIL-MARSHMALLOW WHIP

1 No. 303 can fruit cocktail
¼ lb. marshmallows, cut into eighths
1 tsp. lemon juice
1 tsp. grated lemon peel
1 c. heavy cream, whipped

Reserve 1/4 cup fruit cocktail for garnish. Combine remaining fruit cocktail and marshmallows. Refrigerate for 1 hour. Just before serving, drain well. Add lemon juice and lemon peel; fold in whipped cream. Garnish with reserved fruit. Yield: 6 servings.

Mrs. James B. Franklin
San Diego, Calif.

FRUIT DELIGHT

Plump green grapes
Plump blueberries
Sour cream
Brown sugar

Mix fruit and berries. Top with sour cream; sprinkle with brown sugar.

Mrs. Lawrence Dennis Ballou
Portsmouth Naval Shipy'd, N.H.

FRUIT DELIGHT

2 c. white cherries, halved and pitted
2 c. diced pineapple, drained
2 c. orange sections, drained
2 c. quartered marshmallows
2 eggs
2 tbsp. sugar

¼ c. light cream
Juice of 1 lemon
1 c. heavy cream, whipped

Combine well drained fruits; add marshmallows. Beat eggs until light; gradually add sugar, light cream and lemon juice. Mix thoroughly; cook in double boiler until smooth and thick, stirring constantly. Cool. Fold in whipped cream. Pour over fruit mixture; mix lightly. Chill for 24 hours. Do not freeze. Yield: 10-12 servings.

Mrs. Raymond F. Jackson
Ft. Greely, Alaska

FRUIT DESSERT

1 can fruit cocktail, drained
Sliced bananas
Black walnuts
Quartered marshmallows
½ pt. heavy cream, whipped

Mix all ingredients except whipped cream. Fold in whipped cream. Chill before serving.

Mrs. Joseph E. Shevlin
Sanford, Fla.

LOW CALORIE FRUIT DESSERT

½ pt. sliced strawberries
½ c. blueberries
1 c. pineapple chunks
1 c. seedless grapes
2 oranges, sectioned and cut into chunks
2 bananas, sliced
1 sm. bottle ginger ale

Several hours before serving, place glass bowls or sherbet dishes in freezer; chill ginger ale. Mix all fruit except bananas 1 hour or more before serving. Add bananas just before serving. Place fruit in glasses; pour 3 tablespoons ginger ale over each serving. Glasses should frost when ginger ale is poured over. Yield: 4 servings.

Mrs. Maxine Cox
Saginaw, Mich.

FRUIT PARFAIT

1 med. can pineapple chunks, drained
1 med. can Bing cherries, drained
1 box frozen strawberries, thawed and drained
1 c. sour cream
½ c. miniature marshmallows
1 tbsp. powdered sugar

Combine fruits. Mix sour cream, marshmallows and sugar. Fill sherbet or parfait glasses with alternating layers of fruit and cream mixture or fold fruit into cream mixture. Chill overnight.

Theresa Geardino
Highland Park, N.J.

FRESH PEACH MELBA

1 ¼ c. sugar
1 c. water
¼ tsp. salt
1 tsp. pure vanilla flavoring
3 lge. or 6 sm. fresh freestone peaches
2 c. fresh raspberries
1 qt. vanilla ice cream

Mix 1 cup sugar, water and salt in saucepan. Bring to boiling point, stirring constantly. Cover and boil for 3 to 4 minutes. Remove from heat. Stir in vanilla. Dip peaches into very hot water; dip into cold water. Slip off skins. Cut into halves; remove stones. Return sugar syrup to heat; add 2 peach halves at a time. Simmer for 3 to 4 minutes or until peaches are tender when pierced with a fork. Remove peaches from syrup with slotted spoon, draining excess syrup back into saucepan. Chill. Wash and put raspberries through a sieve. Blend in remaining sugar; chill. Place ice cream in each serving dish when ready to serve. Place chilled peaches, cut-side down, on ice cream. Top with raspberries. Yield: 6 servings.

Photograph for this recipe above.

SCALLOPED PEACHES

1 ½ c. sliced peaches
4 c. sliced apples

¼ tsp. salt
¼ c. brown sugar
¼ c. bread or cake crumbs
¼ c. water

Arrange layer of peaches in bottom of greased baking dish. Place one-half of the apples over peaches. Sprinkle with salt. Add remaining peaches and apples. Spread sugar over fruits; sprinkle crumbs over top. Add water. Cover and bake at 350 degrees for 30 minutes. Remove cover; continue baking for 15 minutes longer. Serve hot or cold. Yield: 6 servings.

Mrs. D. C. Thompson
Miami, Fla.

PINEAPPLE-MINT SURPRISE

CRUST:
1 c. flour
½ c. chopped walnuts
¼ c. brown sugar
½ c. butter

Combine flour, nuts and brown sugar; cut in butter. Press into bottom of pan. Bake at 400 degrees for 10 minutes. Cool.

FILLING:
1 1-lb. 4-oz. can crushed pineapple
1 pkg. lime gelatin

(Continued on next page)

1 c. cream cheese
1 c. sugar
⅔ c. evaporated milk
⅛ tsp. peppermint flavoring

Drain and reserve pineapple juice. Heat pineapple juice; dissolve gelatin in hot juice. Cool. Blend cream cheese with sugar. Mix into gelatin; stir in pineapple. Chill only until thick. Chill evaporated milk with peppermint flavoring in a small bowl until crystals form; beat until thick. Fold into pineapple mixture; spoon over crust. Refrigerate.

GLAZE:
½ c. chocolate pieces
⅓ c. evaporated milk
1 tsp. butter
¼ tsp. peppermint flavoring

Melt chocolate pieces in milk. Add butter and flavoring. Spoon glaze carefully over filling. Chill for 4 hours before serving.

Mrs. Sally Sparkman
London, Ky.

SNOWFLAKE FRUIT BOWL
FRUITS:
3 oranges, pared and sectioned
2 bananas, sliced
1 can pineapple chunks, drained
1 sm. can fruit cocktail
½ c. grated coconut

Combine all ingredients; chill.

EGGNOG CUSTARD:
2 c. light cream
1 c. milk
2 tbsp. sugar
1 tsp. rum flavoring
½ tsp. vanilla flavoring
1 pkg. instant vanilla pudding

Combine all ingredients; beat for 1 minute. Let stand for 5 minutes or until set. Chill. Stir until creamy; serve over fruit or as fruit parfait. Yield: 8 servings.

Mrs. C. K. Stubbs
Key West, Fla.

SPICED FRUIT
1 can pears
1 can peaches
1 can pineapple chunks
1 can red sour cherries, drained
4 to 6 sticks cinnamon
½ tsp. cloves
½ tsp. nutmeg

Drain all fruits, saving juice from pears, peaches and pineapple. Cut fruits into large bite-sized pieces. Heat juices in large saucepan. Add cinnamon sticks, cloves and nutmeg.

Pour hot juice over fruits in large bowl. Yield: 10-12 servings.

Mrs. A. J. Campbell
Lexington-Bluegrass Army Depot, Ky.

STRAWBERRY-ORANGE PIQUANT
1 1-lb. pkg. frozen whole strawberries, thawed
4 sticks cinnamon, broken
2 to 4 tbsp. sugar
Kirsch
2 7-oz. cans Mandarin orange slices, drained

Drain strawberries, reserving juice. Add enough water to juice to make 1 1/2 cups liquid. Combine strawberry liquid, cinnamon sticks and sugar in saucepan. Boil until sugar is dissolved; cool. Remove cinnamon sticks. Add several tablespoons Kirsch to taste. Pour syrup over combined strawberries and oranges. Yield: 4-5 servings.

Mrs. L. R. Phillips
Syracuse, N.Y.

SURPRISE DESSERT
4 oranges, peeled and diced
1 No. 2 can pineapple
1 4-oz. pkg. coconut
½ lb. pkg. marshmallows, cut up
½ pt. sour cream

Combine oranges, pineapple, coconut and marshmallows; fold in sour cream. Refrigerate for 8 hours before serving. Yield: 8 servings.

Zenia Johnson
Elkhart, Ind.

TRIFLE
1 tbsp. jam
2 sponge cakes, cubed
1 sm. can fruit cocktail
½ pt. thin vanilla custard, cooled
1 3-oz. pkg. gelatin
Whipped cream

Spread jam in baking dish. Place cake cubes over jam. Pour fruit cocktail over cake; let stand to soak. Pour custard over cake. Prepare gelatin according to package directions; chill until slightly thickened. Pour over custard; chill. Top with whipped cream. Decorate with fruits. Yield: 6-8 servings.

Mrs. Ann French
Winter Harbor, Me.

Frozen
Desserts

RECIPE FOR RASPBERRY PARFAIT ON PAGE 260

Freezing Desserts . . .

. . . is so easy that you'll want to plan desserts for weeks rather than days ahead. You'll save time by preparing desserts for tomorrow while cooking today. The only exceptions are those desserts with cream fillings, cream puddings, or some custard pies which are not recommended for freezing.

The first thing to consider when freezing desserts is quality, since quality of the frozen dessert can never be better than the quality of the dessert chosen for freezing. Quality also demands that care be taken to freeze and keep desserts at 0° F. or below.

The second thing to consider is the amount of space you have in your freezer. Desserts take up considerable space and shouldn't be crushed by crowding into a small space.

Careful wrapping is the third rule as all frozen desserts must be wrapped in moisture-vapor-proof material to keep out as much air as possible. Be sure to label your packages with the contents, number of servings and the date frozen. Finding what you want in the freezer is much easier when you do this.

FREEZING CHART

DESSERT	PREPARATION	PACKAGING AND APPROXIMATE STORAGE TIME	SERVING
CAKES			
1. Butter or Sponge	Baking before freezing is recommended. Cool on rack after baking.	Wrap in moisture-vapor-proof paper. Freeze in amounts for meal. Store up to 4 months.	Unwrap frosted cakes while defrosting. Allow 30 minutes for angel or sponge, others 2 hours.
2. Fruit	Bake and age before freezing.	Wrap as above and store up to 1 year.	
3. Frostings	Uncooked or butter icings are recommended.		
CANDIES	Prepare according to recipe. Cool.	Freeze in container or wrap in foil with waxed paper between layers. Store up to 1 year.	Remove from freezer before serving time and defrost in container.
COOKIES			
1. Baked	Use desired recipe. Cool before wrapping.	Place in layers with waxed paper between layers. Freeze in container or in freezer wrap. Store up to 6 months.	Thaw at room temperature about 15 minutes.

DESSERT	PREPARATION	PACKAGING AND APPROXIMATE STORAGE TIME	SERVING
2. Unbaked			
a. Rolled	Cut and stack with waxed paper between layers.	Wrap and store as above for 1 to 2 months.	Bake without thawing.
b. Dropped	Shape on cookie sheet and then freeze.	Remove from cookie sheet and store in moisture-vapor-proof box or bag for 1 to 2 months.	Bake without thawing.
FRUITS			
Apples, Baking	Prepare firm, ripe-apples; bake according to recipe. Cool quickly.	Wrap in foil or freezer paper. Store 8 to 12 months.	If wrapped in foil, place directly in 300° F. oven for heating.
Other Fruits To Serve Uncooked	Select fully ripened fruit. To prevent light colored fruit from turning brown, when exposed to air, ascorbic acid may be added to the sugar or cool syrup before combining with the fruit.	Package in freezer containers. Store up to 1 year.	Defrost quickly in unopened container for 30 to 60 minutes. Serve icy cold.
ICE CREAM AND SHERBET	Prepare according to recipe. Proper crystal formation is necessary for smoothness.	Store in carton wrapped in moisture-vapor-proof paper. Store up to 2 months.	Do not defrost before serving or refreeze ice cream or sherbet that has melted.
NUTS	Fresh nuts and those in the shell can be frozen, but salted nuts do not freeze well.	Pack in freezer container to keep out air.	Defrost for serving.
PIES			
1. Baked: Chiffon	Prepare filling according to recipe and pour into baked or crumb crust. Cool until set.	Press plastic wrap down on filling. Wrap pie in freezer wrap. Store up to 1 or 2 months.	Defrost in refrigerator 4 to 6 hours before serving.
2. Unbaked: Fruit, Pecan, Mincemeat, Pumpkin, Sweet Potato	It is recommended that these pies be frozen before baking. Prepare according to recipe.	Use metal, foil or glass pie plates. Press plastic wrap on filling of one-crust pies. Wrap in moisture-vapor-proof material. Store up to 6 months.	Remove from freezer and cut steam vent in top crust. Bake, unthawed, in preheated oven. Using dull aluminum or glass pans with sufficient time for baking will prevent an underbaked bottom crust.
WHIPPED CREAM	Whip until stiff. Add sugar and flavoring. Make rosettes on cookie sheet, using pastry tube and rapidly freeze, unwrapped.	When frozen remove from cookie sheet and store in moisture-vapor-proof bags or box.	Do not defrost before serving.

ANGEL FOOD-ICE CREAM CAKE

1 lge. angel food cake
⅔ can chocolate fudge sauce
1 gal. ice cream, softened
½ pt. heavy cream, whipped

Tear cake into large pieces. Stir in chocolate sauce. Mix in ice cream. Put in angel food cake pan. Freeze for 3 to 4 hours. Turn out on large plate. Frost with whipped cream. Decorate as desired; refreeze. Yield: 20-30 servings.

Mrs. Richard P. Shay
Westby, Mont.

ANGEL MINT LOAF

1 angel food loaf cake
½ gal. peppermint ice cream, softened
1 or 2 squares unsweetened chocolate
18 to 24 after dinner mints (opt.)

Slit cake into three layers horizonally. Spread ice cream between layers, ending with ice cream. Spread remaining ice cream on sides. Garnish with curls of shaved chocolate; decorate with mints on top and sides. If prepared ahead of time, wrap in foil and freeze. Let stand at room temperature for 10 to 15 minutes before serving. NOTE: For variation use two layers of strawberry ice cream and spread with 1 cup whipped cream; garnish with fresh strawberries. Yield: 12 servings.

Mrs. E. C. Hines, Jr.
Norfolk, Va.

ICE BOX CAKE

2 c. powdered sugar
½ c. butter
2 squares chocolate, melted
1 tsp. vanilla flavoring
½ c. chopped pecans
3 eggs, separated
Crushed vanilla wafers
1 qt. vanilla ice cream

Cream sugar, butter and chocolate. Add vanilla and pecans. Beat in beaten yolks; fold in beaten whites. Line a 9 x 13-inch pan with wafer crumbs. Pour chocolate mixture over crumbs; cool. Spoon softened ice cream over chocolate layer. Top with remaining crumbs. Cover; store in freezer. Cut into squares to serve. Yield: 9 servings.

Mrs. Carl F. Martin
Tarkio, Mo.

ICE CREAM CAKE

1 lge. angel food cake, crumbled
1 qt. lime sherbet
1 qt. orange sherbet
1 qt. strawberry ice cream
1 qt. vanilla ice cream
1 pt. heavy cream, whipped

Cover bottom of large tube pan with crumbled cake, using about one-third of cake. Using an ice cream dipper, cover cake with all varieties of sherbet and ice cream, making desired designs. Press down; fill spaces with one-half of whipped cream. Repeat layers. Top with crumbs. Freeze overnight.

Mrs. Ralph Castle
Crystal River, Fla.

ALMOND TORTONI

1 egg white
6 tbsp. granulated sugar
1 tbsp. brown sugar
½ pt. heavy cream
1 tsp. almond flavoring
2 tbsp. chopped coconut
2 tbsp. chopped almonds
Maraschino cherries

Beat egg white until frothy; beat in 2 tablespoons granulated sugar and brown sugar. Beat cream until stiff. Add remaining 4 tablespoons granulated sugar and almond flavoring. Add egg white mixture; add 1 tablespoon coconut and 1 tablespoon almonds. Spoon into paper cups; top with remaining coconut and almonds. Decorate with cherry. Place in muffin tin to keep shape. Freeze for at least 3 hours. Yield: 8 servings.

Mrs. John L. Clancy
Fort Benjamin Harrison, Ind.

BRITTLE WHIP

1 pt. heavy cream
1 lb. fresh peanut brittle, crushed

Whip cream until stiff; fold in crushed peanut brittle. Place in 11 x 7 x 1 1/2-inch pan. Freeze for 3 hours. Yield: 8 servings.

Mrs. Michael Bouchard
Oak Harbor, Wash.

DELIGHTFUL FROZEN DESSERT

3 eggs, separated
½ c. sugar
Juice of 1 lemon
1 tsp. grated lemon rind
¼ tsp. salt
1 c. heavy cream
2 c. vanilla wafer crumbs

Beat egg yolks in top of double boiler over hot water; add sugar. Beat until thickened. Remove from heat; add lemon juice and lemon rind. Cool. Add salt to egg whites; beat until stiff. Fold into lemon mixture. Whip cream; fold into mixture. Press 1 cup wafer crumbs into 8 or 9-inch square dish; add lemon filling. Sprinkle on remaining crumbs; freeze. Yield: 9 servings.

Mrs. C. Allan Urban
Glastonbury, Conn.

242

COFFEE FRAPPE

Sugar to taste
8 c. strong coffee
1 pt. heavy cream, whipped
1 tsp. vanilla flavoring
1 tbsp. brandy

Dissolve sugar in hot coffee; chill. Add whipped cream. Add vanilla and brandy; freeze. Serve in parfait glasses topped with whipped cream and crumbled macaroons, if desired. Yield: 8 servings.

Mrs. Marshall Cohen
San Francisco, Calif.

FROZEN CHOCOLATE AU CREME

8 eggs, separated
1 ½ c. sugar
2 pkg. semi-sweet chocolate, melted
4 c. heavy cream, whipped
2 tsp. vanilla flavoring

Add well beaten egg yolks to sugar. Fold in chocolate; fold in whipped cream. Carefully fold mixture into beaten egg whites; add vanilla. Pour into mold; pack in ice and salt for 4 hours. Garnish with whipped cream.

Mrs. Feliz B. Stump
White Stone, Va.

WALNUT-CREAM FREEZE

1 qt. heavy cream, whipped
½ c. honey
1 c. chopped walnuts

Combine all ingredients; pour into two or three ice cube trays. Freeze. Yield: 8-10 servings.

Mrs. Roger D. Williams
Honolulu, Hawaii

FROZEN AMBROSIA

4 c. orange juice
½ c. lemon juice
3 c. powdered sugar, sifted
2 c. heavy cream
2 tbsp. sugar
1 tsp. vanilla flavoring

Mix orange juice, lemon juice and powdered sugar. Whip cream; blend in sugar and vanilla. Pour fruit juice mixture into two refrigerator trays; spoon whipped cream over top. Do not mix. Freeze until firm. Spoon into sherbet dishes or compote; garnish with slivered salted almonds or peanuts. Yield: 8-10 servings.

Mrs. Pearl Harris
Tribune, Kans.

CANDY-APPLE CREAM

¼ c. red cinnamon candies
¼ c. lemon juice
¼ c. sugar
1 ½ tsp. plain gelatin
2 tbsp. cold water
1 c. applesauce
1 c. light cream

Combine candies, juice and sugar in pan. Simmer until candy dissolves. Add gelatin softened in cold water. Stir until dissolved. Combine syrup, applesauce and cream. Pour into an ice cube tray. Freeze until firm. Remove; beat until smooth. Refreeze. Yield: 4 servings.

Mrs. Walter N. Mott
Pine Bluff Arsenal, Ark.

BLUEBERRY FROZEN TORTE

½ box powdered sugar
¼ lb. butter
2 eggs, separated
1 box vanilla wafers, crushed
1 can blueberry pie filling
½ c. heavy cream, whipped

Cream sugar and butter; add egg yolks. Fold in beaten egg whites. Sprinkle three-fourths of the crumbs in 7 x 10-inch pan; spread pie filling over crumbs. Pour in egg mixture; spread whipped cream over top. Sprinkle with remaining crumbs. Freeze for 2 hours. Yield: 8 servings.

Mrs. Asa Klingaman
Dunedin, Fla.

CRANBERRY FREEZE

2 c. cranberry sauce
2 tbsp. sugar
1 c. heavy cream, whipped
½ tsp. almond flavoring

Combine all ingredients. Freeze in refrigerator trays. Stir once or twice while freezing. Yield: 6-8 servings.

Mrs. Laurence Deehr
Tolna, N.D.

CRANBERRY YUM YUM DESSERT

1 lb. fresh cranberries, ground
1 lb. miniature marshmallows
2 c. sugar
1 No. 2 can crushed pineapple, drained
¾ c. chopped nuts
1 pt. heavy cream

Combine cranberries, marshmallows and 1 1/2 cups sugar; chill overnight. Mix pineapple and nuts; fold in cream whipped with remaining 1/2 cup sugar. Blend with cranberry mixture. Pour into an 11 x 7 x 2-inch pan; freeze until firm. Yield: 12 servings.

Mrs. H. M. Brown, Jr.
Norfolk, Va.

FROZEN CRANBERRY DESSERT

1 can whole cranberries, drained
1 No. 2½ can crushed pineapple, drained
1 c. chopped pecans
½ pt. sour cream

Combine all ingredients. Freeze. NOTE: Can also be used as a salad. Yield: 10-12 servings.

Mrs. Harvey Eckman
New Haven, Mo.

RED AND WHITE CRANBERRY FREEZE

1 No. 2 can cranberry sauce
2 tbsp. lemon juice
¼ c. powdered sugar
1 tsp. vanilla flavoring
1 c. chopped nuts
2 c. heavy cream, whipped

Blend cranberry sauce and lemon juice. Spread in baking dish. Add sugar, vanilla and nuts to whipped cream. Spread over berries; freeze. NOTE: Canned grapes or other fruit may be substituted for cranberries. Yield: 6 servings.

Mrs. Hollis Dunham
Erie, Kans.

FROZEN DATE SOUFFLE

1 8-oz. pkg. cream cheese
¼ c. maple syrup
1 tbsp. lemon juice
1 banana, mashed
1 8¾-oz. can crushed pineapple, drained
½ c. finely chopped dates
½ c. chopped pecans
1 c. heavy cream, whipped
Pineapple slices

Cream the cheese; beat in syrup, lemon juice and banana. Stir in pineapple, dates and pecans. Fold in whipped cream. Place in eight paper muffin cups; freeze until firm. Serve on pineapple slice; top with whipped cream and a cherry, if desired. Yield: 8 servings.

Mrs. Donald N. Edmond
Selfridge AFB, Mich.

GRAPE JUICE DESSERT

½ lb. marshmallows, cut up
1 pt. grape juice
1 tbsp. powdered sugar
½ pt. heavy cream, whipped
½ c. chopped nuts

Mix marshmallows, grape juice and sugar; soak overnight. Add whipped cream and nuts. Place in refrigerator tray. Freeze, stirring once. Yield: 6-8 servings.

Mrs. R. L. Crouch
Bainbridge, Md.

CHOCO-LEMON FROZEN DESSERT

1 lb. cream-filled chocolate cookies
Juice of 2 lemons
2 15-oz. cans sweetened condensed milk
2 c. heavy cream, whipped

Crush cookies; spread one-half of the crumbs in bottom of 13 x 9-inch cake pan. Slowly stir lemon juice into condensed milk; do not beat. Stir slowly until it begins to thicken. Fold in whipped cream. Pour onto cookie crumbs; top with remaining crumbs. Yield: 12 servings.

Mrs. John N. Mork
Warrenton, Va.

FROZEN LEMON CRACKLE

¼ c. butter
½ c. brown sugar
1½ c. Wheaties
⅓ c. finely chopped nuts
3 eggs, separated
½ c. sugar
Juice of 1 lemon
1 c. heavy cream, whipped

Melt butter in a skillet. Add brown sugar; cook to crackle stage, stirring constantly. Fold in Wheaties and nuts. Spread on cookie sheet to cool. Beat egg whites until stiff; add 1/4 cup sugar. Beat egg yolks; add remaining 1/4 cup sugar. Fold whites into yolks; fold in lemon juice and whipped cream. Break crackle mixture into small pieces. Spread one-half of the mixture into ice cube tray. Pour in lemon mixture; top with remaining crackle. Freeze. Yield: 6-8 servings.

Mrs. Wynn F. Foster
Lemoore, Calif.

FROZEN LEMON DESSERT

3 eggs
1 c. sugar
2 lemons
½ pt. heavy cream, whipped
1 box vanilla wafers, crushed

Beat eggs with mixer until thick; add sugar. Beat. Add juice and pulp of lemons; beat well. Fold in whipped cream. Place vanilla wafer crumbs in bottom of an 8-inch square pan, reserving some crumbs for topping. Pour in lemon mixture; top with reserved crumbs. Freeze for 6 to 8 hours. Yield: 6 servings.

Mrs. George Bibb Pickett, Jr.
Fort Belvoir, Va.

FROZEN LEMON DESSERT

3 eggs, separated
¾ c. sugar
¼ c. lemon juice

(Continued on next page)

½ pt. heavy cream, whipped
1 tbsp. lemon rind
1 graham cracker crust

Beat egg whites, gradually adding sugar. Beat egg yolks until thick; add lemon juice. Fold in whipped cream. Fold in egg whites. Add rind. Pour into crust; freeze. Yield: 12 servings.

Mrs. W. B. Roach
Victoria, Va.

LEMON BISQUE

¾ c. sugar
5 tbsp. lemon juice
Grated rind of 1 lemon
Pinch of salt
2 eggs, separated
1 ⅔ c. evaporated milk
Vanilla wafers

Combine all ingredients except egg whites, milk and vanilla wafers. Boil, stirring constantly, until thickened; cool. Beat egg whites until stiff; mix with cooled custard. Whip evaporated milk and fold into custard. Line ice cube tray with vanilla wafers. Pour mixture into tray; sprinkle wafer crumbs over top. Freeze. Serve in squares. NOTE: Additional lemon rind may be used if extra tartness is desired. Yield: 6 servings.

Mrs. Nina D. Carson
Miami, Fla.

LEMON ICEBOX DESSERT

3 eggs, separated
¾ c. sugar
Dash of salt
Juice of 3 lemons
Grated lemon rind
1 c. heavy cream. whipped
5 graham crackers, crushed

Beat egg yolks; add sugar, salt, lemon juice and rind. Cook in double boiler until thickened. Fold in stiffly beaten egg whites and whipped cream. Sprinkle buttered refrigerator tray with crumbs, reserving small amount of crumbs. Pour in lemon mixture. Top with crumbs. Freeze and serve. Yield: 8 servings.

Mrs. Ralph N. Dyer
Aiken, S.C.

LEMONADE LOAF

1 10 x 4 x 2-in. loaf angel cake
1 qt. vanilla ice cream
1 6-oz. can frozen pink lemonade concentrate
1 c. heavy cream, whipped (opt.)

Slice cake lengthwise into three even layers. Stir ice cream to soften. Zigzag lemonade concentrate through ice cream until marbled;

spread between cake layers. Freeze. Spread top and sides of loaf with whipped cream 1 hour before serving. Return to freezer. NOTE: Whipped cream frosting may be omitted. If so, the top layer of the cake should be frosted with part of the ice cream-lemonade mixture. Yield: 8-10 servings.

Mrs. W. T. Lincoln
West Point, N.Y.

LUSCIOUS LEMON FROST

1 egg white
⅓ c. water
⅓ c. nonfat dry milk powder
1 egg yolk, slightly beaten
⅓ c. sugar
¼ tsp. grated lemon peel
4 tbsp. graham cracker crumbs

Combine egg white, water and dry milk powder; beat to stiff peaks. Mix egg yolk, sugar and lemon peel; gradually beat into egg white. Sprinkle 3 tablespoons crumbs into a refrigerator tray; spoon in lemon mixture. Dust with remaining 1 tablespoon crumbs. Freeze. Cut into six wedges. NOTE: Contains 50 calories per serving. If desired, 1/4 teaspoon banana flavoring may be substituted for lemon peel. Yield: 6 servings.

Mrs. Harold Riddering
Selma, Ala.

MELON COUPE

2 ripe cantaloupes
1 c. sugar
1 c. water
1 envelope unflavored gelatin
Juice of 2 lemons
Juice of 2 limes
2 tbsp. light corn syrup
¼ tsp. salt
2 ripe honeydew melons
Whipped cream

Put enough cantaloupe through a blender to make 3 cups puree. Slowly heat sugar, water and gelatin until dissolved, stirring frequently. Remove from heat; add juices, puree, corn syrup and salt. Mix well. Pour into two refrigerator trays; partially freeze. Remove mixture from trays; beat until light and fluffy. Pack into 6-cup melon or fluted mold. Freeze until firm. Unmold onto a large plate; surround with honeydew melon balls and fluffs of whipped cream. Center of mold may be filled with lime ice and strawberries. Garnish coupe with crisp mint sprigs. Yield: 8 servings.

Mrs. Frederic J. Brown
San Francisco, Calif.

FROSTED ORANGE

6 lge. oranges
½ gal. orange sherbet
1 sm. bottle ginger ale

(Continued on next page)

Carefully remove pulp of oranges. Freeze orange shells. Mix orange pulp, sherbet and ginger ale. Fill shells with mixture. Freeze. Yield: 6 servings.

Mrs. William H. Ernst
Columbus, O.

ORANGE-LEMON CREAM

1 ½ c. sugar
2 eggs
¼ c. lemon juice
½ c. orange juice
Vanilla wafers
1 pt. cream, beaten

Beat sugar into eggs; add juices. Cook until melted, stirring constantly. Roll enough vanilla wafers to spread on bottom of tray to the thickness of a pie crust. Fold cream into egg mixture. Pour cream mixture over crumbs. Sprinkle wafer crumbs on top; freeze until mixture is solid. Yield: 8 servings.

Mrs. Ruth Davis
Berea, Ky.

FROZEN ORANGE DESSERT

3 eggs, separated
½ tsp. salt
½ c. plus 2 tbsp. sugar
¼ c. orange juice
1 tbsp. orange rind
1 pkg. dessert topping mix, prepared
1 c. vanilla wafer crumbs

Beat egg yolks until foamy; add salt, 1/2 cup sugar, orange juice and rind. Cook until thick; cool. Beat egg whites until stiff, gradually adding 2 tablespoons sugar. Fold into yolk mixture; fold in prepared dessert topping. Spoon onto a layer of vanilla wafer crumbs in a square pan. Sprinkle top with crumbs. Freeze for 24 hours. Cut into squares to serve.

Mrs. James L. Chapman
Point Arena AFS, Calif.

FROZEN ORANGE-CRANBERRY DESSERT

1 1-lb. can jellied cranberry sauce
1 6-oz. can frozen orange juice concentrate
¼ c. sugar
⅛ tsp. salt
1 c. heavy cream, whipped
⅛ tsp. (or more) red food coloring

Combine cranberry sauce, undiluted orange juice concentrate, sugar and salt. Beat with an electric beater or a rotary beater to blend thoroughly. Fold in whipped cream and food coloring. Pour mixture into a 1-quart mold or into two refrigerator trays. Freeze until firm. Yield: 6 servings.

Mrs. Edward R. Dixon
Eglin AFB, Fla.

PATIO FREEZE

1 c. sugar
2 c. mashed bananas
2 c. orange juice
2 tbsp. lemon juice
1 No. 2 can crushed pineapple and juice
10 to 12 Maraschino cherries, cut up
Salt

Combine sugar and bananas; mix well. Add juices, pineapple, cherries and salt. Place in two refrigerator trays. Freeze until solid. Beat until fluffy. Return to trays; freeze. Yield: 6 servings.

Mrs. George E. Murray
Port Allen, La.

MRS. EISENHOWER'S FROSTED MINT DELIGHT

2 1-lb. cans crushed pineapple
1 pkg. unflavored gelatin
¾ c. mint flavored apple jelly
1 pt. heavy cream
2 tsp. confectioners sugar

Drain pineapple; reserve syrup. Chill all ingredients. Dissolve gelatin in 1 cup pineapple syrup. Melt jelly; stir in pineapple. Add gelatin mixture. Whip cream with sugar; fold into gelatin mixture. Pour into mold. Freeze until firm but not solid. Yield: 10-12 servings.

Mrs. Dwight D. Eisenhower

PINEAPPLE FREEZE

8 marshmallows
1 c. crushed pineapple and juice
½ c. shredded coconut
½ pt. heavy cream, whipped
2 c. vanilla wafer crumbs

Combine marshmallows, pineapple, juice and coconut; let stand overnight or until marshmallows soften. Fold in whipped cream; pour into a pie pan lined with vanilla wafer crumbs. Sprinkle top with wafer crumbs. Freeze.

Mrs. R. B. Burgess
Patrick AFB, Fla.

RASPBERRY DELIGHT

1 pkg. frozen raspberries, thawed
2 tbsp. lemon juice
½ c. sugar
1 c. thick sour cream

Crush raspberries. Add all remaining ingredients. Pour into freezing trays; freeze for 2 hours. Stir twice during freezing. NOTE: This recipe may also be made with frozen strawberries. Yield: 6 servings.

Mrs. W. T. Doyel
Portsmouth, Va.

STRAWBERRY BALL

1 qt. strawberry ice cream
3 egg whites, beaten
1 pt. freshly grated coconut
8 sprigs mint

Roll each scoop of strawberry ice cream in egg white; cover with coconut. Store in deep freeze. When ready to serve, garnish each ball with a sprig of mint.

Mrs. Walter V. Kirkwood, Jr.
San Francisco, Calif.

WHITE DESSERT

4 egg yolks
4 tbsp. tarragon vinegar
4 tbsp. sugar
½ pt. heavy cream, whipped
½ lb. shelled blanched almonds
1 lge. can pineapple chunks
2 c. miniature marshmallows
1 c. white grapes

Cook egg yolks, vinegar and sugar in double boiler until thick; cool. Add all remaining ingredients; freeze for several hours. Yield: 12 servings.

Mrs. James W. Holt
Newburgh, N.Y.

FROZEN FRUIT DELIGHT

1 6-oz. pkg. cream cheese
1 c. mayonnaise
½ pt. cream, whipped
1 lge. can crushed pineapple, drained
2 lge. cans fruit cocktail, drained
1 c. cherries, chopped
24 marshmallows, chopped

Blend cream cheese and mayonnaise. Blend in whipped cream; add fruits and marshmallows. Place mixture in empty fruit cans or other containers. Freeze until hard. Slice; serve. Yield: 10 servings.

Agnes C. Napier
Hialeah, Fla.

FROZEN FRUIT MALLOW

1 9-oz. can crushed pineapple
1 3-oz. pkg. cream cheese, softened
1 7-oz. bottle lemon-lime beverage
2 10-oz. pkg. frozen sliced peaches
1 c. halved green grapes
1 c. heavy cream, whipped
1 ½ c. colored miniature marshmallows

Blend undrained pineapple and cream cheese. Stir in beverage; add fruits. Freeze until partially set. Fold in whipped cream and marshmallows. Pour into 9-inch square pan

or 2-quart refrigerator dish. Freeze until firm. Yield: 6-8 servings.

Mrs. James Born
Frankfort, S.D.

FROZEN RUM-FRUIT DESSERT

1 c. chopped candied fruits
Brandy
1 qt. vanilla ice cream
¼ c. rum

Cover fruits with brandy. Soak for several hours; drain. Remove ice cream from freezer; let stand at room temperature until soft enough to mix in fruits and rum. Refreeze immediately in ice trays or in individual sherbets. Garnish with Maraschino cherry and or mint leaves. Yield: 10-12 servings.

Mrs. Robert C. Umphress
Beale AFB, Calif.

SLUSH

3 med. bananas
1 c. sugar
1 No. 2 can crushed pineapple and juice
Juice of 2 med. lemons
2 c. orange juice
2 c. ginger ale

Mash bananas. Blend in sugar, mixing thoroughly. Add remaining ingredients; mix well. Pour mixture into freezing cartons or ice cube trays. Freeze until firm. NOTE: This dessert may be served firmly frozen or allowed to stand at room temperature for an hour or longer and served in the slushy state. Yield: 10 servings.

Mrs. John A. Toth
Mather AFB, Calif.

WAFER-FRUIT FREEZE

2 doz. chocolate or vanilla wafers
1 c. heavy cream, whipped
1 tsp. vanilla flavoring
1 tbsp. sugar
1 No. 2 ½ can fruit cocktail, strained
1 banana, sliced
½ c. miniature marshmallows
¼ c. chopped walnuts

Line 8 x 8 x 2 1/2-inch pan with wafers. Combine whipped cream, flavoring and sugar; fold in fruits, marshmallows and nuts. Pile into pan; freeze. Yield: 6 servings.

Mrs. Joseph A. Macri
Seattle, Wash.

CREME DE MENTHE ICE

1 ½ c. sugar
3 c. water
½ c. lemon juice
¼ c. creme de menthe
Few grains of salt

Boil sugar and water for 5 minutes. Remove from heat; cool in pan. Add all remaining ingredients; stir. Pour into ice tray. Freeze quickly; stir three or four times during freezing. Yield: 6 servings.

Mrs. Douglas C. Plate
Coronado, Calif.

FRUIT ICE

1 c. water
1 c. sugar
Juice of 3 oranges
Juice of 3 lemons
3 bananas, mashed
1 c. crushed pineapple
½ c. Maraschino cherry halves

Make syrup by boiling water and sugar for 3 minutes; cool. Mix orange and lemon juices; add bananas and pineapple. Mix with syrup. Pour into freezer tray; freeze. Add cherries to each serving. Yield: 8 servings.

Mrs. Helen E. Roux
Alameda, Calif.

ALASKAN SNOW ICE CREAM

1 pkg. instant pudding mix
2 ¾ c. milk
2 tsp. vanilla flavoring
1 ½ c. sugar
Dash of salt
3 qt. new clean snow

Combine all ingredients except snow, mixing well. Pour over snow.

Marie Strutz
Seward, Alaska

AVOCADO ICE CREAM

1 pt. vanilla ice cream
1 sm. ripe avocado, well mashed
½ tsp. vanilla flavoring
Chocolate sauce

Slightly soften ice cream; blend in avocado and vanilla. Refreeze. Serve topped with chocolate sauce. Yield: 4 servings.

Mrs. Harold R. Everett
Fort Polk, La.

BURNT ALMOND ICE CREAM

⅓ c. almonds
2 egg whites
⅛ tsp. salt
⅓ c. sugar
½ pt. heavy cream

Blanch almonds; remove skins. Chop almonds very fine. Put in medium hot fry pan. Keep mixing until medium brown or toast on cookie tray in slow oven. Beat egg whites and salt until stiff; slowly add sugar. Whip cream until softly stiff. Add cream and cooled nuts to meringue; fold to combine. Pour into tray; freeze. Leave refrigerator at coldest temperature for 3 to 4 hours; turn refrigerator temperature to normal. Yield: 6 servings.

Mrs. K. E. Jackson
Duluth Air Base, Minn.

HOMEMADE BUTTER-PECAN ICE CREAM

3 qt. sweet milk
3 c. sugar
10 eggs
4 tsp. vanilla flavoring
1 c. finely chopped toasted pecans
3 tsp. butter
½ tsp. salt

Scald milk. Caramelize 1 cup sugar in skillet until golden brown; gradually stir into scalded milk. Beat eggs until light with electric mixer; gradually add remaining sugar. Stir into milk mixture. Cook over hot but not boiling water, stirring often, until it coats a spoon well. Cool. Add vanilla. Season nuts with butter and salt; add to cooled mixture. Freeze mixture in 1-gallon freezer, using ice cream salt and plenty of crushed ice. Yield: 15-20 servings.

Mrs. David Givens
Somerville, Tenn.

CARAMEL ICE CREAM

2 c. sugar
2 c. milk
Pinch of salt
2 tbsp. flour
3 eggs, beaten
3 cans milnot milk

Caramelize 1 cup sugar. Cook milk, remaining sugar, salt and flour in pan over low heat until mixture begins to thicken. Add eggs to milk mixture. Cool; pour into freezer can. Add caramel syrup and milnot milk. Freeze in hand or electric freezer. Yield: 1 gallon.

Mrs. Delmar Jaeger
Slater, Mo.

CHOCOLATE-MALT ICE CREAM

2 qt. plus 1 c. milk
¼ c. sifted cocoa
¼ c. flour
½ tsp. salt
4 eggs, beaten
2 ½ c. sugar
1 c. sifted instant malt
1 tbsp. vanilla flavoring
3 c. heavy cream

Scald 2 1/2 cups milk. Mix cocoa, flour, salt and 1/2 cup milk. Add eggs and sugar. Combine mixture with scalded milk; cook over low heat until thick. Cool. Add malt, vanilla, cream and remaining milk. Place in 1-gallon ice cream freezer; freeze. Yield: 1 gallon.

Mrs. Donald Hallquist
Stanton, Iowa

CHOCOLATE-MINT ICE CREAM

1 pkg. chocolate pudding mix
¼ c. sugar
2 c. milk
¼ tsp. peppermint flavoring
1 c. heavy cream, whipped

Combine pudding mix, sugar and milk. Bring to boil; cook until thickened. Stir in peppermint flavoring. Cool and pour into freezing tray. Chill for 30 minutes. Return to bowl; fold in whipped cream. Freeze for 1 hour. Return to bowl; beat until smooth but not melted. Return to tray; freeze until firm. Yield: 6 servings.

Mrs. John D. Gorham
Lubbock, Tex.

FRUIT ICE CREAM

3 bananas, mashed
Juice of 3 oranges
Juice of 3 lemons
3 c. sugar
3 c. cream
3 c. milk

Combine bananas and fruit juices. Add sugar; stir until dissolved. Add cream and milk. Pour into 1-gallon ice cream freezer. Freeze. Yield: 16 servings.

Mrs. Walter H. O'Hare
Pattonsburg, Mo.

GRAPE ICE CREAM

40 marshmallows
2 c. grape juice
1 pt. heavy cream, whipped

Heat marshmallows and grape juice in a double boiler until melted; cool. Add whipped cream. Put into freezer tray; partially freeze.

Remove from freezer; stir with a spoon to mix partially frozen ingredients. Return to freezer until firm. Yield: 4 servings.

Mrs. C. A. Richmond, Jr.
St. Petersburg, Fla.

HOMEMADE ICE CREAM

4 eggs, beaten
2 c. sugar
4 c. heavy cream, whipped
1 tsp. vanilla flavoring
¼ tsp. almond flavoring
Milk

Beat eggs until thick and lemon colored; add sugar. Fold in whipped cream; add flavorings. Put in freezer; add milk to desired fullness. Freeze in ice cream freezer.

Mrs. Doris Cass
Burwell, Nebr.

HOMEMADE ICE CREAM

6 eggs
2 c. sugar
Pinch of salt
2 tbsp. vanilla flavoring
1 qt. cream
Milk

Beat eggs; add sugar, salt and vanilla, beating well. Mix in cream. Pour into freezer can; fill with milk. Freeze in ice cream freezer. Yield: 1 gallon.

Mrs. Albert Breuler
Harris, Iowa

FRESH PEACH ICE CREAM

6 eggs
2 c. sugar
1 14 ½-oz. can sweetened condensed milk
1 pt. half and half cream
8 lge. ripe peaches, well mashed
Milk

Beat eggs; add sugar. Beat well. Add condensed milk and cream. Add peaches. Pour into gallon freezer; finish filling freezer with milk. Freeze in hand or electric freezer, using plenty of coarse salt with crushed ice. Yield: 16 servings.

Mrs. D. R. McMurtry
Springfield, Ky.

PEACH ICE CREAM

1 pkg. peach gelatin
1 c. boiling water
½ tsp. (scant) salt
1 pkg. frozen peach slices, diced
1 c. milk
1 c. heavy cream, whipped

(Continued on next page)

Dissolve gelatin in boiling water. Stir in salt and peaches with their syrup. Chill until slightly thickened or of consistency of beaten egg whites. Slowly stir in milk; fold in whipped cream. Pour into 8 or 9-inch square pan or freezing trays; freeze until firm. Yield: 8 servings.

Mrs. G. I. Chegin
Barbers Point NAS, Hawaii

PRIZE PEANUT BUTTER ICE CREAM

1 ½ tbsp. flour
¼ tsp. salt
½ c. sugar
2 c. scalded milk
½ c. peanut butter
¾ c. cold milk
1 tsp. vanilla flavoring

Mix flour, salt and sugar; gradually add to scalded milk. Cook in double boiler for 15 minutes; strain and cool. Beat peanut butter and milk until smooth; stir in vanilla. Add to custard. Place in freezing tray. Freeze until mushy; place in a bowl. Beat until creamy. Freeze for several hours before serving. Yield: 6 servings.

Dorothy Hart
Claremont, N.H.

REFRIGERATOR ICE CREAM

2 eggs, separated
6 tbsp. sugar
4 tbsp. white syrup
1 c. milk
1 c. light cream
1 tsp. vanilla flavoring

Beat egg yolks, sugar and syrup until thick and creamy. Add milk, cream and vanilla. Freeze until firm about 1/4 inch from edges. Remove. Add unbeaten egg whites; beat until fluffy. Return to freezer for 45 minutes or until frozen, stirring occasionally. Yield: 6-8 servings.

Mrs. H. R. Montague
Patrick AFB, Fla.

FRESH STRAWBERRY ICE CREAM

1 c. sliced strawberries
1 whole egg
1 tbsp. lemon juice
¾ c. sugar
1 c. heavy cream, whipped

Whip all ingredients except cream at low speed on mixer for 20 minutes. Fold in whipped cream. Pour into tray; freeze. Yield: 6 servings.

Mrs. B. J. Davis
U.S. Naval Sta., Bermuda

HOMEMADE FREEZER STRAWBERRY ICE CREAM

8 eggs
2 ½ c. sugar
Dash of salt
1 qt. half and half cream
1 tsp. vanilla flavoring
2 pkg. frozen strawberries, thawed

Beat eggs well; stir in sugar and salt. Add cream and vanilla. Blend in strawberries. Freeze in gallon freezer. Yield: 12-16 servings.

Mrs. Juanita Leach
Springfield, Mo.

SWEET POTATO ICE CREAM

1 c. mashed sweet potatoes
¾ c. sugar
1 tsp. vanilla flavoring
½ tsp. salt
2 egg whites
1 c. heavy cream, whipped

Combine sweet potatoes and one-half the sugar; add vanilla and salt. Beat egg whites until stiff; add remaining sugar, beating until it will hold its shape. Fold meringue and whipped cream into potato mixture until mixed. Pour into pan. Place in freezer for 1 hour to 1 hour and 30 minutes or until frozen. NOTE: Chopped nuts and Maraschino cherries may be added. Yield: 6-8 servings.

Mrs. Blake W. Lambert
San Antonio, Tex.

TANGERINE CREME

1 6-oz. can frozen tangerine juice
    concentrate, thawed
1 c. heavy cream, whipped
2 egg whites
½ c. sugar
Few drops food coloring (opt.)

Fold undiluted tangerine concentrate into the whipped cream. Beat egg whites until soft peaks form; gradually add sugar, beating until stiff peaks form. Fold in whipped cream mixture. Tint with food coloring. Pour into 1-quart refrigerator tray; freeze until firm. Yield: 6-8 servings.

Mrs. Morris J. Lucree
Arlington Hall Sta., Va.

TUTTI-FRUTTI ICE CREAM

2 pkg. strawberry gelatin
Boiling water
3 c. sugar
6 eggs
3 tbsp. vanilla flavoring
1 tsp. salt
1 ½ pt. heavy cream
1 ⅛ gal. whole milk
1 No. 2 can crushed pineapple

Add enough boiling water to gelatin to dissolve; set aside to cool. Cream sugar and eggs; add vanilla, salt, cream and one-half of the milk. Mix in cooled gelatin mixture, pineapple and enough remaining milk to fill 1 1/2-gallon freezer. Freeze.

Mrs. Ernest Schmidt
Topeka, Kans.

JIFFY VANILLA ICE CREAM

2 pkg. instant vanilla pudding mix
1 lb. powdered sugar
1 can evaporated milk
2 ½ qt. milk

Combine pudding mix, powdered sugar and evaporated milk; mix with beater. Pour into freezer can; add enough milk to make 1 gallon. Freeze until firm. Yield: 10 servings.

Ruth Dikeman
Ft. Scott, Kans.

BONBON VERT

1 qt. vanilla ice milk
1 6-oz. can crushed pineapple
1 pkg. dessert topping mix, prepared
1 4-oz. can shredded coconut
1 4-oz. pkg. pecans
8 oz. creme de menthe

Into each of 8 goblets, place a scoop of ice milk. Add 1 tablespoon pineapple; top with a tablespoon of dessert topping. Add a tablespoon of coconut; top with more dessert topping. Add a tablespoon of pecans; top with another tablespoon of dessert topping. Pour 1 jigger of creme de menthe over each goblet. Yield: 8 servings.

Mrs. Aubrey P. Nathan
Warren, Mich.

BROWNIE ALASKA

1 box brownie mix
2 pt. vanilla ice cream
6 egg whites
¼ tsp. cream of tartar
⅛ tsp. salt
¾ c. sugar

Cook brownie mix according to directions on package; cool. Cut into eight servings. Place on cookie sheet. Cut ice cream into similar size squares; place on top of brownies. Freeze for 2 hours or until firm. Have egg whites at room temperature; whip with cream of tartar and salt at high speed of mixer until soft peaks form. Continue beating, adding sugar gradually until meringue stands in stiff peaks, but not dry. Cover each ice cream-topped brownie with meringue, sealing the sides well. Return to freezer. May be stored up to two days. At serving time, remove from freezer. Bake immediately at 450 degrees for 5 minutes or until meringue is golden brown. Serve immediately. Yield: 8 servings.

Mrs. W. E. Aymond
Pearl Harbor, Hawaii

FROZEN CHOCOLATE CRUNCH

1 c. chopped pecans
3 c. chocolate cake or brownie crumbs
1 qt. vanilla ice cream

Mix nuts with crumbs. Shape ice cream into balls; roll in crumb mixture. Freeze. Remove from freezer several minutes before serving. Serve with sweetened, vanilla flavored whipped cream. NOTE: This may be stored for several days in freezer if tightly covered. Yield: 8 servings.

Mrs. Donald W. Leininger
Westover AFB, Mass.

FROZEN CHOCOLATE DESSERT

⅔ c. butter
2 c. powdered sugar
3 eggs, separated
2 squares chocolate, melted
Pinch of salt
1 tsp. vanilla flavoring
½ c. chopped nuts
30 graham crackers, crushed
1 qt. vanilla ice cream, softened (opt.)

Cream butter and powdered sugar; add beaten egg yolks, chocolate, salt, vanilla and nuts. Fold in well beaten egg whites. Pat one-half of the crumbs into a 9 x 13-inch greased pan; pour chocolate mixture over top. Freeze for 2 hours; spread ice cream over top. Sprinkle with remaining crumbs and additional nuts; freeze. Yield: 12 servings.

Mrs. Eldon MacVey
Plover, Iowa

FROZEN CHOCOLATE JUBILEE

2 ½ c. vanilla wafer crumbs
4 tbsp. melted butter

(Continued on next page)

¼ tsp. cinnamon
½ c. butter or margarine
2 c. powdered sugar
2 squares chocolate, melted
1 tsp. vanilla flavoring
3 eggs, separated
1 qt. vanilla ice cream, softened
¾ c. chopped nuts (opt.)

Mix wafer crumbs, melted butter and cinnamon thoroughly; press firmly into 8-inch square pan. Cream remaining butter; gradually add powdered sugar, beating until light and fluffy. Add chocolate, vanilla and beaten egg yolks, beating until well blended. Fold in beaten egg whites. Spread on wafer crust; chill. Spread ice cream over chocolate layer; sprinkle with nuts. Freeze. Yield: 9 servings.

Lucile Burnside
Kinderhook, Mich.

CREME DE MENTHE PARFAIT

⅔ c. cocoa
3 c. sugar
⅛ tsp. salt
1 ¼ c. light cream
4 ½ tbsp. butter
1 tsp. vanilla flavoring
French vanilla ice cream
Green creme de menthe
Whipped cream

Combine cocoa, sugar and salt. Add cream; bring to boil, stirring constantly. Cook until mixture forms a very soft ball when dropped in cold water. Remove from heat; drop in butter. Cool to lukewarm. Add vanilla; beat until thick and creamy. Chill parfait glasses. Alternate layers of ice cream with fudge mixture until almost to top of glass. Pour creme de menthe over all. Top with a spoon of whipped cream. Place in freezer until 30 minutes before serving time. Yield: 12 servings.

Mrs. S. T. DeLaMater
Norfolk, Va.

FESTIVE ICE CREAM CUPS

6 oz. semi-sweet chocolate pieces
2 tbsp. butter
1 pt. ice cream
¼ c. crushed peppermint candy

Melt chocolate and butter over hot water. Line six fluted paper baking cups with chocolate mixture. Set in muffin pan to keep shape. Chill for at least 1 hour. Peel paper, leaving chocolate cups. Fill with ice cream; sprinkle with peppermint candy. Yield: 6 servings.

Mrs. Gerard Barton
Mobile, Ala.

FROZEN DESSERT

Graham cracker crumbs
½ lb. butter
2 c. powdered sugar
3 eggs, beaten
1 tsp. vanilla flavoring
3 squares bitter chocolate, melted
1 c. nuts
1 qt. softened mint ice cream

Make a graham cracker crust in a 9 x 13-inch pan. Cream butter and sugar. Add eggs and vanilla; mix well. Add chocolate and nuts. Pour one-half of the mixture into crust. Spread ice cream over chocolate layer; top with remaining chocolate mixture. Sprinkle with graham cracker crumbs. Freeze. Yield: 25 servings.

Mrs. Marcella Kropp
LaValle, Wisc.

ELEGANT ICE CREAM DESSERT

3 c. vanilla wafer crumbs
¾ c. melted butter
1 c. chopped nuts
5 eggs, separated
2 ½ c. powdered sugar
3 1-oz. squares chocolate, melted
1 tsp. vanilla flavoring
½ gal. vanilla ice cream

Combine crumbs, butter and nuts. Put one-half of the mixture in a 13 x 9 x 2-inch pan. Combine beaten egg yolks, powdered sugar, chocolate and vanilla; mix well. Cool; add stiffly beaten egg whites. Put one-half of the chocolate mixture on top of crumbs. Slice ice cream over chocolate mixture. Add remaining chocolate mixture; cover with remaining crumbs. Freeze for 8 hours. Yield: 12 servings.

Mrs. Alvan H. Hansen
Manning, Iowa

ICE CREAM CRUNCH

½ c. slightly crushed corn flakes
2 tbsp. butter
3 tbsp. brown sugar
½ c. chopped nuts
1 qt. ice cream, softened

Combine corn flakes, butter, sugar and nuts. Mix well; place in frying pan. Cook over low heat, stirring constantly, until sugar is melted and mixture crumbly; cool. Stir into ice cream. Spread in refrigerator tray; freeze. Cut into bars or scoop out. Yield: 6-8 servings.

Mrs. Alice J. Hladky
Litchfield, Nebr.

ICE CREAM-PECAN BALLS WITH FUDGE SAUCE

1 pt. vanilla ice cream
1 c. coarsely chopped toasted pecans

Form ice cream into balls. Roll in pecans; wrap in waxed paper or moisture proof wrap. Store in freezer.

FUDGE SAUCE:
½ c. butter
2 ¼ c. confectioners sugar
⅔ c. evaporated milk
6 squares bitter chocolate

Mix butter and sugar in top of double boiler; add evaporated milk and chocolate. Cook over hot water for 30 minutes; do not stir while cooking. Remove from heat; beat. Serve with ice cream balls. NOTE: Store in refrigerator and reheat as needed. Yield: 4 servings.

Mrs. Wilbur E. Fleck
Tucson, Ariz.

ICE CREAM ROLL

1 pkg. angel food cake mix
2 ½-gal. cartons ice cream, softened
1 pt. heavy cream, whipped

Mix cake mix as directed on box; pour into two jelly roll pans lined with waxed paper. Bake at 350 degrees for 15 minutes or until brown. Let cool; spread with ice cream. Roll up like jelly roll. Frost roll with whipped cream. Freeze. Yield: 12 servings.

Mrs. James Bloom
Clay City, Ky.

ICE CREAM-WICH SUNDAES

1 ½ c. rice cereal
¼ c. (packed) brown sugar
¼ c. butter
1 c. flaked coconut
½ c. chopped walnuts
1 ½ to 2 qt. vanilla ice cream, slightly softened
Strawberry or raspberry pie filling

Mix cereal, sugar, butter, coconut and nuts. Put one-half of the mixture in a buttered 8-inch pan. Spread evenly with ice cream. Sprinkle with remaining cereal mixture; press lightly. Cover and freeze until firm. Serve with strawberry pie filling over top of each piece. Yield: 9 servings.

Mrs. Richard King
Minneapolis, Minn.

PINEAPPLE-DE MENTHE SUNDAE

1 30-oz. can sliced pineapple
1 qt. vanilla ice cream
¼ c. green creme de menthe

Freeze unopened can of pineapple for at least 4 hours. Make eight ice cream balls; freeze. When ready to serve, dip can of pineapple into hot water for 30 seconds. Open both ends of can; force out frozen pineapple. Cut crosswise into eight sections. Top each slice with one ice cream ball; spoon 2 or 3 teaspoons creme de menthe over top. Serve. Yield: 8 servings.

Mrs. Robert J. Parr
Fort Richardson, Alaska

FROZEN STRAWBERRY CREAM

½ gal. strawberry ice cream
1 c. crumbled chocolate sandwich cookies, frosting removed
1 c. miniature marshmallows
½ c. chopped walnuts
½ c. heavy cream, whipped

Soften ice cream; add cookie crumbs, marshmallows, walnuts and whipped cream. Mix well; freeze in a mold. Top each serving with a strawberry or chocolate syrup. Lime sherbet or chocolate ice cream may be used.

Mrs. Lloyd Rock
Hope, Kans.

SURPRISE DESSERT

1 stick butter
2 c. graham cracker crumbs or oats
½ c. brown sugar
1 c. walnuts
1 c. caramel sauce
½ gal. softened ice cream

Combine butter, crumbs and brown sugar; brown slightly on cookie sheet. Place three-fourths of the crumbs in 9 x 13-inch pan. Cool. Cover with nuts and softened caramel sauce. Beat ice cream slightly until soft enough to spread. Spread over sauce; sprinkle with remaining crumbs. Freeze. Yield: 16-20 servings.

Mrs. Gladys Pelley
Linn Grove, Iowa

CREME DE MENTHE MOUSSE

16 marshmallows
⅔ c. creme de menthe
1 pt. heavy cream, whipped

Melt marshmallows in creme de menthe; cool. Blend with whipped cream. Freeze; serve like ice cream. NOTE: Can be molded and served with strawberries. Yield: 4-6 servings.

Mrs. M. A. Feher
Cecil Field, Fla.

FROZEN PUMPKIN PARFAIT SQUARES

1 ½ c. graham cracker crumbs
¼ c. butter, melted
¼ c. sugar
½ c. finely chopped pecans
1 qt. vanilla ice cream
1 ½ c. canned pumpkin
½ c. brown sugar
½ tsp. salt
1 tsp. cinnamon
¼ tsp. ginger
⅛ tsp. cloves

Combine crumbs, butter, sugar and nuts. Press mixture firmly against sides and bottom of a 9-inch square pan. Bake at 375 degrees for 8 minutes. Cool. Soften ice cream to custard consistency. Stir in mixture of pumpkin, brown sugar and spices. Pile into cooled crumb crust. Freeze until hard. Remove from freezer 20 minutes before serving. Cut into squares. Garnish with whipped cream and additional chopped nuts if desired.

Photograph for this recipe above.

TRI-COLORED GLACE

½ pt. lemon sherbet, softened
Green food coloring
1 No. 1 can crushed pineapple, drained

½ pt. macadamia nut ice cream, softened
½ pt. orange sherbet, softened
2 tbsp. chopped crystalized ginger

Blend lemon sherbet with food coloring and pineapple. Spread in 6-cup ring mold; freeze. Spread macadamia nut ice cream evenly on top; freeze. Combine orange sherbet and ginger; spread over ice cream. Freeze. Unmold to serve; center may be filled with sugared grapes. NOTE: If macadamia nut ice cream is not available, use 1/2 pint vanilla ice cream blended with 2 tablespoons melted butter and 1/4 cup chopped pecans. Yield: 8 servings.

Mrs. J. F. O'Connell
Pearl Harbor, Hawaii

FROZEN FRUIT MOUSSE

1 pkg. frozen raspberries, strawberries or peaches
1 c. sugar
1 tsp. vanilla flavoring
1 pt. sour cream

Whip all ingredients in blender. Freeze in ice tray. Yield: 6 servings.

Mrs. J. F. Thorlin
White Sands Missile Range, N.M.

HONEY MOUSSE

6 eggs, separated
1 ½ c. strained honey
Whipped cream
Finely chopped pistachio nuts or almonds

Beat egg yolks and honey; heat in double
boiler until thickened. Chill. Fold in stiffly
beaten egg whites. Fold in whipped cream.
Pour into molds; freeze. Garnish with nuts.
Yield: 4-6 servings.

Louvanna Monders
Lebanon, Oreg.

STRAWBERRY MOUSSE

1 egg white
⅛ tsp. salt
¾ c. powdered sugar
1 c. heavy cream
1 ¼ c. fresh strawberries

Beat egg white and salt until foamy. Gradually add sugar; beat until stiff. Whip cream
until stiff; add to egg white. Wash, hull and
mash strawberries; fold into mixture. Pour
into refrigerator tray. Freeze, without stirring, until firm. Let stand at room temperature for a few minutes before serving.
Yield: 4 servings.

Mrs. Robert L. Pfluger
Corvallis, Oreg.

EASY VANILLA MOUSSE

¼ c. sugar
¼ c. milk
⅛ tsp. salt
1 tsp. vanilla flavoring
1 c. heavy cream, whipped

Combine sugar, milk, salt and vanilla in
mixing bowl; stir until sugar is almost dissolved. Fold in whipped cream until well
blended. Place in fluted cups inserted in
muffin pan. Place muffin pan directly on
surface of freezer. Freeze for 1 hour and 30
minutes to 2 hours. Leave at room temperature for 10 to 15 minutes before serving.
Yield: 6 servings.

Mrs. R. A. Powell
Whidbey Island, Wash.

COFFEE-ICE CREAM PIE

2 squares unsweetened chocolate
2 tbsp. butter or margarine
2 tbsp. hot milk
⅔ c. sifted powdered sugar
1 ½ c. shredded coconut
1 qt. coffee ice cream
¼ c. pecans

Blend chocolate and butter over hot water.
Stir milk into powdered sugar; blend into
chocolate mixture. Stir in coconut. Press into
bottom and sides of buttered pie pan. Chill.
Stir ice cream to soften; add pecans. Fill
pie shell. Decorate with pecans or grated
chocolate; freeze. Yield: 6 servings.

Mrs. Chandler Swanson
Sanford, Fla.

CREME DE MENTHE PIE

¾ c. chocolate wafer crumbs
¼ c. butter
24 marshmallows
⅔ c. creme de menthe
1 c. heavy cream, whipped

Combine crumbs and butter; press into 9-
inch pan. Freeze. Melt marshmallows in
double boiler; add creme de menthe. Cool.
Fold in whipped cream; pour over crumb
crust. Place in freezer for 2 hours. Garnish
with crumbs, shaved chocolate, whipped
cream, cherries, strawberries or mint
leaves. Yield: 8 servings.

Mrs. Louise De Carlo
Ironwood, Mich.

CREME DE MENTHE PIE

20 marshmallows
¼ c. milk
12 chocolate cookies, crushed
2 tbsp. margarine, melted
½ pt. heavy cream
8 tsp. creme de menthe
Pinch of salt

Melt marshmallows in milk; cool. Sprinkle
three-fourths of crumbs into lightly greased
pie plate. Pour margarine over cookie
crumbs. Whip cream; fold in marshmallows,
creme de menthe and salt. Spoon mixture
into pie pan. Sprinkle remaining crumbs on
top. Keep in freezer. Yield: 8 servings.

Mrs. Gay Russell
Boston, Mass.

EGGNOG PIE

3 eggs, separated
5 tbsp. bourbon
½ c. sugar
½ tsp. nutmeg
1 c. heavy cream, whipped
1 10-in. graham cracker crust

Beat egg yolks; add bourbon gradually. Beat
egg whites, adding sugar and nutmeg. Fold
into yolk mixture. Fold in whipped cream.
Pour into crust; freeze overnight. Garnish
with additional whipped cream or sprinkle
top of pie with graham cracker crumbs.
Yield: 8 servings.

Mrs. Wilmer G. Morgan
Pueblo Army Depot, Colo.

CHOCOLATE-MARSHMALLOW PIE

15 Chiparoons, finely rolled
¼ c. butter or margarine, softened
¼ c. sugar
1 qt. chocolate ice cream
1 c. marshmallow creme
2 tbsp. water
¼ c. walnut halves

Blend Chiparoon crumbs, butter and sugar. Press firmly against bottom and sides of 9-inch pie plate. Bake at 375 degrees for 5 minutes. Cool and freeze. Soften ice cream slightly; pack into pie shell. Freeze. Just before serving, mix marshmallow creme with water; spoon over pie. Sprinkle with walnut halves. Allow to stand at room temperature for a few minutes before serving. Yield: 8 servings.

Photograph for this recipe above.

DATE-NUT-ICE CREAM PIE

1 7¼-oz. pkg. pitted dates
½ c. sugar
1 c. water
1 tsp. lemon juice
1 tbsp. unflavored gelatin
¼ c. chopped pecans
1 4¾-oz. pkg. vanilla wafers, crushed

⅓ c. butter, melted
1 qt. vanilla ice cream

Cut dates into fourths; combine with sugar, 1/2 cup water and lemon juice. Cover; cook slowly until dates are soft. Remove from heat; add gelatin which has been dissolved in remaining cold water. Add nuts; let mixture cool. Mix wafers with butter; press mixture into bottom and sides of 9-inch pie plate. Spread 1 pint ice cream over crust. Spread cooled date mixture on ice cream. Top with remaining ice cream which has been slightly softened. Freeze. Let stand at room temperature for 5 to 10 minutes before serving. Yield: 8 servings.

Mrs. Hubert Prudoehl
Rushford, Minn.

FROZEN LEMON PIE

1 ¼ c. finely crushed corn flakes
¼ c. butter, melted
⅔ c. sugar
⅛ tsp. salt
3 eggs, separated
¼ c. lemon juice
1 tbsp. grated lemon rind
1 c. heavy cream, whipped

(Continued on next page)

Mix corn flake crumbs and butter; press 1 cup of the mixture into bottom of refrigerator tray. Combine sugar, salt, slightly beaten egg yolks, lemon juice and rind; cook over boiling water until thickened, stirring constantly. Chill. Fold in beaten egg whites and whipped cream. Pour over crumb mixture in tray; top with remaining crumbs. Freeze. Yield: 6 servings.

Mrs. H. F. Guffey
Holloman AFB, N.M.

FROZEN LEMON PIE

3 eggs, separated
⅛ tsp. salt
½ c. sugar
¼ c. lemon juice
½ tsp. grated lemon rind
1 c. heavy cream
¾ c. graham cracker or vanilla wafer crumbs

Beat egg yolks; add salt and sugar. Place mixture in top of double boiler. Stir in lemon juice and rind. Cook until mixture thickens and coats spoon; chill. Whip cream. Beat egg whites until stiff; fold cream into egg whites. Fold in chilled lemon mixture. Sprinkle one-half of the crumbs in freezer tray; pour in mixture. Sprinkle remaining crumbs on top. Freeze and serve. NOTE: This pie can be kept in freezer for 24 hours before serving. Yield: 6 servings.

Mrs. Ethel S. Butchart
Kahului, Maui, Hawaii

FROZEN LIME PIE

2 eggs
½ c. sugar
Green food coloring
1 c. light cream
½ c. lime juice
1 tbsp. grated lime peel
1 pt. vanilla ice cream
Graham cracker crust

Beat eggs until light. Add sugar gradually; continue beating until mixture is light and fluffy. Add food coloring, cream, lime juice and lime peel; mix well. Pour into freezing tray; freeze. Put in bowl; beat. Return to tray; partially freeze again. Whip ice cream smooth; spread on crust. Top with mixture; garnish with grated lime peel. Freeze until firm. Yield: 6 servings.

Mrs. E. L. Mapp, Jr.
Boston, Mass.

ICE CREAM PIE

2 c. Rice Krispies
½ c. melted butter
½ c. brown sugar
1 qt. ice cream
½ c. slivered almonds
1 can shredded coconut

Combine Rice Krispies and butter; blend in sugar. Press in bottom and on sides of pie pan. Spread ice cream evenly over crust. Top with almonds and coconut. Freeze until firm. NOTE: To soften ice cream after placing on crust, place in 325 degree oven for 5 minutes. Yield: 8 servings.

Mrs. Arthur Anderson
Muskegon, Mich.

MILE HIGH STRAWBERRY PIE

1 10-oz. pkg. frozen strawberries
1 c. sugar
2 egg whites
1 c. heavy cream, whipped
1 10-in. meringue shell, baked

Break berries apart with a fork; do not thaw. Add sugar and egg whites; beat until stiff. Add whipped cream. Pile high into cooled meringue shell. Freeze overnight. Yield: 6-8 servings.

Mrs. Mervin S. Waters
Warren, Mich.

QUICK AND EASY ICE CREAM PIE

1 qt. vanilla or other ice cream
1 9-in. crumb crust or baked pastry shell
1 lge. pkg. frozen strawberries
Meringue topping

Spread slightly softened ice cream evenly into pie crust. Freeze for 30 minutes or until ice cream hardens. Place strawberries over ice cream. Cover with meringue; return to freezer. Remove from freezer 15 minutes before serving. NOTE: Any other fruit or filling may be substituted for strawberries. Yield: 8 servings.

Mrs. William F. Miller, Jr.
Dover-Foxcroft, Me.

FROZEN CHRISTMAS PUDDING

10 graham crackers, rolled
¼ c. chopped Maraschino cherries
½ c. chopped nuts
2 tbsp. peanut butter
1 qt. vanilla ice cream

Mix crumbs, cherries, nuts and peanut butter; blend well. Line pan with waxed paper; spread

(Continued on next page)

one-half of the mixture over bottom. Spread ice cream over base; top with remaining mixture. Freeze; slice and serve. Yield: 6 servings.

Mrs. Martha Hopkins
Apollo, Pa.

FROZEN CRANBERRY PUDDING

Rind of 1 orange
2 c. cranberries
¾ c. sugar
½ c. chopped pecans
1 pt. vanilla ice cream, softened

Put orange rind and cranberries through food chopper; mix with sugar and pecans. Stir into ice cream. Put in freezer tray. Freeze until firm. Yield: 6 servings.

Betty Duff
Harvard, Ill.

FROZEN FRUIT PUDDING

1 lge. can fruit cocktail
16 lge. marshmallows
¼ tsp. salt
½ c. evaporated milk, chilled

Drain juice from fruit cocktail, reserving 1/2 cup liquid. Combine juice, marshmallows and salt; heat over boiling water until marshmallows are melted, stirring occasionally. Add fruit cocktail; chill thoroughly. Whip milk until stiff; fold into chilled fruit. Pour into oblong dish; freeze at lowest temperature. Yield: 8 servings.

Leffa M. Coble
Denver, Colo.

FROZEN PARADISE PUDDING

1 7-oz. pkg. sugar wafers
½ c. butter or margarine
1 ½ c. sifted powdered sugar
2 eggs
1 c. heavy cream, whipped
1 10-oz. pkg. frozen red raspberries, partially thawed

Set aside 10 wafers. Crush remaining wafers. Press crumbs on bottom of 9-inch cake pan. Cream butter and 3/4 cup sugar until light and fluffy. Add an egg at a time, beating after each addition. Gradually beat in remaining sugar. Fold in whipped cream. Spread 1/2-inch layer of the mixture over crumbs. Add raspberries in an even layer. Top with remaining cream mixture. Freeze until needed. Let stand at room temperature. Decorate with reserved wafers. Yield: 10 servings.

Mrs. R. V. Harmon
Page, Nebr.

FROZEN PINEAPPLE PUDDING

½ lb. vanilla wafers, crushed
½ b. butter, softened
1 ½ c. powdered sugar
2 eggs
1 c. heavy cream
⅓ c. granulated sugar
1 c. drained crushed pineapple
¾ c. chopped nuts

Place wafer crumbs in two freezing trays. Cream butter and powdered sugar. Add eggs; beat well. Pour over crumbs. Whip cream; add granulated sugar. Fold in pineapple and nuts. Pour over egg mixture. Freeze. Yield: 8-10 servings.

Mrs. Ted Miller
Danbury, Nebr.

TIFFIN FRENCH PUDDING

1 2-lb. box vanilla wafers, crushed
1 lb. butter
4 c. powdered sugar
8 eggs
1 qt. heavy cream, whipped
2 c. chopped walnuts
2 c. Maraschino cherries
2 tsp. vanilla flavoring
Pinch of salt

Line two 13 x 9-inch cake pans with one-half of the wafer crumbs. Cream butter well; slowly add powdered sugar. Add an egg at a time; beat until fluffy. Put mixture in wafer-lined pan; chill for 15 minutes or until fairly hard. Combine all remaining ingredients; spread over egg mixture. Top with remaining wafer crumbs. Freeze for 24 hours. Let stand at room temperature for 1 hour before serving. Yield: 14-24 servings.

Mrs. Barney A. Grimes, Jr.
Offutt AFB, Nebr.

BUTTERMILK SHERBET

2 c. buttermilk
½ c. sugar
1 c. crushed pineapple
1 egg white
1 ½ tsp. vanilla flavoring

Mix buttermilk, sugar and pineapple thoroughly; pour into ice cube tray. Place in freezer until of mushy consistency. Place in bowl; add egg white and vanilla. Beat until light and fluffy; return to ice cube tray. Wet bottom of tray; place in freezer until firm. Yield: 4-6 servings.

Mrs. Thomas S. Johnson
Brooklyn, N.Y.

CHAMPAGNE SHERBET

½ lb. lemon gelatin
2 qt. hot water
2 qt. cold water
Juice of 6 lemons
1 pt. grapefruit juice
1 lb. sugar
3 or 4 egg whites
½ bottle Champagne

Dissolve gelatin in hot water. After 30 minutes, add cold water, lemon juice, grapefruit juice and sugar dissolved in a small amount of hot water. Add unbeaten egg whites and Champagne. Mix well; freeze to thick mush. Mix again; return to freezer. Cover if not used immediately. Yield: 10 servings.

Mrs. B. W. Poor, Jr.
Key West, Fla.

CRANBERRY SHERBET

4 c. cranberries
2 ½ c. water
2 c. sugar
1 tsp. gelatin
½ c. cold water
Juice of 1 lemon
Juice of 1 orange

Cook berries in water until they stop popping; strain. Add sugar; cook until sugar dissolves. Add gelatin softened in cold water. Cool. Stir in fruit juices; pour into refrigerator tray. Stir twice during freezing. Yield: 8 servings.

Mrs. George Miller
Norman, Okla.

GRAPEFRUIT SHERBET

2 tsp. gelatin
1 ½ c. water
1 c. sugar
½ c. lemon juice
2 c. grapefruit juice
⅓ c. orange juice
½ tsp. salt
2 egg whites, stiffly beaten

Soak gelatin in 1/2 cup water. Boil sugar and 1 cup water for 10 minutes. Dissolve gelatin in hot syrup; cool. Add fruit juices and 1/4 teaspoon salt. Chill mixture for 45 minutes. Whip in chilled bowl. Fold in egg whites and remaining salt. Freeze. Yield: 6 servings.

Mrs. W. S. Antle, Jr.
New London, Conn.

LEMON-MILK SHERBET

⅓ c. lemon juice
1 ¼ c. sugar
Grated rind of 1 lemon
¼ tsp. lemon flavoring
2 c. milk

Combine lemon juice, sugar, rind and flavoring. Add milk; stir until sugar dissolves. Pour into refrigerator tray; freeze until firm. Remove from refrigerator when it starts to freeze; beat until light and creamy. Return to freezer and finish freezing. Yield: 12 servings.

Mrs. R. O. Mosher
Laughlin AFB, Tex.

LEMON SHERBET

2 c. sugar
Juice of 4 lemons
1 qt. milk

Combine sugar and lemon juice; add milk. Freeze for 1 hour to 1 hour and 30 minutes. Stir with fork. Freeze until ready to serve. Yield: 4 servings.

Ella Hill
Alexandria, Va.

HOMEMADE ORANGE SHERBET

6 bottles carbonated orange drink
1 8-oz. can crushed pineapple, drained

Mix orange drink and pineapple in 1-gallon freezer. Freeze until firm. Yield: 8-10 servings.

Ouida Jackson
College Sta., Tex.

LOW CALORIE ORANGE-PINEAPPLE SHERBET

1 6-oz. can frozen unsweetened orange juice concentrate
1 6-oz. can frozen unsweetened pineapple juice concentrate
3 ½ c. cold water
2 tbsp. liquid sugar substitute
1 c. nonfat dry milk solids

Combine all ingredients in 2-quart mixing bowl. Beat just enough to blend. Pour into ice cube trays; freeze for 1 to 2 hours or until half frozen. Remove to large chilled mixer bowl; beat on low speed until mixture is softened. Beat on high speed for 3 to 5

(Continued on next page)

minutes until creamy but not liquid. Pour into freezer containers or ice cube trays. Freeze. Yield: 20 servings.

Mrs. Delia Hinojosa
Boron AFS, Calif.

ORANGE-PINEAPPLE SHERBET

Juice of 1 lemon
Juice of 2 oranges
1 sm. can crushed pineapple
1 ½ c. sugar
Pinch of salt
1 pt. milk
½ pt. cream

Combine juices and pineapple; add sugar and salt, stirring to dissolve. Pour in milk and cream, stirring constantly until thoroughly combined. Pour into ice cube tray and freeze, stirring several times. Yield: 6-8 servings.

Mrs. Frank Derbyshire
Oscoda, Mich.

ORANGE SHERBET

1 lge. can crushed pineapple
1 can sweetened condensed milk
6 carbonated orange drinks

Mix pineapple and condensed milk; add orange drinks. Freeze until firm.

Mrs. J. A. Royal
Waycross, Ga.

PAPAYA SHERBET

1 c. sieved papaya pulp
Juice of 1 orange
Juice of 1 lemon
½ c. sugar
1 c. milk

Combine papaya pulp and fruit juices. Dissolve sugar in milk; add to fruit mixture. Freeze in ice trays. Beat until soft and fluffy; freeze. Beat again just before serving. Yield: 6 servings.

Mrs. Reinhold Julich
Honolulu, Hawaii

PASSION FRUIT SHERBET

1 pkg. orange gelatin
1 c. boiling water
1 ½ c. sugar
½ c. passion fruit or lilikoi juice
3 c. whole milk
1 c. evaporated milk

Dissolve gelatin in water. Add sugar; stir until dissolved. Add fruit juice; mix well. Slowly stir in milks. Freeze in refrigerator trays until mushy; beat well with electric mixer. Freeze until firm.

Mrs. Lillian Maeda
Wailuku, Maui, Hawaii

PINEAPPLE SHERBET

¾ c. powdered sugar
¾ c. water
3 ½ tbsp. lemon gelatin
2 c. crushed pineapple
4 tbsp. lemon juice
½ pt. light cream, whipped
3 egg whites, stiffly beaten

Dissolve sugar in water; boil for 2 minutes. Pour over gelatin; stir until gelatin is dissolved. Cool. Add to pineapple and lemon juice. Fold cream into egg whites; fold in fruit mixture. Pour into freezer pans; stir well at least two times during the first hour of freezing. Yield: 16 servings.

Mrs. Carrie M. Lee
Decorah, Iowa

RASPBERRY PARFAIT

1 pt. fresh raspberries
Sugar to taste (opt.)
1 6 ½-oz. pkg. sugar wafers, crushed
1 pt. lemon sherbet

Crush raspberries, saving a few for garnish. Add sugar if berries are tart. Layer crushed berries with wafers and lemon sherbet in four parfait glasses. Freeze. Yield: 4 servings.

Photograph for this recipe on page 239 .

TANGERINE SHERBET

1 c. sugar
1 ½ c. water
Grated rind of 4 tangerines
4 c. tangerine juice
Juice of 2 lemons

Boil sugar and water for 10 minutes. Add rind to hot syrup. Cool slightly; add tangerine juice and lemon juice. Add more sugar if needed. Chill thoroughly; strain and freeze.

Mrs. Alyce Tincher
Anthony, Fla.

Chilled
Desserts

RECIPE FOR ANGEL FOOD DELIGHT ON PAGE 266

BOSTON CREAM PIE

2 eggs
1 c. sugar
¼ tsp. salt
1 tsp. vanilla flavoring
1 tbsp. butter, melted
½ c. boiling milk
1 c. sifted all purpose flour
1 tsp. baking powder
1 pkg. instant or regular vanilla pudding

Beat eggs until very light; beat in sugar, salt and vanilla. Beat in butter and boiling milk. Sift flour with baking powder; beat in quickly. Pour into a greased and floured 9-inch cake pan. Bake at 350 degrees for 25 to 30 minutes until cake tests done. Cool. Remove from pan; split the layer in half. Prepare pudding according to package directions. Cool; spread between cake layers.

TOPPING:
1 ½ c. powdered sugar
¼ c. cocoa
¼ c. soft butter
3 tbsp. milk
½ tsp. vanilla flavoring

Sift powdered sugar and cocoa. Cream butter; add sugar mixture alternately with milk, beating thoroughly. Stir in vanilla. Pour frosting into saucepan. Place over low heat for 5 minutes or until dark and glossy, stirring constantly. Spread on cake. Refrigerate until needed. Yield: 8-10 servings.

Mrs. Betty Whitehair
Almaden AFS, Calif.

BROKEN GLASS CAKE

1 pkg. raspberry gelatin
1 pkg. lemon gelatin
1 pkg. lime gelatin
Water
Sugar
1 c. pineapple juice
1 tbsp. unflavored gelatin
1 pt. heavy cream, whipped
30 graham crackers, crushed
¼ c. butter, melted

Dissolve each package of flavored gelatin in 1 cup hot water; add 1/2 cup cold water to each. Add a small amount of sugar to each; chill until firm. Cut into small pieces. Boil pineapple juice with 1 tablespoon sugar; add unflavored gelatin dissolved in 1/4 cup cold water. Cool. Fold pineapple mixture and cubed gelatins into whipped cream. Combine cracker crumbs, butter and 1/2 cup sugar. Line cake pan with one-half of the mixture. Pour whipped cream mixture into pan. Top with remaining crumb mixture. Chill overnight.

Mrs. Lois Hanson
Truax Field, Wisc.

BANANA-CHEESE CAKE

1 pkg. pineapple gelatin
1 c. boiling water
1 8-oz. pkg. cream cheese
1 c. sugar
1 tsp. vanilla flavoring
2 bananas, broken into pieces
1 c. graham cracker crumbs
3 tbsp. butter or margarine, melted
1 14-oz. can evaporated milk, well chilled
3 tbsp. lemon juice

Dissolve gelatin in boiling water; cool. Blend cream cheese, sugar and vanilla; add bananas. Beat until fluffy. Add gelatin gradually; blend thoroughly. Chill until thick, stirring occasionally. Mix graham cracker crumbs and butter. Press one-half of the mixture evenly in bottom of a 12 x 7 x 2 1/2-inch baking dish. Whip evaporated milk until thick; add lemon juice. Beat until mixture will hold peaks. Beat gelatin mixture slightly; fold into whipped evaporated milk. Turn into crumb-lined dish; sprinkle remaining crumbs evenly over top. Cover with plastic wrap; chill for 2 to 3 hours or until firmly set. Yield: 12 servings.

Mrs. Frank H. Tryon
White Sands Missile Range, N.M.

CHEESE CAKE

¼ pkg. graham crackers, crushed
2 tbsp. sugar
1 stick margarine
1 pkg. lemon gelatin
1 lge. pkg. cream cheese
1 c. powdered sugar or ¾ c. sugar
1 tsp. vanilla flavoring
1 box dessert topping mix, prepared
¾ c. milnot milk
¼ c. chopped nuts

Mix cracker crumbs, 2 tablespoons sugar and margarine until crumbly; spread into a 13 x 9 x 1 1/2-inch pan reserving part of crumbs for top. Prepare lemon gelatin as directed on package; let set until creamy. Mix cheese and powdered sugar; beat until creamy. Add vanilla. Beat dessert topping mix and milnot milk until it resembles whipped cream. Mix gelatin with cheese mixture; fold into whipped cream. Add nuts; pour into pan lined with crumbs. Top with crumbs. Yield: 10-12 servings.

Mrs. Kathryn Bryant
Bowling Green, Ind.

BLUEBERRY CHEESE CAKE

1 ½ c. fine graham cracker crumbs
2 ½ c. sugar
1 stick butter
2 8-oz. pkg. cream cheese, softened
4 eggs, slightly beaten
2 tsp. vanilla flavoring
1 1-lb. 6-oz. can blueberry pie filling
½ tsp. grated lemon rind
2 tbsp. lemon juice

Combine crumbs, 1/2 cup sugar and butter; blend well. Pack firmly into bottom of a 13 x 9 x 2-inch baking pan. Beat cream cheese until smooth. Add eggs, vanilla and remaining sugar; beat until fluffy. Spread over crumb mixture. Bake at 375 degrees for 20 minutes or until done. Remove from oven; cool. Combine blueberry filling, lemon rind and lemon juice in a saucepan. Place over low heat; bring to boiling point, stirring constantly. Cool. Spread over cheese mixture; chill.

Photograph for this recipe above.

LEMON-CHEESE CAKE

1 3-oz. pkg. lemon gelatin
1 c. hot water
1 ¼ c. sugar
1 8-oz. pkg. cream cheese

1 tsp. vanilla flavoring
1 ⅔ c. evaporated milk, chilled and whipped
Graham cracker crumbs

Dissolve gelatin in hot water; chill until consistency of egg whites. Beat sugar, cream cheese and vanilla; fold in gelatin and whipped milk. Pour into a 9 x 13-inch pan lined with graham cracker crumbs. Chill overnight. Yield: 12 servings.

Mrs. Bruce Gethen
Hebron, Ill.

MANDARIN ORANGE-CHEESE CAKE

1 c. zwieback or graham cracker crumbs
2 ¼ c. sugar
¼ c. butter, melted
5 8-oz. pkg. cream cheese, softened
6 eggs
½ c. heavy cream
1 tsp. lemon flavoring
¼ c. flour
¼ tsp. salt
1 11-oz. can Mandarin orange segments, drained
1 sm. jar apple jelly, melted

Combine crumbs, 1/4 cup sugar and butter; press into bottom of greased 9-inch spring form pan. Beat cheese until fluffy. Add an

(Continued on next page)

egg at a time; add cream and lemon flavoring. Mix remaining 2 cups sugar with flour and salt; add to mixture, beating until smooth. Pour into crumbs in tin. Bake at 475 degrees for 15 minutes. Reduce heat to 250 degrees; continue baking for 1 hour and 15 minutes. Remove from oven; cool. Arrange orange segments over top. Spoon jelly over oranges; refrigerate. NOTE: Other fruits and glazes may be substituted. Yield: 12 servings.

Mrs. Herbert T. King
Key West, Fla.

PEACHY-CHEESE CAKE

⅔ c. finely crushed graham crackers
½ c. plus 2 tbsp. sugar
¼ c. butter, melted
2 3-oz. pkg. peach gelatin
2 c. boiling water
1 c. cold water
2 tbsp. lemon juice
1 8-oz. pkg. cream cheese, softened
1 6-oz. can evaporated milk, chilled
1 ½ c. diced fresh peaches, sweetened and drained

Combine crumbs and 2 tablespoons sugar; stir in butter. Press into bottom of pan. Dissolve gelatin in boiling water; stir in cold water and lemon juice. Chill until partially set. Cream remaining sugar and cheese until light and fluffy; beat in milk. Whip gelatin until light and fluffy; fold in cheese mixture. Chill until partially set; fold in peaches. Pour over graham crust; chill until firm. Unmold to serve. Yield: 8-10 servings.

Mrs. Helen Freeman
Lake City, Kans.

CHERRY-PINEAPPLE DREAM CAKE

1 ½ tsp. vanilla flavoring
1 tsp. vinegar
8 egg whites
2 c. sifted sugar
2 c. heavy cream
1 c. crushed pineapple, drained
¾ c. Maraschino cherries

Add vanilla and vinegar to egg whites; whip until mixture forms peaks. Add sugar, 1 tablespoon at a time, beating until stiff and sugar is dissolved. Pour into two round layer cake pans lined with aluminum foil. Bake at 300 degrees for 1 hour and 15 minutes. Cool well in pans. Whip cream; add pineapple and cherries. Frost layers with cream-fruit mixture. Chill for 12 hours or overnight. Yield: 12 servings.

Mrs. Vernon W. Tuxbury
Philadelphia, Pa.

PINEAPPLE-CHEESE CAKE

15 to 18 graham crackers, crushed
½ c. sugar
¼ c. melted margarine
1 c. pineapple juice
1 pkg. lemon gelatin
2 3-oz. pkg. cream cheese
⅔ c. sugar
1 tsp. vanilla flavoring
1 ⅔ c. evaporated milk, chilled
1 sm. can crushed pineapple, drained

Combine graham cracker crumbs with 1/2 cup sugar and melted margarine; press in bottom of 9-inch pie pan. Bake at 375 degrees for 8 minutes; cool. Bring pineapple juice to a boil; add gelatin. Cool. Blend cream cheese with sugar and vanilla; combine with gelatin mixture. Whip evaporated milk until thick; add gelatin mixture. Pat pineapple over graham cracker crust; pour in filling. Sprinkle a few graham cracker crumbs over top. Chill for 3 hours. Yield: 8 servings.

Mrs. Juanita Miller
Austin, Tex.

LEMON CHIFFON ICEBOX CAKE

8 eggs, separated
1 ½ c. sugar
Juice of 2 lemons
Grated rind of 2 lemons
2 tbsp. unflavored gelatin
½ c. cold water
½ c. boiling water
½ lb. ladyfingers
½ pt. heavy cream, whipped

Combine beaten egg yolks, 1/2 cup sugar, lemon juice and rind. Cook in double boiler, stirring constantly, until slightly thickened. Set aside to cool. Soften gelatin in cold water; dissolve in boiling water. Cool; add to lemon mixture. Beat egg whites, adding remaining sugar gradually. Fold into custard. Line sides and bottom of lightly buttered sponge form mold with ladyfingers; pour in custard. Chill until firm. Serve topped with whipped cream. Yield: 12 servings.

Ilsa Potvin
Huntington Park, Calif.

PINEAPPLE CHIFFON CAKE

1 envelope unflavored gelatin
⅓ c. sugar
⅛ tsp. salt
3 eggs, separated
1 ¼ c. crushed pineapple and syrup
2 tbsp. lemon juice
1 c. heavy cream, whipped
Thin chocolate cookies

Mix gelatin, 2 tablespoons sugar and salt in top of double boiler. Add beaten egg yolks and pineapple and syrup. Cook for 5 minutes,

(Continued on next page)

stirring constantly. Remove from heat. Add lemon juice; chill. Add remaining sugar to stiffly beaten egg whites; fold in gelatin mixture. Fold in whipped cream. Spoon one-fourth of the mixture into a waxed paper-lined 9 x 15-inch loaf pan. Cover with cookies; repeat three times, ending with gelatin mixture. Chill until firm. Unmold; top with whipped cream. Yield: 8-10 servings.

Mrs. Joan Bowman
Marion, Ind.

CHOCOLATE ICEBOX CAKE

½ lb. butter
1 lb. confectioners sugar
3 tbsp. cocoa
6 eggs, separated
1 tsp. vanilla flavoring
1 lb. vanilla wafers

Cream butter, sugar and cocoa; add well beaten egg yolks. Fold in stiffly beaten egg whites and vanilla. Put a layer of wafers in dessert dish; cover with a layer of chocolate mixture. Continue alternating layers, ending with wafers. Refrigerate overnight. Serve with whipped cream. Yield: 10-12 servings.

Mrs. Cora Hyde
Nauvoo, Ala.

CHOCOLATE ICEBOX CAKE

1 cake German's sweet chocolate
2 tbsp. water
2 eggs, separated
2 tbsp. sugar
½ c. nuts
1 c. heavy cream, whipped
½ lb. vanilla wafers

Melt chocolate in water; remove from heat. Add egg yolks, sugar and nuts; cool. Add stiffly beaten egg whites and whipped cream. Put a thin layer of mixture in pan; add a layer of wafers. Alternate layers until all is used. Refrigerate for 24 hours. Yield: 6 servings.

Mrs. J. Turner
Virginia Beach, Va.

ORANGE ICEBOX CAKE

1 tbsp. unflavored gelatin
2 tbsp. cold water
2 c. milk
2 tbsp. cornstarch
1 c. sugar
2 eggs
¾ c. orange juice
1 tsp. grated orange rind
1 pt. heavy cream, whipped
1 ½ doz. ladyfingers, split

Soak gelatin in cold water. Heat milk in double boiler. Mix cornstarch, sugar and eggs thoroughly. Pour hot milk over egg mixture; return to double boiler. Cook for 10 minutes or until thickened. Add gelatin, orange juice and rind in order. Cool until slightly thickened; fold in whipped cream. Line a 13 x 9 x 2-inch pan with ladyfingers. Alternate layers of custard and ladyfingers until all is used. Serve in squares; top with whipped cream and a cherry, if desired. Yield: 12 servings.

Mrs. Mary L. Calhoun
Jacksonville, Fla.

ANGEL AFFINITY

1 tsp. unflavored gelatin
¼ c. cold water
6 eggs, separated
1 ½ c. sugar
½ c. lemon juice
1 lge. angel food cake, broken into pieces
1 pt. whipped cream

Dissolve gelatin in water. Combine egg yolks, 3/4 cup sugar and lemon juice; cook until thickened. Remove from heat. Add gelatin; cool. Gradually add remaining sugar to egg whites, beating until stiff. Gently fold egg whites and cake pieces into cooled custard. Pour into waxed paper-lined angel cake pan. Chill for several hours or overnight. Frost with whipped cream just before serving. Yield: 12-16 servings.

Mrs. Sheila K. Whorton
Lone Pine, Calif.

ANGEL CAKE WITH COFFEE-CREAM TOPPING

⅔ c. sugar
2 c. heavy cream
3 tbsp. instant coffee
1 angel food cake
½ c. chopped pecans

Combine sugar, cream and instant coffee; chill for 1 hour. Whip until stiff. Split cake into three layers. Add nuts to one-half of the cream mixture; spread between layers. Cover top and sides with remaining mixture. Chill. Yield: 8-10 servings.

Mrs. William B. Campbell
Grand Forks AFB, N.D.

ANGEL DELIGHT

2 envelopes gelatin
4 tbsp. cold water
1 c. boiling water
2 sm. cans crushed pineapple with juice
1 c. (scant) sugar
½ tsp. salt

(Continued on next page)

265

Juice of 1 lemon
2 lge. boxes dessert topping mix
1 lge. angel food cake
½ pt. heavy cream, whipped
Coconut

Soften gelatin in cold water. Add hot water, pineapple, sugar, salt and lemon juice. Mix well. Refrigerate until partially set. Prepare dessert topping mix; fold into gelatin. Cut off all brown from cake. Tear white cake into small pieces. In a 9 x 15-inch or two 9-inch square pans, put a layer of filling; add a layer of cake. Continue layers until all is used. Refrigerate overnight. Frost top with whipped cream and coconut 1 hour before serving. Refrigerate until ready to serve. Yield: 10-12 servings.

Mrs. M. J. Dross
Tallahassee, Fla.

ANGEL FOOD DELIGHT

1 3-oz. pkg. chocolate pudding and pie
   filling mix
1 c. milk
½ c. sour cream
1 10-in. round unfrosted angel food cake
1 c. heavy cream, whipped
2 to 3 tbsp. confectioners sugar

Combine pudding mix with milk. Cook over medium heat, stirring constantly, until smooth and mixture bubbles. Cool slightly; stir in sour cream. Chill thoroughly. Split cake into two layers. Spread chocolate filling between layers. Reassemble cake. Beat whipping cream until stiff; sweeten with confectioners sugar. Spread top and sides of cake with whipped cream. Garnish with shaved chocolate or chocolate shots if desired. Keep refrigerated until ready to serve. Yield: 10-12 servings.

Photograph for this recipe on page 261.

CHOCOLATE ANGEL FOOD DESSERT

2 pkg. chocolate pieces
1 tbsp. hot water
4 eggs, separated
½ pt. heavy cream, whipped
1 lge. angel food cake, broken into pieces

Melt chocolate; add hot water. Add beaten egg yolks; remove from heat. Fold in stiffly beaten egg whites and whipped cream. Pour over cake; mix. Chill; serve with whipped cream. Yield: 8-10 servings.

Mrs. Walter Klimoski
Phlox, Wisc.

CHOCOLATE ANGEL DELIGHT

2 6-oz. pkg. sweet chocolate pieces
4 tbsp. sugar
3 eggs, separated
2 c. heavy cream, whipped
1 med. angel food cake
1 5-oz. pkg. almonds, slivered (opt.)

Melt chocolate in double boiler. Add sugar; stir. Remove from heat. Add a small amount of hot mixture to beaten egg yolks. Add yolks to hot mixture; cool. Mixture will be grainy. Fold in beaten egg whites; cool completely. Gently fold in whipped cream. Tear cake into bite-sized pieces. Place a layer of cake in a buttered 9 x 13-inch baking dish; add a layer of chocolate sauce. Lightly mix with a fork; repeat layers. Top with almonds. Refrigerate for at least 12 hours. Yield: 15-18 servings.

Mrs. Dorothea Mansfield
San Clemente, Calif.

GELATIN ANGEL CAKE

1 pkg. lime gelatin
1 c. hot water
¼ c. pineapple juice
¼ c. lemon juice
¼ c. orange juice
1 can crushed pineapple, drained
1 angel food cake
1 pt. heavy cream
4 tbsp. sugar
Dash of green food coloring

Dissolve gelatin in hot water. Add pineapple, lemon and orange juices and crushed pineapple. Chill until partially jelled. Break angel food cake into 1-inch cubes. Whip gelatin. Whip 1/2 pint heavy cream with 2 tablespoons sugar. Fold whipped cream into gelatin mixture. Put layer of cake cubes in bottom of angel cake pan. Cover with layer of gelatin-cream mixture, soaking up liquid with cubes. Continue layers, ending with gelatin mixture. Refrigerate for 8 hours or more. Remove from pan. Frost with remaining cream whipped with 2 tablespoons sugar and food coloring. Yield: 12 servings.

June Marquis
Melbourne, Fla.

RASPBERRY GELATIN CAKE

2 pkg. raspberry gelatin
2 c. boiling water
2 pkg. frozen raspberries
1 pt. heavy cream, whipped
1 med. angel food cake

Dissolve gelatin in boiling water. Immediately add frozen raspberries; blend well. Refrigerate until slightly jelled. Add whipped cream. Tear cake into pieces; fold into mix-

(Continued on next page)

ture. Pour mixture into ungreased angel food cake pan; refrigerate for about 3 hours. Remove from pan; slice and serve. NOTE: Cake does not keep well overnight. Yield: 8 servings.

Mrs. Harry K. Woodward
Tooele Army Depot, Utah

RUM ANGEL CAKE

1 stick margarine
1 ½ c. powdered sugar
5 egg yolks, beaten
4 tbsp. rum or 2 tsp. rum flavoring
½ c. chopped almonds (opt.)
1 angel food cake
½ pt. heavy cream, whipped

Cream margarine and sugar. Add egg yolks, rum and almonds, mixing well. Slice cake crosswise into four layers. Spread mixture between layers. Frost with whipped cream. Chill for 24 hours. Yield: 8 servings.

Mrs. William J. Crandall
Waco, Tex.

APRICOT SHORTCAKE

1 c. dried apricots
2 ½ c. water
⅓ c. sugar
1 tsp. unflavored gelatin
1 tbsp. cold water
2 tbsp. honey
½ tsp. vanilla flavoring
1 c. heavy cream, whipped
1 angel food cake

Cook apricots in water for 25 minutes. Add sugar; beat to a pulp. Soften gelatin in water; add to hot apricots. Chill until mixture begins to thicken. Add honey and vanilla to whipped cream. Arrange 1/4-inch layer of cake in rectangular pan. Cover with apricot mixture; top with whipped cream. Chill. Yield: 6 servings.

Mrs. Donald Badura
Ashton, Nebr.

EASY GELATIN DESSERT

2 pkg. strawberry gelatin
2 c. heavy cream, whipped
1 can crushed pineapple
1 sm. angel cake, broken into pieces

Prepare gelatin according to package directions; chill to consistency of egg whites. Whip until fluffy. Fold in whipped cream, reserving small amount for topping. Fold in pineapple; pour one-half of mixture into 13 x 9 x 2-inch pan. Cover with one-half of cake; add remaining mixture. Add remaining cake. Top with

remaining whipped cream; chill until firm. Yield: 12 servings.

Mrs. Dorothy Pearson
Clyde, Kans.

HEAVENLY DELIGHT

1 ½ c. heavy cream, whipped
1 5 ½-oz. can caramel sauce
½ tsp. vanilla flavoring
¾ lb. English toffee, crushed
1 lge. angel food cake

Combine whipped cream, caramel sauce and vanilla; add 1/2 pound English toffee. Cut angel cake into three layers; spread mixture between layers and over cake. Sprinkle with remaining crushed toffee. Refrigerate. Yield: 12 servings.

Mrs. Helen Jacobson
Sioux Falls, S.D.

LEMON ANGEL CAKE DESSERT

Juice of 4 lemons
½ c. sugar
1 c. sweetened condensed milk
1 pt. heavy cream, whipped
1 angel food cake

Fold juice, sugar and condensed milk. Fold in whipped cream. Tear or cut cake into bite-sized pieces; place in bottom of 9 x 12-inch pan. Pour whipped cream mixture over cake; chill for 24 hours. Yield: 12 servings.

Mrs. Joseph Poynter
Memphis, Tenn.

ORANGE FLUFF

1 pkg. lemon gelatin
¾ c. (scant) boiling water
1 c. orange juice
Juice of 1 lemon
Grated rind of 1 lemon
1 c. sugar
1 pt. heavy cream, whipped
1 angel food cake, broken into pieces
Slivered almonds

Dissolve gelatin in boiling water; add orange juice, lemon juice, rind and sugar. Cool until partially set. Fold in whipped cream. Alternate layers of cake and mixture in 9 x 12-inch pan. Chill overnight. Sprinkle with slivered almonds. Yield: 15 servings.

Mrs. Oscar Mohn
Minneapolis, Minn.

SPONGE LAYER DESSERT

1 5½-oz. can chocolate syrup
1 egg, separated
½ pt. heavy cream, whipped
2 sponge cake layers

Mix chocolate syrup with egg yolk. Add to stiffly beaten egg white. Add mixture to whipped cream. Split sponge cake layers. Frost between layers and on top. Chill overnight. Yield: 6 servings.

Mrs. Robert W. Clark
Kittery, Me.

STRAWBERRY DESSERT

2 pkg. strawberry gelatin
2 c. hot water
2 c. frozen strawberries, thawed
1 c. heavy cream, whipped
1 angel cake, cubed

Dissolve gelatin in hot water. Drain berries; add water to juice to measure 2 cups. Add to gelatin. Chill until partially set. Whip until fluffy; fold in whipped cream and strawberries. Fold in cake. Pour into shallow pan. Chill until firm. NOTE: Raspberry gelatin and raspberries may be substituted. Yield: 12-15 servings.

Mrs. Howard Haas
Veteran, Wyo.

FRUIT CHARLOTTE

1 No. 2 can fruit cocktail
1 pkg. lemon gelatin
¾ c. evaporated milk, chilled
16 marshmallows
¼ tsp. salt
1 tbsp. lemon juice

Drain fruit cocktail; add water to juice to make 1 cup liquid. Heat to boiling; add gelatin. Dissolve. Combine 1/4 cup milk, marshmallows and salt over boiling water; melt. Fold into gelatin; cool. Add fruit; chill until almost firm. Whip remaining milk until fluffy. Add lemon juice; whip stiff. Fold into gelatin. Pour into mold; chill. Yield: 6 servings.

Mrs. Laura Harter
Morrisville, N.Y.

STRAWBERRY CHIFFON SQUARES

1 3-oz. pkg. strawberry gelatin
1 c. boiling water
1 tsp. lemon juice
1 10-oz. pkg. frozen sliced strawberries
1 3-oz. pkg. strawberry chiffon pie filling
10 slices angel food cake, cut ½-in. thick
1 pkg. dessert topping mix, whipped

Dissolve gelatin in boiling water; add lemon juice and strawberries, stirring until thawed. Let stand until set. Prepare chiffon filling according to package directions. Line bottom of 10 1/2 x 14-inch pan with cake. Spoon 1 tablespoon of gelatin mixture over each slice; top with 1 tablespoon pie filling. Cover with remaining gelatin mixture. Chill. Cut into squares; top with dessert topping mix. Yield: 15 servings.

Allie Stonehill
Brook, Ind.

ORANGE CHARLOTTE RUSSE

½ lb. marshmallows, cut up
1 6-oz. can frozen orange juice, thawed
Few grains of salt
2 egg whites, at room temperature
¼ c. sugar
½ pt. heavy cream, whipped
1 tbsp. Sherry (opt.)
Ladyfingers

Melt marshmallows over boiling water; add orange juice. Cool until consistency of unbeaten egg white. Add salt to egg whites; beat until soft peaks form. Add sugar gradually; beat until stiff. Fold whipped cream and marshmallows into egg whites. Fold in Sherry. Line bowl with ladyfingers; pour in pudding. Chill. Yield: 4-6 servings.

Mrs. Virginia L. Paris
Chicago, Ill.

AMBROSIA CREAM

½ c. crushed pineapple, drained
1 c. sour cream
¾ c. miniature marshmallows
½ c. flaked coconut
½ c. chopped walnuts
1 11-oz. can Mandarin oranges
1 c. seedless grapes

Combine all ingredients; mix well. Chill for 8 hours. Yield: 4 servings.

Mrs. Charles W. Geha
Toledo, O.

APRICOT BAVARIAN CREAM

1 tbsp. unflavored gelatin
¼ c. cold water
½ c. boiling water
½ c. honey
Pinch of salt
1 c. apricot puree or crushed apricots
1 tbsp. lemon juice
1 c. cream, stiffly whipped (opt.)
Fresh apricot halves
Pecan halves

(Continued on next page)

268

Moisten gelatin in cold water; dissolve in boiling water. Add honey, salt, apricot puree and lemon juice. Fold in whipped cream; chill. Garnish with apricot halves and pecan halves. Yield: 6 servings.

Mrs. May E. Paulsen
Eureka, Calif.

BAVARIAN CREAM

1 pkg. cherry or raspberry gelatin
1 c. heavy cream, whipped
¼ lb. marshmallows, cut up
3 bananas, sliced
½ c. walnuts

Dissolve gelatin in 1 cup hot water; add 1 cup cold water. Set in cool place until mixture begins to thicken. Beat with dover egg beater until twice in bulk. Gently fold in whipped cream, marshmallows, bananas and walnuts. Pour into oiled mold; refrigerate until firm. May be served with whipped cream. Yield: 8-10 servings.

Mrs. James V. Reardon
Castle AFB, Calif.

BAVARIAN CREAM

1 c. milk
1 tbsp. gelatin
2 eggs, separated
¼ c. sugar
½ tsp. salt
½ c. heavy cream, whipped
½ tsp. vanilla flavoring

Scald milk in top of double boiler with gelatin. Beat egg yolks slightly with sugar and salt. Add hot milk slowly, stirring constantly. Return to double boiler; stir and cook until coating forms on spoon. Strain onto stiffly beaten egg whites. When beginning to thicken, fold in whipped cream and vanilla. Pour into molds; chill. Yield: 4 servings.

Mrs. George B. Dany
Travis AFB, Calif.

ORANGE OR PINEAPPLE BAVARIAN CREAM

1 tbsp. unflavored gelatin
¼ c. cold water
1 c. orange juice or grated pineapple
Juice of ½ lemon
½ c. sugar
Dash of salt
1 c. heavy cream

Soak gelatin in water. Heat orange juice; add lemon juice, sugar and salt. Pour over gelatin. Set in pan of ice water. Stir until mixture begins to thicken; fold in cream.

Whip until stiff. Turn into mold; chill. Yield: 6 servings.

Elsie Sluder
Napanoch, N.Y.

CAFE AU CREME

24 marshmallows, quartered
1 c. strong hot coffee
1 c. heavy cream
2 tbsp. crushed pecans
2 tbsp. shaved chocolate

Melt marshmallows in coffee; cool. Whip cream; fold in coffee mixture. Pour into sherbet or parfait glasses. Top with pecans and chocolate. Chill and serve. Yield: 4 servings.

Mrs. Charles E. Weakley
Norfolk, Va.

CHOCOLATE-MACAROON CREAM

1 1-oz. square unsweetened chocolate
1 ½ c. milk
1 tbsp. unflavored gelatin
2 tbsp. cold water
½ c. sugar
¼ tsp. salt
½ c. heavy cream, whipped
½ tsp. vanilla flavoring
¾ c. macaroon cookies, crushed
Walnut halves

Heat chocolate and milk in double boiler. Dissolve gelatin in cold water; add to chocolate mixture. Add sugar and salt. Chill until partially set. Add whipped cream, vanilla and one-half of the macaroon crumbs. Pour into 9 x 9-inch pan. Garnish with remaining crumbs and nuts. Chill.

Mrs. Olga Vannurden
Litchfield, Minn.

MOLDED CINNAMON CREAM

1 ½ c. light cream
1 c. sugar
¼ tsp. salt
2 sticks cinnamon, 2 inches long
1 envelope unflavored gelatin
¼ c. cold water
1 c. sour cream
1 tsp. vanilla flavoring

Combine cream, sugar, salt and cinnamon in a saucepan. Heat until sugar is dissolved. Soften gelatin in cold water for 5 minutes. Add hot cream mixture, stirring until dissolved. Cool; chill until mixture begins to thicken. Remove cinnamon. Beat sour cream until smooth and fluffy; fold into sugar-cream mixture along with vanilla. Turn into

(Continued on next page)

lightly oiled individual molds or a lightly oiled 1-quart mold. Chill until firm and ready to serve. Unmold; serve with sweetened fresh, frozen or canned fruit. Yield: 6 servings.

Mrs. Russell G. Henneberger
Newport, Ky.

MOCHA CREAM

1 ¾ c. vanilla wafer crumbs
½ c. chopped pecans
½ c. butter, melted
1 3-oz. pkg. regular chocolate pudding mix
1 tbsp. instant coffee
1 ⅔ c. evaporated milk
⅓ c. water
1 3-oz. pkg. cream cheese, softened

Combine crumbs, pecans and butter in bottom of 8 or 9-inch square pan. Reserve 1/2 cup of the mixture; press remaining mixture firmly into bottom of pan. Place pudding mix and instant coffee in 2-quart saucepan. Gradually stir in evaporated milk, then water. Cook over medium heat, stirring constantly, until thickened. Remove from heat; beat in cream cheese until smooth and well blended. Pour into crumb-lined pan, smoothing into an even layer. Sprinkle with remaining crumb mixture. Chill for 2 to 3 hours. Yield: 9 servings.

Mrs. M. E. Webb
Chanute AFB, Ill.

ORANGE CREAM

1 c. heavy cream
2 tbsp. sugar
Dash of nutmeg
¼ tbsp. almond flavoring
1 c. orange sections, drained and diced or
    1 can Mandarin oranges
2 tbsp. Cointreau
¾ c. miniature marshmallows
⅓ c. chopped pecans
⅓ c. chopped Maraschino cherries

Combine heavy cream, sugar, nutmeg and almond flavoring; beat with rotary beater until mixture forms soft peaks. Fold in remaining ingredients. Chill for at least 1 hour. Yield: 6-8 servings.

Mrs. Roy W. Olson
Columbus, O.

SPANISH CREAM

2 envelopes unflavored gelatin
3 ½ c. milk
4 eggs, separated
½ c. sugar
1 tbsp. vanilla flavoring
Whipped cream

Soak gelatin in milk for at least 10 minutes; scald, stirring constantly. Add yolks beaten with 1/4 cup sugar. Beat whites until stiff; add remaining sugar. Combine mixtures; beat thoroughly. Add vanilla. Pour into a mold; chill. Unmold; serve with whipped cream. Yield: 8 servings.

Mrs. Lewis C. Conant
Ft. Myers, Fla.

STRAWBERRY BAVARIAN CREAM

1 envelope unflavored gelatin
¼ c. cold water
½ c. hot water
1 c. crushed strawberries
¾ c. confectioners sugar
1 tbsp. lemon juice
1 c. heavy cream, whipped
Whole berries

Soften gelatin in cold water; dissolve in hot water. Chill until partially set; beat until frothy. Mix crushed strawberries, sugar and lemon juice; add to gelatin, mixing well. Fold in whipped cream. Pour into large or individual oiled molds; chill until set. Unmold and garnish with whole berries. Yield: 6 servings.

Mrs. Marshall E. Baker
Montgomery, Ala.

VELVET CREAM

CRUST:
1 ½ c. finely crushed chocolate wafers
⅓ c. melted margarine

Combine wafers and butter; press into 9-inch spring pan. Bake at 325 degrees for 10 minutes.

FILLING:
1 8-oz. pkg. cream cheese, softened
½ c. sugar
1 tsp. vanilla flavoring
2 eggs, separated
1 16-oz. pkg. semi-sweet chocolate pieces
1 c. heavy cream, whipped
¾ c. chopped pecans

Combine cream cheese, 1/4 cup sugar and vanilla; stir in egg yolks. Melt chocolate pieces; stir into cheese mixture. Beat egg whites until stiff, gradually adding remaining sugar. Fold into chocolate mixture. Fold in whipped cream and pecans. Pour over crust; freeze. Yield: 8-10 servings.

Helen R. Hodge
Yampa, Colo.

APRICOT CRUNCH DESSERT

1 ½ c. apricot juice
1 pkg. lemon gelatin
½ c. plus 2 tbsp. sugar
1 ⅔ c. evaporated milk, chilled
1 tbsp. almond flavoring
1 No. 2 can peeled apricots, drained and
    mashed
Blanched almonds (opt.)
3 c. crushed corn flakes
⅓ c. melted butter

Heat apricot juice; dissolve gelatin in juice.
Add 1/2 cup sugar; cool until syrupy. Whip
evaporated milk; whip cooled gelatin mixture. Combine gelatin mixture, whipped milk,
flavoring, apricots and nuts lightly. Combine
crumbs, remaining sugar and butter; press
one-half of the crumb mixture into 9 x 13-
inch pan. Pour in filling; press remaining
crumbs on top. Serve with whipped cream
and a cherry, if desired. Yield: 12 servings.

Mrs. Clara Knapton
Yuma, Ariz.

BERRY AND RHUBARB GELATIN

2 lb. rhubarb, coarsely chopped
4 c. water
1 c. sugar
2 pkg. red gelatin

Place rhubarb and water in heavy pan.
Simmer, covered, until tender. Add sugar;
simmer for 7 minutes longer. Dissolve gelatin in mixture. Chill until firm. Yield: 12
servings.

Mildred Botkin
Meridian, Idaho

BRIDE'S DESSERT

1 can white cherries, chopped
1 can sliced pineapple, chopped
1 c. chopped nuts
¼ c. mayonnaise
1 c. heavy cream, whipped
1 tbsp. gelatin

Drain cherries and pineapple; reserve juices.
Fold cherries, pineapple, nuts and mayonnaise into whipped cream. Dissolve gelatin
in pineapple juice over hot water; add cherry
juice. Fold gelatin mixture into cream. Chill
overnight. Yield: 10-12 servings.

Mrs. Sadie Eckelberg
Bellville, Tex.

CHERRY-EGGNOG MOLD

1 envelope unflavored gelatin
½ c. sugar

3 eggs, separated
1 ½ c. milk
½ tsp. vanilla flavoring
½ c. thinly sliced Brazil nuts
½ c. sliced Maraschino cherries, drained
½ c. heavy cream, whipped
Rum flavoring to taste

Mix gelatin and 1/4 cup sugar; add slightly
beaten egg yolks and milk. Heat until mixture thickens; stir constantly. Add vanilla;
chill until partially set. Beat until fluffy.
Beat egg whites until soft peaks form. Add
remaining sugar; beat stiff. Fold egg whites
and remaining ingredients into gelatin; pour
into 5-quart mold. Chill overnight. Yield: 6
servings.

Rita M. Ryan
Shortsville, N.Y.

COFFEE COUPE TOPAZ

2 envelopes unflavored gelatin
½ c. cold water
4 c. strong hot coffee
⅔ c. sugar
½ tsp. vanilla flavoring

Soften gelatin in cold water; add hot coffee
and sugar. Stir until dissolved; add flavoring. Rinse shallow pan in cold water. Pour
mixture into pan to a depth of 1/2 inch.
Chill; cut into cubes.

CUSTARD SAUCE:

¾ c. milk
1 ½ tbsp. sugar
⅛ tsp. salt
2 egg yolks, beaten
½ tsp. vanilla flavoring

Scald milk; add sugar, salt and egg yolks.
Cook over hot water until mixture coats
spoon. Stir in flavoring. Chill until serving time; spoon over gelatin cubes in individual serving dishes. Yield: 6 servings.

Ida C. James
Kellogg, Idaho

DATE DESSERT OR SALAD

1 can crushed pineapple
Water
2 pkg. orange or lemon gelatin
1 8-oz. pkg. dates, cut up
Nuts (opt.)
¼ pt. heavy cream, whipped

Drain pineapple; reserve juice. Combine
pineapple liquid and enough water to make 2
cups liquid; heat. Add gelatin; stir until dissolved. Add 1 1/2 cups cold water; cool. Place
pineapple and dates in 9 x 13 x 2-inch glass
dish or pan. Pour gelatin over fruit; sprinkle
with nuts. Chill; top with whipped cream.

(Continued on next page)

NOTE: For salad, add 1 tablespoon salad dressing to whipped cream for topping. Yield: 6 servings.

Mattie Griffin
Naples, Fla.

FROST BITE

2 squares semi-sweet chocolate, grated
3 eggs, separated
¾ c. sugar
1 ½ c. milk
1 envelope unflavored gelatin
¼ c. cold water
1 tsp. vanilla flavoring
Dash of salt
1 c. heavy cream, whipped

Sprinkle chocolate in 8 x 8 x 2 or 7 1/2 x 11-inch glass dish. Reserve some for top. Beat egg yolks with 1/2 cup sugar; add milk. Cook in double boiler until mixture coats spoon. Soften gelatin in cold water. Add to hot mixture; cool. Add vanilla and salt. Beat egg whites, slowly adding remaining sugar. Fold into cooled custard. Fold in whipped cream. Pour mixture over chocolate; sprinkle with remaining chocolate. Chill. Yield: 8-12 servings.

Mrs. Janet DeWaal
Ft. Lauderdale, Fla.

GELATIN WHIP

1 lge. box lime gelatin
2 c. boiling water
1 c. cold water
1 c. creme de menthe
2 c. heavy cream, whipped

Dissolve gelatin in boiling water. Add cold water and creme de menthe; mix well. Refrigerate until firm. Beat until mixture is frothy. Add whipped cream; blend at low speed on mixer. Spoon into goblets. Refrigerate. Serve with tea cakes. Yield: 8 servings.

Mrs. Paul H. Thurn
Selfridge AFB, Mich.

LIME-CHOCOLATE DELICIOUS

1 ⅔ c. evaporated milk
1 3-oz. pkg. lime flavored gelatin
1 ¾ c. hot water
¼ c. lime juice
2 tsp. lemon juice
1 c. sugar
2 c. chocolate wafer crumbs
⅓ c. butter, melted
Shaved semi-sweet chocolate
Walnut halves

Chill evaporated milk in freezing compartment until icy cold. Dissolve gelatin in hot water; chill until partially set. Whip until fluffy. Stir in lime juice, lemon juice and sugar. Whip milk; fold into gelatin. Combine crumbs and butter; press into bottom of 13 x 9 1/2 x 2-inch pan. Pour in gelatin mixture. Top with shaved chocolate. Chill until firm. Cut into squares; top with a walnut half. Yield: 9 servings.

Mrs. William T. Greenhalgh
Albuquerque, N.M.

GELATIN-ORANGE DESSERT

2 cans Mandarin oranges
1 tbsp. unflavored gelatin
¼ c. cold water
2 pkg. orange gelatin
2 c. boiling water
1 pt. orange sherbet

Drain oranges, reserving syrup. Soften unflavored gelatin in cold water. Dissolve orange gelatin in boiling water. Combine gelatin mixtures; stir. Add sherbet and orange syrup; stir until sherbet melts. Chill until partially thickened. Fold in oranges. Pour into large mold; chill. Yield: 12 servings.

Mrs. Mary E. Niemi
Ishpeming, Mich.

MANDARIN ORANGE DELIGHT

1 pkg. orange or lemon gelatin
1 c. boiling water
1 pt. orange sherbet
1 can shredded pineapple (opt.)
1 can Mandarin oranges (opt.)
½ c. shredded coconut (opt.)
1 pkg. dessert topping, prepared (opt.)

Dissolve gelatin in boiling water; add sherbet. Add remaining ingredients; place in a 6 x 8-inch flat pan. Chill for 4 to 6 hours or until set. Yield: 6-8 servings.

Marie B. Savard
Duarte, Calif.

ORANGE FROST

2 3-oz. pkg. orange gelatin
1 c. miniature marshmallows
1 ½ c. boiling water
1 sm. can Mandarin oranges
1 pt. orange sherbet
1 c. heavy cream, whipped

Dissolve gelatin and marshmallows in boiling water; cool slightly. Add Mandarin oranges and sherbet; allow to set until of egg white

(Continued on next page)

consistency. Fold in whipped cream; chill. Yield: 10 servings.

Mrs. Bessie Rook
Vevay, Ind.

PECAN SANDIES DESSERT

⅔ pkg. pecan sandies cookies, crushed
4 eggs, separated
1 c. sugar
Salt
1 8¼-oz. can crushed pineapple
1 pkg. lemon gelatin

Line a 13 x 9 x 2-inch dish with three-fourths of the cookie crumbs. Combine egg yolks, 1/2 cup sugar, salt and pineapple. Cook for 1 minute, stirring constantly. Add lemon gelatin; cool. Beat egg whites until stiff; add remaining 1/2 cup sugar. Fold in gelatin mixture. Pour over cookie crumbs; top with remainder of crumbs. Chill for 2 hours. Yield: 12 servings.

Mrs. Janet Lueders
Elk Creek, Nebr.

APPLE MYSTERY DESSERT

2 c. graham cracker crumbs
½ c. butter or margarine, melted
¼ c. sugar
3 eggs, separated
1 c. thick applesauce
1 15-oz. can sweetened condensed milk
⅓ c. lemon juice
1 tbsp. grated lemon rind

Mix crumbs with butter and sugar; reserve 1/2 cup of the mixture for topping. Press remaining crumbs into bottom and sides of an 8 x 12-inch pan. Combine well beaten yolks, applesauce, milk, lemon juice and lemon rind. Fold in well beaten egg whites. Pour into crumb crust. Top with remaining crumbs. Chill for several hours or overnight. Serve with a whipped cream topping. Yield: 12 servings.

Marcella B. Huber
Sarasota, Fla.

BLUEBERRY DELIGHT DESSERT

1 c. graham cracker crumbs
1 stick butter or margarine
1 c. sugar
2 eggs, beaten
8 oz. cream cheese
1 can blueberry pie filling
1 tbsp. lemon juice (opt.)
Whipped cream (opt.)

Mix crumbs, butter and 1/2 cup sugar; press into a 9 x 13-inch pan. Combine eggs, remaining 1/2 cup sugar and cheese; pour over crumbs. Bake at 350 to 375 degrees for 20 minutes. Cool. Cover with blueberry pie filling mixed with lemon juice; top with whipped cream. Yield: 15 servings.

Rosalee Wade
Clear Lake, Wisc.

BLUEBERRY DELIGHT DESSERT

18 graham crackers, crushed
½ stick butter
¼ c. sugar
1 pkg. instant vanilla pudding mix
1 can blueberry pie mix
1 pkg. dessert topping mix, prepared

Combine crumbs, butter and sugar; press into an 8-inch square pan. Bake at 375 degrees for 8 minutes. Cool. Prepare pudding according to package directions; pour over crust. Heat pie mix until thickened; pour over pudding. Cool. Top with dessert topping; chill. Yield: 9 servings.

Mrs. Bessie Ross
Wellsburg, Iowa

BLUEBERRY DESSERT

24 graham crackers
1 c. sugar
½ c. butter, melted
8 oz. cream cheese
2 eggs
1 can blueberry pie filling

Crush graham crackers; add 1/2 cup sugar and butter. Pat mixture into a 9 x 13-inch greased pan. Blend cream cheese, eggs and 1/2 cup sugar. Spread on crust. Bake at 350 degrees for 15 minutes. Cool; spread pie filling on top. Cover and chill. Yield: 12 servings.

Mrs. LaVerne Junkmann
Eielson AFB, Alas.

BLUEBERRY DESSERT

1 pkg. lemon gelatin
¾ c. boiling water
1 ⅔ c. evaporated milk
Juice of 1 lemon
1 c. sugar
Graham cracker crumbs
1 can blueberry pie mix

Dissolve gelatin in boiling water; cool. Combine milk, lemon juice and sugar; whip. Add gelatin; continue to whip. Line a 9 x 13-inch pan with cracker crumbs. Add one-half of the whipped mixture. Add pie mix and remaining whipped mixture. Cover with cracker crumbs. Chill. Yield: 8 servings.

Mrs. Herb Schons
Pipestone, Minn.

BOYSENBERRY DELIGHT

15 graham crackers, crushed
¼ c. melted butter
½ lb. marshmallows
½ c. milk
1 c. heavy cream, whipped
1 can boysenberries and juice
2 tbsp. cornstarch
¼ c. sugar
1 tbsp. lemon juice

Combine cracker crumbs and butter; press into a pan. Dissolve marshmallows in milk over boiling water. Cool; fold in whipped cream. Mix juice from boysenberries, cornstarch, sugar and lemon juice. Cook until thickened; add boysenberries. Pour one-half of the marshmallow mixture over crumbs. Cover with boysenberry mixture; top with remaining marshmallow mixture. Chill. Yield: 6-8 servings.

Mrs. Myrl Miller
Thorton, Iowa

CHERRY CHA CHA

4 c. miniature marshmallows
½ pt. heavy cream, whipped
1 8 x 13-in. graham cracker crust, baked
1 c. cherry pie filling
Buttered graham cracker crumbs

Fold marshmallows into whipped cream. Spread one-half of the mixture in baked crust. Pour pie filling over mixture. Add remaining cream mixture; sprinkle buttered crumbs over top. Refrigerate for several hours. NOTE: Pie may be made in 9-inch pan.

Mrs. Clement D. Eagan
Sandia Base, N.M.

CHERRY DELIGHT

1 ½ c. crushed graham crackers
3 tbsp. melted butter
Sugar
1 c. miniature marshmallows
1 c. heavy cream, whipped
1 can cherry pie filling

Mix graham crackers, butter and 3 tablespoons sugar; pat into bottom of 8 x 10-inch baking pan. Fold marshmallows into sweetened whipped cream; spread over graham cracker mixture. Spread cherry pie filling over cream mixture. Chill for 24 hours. Yield: 10-12 servings.

Edelyne Berry
Pilot Rock, Oreg.

CHERRY DREAM DELIGHT

½ c. melted butter or margarine
3 tbsp. sugar

1 ½ c. graham cracker crumbs
1 envelope dessert topping mix
3 tbsp. powdered sugar
1 8-oz. pkg. cream cheese, softened
1 can cherry pie filling

Mix melted butter and sugar with graham cracker crumbs. Press into 9 x 12 or 13-inch pan; chill. Prepare dessert topping mix according to directions. Add powdered sugar and cream cheese. Beat at high speed until firm. Pour into chilled shell. Spread pie filling over top; chill. Yield: 12 servings.

Carol Peludat
South Daytona, Fla.

CHERRY YUM YUM

3 c. graham cracker crumbs
1 ½ sticks margarine, melted
1 8-oz. pkg. cream cheese, softened
¾ c. sugar
1 tsp. vanilla flavoring
2 pkg. dessert topping mix
1 c. half and half cream
2 cans cherry pie filling

Combine cracker crumbs and margarine; line 9 x 15-inch dish with one-half the mixture. Blend cream cheese, sugar and vanilla. Whip topping mix with cream; fold into cream cheese mixture. Spread one-half this mixture over cracker crumbs; top with cherry filling. Add remaining cream cheese mixture; top with remaining crumbs. Refrigerate overnight. Yield: 15 servings.

Mrs. Jessie Edwards Hill
Sparta, N.C.

CHERRY YUM YUM

3 c. graham cracker crumbs
1 ½ sticks butter or margarine, melted
2 pkg. dessert topping mix
1 lge. pkg. cream cheese
1 c. cold milk
¾ c. sugar
2 cans cherry pie filling

Mix graham cracker crumbs with butter. Spread one-half of the mixture in large pan. Beat dessert topping mix with cream cheese, milk and sugar. Spread one-half of the mixture on cracker crust; add cherry pie filling. Spread remaining cream mixture over filling. Top with remaining crumb mixture. Chill for 24 hours. Yield: 12 servings.

Mrs. Valerie Hyman
Ft. Jackson, S.C.

FAVORITE CHERRY DESSERT

CRUST:
⅔ c. crushed graham crackers
½ c. confectioners sugar
¼ c. melted butter

(Continued on next page)

Combine cracker crumbs, sugar and butter; press into 8-inch square pan.

FILLING:
1 c. powdered sugar
1 6-oz. pkg. cream cheese
1 2-oz. pkg. dessert topping mix, whipped
1 can cherry pie filling

Cream powdered sugar with cream cheese; fold in dessert topping. Spread over crust. Top with cherry filling. Chill for 6 hours or overnight. Yield: 10-12 servings.

Shirley Lantz
Calhoun, Nebr.

UNCOOKED DATE DESSERT

½ lb. graham crackers, crushed
2 c. dates, chopped
½ lb. marshmallows, chopped
1 tsp. vanilla flavoring
1 c. chopped nuts
1 c. heavy cream, whipped

Combine one-half of crumbs, dates, marshmallows, vanilla and nuts; moisten with whipped cream. Shape into a roll. Roll in remaining crumbs; chill. Serve in slices; top with whipped cream. Yield: 8-10 servings.

Mrs. LaVerne Olson
Wyndmere, N.D.

GRAHAM CRACKER FLUFF

2 eggs, separated
½ c. sugar
¾ c. milk
1 pkg. unflavored gelatin
⅓ c. cold water
1 tsp. vanilla flavoring
1 c. heavy cream, whipped
3 tbsp. butter, melted
12 graham crackers, crushed
3 tsp. brown sugar

Beat egg yolks; add sugar and milk. Cook mixture in top of double boiler until slightly thickened. Soak gelatin in cold water. Pour hot mixture over softened gelatin; stir until smooth. Chill until slightly thickened. Add stiffly beaten egg whites, vanilla and whipped cream to chilled mixture. Combine butter, cracker crumbs and brown sugar; mix to make crumbs. Sprinkle one-half of mixture in bottom of serving dish; pour liquid mixture into dish. Sprinkle with remaining crumbs; chill until thickened. Yield: 8 servings.

Savilla Yoder
Blountstown, Fla.

GRAHAM CRACKER-GELATIN DESSERT

Graham cracker crumbs
¼ c. butter
½ c. sugar
1 egg, slightly beaten
½ c. crushed pineapple, drained
½ c. chopped nuts
1 pkg. strawberry gelatin

Line 8-inch square pan with crumbs. Cream butter and sugar; add egg, pineapple and nuts. Pour one-half of the mixture over crumbs; add a layer of crumbs. Add remaining sugar mixture; add a layer of crumbs. Prepare gelatin according to package directions; let stand until slightly thickened. Pour gelatin mixture over crumbs. Chill until set. Yield: 6 servings.

Svea Boatright
Rodeo, Calif.

ICE BOX DREAM SQUARES

Whole graham crackers
2 ¾ sticks margarine
1 egg
½ c. plus 3 tbsp. milk
1 c. sugar
1 c. nuts
1 c. shredded coconut
1 c. graham cracker crumbs
2 c. sifted confectioners sugar
1 tsp. vanilla flavoring

Place a layer of whole graham crackers on bottom of 9 x 13-inch pan. Melt butter; beat egg, milk and sugar. Mix egg mixture with margarine; bring to a boil. Remove from heat; add nuts, coconut and graham cracker crumbs. Pour over graham crackers; top with another layer of whole graham crackers. Combine remaining ingredients; heat until smooth. Spread over graham crackers. Place in refrigerator for 2 hours; cut into squares.

Sue Horton
Pageland, S.C.

IDIOT'S DELIGHT

1 lb. marshmallows
1 c. milk
1 No. 2 can crushed pineapple, drained
1 c. finely chopped nuts
1 pt. heavy cream, whipped
15 double graham crackers, crushed

Cook marshmallows in milk until melted; cool. Mix in pineapple and nuts; fold in whipped cream. Line a shallow oblong pan with one-half of the crumbs; add filling. Top with remaining crumbs. Chill for 2 hours before serving. Yield: 8 servings.

Mrs. Del Clark
Astoria, Oreg.

LEMON FROTH

1 ⅔ c. evaporated milk
1 pkg. lemon gelatin
1 c. sugar
1 c. boiling water
½ c. cold water
Juice of 2 lemons
Grated rind of 2 lemons
12 graham crackers, finely rolled
1 tbsp. soft butter
2 tbsp. brown sugar

Chill milk, bowl and beaters thoroughly. Dissolve gelatin and sugar in boiling water. Add cold water, lemon juice and rind. Refrigerate until it begins to jell. Whip milk; add gelatin mixture gradually, beating with electric mixer until light and frothy. Combine all remaining ingredients; spread one-half of the mixture on bottom of 13 x 9 x 2-inch pan. Spread whipped mixture over crust; sprinkle remaining crust mix over top. Chill until set. Yield: 10 servings.

Mrs. David P. Sherrell
Pearl Harbor Naval Sta., Hawaii

MARSHMALLOW DELIGHT

24 graham crackers, rolled
5 tbsp. melted butter
1 lb. marshmallows
1 c. milk
1 c. heavy cream, whipped
½ c. pecans
1 can crushed pineapple, drained

Mix crackers with butter. Cover bottom of pan with one-half of the crackers. Melt marshmallows in milk; cool. Add whipped cream, pecans and pineapple. Pour over cracker crumbs; add remaining crumbs. Chill until set. Yield: 8-10 servings.

Mrs. Mayme Gordon
Rancom, Ill.

PEPPERMINT WHIP

14 chocolate covered graham crackers, finely crushed
1 ¼ c. miniature marshmallows
½ c. crushed peppermint candy
½ pt. heavy cream, whipped

Cover bottom of 9-inch square pan with one-half of the cracker crumbs. Fold marshmallows and peppermint candy into whipped cream. Carefully spoon onto the crumbs. Sprinkle with remaining crumbs; refrigerate for at least 12 hours. Yield: 9 servings.

Mrs. Francis J. Henggeler
Richmond, Va.

FRESH PEACH DELIGHT

1 ½ c. graham cracker crumbs
¼ c. butter, melted
2 tbsp. fresh orange juice
1 tbsp. lemon juice
½ lb. marshmallows
2 c. crushed fresh peaches
1 c. heavy cream, whipped
Maraschino cherries

Combine cracker crumbs with butter; pat evenly over sides and bottom of individual dessert dishes. Cool. Heat orange and lemon juices to boiling point; add marshmallows. Reduce heat; stir until melted. Cool slightly; mix in drained peaches. Fold in whipped cream; pour into crusts. Place in freezer until almost time to serve. Top with a cherry. Yield: 6-8 servings.

Rosa Nelle Hilton
Crestview, Fla.

PINEAPPLE-MARSHMALLOW DESSERT

15 graham crackers, crushed
⅛ lb. butter, melted
1 lb. marshmallows
1 c. hot milk
1 c. crushed pineapple, drained
1 pkg. dessert topping mix, prepared

Mix graham cracker crumbs with melted butter. Sprinkle one-half of the mixture in bottom of 9-inch square glass baking dish. Melt marshmallows in hot milk; cool. Add pineapple and dessert topping mix; pour over crumb mixture. Top with remaining crumbs. Chill. Yield: 8 servings.

Mrs. Louise Harmless
Groveland, Ind.

PEPPERMINT SURPRISE

2 c. graham cracker crumbs
1 pt. heavy cream
2 tsp. vanilla flavoring
1 c. crushed peppermint cream stick candy
½ c. broken nuts
1 c. miniature marshmallows

Put 1 cup crumbs in bottom of buttered 8-inch square pan. Whip cream; add vanilla. Fold in crushed candy, nuts and marshmallows. Pour into graham crust; sprinkle with remaining cracker crumbs. Chill for 24 hours. Yield: 6-8 servings.

Mrs. Delbert E. Smith
Waco, Tex.

RIBBON ICEBOX DESSERT

14 graham crackers, crushed
⅓ c. soft butter

(Continued on next page)

1 ½ c. powdered sugar
¾ c. plus 3 tbsp. sweetened condensed milk
1 ½ pkg. strawberry gelatin
3 c. canned fruit cocktail and juice
Water

Line bottom of medium loaf pan with one-half of the crackers. Cream butter, sugar and 3 tablespoons milk; spread on crackers. Cover with remaining crackers; chill. Dissolve gelatin in hot fruit juice; add water to obtain correct amount liquid. Cool to room temperature; divide into two equal portions. Allow one to remain uncongealed; to the other, add 3/4 cup condensed milk. Chill until thickened; beat until fluffy. Pour over crackers; chill until firm. Combine drained fruit with uncongealed gelatin; add to congealed layer. Chill until firm; top with whipped cream if desired. Yield: 6 servings.

Miriam B. Fulkerson
Knollwood, O.

VANILLA-CREAM BARS

CRUST:
5 tbsp. sugar
¼ c. cocoa
1 egg, beaten
½ c. melted butter
1 tsp. vanilla flavoring
2 c. crushed graham crackers
1 c. flaked coconut
½ c. broken nuts

Mix sugar with cocoa; stir in all remaining ingredients. Press into ungreased 9 x 13 x 2-inch pan; chill.

FILLING:
3 tbsp. milk
2 tbsp. vanilla instant pudding mix
¼ c. plus 1 tbsp. melted butter
2 c. powdered sugar
4 squares semi-sweet chocolate

Blend milk, pudding mix, 1/4 cup melted butter and powdered sugar; spread on crust. Chill. Melt chocolate with remaining butter; spread over sugar mixture. Chill. Cut into small bars; keep refrigerated.

Mrs. Arch Correll
Linden, Wisc.

ANGEL MOUSSE

3 eggs, separated
½ c. sugar
2 tbsp. cognac
2 tbsp. rum
1 tbsp. gelatin
¼ c. cold water

1 c. heavy cream, whipped
1 tsp. vanilla flavoring

Beat egg yolks until light and lemon colored. Gradually add sugar, beating mixture until creamy. Stir in cognac and rum. Soften gelatin in cold water for 5 minutes. Dissolve over hot water; stir into egg yolk mixture. Fold in stiffly beaten egg whites and whipped cream. Flavor with vanilla. Pour into cocktail glasses; chill for 2 hours.

Mrs. Donald J. Hopkins
Clovis, N.M.

SIMPLE APRICOT MOUSSE

1 28-oz. can apricots
1 pkg. lemon flavored gelatin
2 tbsp. brandy
1 c. heavy cream, whipped
1 c. crumbled vanilla wafers

Drain apricots; mash through a sieve. Add enough water to apricot juice to make 1 3/4 cups liquid. Heat liquid to boiling. Add gelatin; stir until dissolved. Cool. Add apricots and brandy; refrigerate until of jelly-like consistency. Beat slightly; fold in whipped cream. Pour one-half of the mixture into 8-inch square pan. Sprinkle crumbs over mixture; add remaining mixture. Refrigerate until firm. Yield: 6-8 servings.

Mrs. Melvin Harper
Concord, Calif.

CHOCOLATE-RUM MOUSSE

1 envelope unflavored gelatin
¼ c. cold water
2 oz. sweet baking chocolate
¾ c. hot strong coffee
2 egg yolks, beaten
¼ tsp. salt
1 tsp. artificial rum flavoring
Liquid sugar substitute to taste
4 egg whites
Pinch of cream of tartar

Sprinkle gelatin on cold water to soften. Melt chocolate in hot coffee. Add gelatin; dissolve over low heat, stirring. Add egg yolks, stirring vigorously. Remove from heat; add salt, rum flavoring and sugar substitute. Cool. Beat egg whites with cream of tartar until stiff peaks form. Fold into chocolate mixture until well blended. Pour into small spring form pan. Refrigerate until firm. Loosen side of form with knife. Unmold; garnish with low calorie whipped cream just before serving. NOTE: Each serving has 60 calories.

Mrs. Francis B. Risser
Long Beach, Calif.

COCONUT MOUSSE

1 ½ pkg. unflavored gelatin
¼ c. cold water
1 ½ c. scalded milk
½ c. sugar
½ can shredded coconut
½ tsp. almond flavoring
1 c. heavy cream, whipped
Strawberries

Dissolve gelatin in cold water; set in pan of hot water. Combine milk and sugar; stir until dissolved. Add gelatin mixture. Remove from heat; add coconut and almond flavoring. Pour into bowl; refrigerate until partially set. Fold in whipped cream. Pour into ring mold; refrigerate until firm. Unmold; fill center with strawberries.

SAUCE:

1 c. sugar
1 c. brown sugar
¼ lb. butter or margarine
1 c. heavy cream

Combine sugars, butter and cream in top of double boiler; cook until creamy and smooth. Serve warm over mousse and berries. Yield: 12 servings.

Mrs. James C. Hare
Nellis AFB, Nev.

COFFEE MOUSSE

24 marshmallows
1 c. strong hot coffee
1 c. heavy cream, whipped
2 tbsp. Jamaica rum

Melt marshmallows in double boiler. Add coffee; mix well. Cool. When it begins to thicken, fold in whipped cream and rum. Pour into mold; chill for 2 to 3 hours. NOTE: If desired, mold may be lined with ladyfingers. Yield: 6 servings.

Mrs. Michael Durant
Sanford, Fla.

CREME DE MENTHE MOUSSE

20 marshmallows
⅔ c. green creme de menthe
1 pt. heavy cream, whipped

Melt marshmallows in creme de menthe in top of double boiler. Cool thoroughly. Fold in whipped cream. Pour into mold or freezing tray; freeze for 3 hours with freezer set at lowest temperature. When firm, reset controls to normal; let it ripen until time to serve. Unmold; serve with fresh strawberries or whipped cream topped with creme de menthe. Yield: 6 servings.

Mrs. C. M. Esler, Jr.
Charleston, S.C.

FRUIT MOUSSE

¾ c. boiling water
1 ½ c. sugar
2 tbsp. grated orange rind
2 tbsp. unflavored gelatin
1 ½ c. orange juice
⅓ c. pineapple juice
¾ c. cold water
¾ c. instant nonfat dry milk
⅓ c. lemon juice
½ c. chopped Maraschino cherries
½ c. drained crushed pineapple
1 ½ c. chopped blanched almonds

Combine boiling water, sugar, orange rind and gelatin in saucepan. Stir and boil for 1 minute. Add orange juice and pineapple juice; cool until mixture is partially set. Pour cold water into a bowl; sprinkle dry milk on top and beat. When mixture is partially whipped, add lemon juice; beat for 10 minutes or until stiff. Fold in gelatin mixture. Fold in cherries, pineapple and nuts. Pour into 2-quart mold; chill until set. Yield: 12 servings.

Mrs. T. Hatzimanolis
Requa, Calif.

MAPLE MOUSSE

2 envelopes unflavored gelatin
¼ c. cold water
1 c. milk
1 c. maple syrup
1 pt. heavy cream, whipped
1 c. chopped nuts
½ lb. vanilla wafers, crumbled

Dissolve gelatin in cold water. Bring milk to boiling point; stir in gelatin. Pour in syrup; cool until slightly thickened. Add whipped cream and nuts. Place one-half of the crumbs in bottom of long casserole; pour in maple mixture. Cover with remaining wafer crumbs. Refrigerate. Yield: 12-16 servings.

Mrs. Rose E. Amis
Covington, Okla.

ORANGE MOUSSE

1 pkg. orange gelatin
1 c. hot water
2 tsp. lemon juice
4 tsp. sugar
Juice of 2 lge. oranges
Grated rind of 1 orange
1 c. heavy cream, whipped
1 sm. angel food cake
2 cans Mandarin oranges, drained

Combine gelatin and hot water. Add lemon juice, sugar, orange juice and rind; let set, but not until completely thickened. Fold in whipped cream. Break cake into pieces the size of walnuts; place in bottom of 13 x 9 x 2-inch baking dish. Pour one-half of juice

(Continued on next page)

mixture over cake; cover with 1 can Mandarin oranges. Repeat, using remaining ingredients. Do not use more cake than can be covered with mixture. Cover tightly; refrigerate for two days. Cut into squares; serve. Yield: 12 servings.

Mrs. W. M. Kurowski
Holloman AFB, N.M.

PINEAPPLE MOUSSE

1 pkg. lemon gelatin
1 c. warm water
1 No. 2 can crushed pineapple
1 c. honey graham crumbs
½ pt. heavy cream, whipped

Dissolve gelatin in warm water. Drain pineapple; add 1 cup pineapple juice to gelatin. Allow to congeal partially. Spread graham cracker crumbs in 8 x 8 x 2-inch pan, reserving some for top. Whip gelatin; fold in pineapple. Fold in whipped cream. Pour into pan; top with remaining crumbs. Refrigerate for 4 to 6 hours. Yield: 10 servings.

Mrs. James A. Hebbeler
Ft. Douglas, Utah

STRAWBERRY MOUSSE

1 qt. strawberries, washed and hulled
½ c. sugar
½ c. rose wine
2 envelopes unflavored gelatin
½ c. cold water
½ c. boiling water
2 c. heavy cream, whipped

Reserve several strawberries for garnish. Mash remaining berries with potato masher. Add sugar and wine; stir well. Chill. Soften gelatin in cold water. Add boiling water; stir to dissolve. Cool. Combine gelatin and strawberry mixture. Beat with rotary beater until fluffy and slightly thickened. Fold in whipped cream. Pour into oiled 2-quart mold. Chill for 3 hours or longer. Unmold onto chilled serving platter. Garnish with reserved whole strawberries. Yield: 8 servings.

Mrs. Frank J. Hess
Arlington, Va.

BANANA PARFAIT

1 egg, separated
2 tbsp. lemon juice
½ tsp. grated lemon rind
4 tbsp. sugar
½ tsp. ground mace
½ c. heavy cream, whipped
2 bananas

Beat egg yolk, lemon juice and rind until slightly thickened. Add 2 tablespoons sugar; mix well. Cook over low heat for 3 to 4 minutes or until mixture thickens, stirring constantly. Stir in mace; cool. Beat egg white to soft peaks; slowly add remaining 2 tablespoons sugar. Beat until stiff; fold into mixture. Fold in whipped cream. Fill parfait glasses with alternate layers of mixture and sliced bananas. Top with sliced bananas; chill. Yield: 6 servings.

Mrs. Betty Ferge
Corvallis, Oreg.

COCONUT-CREAM PUDDING PARFAIT

2 pkg. instant coconut cream pudding
1 pkg. frozen strawberries, thawed
Whipped cream

Prepare pudding according to package instructions. Alternate layers of pudding and strawberries in parfait glasses. Top with whipped cream and a strawberry. Chill before serving. Yield: 8 servings.

Mrs. Benjamin Berry
North Island, Calif.

COFFEE PARFAIT

½ lb. marshmallows
1 c. hot strong coffee
½ pt. heavy cream
1 qt. vanilla or coffee ice cream
Finely chopped black walnuts

Dissolve marshmallows in hot coffee over hot water in double boiler. Cool to lukewarm. Whip cream until it stands in stiff peaks; add to coffee mixture. Spoon a small amount of mixture into parfait glasses; add ice cream to fill glasses two-thirds full. Spoon coffee mixture over ice cream to fill glasses. Sprinkle with small amount of chopped nuts. Place glasses in ice chest of refrigerator until ready to serve. Yield: 10-12 servings.

Mrs. Robert E. Walsh
Brooklyn, N.Y.

FRUIT PARFAIT

¾ c. sugar
½ c. water
2 eggs, separated
½ pt. heavy cream, whipped
1 No. 2 can fruit cocktail
1 sm. bottle cherries

Boil sugar and water until it spins a thread; beat until cool. Add egg yolks; beat again. Beat egg whites until stiff; fold in. Add whipped cream. Add fruit cocktail and cherries. Refrigerate. Yield: 6-8 servings.

Gerri Combes
Sarasota, Fla.

BANANA SPLIT PIE

1 stick margarine
½ c. powdered sugar
2 eggs
1 tsp. vanilla flavoring
2 bananas, sliced
Lemon juice
½ c. chocolate pieces, shaved
¼ c. nuts
1 pie shell, baked

Cream margarine with powdered sugar. Add an egg at a time, beating for 3 minutes after each addition. Add vanilla. Place bananas in lemon juice to keep from turning brown. Add bananas to filling; add chocolate pieces and nuts. Pour into pie shell; decorate with chocolate, nuts or bananas. Chill for 3 to 4 hours before serving. Yield: 6 servings.

Mrs. Norma Hamilton
Pittsboro, Ind.

BAVARIAN PIE

1 pkg. unflavored gelatin
¼ c. cold water
3 eggs, separated
½ c. sugar
¼ tsp. salt
1 c. milk, scalded
1 tsp. vanilla flavoring
½ pt. heavy cream, whipped

Soften gelatin in water; set aside. Cook slightly beaten yolks, sugar, salt and milk in double boiler until mixture coats a spoon. Add gelatin mixture; cool until slightly thickened. Fold in vanilla, beaten egg whites and whipped cream. Pour into graham cracker crust. Sprinkle crumbs on top.

CRUST:
16 graham crackers
1 tsp. cinnamon
⅓ c. sugar
⅓ c. melted butter

Mix all ingredients; press into pie plate, reserving a few crumbs for top. Yield: 8 servings.

Mrs. Thressa Christl
Oconto, Wisc.

BITTERSWEET MINT PIE

1 envelope gelatin
½ c. cold milk
1 c. milk, scalded
¾ c. sugar
3 eggs, separated
2 squares chocolate, melted

½ c. heavy cream, whipped
1 crumb crust
¼ c. creme de menthe

Soften gelatin in cold milk. Pour a small amount of scalded milk into sugar and beaten egg yolks; gradually stir in remaining milk. Cook, stirring constantly, until mixture thickens. Stir in softened gelatin. Divide custard mixture into halves. To one-half, blend in slightly cooled chocolate. Chill until partially set. Fold in whipped cream. Spoon into crumb crust; chill until slightly firm. Keep remaining one-half of custard at room temperature. Fold in stiffly beaten egg whites and creme de menthe. Pour over chocolate layer; chill until firm. Yield: 8 servings.

Mrs. Antone M. Swanda
Denver, Colo.

BUTTER CRUNCH-LEMON CHIFFON PIE

BUTTER CRUNCH CRUST:
½ c. butter or margarine
¼ c. (packed) brown sugar
1 c. sifted flour
½ c. chopped walnuts

Mix all ingredients until crumbly. Spread in 13 x 19 x 2-inch pan. Bake at 400 degrees for 15 minutes. Take from oven; stir. Save 3/4 cup for topping. Press remaining mixture against bottom and sides of 9-inch pie pan. Cool.

LEMON CHIFFON FILLING:
1 c. sugar
1 envelope unflavored gelatin
⅔ c. water
⅓ c. fresh lemon juice
4 eggs, separated
1 tbsp. grated lemon rind
½ tsp. cream of tartar

Blend 1/2 cup sugar, gelatin, water, lemon juice and slightly beaten egg yolks thoroughly in saucepan. Cook over low heat, stirring constantly, just until mixture comes to a boil. Stir in lemon rind. Place pan in cold water; cool until mixture mounds slightly when dropped from a spoon. Beat egg whites with cream of tartar until frothy. Gradually beat in remaining sugar until stiff and glossy. Fold lemon mixture into meringue; pour into cooled crust. Sprinkle with reserved crumbs; chill. Yield: 6-8 servings.

Mrs. Warren F. Brown
Concord, Calif.

CARIBBEAN CHIFFON PIE

1 envelope gelatin
½ c. sugar
⅛ tsp. salt
3 eggs, separated
1 c. milk
⅓ c. unsulphured molasses
1 ½ tsp. rum flavoring
1 c. heavy cream, whipped
1 9-in. baked pastry shell

Mix gelatin, 2 tablespoons sugar and salt in top of double boiler. Beat egg yolks and milk; add to gelatin mixture with unsulphured molasses. Cook over boiling water, stirring occasionally, until mixture is slightly thickened. Remove from heat; stir in rum flavoring. Chill until slightly thicker than the consistency of unbeaten egg whites. Beat egg whites until stiff but not dry. Gradually add remaining sugar; beat until very stiff. Fold in gelatin mixture. Fold in whipped cream. Turn into baked pastry shell; chill. Garnish with whipped cream if desired. Yield: One 9-inch pie.

Photograph for this recipe above.

BRIDE'S PIE

2 eggs, separated
¾ c. sugar

1 ½ c. milk, scalded
1 tbsp. unflavored gelatin
Cold water
½ pt. heavy cream, whipped
Vanilla flavoring
2 squares bitter baking chocolate

Cream egg yolks and sugar; add milk. Cook in top of double boiler until thickened. Dissolve gelatin in a small amount of cold water; add to cooked custard. Cool. Beat egg whites until stiff; add to custard. Add cream and vanilla. Grate 1 1/2 squares chocolate in bottom of 8 x 10-inch pan. Pour in custard; grate 1/2 square of chocolate over top. Chill well or overnight before serving.

Mrs. Newton M. Benzing
Monona, Iowa

BROWNIE PIE

3 egg whites
Dash of salt
¾ c. sugar
¾ c. chocolate wafer crumbs
½ c. chopped walnuts
½ tsp. vanilla flavoring
Sweetened whipped cream

Beat egg whites and salt until soft peaks form. Gradually add sugar, beating until

(Continued on next page)

stiff peaks form. Fold in crumbs, nuts and vanilla. Pour into buttered 9-inch pie plate. Bake at 325 degrees for 35 minutes. Cool. Top with whipped cream. Chill for 3 to 4 hours. Trim with curls of shaved unsweetened chocolate, crumbs or candies. Yield: 6-8 servings.

Betty Bielenberg
Jefferson, Iowa

CHOCOLATE-PECAN PIE

½ lb. butter
¾ c. extra fine sugar
1 ½ squares unsweetened chocolate, melted
2 eggs
1 tsp. vanilla flavoring
1 baked pie crust
¼ c. broken pecans
¼ pt. heavy cream, whipped

Cream butter and sugar until smooth. Add melted chocolate, 1 egg and vanilla; beat for 5 minutes. Add remaining egg; beat for 5 minutes longer. Pour filling into pie crust; sprinkle with pecans. Use whipped cream to garnish edge and center. Chill for at least 6 hours before serving. Yield: 8 servings.

Jackie McGregor
Iron Mountain, Mich.

LEMON-ORANGE CHIFFON PIE

4 eggs, separated
1 c. sugar
⅓ c. fresh lemon juice
¼ c. fresh orange juice
½ tsp. salt
1 tbsp. unflavored gelatin
¼ c. cold water
1 tsp. grated lemon rind
1 tsp. grated orange rind
1 baked 9-in. pastry shell, cooled
½ c. heavy cream, whipped
1 tbsp. grated walnuts

Combine beaten egg yolks, 1/2 cup sugar, juices and salt; cook in double boiler until thick, stirring constantly. Add gelatin softened in cold water; stir until gelatin dissolves. Add rinds; cool until partially set. Beat egg whites until frothy. Gradually add remaining 1/2 cup sugar; beat until stiff. Fold lemon-orange mixture into egg whites. Pour into cooled baked shell; chill until firm. Spread with sweetened whipped cream; top with walnuts. Yield: 6 servings.

Mrs. Frank Villaescusa
Tacoma, Wash.

COCONUT CHIFFON PIE

1 c. sugar
3 tbsp. flour

2 eggs, separated
1 ½ c. sweet milk
1 envelope unflavored gelatin
½ c. cold water
1 ½ c. grated coconut
2 tbsp. confectioners sugar
1 tsp. vanilla flavoring
1 9-in. pie shell, baked
1 2-oz. pkg. dessert topping mix

Beat sugar, flour and egg yolks until lemon colored. Add milk; cook in top of double boiler until thickened. Dissolve gelatin in water; fold into custard with 1 cup coconut. Beat egg whites until stiff; add confectioners sugar and vanilla flavoring. Fold into custard; pour into pie shell. Chill. Prepare topping mix according to package instructions; spoon over chilled custard. Sprinkle with remaining coconut. Yield: 6 servings.

Mrs. Bertha Shook
Celina, Tex.

CRANBERRY PIE

24 marshmallows
½ c. milk
1 1-lb. can cranberry sauce
2 tbsp. crushed pineapple, drained
1 c. heavy cream, whipped
1 9-in. baked pie shell

Melt marshmallows in milk in top of double boiler; remove from heat. Add cranberry sauce and pineapple; cool. Fold stiffly whipped cream into cranberry mixture. Pour into pie shell; chill for 4 hours.

Mrs. Daryl Davidson
Schenectady, N.Y.

CREME DE MENTHE PIE

22 chocolate cookies, finely crushed
¼ c. butter, melted
4 egg yolks
¾ c. sugar
1 tbsp. gelatin
¼ c. cold water
¼ c. creme de menthe
1 ½ c. heavy cream, whipped
Grated bitter chocolate

Combine cookie crumbs and butter; press into pie plate. Chill. Beat yolks with sugar until thick and yellow. Soak gelatin in cold water for 5 minutes; dissolve over hot water. Add to egg mixture. Add creme de menthe; stir. Cool until it begins to thicken. Fold in whipped cream. Pour into crust-lined plate; refrigerate. Sprinkle with grated chocolate. Yield: 8 servings.

Mrs. Robert W. Gentleman
Ft. Story, Va.

CREME DE MENTHE PIE

28 lge. marshmallows
½ c. milk
2 tbsp. creme de menthe
18 cream filled chocolate cookies, crushed
⅓ stick butter
½ pt. heavy cream, whipped

Combine marshmallows and milk in double boiler; cook until dissolved. Cool; add creme de menthe. Cool thoroughly. Combine cookies and butter; mix well. Press into 8-inch pie pan. Fold whipped cream into marshmallow mixture; pour into pie shell. Sprinkle with additional cookie crumbs; chill for at least 5 hours before serving. Yield: 8-9 servings.

Mrs. Margaret Wade
Midland, Mich.

DREAM PIE

1 No. 2 can red sour cherries
1 No. 2 can crushed pineapple
¼ c. flour or cornstarch
⅔ c. sugar
1 pkg. orange gelatin
3 mashed bananas
1 c. chopped pecans
¼ tsp. red food coloring
2 baked pie shells
2 cartons heavy cream, whipped

Heat cherries, pineapple and juices, reserving 1/2 cup cherry juice. Mix reserved juice with flour and sugar. Add to fruit mixture; stir until thick over medium heat. Add orange gelatin; mix well and cool. Add bananas, nuts and food coloring. Pour mixture into pie shells; chill. Top with whipped cream. Yield: 2 large pies.

Mrs. J. C. Reavis, Jr.
Texarkana, Tex.

EGGNOG-MINCE PIE

1 stick pie crust mix or 1 recipe pastry
1 c. mincemeat
1 med. apple, pared, cored and diced
1 pkg. dessert topping mix
1 ¾ c. milk
½ tsp. orange flavoring
1 pkg. instant vanilla pudding
½ tsp. rum flavoring
2 tbsp. sugar
2 tbsp. grated orange rind

Prepare pie crust mix according to package directions. Roll out to 11-inch round on lightly floured board; fit into 9-inch pie plate. Combine mincemeat and apple; spoon into pie shell. Bake at 400 degrees for 20 minutes or until crust is golden brown. Cool completely on wire rack. Prepare dessert topping mix with 1/2 cup milk and orange flavoring.

Measure 1 cup pudding mix; combine with remaining milk and rum flavoring. Beat for 1 minute or until well blended with rotary beater. Pour over cooled mincemeat. Spoon dessert topping mix in soft swirls over top. Sprinkle with sugar and rind. Chill until ready to serve. Yield: 8 servings.

Dottie C. Bosworth
Pawtucket, R.I.

FLORIDA FRUIT PIE

½ lb. vanilla wafers
¼ lb. butter or margarine
1 lb. confectioners sugar
2 eggs
1 pt. fresh or frozen strawberries, sliced
1 orange, thinly sliced
½ pt. heavy cream, whipped

Place one-half of the wafers in buttered baking dish. Cream butter and sugar. Beat eggs; add. Spread mixture over wafers; add drained fruit. Add remaining wafers. Refrigerate for 8 hours. Serve with whipped cream. Yield: 12 servings.

Mrs. Ernest R. Elliott
Lakeland, Fla.

FRENCH PINEAPPLE PIE

¾ lb. vanilla wafers
½ c. butter
1 ½ c. powdered sugar
2 eggs
½ pt. heavy cream
12 marshmallows, cut up
½ c. pecans or walnuts
1 med. can pineapple chunks, drained and chopped
1 sm. bottle Maraschino cherries, halved or quartered

Put one-half of the wafer crumbs in bottom of large pan. Cream butter. Add powdered sugar; cream well. Add an egg at a time; beat well after each addition. Pour mixture carefully over wafer crumbs in pan. Whip cream; add marshmallows, nuts, pineapple and cherries. Pour over butter mixture. Sprinkle remaining crumbs on top. Refrigerate for 24 hours. Yield: 14 servings.

Mrs. Forrest E. Asher
Texarkana, Tex.

FRENCH SILK CHOCOLATE PIE

½ c. butter
¾ c. sugar
1 square chocolate, melted and cooled
1 tsp. vanilla flavoring
2 eggs
1 8-in. baked pie shell, cooled
Whipped cream

(Continued on next page)

Cream butter and sugar; blend in chocolate and vanilla. Add an egg at a time, beating for 5 minutes with electric mixer after each addition. Pour into shell. Top with whipped cream; garnish with chopped pecans. Yield: 6 servings.

Mrs. Thomas E. Curry
Jacksonville, Fla.

FROZEN DAIQUIRI PIE

1 envelope gelatin
1 c. sugar
½ tsp. salt
3 eggs, separated
¼ c. water
½ c. lime juice
1 tsp. grated lime rind
Green food coloring
⅓ c. rum
1 9-in. baked pie shell
Whipped cream (opt.)

Combine gelatin, 2/3 cup sugar and salt. Add egg yolks, water and lime juice. Beat with rotary beater until blended. Simmer in double boiler, stirring constantly, until mixture coats spoon. Remove from heat; add rind. Tint until pale green with food coloring; cool. Add rum. Refrigerate until slightly thicker than an unbeaten egg white. Beat egg whites; add remaining sugar. Fold in gelatin mixture. Pour into pie shell. Refrigerate. Just before serving, top with whipped cream. Yield: 6 servings.

Mrs. Renetta Friesen
Alamogordo, N.M.

GELATIN-ICE CREAM PIE

CRUMB CRUST:
1 ½ to 2 c. graham cracker crumbs
¼ c. melted butter
1 tbsp. sugar

Combine all ingredients; press into 8-inch pie pan.

FILLING:
1 pkg. strawberry gelatin
1 ¼ c. boiling water
1 pt. vanilla ice cream
1 c. sliced fresh strawberries, sweetened and drained, or 1 10-oz. pkg. frozen strawberries, thawed and drained

Dissolve gelatin in boiling water. Stir in ice cream until melted. Chill until thick. Fold in strawberries. Pour into crumb crust. Chill until firm. Garnish with whole berries. NOTE: Peaches, Bing cherries, red or black raspberries may be substituted for strawberries. Yield: 6 servings.

Mrs. Herman F. Mayes
Watseka, Ill.

GINGER PIE

¼ lb. butter
¾ c. confectioners sugar
2 tbsp. coffee cream
1 tbsp. ginger
2 c. heavy cream, whipped
1 10-in. layer of yellow cake, ¼-in. thick
1 tbsp. grated semi-sweet chocolate

Cream butter and sugar; slightly thin with coffee cream. Mix thoroughly; add ginger. Fold whipped cream into mixture. Place cake layer in 9-inch pan to form side crust for pie. Pile filling onto cake; smooth top surface. Sprinkle top with chocolate. Refrigerate. NOTE: Chocolate may be melted and drizzled over top. Yield: 8-10 servings.

Mildred Bowers
New Cayama, Calif.

GRAHAM-WALNUT PIE

3 eggs, separated
1 c. sugar
½ c. nuts
1 c. graham cracker crumbs
Dash of salt
1 tsp. vanilla flavoring

Combine yolks, 1/2 cup sugar, nuts, crumbs, salt and vanilla. Beat egg whites until fluffy; gradually add remaining sugar to whites. Fold into egg yolk mixture. Pour into 8 x 8 x 2-inch pan. Bake at 350 degrees for 20 minutes. Cut into squares. Serve with whipped or ice cream. Yield: 8 servings.

Mrs. Florence E. Flower
Marion, Mass.

GRAPEFRUIT PIE

1 pkg. pink grapefruit gelatin
1 c. boiling water
1 pt. grapefruit or lime sherbet
1 No. 2 can sweetened grapefruit, finely cut
Sugar to taste
Fruit coloring (opt.)
Baked pastry shell or graham cracker crust
Dessert topping mix, prepared or heavy cream, whipped

Dissolve gelatin in boiling water. Stir sherbet into hot gelatin. When nearly dissolved, add grapefruit, sugar and coloring. Chill until congealed. Spoon into baked pie shell or graham cracker crust. Return to refrigerator until set. When ready to serve, cover with dessert topping. NOTE: If grapefruit sherbet is not available, lime or lemon sherbet can be substituted. Yield: 6 servings.

Fannie R. Weale
Leesburg, Fla.

HOLIDAY PIE

PIE SHELL:
1 ¼ c. Brazil nuts
3 tbsp. sugar

Put nuts through meat grinder, using fine knife. Add sugar; blend. Press mixture into bottom and sides of 9-inch pie plate up to rim. Bake at 400 degrees for 8 minutes or until lightly browned.

FILLING:
1 envelope unflavored gelatin
¼ c. water
3 eggs, separated
½ c. sugar
⅛ tsp. salt
1 ½ c. milk, scalded
½ c. thinly sliced glazed cherries
2 tbsp. light rum

Soak gelatin in water. Beat egg yolks; add 1/4 cup sugar and salt. Gradually stir in scalded milk. Cook in double boiler over very hot water until mixture coats metal spoon. Remove from heat; stir in gelatin. Chill until custard mounds when some is dropped from spoon. Whip until smooth. Add cherries and rum. Whip egg whites until peaks form; add remaining sugar gradually. Whip until stiff; fold into custard mixture. Pour into cooled pie shell. Chill overnight.

TOPPING:
¼ c. Brazil nuts
¾ c. heavy cream
Sugar to taste

Soak Brazil nuts in boiling water for 30 minutes. Whip cream; sweeten to taste. Spoon around edge of pie. Drain nuts; with sharp knife, shave over pie. Refrigerate until serving time. Yield: 6-8 servings.

Mrs. R. E. Sink
San Diego, Calif.

LIME CHIFFON PIE

1 tbsp. gelatin
½ c. cold water
4 eggs, separated
1 c. sugar
⅛ tsp. salt
⅓ c. lime juice
½ tsp. lemon rind
1 drop green coloring
1 9-in. pastry shell, baked

Soften gelatin in cold water. Combine slightly beaten egg yolks, 1/2 cup sugar, salt, lime juice, lime and lemon rinds in top of double boiler; blend well. Cook over boiling water until thick and foamy, beating constantly for 5 minutes. Remove from heat; add gelatin mixture. Mix well; add green coloring. Cool until mound will drop from spoon. Beat egg whites until stiff but not dry. Gradually add remaining sugar. Fold into cooked mixture. Pile lightly into baked shell. Decorate with additional grated lime rind; chill. Yield: 5-6 servings.

Alice C. Wilson
Orlando, Fla.

MACAROON-CREAM PIE

12 macaroon cookies
1 ½ tbsp. gelatin
¼ c. cold water
3 c. milk, scalded
½ c. sugar
¼ tsp. salt
3 eggs, separated
1 tsp. vanilla flavoring
Whipped cream

Crumble macaroons over bottom of 8 x 12-inch baking dish. Soak gelatin in cold water. Stir into scalded milk. Add sugar and salt; pour slowly on slightly beaten egg yolks. Cook in double boiler until slightly thickened, stirring constantly. Remove from heat; add vanilla. Fold in stiffly beaten egg whites. Pour at once over macaroons. Cool; refrigerate. Before serving, top with whipped cream. Yield: 10 servings.

Mrs. J. D. Hunter
Miramar, Calif.

PEACH PIE

6 c. sliced ripe peaches
¾ c. sugar
2 tbsp. butter
⅛ tsp. salt
3 tbsp. cornstarch
1 9-in. baked pastry shell

Cook 3 cups peaches with 1/4 cup sugar until mixture comes to a boil; add remaining sugar, butter, salt and cornstarch. Cook until clear and glossy. Place remaining peaches in pastry shell. Pour hot mixture over peaches. Chill until cold. Serve with whipped cream or ice cream. Yield: 6 servings.

Mrs. Anita Ellis
Forks, Wash.

ICEBOX PECAN PIE

1 c. sugar
2 tsp. baking powder
3 egg whites, stiffly beaten
1 c. finely chopped pecans
11 graham crackers, finely rolled

(Continued on next page)

Fold sugar and baking powder slowly into stiffly beaten egg whites. Fold in pecans and cracker crumbs. Pour into buttered pie plate. Bake at 300 degrees for 30 minutes. Cool thoroughly; refrigerate for 3 to 4 hours before serving. Garnish entire top with sweetened whipped cream. Yield: 6-8 servings.

Mrs. Hubert E. Wrenn
Shaw AFB, S.C.

PERSIMMON-BANANA PIE

4 ripe bananas
3 ripe persimmons
1 unbaked graham cracker pie crust
½ c. shredded coconut
Dessert topping mix or whipped cream

Peel and thinly slice bananas. Remove outside skin of persimmons and mash. Arrange persimmons and bananas alternately in pie shell. Cover with coconut; chill. Top with whipped cream. Yield: 6 servings.

Mrs. Beulah Swayne
Tucson, Ariz.

PINEAPPLE ICEBOX PIE

1 can sweetened condensed milk
Few drops of yellow coloring
¼ c. lemon juice
Pinch of salt
1 c. crushed pineapple, drained
1 baked pie shell
Whipped cream

Empty milk into mixing bowl. Add combined coloring, lemon juice and salt; stir until thickened. Add pineapple; mix well. Pour into baked pie shell. Top with whipped cream. Yield: 6 servings.

Mrs. Marie Forbes
Ralston, Okla.

PINK LADY PIE

1 ½ c. finely crushed vanilla wafers
¼ c. softened butter
¼ c. sugar
¾ c. orange juice
¾ lb. marshmallows
1 ¼ c. heavy cream, whipped
1 10-oz. pkg. frozen raspberries or strawberries, thawed and drained

Blend wafers with butter and sugar; press into 9-inch pie pan. Bake at 375 degrees for 5 minutes. Cool thoroughly. Heat orange juice in double boiler. Add marshmallows; stir until melted. Cool mixture; chill until partially set. Fold in whipped cream and raspberries. Pour into pie shell. Chill until

set; top with additional whipped cream. Yield: 6-8 servings.

Mrs. Wanda Mauree Hall
Onida, S.D.

ICEBOX PUMPKIN PIE

1 ⅓ c. graham cracker crumbs
½ tsp. cinnamon
¼ c. sugar
¼ c. margarine or butter, softened
1 ¾ c. canned pumpkin
1 15-oz. can sweetened condensed milk
2 eggs, beaten
1 tsp. cinnamon
¼ tsp. nutmeg
⅛ tsp. allspice
1 tbsp. molasses (opt.)

Combine cracker crumbs, cinnamon and sugar; blend thoroughly with margarine. Pour into lightly oiled pie plate; press firmly against sides and bottom of plate. Chill for 1 hour. Mix pumpkin, condensed milk, eggs, spices and molasses thoroughly in large mixing bowl. Pour into top of double boiler; cook until thick. Filling will thicken even more when it is chilled, so do not overcook. Cool; pour into crust. Chill for at least 3 hours. Top with whipped cream before serving. NOTE: May be made the day before it is to be served. Yield: 8 servings.

Mrs. Jack Tiller
Fort Jackson, S.C.

MARSHMALLOW-PUMPKIN PIE

1 c. cooked mashed pumpkin, drained
½ lb. marshmallows
½ tsp. cinnamon
¼ tsp. ginger
¼ tsp. salt
1 c. heavy cream, whipped
1 9-in. baked pie shell

Combine pumpkin, marshmallows, cinnamon, ginger and salt in top of double boiler. Stir over boiling water until marshmallows melt and mixture is smooth. Remove from heat; cool slightly. Fold in whipped cream. Pile into 9-inch pie shell. Chill or freeze. Garnish with whipped cream. Yield: 6 servings.

Mrs. Frank K. Stone
Maryville, Tenn.

GRAPEFRUIT-CREAM PIE

CRUST:
3 c. bite-sized toasted corn cereal
¼ c. butter or margarine
1 c. marshmallow creme
⅛ tsp. rum flavoring
½ c. finely shredded coconut

(Continued on next page)

Crush cereal to measure 1 cup. Heat and stir butter and marshmallow creme over hot water until syrupy. Stir in rum flavoring, coconut and cereal crumbs. Press into 8 or 9-inch pie plate.

FILLING:
1 c. sugar
3 eggs, separated
¼ tsp. salt
⅔ c. plus 4 tbsp. grapefruit juice
2 tsp. grated grapefruit peel
1 envelope unflavored gelatin
1 c. grapefruit segments, quartered
½ tsp. rum flavoring
2 drops yellow food coloring
Toasted coconut (opt.)

Mix sugar, egg yolks, salt, 1/3 cup grapefruit juice and grapefruit peel in top of double boiler. Cook, stirring constantly, until thickened. Soften gelatin in 1/4 cup grapefruit juice. Add to cooked mixture; stir to mix thoroughly. Cool; add remaining grapefruit juice, grapefruit segments and rum flavoring. When mixture begins to stiffen, fold in stiffly beaten egg whites and food coloring. Pour into marshmallow crust. Chill. Sprinkle top with toasted coconut before serving. Yield: 6-8 servings.

Mrs. Leo R. Kallinger
Largo, Fla.

RUM-CREAM PIE

1 pkg. unflavored gelatin
½ c. cold water
6 egg yolks
1 c. (scant) sugar
1 pt. heavy cream, whipped
¼ c. dark Jamaican rum
1 graham cracker crust
Grated bittersweet chocolate

Melt gelatin with cold water over boiling water. Beat egg yolks and sugar well; add gelatin mixture. Add whipped cream; fold in rum. Pour into graham cracker crust; sprinkle with grated chocolate. Place in refrigerator for 24 hours. Yield: 12 servings.

Mrs. Lorraine Douglas
Corpus Christi, Tex.

SHERRY-ALMOND PIE

2 c. finely ground almonds
⅔ c. plus 3 tbsp. sugar
1 envelope unflavored gelatin
¼ c. cold water
1 ½ c. milk
2 eggs, separated
⅛ tsp. salt
1 c. heavy cream, whipped
2 tbsp. Sherry wine
1 pie shell

Combine 1 1/2 cups ground almonds with 3 tablespoons sugar; press into bottom and sides of 9-inch pie plate. Bake at 400 degrees for 8 minutes; cool. Soften gelatin in cold water. Scald milk in top of double boiler. Combine egg yolks, salt and 1/3 cup sugar; add milk slowly, stirring constantly. Return mixture to double boiler. Cook over hot water, stirring constantly, until thick enough to coat spoon with thin film of custard. Remove from heat; stir in gelatin. Cool; refrigerate until thick, but not lumpy. Beat egg whites until stiff; beat in remaining sugar. Fold egg whites, whipped cream, Sherry and remaining almonds into custard. Pour into shell; chill. Just before serving, top with additional whipped cream and shaved chocolate. Yield: 10 servings.

Mrs. Royal Hatch
Stewart AFB, N.Y.

STRAWBERRY ICE BOX PIE

1 c. flour
1 tsp. salt
1 tbsp. sugar
2 tbsp. shortening
3 tbsp. cold water

Sift flour, salt and sugar; cut in shortening. Sprinkle with water, tossing gently to moisten. Roll out and fit into pie plate. Bake in hot oven until golden brown. Cool.

FILLING:
1 17-oz. pkg. marshmallows
1 box frozen or 2 c. fresh sweetened strawberries
1 c. heavy cream, whipped

Place marshmallows in double boiler; add 2 tablespoons strawberry juice. Cook until marshmallows are dissolved. Fold in strawberries. Chill for about 2 hours. Fold in whipped cream; pour into cool pastry shell. Chill until firm.

Mrs. Lyndon B. Johnson

OPEN STRAWBERRY PIE

1 3-oz. pkg. cream cheese, softened
1 baked pie shell
1 qt. fresh strawberries, sliced
Few drops of red food coloring
1 c. sugar
1 pt. fresh berries, crushed
3 tbsp. (heaping) cornstarch

Spread cream cheese on baked pie shell. Add strawberries; set aside. Add food coloring and sugar to berries. Add cornstarch; boil over low heat until thickened. Pour mixture over

(Continued on next page)

strawberries in pie shell; chill. Serve with whipped cream. Yield: 8 servings.

Mrs. C. A. Knight
Starke, Fla.

CHERRY PINK SPONGE

1 6-oz. pkg. cherry gelatin
3 c. boiling water
2 c. cooked rice
½ tsp. salt
½ c. sugar
1 tsp. vanilla flavoring
2 tsp. almond flavoring
2 c. heavy cream, whipped

Dissolve gelatin in boiling water; add rice, salt, sugar and flavorings. Chill until partially thickened. Fold in whipped cream; turn into individual molds or 2-quart mold. Chill until firm. Yield: 8-12 servings.

Mrs. S. E. Ward, Sr.
Iaeger, W. Va.

GLORIFIED RICE

1 c. rice
2 ½ c. water
1 tsp. salt
1 c. crushed pineapple, drained
½ c. chopped pecans
½ c. chopped Maraschino cherries
½ c. shredded coconut
½ pt. heavy cream
⅓ c. sugar
Few drops of rum flavoring
1 c. miniature marshmallows

Cook rice in water with salt until fluffy and soft. Rinse with cold water; drain well. Mix pineapple, pecans, cherries and coconut. Add to rice; mix well. Whip cream until thick but not stiff. Add sugar and flavoring; blend thoroughly. Add rice mixture and marshmallows. Garnish with pecan halves, cherries and coconut. Yield: 16 servings.

Mrs. Ruth C. Turner
Fort Wolters, Tex.

HEAVENLY HASH

1 pkg. lemon gelatin
1 c. sugar
1 sm. can crushed pineapple
2 c. cooked rice
1 c. heavy cream, whipped

Prepare gelatin; add sugar to hot mixture. Let stand until thickened but not set. Add pineapple and rice; blend well. Fold in whipped cream. Refrigerate for several hours. Serve plain or with whipped cream topped with a Maraschino cherry. Yield: 8-10 servings.

Mrs. A. B. Joyner, Jr.
Southport, N.C.

ICEBOX PUDDING

¾ lb. sweet chocolate
3 tbsp. hot water
3 tbsp. powdered sugar
3 eggs, separated
¾ pt. heavy cream, whipped
1 pkg. miniature marshmallows
½ c. nuts
Ladyfingers

Combine chocolate and water. Add sugar to beaten egg yolks; beat until fluffy. Fold into chocolate; cool. Fold in stiffly beaten egg whites and whipped cream. Add marshmallows and nuts. Pour into pan lined with ladyfingers. Chill for 24 hours. NOTE: Chocolate pieces may be used; add 2 tablespoons sugar. Graham cracker crust may replace ladyfingers.

Mrs. Darrell Billett
Red Lion, Pa.

TROPICAL RICE

1 c. cooked rice, cold
1 ½ c. crushed pineapple, drained
½ c. sugar
½ tsp. vanilla flavoring
8 marshmallows, diced
¼ c. Maraschino cherries
1 c. heavy cream, whipped

Combine rice, pineapple, sugar and vanilla; blend well. Fold in marshmallows, cherries and whipped cream. Chill for 1 hour. Serve in dessert dishes. Yield: 6-8 servings.

Mrs. Franklin Swartz
Portage, O.

SNOW PUDDING WITH VANILLA SAUCE

3 envelopes unflavored gelatin
3 c. water
1 c. sugar
¼ c. fresh lemon juice
3 egg whites, stiffly beaten

Soak gelatin in 1/4 cup cold water; dissolve in 2 3/4 cups boiling water. Add sugar and lemon juice; strain and set aside in cool place. Occasionally stir mixture until quite thick. Beat with egg beater until frothy; add egg whites. Continue beating until stiff enough to hold shape. Place in molding dish or pan and refrigerate.

VANILLA SAUCE:

1 c. sugar
3 egg yolks
½ tsp. salt
1 c. milk, heated
1 tsp. vanilla flavoring

Mix sugar, egg yolks and salt; beat with egg beater. Add hot milk. Cook in double boiler

(Continued on next page)

for 20 minutes; add vanilla. Chill; serve over pudding. Yield: 6 servings.

Mrs. Edmund B. Taylor
Norfolk, Va.

TWENTY-FOUR HOUR FRUIT DESSERT

1 sm. can crushed pineapple
1 sm. can sliced peaches
1 lge. can fruit cocktail
1 pkg. vanilla pudding mix
1 c. heavy cream, whipped
Sugar
1 pkg. miniature marshmallows

Drain fruits for 3 hours. Prepare pudding mix according to package directions; cool. Fold in whipped cream. Add small amount of sugar. Fold in fruits and marshmallows. Refrigerate for 24 hours. NOTE: Cherries and nuts may be added if desired. Yield: 10-12 servings.

Mrs. Ed Brown
Denbigh, N.D.

APPLE-BUTTER REFRIGERATOR ROLL

⅓ c. apple butter
1 c. heavy cream, whipped
15 vanilla wafers
½ c. chopped nuts

Fold apple butter gradually into whipped cream. Spread wafers with mixture; arrange in piles or form into roll. Cover top and sides with remaining filling. Sprinkle with chopped nuts; chill for 3 hours. Cut roll into diagonal slices; serve on individual plates. NOTE: For frozen roll, place roll in refrigerator tray; freeze for 3 hours. Slice as above. Use apricot or raspberry jam instead of apple butter. Add chopped Maraschino cherries. May use chocolate wafers or graham crackers instead of vanilla wafers. Yield: 4 servings.

Mrs. William E. Zielinski
Keyport, Wash.

CHOCOLATE ROLL

5 eggs, separated
¾ c. sugar
2 tbsp. (heaping) cocoa
¼ tsp. salt
1 tbsp. (heaping) flour
½ tsp. vanilla flavoring
1 c. heavy cream, whipped

Beat egg yolks until thick and lemon colored. Blend sugar, cocoa, salt and flour; add gradually to yolks, beating until smooth. Fold in stiffly beaten egg whites. Flavor with vanilla. Spread evenly in long shallow pan lined with buttered waxed paper. Bake at 350

degrees for 15 minutes or until firm. Turn onto cloth wrung out with water. Remove paper; roll up in damp towel. Cool; unroll and spread with sweetened whipped cream. Roll again.

SAUCE:
1 c. cocoa
1 c. sugar
½ c. boiling water

Mix cocoa and sugar. Thin with boiling water; cook for a few minutes. Serve warm over roll. Yield: 8 servings.

Mrs. George Fleeson
Fort Riley, Kans.

GRAHAM CRACKER-NUT ROLL

1 lb. graham crackers, finely rolled
1 lb. dates, finely chopped
1 lb. marshmallows, finely cut
1 lb. nuts, finely chopped
1 c. pineapple juice or cream

Mix all ingredients; shape into roll. Refrigerate. Slice; serve with whipped cream.

Mrs. Robert G. Frye
Syracuse, N.Y.

MARSHMALLOW ROLL

2 squares unsweetened chocolate
2 squares sweet chocolate
2 tsp. butter
1 ½ c. powdered sugar
1 egg, beaten
1 c. coconut
1 pkg. colored or white miniature marshmallows

Melt chocolate and butter in double boiler. Add powdered sugar, egg and coconut. Spread on waxed paper; put marshmallows on top. Roll up as jelly roll. Chill; slice. NOTE: This cuts well when frozen. Yield: 10 servings.

Mrs. John Vlasaty
Lidgerwood, N.D.

BOURBON SOUFFLE

8 eggs, separated
¾ c. bourbon
1 c. sugar
2 ½ envelopes gelatin
½ c. cold water

Combine well beaten yolks and bourbon. Combine stiffly beaten whites and sugar. Dissolve gelatin in cold water; heat in double boiler. Pour slowly over whites, beating constantly until mixture is like divinity. Fold yolks into whites. Pour into 2-quart mold;

(Continued on next page)

chill. Unmold; garnish with mint leaves and rose bloom. Yield: 10 servings.

Mrs. James A. Zimmerman
Fort Sam Houston, Tex.

COLD MANDARIN SOUFFLE

¼ c. plus 2 tbsp. sugar
1 envelope gelatin
4 eggs, separated
¾ c. tangerine or orange juice
2 tbsp. lemon juice
2 tsp. grated orange peel
1 c. heavy cream, whipped
Mandarin orange sections
Sweetened whipped cream

C o m b i n e 1/4 cup sugar and gelatin in saucepan. Blend in beaten egg yolks, tangerine and lemon juices. Cook and stir over low heat until gelatin dissolves and mixture thickens slightly. Stir in orange peel; cool to room temperature. Beat egg whites to soft peaks, gradually adding 2 tablespoons sugar. Beat to stiff peaks. Fold in gelatin mixture; fold in whipped cream. Pour into 5-cup mold; chill overnight until set. Unmold onto serving dish; garnish with Mandarin orange sections and sweetened whipped cream. Yield: 6-8 servings.

Mrs. John E. Clark
Pt. Mugo, Calif.

MINT SOUFFLE WITH MELON BALLS

1 pkg. lime gelatin
1 c. hot water
1 c. cold water
Oil of peppermint or mint flavoring
Watermelon balls
Honeydew balls

Dissolve gelatin in hot water. Add cold water and a few drops of oil of peppermint to flavor delicately. Chill until it begins to thicken; beat with egg beater until frothy and thick. Pour into ring mold which has been rinsed with cold water but not dried. Chill until firm. Unmold; fill center or serve with watermelon and honeydew balls. Garnish with fresh mint. NOTE: Unhulled strawberries may be used instead of melon balls. Yield: 8 servings.

Mrs. John J. Hilton, Jr.
Glynco, Ga.

CHOCOLATE SPONGE

4 eggs, separated
1 c. sugar
2 squares unsweetened chocolate, melted
1 ½ tsp. gelatin
1 tbsp. cold water
5 tbsp. boiling water

Beat egg yolks until light; add sugar. Beat again; add chocolate. Soften gelatin in cold water; add boiling water. Mix with chocolate mixture; beat v i g o r o u s l y. Fold in stiffly beaten egg whites; chill until set. Serve with whipped cream. Yield: 6 servings.

Mrs. Bryan Gruver, Jr.
Fort Devens, Mass.

POPPY SEED TORTE

CRUST:
1 c. graham cracker crumbs
1 c. flour
½ c. butter, melted
½ c. chopped nuts

Combine all ingredients; press into 9 x 13-inch pan. Bake at 325 degrees for 10 to 15 minutes or until light brown.

FILLING:
1 ½ c. milk
5 eggs, separated
1 ½ c. sugar
2 tbsp. cornstarch
¼ c. poppy seed
¼ tsp. salt
1 ½ tbsp. unflavored gelatin
¼ c. cold water
½ tsp. vanilla flavoring
½ tsp. cream of tartar

Combine milk, egg yolks, 1 cup sugar and cornstarch; cook in double boiler until thick. Remove from heat; add poppy seed and salt. Cool. Dissolve gelatin in cold water; stir into custard until dissolved. Beat egg whites, vanilla and cream of tartar until stiff; fold into custard. Pour over graham crust; refrigerate until set. Serve plain or with whipped cream.

Coralie Lemcke
Middleton, Wisc.

BUTTER SQUARES

1 lb. butter
1 ½ c. sugar
2 tsp. vanilla flavoring
1 lb. vanilla wafers, finely crumbled
6 eggs
Whipped cream (opt.)

Cream butter and sugar for 10 minutes. Add vanilla; beat well. Beat eggs until light; add slowly to creamed mixture. Put one-half of crumbs into bottom of 10-inch square pan. Spread butter mixture evenly over crumbs. Cover with remaining crumbs; chill. Cut into squares; top with whipped cream. Yield: 8 servings.

Mrs. Jack Silmser
Massena, N.Y.

CHOCOLATE-NUT CRUNCH

½ lb. sweet chocolate or 1 ½ to 2 pkg.
   chocolate pieces
2 ½ tsp. water
4 eggs, separated
6 tsp. confectioners sugar
1 c. chopped nuts
½ pt. heavy cream, whipped
Crushed vanilla wafers or graham crackers

Melt chocolate in double boiler; add water. Blend well. Remove from heat; add egg yolks, beating vigorously until blended. Add confectioners sugar and nuts; blend. Fold in stiffly beaten egg whites and whipped cream. Sprinkle crumbs in bottom of 8 x 10-inch pan; pour in chocolate mixture. Chill for 24 to 48 hours. Yield: 6-8 servings.

Mrs. Malcolm A. Moore
Newburgh, N.Y.

GRAPE REFRIGERATOR DESSERT

1 pt. grape juice
½ c. instant tapioca
1 c. sugar
1 c. crushed pineapple
1 tsp. vanilla flavoring
1 tsp. orange juice
Vanilla wafers

Mix grape juice, tapioca and sugar. Let stand for 5 to 10 minutes. Cook until tapioca is softened and mixture is thickened; cool. Add pineapple, vanilla and orange juice. Arrange wafers in a pan; add tapioca mixture. Chill. Yield: 6-8 servings.

Mrs. Ruth Hartzler
Haven, Kans.

HONEY-LEMON BISQUE

1 ⅔ c. evaporated milk
1 3-oz. pkg. lemon gelatin
1 ¼ c. boiling water
⅓ c. honey
⅛ tsp. salt
3 tbsp. lemon juice
Grated rind of 1 lemon
2 ½ c. vanilla wafer crumbs

Chill evaporated milk overnight. Dissolve gelatin in boiling water. Add honey, salt, lemon juice and rind. Chill until mixture is slightly congealed. Whip milk until stiff; add gelatin mixture. Spread one-half of the wafer crumbs in 10 x 13 1/2-inch pan; pour in lemon mixture. Top with remaining crumbs. Chill for 3 hours. Cut into squares to serve. Yield: 15-18 servings.

Mrs. Charles W. Brown
Santa Maria, Calif.

LEMON BISQUE

1 pkg. lemon gelatin
1 ⅓ c. hot water
½ c. sugar
½ tsp. salt
3 tbsp. lemon juice
1 tsp. grated lemon rind
1 sm. can evaporated milk
2 c. vanilla wafer crumbs

Dissolve gelatin in water. Add sugar, salt, lemon juice and rind; congeal slightly. Stir and scrape bottom of bowl. Chill milk until it freezes around edge of tray; whip until stiff. Add to gelatin mixture; mix well. Spread one-half of the crumbs in large pan. Pour mixture in; top with remaining crumbs. Chill for 3 hours or longer. Yield: 6 servings.

Mrs. Betty R. Kuhns
Staten Island, N.Y.

LEMON FLUFF

1 pkg. lemon gelatin
1 ¾ c. water
1 ⅔ c. evaporated milk, chilled
1 c. sugar
¼ c. lemon juice
1 lge. pkg. vanilla wafers, crushed

Combine gelatin and water; let set until syrupy. Whip milk until stiff; add sugar and lemon juice. Fold in gelatin mixture. Line 9 x 12 x 2-inch pan with crushed wafers; pour cream mixture over crumbs. Refrigerate until set. Cut into squares and serve.

Letitia G. Thompson
Green River, Utah

MARSHMALLOW-FRUIT DESSERT

1 lb. marshmallows
1 c. milk
1 pt. heavy cream, whipped
1 sm. can pineapple
1 sm. bottle Marschino cherries, chopped
Chopped nuts
Vanilla wafer or graham cracker crumbs

Melt marshmallows with milk in double boiler; cool. Add whipped cream, pineapple, cherries and nuts. Spread crumbs in dish; cover with fruit mixture. Top with crumbs. Chill for 1 hour. Yield: 6 servings.

Mrs. Norman Teten
Talmage, Nebr.

PINEAPPLE DELIGHT

1 lb. vanilla wafers
½ c. butter
1 ½ c. powdered sugar
2 eggs
1 med. can crushed pineapple, drained
1 c. heavy cream, whipped

(Continued on next page)

Grind vanilla wafers; put one-half of wafers into bottom of greased 10 x 14-inch pan. Cream butter, sugar and eggs; pour over wafers. Mix pineapple and whipped cream; spread over egg mixture. Cover with remaining crumbs; refrigerate for 24 hours. Serve with whipped cream topping; trim with a cherry if desired.

Mrs. B. L. Feaster
St. Petersburg, Fla.

PINEAPPLE FLUFF

1 No. 2 can crushed pineapple
1 ⅔ c. evaporated milk
1 pkg. lemon gelatin
1 ½ c. hot water
½ to ¾ c. sugar
2 ½ c. vanilla wafer crumbs

Drain pineapple, reserving liquid. Chill milk for 3 to 4 hours. Dissolve gelatin in hot water; add enough water to pineapple liquid to make 1/2 cup. Add liquid to gelatin; chill until partially set. Whip gelatin until light and fluffy, adding sugar gradually. Whip milk; fold into gelatin. Fold in pineapple. Line bottom of pan with part of wafer crumbs; spread gelatin mixture over crumbs. Spread remaining crumbs over top. Chill until firm. Cut into squares; top each square with a cherry. Yield: 12 servings.

Mrs. Olive Clark
Plain City, O.

PINEAPPLE ICEBOX SQUARES

1 ½ c. confectioners sugar
½ c. butter
2 tbsp. lemon juice
2 eggs
½ lb. vanilla wafers, finely crumbled
1 9-oz. can crushed pineapple, drained
1 c. cream, whipped
Chopped nuts

Cream sugar and butter well. Add lemon juice to eggs; beat lightly. Blend into creamed mixture. Spread one-half of the wafer crumbs in an 8-inch square dish. Pour creamed mixture over crumbs. Fold pineapple into whipped cream; spread over creamed mixture. Top with remaining crumbs; sprinkle with nuts. Chill overnight. Yield: 8 servings.

Mrs. George G. Herck
Syosset, N.Y.

SNOWBALLS

1 lb. apricots
1 to 1 ½ c. brown sugar
1 8-oz. pkg. almonds, finely ground
1 pt. heavy cream
1 tsp. vanilla or almond flavoring
Sugar to taste
1 box vanilla wafers
2 pkg. flaked coconut

Combine apricots and brown sugar; cook to jam consistency. Blend in almonds; refrigerate for three days. Whip cream with flavoring and sugar. Spread apricot mixture between vanilla wafers, sandwich-style, using four wafers per stack. Ice generously with whipped cream; coat heavily with coconut. Place in container; cover tightly. Refrigerate for 24 hours before serving.

Mrs. Roy F. Claytor
Grand Forks AFB, N.D.

SNOWBALLS

½ c. butter
½ c. sugar
2 eggs, separated
1 c. crushed pineapple, well drained
1 c. chopped nuts
64 vanilla wafers
1 pt. heavy cream, whipped
1 tsp. vanilla flavoring
Coconut

Cream butter and sugar; add egg yolks, pineapple and nuts. Add stiffly beaten egg whites. Spread between wafers; stack four wafers high. Refrigerate for 24 hours. Spread with whipped cream flavored with vanilla. Roll or sprinkle with coconut. NOTE: Tint coconut yellow, green and pink for Easter. Yield: 16 servings.

Ann Gher
Columbus, Nebr.

WHANG DOODLE

⅔ lb. vanilla wafers, ground
¼ lb. butter
2 c. sifted powdered sugar
2 eggs, separated
1 tsp. vanilla flavoring
½ pt. heavy cream
1 No. 2 can crushed pineapple, well drained
1 sm. bottle Maraschino cherries, chopped

Sprinkle one-half of the wafer crumbs on bottom of 8 x 10-inch baking dish. Mix creamed butter, powdered sugar and egg yolks; beat until light. Add beaten egg whites and vanilla. Spread mixture over crumbs. Whip cream; add pineapple and cherries. Spread over first layer. Sprinkle with remaining crumbs. Refrigerate for 12 to 24 hours. NOTE: Do not freeze. Yield: 8-10 servings.

Mrs. Richard E. Knapp
Denver, Colo.

Jiffy Desserts

RECIPE FOR MOCK INDIAN PUDDING ON PAGE 303

APPLE CAKE

2 c. peeled chopped apples
1 c. sugar
1 c. flour
1 tsp. cinnamon
1 tsp. baking soda
1 egg, beaten
1 c. chopped nuts
1 tsp. vanilla flavoring

Mix apples and sugar; let stand for 15 minutes. Sift flour, cinnamon and baking soda. Add beaten egg to apple mixture; add flour mixture. Add nuts and vanilla. Pour into 8-inch glass baking dish. Bake at 325 degrees for 30 minutes. Serve with ice cream or whipped cream. Yield: 8 servings.

Mrs. W. K. Ramm
Seattle, Wash.

CHOCOLATE FUDGE CAKE

½ pkg. cake mix
⅛ c. cocoa
½ c. brown sugar
1 c. hot water

Prepare cake mix according to package directions. Pour into 9 x 12-inch pan; sprinkle with cocoa and brown sugar. Pour hot water over mixture. Bake at 350 degrees for 22 minutes. Serve warm with whipped cream or ice cream. Yield: 8 servings.

Sister M. Luke, O.S.B.
Salem, S.D.

EASY FRUIT CAKE

1 ¼ c. sugar
2 c. flour
1 ¼ tsp. soda
¼ tsp. salt
2 c. fruit with juice
2 eggs

Mix all dry ingredients; make a hole in dry ingredients. Add fruit, juice and eggs. Beat well; put into floured pan. Bake at 375 degrees for 40 minutes. NOTE: Topping of 1 cup brown sugar and 1/2 cup nuts may be added before baking if desired. Fruit may be fruit cocktail, cooked apples, peaches, rhubarb or leftovers. Yield: 18 servings.

Mrs. John Lidmila
Platteville, Colo.

QUICK FRUIT CAKE

1 egg, beaten
1 c. sugar
½ tsp. salt
1 tsp. soda

1 tsp. vanilla flavoring
½ tsp. almond flavoring
1 c. sifted flour
1 No. 303 can fruit cocktail
½ c. brown sugar
½ c. chopped nuts

Mix all ingredients except brown sugar and nuts. Turn batter into greased 9-inch square pan. Sprinkle with brown sugar and nuts. Bake at 350 degrees for 40 minutes. Serve warm or cool, topped with whipped cream. Yield: 9 servings.

Mrs. Bessie Short
Macdoel, Calif.

FRUIT COCKTAIL CAKE

2 c. flour
2 c. sugar
2 tsp. soda
½ tsp. salt
2 eggs, beaten slightly
2 cans. No. 303 fruit cocktail
Brown sugar

Mix dry ingredients; add eggs and fruit cocktail. Pour into greased 9 x 13 x 2-inch pan; sprinkle with brown sugar. Bake at 350 degrees for 30 to 35 minutes. Serve with whipped cream. Yield: 10 large servings.

Mrs. Clarence Wasinger
Mankato, Minn.

LEMON GELATIN CAKE

¾ c. cooking oil
¾ c. water
4 eggs
1 box lemon gelatin
1 box yellow cake mix

Beat oil, water and eggs. Mix gelatin and cake mix; add to egg mixture. Beat. Pour into hot greased and floured oblong pan. Bake at 350 degrees for 20 to 25 minutes. When done, prick top of hot cake with toothpick; pour on glaze.

GLAZE:
½ c. lemon juice
2 c. confectioners sugar

Combine ingredients; pour over hot cake. Yield: 14 servings.

Mrs. Donald Cain
McCrory, Ark.

SLAPPED TOGETHER CAKE

1 egg, beaten
1 c. sugar
1 c. flour

(Continued on next page)

1 tsp. soda
1 tsp. vanilla flavoring
1 sm. can fruit cocktail, drained
1 c. brown sugar
½ c. pecans

Mix all ingredients except fruit, brown sugar and pecans. Add fruit; mix well. Pour into greased and floured 8 or 9-inch pan. Sprinkle brown sugar and pecans on top. Bake at 350 degrees for 45 minutes. Yield: 16 servings.

Mrs. Orval R. Krone
Edwards AFB, Calif.

WACKY CAKE

1 ½ c. cake flour
1 c. sugar
3 tbsp. cocoa
1 tsp. soda
½ tsp. salt
6 tbsp. cooking oil or melted shortening
1 tbsp. vinegar
1 tsp. vanilla flavoring
1 c. cold water

Sift flour with sugar, cocoa, soda and salt. Put mixture into 8-inch square baking dish. Make one large, one medium and one small hole in dry ingredients. Pour oil into the large hole, vinegar into medium hole and vanilla into small hole. Pour water over all; mix well with a fork. Bake at 350 degrees for 25 minutes. When cake is cool frost it in baking dish. Yield: 6 servings.

Mrs. C. V. Davis
Chapel Hill, N.C.

ZWIEBACK CAKE

2 eggs
1 c. sugar
1 c. rolled zwieback
1 c. chopped nuts
1 ½ tsp. baking powder
1 tbsp. flour
½ tsp. almond flavoring
Apricot or berry jam
Whipped cream

Beat eggs and sugar. Combine remaining ingredients except jam and whipped cream; add to egg mixture. Place in 9-inch square baking pan. Bake at 350 degrees for 25 minutes. Top with jam and whipped cream. Yield: 9 servings.

Mrs. Richard H. Sproule
Vallejo, Calif.

SEVEN LAYER WONDERS

1 stick margarine, melted
1 c. graham cracker crumbs
1 c. flaked coconut

1 c. chocolate pieces
1 c. butterscotch pieces
1 c. chopped nuts
1 can sweetened condensed milk

Pour margarine into 9 x 13-inch pan; cover with alternate layers of graham cracker crumbs, coconut, chocolate pieces, butterscotch pieces and nuts. Spoon condensed milk over nuts. Bake at 325 degrees for 25 minutes. Cool and cut into small squares.

Carmen E. Jones
Perry, Iowa

FILLED ANGEL FOOD CAKE

1 10-in. angel food cake
1 pkg. instant chocolate pudding
½ pt. heavy cream, whipped

Slice cake horizontally into four layers. Prepare pudding, using one-half amount of liquid called for on package. Fold one-half of whipped cream into pudding mixture. Spread between layers, reserving one-third of pudding mixture. Add remaining whipped cream. Frost top and sides of cake with remaining pudding mixture. Refrigerate until ready to serve. Yield: 12-16 servings.

Mrs. Virgil A. Ganz
Fort Polk, La.

BAKED ALASKA

4 egg whites
¼ tsp. cream of tartar
½ c. sugar
½ tsp. vanilla flavoring
1 pt. ice cream
1 cake layer

Beat egg whites with cream of tartar until stiff but not dry. Gradually beat in sugar until whites stand in peaks. Add vanilla. Spoon ice cream on cake. Cover with meringue. Bake at 450 degrees for 5 minutes. Serve at once. Yield: 8 servings.

Mrs. D. M. Anderson
Davison, Mich.

BANANA-CREAM CAKE

1 angel food cake
2 pkg. banana cream instant pudding mix
2 c. cold milk
1 c. heavy cream, whipped
1 banana, sliced

Split angel food cake to make four layers. Add pudding mix to cold milk; beat slowly for

(Continued on next page)

1 minute. Let stand for 2 minutes; fold into whipped cream. Spread between layers and on top; chill. Place sliced bananas on top. Yield: 12 servings.

Mrs. Thomas C. Piddington
Fort Jay, Governors Island, N.Y.

BANANA DELIGHT

1 pound cake
2 lge. bananas
1 pkg. vanilla pudding mix
4 Maraschino cherries

Slice cake into four equal parts. Cut bananas into four lengthwise slices; place on cake slices. Prepare pudding according to package directions. Chill slightly. Spoon pudding over cake and bananas. Place cherries on top; serve. Yield: 4 servings.

Mrs. Gwendolyn Mathews
Daytona Beach, Fla.

KING RICHARD'S CAKE

1 angel food cake
½ pt. heavy cream
¼ c. sugar
½ tsp. vanilla flavoring
Crushed peanut brittle

Place cake on large sheet of waxed paper. Whip cream until stiff; fold in sugar and vanilla. Ice cake with mixture. Sprinkle iced cake with peanut brittle. Collect from waxed paper loose brittle which does not stick; sprinkle again over cake. Repeat until icing is thoroughly coated with brittle. Refrigerate cake until served. Yield: 8 servings.

Mrs. Cyril P. Williams
Sidney, Nebr.

ORANGE-CHEESE CAKE

1 11-oz. can Mandarin oranges
1 7-in. frozen cream cheese cake
4 tsp. cornstarch
½ c. orange juice

Drain oranges, reserving liquid. Let frozen cheese cake stand at room temperature as label directs. Pour 1/2 cup liquid from Mandarin oranges into saucepan; stir in cornstarch. Add orange juice; cook until thickened. Chill sauce and oranges. Garnish cheese cake with oranges; spoon sauce over all.

Mrs. Whittier G. Davis
Pearl Harbor, Hawaii

APPLE QUICKIE

1 17-oz. can sliced apples
¾ c. sugar
½ tsp. cinnamon
½ tbsp. butter
½ box yellow cake mix

Spread apples into buttered baking dish; sprinkle with sugar and cinnamon. Dot with butter. Spread dry cake mix over top; press gently with fingertips. Bake at 375 degrees for 30 minutes. Serve warm or cold with or without whipped cream or ice cream. Yield: 6 servings.

Mrs. Bernard Cotner
Arlington, O.

BUTTER-PECAN-FRUIT RING

½ c. pecans
¼ c. butter
½ c. brown sugar
1 white cake mix
1 c. heavy cream
3 tbsp. powdered sugar
1 tsp. vanilla flavoring
2 ½ c. cut up fruit

Break pecans and butter into greased 10-inch mold; sprinkle with sugar. Prepare cake mix according to package directions; place on top. Bake at 350 degrees for 35 to 40 minutes. Remove at once; cool. Whip cream; add powdered sugar and vanilla. Fold in fruit; pile mixture into center of cake ring. Serve. Yield: 12-14 servings.

Eunice M. Steiner
Bangor, Wisc.

CHERRY-CREAM CRUMB

1 jar prepared cherries
1 9-in. prepared pie shell
1 sm. box white cake mix
¼ c. sugar
¼ c. flour
3 tbsp. margarine

Pour cherries into pie shell. Bake at 425 degrees for 15 minutes. Add cake mix. Combine all remaining ingredients; sprinkle mixture on top. Bake at 350 degrees for 45 minutes. Yield: 8 servings.

Mrs. Floyd R. Cox
Orlando, Fla.

QUICK AND EASY CHERRY CRUNCH

1 can cherry pie filling
1 tsp. lemon juice (opt.)
1 c. white cake mix
½ stick butter, melted

(Continued on next page)

Pour cherry pie filling into 9-inch pie plate; sprinkle lemon juice over filling. Sprinkle cake mix on top; drizzle with butter. Bake at 325 to 350 degrees for 30 to 45 minutes. Serve warm with vanilla ice cream or whipped cream. Yield: 6 servings.

Mrs. James W. Twaddell, Jr.
Madison, Wisc.

QUICK LEMON CAKE

1 pkg. lemon cake mix
4 eggs
¾ c. water
¾ c. salad oil
Juice of 2 lemons
Grated rind of 2 lemons
1 stick butter, melted
2 c. powdered sugar

Blend cake mix, eggs, water and oil. Pour into angel cake pan. Bake at 350 degrees for 40 minutes or until done. While hot carefully remove from pan and place on cake plate. Mix lemon juice, lemon rind, butter and powdered sugar. Spoon over cake and allow to soak in. NOTE: Cake freezes well. Yield: 12 servings.

Mrs. Le Roy G. Miller
Vandenburg AFB, Calif.

APPLE COBBLER

1 stick butter
1 c. sugar
1 c. flour
2 tsp. baking powder
½ c. milk
1 tsp. salt
1 can pie fruit

Melt butter in 9 x 5 x 2 3/4-inch loaf pan. Combine remaining ingredients except fruit. More milk may be added if necessary. Pour batter over butter; add fruit. Bake at 350 degrees for 30 to 40 minutes or until crust is golden brown. Yield: 6-8 servings.

Mrs. Patrick T. Donohue
Point Arena AES, Calif.

QUICK APPLE COBBLER

2 c. applesauce
½ c. seedless raisins (opt.)
½ c. light brown sugar
½ c. chopped walnuts
½ tsp. cinnamon
¼ tsp. nutmeg
1 c. biscuit mix
½ c. sugar
¼ c. butter

Combine applesauce, raisins, brown sugar, walnuts, cinnamon and nutmeg. Pour into greased 9-inch pie pan. Combine biscuit mix and sugar; cut in butter. Sprinkle evenly over apple mixture. Bake at 400 degrees for 25 to 30 minutes. Serve warm or cold with cream. Yield: 5-6 servings.

Mrs. John Wolf
Eustis, Nebr.

CHERRY COBBLER

1 c. prepared biscuit mix
1 tbsp. cooking oil
1 tbsp. sugar
½ c. milk
1 No. 2 can cherries
1 c. sugar

Mix prepared biscuit mix, oil, sugar and milk. Pour into pie plate. Pour cherries over batter; sprinkle with sugar. Bake at 350 degrees for 30 minutes. Serve plain or with whipped cream. Yield: 8 servings.

Mrs. Sherrill Williams
Licking, Mo.

MODERN CHERRY COBBLER

1 can red pie cherries
1 can cherry pie filling
½ to 1 tsp. red food coloring
1 pkg. white cake mix
1 stick butter, melted

Mix cherries, pie filling and coloring in 9 x 12 or 13-inch cake pan. Spread evenly in bottom of pan. Cover with dry cake mix. Dribble butter over mixture. Bake at 350 degrees for 20 to 30 minutes. Serve with whipped cream or ice cream. Yield: 12 servings.

Mrs. R. B. Jarnagin
Pearl Harbor, Hawaii

QUICK AND EASY CHERRY COBBLER

1 stick butter
1 c. sugar
1 c. flour
1 c. milk
1 tsp. baking powder
1 can cherry pie filling

Melt butter in baking dish. Combine sugar, flour, milk and baking powder; pour into baking dish. Place cherries on top of batter. Bake at 350 degrees for 25 minutes. Yield: 8 servings.

Mrs. Henry M. Best
Roanoke Rapids, N.C.

FRUIT COBBLER

1 c. flour
1 c. sugar

(Continued on next page)

1 tsp. baking powder
1 c. milk
¼ lb. melted butter
1 No. 303 can fruit

Mix all dry ingredients. Add milk and butter. Pour into 8 x 10-inch pan. Add fruit. Bake at 350 degrees until golden brown. Yield: 6 servings.

Barbara Cuthbert
Flagler, Colo.

QUICK FRUIT COBBLER

3 tbsp. butter or margarine
½ c. flour
1 tbsp. baking powder
¼ tsp. salt
½ c. milk or cream
2 c. fruit
¾ c. sugar
2 tbsp. water

Melt butter in baking dish. Combine flour, baking powder, salt and milk; pour over butter. Cook fruit with 1/2 cup sugar and water. Pour over flour mixture. Sprinkle with remaining sugar. Bake at 400 degrees for 30 minutes. Yield: 4 servings.

Flo Igo
McCamey, Tex.

PEACH COBBLER

½ stick margarine
¾ c. flour
¾ c. sugar
¾ c. milk
1 lge. can peaches or other fruit

Melt margarine in 1 1/2-quart dish. Mix flour, sugar and milk. Pour into melted margarine. Do not stir. Add fruit. Do not stir. Bake at 350 degrees for 45 minutes. Top with ice cream; serve hot. Yield: 5 servings.

Mrs. Ronald H. Holmes
Cape Charles AFS, Va.

BANANA-FUDGE COOKIES

1 ripe banana
1 egg
2 tbsp. water
1 pkg. chocolate cake mix
1 c. chocolate pieces

Mash banana; add egg, water and cake mix. Mix thoroughly; mix in chocolate pieces. Drop by spoonfuls onto cookie sheet. Bake at 350 degrees for 10 minutes. NOTE: For variety, mint chocolate pieces or 1/2 teaspoon mint flavoring may be added. Yield: 3 dozen cookies.

Betty Welty
Gervais, Oreg.

QUICK BROWNIES

24 graham crackers, crushed
1 c. chopped black walnuts
½ pkg. chocolate pieces
1 tsp. vanilla flavoring
1 can sweetened condensed milk

Thoroughly mix all ingredients. Bake in 325 degree oven for 25 minutes. Cut into squares. Yield: 18 squares.

Mrs. Helen Gugliotta
Dilliner, Pa.

QUICK AND EASY BROWNIES AND FROSTING

1 c. sugar
1 stick margarine
4 eggs
1 c. unsifted flour
1 1-lb. can chocolate syrup
½ c. chopped nuts

Cream sugar, margarine and eggs; add flour, syrup and nuts. Pour into greased and floured pan. Bake at 350 degrees for 30 minutes; cool.

FROSTING:
1 ½ c. sugar
6 tbsp. margarine
6 tbsp. milk
½ c. chocolate pieces

Combine sugar, margarine and milk; boil for 30 seconds. Remove from heat; add chocolate pieces. Beat until melted; frost brownies.

Mrs. Harold Hilpipre
Elmore, Minn.

BUTTERSCOTCH BARS

½ c. melted butter
2 c. brown sugar
2 eggs
2 tsp. vanilla flavoring
1 c. flour
2 tsp. baking powder
1 tsp. salt
1 c. chopped nuts

Combine butter and sugar; add eggs and vanilla. Add dry ingredients and nuts. Mix well; pour into greased 11 x 17-inch pan. Bake at 350 degrees for 20 to 25 minutes. Cut into 1 x 2 1/2-inch bars while still warm. Yield: 40 bars.

Mrs. Ed Williams
West Columbia, Tex.

CHOCOLATE-WHEAT GERM BARS

2 c. graham cracker crumbs
¼ c. wheat germ
1 6-oz. pkg. chocolate pieces
1 15-oz. can sweetened condensed milk
1 tsp. vanilla flavoring

Mix all ingredients; spread mixture evenly in greased 8-inch pan. Bake at 350 degrees for 30 to 35 minutes. Cool; cut into bars or small squares. Yield: 16 bars.

Mrs. Eileen Krody
Bethel, O.

DATE BALLS

1 c. melted margarine or butter
1 ½ c. sugar
2 c. chopped dates
2 tbsp. milk
2 eggs
1 tsp. salt
1 tsp. vanilla flavoring
4 c. Rice Krispies
1 c. chopped walnuts
Coconut

Combine butter and sugar; stir until melted. Add dates. Cook until well done. Remove from heat; add milk, eggs, salt and vanilla. Boil for 2 minutes; remove from heat. Add Krispies and nuts; cool. Shape into balls; roll in coconuts. Yield: 36 servings.

Mrs. E. F. Sandleback
Dodgeville, Wisc.

DATE-NUT BARS

4 eggs
1 c. sugar
1 tsp. vanilla flavoring
1 c. flour
1 tsp. baking powder
½ tsp. salt
6 c. finely cut dates
2 c. chopped nuts

Beat eggs; add sugar and vanilla. Beat until thick. Fold in dry ingredients. Pour mixture over dates and nuts; mix lightly. Spread in well greased 9 x 13 x 2-inch pan. Bake at 325 to 350 degrees for 25 to 30 minutes or until top springs back when touched. Cut while warm; cool and remove from pan. NOTE: Do not pack dates when measuring. If desired 1/2 cup sugar plus 1/2 cup honey may be substituted for 1 cup sugar. Yield: 36 servings.

Mrs. Carl Faulkner
Yuma, Ariz.

GOLDEN BARS

1 ½ c. sifted cake flour
2 tsp. baking powder
¼ tsp. salt
⅔ c. shortening, melted
2 c. brown sugar
2 eggs
1 tsp. vanilla flavoring
⅔ c. chopped nuts

Sift flour with baking powder and salt. Combine shortening and sugar in saucepan; add sifted ingredients, mixing well. Add an egg at a time, beating well; add vanilla and nuts. Spread in 9 x 12-inch pan. Bake at 350 degrees for 30 minutes. Cool; cut into 2 x 1-inch bars. NOTE: Do not bake in shallow pan. Yield: 4 dozen.

Mrs. Margaret C. Swanson
Erwin, N.C.

GRAHAM CRACKER BARS

2 eggs, beaten
⅔ c. butter
1 c. sugar
1 tsp. vanilla flavoring
3 c. crushed graham crackers
2 ½ c. miniature marshmallows
½ c. nuts
½ c. coconut

Mix eggs, butter and sugar. Heat until butter is melted. Add vanilla; cool. Pour over remaining ingredients; mix well. Pat into 8 x 10-inch pan. Cut into bars; refrigerate. Yield: 24-27 servings.

Hildegarde Anderson
Leal, N.D.

NO-BAKE COOKIES

½ lb. margarine
4 c. sugar
6 to 8 tbsp. cocoa
1 c. milk
6 c. oats
1 c. peanut butter
2 tbsp. vanilla flavoring
1 c. coconut(opt.)

Combine margarine, sugar, cocoa and milk in saucepan; cook for 1 minute. Bring to a full boil. Mix oats, peanut butter, vanilla and coconut in large bowl. Cool first mixture for 30 minutes; pour over second mixture. Blend well; drop by teaspoonfuls onto waxed paper. Yield: 3 dozen.

Mrs. Alfred E. Statzer
Norwalk, O.

NO-BAKE FUDGE COOKIES

4 c. sugar
¾ cocoa
1 c. milk
¼ lb. butter
1 c. peanut butter
6 c. oats

(Continued on next page)

Mix sugar, cocoa and milk; boil for 1 minute. Remove from heat; add butter and peanut butter. Stir until melted; stir in oats. Drop from teaspoon onto waxed paper; cool. Yield: 5 dozen.

Mrs. Charles Kalous
Cincinnati, O.

NO-BAKE OATMEAL COOKIES

2 c. sugar
3 tbsp. cocoa
1 stick margarine
½ c. milk
½ c. peanut butter
3 c. quick cooking oats
1 tsp. vanilla flavoring

Mix sugar, cocoa, margarine and milk; boil for 1 minute. Remove from heat; add at once all remaining ingredients. Stir well; drop onto waxed paper. Yield: 3 dozen cookies.

Mrs. Elmer J. Riehl
Canfield, O.

OATMEAL COOKIES

½ c. butter
2 c. sugar
⅓ c. cocoa
½ c. milk
1 tsp. vanilla flavoring
3 c. oats

Mix butter, sugar, cocoa and milk; boil hard for 1 minute. Remove from heat; add vanilla and oats. Drop by spoonfuls onto waxed paper. NOTE: One-third cup peanut butter may be added if desired.

Mrs. Wallace Gilliam
Lexington, Tenn.

OATMEAL CRISPIES

1 c. shortening
1 c. sugar
1 c. brown sugar
2 eggs, well beaten
1 tsp. vanilla flavoring
1 ½ c. sifted flour
1 tsp. salt
1 tsp. soda
3 c. oats
½ c. coconut or nuts

Cream shortening and sugars; add eggs and vanilla. Beat well. Add sifted flour, salt and soda. Mix in oats and coconut. Bake at 350 degrees for 10 minutes. Yield: 40 servings.

Mrs. Alyce Holton
Delmont, S.D.

PEANUT CLUSTERS

1 6-oz. pkg. chocolate pieces
1 6-oz. pkg. caramel pieces
1 3-oz. can Chinese noodles
1 7 to 8-oz. can skinless salted peanuts

Melt chocolate and caramel pieces in top of double boiler. Add Chinese noodles and peanuts; blend well. Remove from heat but keep mixture over hot water; drop by teaspoonfuls onto waxed paper. Cool. Yield: 30-36 servings.

Mrs. Elsie D. Smith
Pomeroy, O.

PRESTO PEANUT BARS

½ c. light corn syrup
¼ c. brown sugar
Dash of salt
1 pkg. butterscotch pieces
½ c. peanut butter
2 c. Rice Krispies
1 c. corn flakes

Bring syrup, brown sugar and salt just to a boil. Remove from heat; quickly add all remaining ingredients. Stir briefly; spread in buttered pan. Cut into bars. Yield: 20 bars.

Mrs. Ken Elliott
Kewanee, Ill.

TOFFEE BARS

1 c. butter or margarine
1 c. brown sugar
1 tsp. vanilla flavoring
2 c. sifted flour
1 c. chocolate pieces
1 c. chopped walnuts

Mix all ingredients in order listed; press mixture into 9 x 13-inch loaf pan. Bake at 350 degrees for 25 minutes. Do not overbake. Cut into bars while warm. Yield: 30 servings.

Mrs. Norman C. Robb
Missoula, Mont.

QUICK ICE CREAM

1 ⅔ c. evaporated milk, chilled
½ c. sugar
1 sm. can concentrated lemon or orange juice

Whip chilled milk to fluff; add sugar and fruit juice. Place in freezer tray; freeze. Yield: 4-6 servings.

Idilla I. Alfson
Woonsocket, S.D.

STINGER PARFAIT

4 oz. creme de menthe
1 pt. vanilla ice cream
4 oz. creme de cacao

Pour 1/2 ounce creme de menthe into bottom of parfait glass; spoon in part of ice cream. Add 1/2 ounce creme de cacao; add layer of ice cream. Repeat layers until glass is full. Put in freezer until serving time. Yield: 4 servings.

Mrs. Francis Beitzer
Yorktown, Va.

BANANA-CREAM PIE

1 pkg. graham cracker crumbs
1 pkg. instant vanilla pudding mix
1 lge. banana

Make graham cracker crust according to directions on cracker crumb package, reserving 2 tablespoons crumbs for topping. Place crust in refrigerator to chill. Prepare pudding according to directions on package. Slice banana into pie crust. Pour in pudding; sprinkle with reserved crumbs. Chill for a few minutes. Yield: 1 pie.

Mrs. Dewey Worden
Robstown, Tex.

QUICK AND EASY CHOCOLATE ICEBOX PIE

1 pkg. instant chocolate pudding
1 c. milk
1 pt. vanilla ice cream, cut into chunks
1 baked 9-in. pie crust
1 c. heavy cream, whipped

Beat pudding and milk with electric mixer; add ice cream. Pour into baked pie shell; top with whipped cream. Refrigerate. Yield: 6 servings.

Mrs. Walter C. Lane
Memphis, Tenn.

QUICK AND EASY CHOCOLATE PIE

2 pkg. chocolate pudding
1 square unsweetened chocolate
¼ tsp. salt
1 qt. milk
4 egg yolks, slightly beaten
2 tbsp. butter
½ tsp. vanilla flavoring
1 8 or 9-in. baked pie shell

Combine chocolate pudding, chocolate, salt and milk; cook to a boil. Slowly add chocolate mixture to egg yolks. Cook for 2 minutes, stirring constantly. Add butter and vanilla; continue stirring until butter is melted and blended. Pour immediately into pie shell. Cool before refrigerating. Yield: 8 servings.

Mrs. Ralph B. Wager
Virginia Beach, Va.

CREME DE MENTHE PIE

20 marshmallows
¼ c. milk
12 chocolate cookies
2 tbsp. margarine, melted
½ pt. heavy cream, whipped
8 tsp. creme de menthe
Pinch of salt

Melt marshmallows in milk; cool. Crush cookies with rolling pin. Sprinkle three-fourths of the crumbs into lightly greased pie plate. Pour melted margarine over cookie crumbs. Whip cream; fold in marshmallows, creme de menthe and salt. Spoon mixture into pie pan. Sprinkle remaining crumbs on top. Store in freezer. Yield: 8 servings.

Mrs. Gay Russell
Boston, Mass.

HOLIDAY CRUMB PIE

½ pkg. pastry mix
2 c. mincemeat
3 c. sliced apples
¾ c. sugar
2 c. flour
3 tbsp. butter

Make pastry for 9-inch pie shell. Place mincemeat in shell. Add apples mixed with 1/2 cup sugar. Mix remaining sugar and flour; add butter, mixing until crumbs are formed. Sprinkle over apples. Place on lower oven rack. Bake at 425 degrees for 30 to 40 minutes. Serve warm.

Mrs. James C. MacGregor
Floyd Bennett Field, N.Y.

QUICK AND EASY ICE CREAM PIE

1 qt. vanilla or other ice cream
1 9-in. crumb crust or baked pastry shell
1 lge. pkg. frozen strawberries
Meringue

Spread slightly softened ice cream evenly into pie crust. Freeze for 30 minutes or until ice cream hardens. Place strawberries over ice cream. Cover with meringue topping; return to freezer. Remove from freezer 15 minutes before serving. NOTE: If desired, any other fruit or filling may be substituted for strawberries. Yield: 8 servings.

Mrs. William F. Miller, Jr.
Dover-Foxcroft, Me.

KRUMMEL PIE

1 c. sugar
11 graham crackers, crushed
1 tsp. baking powder
¼ tsp. salt
3 egg whites
1 tsp. vanilla
¾ to 1 c. chopped nuts

Mix all dry ingredients; fold into beaten egg whites. Add vanilla and nuts. Pour into greased pie pan. Bake at 350 degrees for 20 to 30 minutes. Serve with ice cream or whipped cream. Yield: 7 servings.

Mrs. James E. Yearty
Mobile, Ala.

SPEEDY PEACH PIE

Butter
½ c. flour
½ c. sugar
½ c. milk
1 tsp. baking powder
2 c. ripe peaches, slightly sweetened

Dot bottom of 1-quart baking dish generously with butter. Mix flour, sugar, milk and baking powder; pour into baking dish. Add peaches. Bake at 350 degrees for 30 minutes. Yield: 4 servings,

Mrs. Marion G. Smith
Joliet, Ill.

PIE

12 graham crackers, rolled
1 c. sugar
½ c. chopped nuts
3 egg whites
½ pt. heavy cream, whipped

Combine cracker crumbs, sugar and nuts. Beat egg whites until stiff; fold into mixture. Pour into well greased pie pan. Bake at 350 degrees for 30 minutes. Cool; spread whipped cream over top. Refrigerate for 24 hours. Yield: 6-8 servings.

Mrs. Frank R. Morrison
Fairchild AFB, Wash.

SURPRISE PIE

1 stick margarine
2 oz. butterscotch or chocolate pieces
½ c. sifted flour
1 c. sugar
2 eggs, slightly beaten
½ c. nuts

Melt margarine and butterscotch in saucepan. Sift flour and sugar; add to mixture. Add eggs; mix well. Add nuts. Pour into greased and floured 9-inch pie plate. Bake at 325 degrees for 25 minutes. Serve frozen, chilled or warmed. Yield: 6 servings.

Mrs. Grayson C. Powell
Valdosta, Ga.

WALNUT PIE

3 eggs
1 c. sugar
1 c. crushed graham crackers
½ c. coarsely chopped walnuts
½ tsp. vanilla flavoring
Dash of salt

Beat eggs, add sugar. Beat well. Fold in cracker crumbs, walnuts, vanilla and salt. Pour into greased 9-inch pie pan. Bake at 350 degrees for 20 to 25 minutes. Cool. Serve topped with whipped cream or ice cream. Yield: 6 servings.

Mrs. C. W. Nickerson
Portsmouth, N.H.

BAKED SHENANDOAH DELIGHT

2 cans baked apples
1 pkg. vanilla pudding
1 tbsp. brandy or rum

Heat apples at 375 degrees for 20 minutes. Make pudding according to directions on package, using 1/2 cup more milk than called for in directions. Add brandy or rum; pour pudding over apples. Serve hot. Yield: 6 servings.

Mrs. Edgar H. Willard
Langley AFB, Va.

CHERRY PUDDING

1 ½ c. sugar
1 can pitted red cherries
3 tbsp. butter
½ c. milk
1 c. flour
2 tsp. baking powder

Heat 1 cup sugar and cherries until sugar is dissolved. Cream butter and remaining sugar; add milk, flour and baking powder. Batter will be thick. Pour into greased 9-inch square cake pan. Pour cherry mixture on top. Bake at 350 degrees for 30 to 40 minutes. Serve with whipped cream or vanilla ice cream. May be served slightly warm. Yield: 9 servings.

Mrs. Jerry L. Case
Philadelphia, Pa.

FRUIT COCKTAIL PUDDING

1 can fruit cocktail
2 tbsp. cornstarch

Drain fruit cocktail, r e s e r v i n g juice. Heat juice and c o r n s t a r c h until thickened. Fold in fruit; chill. Yield: 6 servings.

Mrs. Marion A. Hackett
Victoria, Tex.

MOCK INDIAN PUDDING

2 eggs
¼ c. sugar
¼ tsp. salt
1 tsp. cinnamon
½ tsp. ginger
½ c. molasses
1 c. fine craham cracker crumbs
1 tbsp. butter or margarine
2 c. milk
1 pt. vanilla ice cream

Beat eggs, sugar, salt, cinnamon, ginger and molasses. Add graham cracker crumbs and butter to milk. Heat; stir into egg mixture. Pour into six 5-ounce custard cups. Set cups in a shallow pan containing water 1/2-inch deep. Bake at 350 degrees for 40 minutes or until an inserted silver knife comes out clean. Serve warm with vanilla ice cream. Yield: 6 servings.

Photograph for this recipe on page 293 .

LEMON-WALNUT SURPRISE

1 pkg. lemon instant pudding mix
½ c. chopped walnuts
Whipped cream

Prepare pudding according to package directions; add nuts. Pour into dessert dishes. Top with whipped cream. Chill. Yield: 4 servings.

Audrey Keene
Ayer, Mass.

VANILLA WAFER PUDDING

1 c. plus 6 tbsp. sugar
12 tbsp. flour
3 eggs, separated
¼ lb. butter, melted
3 c. milk
1 tsp. vanilla flavoring
½ lb. vanilla wafers

Sift 1 cup sugar and flour; mix well. Add egg yolks, butter, milk and vanilla. Cook until thick, stirring constantly. Alternate layers of wafers and pudding in baking dish. Beat egg whites until stiff; gradually beat in re-

maining 6 tablespoons sugar. Pile on top of pudding. Brown in oven. Yield: 12 servings.

Mrs. Everett Quiggins
Yeaman, Ky.

APPLE MUFFINS

1 egg
½ c. milk
¼ c. cooking oil
1 c. grated unpared tart apples
1 ½ c. sifted flour
½ c. sugar
2 tsp. baking powder
½ tsp. salt

Combine all ingredients; pour into greased muffin tins.

NUT CRUNCH TOPPING:
⅓ c. brown sugar
⅓ c. chopped nuts
½ tsp. cinnamon

Mix sugar, nuts and cinnamon; sprinkle over batter. Bake at 400 degrees for 20 to 25 minutes. Yield: 12 servings.

Mrs. Edward J. McLaughlin
Norfolk, Va.

JIFFY APPLE CRUMBLE

½ pkg. orange muffin mix
½ tsp. cinnamon
½ tsp. nutmeg
¼ c. butter or margarine
1 No. 2 can sliced apples
1 tbsp. lemon juice

Combine muffin mix and spices; cut in butter until crumbly. Pour apples into 8 x 8 x 2-inch pan. Sprinkle with lemon juice; top with crumb mixture. Bake at 375 degrees for 40 to 45 minutes. Yield: 6 servings.

Mrs. George W. Marshall
Tooele Army Depot, Utah

COFFEE DREAMS

1 can biscuits
Butter
1 c. brown sugar
1 c. chopped nuts

Stretch biscuits into 4-inch circles. Place on cookie sheet. Butter generously. Press brown sugar and nuts into each circle. Bake at 450 degrees for 8 minutes. Yield: 12 servings.

Mrs. Jennie Coleman
Rossville, Kans.

TAPIOCA CREAM

2 eggs, separated
1 qt. milk
⅓ c. quick cooking tapioca
½ c. sugar
¼ tsp. salt
1 tsp. vanilla flavoring

Mix egg yolks with a small amount of milk; add tapioca, sugar, salt and remaining milk. Cook in double boiler over boiling water for 10 to 12 minutes, stirring frequently. Or bring quickly to a boil over direct heat, stirring constantly. Remove from heat; mixture will be thin. Fold hot mixture into stiffly beaten egg whites. Cool slightly. Add vanilla; chill thoroughly. This pudding is delicious poured over fresh or canned fruit or berries. Raisins, prunes, figs, dates, coconut or nuts may be added while cooling. Yield: 8 servings.

CHOCOLATE MINT SAUCE:
1 c. light corn syrup
1 c. sugar
¼ c. water
Pinch of salt
4 1-oz. squares semi-sweet chocolate
1 c. light cream
2 tbsp. butter
1 tsp. vanilla flavoring
¾ tsp. peppermint flavoring

Heat corn syrup, sugar, water and salt until sugar is dissolved, stirring constantly. Bring to full rolling boil; boil for 3 minutes. Remove from heat. Add chocolate; stir until melted. Stir in cream, butter, vanilla and peppermint flavoring. Beat with rotary beater until smooth. Yield: 3 cups.

Photograph for this recipe above.

YUMMIES

2 c. biscuit mix
2 tbsp. sugar
¼ c. shredded coconut
¼ c. chocolate pieces
⅔ c. milk

Mix all ingredients. Fill muffin tins about two-thirds full. Bake at 450 degrees for 10 to 12 minutes. Serve hot. Especially good with chilled canned fruit. Yield: 4-6 servings.

Mrs. Lillian Englmann
Battle Ground, Wash.

BAKED AMBROSIA

1 No. 2 can fruit cocktail
1 9-oz. can crushed pineapple
3 bananas, sliced

(Continued on next page)

6 marshmallows, quartered
¾ c. shredded coconut

Combine fruits and marshmallows. Spoon into 10 x 6 x 1 1/2-inch baking dish. Sprinkle with coconut. Bake at 350 degrees for 20 minutes. Serve hot with sweetened whipped cream. Yield: 6 servings.

Mrs. Richard W. Huxford
Patuxent River, Md.

APPLE CRISP

1 c. sugar
1 c. flour
1 tsp. cinnamon
1 stick margarine
2 cans sliced apples
½ c. nuts
½ c. water

Combine all dry ingredients; cut in margarine to make a crumbly mixture. Arrange apples in a shallow baking dish 11 x 7 x 2-inches. Distribute crumbly mixture over apples; sprinkle nuts and water over top. Bake at 375 degrees for 30 minutes or until brown and crunchy. Serve warm or cold with a lemon sauce or whipped cream. Yield: 6 servings.

Mrs. H. T. Whitlock
San Francisco, Calif.

APPLE GOODIE

3 c. sliced apples
1 c. (scant) sugar
1 tbsp. (heaping) flour
Salt
Cinnamon
¼ tsp. soda
¼ tsp. baking powder
⅓ c. melted butter
1 c. oats
¾ c. flour
¾ c. brown sugar

Mix apples, sugar, flour, salt and cinnamon; place in pan. Mix all remaining ingredients until crumbly; sprinkle over apples. Bake at 350 degrees for 30 to 40 minutes. Cut into squares. Serve with whipped cream or vanilla ice cream. Yield: 6 servings.

Mrs. Evan A. McNear
Warrenton, Va.

APPLESAUCE CRUNCH

1 No. 303 can applesauce
½ c. brown sugar
½ tsp. nutmeg
¼ tsp. mace
1 tbsp. flour
¼ tsp. cinnamon
2 tbsp. lemon juice
1 ½ c. quick cooking oats
⅓ c. white sugar
⅓ c. melted butter

Mix applesauce, brown sugar, nutmeg, mace, flour and cinnamon. Pour into greased 8-inch square pan or 1 1/2-quart baking dish. Sprinkle lemon juice over top. Mix oats, sugar and melted butter; arrange mixture over applesauce mixture. Bake at 350 degrees for 30 minutes or until top is browned and crunchy. Serve with or without cream. Yield: 6 servings.

Mrs. John G. Dillon
Budocks, Wash., D.C.

APRICOT-COCONUT BALLS

1 ½ c. ground dried apricots
2 c. shredded coconut
⅔ c. sweetened condensed milk
Powdered sugar

Mix apricots and coconut. Add condensed milk; blend well. Shape into balls; roll in powdered sugar. Let stand until firm. Yield: 32 balls.

Mrs. A. L. Dodson
Memphis, Tenn.

CREAM CHEESE-CHERRY DESSERT

1 4-oz. pkg. cream cheese
2 c. powdered sugar
1 envelope dessert topping mix
½ c. milk
1 graham cracker crust
½ can cherry pie mix
Coconut or pecans (opt.)

Combine cream cheese and 1 cup sugar. Mix well; set aside. Whip dessert topping mix with milk and remaining sugar until well mixed. Combine with cream cheese mixture; mix well. Pour mixture into crust. Top with cherry pie mix; sprinkle with coconut. Yield: 6 servings.

Mrs. Delores Banik
Tolstoy, S.D.

FOUR-LAYER CHERRY DESSERT

1 graham cracker crust
1 8-oz. pkg. cream cheese
1 c. powdered sugar
½ pt. heavy cream, whipped
1 c. chopped pecans
1 can cherry pie filling

Line bottom of 9-inch cake pan with graham cracker crust. Mix cream cheese and sugar; spread over crust. Mix whipped cream and pecans; spread over cream cheese. Pour cherry filling over top. Chill for 4 hours.

Mrs. Edward A. Martens
Crystal Springs, Miss.

JIFFY DESSERTS

DATE SOUFFLE

2 c. sugar
4 eggs, separated
4 tbsp. flour
2 tsp. baking powder
Dash of salt
1 tsp. vanilla flavoring
1 ½ c. chopped dates
1 ½ c. chopped English walnuts

Beat sugar with egg yolks. Add flour, baking powder and salt. Add vanilla. Fold in stiffly beaten egg whites, dates and walnuts. Pour into ungreased pan. Bake at 300 degrees for 35 minutes. Yield: 12 servings.

Mrs. Louis H. Bauer
Miramar, Calif.

FRENCH CHOCOLATE-MINT DESSERT

2 c. crushed vanilla wafers
1 ¼ c. butter or margarine
2 c. powdered sugar
4 squares chocolate, melted
4 eggs, beaten
1 tsp. peppermint flavoring
2 tsp. vanilla flavoring

Mix vanilla wafer crumbs and 1/4 cup butter. Place mixture in pie pan or individual muffin paper cups, reserving some for topping. Beat remaining butter and powdered sugar; add melted chocolate. Add eggs and flavorings. Pile into pie plate. Sprinkle remaining crumb mixture on top. Serve with whipped cream and a green cherry. NOTE: This freezes well. Yield: 12 servings.

Mrs. Howard Persons
Redstone Arsenal, Ala.

FROZEN DESSERT SHELLS

1 pkg. dessert topping mix
Ice cream or fruit
Sauce or whipped cream

Prepare topping mix according to directions on box. Drop 1/4 cup at a time onto waxed paper. Make depression in top of each mound with spoon. Freeze for 3 hours or until firm. Fill with ice cream or fruit; top with favorite sauce or whipped cream. NOTE: Shells may be made days ahead and kept frozen until ready to serve. Yield: 8 servings.

Mrs. W. N. Pace, Jr.
Reno, Nev.

CINNAMON FLOP

4 tbsp. shortening
1 c. sugar
1 c. milk
½ tsp. salt
2 tsp. baking powder
2 c. sifted flour
¼ c. brown sugar
1 tsp. cinnamon
Butter

Cream shortening and sugar. Add milk, salt, baking powder and flour; beat well. Pour into greased and floured square pan. Sprinkle with brown sugar and cinnamon. Dot with butter. Bake at 400 degrees for 35 to 40 minutes. Good served warm. Yield: 8 servings.

Mrs. Henry Leininger
Longmont, Colo.

COMPANY DESSERT

½ c. shortening
1 ½ c. sugar
4 eggs, separated
1 tsp. vanilla flavoring
1 c. flour
1 tsp. baking powder
¼ tsp. salt
5 tbsp. milk
1 c. chopped nuts

Cream shortening and 1/2 cup sugar. Add beaten egg yolks and vanilla. Sift flour with baking powder and salt. Add alternately with milk to sugar mixture. Spread in two greased and floured 8-inch pans. Beat egg whites until stiff; gradually add remaining sugar. Spread over batter; sprinkle with nuts. Bake at 325 degrees for 30 minutes. Cool; frost with lemon or cream filling. Yield: 12 servings.

Mrs. Donald Bakken
Fertile, Minn.

FIVE-IN-ONE FRUIT DESSERT

1 c. sliced bananas
1 c. Mandarin oranges
1 c. coconut
1 c. sour cream
1 c. pineapple chunks

Combine all ingredients just enough to blend with the cream. Serve immediately. Yield: 6-8 servings.

Ann Eddington
Waldport, Oreg.

FRUIT FRAPPE

½ c. sugar
1 c. water
½ c. fresh orange juice
¼ c. fresh lemon juice

Boil sugar and water to make syrup; cool. Combine syrup with fruit juices; pour into freezer trays. Freeze. Yield: 4-6 servings.

Mrs. Leon M. Mesropian
Newburgh, N.Y.

QUICK PEANUT BUTTER-COFFEE RING

2 tbsp. peanut butter
2 tbsp. jelly or jam
1 tbsp. milk
1 pkg. refrigerated unbaked raisin cinnamon
   rolls

Combine peanut butter, jelly and milk. Separate rolls; spread one side of each roll generously with peanut butter mixture. Slightly overlap rolls, spread-side up, to form a circle on a lightly greased cookie sheet. Press rolls together lightly where rolls overlap. Bake in a preheated 375 degree oven for 20 minutes. Frost with icing that is included in cinnamon roll package. Serve hot.

Photograph for this recipe above.

CRUNCHY COFFEE CAKE

2 c. plus 2 tbsp. sifted flour
⅔ c. light brown sugar
2 tbsp. butter
1 c. chopped nuts
¾ c. sugar
2 tsp. baking powder
½ tsp. salt
1 tsp. cinnamon
¼ tsp. nutmeg
⅓ c. shortening
1 c. milk
2 eggs

Combine 2 tablespoons flour and brown sugar; cut in butter. Add nuts; chill until ready to use. Combine and sift sugar with remaining 2 cups flour, baking powder, salt, cinnamon and nutmeg; add shortening and milk. Beat for 1 minute and 30 seconds with electric mixer. Add eggs; beat until mixed. Pour one-half of the batter into greased 9 x 13 x 2-inch pan; sprinkle one-half of nut topping over batter. Pour in remaining batter; sprinkle with remaining topping. Bake at 350 degrees for 35 minutes. Yield: 8 servings.

Mrs. Howell W. Crawford
Waynesville, N.C.

LOW CHOLESTEROL FRUIT WHIP

3 egg whites
2 tbsp. sugar
2 jars baby food strained fruit

Beat egg whites until stiff. Fold sugar into egg whites. Fold fruit into mixture. Pour into baking dish. Bake at 300 degrees for 25 minutes. NOTE: Also can be used in salt-free diets. Yield: 6 servings.

Mrs. Merle K. Heckler
Windber, Pa.

HEAVENLY GRAPES

4 c. green seedless grapes
1 c. sour cream
Brown sugar

Wash grapes; drain well. Combine grapes and sour cream. Put into large bowl or individual dishes. Sprinkle top generously with brown sugar. Yield: 8 servings.

Mrs. Suzanne Lockard
New Florence, Pa.

ONE-CUP DESSERT

1 c. shredded coconut
1 c. Mandarin oranges
1 c. miniature marshmallows
1 c. nuts
1 c. sour cream
1 tbsp. sugar

Combine all ingredients; refrigerate for 8 to 10 hours. Yield: 8 servings.

Mrs. Frank W. Clift, III
Norfolk, Va.

NUTTY NOODLES

1 6-oz. pkg. egg noodles
½ c. chopped walnuts
⅓ c. melted butter

Cook noodles according to package directions. Brown walnuts in butter; add to noodles. Toss lightly. Place in greased casserole.

TOPPING:
⅓ c. melted butter
1 c. bread crumbs
½ c. sugar
1 tsp. cinnamon
¼ c. chopped walnuts

Mix all ingredients until crumbs are coated; sprinkle over noodles. Bake at 350 degrees for 15 minutes or until crumbs are browned. Yield: 6-8 servings.

Mrs. Gerald F. Ryan
Virginia Beach, Va.

PEACH-CARAMEL SUNDAE

2 ½ c. fresh peaches
1 ½ c. self-rising flour
¼ c. sugar
½ c. brown sugar
½ tsp. cinnamon
⅓ c. butter

Spread peaches in baking dish. Sift flour with sugar, brown sugar and cinnamon. Cut in butter to consistency of corn meal. Spread over peaches. Bake at 325 to 350 degrees for 30 minutes or until golden brown. Serve warm. Yield: 6-8 servings.

Mrs. Mozelle White
Granite Falls, N.C.

PINEAPPLE DESSERT

1 lge. can pineapple chunks
¾ c. sugar
2 eggs, beaten
2 tbsp. (heaping) flour
¾ lge. pkg. miniature marshmallows
½ c. chopped pecans

Drain pineapple, reserving juice. Combine juice, sugar, eggs and flour in saucepan. Cook until thickened. Fold in pineapple and marshmallows. Spread in 8-inch square pan; top with nuts. Yield: 6 servings.

Mrs. Jack Holthues
Edon, O.

PINEAPPLE SURPRISE

1 sm. pkg. miniature marshmallows
1 No. 2 can crushed pineapple
½ pt. heavy cream, whipped

Mix marshmallows and pineapple; let stand for 30 minutes. Fold in whipped cream; chill. Yield: 6 servings.

Mrs. Betty L. Evans
Baltimore, Md.

STRAWBERRY FLUFF

2 egg whites
1 tbsp. unflavored gelatin
1 10-oz. pkg. frozen sliced strawberries

Beat egg whites in blender until frothy. Add gelatin; continue beating. Add frozen strawberries, one piece at a time. When thoroughly blended, pour mixture into four dessert dishes; put into freezer for 5 minutes. Garnish with finely ground nuts, semi-sweet chocolate curls or whipped cream. Yield: 4 servings.

Mrs. George J. McCartin, Jr.
Schofield Barracks, Hawaii

SUNSHINE SPECIAL

¼ c. orange marmalade
2 tbsp. melted butter
Coconut
4 thick slices pound cake
4 slices pineapple

Spoon mixture of marmalade, butter and coconut over pound cake. Top with slice of pineapple; broil until bubbly. Garnish with candied cherry. Yield: 4 servings.

Mrs. Hendrick J. Arnold
U.S. Air Force Acad., Colo.

RECIPE FOR KILLARNEY CHERRY CAKE (IRELAND) ON PAGE 323

BENNE COOKIES (AFRICA)

1 ¼ c. butter or margarine
1 ½ c. light brown sugar
1 tsp. vanilla flavoring
2 eggs
1 ¾ c. sifted flour
1 tsp. baking powder
¼ tsp. salt
⅓ c. toasted benne seed (sesame seed)

Cream butter and sugar until light and fluffy. Add vanilla and eggs; beat until smooth and creamy. Sift flour with baking powder and salt; add to creamed mixture. Stir in sesame seed. Drop by teaspoonfuls 2 inches apart onto greased cookie sheets. Bake at 400 degrees for 11 minutes. Cookies should be very pale with delicately tanned edges. Remove from sheets at once; cool on wire racks. While warm, they may be bent over a rolling pin for interesting tea shape. These cookies are very thin and fragile but store well in covered tin. NOTE: To toast sesame seed, spread seed out on large pan. Toast in preheated 350 degree oven for 25 minutes or until lightly browned. Yield: 7 dozen.

Mrs. Charles Ostrom, Jr.
Aberdeen Proving Ground, Md.

VIENNESE CHOCOLATE-CHERRY KUCHEN (AUSTRIA)

1 ½ c. butter
6 squares unsweetened chocolate
3 c. sugar
6 eggs, beaten
3 c. sifted cake flour
¾ tsp. baking powder
¾ tsp. salt
1 No. 303 can pitted sour red cherries, drained
1 tbsp. vanilla flavoring

Melt butter and chocolate over hot water. Gradually add sugar to eggs. Add chocolate mixture; beat hard for 1 minute. Sift flour with baking powder and salt; add cherries. Fold into chocolate mixture. Add vanilla. Pour into three greased 9-inch square cake pans. Bake at 350 degrees for 35 to 40 minutes. Cool. Circle with ribbon of whipped cream. Yield: 36 servings.

Mrs. Henry J. Sulkowski
St. Louis, Mo.

VIENNA DREAM BARS (AUSTRIA)

BARS:
½ c. soft margarine
½ c. brown sugar
1 c. sifted flour

Cream margarine and sugar until fluffy. Stir in flour. Press into 8 x 10-inch pan. Bake at 350 degrees for 10 minutes. Cool slightly.

TOPPING:
2 eggs, well beaten
1 c. brown sugar
1 tsp. vanilla flavoring
2 tbsp. flour
1 tsp. baking powder
½ tsp. salt
1 c. coconut
1 c. chopped nuts

Beat eggs, sugar and vanilla until fluffy. Sift all dry ingredients; add to egg mixture. Fold in coconut and nuts. Spread over baked mixture. Bake at 350 degrees for 25 minutes. Cool before cutting. Yield: 10 servings.

Mrs. Sharol Knobel
Daykin, Nebr.

BOLO DE LARANJA--ORANGE CAKE (BRAZIL)

5 eggs, separated
8 tbsp. orange juice
2 c. flour
2 c. sugar
1 tsp. baking powder
½ tsp. vanilla flavoring

Combine and mix egg yolks and orange juice. Mix flour with sugar and baking powder; add slowly to egg yolk mixture. Beat or mix for 2 minutes. Add vanilla; fold in beaten egg whites. Pour into well greased pan. Bake at 325 to 350 degrees for 25 minutes. May be served with desired topping or just plain orange juice. Yield: 6 servings.

Louise Figueiredo
Leonville, La.

FLAMING BANANAS AND RUM (BRITISH WEST INDIES)

4 tbsp. butter
½ c. plus 3 tbsp. sugar
½ c. plus 2 tbsp. dark rum
4 green-ripe bananas

Melt butter in saucepan or chafing dish. Add 5 tablespoons sugar and 7 tablespoons rum. Bring to a slow boil; beat until syrupy but not thick. Slice peeled bananas into halves, lengthwise. Place in simmering syrup. Simmer on each side until bananas are translucent. Do not overcook. Remove from heat. Add remaining rum mixed with remaining sugar. Ignite; serve flaming. Yield: 4 servings.

Mrs. Vernon P. O'Neil
Dallas NAS, Tex.

PETITS FOURS--LITTLE COOKIES (CANADA)

1 egg, separated
4 tsp. powdered sugar
½ c. butter or margarine

(Continued on next page)

¼ c. brown sugar
1 c. flour
1 tsp. baking powder
Pinch of salt
Grape, apple or strawberry jelly

Beat egg white until foamy; add powdered sugar. Beat until soft peaks form to make a meringue. Blend butter and brown sugar; beat in egg yolk. Add sifted dry ingredients; mix well. Shape dough into balls the size of egg yolks. Place 1 inch apart on lightly greased cookie sheet. Press down with finger in center of each ball. Bake at 375 to 400 degrees for 5 to 7 minutes or until lightly browned. Do not overbake. Remove from oven. Put jelly in center of each cookie. Place a drop of meringue on top of jelly; spread to cover jelly completely. Return to oven until meringue is golden brown. Yield: 24 cookies.

Mrs. Gisele Beaudet
Fort Benjamin Harrison, Ind.

ALMOND CAKES (CHINA)

¼ c. butter
¼ c. shortening
1 c. sifted flour
½ tsp. salt
¼ c. plus 2 tbsp. sugar
½ tsp. almond flavoring
1 egg yolk
1 tbsp. water
¼ c. blanched almond halves

Cut butter and shortening into flour until mixture is fine. Use hands to work in salt, sugar and flavoring. Shape into long roll, 1 inch in diameter. Wrap in waxed paper. Chill for 1 hour. Cut roll into 1/4-inch slices; place 1 inch apart on lightly greased baking sheets. Brush with mixture of egg yolk and water. Press almond half into top of each slice. Bake in preheated 400 degree oven for 8 to 10 minutes or until light brown. NOTE: Perfect with fresh fruit or with orange ice to finish a chow mein supper. Yield: 2 dozen cookies.

Mrs. T. Alan Bennett
Hill AFB, Utah

FRUIT CAKE (CHINA)

1 c. sweetened condensed milk
1 c. chopped pecans
1 c. dates
1 c. candied cherries
1 c. flaked coconut

Mix all ingredients. Pour into greased pan. Bake at 300 degrees for 35 minutes. Yield: 8 servings.

Mrs. Gertrude Nash
Muskogee, Okla.

BAR COOKIES (CZECHOSLOVAKIA)

2 sticks margarine
1 c. sugar
2 egg yolks
2 c. flour
1 c. pecans
½ c. strawberry jam

Cream margarine and sugar; add egg yolks, flour and pecans. Mix thoroughly. Divide batter in half; spread one-half of the mixture into brownie pan. Finely mash jam; spread on top of first layer. Press remaining batter on top of jam layer. Bake at 375 degrees for 1 hour. Cut into squares. Yield: 2 dozen.

Mrs. Lucy B. Taylor
Warren, Ark.

ICEBOX KOLACHKI (CZECHOSLOVAKIA)

CRUST:
1 8-oz. pkg. cream cheese, softened
2 c. shortening or butter
6 c. flour
¼ tsp. salt
Powdered sugar

Combine all ingredients except sugar; mix well. Shape mixture into seven flat patties; put waxed paper between layers. Place in refrigerator overnight. Remove from refrigerator 30 minutes before using. Roll out crust in powdered sugar; cut into 1 1/2-inch squares.

FILLING:
1 c. ground nuts or dates
1 tbsp. milk
¼ tsp. salt
1 tbsp. butter

Combine all ingredients; simmer until mixture forms a paste. Spread filling over crust; roll up. Place pastries on foil or brown paper on cookie sheet. Bake at 325 degrees until lightly browned. Yield: 50 cookies.

Mrs. Ralph Sandike
Binghamton, N.Y.

KOLECHI (CZECHOSLOVAKIA)

½ lge. cake yeast
½ tsp. salt
½ c. sugar
1 c. butter, melted
1 c. lukewarm milk
4 c. flour
3 eggs

Crumble yeast into mixture of salt, sugar, butter and milk; mix until blended. Add flour and eggs alternately, mixing well after each addition. Refrigerate overnight.

(Continued on next page)

NUT FILLING:
1 lb. finely ground walnuts
½ c. honey
3 eggs
⅓ c. butter

Combine all ingredients, mixing well. Shape dough into six loaves; press an indention into top of each loaf. Spoon filling into indention; let dough rise for 1 hour. Bake at 350 degrees for 35 to 45 minutes. Yield: 6 loaves.

Mrs. Mary E. Leyba
Carswell AFB, Tex.

AGNETE'S LAYER CAKE (DENMARK)
½ lb. butter
1 c. sugar
4 egg yolks
1 c. flour
2 tsp. baking powder
1 tsp. vanilla flavoring
6 egg whites

Mix all ingredients except egg whites until smooth. Fold in beaten egg whites; pour into four layer cake tins. Bake at 350 degrees for 12 to 15 minutes.

CUSTARD:
1 c. milk
2 egg yolks
2 tbsp. cornstarch
1 tbsp. sugar
½ tsp. vanilla flavoring
Raspberry jam

Boil milk; stir in remaining ingredients except jam. Cook until custard begins to thicken. Remove from heat. Spread custard and jam between layers of hot cake. Frost with a butter-almond frosting or whipped cream. Yield: 8-10 servings.

Mrs. F. E. Leek
El Toro, Calif.

APPLE PUDDING (DENMARK)
1 ½ c. fine dry bread crumbs
⅓ c. butter
2 c. or 1 lb. applesauce
¼ tsp. salt
1 tbsp. lemon juice
4 tsp. cinnamon
Whipped cream

Saute crumbs in butter until evenly browned. Line greased 8 x 8 x 2-inch pan with one-half of the crumbs. Mix applesauce, salt, lemon juice and cinnamon. Pour one-half of the mixture over crumbs. Repeat layers. Top with sweetened whipped cream. Chill for several hours. Serve in squares decorated with bits of red jelly, if desired. Yield: 8 servings.

Mrs. A. G. Meyer
Sparta, Mich.

APPLE SQUARES (DENMARK)
2 ½ c. sifted flour
1 tsp. salt
1 c. shortening
1 egg, separated
Milk
1 c. corn flakes, crushed
6 lge. cooking apples, peeled and sliced
1 ½ c. sugar
1 tsp. cinnamon

Sift flour and salt; cut in shortening with pastry blender. Combine beaten egg yolk and enough milk to make 2/3 cup liquid. Add to flour-shortening mixture. Mix like pie pastry. Divide dough in half. Roll one-half of dough into a 12 x 17-inch rectangle. Place in greased jelly roll pan; bring pastry up the sides. Sprinkle crushed corn flakes over pastry. Arrange apples, sugar and cinnamon mixture evenly over corn flakes. Roll out remaining pastry. Place over apples. Moisten edges with milk; pinch top layer to bottom. Beat egg white until stiff. Brush evenly over top crust. Bake at 400 degrees for 40 minutes. While still warm, ice with powdered sugar glaze.

Mrs. Ed J. Bredehoeft
Emmetsburg, Iowa

BAKELESS DESSERT (DENMARK)
½ lb. vanilla wafers, crushed
½ c. butter
1 c. sugar
1 No. 2 can crushed pineapple, drained
4 eggs, separated
1 c. chopped nuts

Line 9-inch square pan with one-third of the crumbs. Cream butter and sugar. Add pineapple, beaten egg yolks and nuts. Fold in stiffly beaten egg whites. Pour one-half of the mixture over crumbs; add one-third of remaining crumbs. Pour over remaining pineapple mixture; top with remaining crumbs. Chill for 12 hours. Yield: 8 servings.

Mrs. Irene Noss
Goodman, Mo.

BUTTER COOKIES (DENMARK)
1 c. soft butter
½ c. powdered sugar
2 c. sifted flour
1 c. coarsely chopped nuts
1 tsp. vanilla flavoring
Granulated sugar
Dash of salt

Combine all ingredients except granulated sugar and salt. Mix well. Shape into small, flat circles. Place on ungreased cookie sheet. Bake at 325 degrees until lightly browned.

(Continued on next page)

Combine sugar and salt. Roll warm cookies in sugar mixture.

Mrs. Dagmar Ingvoldstad
Decorah, Iowa

NEVER-FAIL COFFEE CAKE (DENMARK)

4 c. sifted flour
1 tbsp. sugar
1 tsp. salt
1 c. butter
1 cake yeast
1 c. milk
3 egg yolks

Sift flour with sugar and salt. Cut in butter. Dissolve yeast in cold milk. When dissolved, add beaten egg yolks. Add egg-yeast mixture to sifted dry ingredients. Place in covered bowl; refrigerate overnight.

FILLING:
3 egg whites, stiffly beaten
1 c. sugar
1 tsp. cinnamon
Chopped nuts

Combine all filling ingredients. Cut dough into three parts; roll each part to 1/4-inch thick. Spread with filling mixture. Roll to crescent shape; let rise for 1 hour. Bake at 350 degrees for 20 to 25 minutes. Frost with a thin powdered sugar frosting while still warm. Yield: Three 8-inch cakes.

Erna Nordstrand
Beecher, Ill.

WIENERBROD (DENMARK)

4 c. unsifted flour
4 tbsp. sugar
2 tsp. salt
1 c. shortening
1 cake yeast
½ c. warm water
3 egg yolks, beaten
1 c. warm milk

Mix flour, sugar and salt; cut in shortening. Dissolve yeast in water; add with egg yolks and milk to flour mixture. Beat until smooth. Place in refrigerator overnight. Remove dough from refrigerator; shape as desired. Let rise for 2 hours or until double in bulk. Place on greased cookie sheet. Bake at 400 to 425 degrees for 15 to 20 minutes. NOTE: Can be used as rolls, coffee cake or tea rings. If used as crescents or horns, fill with strawberry or pineapple preserves. Yield: 2 dozen.

Kirstine Jensen Thal
Cincinnati, O.

ENGLISH TEA SCONES (ENGLAND)

2 c. sifted flour
3 tsp. baking powder
1 tsp. salt
2 tbsp. sugar
4 tbsp. shortening
2 eggs, beaten
¼ c. plus 2 tbsp. milk

Sift all dry ingredients; cut in shortening until consistency of coarse corn meal. Combine eggs and milk; add to mixture, stirring to blend. Turn out onto lightly floured board. Roll to 1/2-inch thickness; cut into 2-inch squares. Fold into triangles. Brush with milk; sprinkle with sugar. Place on greased baking sheet. Bake at 400 degrees for 25 minutes or until brown. Serve with butter and marmalade or jam. Yield: 12 scones.

Mrs. Beryl E. Heaton
Fairchild AFB, Wash.

DEEP-DISH APPLE PIE (ENGLAND)

5 c. sliced apples
½ c. sugar
½ c. water
1 c. brown sugar
½ c. butter
½ c. milk
1 c. flour
1 tsp. vanilla flavoring
½ c. chopped nuts

Combine apples, sugar and water; line 8-inch square pan with apple mixture. Cream brown sugar and butter; add milk, flour and vanilla. Mix well; fold in nuts. Pour over apples. Bake at 375 degrees until apples are tender. Yield: 6 servings.

Mrs. Elaine Geilenkirchen
Lindsay, Nebr.

FLAPJACKS (ENGLAND)

4 oz. margarine or butter
4 oz. brown sugar
6 oz. oats

Melt margarine in saucepan. Stir in brown sugar and oats. Spread in greased pan about 1/2-inch thick. Bake at 350 degrees until golden brown, about 20 minutes. Cool for 5 minutes before cutting. Yield: 2 dozen.

Mrs. Joseph M. Kelly
Clinton-Sherman AFB, Okla.

FRUIT CAKE (ENGLAND)

½ lb. butter
½ lb. lard
2 lb. sugar

(Continued on next page)

1 tsp. nutmeg
1 tsp. cinnamon
1 tsp. allspice
1 c. molasses
4 eggs, beaten
1 box currants
1 box seedless raisins
1 pkg. candied citron
1 pkg. candied pineapple
2 pkg. candied lemon peel
2 pkg. candied orange peel
2 pkg. candied cherries
1 lb. walnuts, chopped
½ tsp. salt
½ tsp. soda
6 c. coffee
14 c. plus 2 tbsp. flour

Line eight bread pans with waxed paper. Cream shortening and sugar. Add spices, molasses and beaten eggs; mix thoroughly. Add currants and raisins. Cut up candied fruits; add. Add walnuts, salt and soda. Alternately add coffee and flour, using only enough coffee to make mixture moist. Bake in 250 degree oven for 2 hours or until toothpick inserted comes out dry. Yield: 8 loaves.

Mrs. William H. Herbert
Athens, O.

GINGERSNAPS (ENGLAND)

1 c. flour
¼ c. margarine
1 c. light brown sugar
2 to 3 tsp. ginger
Dark or light corn syrup

Mix flour and margarine until crumbly; add sugar and ginger. Add just enough syrup to make a stiff dough. Shape into long small rolls. Pinch off marble-sized balls; place far apart on well greased cookie sheet. Bake at 350 degrees until done. Cookies will be hard and porous when done.

Mrs. Clyde H. Landreth
Jacksonville, Ill.

HOT CROSS BUNS (ENGLAND)

1 ¼ c. milk
1 cake yeast
⅛ tsp. salt
Sugar
¼ c. margarine
2 eggs
⅓ c. raisins
Flour
1 c. powdered sugar
½ tsp. vanilla flavoring

Scald milk; cool to lukewarm. Crumble in yeast; add salt, 1/3 cup sugar, margarine, 1 beaten egg and raisins. Mix well; add enough flour to make dough easy to handle. Place in greased bowl; cover and let rise in warm place until double in bulk. Pinch off rolls the size of small walnuts; place on greased cookie sheet 1 1/2 inches apart. Let rise for 30 minutes. With scissors, snip top of each raised bun twice, forming cross. Brush with remaining egg diluted with 2 tablespoons water. Bake at 400 degrees until brown. Remove from oven; brush with mixture of 1/4 cup sugar and 2 tablespoons water. When cool, make icing with powdered sugar moistened with enough water to make proper consistency. Add vanilla and fill cross. Yield: 36 servings.

Eva J. Dodd
Moorefield, W. Va.

MARLBOROUGH PUDDING (ENGLAND)

PASTRY:
2 c. flour
7 tbsp. milk
¾ tsp. salt
¾ c. shortening

Mix flour, milk, salt and shortening like pie dough. Roll into ball; place in refrigerator while preparing filling.

FILLING:
1 c. sugar or 1 tbsp. artificial sweetener
4 eggs
2 tbsp. lemon juice
½ tsp. nutmeg
2 ½ c. applesauce
1 c. heavy cream

Combine ingredients in order given. Place pastry in two 9-inch greased pie pans. Pour filling into pie shells. Bake at 350 degrees for 45 minutes. Yield: 12-16 servings.

Earlene Nofziger
Goshen, Ind.

MINCEMEAT FOR TARTS (ENGLAND)

1 lb. suet, finely cut
1 lb. seeded muscat raisins
1 lb. seedless golden raisins
1 lb. currants
1 lb. apples, peeled and cored
1 lb. sugar
2 oz. candied peel mix
1 tsp. cinnamon
1 tsp. nutmeg
1 tsp. cloves
Juice of 2 oranges

Put all ingredients through food grinder; mix well. Do not cook. Pack into jars; store in cool place until ready to use. A tablespoon of cooking Sherry or whiskey may be added to improve flavor when ready to use. Fill pastry-lined tart or pattie tins half full of mincemeat; cover with top crust. Bake in 400 degree oven for 15 minutes.

Mrs. Roberta Johnson
Moline, Ill.

TOFFEE DESSERT (ENGLAND)

½ c. butter
1 c. powdered sugar
1 tsp. vanilla flavoring
3 eggs, separated
2 squares chocolate, melted
½ pkg. vanilla wafers, crushed
1 c. chopped pecans

Cream butter, sugar, vanilla, beaten egg yolks and chocolate. Fold in stiffly beaten egg whites. Mix crumbs and nuts; spread one-half of the crumb mixture into 8-inch square pan. Pour in chocolate mixture; top with remaining crumbs. Chill overnight. Serve with whipped cream.

Mrs. Arleen Volovsek
Greenwood, Wisc.

STEPHANIE'S ENGLISH TRIFLE (ENGLAND)

2 pkg. vanilla instant pudding
1 lb. cake or sponge cake
1 c. Sherry
1 lge. can apricots
2 bananas, sliced
2 8-oz. cans Mandarin oranges
1 lge. can chunk pineapple
1 pt. heavy cream, whipped

Mix vanilla pudding as directed on package; chill. Slice cake lengthwise; line 3-quart bowl with cake. Soak cake with Sherry. Cover with apricots; spread with one-half of the vanilla pudding. Add layers of bananas, Mandarin oranges and pineapple. Cover with remaining vanilla pudding. Spread sweetened whipped cream over top, sealing the edges. Chill for at least 1 hour. Yield: 12 servings.

Mrs. James R. Backus
New Cumberland Army Depot, Pa.

TRIFLE (ENGLAND)

1 jelly roll or 1 doz. ladyfingers
½ c. Sherry wine
1 pkg. custard dessert or vanilla pudding
Almond macaroons, broken into pieces
1 c. heavy cream, whipped
Maraschino cherries

Line cut glass or other pretty bowl with slices of jelly roll. Dribble wine over jelly roll. Prepare pudding according to package directions; cool. Spoon over jelly roll. Sprinkle macaroons over pudding. Top with sweetened whipped cream; garnish with cherries. NOTE: If ladyfingers are used, spread halves with raspberry jelly and put back together. Yield: 12 servings.

Mrs. Edythe Anderson
Howell, Mich.

FINNISH COOKIES (FINLAND)

2 ⅓ c. margarine
1 ½ c. sugar
2 eggs
4 tbsp. syrup
1 tsp. cinnamon
½ tsp. cloves
1 tsp. cardamom
½ tsp. soda
3 ½ c. flour

Cream margarine and sugar; add eggs, syrup, spices and soda mixed with flour. Let dough stand in covered bowl in refrigerator overnight. Roll on floured surface 1/4-inch thick. Cut with cookie cutter. Place on greased cookie sheet. Bake at 350 degrees until light brown. Yield: 8 dozen.

Mrs. Ritva Dillard
Ketchikan, Alaska

FRENCH PASTRIES (FRANCE)

3 tbsp. butter
5 eggs
1 c. minus 1 tbsp. sugar
¼ tsp. vanilla flavoring
⅛ tsp. almond flavoring
1 ¼ c. sifted cake flour
Raspberry jam

Melt butter over hot water; cool. Combine eggs and sugar in top of 3-quart double boiler; set over simmering water. Beat constantly for 10 minutes with electric mixer or until mixture is thick and piles softly, or for 20 to 25 minutes with hand rotary beater. Remove from heat; continue beating until mixture is cold. Blend in flavorings. Divide cake flour into four portions. Sift one portion at a time over egg mixture; gently fold in until just blended. Gradually add melted butter, folding only until blended. Pour batter into buttered 10 1/2 x 15 1/2 x 1-inch pan lined with buttered waxed paper cut to fit. Bake at 325 degrees for 40 to 45 minutes or until cake springs back when lightly touched at center. Loosen edges with spatula; remove immediately from pan. Carefully peel off paper. Cool on rack, top-side up. Cut into six rectangles, four squares, six rounds, six ovals or diamonds. Spread one-half of the pastry shapes thinly with jam.

CHOCOLATE-BUTTER FROSTING:
6 oz. semi-sweet chocolate
¼ c. strong coffee
1 ½ c. firm unsalted butter
1 ½ tsp. vanilla flavoring
¾ c. white corn syrup
4 egg yolks
Flaked coconut

Melt chocolate in coffee over low heat. Remove from heat; blend well. Cool. Cream butter and vanilla until light and fluffy.

(Continued on next page)

Gently heat syrup to 234 degrees. Beat egg yolks until thick and lemon colored. Slowly pour syrup into egg yolks, beating constantly with rotary beater. Beat until of consistency of whipped butter; cool completely. Beat egg yolk mixture into butter, 2 tablespoons at a time, just until blended. Gradually blend in chocolate mixture. Spread frosting over jam on pastries. Cover each with remaining pastries. Frost top and sides with remaining frosting. Sprinkle with coconut. Garnish with nuts or cherries, as desired. Yield: 22 servings.

Mrs. Macey M. Casebeer
White Sands Missile Range, N.M.

TINY CREAM PUFFS (FRANCE)

½ c. butter
1 c. boiling water
1 c. sifted flour
½ tsp. salt
4 eggs

Melt butter in boiling water; add flour and salt all at once. Cook over medium heat for 2 minutes, stirring constantly, until mixture leaves sides of pan and is smooth and compact. Remove from heat. Blend in an egg at a time, beating vigorously after each addition until mixture is smooth and glossy. Drop by one-half teaspoonfuls onto greased baking sheet. Shape to a point. Bake at 425 degrees for 18 to 20 minutes or until golden brown. Turn off heat; prick puffs to allow steam to escape. Leave puffs in oven for 10 minutes to dry out centers. Cool.

FILLING:
½ c. sugar
¼ c. flour
2 tbsp. cornstarch
¼ tsp. salt
2 egg yolks, slightly beaten
1 c. hot milk
½ c. hot cream
2 tbsp. butter
1 square unsweetened chocolate (opt.)
1 ½ tsp. vanilla flavoring

Mix sugar, flour, cornstarch and salt. Beat egg yolks and milk; add to dry ingredients. Stir until smooth. Blend in cream and milk. Cover and cook in double boiler for 5 minutes, stirring constantly. Remove from heat; add butter and melted chocolate. Cover and cool; add vanilla. Split cream puffs; fill with cream filling. Yield: 4 dozen.

Mrs. Gordon Culver
Shelbyville, Mich.

POTS DE CREME A LA CREME DE CACAO (FRANCE)

2 c. heavy cream
½ c. sugar
6 egg yolks
2 tbsp. creme de cacao

Scald cream with sugar; cool slightly. Beat egg yolks until light and lemon colored; add cream, stirring constantly. Add creme de cacao. Strain mixture through fine sieve into six small earthenware pots or custard cups. Set pots in pan of water; cover pan. Bake at 325 degrees for 15 minutes or until knife inserted near center comes out clean. Serve chilled. Yield: 6 servings.

Mrs. R. E. Skinner
Beaufort, S.C.

CHRISTSTOLLEN (GERMANY)

5 c. raisins
1 ½ c. mixed fruit
1 c. rum
3 cakes yeast
4 c. milk
10 c. flour
1 c. sugar
2 ½ c. butter or margarine
½ tsp. nutmeg
Rind of 1 lemon
1 ½ c. chopped almonds
1 tsp. almond flavoring

Soak raisins and fruit in rum overnight. Dissolve yeast in 1 cup of lukewarm milk. Stir in 1 cup of flour. Cover sponge; let rise in a warm place for 30 minutes. Heat remaining milk; add sugar, butter, nutmeg and rind. Stir until fat and sugar are dissolved. Cool to hand warmth. Add liquid to yeast sponge. Beat in 6 cups flour gradually. Put a third of dough in a separate bowl; add remaining flour. Mix until dough is stiff. Add fruit, almonds and flavoring to remaining dough. Knead in flour until dough is stiff. It may require additional flour. Cover the two bowls; let dough rise until double in bulk. Divide each piece of dough into two parts. Shape fruit dough into two loaves. Roll out remaining dough; wrap around loaves. Let rise to double in size. Bake at 325 degrees for 1 hour. Brush with melted butter; sprinkle with powdered sugar. Cool; wrap in plastic paper. Ripen for two weeks before serving. Yield: 2 loaves.

Friedel Schweitzer
Bloomington, Ind.

APFELKUCHEN--APPLE CAKE (GERMANY)

1 egg
½ c. butter, melted
1 c. milk
¼ tsp. salt
2 tbsp. sugar
2 c. flour
2 tsp. baking powder
Sliced apples

Mix all ingredients except apples; spread into two buttered 8-inch square pans. Cover with apples. Press into top of dough. Bake at 350 to 375 degrees for 20 minutes or until fruit is done.

(Continued on next page)

TOPPING:
½ c. sour cream
2 or 3 eggs, well beaten
3 tbsp. sugar

Combine all ingredients; pour over cake. Bake for 10 minutes longer. Yield: 12-18 servings.

Mrs. William H. Koenig
El Centro, Calif.

APPLE CAKE (GERMANY)
BATTER:
½ c. margarine
½ c. sugar
1 egg
2 c. flour, sifted
2 tsp. baking powder
Pinch of salt
¼ c. milk

Cream margarine with sugar and egg; add all dry ingredients. Stir in enough milk to make batter smooth. Mix well; spread into two greased 9-inch pans.

FILLING:
4 or 5 apples, peeled and sliced
½ c. sugar
Grated rind of 1 lemon
1 tsp. cinnamon

Stew apples with sugar and rind for 5 minutes. Place on batter; sprinkle with cinnamon.

TOPPING:
½ c. shortening
½ c. sugar
½ c. flour

Combine all ingredients; mix well. Spread over apples. Bake cake at 350 degrees for 30 to 35 minutes. Yield: 6 servings.

Mrs. Vlasta Schwarz
Jefferson, N.Y.

BAVARIAN SPICE CAKE (GERMANY)
2 c. brown sugar
1 c. shortening
2 eggs
1 c. chopped nuts
2 c. chopped dates
1 tsp. cinnamon
½ tsp. allspice
½ tsp. cloves
3 c. sifted flour
2 tsp. soda
½ tsp. salt
2 c. beer or ale

Cream sugar and shortening; stir in eggs, nuts, dates and spices. Sift flour with soda and salt; stir in beer. Combine beer mixture with creamed mixture; mix until well blended.

Pour into 2 1/2-quart tube pan. Bake at 350 degrees for 1 hour and 15 minutes. NOTE: Batter may be baked in 9 x 13-inch loaf pan or two loaf pans at the same temperature and time.

Mrs. Mardy Coons
Sunnyvale, Calif.

BLACK FOREST CAKE (GERMANY)
1 ¼ c. egg whites
½ c. plus 2 tbsp. sugar
1 ½ c. finely ground blanched almonds
2 tbsp. flour

Beat egg whites with sugar until stiff. Carefully fold in almonds and flour. Spread into three 10-inch cake pans lined with waxed paper. Bake at 250 degrees for 1 hour and 30 minutes. Remove from pans; cool.

FILLING:
1 envelope unflavored gelatin
2 tbsp. hot water
3 c. heavy cream, whipped
1 c. sugar
1 tbsp. vanilla flavoring
Shaved dark sweet chocolate
Confectioners sugar

Dissolve gelatin in hot water; cool slightly. Combine whipped cream, sugar and vanilla; add gelatin, mixing carefully. Spread on cake layers. Stack layers; cover top and sides with whipped cream mixture. Sprinkle with shaved chocolate. Sift confectioners sugar over chocolate. Yield: 10-12 servings.

Mrs. George P. Chopin
Dover AFB, Del.

FASTNACHTS--RAISED DOUGHNUTS (GERMANY)
1 c. mashed potatoes
½ c. shortening
2 tsp. salt
2 c. sugar
3 eggs, beaten
1 qt. warm milk
1 ½ cakes yeast
½ c. warm water
5 lb. flour

Mix hot mashed potatoes, shortening, salt, sugar and eggs. Add milk. Dissolve yeast in warm water; add to mixture. Add flour gradually. Let dough rise overnight or for a few hours. Knead dough; roll on floured board to 1/2-inch thickness. Cut into squares or with doughnut cutter. Let dough rise for 1 hour before frying. Fry in deep hot fat at 350 degrees until golden brown. Drain excess fat; roll in sugar. Yield: 10 dozen.

Mrs. Harold Schatz
Pottstown, Pa.

GUTTEKUCHEN (GERMANY)

2 c. sifted flour
1 tsp. baking powder
¾ c. sugar
¾ c. shortening
1 egg
1 tsp. vanilla flavoring
½ tsp. cinnamon
2 tbsp. milk
Jam

Mix all ingredients except jam; knead. Roll one-half of the dough on greased cookie sheet. Spread with jam. Make lattice work of remaining dough; cover jam. Bake at 400 degrees for 20 minutes. Yield: 24 pieces.

Mrs. Robert Parker
Pittsfield, Me.

KUKEN--COFFEE CAKE (GERMANY)

1 yeast cake
¼ c. lukewarm water
2 c. milk or 1 c. milk plus 1 c. water
4 tbsp. butter
⅓ c. sugar
2 tsp. salt
1 or 2 eggs, beaten
4 c. sifted flour

Crumble yeast into water. Combine milk, butter and sugar. Heat only enough to melt butter and sugar; cool to lukewarm. Add yeast mixture, salt and eggs. Add flour to make a soft dough; knead gently. Let rise until double in size. Knead gently. Spread thinly over bottom of pan.

STREUSEL:
1 c. sugar
2 tbsp. flour
2 to 3 tsp. cinnamon
1 stick butter

Combine sugar, flour and cinnamon; add enough butter to make a crumbly mixture. Spread mixture thickly over dough. Let rise. Bake at 350 degrees for 15 to 20 minutes. Yield: 10 servings.

Mary Lawrence
Big Spring, Tex.

LEBKUCHEN (GERMANY)

1 c. lard
1 c. sorghum molasses
1 c. wine or sour milk
2 c. sugar
1 c. nuts
1 c. coconut
2 oranges, diced
2 lemons, diced
6 tsp. soda
1 tbsp. cinnamon
1 tsp. nutmeg
1 tsp. cloves
1 tsp. salt
Flour

Combine lard, molasses, wine and sugar. Add nuts, coconut and fruits. Add sifted soda, cinnamon, nutmeg, cloves and salt. Mix well; add flour until dough is stiff enough to roll. Mix well. Roll dough to 1/4-inch thickness; cut with cookie cutter. Bake in 350 degree oven for 12 to 15 minutes. NOTE: These may also be formed into rolls or stored in refrigerator and sliced before baking. Yield: 5-6 dozen large cookies.

Mrs. Harry Daniel
Carmi, Ill.

PFEFFERNUESSE--CHRISTMAS COOKIES (GERMANY)

¼ c. butter
¾ c. lard
½ c. brown sugar
1 qt. sorghum molasses
4 tsp. allspice
1 tsp. ginger
1 can anise seed
4 tsp. soda
2 tsp. salt
Flour

Cream shortenings and sugar; add molasses. Add spices, soda and salt to 1 cup flour. Mix well; add to creamed mixture. Add enough flour to make stiff dough. Chill well. Roll into rolls the size of a pencil; slice into small pieces. Bake at 300 degrees for 15 minutes or until golden brown.

Mrs. Dorothy Elliott
Laporte City, Iowa

SPITZKUCHEN--CHOCOLATE-COVERED FRUIT COOKIES (GERMANY)

1 pkg. gingerbread mix
½ tsp. allspice
½ c. finely chopped citron
½ c. finely chopped candied orange peel
⅓ c. finely chopped almonds
3 6-oz. pkg. semi-sweet chocolate pieces
3 tbsp. hot water

Prepare gingerbread mix according to package directions, but adding allspice, citron, candied orange peel and almonds before adding liquid. Pour batter into greased rectangular baking pan. Bake at 350 degrees for 25 to 30 minutes. Place on cooling rack to cool. Cut into 2-inch squares. Melt chocolate with water in double boiler over hot, but not boiling, water. Pour over cooled cookie squares. Cool until chocolate is firm. Yield: 35 servings.

Mrs. Anni L. Cummins
Kirksville AFS, Mo.

RAISIN POT CAKE (GERMANY)

2 c. dark or golden raisins
1 c. finely cut citron
1 ½ c. currants
2 ½ c. sifted cake flour
1 ¼ c. butter or margarine
1 ¼ c. sugar
5 eggs
1 tsp. grated lemon rind
1 tbsp. vanilla flavoring
¾ tsp. baking powder
¼ tsp. salt

Chop raisins coarsely. Combine with citron, currants and 1/2 cup flour; mix until coated. Beat butter until soft. Add sugar gradually, beating until mixture is fluffy. Add an egg at a time, beating vigorously after each addition. Blend in lemon rind and vanilla. Resift remaining flour with baking powder and salt. Add to batter all at once; beat vigorously for 1 minute. Fold in floured fruit. Turn into greased and floured 2-quart baking mold or 9-inch tube pan. Bake at 325 degrees for 1 hour and 30 minutes. Cool cake in pan for 10 minutes; turn out onto cake rack. Frost with dark chocolate icing when cake is cold.

DARK CHOCOLATE ICING:

2 1-oz. squares unsweetened chocolate
¼ c. butter
¼ c. boiling water
3 c. sifted powdered sugar
⅛ tsp. salt
½ tsp. vanilla flavoring

Melt chocolate and butter in saucepan. Add boiling water, powdered sugar, salt and vanilla. Beat until smooth and thick.

Photograph for this recipe above.

SPRINGERLE--CHRISTMAS COOKIE (GERMANY)

4 eggs
2 c. sugar
8 drops anise oil
4 ½ c. sifted cake flour

Beat eggs until thickened; gradually add sugar, beating well after each addition. Beat for 15 minutes with electric mixer; blend in anise oil. Fold in flour lightly; dough will be stiff. Roll 1/4-inch thick on lightly floured board. Roll floured springerle rolling pin firmly over dough; cut cookies along imprinted edges. Place on buttered cookie sheet; let dry overnight in cool place. Bake at 300 degrees for 30 minutes. Yield: 3 dozen.

Margaret Schluckebier
Douglas, Wyo.

TORTE (GERMANY)

½ c. butter
2 c. sugar
4 eggs, separated
1 ¾ c. sifted cake flour
½ tsp. salt
2 tsp. baking powder
½ c. milk
1 tsp. vanilla flavoring
1 c. chopped nuts

Cream butter and 1 cup sugar; add egg yolks. Mix well. Sift flour with salt and baking powder; add alternately with milk. Spread in two greased and floured 9-inch layer cake pans. Beat egg whites until stiff. Gradually beat in remaining sugar and vanilla. Carefully fold in nuts. Spread egg white mixture over dough. Bake at 375 degrees for 25 to 30 minutes. Yield: 16 servings.

Mrs. Bruno Block
Neponset, Ill.

ALMOND CRESCENT COOKIE (GREECE)

1 lb. unsalted butter, softened
½ c. shortening
¾ c. powdered sugar
2 egg yolks
1 tsp. almond flavoring
6 c. flour
1 tsp. baking powder
1 c. toasted blanched almonds, finely
  chopped

Cream butter and shortening well; add powdered sugar, egg yolks and almond flavoring. Beat until light and creamy. Sift flour with baking powder; add to butter mixture. Add almonds. Form into crescent shapes. Bake at 370 degrees for 15 minutes. Immediately upon removing cookies from oven, place on waxed paper which has been generously sprinkled with powdered sugar. Sift sugar over cookies until completely covered. Cool; store in refrigerator. NOTE: Will keep indefinitely in covered container. Yield: 5 dozen.

Mrs. Helen M. Stanley
Madison, Wisc.

BRANDIED STRAWBERRIES (GREECE)

2 baskets fresh strawberries or 2 boxes
  frozen berries
1 ½ c. sugar
Brandy to taste

Clean berries; place in large bowl. Add sugar. Place in individual serving dishes. Add brandy; serve. Yield: 6 servings.

Mrs. Joseph W. Leech
Norfolk, Va.

KARIDOPITA--HONEY CAKE (GREECE)

1 c. flour
2 tsp. (heaping) baking powder
½ tsp. salt
¼ tsp. cinnamon
¼ tsp. ground cloves
6 eggs, separated
3 c. sugar
1 lb. walnuts, chopped
2 c. water

Sift flour; add remaining dry ingredients except sugar. Set aside. Whip egg whites until stiff; gradually add 1 cup sugar. Add yolks. Fold in dry ingredients and chopped walnuts; mix well. Pour into 9 x 13-inch greased baking dish. Bake at 350 degrees for 35 minutes. Combine remaining sugar and water. Boil for 12 to 15 minutes or until syrupy. Pour hot syrup over warm cake. Cool; cut into diamond-shaped pieces.

Christine A. Petsas
Munster, Ind.

KRECAMBYETHES-- POWDERED SUGAR COOKIES (GREECE)

1 egg yolk
1 lb. butter, softened
½ c. powdered sugar
¾ c. finely chopped toasted almonds or
  walnuts
1 oz. whiskey
4 c. cake flour

Add egg yolk to soft butter; beat for 30 minutes or until light and fluffy. Add sugar, nuts and whiskey; mix well. Blend in flour, a little at a time, working it in until dough can be handled without sticking to fingers. Shape into crescents. Place on greased cookie sheet. Bake at 325 degrees for 25 minutes or until lightly browned. Remove from cookie sheet with table knife; place on waxed paper which has been sprinkled with powdered sugar. Sift powdered sugar on top of cookies. Cool before moving again. Yield: 40 cookies.

Mrs. Evangeline Auxier
Itasca, Ill.

MELOMACARONA--BROWN COOKIE (GREECE)

2 c. oil
1 stick butter
1 egg
Juice of 1 orange
Sugar
¾ c. nuts
1 tsp. vanilla flavoring
1 tsp. ground cinnamon
1 tsp. ground cloves
1 tsp. ground nutmeg
6 c. flour
1 1-lb. jar honey
½ honey jar hot water

(Continued on next page)

Combine oil and butter; bring to a boil. Cool; add egg, juice, 1 cup sugar, nuts, vanilla and spices. Mix well. Add flour; mix to form dough. Shape into ovals. Place on waxed paper-lined pans. Bake at 350 degrees for 25 minutes or until done. Combine honey with hot water. Dip cookies into mixture. Sprinkle with sugar and cinnamon. Yield: 3 dozen cookies.

Mrs. Steven P. Pakes
Pine Bluff Arsenal, Ark.

SIPHNIAC--HONEY SQUARES (GREECE)

6 tbsp. butter
1 c. sifted flour
1 tbsp. ice water
2 3-oz. pkg. cream cheese
¼ c. plus 1 tbsp. sugar
2 eggs
¼ c. honey
Powdered cinnamon

Work butter into flour until the size of peas; add ice water. Mix until particles stick together. Roll out dough 1/8-inch thick on floured board. Line bottom and 1 inch up sides of 8 x 8 x 2-inch baking dish with pastry. Blend cream cheese with 1/4 cup sugar and eggs until light with electric mixer at medium speed. Add honey and 1/2 teaspoon cinnamon; mix well. Spread mixture over dough; sprinkle with 1 tablespoon sugar mixed with 1/4 teaspoon cinnamon. Bake at 350 degrees for 30 minutes or until golden. Yield: 12 squares.

Mrs. Anthony C. Dias
Beaufort, S.C.

SCANDINAVIAN COOKIE (GREENLAND)

¼ c. powdered sugar
½ c. shortening
1 egg, separated
1 c. flour
Chopped walnuts
Currant or mint jelly

Mix sugar, shortening, egg yolk and flour; form into walnut-sized balls. Roll in slightly beaten egg white; roll in walnuts. Place 2 inches apart on greased cookie sheet. Make a depression in each cookie with thumb. Bake at 350 degrees for 12 to 15 minutes. Cool on rack. Before serving fill depression in each cookie with jelly.

Martha Loy
Kingston, Ill.

ALMOND PASTRY (HOLLAND)

FILLING:
1 lb. almond paste
2 c. sugar
3 eggs, slightly beaten

Juice of 1 orange
Grated rind of 1 orange

Blend all ingredients; mix well. Refrigerate overnight.

CRUST:
4 c. flour
½ tsp. baking powder
1 lb. butter
1 c. water
Beaten egg white

Sift dry ingredients; cut in butter. Add water; mix well. Refrigerate overnight. Divide dough into eight pieces. Roll each piece into a 10 x 8-inch rectangle. Spread with 3 tablespoons filling; roll up, sealing edges tightly. Place on baking sheet; brush with beaten egg white. Slash top every 2 inches. Bake at 300 degrees for 30 minutes. Yield: 8 pastries.

Mrs. Jake Van Der Veen
Willmar, Minn.

SCHUIMIGE CITROENVLA--FOAMY LEMON CUSTARD (HOLLAND)

3 lge. eggs, separated
½ c. sugar
Juice of 2 lemons
½ c. Rhine wine

Stir egg yolks and sugar until mixture becomes thick and white. Add lemon juice and wine. Place over boiling water and stir until mixture thickens; do not boil. Remove from heat; fold in stiffly beaten egg whites. This must be done immediately so egg whites will cool mixture. Turn into serving bowl or individual bowls. Chill. Yield: 6 servings.

Mrs. Leo P. Kendall
Bainbridge, Md.

ST. NICHOLAS COOKIES (HOLLAND)

1 c. butter
1 c. lard
2 c. sugar
4 c. flour
4 tsp. cinnamon
½ tsp. nutmeg
½ tsp. cloves
½ tsp. soda
½ c. sour cream
½ c. finely sliced almonds

Cream butter and lard. Add sugar; continue to cream. Add sifted dry ingredients alternately with sour cream; add almonds. Knead into loaves. Put into greased bread pans; chill overnight. Slice into desired thickness. Bake at 350 degrees for 10 minutes or until edges are brown. Yield: 8-9 dozen.

Mrs. A. H. Bennett
Esmond, R. I.

BUBBLE LOAF COFFEE CAKE (HUNGARY)

1 c. sour cream
1 ½ c. sugar
1 tsp. salt
2 cakes fresh yeast
3 eggs
1 c. butter
4 ½ c. flour
1 c. chopped walnuts
¾ tsp. cinnamon

Mix sour cream, 1/2 cup sugar, salt and yeast; stir until dissolved. Add eggs, 1/2 cup softened butter and 2 1/4 cups flour; mix well. Add remaining flour. Place dough on floured board; knead until smooth. Place in greased bowl; cover and let rise for 1 hour and 30 minutes to 2 hours. Punch down; turn over. Let rise for 45 minutes. Form into walnut-sized balls. Melt remaining butter; combine remaining sugar, nuts and cinnamon. Dip balls into butter; roll in sugar mixture. Place in layers in 10-inch tube pan; let rise for 45 minutes. Bake at 375 degrees for 40 to 50 minutes. Yield: 10-12 servings.

Mrs. Milford F. Saunders
Sheridan, Wyo.

CSOREGE--DEEP FRIED COOKIES (HUNGARY)

2 c. sifted flour
1 tbsp. sugar
½ tsp. salt
3 egg yolks, slightly beaten
½ c. thick sour cream
⅓ tsp. vanilla flavoring
2 to 3 tbsp. confectioners sugar

Sift flour, sugar and salt into bowl; make a well in center of mixture. Combine egg yolks, sour cream and vanilla; pour into dry ingredients. Blend until all flour is moistened. Let dough rest for 1 to 2 minutes. Turn dough onto lightly floured surface; knead only until well blended. Shape into smooth ball; roll into rectangle 1/8-inch thick. Cut into diamond-shaped pieces 2 inches wide at center and 6 inches long. Make a 1-inch lengthwise cut in center of each diamond; pull one end through slit, twisting slightly. Deep fry one layer at a time in 365 degree deep fryer. Turn cookies several times with fork as they rise to the surface; do not pierce. Fry for 3 minutes or until lightly browned. Drain briefly on absorbent paper. Sprinkle with confectioners sugar. Yield: 2 1/2 dozen cookies.

Mrs. Robert H. Lang
San Antonio, Tex.

CHRISTMAS CAKE (ICELAND)

FILLING:
2 lb. dried prunes
1 c. sugar
½ tsp. cardamom seed
1 tsp. vanilla flavoring
¼ tsp. salt

Cover prunes with water. Cook until tender; drain, reserving 1/2 cup liquid. Remove pits; put prunes through grinder or cut into fine pieces. Add prune liquid, sugar and cardamom seed to prunes. Cook until filling is as thick as jam. Cool; add vanilla and salt.

CAKE:
1 c. butter
1 c. sugar
2 eggs, slightly beaten
1 tsp. vanilla flavoring
4 c. sifted flour
2 tsp. baking powder
½ tsp. salt
¼ c. milk

Cream butter until soft; gradually add sugar. Continue mixing until very creamy. Stir in eggs and vanilla. Sift flour with baking powder and salt; add alternately with milk to butter mixture. The dough should be firm but not stiff; it can be chilled for easy handling. Divide dough into seven equal portions. Roll each portion out thinly on pan upside-down; trim edges. Bake at 350 degrees for 20 minutes or until brown. Remove from oven; slide cake off bottom of pan. Cool on wire rack. Repeat until all seven layers are baked. Layers will be very hard. Spread a generous amount of filling between layers. Yield: 14 servings.

Georgia Thomas
Lenoir City, Tenn.

CARROT COOKIES (INDIA)

¾ c. butter or margarine
¾ c. sugar
1 egg, beaten
1 c. cooked carrots, mashed
1 orange rind, grated
3 c. sifted flour
2 tbsp. baking powder
¼ tsp. salt
½ tsp. lemon flavoring
1 tsp. vanilla flavoring

Cream shortening and sugar well; add egg. Beat in carrots and grated rind. Sift all dry ingredients; stir into creamed mixture. Add flavorings. Drop by teaspoonfuls onto lightly greased cookie sheet. Bake at 375 degrees until cookies begin to brown. Watch closely; cookies brown easily.

FROSTING:
Grated rind of 1 orange
2 tsp. butter, softened
2 c. powdered sugar
Orange juice

Combine orange rind, butter and sugar. Add enough orange juice to make of spreading

(Continued on next page)

consistency. Spread on cookies while cookies are still warm. Yield: 2-4 servings.

Mrs. George W. Wier
Austin, Tex.

CHILDREN'S CHRISTMAS CAKE (IRELAND)

½ lb. butter
1 ½ c. sugar
8 eggs
½ c. orange juice
1 lb. jar mixed peelings from citron, lemon, orange and cherries
1 lb. box seeded raisins
½ lb. box white raisins
¼ lb. box currants
½ c. broken walnuts
3 ½ c. flour
1 tsp. baking powder

Cream butter and sugar well; add 2 eggs at a time, beating well after each addition. Add juice and citric peel. Add raisins and currants which have been washed in hot water. Add nuts; add flour and baking powder. Place in two paper-lined loaf pans. Bake at 275 degrees for 2 hours or until there is no cracking sound when cake is held to ear. Yield: 50 servings.

Rita M. White
Hialeah, Fla.

FRECKLE BREAD (IRELAND)

2 pkg. dry yeast
1 c. warm potato water
¼ c. mashed potatoes
1 tsp. salt
8 tbsp. sugar
5 ¼ c. flour
2 eggs, beaten
½ c. margarine
1 c. dark seedless raisins

Sprinkle yeast into potato water; stir until dissolved. Add mashed potatoes, salt,2 tablespoons sugar and 1 cup flour. Beat until smooth. Cover; let rise about 30 minutes. Stir down; add remaining sugar. Gradually add remaining flour. Stir in eggs and melted margarine. Stir in raisins and enough flour to make soft dough. Knead about 5 minutes or until soft and elastic. Place in greased bowl. Cover; let rise for 1 hour. Punch down; divide into four parts. Let rest for 5 minutes. Shape into small loaves. Place two loaves in 9 x 5 x 3-inch pan. Let rise for 40 minutes. Bake at 350 degrees for 45 minutes. Yield: 20 servings.

Mrs. Loraine Griffin
Malvern, Iowa

KILLARNEY CHERRY CAKE (IRELAND)

1 1-lb. 2 ½-oz. pkg. chocolate fudge cake mix
¼ c. plus 3 tbsp. creme de menthe or 1 ½ tsp. peppermint flavoring
½ c. chopped green Maraschino cherries
1 ½ c. heavy cream
2 tbsp. confectioners sugar
¼ c. whole green Maraschino cherries
Chocolate curls

Prepare cake according to package directions, substituting 1/4 cup creme de menthe for 1/4 cup water or adding 1 teaspoon peppermint flavoring. Stir in chopped cherries; pour into two greased 9-inch layer pans. Bake as directed on package. Cool. Whip cream with remaining creme de menthe or 1/2 teaspoon peppermint flavoring and confectioners sugar. Spread one-third of the whipped cream between cake layers. Heap remaining whipped cream on top. Arrange whole cherries and chocolate curls over whipped cream. Yield: One 9-inch layer cake.

Photograph for this recipe on page 309 .

PONETONE--CHRISTMAS BREAD (ITALY)

2 c. milk, scalded
1 cake yeast
6 c. flour
5 tbsp. shortening
1 c. sugar
3 eggs
1 ½ tsp. salt
1 tsp. nutmeg
½ c. raisins
½ c. finely sliced citron
1 c. chopped walnuts
Olive oil

Cool milk to lukewarm. Crumble in yeast; stir until dissolved. Add 2 cups flour; beat well. Cream shortening and sugar; add 2 beaten eggs. Add milk, salt and remaining flour; knead well. Cover and let rise for 1 hour and 30 minutes. Work in remaining ingredients; knead on floured board until smooth and elastic. Place in greased bowl; rub with olive oil. Cover and let rise until doubled in bulk. Knead; shape into loaves. Place on greased cookie sheet. Beat remaining egg; brush on loaves. Let rise until doubled. Bake at 400 degrees for 15 minutes. Reduce heat to 350 degrees; bake for 25 minutes.

Mrs. Lee Hacker
Pasco, Wash.

CHRISTMAS BREAD (ITALY)

1 pkg. active dry yeast
1 ¼ c. warm water
2 tbsp. soft shortening

(Continued on next page)

2 tsp. salt
2 tbsp. sugar
3 c. sifted flour
¼ c. raisins
¼ c. candied fruit
¼ c. chopped nuts
¾ tsp. anise
¼ tsp. vanilla flavoring

Dissolve yeast in warm water. Add shortening, salt, sugar and one-half the flour. Beat for 2 minutes at medium speed or 300 strokes by hand. Scrape sides of bowl frequently. Add remaining flour, fruits, nuts and flavorings; blend thoroughly with spoon. Scrape batter from sides of bowl; cover. Let rise in warm place about 85 degrees for 30 minutes or until double in size. Stir down by beating 25 strokes. Spread evenly in greased 9 x 5 x 3-inch loaf pan. Batter will be sticky; smooth with floured hands. Let rise until batter reaches 1 inch from top of pan. Bake at 375 degrees for 45 to 50 minutes. Yield: 12-16 servings.

Mrs. Charles Pope
Tarpon Springs, Fla.

PANATUNG--CHRISTMAS CAKE (ITALY)

¼ lb. butter
1 c. sugar
3 eggs
3 c. flour
1 ⅓ c. milk
Grated rind of 1 lemon
1 tsp. vanilla flavoring
2 oz. candied fruit
1 c. white raisins
1 tsp. baking soda
1 tsp. cream of tartar

Cream butter and sugar. Add eggs, flour, milk, lemon rind and vanilla. Mix for 10 minutes; add fruits, soda and cream of tartar. Mix well; pour batter into angel food pan, greased and dusted with a mixture of flour, sugar and cinnamon. Bake at 325 degrees for 45 minutes. Increase heat to 350 degrees; bake for 30 minutes. NOTE: Cake can be frozen. Yield: 6 servings.

Mrs. Michael J. Bussone
Negaunee, Mich.

CHRISTMAS COOKIES (ITALY)

2 c. red wine
2 c. cooking oil
½ c. water
5 to 6 c. flour
3 eggs
2 tsp. baking powder

Heat wine, oil and water to boiling. Remove from heat. Add flour; mix until dough leaves bowl clean. Cool; add eggs, baking powder and additional flour if needed. Dough should resemble soft pie crust dough. Roll to 6 x 20 inches.

FILLING:
1 lb. walnuts, ground
2 lb. raisins, ground

Combine nuts and raisins; spread over dough. Roll as a jelly roll. Cut into 1 1/2-inch slices. Bake at 350 degrees for 30 minutes. When cool drop into syrup.

SYRUP:
4 c. sugar
2 c. water
2 c. honey
Juice of 1 lemon

Boil sugar, water and honey for 10 minutes; add juice.

Mary Vigor
Helper, Utah

CROSTATA (ITALY)

3 c. flour
½ c. sugar
3 tbsp. baking powder
Dash of salt
½ lb. butter
¼ c. milk
2 eggs, slightly beaten
1 tsp. vanilla flavoring
1 8-oz. jar of grape, apricot or strawberry jam

Sift all dry ingredients; cut in butter. Combine milk, eggs and vanilla. Add to dry ingredients; mix well. Knead on floured board until smooth. Roll three-fourths of dough 1/2-inch thick. Place on 15 x 10 x 2-inch baking sheet; spread with jam. Roll remaining dough 1/4-inch thick; cut into strips. Form lattice over jam. Bake at 400 degrees for 25 minutes. Yield: 15 servings.

Mrs. Aldo J. Cardorri
Scranton, Pa.

FRETTURA DOLCE--LEMON-ALMOND FRITTERS (ITALY)

½ c. farina
½ c. sugar
2 c. milk, scalded
Grated rind of 1 lemon
1 tsp. almond flavoring
1 egg, beaten
Cracker crumbs

Slowly add farina and sugar to hot milk; stir in lemon rind. Add almond flavoring; pour into dinner plate or pan. Allow mixture to set. Cut into diamond or oblong-shaped pieces. Roll each piece in beaten egg; roll in cracker crumbs. Fry on all sides until golden brown.

Mrs. S. James Bessolo
Negaunee, Mich.

MACAROONS (ITALY)

2 egg whites
¼ tsp. salt
1 c. sugar
¾ c. almonds, ground
½ tsp. almond flavoring

Cover cookie sheet with unglazed paper. Beat egg whites and salt. Add sugar, 1 tablespoon at a time, beating thoroughly after each addition. Fold in almonds and flavoring. Drop by teaspoonfuls 1 inch apart on cookie sheet. Bake at 350 degrees for 20 minutes or until light brown. Yield: 12 servings.

Mrs. Margaret Carberry
Glenolden, Pa.

PLUM CAKE (ITALY)

3 ½ sticks margarine
2 ½ c. sugar
1 egg
4 c. self-rising flour
2 lb. fresh Italian prune plums, quartered
¼ tsp. cinnamon
½ tsp. vanilla flavoring

Cream 1 1/2 sticks margarine and 1 cup sugar; add egg and 2 cups flour. Spread in 11 x 13-inch pan; cover evenly with plum quarters. Sprinkle with cinnamon. Combine remaining margarine, sugar, flour and vanilla, mixing until crumbly; sprinkle over plums. Bake at 350 degrees for 45 minutes. May be served warm or cold. Yield: 20 servings.

Mrs. Ruth B. Waits
New Orleans, La.

FRUIT CAKE (JAPAN)

1 c. butter
2 c. sugar
6 eggs, separated
3 c. flour
4 tbsp. baking powder
2 tsp. cinnamon
1 tsp. cloves
1 tsp. nutmeg
1 c. milk
½ lb. coconut
1 box seedless raisins
1 c. pecans or black walnuts

Cream butter and sugar. Add egg yolks. Sift all dry ingredients. Add to batter alternating with milk. Add coconut, raisins and nuts which have been rolled in flour. Beat egg whites until stiff; fold into batter. Pour into four layer pans. Bake at 350 degrees for 30 minutes. Cool.

FILLING:

2 c. sugar
9 tbsp. flour
2 peeled lemons, chopped
2 peeled oranges, chopped
1 ½ c. boiling water
½ lb. coconut

Mix sugar and flour; add lemons, oranges and water. Cook until thick. Add coconut. Cook for 2 minutes. Cool; spread on layers of cake.

Mrs. Kyle S. Ford
Newport News, Va.

SUMBUSIC--COOKIES (LEBANON)

2 c. melted butter
8 c. sifted flour
1 c. sugar
¼ tsp. salt
½ tsp. dry yeast
½ c. warm water
½ c. warm milk
Nut filling
Powdered sugar

Cut butter into flour, sugar and salt; add yeast, water and milk. Blend. Let rest for 30 minutes. Roll into small balls; pat out. Fill with nut filling; form into crescent shapes. Prick cookies before baking. Bake at 350 degrees for 20 minutes. Sprinkle with powdered sugar after baking. Yield: 100 cookies.

Jeanette R. Nemer
Lead, S.D.

MEXICAN WEDDING CAKE COOKIES (MEXICO)

1 lb. butter
Powdered sugar
2 ½ c. flour
1 tbsp. vanilla flavoring
1 ½ to 2 c. pecans

Cream butter and 1/2 cup powdered sugar well. Add flour, vanilla and pecans. Drop by teaspoonfuls onto ungreased cookie sheet; press down slightly with fork tines. Bake at 350 degrees for 20 minutes. Cool; roll in powdered sugar.

Mrs. Joe B. Ballew
Pine Bluff Arsenal, Ark.

PLUM PUDDING (NEW ZEALAND)

1 lb. flour
2 tsp. baking powder
8 oz. chopped lard
8 oz. sugar
1 c. currants

(Continued on next page)

1 c. raisins
2 tsp. spice
1 tsp. ground ginger
2 oz. orange or lemon peel
Milk

Mix flour and baking powder; add remaining ingredients, using enough milk to mix well. Put into pudding basin or cloth; boil for 3 hours. Serve with custard sauce.

Mrs. Pamela L. Cunningham
Bainbridge, Md.

APPLE PIE (NORWAY)

1 c. flour
2 tsp. baking powder
½ tsp. salt
1 ⅓ c. sugar
2 c. apples
½ tsp. lemon juice
1 tsp. vanilla flavoring
1 c. chopped pecans
3 eggs, slightly beaten

Mix all dry ingredients. Mix apples, lemon juice, vanilla, nuts and eggs; add to dry ingredients. Mix well. Bake in well greased pie plates. Bake at 325 degrees for 30 to 35 minutes. Yield: 6 servings.

Mrs. Angelina B. Menilolia
Pearl River, N.Y.

ARISTOCRATS (NORWAY)

2 c. sifted flour
1 c. butter
½ c. sugar
½ c. ground almonds
1 egg, beaten
½ tsp. vanilla flavoring

Combine flour and butter; add sugar and almonds. Blend egg and vanilla into mixture. Shape into balls; wrap in waxed paper. Refrigerate for 24 hours; slice thin. Place on greased cookie sheet. Bake at 350 degrees for 8 to 10 minutes. Yield: 48 cookies.

Mary C. Parkinson
Waynesburg, Pa.

ROMMEGROT--CREAM PUDDING (NORWAY)

1 pt. thick cream, slightly soured
½ c. water
½ c. sifted flour
½ tsp. salt
1 pt. hot milk
Sugar
Cinnamon

Simmer cream and water for 45 to 60 minutes, stirring occasionally. Combine flour and salt; sift into hot cream, beating until smooth. Cook until mixture is thick and butter

fat rises to top. Remove fat and save. Stir in hot milk; beat well. Pudding should be smooth and creamy. Pour into bowl; make depressions on top for butter fat. Serve hot in dessert dishes with sugar and cinnamon sprinkled on top. NOTE: The pudding is not a success unless butter fat rises to top after flour is added. Yield: 6-8 servings.

Mrs. Mary Bottolfson
Glenwood, Minn.

SOTSUPPE--FRUIT SOUP (NORWAY)

3 c. mixed dried fruits
1 c. chopped mixed apples and oranges
7 c. mixed fruit juice and water
1 lemon, sliced
2 tbsp. tapioca
½ tsp. salt
1 to 1 ⅓ c. sugar
2 or 3 cinnamon sticks

Mix all ingredients; cook, covered, for 30 to 40 minutes or until tender. Serve hot or cold as a main dish, meat accompaniment, appetizer or frozen dessert served with cream. Yield: 8 servings.

Mrs. Kristine Paulson
Hanska, Minn.

PRUNE PUDDING (NORWAY)

1 lb. prunes
¾ c. sugar or to taste
Juice of 1 lemon
Pinch of salt
2 tbsp. cornstarch

Soak prunes overnight. Cook until tender, keeping prunes well covered with water. Remove stones; put prunes back into liquid. Simmer for 5 minutes. Add sugar, lemon juice and salt. Remove from heat; cool. Blend cornstarch into 1 cup prune liquid; add to pudding. Return pudding to heat; cook until thickened. Chill. Serve with whipped cream and chopped nuts. Yield: 6 servings.

Mrs. Richard Goward
San Francisco, Calif.

SPRITZ COOKIES (NORWAY)

1 c. butter, softened
⅔ c. sugar
3 egg yolks
1 tsp. vanilla, almond or lemon flavoring
2 ½ c. sifted flour
¼ tsp. salt
Candies or cherries to decorate

Cream butter and sugar until fluffy. Blend in egg yolks and flavoring. Gradually add sifted

(Continued on next page)

flour and salt; mix thoroughly. Chill dough for 5 to 15 minutes. Force dough through cookie press onto ungreased sheets; decorate. Bake at 400 degrees for 7 to 10 minutes or until set but not brown. Yield: 6-7 dozen.

Mrs. Arlene Thorsness Kostoch
Coronado, Calif.

FIRNI--RICE PUDDING (PAKISTAN)

¼ c. long grain rice
1 qt. milk
1 c. sugar
¼ c. silver cake dusting
1 c. finely sliced pistachio nuts

Soak rice in cold water for 1 hour; drain. Heat milk to near boiling point; add rice. Reduce heat; cover and simmer slowly, stirring occasionally. When mixture begins to thicken, add sugar; mix well. Simmer for 1 minute; remove from heat. Cool; pour into a large bowl. Decorate top with silver dusting and nuts. Chill before serving. Yield: 4 servings.

Mrs. Albert J. Fleming
Burns AFS, Oreg.

CHRUSCIKI--ANGEL WINGS (POLAND)

2 ½ c. sifted flour
¼ tsp. salt
5 egg yolks
3 tbsp. sugar
¼ tsp. grated lemon rind
1 ½ tsp. almond flavoring
5 tbsp. sour cream
1 qt. cooking oil
Powdered sugar

Sift flour with salt. Beat egg yolk, sugar, lemon rind and flavoring until thick. Add sour cream; mix well. Gradually stir in flour; knead in bowl until dough is pliable. Cover and let stand for 1 hour. Half dough; roll out each part paper thin. Cut with pastry wheel into 2 x 5-inch strips. Cut a 2-inch slit in center of each strip. Pass one end of strip through slit. Fry in deep oil at 370 degrees. Fry three at a time; turn once. Drain; sprinkle with powdered sugar. Yield: 25 servings.

Donna L. Wyland
Berkley, Mich.

BLUEBERRY PIEROGI (POLAND)

2 c. plus 2 tbsp. flour
1 egg
Water
1 qt. fresh or frozen blueberries
½ c. sugar

Sift 2 cups flour into a bowl. Add egg; mix. Add at least 1/2 cup water; mix. If dough is not sticky, add more water to look like bread dough. Knead dough until smooth. Roll to 1/4-inch thick; cut into 4-inch circles. Combine blueberries, sugar and remaining 2 tablespoons flour. Place 2 tablespoons of mixture on circle; fold in half and pinch edges to seal. Boil for 5 minutes in water.

Louise Bartos
South Deerfield, Mass.

CHRUSTI--LOVERS' KNOTS (POLAND)

3 tbsp. sugar
2 tbsp. butter
2 eggs
4 egg yolks
2 tbsp. rum or 1 tsp. vanilla flavoring
2 ½ c. flour
Powdered sugar

Mix sugar and butter; add eggs and rum. Beat until light and frothy. Mix thoroughly into flour. Knead on lightly floured board for 3 minutes. Roll dough 1/8-inch thick; cut 1 1/2 x 4-inch strips. Make 1-inch slash in center of each. Slip one end through slit to form knot. Drop into 375 degree deep fat. Brown each side. Drain; sprinkle with powdered sugar. Yield: 4 dozen.

Antoinette Formanski
New Haven, Conn.

MAZUREK--FRUIT BARS (POLAND)

2 c. flour
1 c. sugar
¼ tsp. salt
½ c. butter, softened
1 egg, beaten
3 tbsp. cream

Sift all dry ingredients; cut in butter until crumbly. Mix egg with cream; add to flour. Mix lightly; spread on buttered 10 x 16-inch cookie sheet. Bake at 350 degrees for 25 to 30 minutes.

TOPPING:
½ lb. raisins, chopped
½ lb. dates, chopped
½ lb. figs, chopped
¼ lb. nuts, chopped
1 c. sugar
2 eggs
Juice of 1 lemon
Juice of 1 orange

Mix all ingredients thoroughly. Spread quickly over hot pastry. Bake at 350 degrees for 15 minutes longer. Cut into squares. Yield: 2 dozen.

Mrs. Peter P. Narsavage
Philadelphia, Pa.

FILOZES--ALMOND DREAMS (PORTUGAL)

1 c. water
1 c. milk
1 ½ tsp. vanilla flavoring
½ c. butter
½ tsp. salt
1 tsp. almond flavoring
1 ½ c. sifted flour
5 eggs
1 tbsp. finely grated orange rind
2 tbsp. finely chopped roasted almonds
2 c. salad oil
2 c. shortening
Sugar
Cinnamon

Put water, milk, vanilla, butter, salt and almond flavoring into pan; bring to a boil. When boiling hard, add flour, stirring constantly with wooden spoon. When mixture starts rolling around spoon and separates from side of pan, remove from heat; cool slightly. Pour mixture into mixing bowl; mix with electric mixer at low speed. Add an egg at a time; mix for 5 minutes until well blended. Fold in orange rind and almonds. Heat oil and shortening to 375 degrees in frying pan. Drop mixture from tablespoon into oil; fry golden brown. Drain on paper towels; sprinkle with sugar and cinnamon while hot. Yield: 4 dozen.

Mrs. Eugene B. Fluckey
Pearl Harbor, Hawaii

CZARINA--GEMS (RUSSIA)

CRUST:
1 c. butter
2 c. flour
4 tbsp. brown sugar

Mix all ingredients; spread in a 15 x 10-inch pan. Bake at 350 degrees for 15 to 20 minutes. Cool.

FILLING:
3 c. brown sugar
4 eggs, well beaten
8 tsp. flour
2 tsp. vanilla flavoring
1 c. chopped nuts
1 c. finely chopped coconut
1 c. chopped dates
1 c. candied red cherries
Powdered sugar

Mix all ingredients except powdered sugar; pour on top of crust. Bake at 350 degrees for 40 minutes. Cool. Cut into diamond shapes. Sprinkle with powdered sugar. Yield: 36 cookies.

Mrs. R. L. McNeely
Portsmouth, Va.

FILLED TARTS (SCANDINAVIA)

½ c. butter
¼ c. brown sugar
1 egg, separated
1 c. flour
½ c. chopped pecans
Jelly

Cream butter and sugar. Add egg yolk; beat. Mix in flour. Roll dough into small balls; dip into unbeaten egg white. Roll in nuts. Place on cookie sheet; make dent in center of each ball. Bake at 350 degrees for 5 minutes. Take out of oven; make dent deeper. Bake for 15 minutes longer. While warm, fill with jelly. Handle with care. Yield: 2 dozen tarts.

Mrs. C. E. Connaway
Fort Richardson, Alaska

RHUBARB PUDDING (SCANDINAVIA)

1 ½ lb. rhubarb
1 ½ c. water
¾ c. sugar
1 ½ tsp. vanilla flavoring
3 tbsp. cornstarch
1 c. heavy cream

Trim rhubarb; cut into 1/2-inch slices. Combine with water and 1/2 cup sugar; simmer until softened. Stir in 1/2 teaspoon vanilla. Blend cornstarch with a small amount of cold water to make a smooth stiff paste. Stir into rhubarb mixture; cook for 5 minutes or until thickened and clear, stirring constantly. Pour rhubarb into glass serving dish; chill. At serving time, whip cream. When frothy, add remaining 1/4 cup sugar and 1 teaspoon vanilla; whip until stiffened. Pipe through pastry tube in decorative swirls on pudding or cover top with spoonfuls of whipped cream. Yield: 4 servings.

Nelda R. Judy
Germantown, O.

PETTICOAT TAILS (SCOTLAND)

1 c. butter
½ c. sugar
1 tbsp. cream
½ tsp. baking powder
2 c. sifted flour
½ tsp. salt

Cream butter and sugar; mix in cream. Add sifted dry ingredients; mix well. Chill. Roll very thin; cut into bite-sized triangles. Bake at 300 to 325 degrees until lightly browned. NOTE: Original recipe was introduced into Mary Queen of Scots' court by the French ladies.

Mrs. F. A. Hansen
Dover, N.J.

PUDDING SAUCE (SCOTLAND)

1 c. sugar
1 tbsp. (heaping) butter
1 egg, separated
¼ c. (scant) water
1 tbsp. lemon juice, vinegar or brandy

Combine sugar, butter, egg yolk and water in double boiler. Cook over hot water until sugar is dissolved. Fold into stiffly beaten egg white to which lemon juice has been added. To reheat cold sauce, add an extra egg yolk and beaten white at the time of reheating.

Mrs. Charles G. Stoll
Lawrenceville, Ill.

FLAN--CUSTARD (SPAIN)

4 eggs
1 can sweetened condensed milk
1 can water
½ tsp. vanilla flavoring
4 drops of lemon flavoring
¼ c. sugar
Nutmeg

Beat eggs thoroughly; add remaining ingredients except sugar and nutmeg. Using top portion of 1 1/2-quart double boiler, caramelize 1/4 cup sugar directly over low heat. Coat sides of container by swirling the melted sugar. When coating has hardened, pour in egg mixture. Sprinkle lightly with nutmeg. Cook, covered, over low heat for 1 hour. Invert into deep serving dish immediately. Chill and serve. Yield: 6-8 servings.

Mrs. R. L. Reed
Paris, Tex.

APPLE CRISP (SWEDEN)

4 c. sliced apples
1 c. sugar
½ c. water
1 tsp. cinnamon
1 c. sifted pastry flour
½ c. oats
½ c. butter
Grated orange

Place apples in 8 x 12-inch pan; add 3/4 cup sugar, water and cinnamon. Add flour to remaining 1/4 cup sugar and oats. Cut in butter; mix well. Spread over apples; add grated orange. Bake at 375 degrees for 40 to 50 minutes. Cut into squares; serve hot or cold with whipped cream or ice cream.

Mrs. William M. Beihl
Grand Haven, Mich.

APPLE PIE (SWEDEN)

½ c. brown sugar
¼ c. sugar
1 lge. egg, beaten
½ c. flour
1 tsp. baking powder
½ tsp. salt
1 ½ c. chopped apples
½ c. chopped nuts
Whipped cream

Add brown and white sugars to beaten egg. Sift flour with baking powder and salt; add to egg-sugar mixture. Add apples and nuts; pour into greased pie tin. Bake at 350 degrees for 25 minutes. Cool; top with whipped cream. Yield: 6 servings.

Mrs. Claude Beasley
Casey, Ill.

KONJAKSKRANSAR--BRANDY RINGS (SWEDEN)

1 ⅓ c. butter
¾ c. sugar
3 ½ c. flour
3 tbsp. brandy

Mix all ingredients; blend until smooth. Turn onto floured baking board. Roll into thin lengths; twist two strips like twine. Cut into 5-inch pieces; shape into rings. Place on buttered baking sheet. Bake at 350 degrees for 10 minutes or until a golden yellow. Yield: 75 cookies.

Mrs. D. E. Carlson
San Diego, Calif.

COFFEE CAKE (SWEDEN)

PIE CRUST:
1 stick margarine
1 c. flour
2 tbsp. water

Cut margarine into flour; add water to form soft dough. Spread in 9 or 10-inch pie pan. Press out evenly.

FILLING:
1 stick margarine
1 c. water
1 c. flour
1 tsp. almond flavoring
3 eggs

Combine margarine and water in saucepan; heat to boiling. Add flour; mix well. Add flavoring and an egg at a time, beating well after each addition. Spread over pie crust. Bake at 400 degrees for 40 minutes. Ice while still hot.

FROSTING:
Powdered sugar
¼ c. milk

(Continued on next page)

Almond flavoring
Toasted almonds

Mix powdered sugar and milk until smooth; add flavoring. Spread over coffee cake. Sprinkle with almonds. Yield: 8 servings.

Mrs. Ella Van Briesen
Stillman Valley, Ill.

DATE CUPS (SWEDEN)
CRUST:
¼ c. butter
1 c. sifted flour
3 tbsp. confectioners sugar

Cream butter; blend in flour and sugar. Press in smallest muffin tins; dough should be about 1/4-inch thick. Bake at 350 to 375 degrees for 15 minutes.

FILLING:
1 lb. dates, washed and quartered
1 c. water
½ c. sugar
Whipped cream

Boil dates with water and sugar to jam consistency. Serve heaping teaspoonful of date filling in each cup; top with whipped cream. NOTE: Cups may be stored in airtight container; filling can be stored in refrigerator for several weeks.

Mrs. John B. Wells
Johnsville Naval Air Dev. Cen., Pa.

KRINGLER (SWEDEN)

1 c. butter
2 c. flour
1 c. plus 1 tbsp. water
3 eggs
½ tsp. almond flavoring

Cut 1/2 cup butter into 1 cup flour; stir in 1 tablespoon water with a fork. Pat mixture on cookie sheet into two long strips each 3 inches wide. Bring remaining water and butter to boiling point; remove from heat. Stir in remaining flour until smooth. Add an egg at a time, beating well after each addition. Add almond flavoring; pour mixture over strips. Bake at 350 degrees for 40 minutes. Cool and frost. Yield: 20 servings.

Mrs. Warren R. Johnson
Salina, Kans.

ALMOND GINGERSNAPS (SWEDEN)

1 c. soft butter
1 c. sugar
½ c. molasses

1 tbsp. ginger
2 tsp. cinnamon
2 tsp. cloves
1 tsp. soda
3 ½ c. flour
1 c. finely chopped blanched almonds

Put all ingredients into large bowl; work with hands until well mixed and dough is smooth. Shape rolls. Wrap in waxed paper; chill thoroughly. Cut into thin slices. Place on greased cookie sheet. Bake at 325 degrees for 8 to 10 minutes.

Evelyn Davis
Eureka, Calif.

GINGERSNAPS (SWEDEN)

1 c. butter
1 c. sugar
2 eggs
1 c. corn syrup
1 tsp. soda
1 tsp. cardamom
1 tsp. ginger
1 tsp. cloves
1 tsp. cinnamon
5 to 6 c. flour

Cream butter and sugar; add eggs and syrup. Add dry ingredients. Refrigerate overnight. Roll out thin; cut with a cookie cutter. Bake at 350 degrees until done. Yield: 3 dozen cookies.

Mrs. Arthur J. Carlson
Wright-Patterson AFB, O.

NAPOLEON FINGERS (SWEDEN)

¾ lb. butter
4 c. sifted flour
½ tsp. baking powder
2 tbsp. sugar
1 egg yolk
4 tbsp. cold water
1 pt. raspberry jam
1 tbsp. butter or margarine
1 tbsp. milk or cream
½ c. confectioners sugar
Vanilla flavoring to taste

Cut butter into flour, baking powder and sugar mixture. Beat egg yolk in water; add to flour mixture. Mix to a stiff paste; divide into three equal portions. Roll one portion thickly on waxed paper. Prick over all with fork; invert onto cookie sheet. Spread with raspberry jam. Repeat with other two portions in layers approximately 8 x 12-inches. Bake at 350 degrees for 30 minutes. Cut into finger shapes. Blend butter and milk; blend in confectioners sugar until of spreading consistency. Flavor with vanilla. Spreading on cookies. Yield: 40 cookies.

Mrs. Robert E. Clarke
Winnemucca, Nev.

RAISIN SWEDISH CHURCH BREAD (SWEDEN)

1 pkg. dry yeast
¼ c. warm water
¼ c. milk
1 ½ c. sifted flour
½ tsp. salt
3 tbsp. sugar
⅓ c. plus 2 tbsp. butter or margarine
1 egg, beaten
½ c. dark or golden raisins

Soften yeast in warm water in a warm bowl. Scald milk; cool to lukewarm. Add to yeast. Resift flour with salt and sugar. Cut in 1/3 cup butter until mixture resembles coarse meal. Add egg, raisins and yeast; mix thoroughly. Turn into a well greased 8-inch round layer cake pan. Sprinkle with sugar; dot with remaining 2 tablespoons butter. Cover; let rise in a warm place for 1 hour or until double in size. Bake at 375 degrees for 25 to 30 minutes. Remove from pan immediately; serve with butter. Yield: One 8-inch coffee cake.

Photograph for this recipe above.

NUT CRESCENTS (SWEDEN)

¼ c. shortening
1 ¼ c. sugar

1 egg
2 tbsp. milk
1 tsp. vanilla flavoring
1 ⅓ c. flour
1 tsp. baking powder
2 tsp. salt
1 c. chopped pecans

Thoroughly mix shortening, 3/4 cup sugar, egg, milk and vanilla. Mix in sifted flour, baking powder and salt. Spread 1/4 cup of dough thinly and evenly on greased inverted 9 x 9 x 2-inch pan. Sprinkle with mixture of remaining 1/2 cup sugar and nuts. Bake one pan at a time at 325 degrees for 10 to 12 minutes. While layer is hot, cut into 4 1/4 x 3/4-inch strips; shape over rolling pin. Repeat until all dough is used. If strips become too brittle to shape, soften in oven. Yield: 9 dozen.

Mrs. Bernice Campen
Union City, N.J.

PASTRY (SWEDEN)

1 c. margarine
1 ½ c. flour
1 c. plus 1 tbsp. water
2 tsp. almond flavoring
3 eggs
Powdered sugar frosting

(Continued on next page)

Mix 1/2 cup margarine and 1 cup flour until crumbly; add 1 tablespoon water. Cover with waxed paper; roll out on cookie sheet. Combine remaining 1/2 cup margarine, remaining 1 cup water and 1 teaspoon flavoring; heat to boiling. Remove from heat; add remaining 1/2 cup flour. Add an egg at a time; beat well after each addition. Spread over rolled pastry. Bake at 350 degrees for 45 to 60 minutes. Frost with powdered sugar frosting flavored with remaining almond flavoring. Yield: 12 servings.

Mrs. Paul Schmid
Monroe, Nebr.

SWEDISH GINGERSNAPS (SWEDEN)

½ c. butter
1 c. sugar
3 eggs
1 tsp. cinnamon
1 tsp. ginger
1 tsp. cloves
1 ¾ c. flour
1 tsp. soda
⅔ c. sour cream

Cream butter and sugar until light and fluffy; add eggs and spices. Sift flour with soda. Add alternately with cream. Stir until well blended; pour into deep round cake pan which has been buttered and sprinkled with bread crumbs. Bake at 325 degrees for 15 minutes. Reduce heat to 250 degrees; continue baking 30 minutes longer. Serve plain or with whipped cream.

Frieda A. Buckingham
Wolfeboro, N.H.

SWEDISH TOSCAS (SWEDEN)

CRUST:
6 tbsp. butter
¼ c. sugar
1 c. flour

Cream butter and sugar; blend in flour. Press into bottom and half way up sides of 12 small ungreased muffin tins. Bake at 350 degrees for 8 to 10 minutes or until edges are golden.

FILLING:
⅓ c. walnuts or almonds
¼ c. sugar
2 tbsp. butter
1 ½ tbsp. evaporated milk or cream
2 tsp. flour

Combine all ingredients; cook over high heat until mixture boils, stirring constantly. Fill baked shells with mixture. Bake at 350 degrees for 8 to 10 minutes until light brown.

Cool for 3 to 5 minutes; carefully remove from pans. Yield: 12 servings.

Mrs. Morris E. Petty
Duluth AB, Minn.

TEA CAKE (SWEDEN)

½ c. shortening
2 c. brown sugar, sifted
2 eggs
1 tsp. vanilla flavoring
2 c. flour
1 tsp. soda
1 tsp. salt
1 c. buttermilk or sour milk

Cream shortening with sugar. Add eggs and vanilla; beat well. Sift flour with soda and salt. Add alternately with buttermilk to egg mixture. Pour into greased and floured 9 x 13-inch pan. Sprinkle with topping. Bake at 350 degrees for 35 to 40 minutes.

TOPPING:
½ c. brown sugar
1 tsp. cinnamon
½ c. chopped nuts (opt.)

Combine all ingredients; sprinkle over batter. Yield: 20-25 servings.

Mrs. Harry E. Davis
Lorain, O.

TOSCAKAKA (SWEDEN)

3 eggs
1 c. sugar
½ c. milk or cream
1 c. sifted flour
1 ½ tsp. baking powder
½ c. melted margarine or butter

Mix thoroughly all ingredients except margarine. Add margarine; beat until smooth. Pour into two 8-inch round cake pans. Bake at 350 degrees for 20 minutes or until lightly browned.

TOPPING:
½ c. margarine or butter
½ c. sugar
1 tbsp. cream
1 tbsp. flour
¼ c. blanched almonds, slivered

Mix all ingredients; heat to boiling. Spread over cakes; broil until golden brown. Remove from pans when cooled. Yield: 12-16 servings.

Patricia Dodgen
Lonoke, Ark.

BASLER LAKERI (SWITZERLAND)

1 tsp. soda
⅓ c. hot honey
3 eggs, well beaten
2 c. brown sugar
¾ c. finely chopped citron
¾ tsp. cloves
2 tsp. cinnamon
3 to 3 ½ c. flour

Mix soda with honey. Combine all ingredients; spread on cookie sheet. Bake at 350 degrees for 12 to 15 minutes.

TOPPING:
1 can evaporated milk
1 ¼ c. powdered sugar

Stir milk into powdered sugar. Brush on cookies while still hot. Cut into squares. Yield: 3 dozen.

Martha Bauman
Longview, Wash.

GRABIE--SHORTBREAD COOKIES (SYRIA)

1 c. butter
1 c. powdered sugar
2 c. flour

Soften butter; gradually blend in sugar. Stir in flour. Roll dough on lightly floured board to 1/4-inch thickness. Cut into desired shapes. Place on a greased cookie sheet. Bake at 300 degrees for 25 minutes. Cookies should be dry but white in color. Do not remove from cookie sheet until cooled. Yield: 3-4 dozen.

Mrs. Hugh Beasley
Robbinsville, N.C.

MEYVA KOMPOSTOSU--FRUIT COMPOTE (TURKEY)

1 ½ tbsp. gelatin
¼ c. cold water
1 ½ c. hot unsweetened grape juice
¾ c. sugar
⅛ tsp. salt
1 tsp. lemon juice
1 tsp. grated lemon rind
⅓ c. Cointreau
1 c. strawberries
1 c. seedless green grapes
1 c. pitted black cherries
1 c. fresh peach halves
Whipped cream

Soften gelatin in cold water; stir in hot grape juice, sugar and salt. Stir until sugar and gelatin are completely dissolved; cool. Stir in lemon juice and rind; chill until beginning to set. Add Cointreau; blend well. Add fruits; pour into an oiled mold. Chill until set.

Unmold; serve with whipped cream flavored with Cointreau. Yield: 8-10 servings.

Mrs. Paul M. Dickens
Moody AFB, Ga.

CHRISTMAS PLUM PUDDING (WALES)

2 c. flour
2 c. brown sugar
2 tsp. baking powder
1 tsp. salt
1 tsp. cinnamon
1 tsp. ginger
1 tsp. cloves
1 tsp. nutmeg
1 tsp. mace
2 c. minced lemon, orange and citron rind
2 c. seedless raisins
2 c. currants
Dates (opt.)
Figs (opt.)
1 c. fruit juice
2 c. ground suet

Thoroughly blend all dry ingredients; stir in fruits. Add fruit juice, suet and 1 cup water. Add additional water to make a thick dough if necessary. Fill greased molds two-thirds full; dip a cloth into boiling water and into flour. Tie over the top of molds. Steam for 5 to 6 hours. NOTE: Pudding is best if made a week ahead.

Mrs. Alun Lewis
Hoquiam, Wash.

CURRENT COOKIES (WALES)

1 c. margarine
3 c. oats
1 c. sugar
¾ c. sifted flour
1 tsp. soda
½ tsp. ground cloves
½ tsp. cinnamon
¼ c. milk
½ c. dried currants

Soften margarine in large mixing bowl. Blend in oats and sugar. Add remaining sifted dry ingredients. Stir in milk and currants; mix well. Shape into small balls about 1 inch in diameter. Place on greased baking sheet about 3 inches apart. Bake at 350 degrees for 15 minutes or until golden brown. Remove from baking sheet; cool. NOTE: Raisins may be substituted for currants. Yield: 3 dozen.

Mrs. M. H. Petersen
Britt, Iowa

CHRISTMAS PLUM PUDDING (WALES)

¾ lb. or 1 c. chopped suet
1 c. plus 2 tbsp. brown sugar
½ c. milk
¼ c. water
2 eggs, well beaten
1 c. seedless raisins
1 ½ c. currants
⅛ c. sliced preserved orange peel
⅓ c. sliced preserved lemon peel
½ c. sliced citron peel
½ c. chopped blanched almonds
1 c. sifted flour
1 tsp. soda
1 tsp. salt
½ tsp. cinnamon
¼ tsp. mace
1 c. stale bread crumbs

Mix suet, brown sugar, milk, water and eggs. Mix fruits, peels and nuts with 1/4 cup flour. Sift remaining 3/4 cup flour with soda, salt and spices. Add fruit mixture, crumbs and flour mixture to suet mixture. Turn into greased 1 1/2-quart mold. Steam for 2 hours and 30 minutes. Use steamer on deep covered kettle with rack. Have water to half the depth of mold; boil rapidly. Keep water boiling constantly; add boiling water as needed. If desired, place in oven for 5 minutes to dry top. NOTE: One-fourth cup evaporated milk may be substituted for 1/2 cup milk. Yield: 8 servings.

Mrs. Jack Peters
Oskaloosa, Iowa

CHRISTMAS COOKIES (YUGOSLAVIA)

½ lb. butter
1 ½ c. sugar
1 egg yolk
¼ to ½ tsp. salt
2 ½ c. sifted flour
4 egg whites
¾ c. finely ground walnuts
1 tsp. lemon flavoring
1 c. blackberry or currant jelly
1 c. chopped walnuts

Cream butter with 1/2 cup sugar; beat until fluffy. Add egg yolk and salt. Stir in flour. Pat dough into a thin layer on a 10 x 15-inch cookie sheet or in a 9 x 13 x 2-inch pan. Beat egg whites until stiff; gradually add remaining 1 cup sugar. Continue beating until of a meringue consistency. Fold in ground walnuts and flavoring. Spread jelly over dough; swirl meringue over jelly. Sprinkle with chopped walnuts. Bake at 350 degrees for 40 to 45 minutes. Cut into squares. Yield: 3-4 dozen cookies.

Mrs. Bryan B. Brown
Sanford, Fla.

KIFLE (YUGOSLAVIA)

1 cake compressed yeast
2 c. sifted flour
1 c. butter
½ c. sour cream
2 eggs, separated
½ c. sugar
1 tsp. vanilla flavoring
1 c. chopped nuts

Add yeast to flour. Mix in butter until crumbly. Add cream and egg yolks. Knead on lightly floured board. Divide into three parts. Wrap in waxed paper; chill. Roll each part into a circle. Divide into eight pie-shaped wedges. Make filling by combining 2 beaten egg whites, sugar, vanilla and nuts. Put a tablespoon of filling on each. Roll wide end to point to form crescent shapes. Bake at 375 degrees for 25 minutes. Yield: 24 servings.

Mrs. Max Landon
Marshalltown, Iowa

WALNUT POTICA--HOLIDAY BREAD (YUGOSLAVIA)

DOUGH:
1 pt. milk, scalded
¾ c. plus 1 tbsp. sugar
1 ½ tsp. salt
1 stick butter
1 yeast cake
4 eggs, well beaten
7 c. sifted flour

Combine milk, 3/4 cup sugar, salt and butter; cool. Dissolve yeast and 1 tablespoon sugar in 1/2 cup lukewarm water; add to milk mixture. Add eggs; add flour, a little at a time, beating thoroughly. Add flour until dough can be handled without sticking. Knead for 20 minutes on floured board. Put dough into greased bowl; let rise in warm place for 2 hours. Do not punch down. Spread dough on floured cloth. Pull out as thin as possible; cut off thick edges. Spread with filling; roll up as a jelly roll. Cut into four loaves 12 inches long. Cover and let rise in greased pans until doubled. Bake at 325 degrees for 1 hour.

FILLING:
½ c. butter
1 c. honey
2 c. sugar
1 pt. top milk
2 lb. ground walnuts
½ tsp. grated lemon rind
1 pt. heavy cream, whipped
3 eggs

Melt butter; add honey. Bring to a rolling boil. Add sugar, milk, walnuts and lemon rind. Remove from heat; add whipped cream and eggs. Mixture must be slightly cooled before spreading on dough. Yield: 4 loaves.

Mrs. Josephine J. Anderson
Soudan, Minn.

Sweet Breads

RECIPE FOR RAISIN BATTER COFFEE CAKE ON PAGE 342

APPLE COFFEE CAKE

2 c. flour
4 tsp. baking powder
½ tsp. salt
½ c. sugar
¾ c. milk
1 egg, beaten
3 tbsp. butter, melted
Apple slices

Sift flour with baking powder and salt. Combine sugar, milk and egg; add slowly to flour mixture. Add butter; beat until thoroughly mixed. Pour into well greased pan. Cover with apple slices.

TOPPING:
2 tbsp. sugar
½ tsp. cinnamon
2 tbsp. finely chopped nuts

Combine all ingredients; sprinkle over apple. Bake at 400 degrees for 20 minutes. Yield: 10-12 servings.

Claire E. Haas
Biloxi, Miss.

APPLE-RAISIN COFFEE CAKE

¾ c. plus 2 tbsp. sugar
¼ c. soft shortening
1 egg
½ c. milk
1 ½ c. flour
2 tsp. baking powder
½ to 1 tsp. salt
½ c. seedless raisins
½ c. chopped nuts (opt.)
Thinly sliced apples
1 tsp. cinnamon

Cream 3/4 cup sugar and shortening; add egg. Stir in milk. Sift flour with baking powder and salt; stir in. Add raisins and nuts; pour into well greased and floured square pan or muffin tins. Slightly press apple slices on top of batter. Sprinkle with mixture of cinnamon and remaining sugar. Bake at 375 degrees for 20 minutes. Yield: 12 servings.

Jennie P. Moulton
Ludlow, Vt.

APPLE TEA RING

6 tbsp. sugar
¾ tsp. salt
3 tbsp. shortening
¾ c. milk, scalded
1 cake or 1 pkg. dry yeast
1 egg, well beaten
2 ¾ c. sifted flour
Melted butter
1 tsp. cinnamon
3 tbsp. chopped walnuts or raisins
1 c. diced apples

Add 3 tablespoons sugar, salt and shortening to milk; cool to lukewarm. Soften yeast in small amount of lukewarm milk; add to milk mixture. Add egg; add one-half flour at a time. Knead in bowl for 5 minutes. Place in greased bowl; cover and let rise in warm place until double in bulk. Roll out; brush with melted butter. Combine remaining sugar with all remaining ingredients; spread over dough. Roll as for jelly roll. Place on greased baking sheet. Cover; let rise for 1 hour and 15 minutes or until doubled. Bake at 375 degrees for 30 minutes or until brown. Frost with powdered sugar icing. Yield: 8 servings.

Mrs. Beatrice Fitzgerald
Shelton, Conn.

BAKING POWDER COFFEE CAKE

1 c. sugar
1 ½ c. sifted flour
2 tsp. baking powder
¼ tsp. salt
¼ tsp. cinnamon
¼ c. margarine or butter
1 egg, well beaten
½ c. milk

Sift all dry ingredients. Add margarine; mix well. Beat egg and milk; add to flour mixture. Mix until well blended; put into 9-inch pie plate.

TOPPING:
½ c. sugar
2 tsp. cinnamon
4 tbsp. melted butter
2 tbsp. flour
¼ c. chopped nuts

Mix all ingredients; spread over batter. Bake at 375 degrees for 35 to 40 minutes. Yield: 8 servings.

Mildred Hartman
Angola, N.Y.

BANANA COFFEE CAKE

½ lb. margarine
2 eggs
5 tbsp. milk
3 bananas, mashed
1 ½ c. sugar
2 c. flour
½ tsp. soda
1 tsp. vanilla flavoring

Mix all ingredients; pour into greased 13 1/2 x 9 1/2 x 2-inch pan.

TOPPING:
1 stick margarine, melted
⅔ c. light brown sugar
1 c. coconut

(Continued on next page)

Combine all ingredients; sprinkle over batter. Bake at 350 degrees for 10 minutes. Reduce heat to 325 degrees; bake for 40 minutes longer.

Vida Davis
Kilgore, Tex.

BANANA-NUT COFFEE CAKE

1 ¾ c. flour
2 tsp. baking powder
¼ tsp. soda
½ tsp. salt
½ c. shortening
⅔ c. sugar
2 eggs, beaten
1 c. mashed bananas

Sift flour, baking powder, soda and salt. Cream shortening; add sugar and eggs. Continue creaming until light and fluffy. Add flour mixture alternately with bananas; mix well after each addition. Pour into greased 9-inch square pan.

TOPPING:
2 tbsp. sugar
¼ tsp. cinnamon
1 tsp. grated orange rind
¼ c. chopped walnuts

Mix all ingredients. Cover top of batter. Bake at 350 degrees for 35 minutes. Cool.

Mrs. Lois Cox
Walhalla, S.C.

BERRY COFFEE CAKE

⅓ c. sugar
2 tsp. shortening, softened
1 egg
½ c. milk
¾ c. plus 2 tbsp. flour
1 tsp. baking powder
¼ tsp. salt
½ c. brown sugar
2 tsp. cinnamon
2 tbsp. margarine
½ c. chopped nuts
1 can drained berries

Mix sugar, shortening and egg. Stir in milk. Sift 3/4 cup flour with baking powder and salt; stir into creamed mixture. Spread batter in greased and floured pan. Combine all remaining ingredients; sprinkle over batter. Bake at 375 degrees for 45 minutes.

Mrs. Eliza Holtz
Houston, Tex.

BOHEMIAN COFFEE CAKE

3 c. sifted flour
1 c. brown sugar
1 c. sugar

½ tsp. salt
½ c. butter or margarine
1 c. chopped dates
1 c. chopped English walnuts
1 c. buttermilk
1 tsp. soda

Combine all dry ingredients except soda. Cut butter into dry mixture until it resembles corn meal. Remove 1/2 cup of the mixture for topping. Add dates and nuts. Add buttermilk to which soda has been added. Spread in greased 8 x 11 x 2-inch pan. Sprinkle crumbly mixture over top. Bake at 350 degrees for 35 to 45 minutes. Yield: 16 servings.

Dorothy Cornelius
Pekin, Ill.

BRAZIL NUT COFFEE CAKE

2 c. sifted flour
2 tsp. baking powder
½ c. sugar
½ tsp. salt
1 c. milk
1 egg, beaten
3 tsp. melted butter
1 c. chopped Brazil nuts

Sift flour with baking powder, sugar and salt. Add milk to egg; beat into dry ingredients. Add melted butter. Add nuts which have been lightly rolled in flour. Pour into buttered loaf or ring pan. Bake at 350 degrees for 45 minutes. Yield: 8 servings.

Mrs. Leon Reed
Heber Springs, Ark.

CHERRY COFFEE CAKE

1 egg, beaten
¼ c. milk
½ c. sugar
⅛ tsp. salt
½ tsp. vanilla flavoring
1 ½ c. biscuit mix
1 can cherries, chopped
¼ c. flour
½ c. brown sugar
½ tsp. cinnamon
3 tbsp. butter
⅓ c. chopped nuts

Combine egg, milk, sugar, salt, vanilla and biscuit mix; stir until smooth. Pour into 8-inch square pan. Sprinkle cherries evenly over batter. Mix flour, brown sugar and cinnamon; cut in butter. Add nuts; sprinkle mixture over cherries. Bake at 375 degrees for 30 minutes. Yield: 6 servings.

Mrs. Nancy A. Brassard
Pawtucket, R.I.

337

CHOCOLATE CHIP COFFEE CAKE

TOPPING:
½ c. sugar
2 tsp. cinnamon
½ c. chopped nuts
1 pkg. chocolate pieces

Thoroughly blend all ingredients.

BATTER:
1 c. sugar
½ lb. butter or margarine
3 eggs
2 ¾ c. sifted flour
3 tsp. baking powder
1 tsp. baking soda
1 c. sour cream
1 tsp. vanilla flavoring

Cream sugar, butter and eggs. Sift dry ingredients; add alternately with sour cream. Add vanilla. Pour one-half of the batter into large tube pan; sprinkle with one-half of the topping. Repeat layers; pat down topping gently. Bake at 350 degrees for 1 hour.

Mrs. John H. Keithline
East Hartford, Conn.

COBBLESTONE COFFEE CAKE

½ c. milk
½ c. shortening
½ c. sugar
½ tsp. salt
1 pkg. dry yeast
¼ c. warm water
3 to 3 ½ c. sifted flour
2 eggs, beaten
¼ c. melted butter or margarine
⅔ c. brown sugar
½ tsp. cinnamon
½ c. raisins
½ c. chopped nuts
½ c. chopped mixed candied fruit

Scald milk; add shortening, sugar and salt. Stir until sugar is dissolved; cool to lukewarm. Dissolve yeast in water; combine with milk mixture. Stir in one-half of the flour; add eggs. Beat well. Add enough of remaining flour to make a soft dough. Turn out onto lightly floured board; knead until smooth and elastic. Place in greased bowl; brush with shortening. Cover and let rise in a warm place about 80 to 85 degrees for 2 hours or until double in size. Punch down; form into 1-inch balls. Roll each ball in butter; roll in mixture of brown sugar and cinnamon. Place a layer of balls in 9-inch pan; sprinkle with raisins, nuts and fruit. Repeat until all dough has been used. Cover and let rise until doubled in size. Bake at 350 degrees for 40 minutes. Yield: 24 pieces.

Mrs. Rogers Whittington
Van Buren, Ark.

COFFEE CAKE RING

½ c. milk, scalded
¼ c. sugar
¼ c. butter
½ cake yeast
2 eggs, beaten
½ tsp. salt
2 c. sifted flour
Cinnamon or fruit filling
Frosting
Nuts or fruit

Mix milk with sugar and butter; cool to lukewarm. Add yeast, eggs, salt and flour; stir until smooth. Roll on floured surface into long oblong shape. Spread evenly with cinnamon or fruit filling. Roll jelly-roll fashion; shape into ring on greased pan. With scissors, cut almost through ring at 1-inch intervals. Turn each slice slightly on its side; cover and let rise until double in bulk. Bake at 375 degrees for 20 to 25 minutes. Frost while warm; decorate with nuts or fruit.

Mrs. James F. Wright
Hunter, Kans.

COFFEE CAKE SUPREME

1 stick margarine, softened
1 c. sugar
2 eggs
1 tsp. vanilla flavoring
1 pt. sour cream
2 c. flour
½ tsp. salt
1 tsp. soda
1 tsp. baking powder

Cream margarine and sugar; add eggs, vanilla and sour cream. Sift flour with salt, soda and baking powder. Gradually add flour mixture to cream mixture. Place one-half of the batter in greased tube pan. Sprinkle with one-half of topping; add remaining batter. Sprinkle with remaining topping. Bake at 350 degrees for 45 minutes.

TOPPING:
½ c. brown sugar
½ c. chopped nuts
2 tbsp. cinnamon

Mix all ingredients well. Sprinkle over batter.

Mrs. Leon A. Davis
Stockton, Calif.

COFFEE-TOFFEE CAKE

2 ¼ c. flour
1 ½ c. sugar
3 ¼ tsp. baking powder
1 tsp. (scant) salt
½ c. shortening
¼ c. milk
1 c. cold coffee

(Continued on next page)

½ c. egg whites
1 tsp. vanilla flavoring

Sift all dry ingredients; add shortening, milk and coffee. Beat thoroughly for 1 minute and 30 seconds. Add egg whites and vanilla; beat for 1 minute and 30 seconds longer. Pour into two 8-inch greased layer pans. Bake at 375 degrees for 30 to 35 minutes. Yield: 20-25 servings.

Mrs. Eugene Blackburn
Syracuse, Ind.

CREAM COFFEE CAKE

1 oz. yeast
½ c. lukewarm water
⅓ c. butter, melted
½ c. plus 2 tbsp. sugar
1 tsp. salt
2 eggs, slightly beaten
8 c. plus 1 tsp. flour
8 oz. sour cream
1 tsp. cinnamon

Dissolve yeast in lukewarm water. Add butter, 1/4 cup sugar, salt and an egg; mix well. Stir in 2 cups flour forming a soft dough. Press onto bottom and sides of 9-inch cake pan. Let rise for 1 hour and 30 minutes to 2 hours. Bake at 375 degrees for 20 minutes. Mix an egg, sour cream, 1/4 cup sugar and remaining flour. Spread filling over pastry; sprinkle with remaining sugar and cinnamon. Yield: 12 servings.

Mrs. Roy Koonce
Lenorah, Tex.

FAMILY FAVORITE COFFEE ROLL

FILLING:
¾ c. sugar
1 tbsp. cinnamon
½ c. soft butter
1 c. raisins

Combine ingredients. Set aside.

BATTER:
1 pkg. yeast
1 c. milk
½ c. sugar
⅓ c. shortening
1 ½ tsp. salt
2 eggs, well beaten
1 tsp. vanilla flavoring
5 to 6 c. flour

Soften yeast in 1/4 cup warm water. Scald milk; add sugar, shortening and salt. Cool to lukewarm. Stir in eggs, vanilla and 2 cups flour; add softened yeast. Beat well. Add remaining flour to make a soft dough. Place dough in greased bowl; cover and let rise in warm place for 1 hour and 30 minutes or until doubled in bulk. Punch down;

divide dough into two portions. Roll each portion out; add one-half of the filling to each portion. Roll up as for jelly roll; make horseshoe curve. Let rise until light. Bake at 350 degrees for 25 to 30 minutes. Ice with confectioners icing.

Mrs. Leo Rooker
Ravenden, Ark.

MAPLE-BUTTER TWIST

FILLING:
¼ c. butter
½ c. brown sugar
⅓ c. sugar
¼ c. maple syrup
2 tbsp. flour
½ tsp. cinnamon
½ tsp. maple flavoring
½ c. walnuts

Combine all ingredients; mix well.

BATTER:
1 pkg. yeast
¼ c. water
½ c. hot milk
¼ c. butter
3 tbsp. sugar
1 ½ tsp. salt
2 eggs
3 ¼ to 3 ½ c. flour

Dissolve yeast in water. Scald milk; add butter, sugar and salt. Cool. Add eggs, yeast and flour. Mix well; let rise for 1 hour and 30 minutes. Place on well floured surface; divide in half. Roll out one portion to 14 x 8-inch rectangle; spread with one-half of the filling. Roll up; cut in half, lengthwise. Twist strips together, cut-sides up; shape into ring in greased pan. Repeat with remaining dough. Let rise for 45 minutes. Bake at 350 degrees for 25 to 30 minutes. Frost. Yield: 2 twists.

Mrs. Florine Irwin
Lohrville, Iowa

MINCEMEAT BREAD RING

1 ¾ c. sifted flour
3 tsp. baking powder
½ tsp. salt
2 eggs
¼ c. milk
½ c. brown sugar
5 tbsp. butter, melted
1 c. prepared mincemeat

Sift flour with baking powder and salt. Beat eggs well; stir in milk, sugar, butter and mincemeat. Add flour mixture; stir until just blended. Pour into greased 8-inch ring mold. Bake at 350 degrees for 1 hour. Cool on cake rack for 10 minutes; remove from pan. Cool thoroughly. Serve with orange

(Continued on next page)

butter made by blending 1/2 cup butter and 1/4 cup orange marmalade, if desired.

Mrs. Nathan I. Reiter
Texarkana, Tex.

MINCEMEAT COFFEE CAKE

5 tbsp. butter
3 tbsp. brown sugar
1 c. mincemeat
1 ½ c. flour
½ c. sugar
2 tsp. baking powder
½ tsp. salt
1 egg, beaten
⅔ c. milk

Melt 2 tablespoons butter in deep cake pan; sprinkle brown sugar over butter. Cover evenly with mincemeat. Sift all dry ingredients. Add egg and milk; beat well. Pour batter over mincemeat. Bake at 350 degrees for 30 minutes.

Mrs. George A. Boston
Fairfield, Conn.

NUTMEG COFFEE CAKE

2 c. flour
2 c. brown sugar
¼ lb. margarine or butter
1 tsp. grated nutmeg
1 egg, beaten
1 tsp. soda
1 c. sour milk

Mix flour, sugar, butter and nutmeg. Reserve 1 cup of the mixture for topping. Add egg, soda and sour milk to remaining crumb mixture. Pour into greased pan; sprinkle top with reserved crumbs. Bake in 350 degree oven for 30 minutes. Serve warm. Yield: 6 servings.

Delores Powell
North Sacramento, Calif.

ORANGE COFFEE RING

¾ c. sugar
1 tbsp. grated orange rind
2 cans refrigerated biscuits
¼ c. butter or margarine, melted
1 oz. cream cheese
¾ c. powdered sugar
1 tbsp. orange juice
¼ tsp. vanilla flavoring
¼ c. flaked coconut

Combine sugar and orange rind. Dip each biscuit into butter; roll in sugar mixture. Arrange in an overlapping circle in greased 9-inch round pan. Bake at 425 degrees for 15 to 20 minutes until golden brown. Blend cheese, powdered sugar, orange juice and vanilla.

Spread frosting over warm cake. Sprinkle with coconut. Serve warm. Yield: 8 servings.

Mrs. Marvyn H. Olson
Winnemucca, Nev.

ORANGE-DATE COFFEE CAKE

¼ c. shortening, softened
¾ c. sugar
1 egg
1 ½ c. sifted flour
2 tsp. baking powder
½ tsp. salt
1 tsp. cinnamon
½ c. milk
¼ c. orange juice
¾ c. chopped dates

Cream shortening, sugar and egg. Sift all dry ingredients. Alternately add dry ingredients with milk and orange juice to creamed mixture. Add dates; mix.

TOPPING:
½ c. brown sugar
⅓ c. flour
½ tsp. cinnamon
¼ c. butter, softened
3 tsp. grated orange rind

Combine all ingredients; sprinkle over batter. Bake at 350 degrees for 35 to 40 minutes.

Mrs. Paul Ulmer
Redlands, Calif.

PARTY COFFEE CAKE

1 c. sugar
½ lb. butter or margarine
3 eggs
1 c. sour cream
2 c. sifted flour
2 tsp. baking powder
1 tsp. soda
Pinch of salt
1 tsp. vanilla flavoring
1 tsp. almond or lemon flavoring

Cream sugar and butter; add an egg at a time. Add sour cream. Gradually mix in dry ingredients; add flavorings. Pour one-half of batter into long narrow greased pan.

TOPPING:
1 c. chopped nuts
½ c. sugar
1 tsp. cinnamon

Combine all ingredients. Sprinkle one-half of the mixture over batter. Top with remaining batter. Sprinkle remaining mixture on top. Bake at 375 degrees for 30 minutes or until done. Yield: 20 servings.

Gustava Zivitz
Panama City, Fla.

PEACH COFFEE CAKE

1 egg, beaten
1 c. sugar
½ c. milk
2 tbsp. shortening, melted
1 c. flour
2 tsp. baking powder
½ tsp. salt
Sliced fresh peaches
½ tsp. cinnamon

Combine egg, 1/2 cup sugar, milk and shortening. Sift flour with baking powder and salt; stir into egg mixture. Pour into greased 8 x 10-inch pan. Cover with peach slices. Bake at 375 degrees for 20 minutes. Sprinkle with cinnamon and remaining sugar. Continue baking until done. Yield: 10 servings.

Geraldine Glover
Plentywood, Mont.

PECAN-SOUR CREAM COFFEE CAKE

½ lb. butter or margarine
1 c. sugar
2 whole eggs
2 c. flour
1 tsp. baking powder
1 tsp. soda
½ tsp. salt
1 c. thick sour cream
1 tsp. vanilla flavoring

Cream butter and sugar until fluffy. Add an egg at a time; beat until smooth. Sift flour with baking powder, soda and salt. Add to creamed mixture with sour cream. Add vanilla. Pour one-half of the batter into well greased and floured 13 x 9-inch pan.

FILLING AND TOPPING:

⅓ c. brown sugar
¼ c. sugar
1 tsp. cinnamon
1 c. chopped pecans or other nuts

Mix sugars, cinnamon and nuts. Sprinkle one-half of topping over batter. Cover with remaining batter. Sprinkle with remaining topping. Bake at 350 degrees for 1 hour.

Dorothy K. Biegert
Tampa, Fla.

TEXAS PECAN COFFEE CAKE

1 ¼ c. sugar
1 c. sour cream
½ c. butter
2 eggs
1 tsp. soda
1 tsp. baking powder
2 c. sifted flour
1 tsp. vanilla flavoring
1 tsp. cinnamon
1 c. chopped pecans, toasted

Cream 1 cup sugar, sour cream, butter and eggs. Add soda, baking powder and flour sifted together and vanilla. Mix well; pour one-half of the batter into 9-inch greased and floured tube pan. Combine remaining sugar, cinnamon and pecans; sprinkle two-thirds of the mixture over batter. Cut topping into batter. Pour in remaining batter; sprinkle with remaining topping. Bake at 350 degrees for 35 minutes. Yield: 6 servings.

Mrs. Arlan L. Fenner
San Angelo, Tex.

TALL PRUNE-APRICOT COFFEE CAKE

CRUMB TOPPING:
¼ c. granulated sugar
¼ c. brown sugar
3 tsp. cinnamon
½ c. chopped pecans

Mix all ingredients well.

CAKE:
¾ c. prunes
¾ c. apricots
4 c. flour
2 tsp. baking powder
2 tsp. soda
½ lb. butter
2 c. sugar
6 eggs
1 pt. sour cream
2 tsp. vanilla flavoring
¼ c. melted butter

Pour boiling water over prunes and apricots; drain well and chop. Sift flour with baking powder and soda three times. Cream butter and sugar; add an egg at a time. Blend in flour mixture and sour cream; add vanilla. Beat for 4 minutes at medium speed of electric mixer. Pour one-third of batter into greased and floured 10-inch tube pan. Top with one-half of the prune-apricot mixture. Sprinkle with one-third of the crumb topping. Repeat layers; top with remaining batter and sprinkle with crumb topping. Drizzle 1/4 cup melted butter over top. Bake at 350 degrees for 1 hour and 10 minutes. Yield: 8-10 servings.

Mrs. Howard L. Johnson
Almaden AFS, Calif.

QUICK COFFEE CAKE

1 c. sugar
½ c. brown sugar
½ c. shortening
1 tsp. cinnamon
1 tsp. ginger
2 c. sifted flour
1 egg
1 c. sour cream
1 tsp. soda

Combine sugars, shortening, spices and flour like pie crust. Reserve 3/4 cup for later use. Add all remaining ingredients; mix well.

(Continued on next page)

Pour into 9-inch square pan. Pour reserved crumbs on top. Bake at 350 degrees for 30 to 35 minutes. Yield: 6 servings.

Mrs. William D. Hays
Seattle, Wash.

QUICK COFFEE CAKE

2 c. sifted flour
2 tsp. baking powder
¾ tsp. salt
½ c. sugar
6 tbsp. shortening
1 egg, well beaten
½ c. milk

Sift dry ingredients; cut in shortening. Add egg and milk; mix well. Place in 9-inch greased layer pan.

TOPPING:
1 ½ tsp. butter, melted
1 tbsp. flour
4 tbsp. sugar
½ tsp. cinnamon

Pour melted butter over top of batter. Mix flour, sugar and cinnamon; sprinkle over butter. Bake at 425 degrees for 25 minutes. Yield: 8 servings.

Mrs. W. Wendell Lowe
Waterbury, Vt.

RAISIN BATTER COFFEE CAKE

½ c. milk
⅓ c. sugar
1 tsp. salt
1 stick margarine
½ c. warm water
2 pkg. active dry yeast
2 eggs, beaten
3 c. unsifted flour
½ c. seedless raisins

Scald milk; stir in sugar, salt and margarine. Cool to lukewarm. Measure warm water into large warm electric mixer bowl. Sprinkle in yeast; stir until dissolved. Add lukewarm milk mixture, eggs and 2 cups flour. Beat at medium speed of electric mixer for 15 seconds or until smooth. Stir in remaining flour and raisins for 1 minute or until well blended. Turn into well greased 10-inch tube pan. Sprinkle with topping. Cover; let rise in warm place, free from draft, for 1 hour or until doubled in bulk. Bake at 400 degrees for 35 minutes or until done. Turn out of pan immediately; let cool on wire rack.

TOPPING:
⅓ c. unsifted flour
⅓ c. sugar
½ stick margarine
1 ½ tsp. cinnamon
½ c. chopped pecans
½ c. seedless raisins

Combine flour, sugar, margarine and cinnamon. Stir in pecans and raisins. Sprinkle over top of dough. Yield: One 10-inch tube cake.

Photograph for this recipe on page 335 .

SOUR CREAM COFFEE CAKE

TOPPING:
¼ c. sugar
½ c. chopped nuts
1 tbsp. cinnamon

Mix all ingredients well; set aside for filling and topping.

CAKE:
½ lb. margarine
1 c. sugar
2 eggs
1 tsp. vanilla flavoring
2 c. flour
1 tsp. baking powder
1 tsp. soda
¼ tsp. salt
1 c. sour cream

Cream margarine and sugar; add eggs and vanilla. Sift all dry ingredients; add alternately with sour cream to mixture. Pour one-half of the batter into greased tube pan; sprinkle with one-half of the filling. Add remaining batter; sprinkle with remaining nut mixture. Bake at 350 degrees for 45 minutes.

Mrs. T. P. Adams
Matthews, N.C.

SUNDAY MORNING COFFEE CAKE

1 egg, thoroughly beaten
½ c. sugar
½ c. milk
2 tbsp. shortening, melted
1 c. sifted flour
2 tsp. baking powder
½ tsp. salt

Combine egg, sugar, milk and shortening. Add flour sifted with baking powder and salt; mix well. Pour into waxed paper-lined 8-inch square pan or 9-inch cake pan.

TOPPING:
¼ c. light brown sugar
1 tsp. cinnamon
1 tbsp. flour
1 tbsp. butter, melted
½ c. broken pecans or almonds

Mix brown sugar, cinnamon and flour. Add butter; mix well. Sprinkle over batter; top with nuts. Bake at 375 degrees for 20 to 25 minutes or until toothpick inserted into center comes out clean. Yield: 6 servings.

Velma Sutherland
Panama City, Fla.

SWEDISH TEA RING

BASIC RECIPE:
2 pkg. dry yeast
¾ c. lukewarm orange juice
½ c. shortening
¾ c. orange juice, heated
½ c. sugar
1 tbsp. salt
3 eggs, well beaten
5 ¾ to 6 c. sifted flour

Sprinkle yeast into lukewarm juice; let stand for 5 to 10 minutes. Stir until yeast is thoroughly dissolved. Add shortening to heated orange juice, stirring until melted. Pour mixture over sugar and salt in mixing bowl; cool to lukewarm. Stir in yeast mixture. Add eggs and 3 cups flour; beat well. Add enough flour to make a soft dough. Turn dough onto floured board; knead gently until smooth and elastic. Divide dough into thirds to make Swedish tea ring and other desired sweet breads. Place remaining two-thirds of the dough in oiled bowl; turn once to bring greased side up. Cover bowl tightly with aluminum foil. Place in refrigerator to be used as desired within three to four days. Place reserved dough in oiled bowl; turn once to bring greased side up. Cover; let rise in warm place until doubled in bulk. Use to make Swedish tea ring. To make rolls from dough stored in refrigerator, punch down and

remove one-half of the dough. Allow dough to come to room temperature.

TEA RING:
⅓ basic recipe
1 tbsp. melted butter
¼ c. sugar
¼ tsp. cinnamon
¾ c. chopped citron, cherries, nuts and raisins

Roll dough into a 12 x 15 x 1/4-inch rectangle. Brush with melted butter; sprinkle with sugar, cinnamon, citron, cherries, nuts and raisins. Roll as for jelly roll. Place on greased baking sheet. Form into a circle; seal ends firmly together. Cut 1-inch slices almost through with scissors. Turn each slice partly on its side. Let rise until doubled in bulk. Bake at 375 degrees for 20 to 25 minutes. While still warm, frost with sugar glaze made from confectioners sugar and water. Garnish with additional citron, raisins and nuts. Yield: One 10-inch ring.

Photograph for this recipe above.

BAKED DOUGHNUTS

¾ c. shortening
½ c. sugar
1 tsp. salt

(Continued on next page)

1 c. milk, scalded
1 c. (scant) mashed potatoes
1 cake yeast
¼ c. warm potato water
2 eggs, well beaten
4 ½ c. flour

Add shortening, sugar and salt to scalded milk; cool to lukewarm. Add mashed potatoes and yeast that has been dissolved in potato water. Blend in eggs. Work in flour gradually. Cover; let rise until light. Place on floured board; knead. Roll 1-inch thick. Cut with doughnut cutter that has large hole. Place on buttered cookie sheets; let rise until light. Bake at 425 degrees until delicately browned. Brush with butter on all sides; roll in sugar. NOTE: Dough mixture freezes well. Yield: 3 dozen.

Frances Diamond
Tekonsha, Mich.

DROP DOUGHNUTS

2 tbsp. soft butter
¾ c. sugar
4 egg yolks, beaten
1 c. milk
1 tsp. vanilla flavoring
3 c. flour
3 tsp. baking powder
¼ tsp. salt

Combine butter, sugar and egg yolks. Add milk and vanilla. Blend in sifted dry ingredients. Drop batter by teaspoonfuls into hot fat. Cook for 2 to 3 minutes on each side. Drain; roll in sugar. NOTE: One-fourth teaspoon nutmeg or 2 tablespoons grated orange rind may be added to batter. Yield: 4 dozen.

Mrs. Don Berger
Wells, Minn.

EASY RAISED DOUGHNUTS

½ c. milk
½ c. plus 1 tbsp. sugar
1 tsp. salt
½ c. soft butter or margarine
2 pkg. active dry yeast
½ c. warm water
2 eggs
4 c. flour
¾ tsp. nutmeg or mace
Salad oil or shortening

Scald milk; remove from heat. Add 1/2 cup sugar, salt and butter. Stir until butter melts; cool to lukewarm. Sprinkle yeast and 1 tablespoon sugar over water; stir until dissolved. Add milk mixture and remaining ingredients; beat until smooth. Cover with towel; let rise in warm place until doubled. Punch down dough; turn out onto floured board. Knead 10 times. Roll out dough to 1/2-inch thick; cut with 3-inch cutter. Let rise again until

doubled. Fry in 2 inches hot oil at 375 degrees in electric skillet until golden brown. Drain quickly.

GLAZE:
¼ c. milk
1 tsp. vanilla flavoring
2 c. sifted confectioners sugar

Combine all ingredients. Dip hot doughnuts into glaze. Yield: 18-20 servings.

Mrs. Gordon F. Wooten
Loring AFB, Me.

INEXPENSIVE DOUGHNUTS

4 c. sifted flour
2 tsp. baking powder
½ tsp. salt
2 tbsp. melted butter
1 c. sugar
2 eggs, beaten
1 c. milk

Sift flour with baking powder and salt three times. Cream butter and sugar; add eggs. Add milk and flour mixture alternately. Roll to 1/2-inch thick; cut. Fry in 375 degree fat until done. Yield: 3 dozen.

Mrs. T. A. Wangseng
Winnett, Mont.

SWEET BREAD DOUGHNUTS

2 c. milk, warmed
½ c. sugar
1 tsp. salt
2 cakes yeast
½ c. shortening, softened
2 eggs
7 to 7 ½ c. flour

Combine warm milk, sugar and salt; dissolve yeast in milk mixture. Add shortening and eggs; mix well. Add 1 cup flour at a time, blending well after each addition. Knead for 3 to 4 minutes. Let rise until doubled in bulk; roll out to 1/2-inch thickness. Cut with doughnut cutter. Let rise for 10 minutes or until doughnuts are light. Fry in deep fat until golden brown. Yield: 4 dozen.

Lois O'Malley
Erie, Kans.

GINGERBREAD

½ c. sugar
½ c. shortening
1 egg
1 c. molasses
2 c. flour
1 tsp. soda
2 tsp. ground ginger
½ tsp. cinnamon
½ tsp. nutmeg
1 c. hot water

(Continued on next page)

Cream sugar and shortening; add egg. Beat well. Add molasses; mix thoroughly. Add sifted dry ingredients. Add hot water; pour into 13 x 8 x 2-inch pan. Bake at 325 to 350 degrees for 35 to 45 minutes.

Mrs. Christine Maddox
Durant, Okla.

GINGERBREAD

¾ c. shortening
1 c. brown sugar
1 c. molasses
3 eggs, beaten
3 c. flour
1 tsp. soda
1 tsp. baking powder
½ tsp. salt
2 tbsp. ginger
½ tsp. cloves
1 tbsp. cinnamon
1 c. sour milk

Cream shortening and sugar. Add molasses and eggs. Sift all dry ingredients. Alternately add dry ingredients and milk to molasses mixture. Turn into well greased 13 x 9 x 2-inch pan. Bake at 350 degrees for about 35 minutes. Yield: 12-15 servings.

Mrs. Troy M. Shearon
Dothan, Ala.

ONE-BOWL GINGERBREAD

1 egg
½ c. sugar
½ c. molasses
1 ½ c. flour
1 tsp. soda
½ tsp. cinnamon
½ tsp. salt
½ c. boiling water
½ c. salad oil

Lightly beat egg. Stir in sugar; add molasses. Add dry ingredients; mix until smooth. Blend boiling water and salad oil. Line 8-inch square baking pan with waxed paper. Pour in batter. Bake at 350 degrees for 35 to 40 minutes. Yield: 9 servings.

Dorothy Brubaker
Elma, N.Y.

ALOHA BREAD

½ c. butter or margarine
1 c. sugar
2 eggs
2 c. flour
1 tsp. soda
½ tsp. salt
3 tbsp. sour milk
¾ c. mashed bananas
¼ c. plus 1 tbsp. drained crushed pineapple
½ c. chopped walnuts

Cream butter and sugar. Add an egg at a time, beating well after each addition. Add milk. Sift flour with soda and salt. Add to creamed mixture alternately with banana-pineapple mixture. Add nuts; pour into greased 9 x 5 x 3-inch pan. Bake at 350 degrees for 55 to 60 minutes. Cool before slicing. Yield: 1 loaf.

Mrs. Oscar Sheppard
Sioux Falls, S.D.

ALOHA BREAD

2 c. sifted flour
1 tsp. soda
½ tsp. salt
2 tsp. baking powder
½ c. butter
1 c. sugar
2 eggs
1 c. mashed bananas
1 c. undrained crushed pineapple
Juice of 1 orange
2 c. chopped nuts

Sift all dry ingredients. Cream butter and sugar; add eggs. Blend well. Add all remaining ingredients. Pour into greased and floured loaf pan. Bake at 350 degrees for 1 hour to 1 hour and 10 minutes. NOTE: This bread freezes well. Yield: 1 loaf.

Mrs. Keith L. Warren
Madison, Ind.

APPLE-CHERRY-NUT BREAD

6 tbsp. butter or margarine
⅔ c. sugar
2 eggs
1 tsp. grated lemon rind
1 c. applesauce
2 tbsp. milk
2 c. sifted flour
1 tsp. baking powder
½ tsp. soda
½ tsp. salt
½ c. chopped nuts
¼ c. chopped Maraschino cherries

Cream butter and sugar until fluffy; add an egg at a time, beating well after each addition. Add lemon rind. Combine applesauce and milk. Sift all dry ingredients; add to creamed mixture alternately with applesauce mixture. Stir in nuts and cherries. Pour into greased 8 1/2 x 4 1/2 x 2 1/2-inch loaf pan. Bake at 350 degrees for 55 minutes or until done. Remove from pan; cool thoroughly. Yield: 4-6 servings.

Mrs. Evelyn Bailey
Dardanelle, Ark.

APPLE-ORANGE TEA BREAD

1 lge. orange
½ c. seedless raisins
1 c. canned applesauce
¾ c. nuts
1 egg, beaten
3 tbsp. margarine, melted
2 c. sifted flour
2 tsp. baking powder
1 tsp. soda
1 c. sugar
¾ tsp. salt

Squeeze and reserve juice from orange. Put orange and raisins through medium blade of food chopper. Add juice, raisins and rind to applesauce and nuts; mix thoroughly. Add egg and margarine; stir until well blended. Stir in dry ingredients. Pour into greased 8 1/2 x 4 1/2 x 2 1/2-inch loaf pan. Bake at 350 degrees for 1 hour and 10 minutes to 1 hour and 20 minutes. Remove from pan; cool on wire rack. NOTE: Bread will slice more smoothly if wrapped in waxed paper overnight. Yield: 15 servings.

Mrs. Edmond F. Cooney
· Lockbourne AFB, O.

APPLE ROLL

¼ c. margarine
1 c. sugar
1 egg
1 c. flour
¼ tsp. salt
1 tsp. soda
½ tsp. cinnamon
½ tsp. nutmeg
2 med. apples, diced

Mix all ingredients except apples in order given; stir in apples. Bake at 350 degrees for 30 minutes. Serve with whipped cream or lemon pudding. NOTE: Batter will seem dry before baking.

Mrs. R. D. Bruce
Springfield, Oreg.

FRESH APPLE BREAD

1 c. flour
1 tsp. soda
½ tsp. salt
½ c. shortening
1 c. plus 3 tbsp. sugar
2 eggs
1 raw apple, grated
1 ½ tbsp. evaporated milk
½ tsp. vanilla flavoring
1 c. chopped nuts
1 tsp. cinnamon

Sift flour, soda and salt. Cream shortening and 1 cup sugar; add eggs. Mix well. Add apple, milk and vanilla; mix well. Add sifted dry ingredients; beat well. Stir in nuts; pour into greased loaf pan. Combine remaining sugar and cinnamon; sprinkle over batter. Bake at 350 degrees for 1 hour. Yield: 6-8 servings.

Dorothy Lawyer
Concordia, Kans.

APRICOT BREAD

3 c. flour
2 ¼ c. sugar
1 ½ tsp. salt
1 ½ tsp. soda
1 ½ tsp. cinnamon
4 eggs
1 ⅓ c. cooking oil
1 ½ c. cooked apricots
1 c. chopped pecans

Combine all dry ingredients; add eggs and oil. Beat until smooth; add apricots. Mix thoroughly; add nuts. Pour into greased and floured loaf pan. Bake at 325 degrees for 1 hour and 15 minutes or until done. Can be baked in two smaller pans. Yield: 18-20 servings.

Mrs. Carl Adams
Perryville, Ark.

APRICOT PINWHEELS

¼ c. sugar
½ tsp. salt
¼ c. margarine
¼ c. scalded milk
1 pkg. dry yeast
¼ c. warm water
2 ¼ to 2 ½ c. flour
1 egg, beaten
⅓ c. apricot preserves
⅓ c. chopped pecans
Cherry halves

Stir sugar, salt and margarine into milk; cool to warm. Sprinkle yeast in warm water; stir until dissolved. Add 1 cup flour. Beat until smooth; add remaining flour to make a soft dough. Knead lightly; let rise for 1 hour. Roll dough; cut into 2-inch squares. Combine apricot preserves and pecans. Place 1 teaspoon of mixture in center of dough. Fold corners of dough to center; top with a cherry half. Bake at 350 degrees until dough is golden brown.

Minnie Behr
Boerne, Tex.

AVOCADO BREAD

1 ½ c. sugar
½ c. shortening
1 lge. egg

(Continued on next page)

1 c. mashed avocado
½ tsp. cinnamon
½ tsp. nutmeg
½ tsp. salt
1 ½ c. flour
1 tsp. soda
½ c. sour milk or buttermilk
8 dates, chopped
½ c. chopped nuts

Cream sugar and shortening until light and fluffy. Add egg; beat well. Add avocado; mix thoroughly. Mix all dry ingredients except soda; dissolve soda in milk. Add milk and dry ingredients alternately to sugar mixture, mixing well; stir in fruit and nuts. Pour into loaf pan. Bake at 325 degrees for 1 hour. Yield: 12 servings.

Mrs. Dorothy Sullivan
Dallas, Tex.

BANANA-NUT BREAD

½ c. butter
1 c. sugar
2 eggs
2 bananas, mashed
¼ c. chopped nuts
2 c. flour
1 tsp. soda
1 tsp. salt

Cream butter; add sugar. Beat in an egg at a time, blending well after each addition. Add bananas and nuts. Sift all dry ingredients; add to banana mixture. Pour into paper-lined loaf pan. Bake at 350 degrees for 45 minutes. Cool in pan.

Mrs. J. Irby Foster
Liberty, S.C.

✓ BANANA-NUT BREAD ✓

¼ c. butter
1 ½ c. sugar
1 ½ c. mashed bananas
2 eggs, well beaten
1 tsp. vanilla flavoring
2 c. flour
2 tsp. baking powder
¾ tsp. salt
½ c. milk
¾ c. nuts

Cream butter and sugar; blend in bananas, eggs and vanilla. Sift flour with baking powder and salt. Add flour mixture to banana mixture alternately with milk; mix thoroughly. Add nuts; mix well. Pour into two loaf pans. Bake at 325 degrees for 1 hour. Yield: 2 loaves.

Mrs. Loveina Nolte
Cave Creek, Ariz.

BANANA-NUT TEA BREAD

⅓ c. shortening, softened
⅔ c. sugar
2 eggs
1 c. mashed bananas
1 ¾ c. sifted flour
2 tsp. baking powder
¼ tsp. soda
½ tsp. salt
1 c. chopped nuts

Mix shortening, sugar and eggs. Add bananas and dry ingredients. Beat just until smooth; add nuts. Pour into 9 x 5 x 3-inch greased loaf pan. Bake at 350 degrees for 55 minutes. Cool well before slicing. Yield: 12-14 servings.

Mrs. Ethan Quakenbush
Sublette, Kans.

✓ BANANA-WALNUT BREAD ✓

¾ c. margarine
1 ½ c. sugar
4 bananas, mashed
2 eggs, well beaten
1 tsp. vanilla flavoring
2 c. sifted flour
1 tsp. soda
¾ tsp. salt
½ c. buttermilk
¾ c. chopped walnuts

Cream margarine and sugar thoroughly; blend in bananas, eggs and vanilla. Sift flour with soda and salt; stir into banana mixture alternately with buttermilk. Add nuts, mixing well. Pour into greased and floured loaf pan. Bake at 325 degrees for 1 hour and 15 minutes or until done. Yield: 1 loaf.

Peggy Wilson
Salisbury, N.C.

BEST BANANA BREAD

1 c. sugar
½ c. shortening
2 eggs
3 bananas, mashed
3 tbsp. sour cream
1 tsp. soda
2 c. flour
½ tsp. salt
½ c. chopped nuts

Blend sugar, shortening, eggs, bananas and sour cream. Sift soda with flour and salt; add nuts. Stir into banana mixture. Pour into greased loaf pan. Bake at 350 degrees for 1 hour. Yield: 1 loaf.

Alta Perkins
Lansing, N.C.

BISHOP'S BREAD

1 c. sugar
3 eggs, beaten
1 ½ c. flour
1 ½ tsp. baking powder
¼ tsp. salt
1 c. nuts
1 c. Maraschino cherries
1 c. dates
1 bar German's sweet chocolate, broken into
    chunks

Combine all ingredients; mix well. Pour
into two greased pans; cover with foil. Bake
at 325 degrees for 1 hour and 20 minutes.
Yield: 2 loaves.

Mrs. Louis Simonton
King, Wisc.

QUICK BLUEBERRY-NUT BREAD

2 eggs
1 c. sugar
1 c. milk
3 tbsp. salad oil
3 c. flour
1 tsp. salt
4 tsp. baking powder
1 c. fresh blueberries
½ c. broken nuts

Beat eggs; gradually add sugar. Add milk
and oil. Sift flour with salt and baking powder; add to liquid mixture. Stir only until
blended. Carefully fold in blueberries and
nuts. Pour into well greased 5 x 12-inch
loaf pan. Bake at 350 degrees for 50 to 60
minutes. Yield: 1 loaf.

Mrs. Malcolm Cross
Calvert City, Ky.

BROWN BREAD

2 tsp. soda
1 c. finely chopped dates
2 c. boiling water
2 tbsp. butter
2 c. sugar
3 eggs, well beaten
4 c. flour
Dash of salt
2 tsp. vanilla flavoring
1 c. chopped nuts

Sprinkle soda over dates; pour boiling water
over mixture. Cool to lukewarm. Cream
butter and sugar; add eggs. Combine with
date mixture; blend well. Add all remaining
ingredients. Fill five or more well greased
soup cans one-half full. Bake at 300 to 325
degrees for 1 hour and 20 minutes.

Mrs. Milo Rediger
Upland, Ind.

BUTTERSCOTCH-WALNUT BREAD

1 tsp. vanilla flavoring
1 c. (firmly packed) brown sugar
1 egg
1 ½ tbsp. butter, melted
2 c. sifted flour
½ tsp. soda
¾ tsp. baking powder
¼ tsp. salt
1 c. buttermilk
½ c. chopped nuts

Mix vanilla, sugar, egg and butter. Add sifted
dry ingredients alternately with buttermilk;
beat for 4 minutes. Add nuts. Pour into 9 x
5 x 3-inch loaf pan. Bake at 350 degrees for
1 hour. Yield: 15-20 servings.

Mrs. Sam W. Hoynes
Custer AFS, Mich.

CARROT BREAD

¾ c. cooking oil
1 c. sugar
2 eggs
1 ½ c. sifted flour
1 tsp. cinnamon
1 tsp. soda
½ tsp. salt
1 ½ c. finely grated raw carrots
¼ c. nuts

Combine oil and sugar; add eggs. Beat well.
Combine all dry ingredients; add to egg mixture, stirring well. Fold in carrots and nuts;
pour into loaf pan. Bake at 350 degrees for 1
hour.

Mrs. Russell Ardery
Copeland, Kans.

CARROT-NUT BREAD

2 eggs
1 c. sugar
¾ c. cooking oil
1 ½ c. sifted flour
1 tsp. soda
1 tsp. baking powder
1 tsp. salt
1 tsp. cinnamon
1 c. grated raw carrots
½ c. nuts

Combine eggs, sugar and oil in large bowl;
beat well. Sift flour with soda, baking powder,
salt and cinnamon; add to sugar mixture.
Add carrots and nuts; mix well. Pour into
greased 9 x 5 x 3-inch loaf pan. Bake at
350 degrees for 1 hour. Yield: 8-10 servings.

Hazel Omdahl
Sheldon, N.D.

FAMILY CHRISTMAS BREAD

2 cakes yeast
¼ c. plus 2 tbsp. sugar
1 c. milk, scalded
1 stick butter
1 tsp. salt
6 oz. red candied cherries, chopped
4 oz. green candied cherries, chopped
1 c. raisins
15 dates, chopped
1 slice candied pineapple, chopped
1 c. chopped nuts
3 eggs, beaten
3 c. flour
2 tbsp. cinnamon
2 tsp. nutmeg
1 egg yolk

Dissolve yeast and 2 tablespoons sugar in 1 cup warm water. Combine milk, butter, salt, 1/4 cup sugar, fruits, nuts and eggs, stirring until butter melts and sugar dissolves. Cool; add yeast mixture. Mix dry ingredients; stir. Knead into fruit mixture. Cover with damp cloth; let rise until doubled. Grease three 6-inch round pans. Cut six strips of wide bias tape 18 inches long; grease tape. Place two strips in each pan at right angles. Knead dough; shape into loaves. Place in pans over strips. Bring strips up and around dough; pin loosely to allow for some rising. Let rise. Tape should hold down some dough across center but allow four bulges to rise. Bake at 375 degrees for 15 minutes. Brush with mixture of egg yolk and 1 tablespoon water. Reduce heat to 350 degrees; continue baking for 20 minutes. Brush on remaining egg mixture; cool. Remove bias tape; replace with ribbons. Frost and decorate bulges. NOTE: May be covered with cellophane wrap and given as gifts at Christmas and Easter. Yield: 3 loaves.

Mrs. Grover L. Johnson
Laramie, Wyo.

JULE KAGE OR CHRISTMAS BREAD

1 egg, slightly beaten
½ c. butter
½ c. milk
1 pkg. or 1 cake yeast
½ c. warm water
¼ c. sugar
1 tsp. salt
1 c. raisins
½ c. chopped candied cherries or candied fruit
½ c. chopped almonds
3 ½ to 4 c. sifted flour

Reserve 1 tablespoon beaten egg. Heat butter and milk; cool to lukewarm. Soften yeast in warm water in mixing bowl; stir in sugar, salt, raisins, cherries, nuts, remaining egg and milk mixture. Add flour gradually to make a stiff dough; knead well. Let rise in warm place for 1 hour and 30 minutes to 2 hours or until doubled in size. Shape into two round loaves; place in greased 8-inch pans or star-shaped pans. Cover; let rise for 1 hour or until doubled in size. Bake at 350 degrees for 30 to 35 minutes. Brush with reserved egg. Yield: 2 loaves.

Mrs. William Peterson
New Effington, S.D.

COCONUT LOAF

1 c. coconut, toasted
3 c. flour
1 tbsp. baking powder
1 c. sugar
½ tsp. salt
1 egg
1 ½ c. milk
1 tsp. vanilla flavoring

Mix all dry ingredients; add egg, milk and vanilla. Stir only until mixed; do not beat. Pour into loaf pan. Bake at 350 degrees for 1 hour. Yield: 20 servings.

Mrs. L. A. Clark
Bedford, Ind.

CRANBERRY-BANANA-NUT BREAD

⅓ c. shortening
⅔ c. sugar
2 eggs
1 ¾ c. sifted flour
2 tsp. baking powder
½ tsp. salt
½ c. coarsely chopped nuts
1 c. mashed ripe bananas
1 c. drained fresh or canned whole cranberry sauce

Cream shortening with sugar. Add an egg at a time, beating well after each addition. Sift all dry ingredients; add nuts. Alternately add flour mixture and bananas to creamed mixture, beating well. Fold in cranberry sauce. Pour into greased loaf pan. Bake in 350 degree oven for 1 hour to 1 hour and 5 minutes or until done. Cool before slicing.

Mrs. M. H. Hatcher
Gray, Ga.

CRANBERRY BREAD

1 c. (heaping) sugar
⅓ c. shortening
1 egg, beaten
1 tsp. grated orange rind
2 c. flour
1 ½ tsp. baking powder
½ tsp. soda
1 tsp. salt
1 sm. can frozen orange juice
½ c. nuts
1 c. chopped cranberries

(Continued on next page)

Cream sugar and shortening; add egg and orange rind. Sift dry ingredients; add alternately to creamed mixture with orange juice. Fold in nuts and cranberries. Pour into loaf pan. Bake at 350 degrees for 1 hour. Yield: 12 servings.

Mrs. Stephen V. Pound
Houston, Tex.

CRANBERRY FRUIT BREAD

2 c. sifted flour
1 c. sugar
1 ½ tsp. baking powder
½ tsp. salt
½ tsp. soda
¼ c. shortening
¾ c. orange juice
1 tbsp. grated orange rind
1 egg, well beaten
½ c. chopped nuts (opt.)
2 c. coarsely chopped fresh cranberries

Sift all dry ingredients; cut in shortening. Combine orange juice, rind and egg; add to dry ingredients, mixing just enough to dampen. Fold in nuts and cranberries. Spoon into 9 x 5 x 3-inch loaf pan. Spread corners and sides slightly higher than center. Bake at 350 degrees for 1 hour. Yield: 10 servings.

Carol Towner
Bath, N.Y.

CRANBERRY- ORANGE BREAD

2 c. flour
1 ½ tsp. baking powder
½ tsp. soda
½ tsp. salt
1 c. sugar
2 tbsp. salad oil
¾ c. orange juice
1 egg, beaten
1 c. sliced raw cranberries
Nuts (opt.)

Sift all dry ingredients. Mix in oil, juice and egg thoroughly. Fold in cranberries and nuts. Pour into oiled loaf pan. Bake at 350 degrees for 1 hour.

Mrs. Wade M. Moncrief, Jr.
Ketchikan, Alaska

CRANBERRY-ORANGE BREAD

4 c. sifted flour
1 ½ c. sugar
1 tbsp. baking powder
2 tsp. salt
1 tsp. soda
2 c. chopped cranberries
1 c. chopped walnuts
2 tsp. grated orange rind
2 eggs, beaten

1 ½ c. orange juice
½ c. salad oil

Sift all dry ingredients. Stir in cranberries, nuts and orange rind. Combine eggs, orange juice and oil; add to dry ingredients, stirring just until moistened. Pour into two greased 9 x 5 x 3-inch loaf pans. Bake at 375 degrees for 50 minutes or until done. NOTE: Bread freezes very well. Yield: 2 loaves.

Mrs. E. A. Lawless
Hueytown, Ala.

FESTIVE CRANBERRY BREAD

2 c. sifted flour
1 c. sugar
2 tsp. baking powder
½ tsp. salt
2 tsp. grated orange rind
⅓ c. orange juice
½ c. water
1 egg, well beaten
2 tbsp. salad oil
1 c. chopped nuts
1 c. cranberry halves

Sift all dry ingredients. Combine rind, juice, water, egg and oil; add to dry mixture. Stir just until thoroughly moistened. Fold in nuts and cranberries. Pour into greased loaf pan; let stand for 10 minutes. Bake at 350 degrees for 1 hour. Cool thoroughly before slicing. Yield: 1 loaf.

Mrs. Arnold Kienas
Kalispell, Mont.

DATE-NUT BREAD

1 pkg. dates, cut up
2 tsp. soda
1 ½ c. boiling water
1 ½ c. sugar
3 ½ c. flour
2 tsp. vanilla flavoring
2 eggs
2 tbsp. butter, melted
1 c. nuts

Sprinkle dates with soda; add boiling water. Let stand. Add remaining ingredients in order listed; mix well. Pour into greased and lined pans; let stand for 10 minutes. Bake at 350 degrees for 1 hour. Yield: 2 loaves.

Mrs. Frances Brandriff
Millville, N.J.

DATE-NUT LOAF

1 ½ c. sugar
1 ½ c. flour

(Continued on next page)

1 ½ tsp. baking powder
⅓ tsp. salt
1 lb. dates, chopped
3 ½ c. chopped pecans
3 sticks butter, melted
6 eggs, separated
Vanilla flavoring

Mix sugar, flour, baking powder and salt with dates and nuts. Add butter, egg yolks and vanilla; mix well. Fold in beaten egg whites. Pour into two greased loaf pans. Bake at 300 degrees for 1 hour. Yield: 2 loaves.

> Mrs. Vernon M. Parker, Jr.
> Georgetown, S.C.

GRAHAM-NUT BREAD

1 c. sour milk
1 c. brown sugar
1 egg
¼ c. (scant) shortening
2 c. graham flour
1 tsp. soda
½ c. sliced dates
½ c. chopped nuts

Blend milk, sugar, egg, shortening, flour and soda. Stir in dates and nuts. Divide batter; pour into two well greased bread pans. Bake at 350 degrees for 45 minutes. Cool for 10 minutes before removing from pans. Yield: 32 servings.

> Mrs. C. L. Zormeir
> Lewistown, Mont.

GRAHAM, NUT AND RAISIN BREAD

2 c. flour
3 c. graham flour
3 tsp. soda
1 c. brown sugar
2 tsp. salt
3 c. sour milk
1 egg
½ c. dark molasses
1 c. broken nuts
1 c. raisins

Mix all dry ingredients. Combine sour milk, egg and molasses; add to first mixture. Add nuts and raisins. Pour into two greased 9 1/2 x 5 1/2 x 2 3/4-inch loaf pans. Bake at 350 degrees for 45 to 55 minutes. Yield: 2 loaves.

> Effie B. Porch
> Lansing, Ind.

GRAPENUT BREAD

1 c. grapenuts
2 c. buttermilk
2 c. sugar

2 eggs
3 ½ c. sifted flour
½ tsp. salt
1 tsp. soda
2 tsp. baking powder

Soak grapenuts in buttermilk for 10 minutes. Cream sugar and eggs. Add milk mixture and combined dry ingredients. Pour into two loaf pans which have been greased and floured. Bake at 350 degrees for 45 minutes. Yield: 2 loaves.

> Mrs. Charles L. Redus
> Columbus, Tex.

GUM DROP BREAD

2 eggs
1 c. sugar
1 c. milk
½ tsp. salt
2 tbsp. shortening, melted
1 c. nuts, chopped
3 ½ c. minus 3 tbsp. flour
3 ½ tsp. baking powder
1 lb. gumdrops, cut up

Beat eggs; combine with remaining ingredients. Put into two greased loaf pans; let stand for 20 minutes before baking. Bake at 350 degrees for 1 hour. Yield: 2 loaves.

> Mrs. Ray Borgeson
> Park River, N.D.

HOMESTEAD PINEAPPLE-NUT BREAD

¾ c. (packed) brown sugar
⅓ c. shortening, softened
2 eggs
1 8 ¾-oz. can crushed pineapple
½ c. chopped nuts
2 ¼ c. sifted flour
3 tsp. baking powder
¼ tsp. soda
Salt
1 tbsp. sugar
¼ tsp. cinnamon

Cream brown sugar, shortening and eggs. Stir in undrained pineapple and nuts. Resift flour with baking powder, soda and salt; blend into pineapple mixture. Spoon into greased and floured 9 x 5 x 3-inch loaf pan. Sprinkle with sugar mixed with cinnamon. Bake at 350 degrees for 1 hour. Slice when cold. Yield: 1 loaf.

> Paula A. Strong
> Syracuse, Nebr.

HONEY-NUT BREAD

½ c. coarsely chopped nuts
2 c. flour
3 tsp. baking powder
½ tsp. salt

(Continued on next page)

1 egg, beaten
½ c. honey
½ c. milk
2 tbsp. butter, melted

Add nuts to sifted dry ingredients. Combine egg, honey, milk and butter; add to flour mixture. Stir until flour mixture is just moistened. Pour into greased loaf pan. Bake at 350 degrees for 45 to 50 minutes.

Mrs. Mary Jo Bingham
Selmer, Tenn.

LEMON BREAD

1 c. sugar
6 tbsp. margarine
2 eggs
1 ½ c. sifted flour
¼ tsp. salt
1 tsp. baking powder
½ c. milk
Grated rind of 1 lemon

Mix all ingredients. Pour into greased loaf pan. Bake at 350 degrees for 1 hour.

TOPPING:
Juice of 1 lemon
⅓ c. sugar

Combine juice and sugar; pour over warm cake. Serve.

Mrs. Nell Orr
Long Beach, Calif.

LEMON-NUT BREAD

2 ¼ c. flour
1 c. sugar
1 tbsp. baking powder
½ tsp. salt
1 c. chopped nuts
1 egg, beaten
¼ c. butter, melted
½ c. water
2 tsp. grated lemon rind
¾ c. evaporated milk

Combine all ingredients; mix until blended. Pour into buttered 9 x 5-inch pan. Bake at 375 degrees for 40 minutes. Cool for 10 minutes before removing from pan. Yield: 1 large loaf.

Mrs. George Stearns
Bellingham, Wash.

LEMON-POPPY SEED BREAD

1 tbsp. grated lemon rind
½ c. lemon juice
½ c. shortening, melted

1 c. sugar
2 eggs, beaten
2 tsp. poppy seed
2 ½ c. sifted flour
4 tsp. baking powder
½ tsp. soda
½ tsp. salt
½ c. water

Combine lemon rind, juice, shortening, sugar, eggs and 1 1/2 teaspoons poppy seed. Sift all dry ingredients; add to sugar mixture alternately with water, mixing well. Pour into greased loaf pan. Sprinkle remaining poppy seed over loaf. Bake at 350 degrees for 1 hour and 15 minutes or until done. Cool and serve. Yield: 1 loaf.

Mrs. Dolores Carr
Cambria AFS, Calif.

SPICY MINCE LOAF

2 eggs, beaten
½ c. brown sugar
1 sm. can evaporated milk
1 c. prepared mincemeat
½ stick butter, melted
½ c. chopped walnuts
2 ¼ c. sifted flour
3 tsp. baking powder
1 tsp. salt

Mix eggs, sugar, milk, mincemeat, butter and nuts. Sift in dry ingredients, stirring just until blended. Pour into greased 9 x 5 x 3-inch loaf pan. Bake at 350 degrees for 1 hour or until top is firm and wooden pick inserted comes out clean. Cool for 5 minutes. Turn out onto wire rack. Wrap in foil when completely cooled. Yield: 6 servings.

Mrs. Robert B. Moore
San Diego, Calif.

NUT BREAD

2 c. flour
⅓ c. sugar
3 tsp. baking powder
½ tsp. salt
1 ½ c. nuts
1 c. milk
2 tbsp. shortening
1 egg

Sift all dry ingredients; stir in all remaining ingredients. Pour into loaf pan. Bake at 375 degrees for 1 hour. Yield: 1 loaf.

Marguerite Le Neve
Gilbert, S.C.

OATMEAL-ORANGE BREAD

2 c. boiling water
1 c. oats
1 pkg. yeast

(Continued on next page)

½ c. warm water
½ c. molasses
3 tsp. salt
2 tsp. butter
5 c. flour
2 tbsp. grated orange rind

Pour boiling water over oats; let stand for 2 hours. Soften yeast in warm water; add to oat mixture. Stir in remaining ingredients. Divide dough into two portions; place in two loaf pans. Let rise until doubled. Bake at 375 degrees for 45 to 50 minutes. Yield: 2 loaves.

Mrs. Philip Mueller
Clearmont, Wyo.

ORANGE-DATE-NUT BREAD

1 lge. orange
1 6½-oz. pkg. pitted dates
1 c. sugar
2 tbsp. salad oil
1 egg
2 c. flour
1 tsp. baking powder
1 tsp. soda
1 tsp. salt
½ c. chopped nuts
1 tsp. vanilla flavoring

Thinly peel rind from orange. Grind or finely chop peeling and dates. Squeeze juice from orange; add enough boiling water to juice to make 1 cup liquid. Pour over peeling and date mixture; stir in sugar, oil and egg. Sift flour with baking powder, soda and salt; blend into orange mixture. Add nuts and vanilla; mix well. Pour into greased and floured loaf pan. Bake at 325 degrees for 1 hour. Yield: 1 loaf.

Mrs. W. H. Wheeler, Jr.
Wadesboro, N.C.

ORANGE MARMALADE BREAD

2½ c. sifted flour
1 tsp. soda
1 tsp. salt
¾ c. sugar
1 egg, beaten
½ c. thick orange marmalade
¼ c. white vinegar
1 c. milk
2 tbsp. melted shortening

Sift flour with soda, salt and sugar. Combine egg and marmalade; stir in vinegar, milk and shortening. Pour into dry ingredients; stir until blended. Pour into greased 9 x 5 x 3-inch loaf pan. Bake at 350 degrees for 1 hour. Yield: 10-12 servings.

Mrs. Jerome Avery, Sr.
Hilton, N.Y.

ORANGE-PECAN BREAD

3 c. sifted flour
4 tsp. baking powder
½ tsp. soda
½ tsp. salt
1 c. chopped pecans
2 eggs, well beaten
½ c. milk
½ c. orange juice
1 tbsp. grated orange rind
¾ c. orange marmalade

Sift all dry ingredients. Stir in pecans. Combine eggs, milk, orange juice, orange rind and marmalade; stir in dry ingredients. Mix well; turn into greased loaf pan. Bake at 350 degrees for 1 hour.

Mrs. S. G. Arnold
Jacksonville, Ark.

QUICK ORANGE BREAD

3 c. sifted flour
4½ tsp. baking powder
¾ tsp. salt
⅓ c. shortening
1 c. sugar
1 egg, beaten
1 c. orange juice
⅓ c. grated orange rind

Sift flour with baking powder and salt. Cream shortening. Add sugar gradually; continue beating until light and fluffy. Add egg; beat well. Add orange juice and rind. Pour into flour mixture; stir enough to moisten dry ingredients. Do not beat. Turn into greased 9 1/2 x 5 1/2-inch loaf pan. Bake at 350 degrees for 1 hour. Yield: 1 loaf.

Clarissa Turner
Mexico, Mo.

PEANUT BUTTER BREAD

2 c. sifted flour
⅓ c. sugar
3 tsp. baking powder
1 tsp. salt
¾ c. peanut butter
1 egg, slightly beaten
1 c. milk

Sift all dry ingredients; cut in peanut butter. Combine egg and milk. Stir into peanut butter mixture lightly. Turn into well greased 9 x 5 x 3-inch loaf pan. Bake at 350 degrees for 1 hour or until done. Yield: 1 loaf.

Rose Collier
Elwood, Ind.

PERSIMMON BREAD

1 ¾ c. flour
¾ tsp. soda
1 ¼ tsp. cream of tartar
Pinch of salt
⅓ c. shortening or margarine
⅔ c. sugar
1 c. persimmon pulp

Mix thoroughly all ingredients. Pour into 8 x 5-inch loaf pan. Bake at 350 degrees for 1 hour.

Mrs. Nadine Long
Martinsville, Ind.

PERSIMMON BREAD

1 c. persimmon pulp
1 c. sugar
½ c. shortening
2 eggs, beaten
1 ¾ c. flour
1 tsp. soda
1 tsp. baking powder
½ tsp. salt
¼ c. chopped walnuts

Put persimmons through colander to remove skins and seed. Cream sugar and shortening; add eggs. Sift all dry ingredients into creamed mixture. Add walnuts and pulp. Pour into an 11 x 8-inch pan. Bake at 325 degrees for 45 minutes. Yield: 12 servings.

Mrs. G. Frank Hall
Aurora, Mo.

PINEAPPLE-NUT BREAD

2 c. sifted flour
½ c. sugar
1 tsp. baking powder
½ tsp. salt
1 c. raisins
½ c. coarsely chopped walnuts
1 egg, beaten
1 tsp. vanilla flavoring
2 tbsp. melted shortening
1 tsp. soda
1 c. crushed pineapple

Sift flour with sugar, baking powder and salt. Add raisins and walnuts. Combine egg, vanilla and melted shortening; add to flour mixture. Dissolve soda in undrained pineapple; add mixture and stir until blended. Pour batter into a greased 8 x 4 x 4-inch loaf pan. Bake in a 350 degree oven for 1 hour or until done. Yield: 1 loaf.

Mrs. Richard Graham, Jr.
Masontown, W. Va.

PINEAPPLE-NUT BREAD

1 c. crushed pineapple
Orange juice
⅔ c. All-Bran
1 egg, well beaten
2 tbsp. melted shortening
2 c. flour
½ c. sugar
2 tsp. baking powder
¼ tsp. soda
1 tsp. salt
½ c. chopped nuts

Drain pineapple; reserve juice. Add enough orange juice to pineapple juice to measure 2/3 cup liquid. Pour liquid mixture over All-Bran; let set for 15 minutes. Mix egg with all remaining ingredients. Add All-Bran mixture. Pour into a well greased bread pan. Bake at 325 degrees for 1 hour and 15 minutes. Cool in pan for 10 minutes. Run knife around pan; turn out onto wire rack to cool. Yield: 1 loaf.

Mrs. Rodger C. Dickinson
De Queen, Ark.

PRUNE BREAD

¼ c. shortening
½ c. sugar
1 egg, beaten
1 c. cooked drained prunes
2 c. flour
3 tsp. baking powder
½ tsp. salt
¾ c. prune juice
½ c. nuts
2 tsp. grated lemon rind

Cream shortening and sugar; blend in egg and fruit. Stir in combined dry ingredients alternately with juice. Add nuts and rind; pour batter into greased loaf pan. Bake at 350 degrees for 55 to 60 minutes. Yield: 20 servings.

Ylovia Williams
Lubbock, Tex.

PRUNE BREAD

2 c. sugar
1 c. oil
3 eggs
2 ½ c. flour
1 tsp. salt
1 jar strained prunes
1 tsp. cinnamon
¼ tsp. nutmeg
1 c. chopped nuts

Mix sugar and oil; beat in eggs. Add all remaining ingredients; mix well. Pour into two greased loaf pans. Bake at 325 degrees for 1 hour. Yield: 16 servings.

Mrs. H. D. Rogers
Enid, Okla.

PUMPKIN BREAD

1 ⅓ c. sugar
⅓ c. butter or margarine
2 eggs
1 c. canned pumpkin
⅓ c. cold water
1 ⅔ c. flour
1 tsp. soda
¾ tsp. salt
1 ¼ tsp. pumpkin pie spices
¼ tsp. baking powder
½ c. raisins
⅔ c. walnuts

Cream sugar and butter. Add eggs, pumpkin and water. Sift all dry ingredients; add to pumpkin mixture. Add raisins and walnuts. Pour into a well greased paper-lined loaf pan. Bake at 325 degrees for 1 hour. NOTE: Coffee may be substituted for cold water. Yield: 18 slices.

Mrs. Edward J. Andresen
Sioux Falls, S.D.

WALNUT BREAD

3 c. flour
1 c. sugar
1 ½ tsp. salt
4 tsp. baking powder
1 egg, beaten
1 c. milk
2 tbsp. melted shortening
1 c. chopped walnuts

Sift flour, sugar, salt and baking powder. Add egg, milk and shortening; beat well. Stir in walnuts. Pour into greased pan; let stand for 20 minutes. Bake at 350 degrees for 1 hour and 5 minutes to 1 hour and 10 minutes. Yield: 6-8 servings.

Marge Crandell
Overland, Mo.

WELSH FRUIT BREAD

1 c. milk
1 c. warm water
1 oz. yeast
2 lb. flour
⅔ c. sugar
½ lb. (scant) lard or 1 c. shortening
2 eggs, beaten
1 tbsp. salt
1 lb. currants and raisins combined, washed
    and drained
1 oz. candied orange and lemon peel
½ tsp. mixed spices (cinnamon, ginger and
    nutmeg)

Scald milk; cool to lukewarm. Combine milk and water; dissolve yeast in milk mixture. Make a nest in flour; add yeast mixture. Mix.

Cover; let rise for 30 minutes. Melt shortening; add to dough. Add all remaining ingredients; knead well. Cover; let rise until double in bulk. Separate into two portions; shape into loaves. Place in two greased loaf pans; let rise. Bake at 350 degrees for 45 to 60 minutes. Yield: 2 loaves.

Mrs. Mary Kinyon
Rosendale, Wisc.

WINCHESTER NUT BREAD

¾ c. hot water
½ c. brown sugar
½ c. molasses
¾ c. milk
2 c. graham flour
1 c. plain flour
2 ½ tsp. baking powder
1 ⅓ tsp. salt
¾ tsp. soda
¾ c. walnuts
½ c. seedless raisins

Pour hot water over brown sugar; add molasses and milk. Mix flours, baking powder, salt and soda; add sugar mixture. Fold in walnuts and raisins. Pour into buttered pan. Bake in 350 degree oven for 1 hour and 30 minutes. Yield: 18-20 slices.

Elizabeth M. McKnight
Richmond, Va.

APPLE JIMS

2 c. flour
3 tsp. baking powder
⅓ c. sugar
1 c. finely chopped apples
1 egg, well beaten
1 c. milk
3 tbsp. butter, melted

Sift all dry ingredients; stir in apples. Combine egg, milk and butter; add to dry ingredients. Pour into greased muffin tins.

TOPPING:
½ c. sugar
½ tsp. cinnamon
⅓ c. nuts

Combine sugar, cinnamon and nuts; sprinkle over batter. Bake at 400 degrees for 15 to 20 minutes. Serve warm. Yield: 12 servings.

Mrs. Sylvia M. Mayfield
Fort MacArthur, Calif.

CLOVE-APPLE CUPS

2 c. sifted flour
2 tsp. double-acting baking powder
1 ¼ tsp. salt
¼ c. plus 2 tbsp. sugar
¼ c. shortening
1 c. milk
1 lge. egg, beaten
½ tsp. pure vanilla flavoring
4 med. ripe cooking apples
¼ tsp. ground cloves
½ tsp. ground cinnamon
2 tbsp. light corn syrup
1 tbsp. melted butter or margarine

Sift flour, baking powder, 1 teaspoon salt and 2 tablespoons sugar into a mixing bowl. Cut in shortening with a pastry blender or two knives until mixture resembles coarse meal. Combine milk, egg and vanilla; stir into dry ingredients. Mix well. Drop a tablespoon of batter into each of 12 well greased muffin tins or custard cups. Peel apples; core and cut into 1/2-inch slices crosswise. Place a slice over each cup of batter. Fill centers with a mixture of remaining 1/4 cup sugar, 1/4 teaspoon salt and spices. Brush top with mixture of syrup and melted butter. Bake in preheated 400 degree oven for 20 to 25 minutes or until tender. Serve warm with sweetened whipped cream or as coffee cake without cream. Yield: 12 servings.

Photograph for this recipe above.

SPICY APPLE MUFFINS

⅔ c. sugar
2 ¼ c. flour
¾ tsp. salt
4 ½ tsp. baking powder
½ tsp. cinnamon
¼ tsp. nutmeg
⅛ tsp. allspice
1 egg, beaten
1 ½ c. milk
⅓ c. shortening, melted
1 tbsp. orange juice
1 c. finely chopped apples

Combine all dry ingredients in bowl. Combine liquids; pour into dry ingredients. Mix just enough to moisten; do not beat. Add apples. Fill greased muffin cups two-thirds full. Bake at 425 degrees for 23 to 24 minutes. Yield: 1 1/2 dozen.

Irene Yerxa
Bridgewater, Me.

CINNAMON-APPLE MUFFINS

1 c. milk
1 egg
¼ c. shortening
2 c. flour
½ tsp. salt
½ tsp. cinnamon
4 tsp. baking powder
½ c. sugar
1 c. finely chopped apples

Mix milk, egg and shortening; add sifted dry ingredients and apples. Pour into greased muffin cups two-thirds full. Bake at 425 degrees for 20 to 25 minutes. Yield: 12 muffins.

Barbara Newell
South Paris, Me.

APRICOT-CORN MEAL MUFFINS

1 ¼ c. sifted flour
1 c. yellow corn meal
¼ c. sugar
1 tsp. soda
1 tbsp. baking powder
1 tsp. salt
2 eggs, beaten
1 ¼ c. buttermilk
¼ c. butter, melted
1 c. chopped cooked dried apricots

Sift all dry ingredients. Combine eggs, buttermilk and butter. Add all at once to dry mixture; blend well. Stir in apricots; spoon mixture into greased muffin tins. Bake at 425 degrees for 15 minutes. Yield: 12 servings.

Mrs. Ernest Jenny
Norfolk, Nebr.

BANANA-NUT MUFFINS

1 c. flour
½ c. sugar
2 ½ tsp. baking powder
½ tsp. salt
¼ tsp. soda
¾ c. oats
1 egg, beaten
3 tbsp. fat, melted
½ c. milk
½ c. mashed banana
⅓ c. chopped nuts

Sift all dry ingredients; add oats. Add all remaining ingredients; stir only until flour is moistened. Fill greased muffin cups two-thirds full. Bake at 400 degrees for 20 to 25 minutes. Yield: 12 servings.

Mrs. James Wagoner
Brevard, N.C.

BLUEBERRY MUFFINS

2 c. flour
¼ c. sugar
2 tsp. baking powder
½ tsp. soda
½ tsp. salt
¼ c. melted shortening
1 c. buttermilk
1 egg, beaten
1 c. fresh or frozen blueberries

Sift all dry ingredients. Add shortening and buttermilk to egg. Add to dry ingredients, stirring just enough to moisten. Fold in blueberries. Spoon into muffin tin. Bake at 400 degrees for 25 minutes. Yield: 12 servings.

Mrs. Sarah Franzen
— Libertyville, Ill.

BLUEBERRY MUFFINS

2 ⅔ c. flour
1 c. blueberries
¼ c. butter
¼ c. sugar
1 egg
½ tsp. salt
4 tsp. baking powder
1 c. milk

Mix 2/3 cup flour with blueberries; let stand for 1 hour. Cream butter, sugar and egg. Sift remaining 2 cups flour with salt and baking powder. Add alternately with milk. Add floured blueberries. Pour into greased muffin cups. Bake at 400 degrees for 25 minutes.

Gertrude Nichols
Eureka, Ark.

CARAMEL-PECAN MUFFINS

1 c. sifted flour
¼ c. sugar
3 tsp. baking powder
½ tsp. salt
¼ c. shortening
1 c. oats
1 egg, beaten
1 c. milk
⅓ c. brown sugar
2 tbsp. melted butter
Pecans

Sift flour with sugar, baking powder and salt. Cut in shortening; blend in oats. Stir in egg and milk. Blend brown sugar and melted butter. Put small amount of sugar and butter in bottoms of 12 greased muffin cups. Arrange 2 or 3 pecan halves in each. Fill cups two-thirds full of mixture. Bake at 425 degrees for 20 minutes. Turn out of pan immediately.

Mary J. Rardin
Elkhart, Ind.

DATE MUFFINS

⅓ c. butter
¼ c. sugar
1 egg, beaten
2 c. sifted flour
3 tsp. baking powder
1 tsp. salt
¾ c. milk
1 c. chopped dates

Cream butter and sugar; add egg. Mix well. Sift flour, baking powder and salt; add to creamed mixture alternately with milk. Stir in dates; pour into greased muffin pans. Bake at 400 degrees for 18 to 20 minutes. Yield: 12 servings.

Martha Morganroth
Burlingame, Kans.

MAGIC MUFFINS

1 pkg. dry yeast
¼ c. warm water
¾ c. lukewarm milk
1 ¼ c. sugar
1 tsp. salt
1 egg
¼ c. soft butter
3 ½ to 3 ¾ c. flour
24 marshmallows
1 c. melted butter
1 tbsp. cinnamon

Dissolve yeast in water. Combine milk, 1/4 cup sugar, salt, egg and soft butter. Gradually add flour; knead well. Let rise for 1 hour and 30 minutes. Punch down; let rise for 30 minutes. Divide dough into 24 small sections. Dip marshmallows into melted butter; dip into mixture of 1 cup sugar and cinnamon. Flatten each piece of dough. Wrap around a marshmallow. Dip into melted butter and sugar mixture. Place sealed-side down in large greased muffin tins. Let rise until light. Bake at 375 degrees for 30 minutes. Yield: 24 servings.

Marilyn Sharp
Mountain View, Mo.

MUFFINS

¼ c. shortening
2 tbsp. sugar
1 egg
1 ½ c. flour
4 tsp. baking powder
½ tsp. salt
1 c. milk

Cream shortening; add sugar gradually. Add egg. Sift flour with baking powder and salt; add alternately with milk to creamed mixture. Pour into muffin tins. Bake at 425 degrees until golden brown. Yield: 12 large or 18 small muffins.

Mrs. W. S. Baird
Clover, S.C.

MUFFINS

1 ½ c. sifted flour
½ c. sugar
2 tsp. baking powder
½ tsp. salt
¼ c. shortening or cooking oil
1 egg
½ c. milk

Sift all dry ingredients; cut in shortening. Add egg and milk; stir just until flour is moistened. Fill greased muffin cups two-thirds full. Bake at 400 degrees for 20 to 25 minutes or until golden brown. Yield: 12 servings.

Mrs. W. M. Steinmeyer
Barnwell, S.C.

OATMEAL MUFFINS

1 c. oats
1 c. buttermilk
⅓ c. soft shortening and butter, mixed
½ c. brown sugar
1 egg
1 c. flour
1 tsp. baking powder
½ tsp. soda
1 tsp. salt

Soak oats in buttermilk for 1 hour. Mix shortening, brown sugar and egg thoroughly. Sift all dry ingredients; stir into shortening mixture alternately with oats and buttermilk. Fill greased muffin cups two-thirds full. Bake at 400 degrees for 20 to 25 minutes or until golden brown. Yield: 12 servings.

Mrs. Maude W. Risinger
Lexington, S.C.

STRAWBERRY MUFFINS

1 egg
⅓ c. melted shortening
½ c. plus 2 tbsp. milk
1 ¾ c. flour
1 tbsp. baking powder
4 tbsp. sugar
¾ tsp. salt
1 c. sliced fresh or ¾ c. well drained
   frozen strawberries

Beat egg until foamy. Add shortening and milk. Sift all dry ingredients; add egg mixture. Mix until dry ingredients are just wet. Fold in strawberries. Fill paper-lined muffin tins two-thirds full, trying to keep only batter on top. Bake at 400 degrees for 25 minutes.

(Continued on next page)

NOTE: If frozen strawberries are used, use only 2 tablespoons sugar. Yield: 12 servings.

Mrs. F. E. Harrington
Abbeville, La.

ORANGE TEA MUFFINS

1 c. ground nuts
1 c. ground raisins
1 ½ c. flour
1 c. sugar
½ c. butter
1 c. buttermilk
1 tsp. soda
2 eggs, well beaten
1 tsp. vanilla flavoring
Juice of 1 orange
Grated rind of 1 orange

Roll nuts and raisins in 1/2 cup flour. Mix all remaining ingredients; add raisin mixture. Pour into tiny muffin tins. Bake at 350 to 375 degrees until done.

GLAZE:
1 c. sugar
Juice of 2 oranges

Combine sugar and juice; dip warm muffins into mixture. Yield: 5 dozen.

Mrs. Lula Nelson
Travis AFB, Calif.

CREAM PUFFS

½ c. water
¼ tsp. salt
¼ c. butter or shortening
½ c. sifted flour
2 eggs

Heat water, salt and butter to boiling. Remove from heat. Add flour; mix well. Heat, stirring constantly, until mixture leaves sides of pan. Beat to cool. Add an egg at a time; beat well after each addition. Drop by spoonfuls onto cookie sheet. Bake at 350 degrees for 20 minutes. Fill with whipped cream or custard. Yield: 6 servings.

Mrs. Charles Gibbons
Fort Pierce, Fla.

DANISH PUFFS

1 c. flour
½ c. butter
2 tbsp. water

Mix all ingredients well. Form into a ball; divide in half. Pat into two 12 x 3-inch strips. Place 3 inches apart on an ungreased baking sheet.

FILLING:
½ c. butter
1 c. water
1 tsp. almond flavoring
1 c. flour
3 eggs

Mix butter and water; bring to a boil. Remove from heat; add flavoring. Quickly beat in flour. Add an egg at a time. Spread evenly over pastry strips. Bake at 350 degrees for 55 to 60 minutes or until dry like cream puffs. Frost with powdered sugar icing; sprinkle with chopped nuts. Add bits of cherries if desired.

Mrs. Robert Hussey
Showhegan, Me.

NEVER-FAIL CREAM PUFFS

½ c. butter
1 c. water
1 c. flour
4 eggs

Heat butter and water until butter melts. Add flour; stir vigorously. Add an egg at a time; beat well after each addition. Drop by tablespoonfuls onto ungreased baking sheet. Bake at 425 degrees for 30 to 40 minutes.

CUSTARD:
2 squares chocolate
2 tbsp. butter
1 c. powdered sugar
4 tbsp. cream

Melt chocolate and butter in top of double boiler. Stir in sugar and cream. Beat until smooth and shiny. Split puffs crosswise; fill. Yield: 8 servings.

Arlis Garmon
Bristol, Ind.

RAISIN SCONES

2 c. flour
½ tsp. salt
3 tsp. baking powder
Pinch of cinnamon
2 tbsp. sugar
6 tbsp. shortening
½ c. raisins
¾ c. milk

Sift all dry ingredients; cut in shortening. Add raisins; add enough milk to make dough just stiff enough to handle. Turn onto floured board; knead lightly. Roll about 1/2-inch thick; cut into triangles. Bake at 400 to 425 degrees until brown.

Mrs. Richard Giannini
Fall River, Mass.

BASIC SWEET ROLLS

2 pkg. dry yeast
½ c. warm water
½ c. sugar
2 tsp. salt
½ c. soft shortening
2 eggs
7 to 7½ c. flour
1½ c. milk, scalded and cooled

Dissolve yeast in warm water. Add sugar, salt, shortening, eggs and one-half of flour to milk; beat well. Add yeast; beat thoroughly. Add enough of remaining flour to handle easily; knead on lightly floured board. Let rise until double in bulk. Punch down; let rise again. Shape dough into rolls. Bake at 375 degrees for 25 to 30 minutes. Yield: 1 1/2 dozen rolls.

Mrs. Emil J. Box
St. Elizabeth, Mo.

DESSERT NUT BUTTERHORNS

4 c. flour
1 tsp. salt
1 cake yeast, crumbled
1¼ c. margarine
3 egg yolks, beaten
1 c. sour cream
1 tsp. vanilla flavoring

Sift flour with salt; cut in yeast and margarine with pastry blender. Combine egg yolks, sour cream and vanilla; stir into flour mixture. Knead until smooth ball is formed. Divide dough into five portions; chill for several hours.

FILLING:
3 egg whites, stiffly beaten
1 c. sugar
2 c. finely ground walnuts
1 tsp. vanilla flavoring

Combine all ingredients. On a board sprinkled with powdered sugar, roll each portion of dough into a 12-inch circle. Cut into 12 wedges. Cover each wedge with filling; roll as cresent roll. Place point down on greased cookie sheets. Bake at 350 degrees for 18 to 20 minutes. Yield: 60 servings.

Mrs. Harriet Hayes
Sheridan, Oreg.

CINNAMON CRISPS

1 pkg. yeast
½ c. warm water
3 tbsp. plus 1 tsp. sugar
3 tbsp. shortening
1 c. milk
2 eggs, beaten
1 tsp. salt
5 c. flour
Melted butter
1 c. brown sugar

Soften yeast in warm water; add 3 tablespoons sugar, shortening, milk, eggs, salt and flour. Mix well. Let rise until double in bulk; roll to 26 x 12-inch rectangle. Brush with butter; sprinkle with 1/2 cup brown sugar and 1/2 teaspoon sugar. Fold dough over; roll again. Brush with butter; roll as a jelly roll. Slice 1-inch thick. Sprinkle with 1/2 cup brown sugar and 1/2 teaspoon sugar. Roll thin; place on cookie sheet, sugar-side up. Let rise for 5 minutes. Bake at 350 degrees for 15 minutes.

Marian Pentico
Pierce, Nebr.

DANISH PASTRIES

4 c. flour
½ c. sugar
1 tsp. salt
1 c. shortening
1 cake yeast
½ c. warm water
½ c. milk
2 eggs, well beaten

Sift all dry ingredients; cut in shortening until mixture becomes crumbly. Dissolve yeast in warm water; add milk and eggs. Add yeast mixture to dry ingredients; mix well. Chill; form into rolls. Bake at 350 degrees until light brown. Cover with icing if desired. Yield: 30 servings.

Mrs. Mildred Sellstrom
Austin, Tex.

PECAN CLUSTER ROLLS

¾ c. milk, scalded
½ c. sugar
2 tsp. salt
½ c. margarine
2 pkg. or cakes yeast
½ c. warm water
1 egg
4 c. sifted flour
Melted butter
½ c. brown sugar
1 tsp. cinnamon
½ c. chopped pecans

Combine milk, sugar, salt and margarine; cool to lukewarm. Dissolve yeast in water. Stir in lukewarm milk mixture. Blend in egg and 2 cups flour; beat until smooth. Stir in remaining 2 cups flour to make a stiff batter. Cover tightly; chill for at least 2 hours. Shape into 1 1/2-inch balls; dip into melted butter and into a mixture of brown sugar and cinnamon. Sprinkle with pecans. Place in alternate rows and layers in a greased angel food cake pan. Let rise until doubled in bulk. Bake at 350 degrees for 45 minutes. Yield: 12-14 servings.

Jane Clark
Greenwood, Ind.

Party
Beverages

RECIPE FOR TEA HOUSE PINEAPPLE PUNCH ON PAGE 376

CHAMPAGNE PUNCH

3 qt. Champagne
1 qt. sparkling water
½ pt. brandy
Strawberries

Mix Champagne and sparkling water; pour over ice. Rest ladle with rim at surface of punch. Pour in brandy; it will float. Serve a strawberry in each glass. Yield: 40 servings.

Mrs. J. M. Masters, Sr.
Parris Island, S.C.

CHAMPAGNE PUNCH

1 6-oz. can frozen lemonade concentrate
6 c. or 1 lge. can unsweetened pineapple juice, chilled
1 bottle Sauterne or Rhine Castle wine, chilled
Orange slices
Maraschino cherries
2 bottles extra dry Champagne, well chilled

Combine frozen lemonade concentrate, pineapple juice and Sauterne in punch bowl. Add a block of ice. Add fruits for garnish just before serving. Pour in Champagne. NOTE: The first ingredients may be made up ahead of time and stored in refrigerator. Yield: 50 cups.

Mrs. Fred G. Phillips
Columbus, O.

CHAPLAIN'S PUNCH

3 qt. unsweetened pineapple juice
4 qt. dry ginger ale
2 qt. Champagne
Juice of 8 lemons
Juice of 4 oranges
Juice of 3 limes
Crushed mint leaves
2 c. sugar
1 pt. strawberries

Mix pineapple juice, ginger ale and Champagne; let stand. Add all remaining ingredients and a block or cubes of ice. Yield: 60-70 servings.

Mrs. R. P. Swofford, Jr.
Montgomery, Ala.

PEACHY CHAMPAGNE PUNCH

1 pkg. frozen peaches
1 bottle peach brandy, chilled
4 bottles Champagne, chilled
4 qt. club soda, chilled
Ice cubes
Chopped Maraschino cherries

Place frozen peaches in large punch bowl. Pour in remaining ingredients except cherries; mix well. Garnish with cherries. Yield: 50 servings.

Mrs. Ernest D. Ficco
Norfolk, Va.

QUICK PRETTY PINK CHAMPAGNE

1 gal. Sauterne
4 qt. soda water
4 bottles pink Champagne
1 fifth of brandy

Freeze one large mold of ice made of water, pink vegetable coloring and fresh mint leaves. Place mold in punch bowl when ready to serve punch; quickly pour all ingredients over ice mold. NOTE: The very cheapest domestic ingredients are just as good as the expensive brands. This is a very clear, bubbly punch and can easily be refilled. Yield: 120 cups.

Mrs. K. R. Klofkorn
Oakland, Calif.

APPLE BLOSSOM PUNCH

1 10-oz. can apple juice
2 qt. ginger ale
1 bottle light rum
Juice of 12 limes
3 oz. Grenadine

Stir apple juice and ginger ale in punch bowl. Add large block of ice or ice cubes; stir. Add rum, lime juice and grenadine. Stir well; decorate with apples, pineapple rings and cherries. Yield: 12-15 servings.

Mrs. John R. Murphy
Point Loma, Calif.

HOLIDAY EGGNOG

6 eggs, separated
1 c. sugar
1 qt. milk
1 pt. rum, brandy or whiskey
1 qt. vanilla ice cream
Nutmeg (opt.)

Beat egg whites until stiff; add 1/2 cup sugar gradually. Beat egg yolks until light and creamy. Add remaining sugar; beat. Add milk to egg yolks; beat slowly with electric mixer. Add rum and ice cream; beat slowly for 1 to 2 minutes. Fold egg whites into batter. Pour into punch bowl; sprinkle top with nutmeg. Yield: 12 servings.

Mrs. George C. Orr
Tullahoma, Tenn.

HOLIDAY PARTY PUNCH

1 6-oz. can frozen orange juice
1 6-oz. can frozen lemonade
½ 6-oz. can frozen limeade
1 lge. can pineapple juice
2 ½ qt. cold water
1 pkg. frozen strawberries
1 c. rum (opt.)

Pour frozen juice concentrates, pineapple juice and water over two trays of ice cubes in large punch bowl. Add frozen strawberries; stir. Add rum. May be garnished with lime or orange slices. Yield: 25 servings.

Mrs. Constantine Mackaronis
New Brunswick, N.J.

NECTAR

1 6-oz. can frozen orange-pineapple juice
⅔ c. lemon juice
2 cinnamon sticks
16 whole cloves
⅔ c. water
⅔ c. sugar
4 tbsp. rum
2 12-oz. bottles ginger ale, chilled

Mix orange-pineapple juice with lemon juice. Combine cinnamon sticks, cloves, water and sugar; cook for 5 minutes. Strain. Add to juice; chill. Add rum and ginger ale when ready to serve. Yield: 15 servings.

Mrs. I. B. Jacobson
Monterey, Calif.

RUM PUNCH

46 oz. grapefruit juice
36 oz. orange juice
18 oz. pineapple juice
8 oz. maple syrup
50 oz. rum

Mix all ingredients well; pour over cake of ice· in punch bowl. Yield: 50 servings.

Mrs. William M. Brown, Jr.
Orlando, Fla.

RUM PUNCH

Juice of 6 oranges
Juice of 6 lemons
Juice of 3 limes
¾ c. powdered sugar
1 6-oz. can undiluted frozen pineapple juice
1 ½ fifths rum
1 sm. bottle cherries
1 lemon, thinly sliced
1 orange, thinly sliced
1 lime, thinly sliced
1 ½ lge. bottles ginger ale

Combine orange, lemon and lime juices with powdered sugar. Add pineapple juice; mix well. Add rum and cherries. Alternate fruit slices in container. Pour in juice mixture; freeze. Before serving, place frozen block in punch bowl; add ginger ale. Yield: 24 servings.

Mrs. Dorothy S. Eviston
Walker AFB, N.M.

CRANBERRY PUNCH

2 1-pt. bottles cranberry juice
1 sm. can frozen lemonade
1 qt. ginger ale
1 qt. vodka

Chill all ingredients well. Combine all ingredients in large punch bowl over block of ice. NOTE: An ice ring made in gelatin mold may be used instead of block of ice. Yield: Twenty-four 4-ounce servings.

Mrs. B. W. Rosenbaum
Dallas, Tex.

SOUTHERN SCUPPERNONG WINE

Scuppernongs
Water
Sugar

Wash scuppernongs; put into 3-gallon churn or jar. Do not fill jar more than three-fourths full. Crush scuppernongs; cover with water. Cover churn with cloth; let stand for nine days. Strain scuppernongs through a cloth. Add 3 pounds sugar to each gallon of juice. Put in fruit jar; cover with cloth. Let stand for 14 days or until mixture stops beading. Seal jars; store until ready to serve. NOTE: Other grapes may be substituted for scuppernongs.

Mrs. J. H. Millsaps, Sr.
West Point, Miss.

PINK WINEADE

1 6-oz. can frozen lemonade concentrate
2 c. Rose wine

Prepare lemonade concentrate as directed on can, omitting 1 can of water to allow for dilution of ice cubes. Blend with wine. Fill 1 1/2-quart pitcher with ice cubes; fill with wine mixture. Stir to blend. Yield: 6-8 servings.

Mrs. J. J. Hoblitzell
Pearl Harbor, Hawaii

ARMOR PUNCH

3 fifths bourbon
1 qt. dry Sherry
1 qt. dry Vermouth
1 c. sugar
6 lemons, sliced
2 tsp. Angostura bitters
6 qt. ginger ale, chilled

Mix all ingredients except ginger ale; chill. Just before serving, pour over block of ice in large punch bowl; add ginger ale. NOTE: The ice block may be treated with special effects appropriate to the occasion. Yield: 80 punch cups.

Mrs. R. J. Adamson
Fort Stewart, Ga.

MAI TAI

2 oz. pineapple juice
1 oz. bar mix (rock candy syrup)
½ oz. orange curacao
1 oz. light rum
1 oz. dark rum
Juice of ½ lemon
Fresh pineapple chunk

Combine all ingredients in blender with a handful of crushed ice. Blend. Serve in large glass with cubes of ice. Yield: 1 serving.

Mrs. J. H. McMillan
Pearl Harbor, Hawaii

RHINE WINE PUNCH

3 qt. Rhine wine
1 qt. soda water, chilled
2 ½ jiggers brandy
3 jiggers creme de menthe
1 c. strong tea
½ lb. powdered sugar

Combine all ingredients in punch bowl; set in bed of crushed ice. Decorate with fruit as desired; serve thoroughly chilled. Yield: 25-30 cups.

Mrs. Darrell V. Fowler
Dover, N.J.

SANGRIA

2 oz. dark rum (opt.)
1 can 7-Up
1 bottle Fanta lemon or low calorie Sprite
1 ½ 7-Up cans of dry wine

Pour rum into glass pitcher or punch bowl. Add 7-Up, lemon and wine. Add 1 tray cracked ice; stir until very cold. Any sliced fruit may be added if desired. Yield: 10 servings.

Mrs. Clyde F. Stein
Kincheloe AFB, Mich.

SANGRIA

2 lemons
1 c. cognac
4 tbsp. sugar
4 cans 7-Up
4 c. red wine
Fresh or canned fruit

Squeeze lemons; cut into pieces. Combine all ingredients.

Mes. Marjorie V. Heavner
Perrin, Tex.

CINNAMON COCOA

1 qt. milk
2 tbsp. cocoa
¼ tsp. vanilla flavoring
Dash of salt
½ c. light corn syrup
¼ c. cinnamon candy

Heat milk. Combine 1/4 cup warm milk with cocoa; mix until well blended. Add vanilla, salt and corn syrup; mix well. Add to remaining hot milk; stir. Add cinnamon candy; mix until dissolved. Serve hot or cold. Yield: 1 quart.

Mrs. Sarah Van Tuinen
Craig AFB, Ala.

FRENCH CHOCOLATE

1 c. cocoa
3 to 4 c. sugar
Cream
1 pt. heavy cream, whipped
Hot milk

Mix cocoa and sugar, adding enough cream to make a thick paste. Fold in stiffly whipped cream. Place 1 spoonful of mixture in cup; pour hot milk over it. Yield: 50-60 servings.

Madge Landis Capel
Nacogdoches, Tex.

INSTANT HOT CHOCOLATE

2 c. instant nonfat dry milk
⅓ c. cocoa
¾ to 1 c. sugar
½ tsp. salt

Sift all ingredients; store in quart jar. Use 3 tablespoons of the mixture in each cup of hot water.

Phyllis J. Shipman
Hanna, Wyo.

CHOCOLATE SURF PUNCH WITH ICE CREAM ISLANDS

1 1-lb. box instant chocolate drink powder
2 qt. cold milk
2 qt. vanilla ice cream
2 1-qt. bottles chilled carbonated water

Place chocolate drink powder in large mixing bowl; stir in milk. Beat with rotary beater until blended. Pour mixture into punch bowl. Add scoops of ice cream to chocolate mixture. Pour in carbonated water. Yield: 48 servings.

Photograph for this recipe above.

COCKTAIL SUPREME

⅓ c. cranberry juice
⅓ c. fresh lemon juice
⅓ c. grenadine
1 c. gin

Combine all ingredients; chill thoroughly. Yield: 4 servings.

Mrs. LuVerne Fenton
Zion, Ill.

CRANBERRY COCKTAIL

½ sm. glass cranberry juice
½ sm. glass 7-Up

Chill cranberry juice in glass in which it will be served. Add 7-Up just before serving. Yield: 1 serving.

Mrs. Grace A. Spain
Lompoc, Calif.

CRANBERRY JUICE COCKTAIL

2 c. cranberries
3 c. water
½ c. sugar
1 sm. can frozen lemon juice, undiluted
1 sm. can frozen orange juice, undiluted
1 sm. can frozen pineapple juice, undiluted
1 sm. bottle 7-Up, chilled

Cook cranberries in water until skins burst; strain. Cook juice drained from cranberries and sugar until sugar is dissolved. Chill; add frozen juices. Add 7-Up. Yield: 6 servings.

Mrs. Merle Weber
Wadsworth, O.

HONEY-TOMATO JUICE COCKTAIL

2 tsp. honey
2 c. tomato juice
4 tbsp. lemon juice
¼ tsp. salt

(Continued on next page)

Mix all ingredients thoroughly. Chill; serve. Yield: 8 servings.

Mrs. Elvira C. Jones
Carnegie, Pa.

SPICED TOMATO JUICE

2 c. tomato juice
½ c. sugar
¼ tsp. cinnamon
Pinch of nutmeg
8 whole cloves
1 c. cold water
¼ c. lemon juice

Simmer tomato juice with sugar, cinnamon, nutmeg and cloves for 15 minutes. Chill. Add cold water and lemon juice just before serving. Stir; serve. Yield: 6 servings.

Mrs. W. Porter Murray
Knob Noster, Mo.

TOMATO COCKTAIL

2 qt. finely cut tomatoes
¼ green pepper, finely chopped
2 med. onions, finely chopped
1 c. water
1 bay leaf
7 whole cloves
1 tbsp. salt
1 tbsp. sugar
½ tsp. pepper
2 tbsp. lemon juice
2 tbps. vinegar

Combine tomatoes, green pepper, onions, water, bay leaf and cloves; simmer for 1 hour. Strain. Stir in all remaining ingredients; heat to boiling. Pour into jars; seal while hot. Chill before serving.

Mrs. Thurman Lutrell
Altheimer, Ark.

TOMATO JUICE COCKTAIL

6 stalks celery
1 med. onion
½ green pepper
4 tbsp. brown sugar
3 tbsp. vinegar
½ c. water
Pinch of salt
Dash of pepper
1 tbsp. Worcestershire sauce
1 lge. can tomato juice

Chop celery, onion and pepper. Mix with all remaining ingredients. Refrigerate for 8 to 10 hours or overnight. Strain and serve. Yield: 10 servings.

Mrs. Ethel E. Stahl
Rochester, N.Y.

TOMATO JUICE COCKTAIL

1 No. 2 can tomato juice
2 tbsp. lemon juice
1 tsp. chopped celery
½ tsp. grated onion
¼ tsp. Worcestershire sauce
½ tsp. sugar
½ tsp. salt
½ tsp. horseradish (opt.)

Combine all ingredients; chill for 1 hour. Strain; serve in glasses.

Glenna Seabolt
Davidson, Okla.

COLD MOCHA DRINK

3 c. milk
1 c. left-over coffee
½ c. chocolate syrup
Whipped cream
Cinnamon or nutmeg

Chill milk, coffee and syrup until serving time. Pour mixture into tall glasses; top with whipped cream. Sprinkle cinnamon over whipped cream. Yield: 4 servings.

Mrs. J. Frank Beall
Nacogdoches, Tex.

COFFEE PUNCH

4 qt. double strength coffee
1 qt. cold milk
1 tbsp. vanilla flavoring
1 c. sugar
2 qt. vanilla ice cream

Chill coffee; blend in all remaining ingredients, adding ice cream last. Yield: 20-25 servings.

Mrs. Hugh Busby
San Marcus, Tex.

CREAMY COFFEE PUNCH

1 gal. strong coffee
1 qt. heavy cream
5 tbsp. sugar
5 tsp. vanilla flavoring
2 qt. coffee, vanilla or chocolate ice cream

Cool coffee. Whip cream; add sugar and vanilla. Place ice cream and most of whipped cream in punch bowl. Add coffee; mix well. Garnish with remaining whipped cream. Yield: 50-60 servings.

Mrs. Frank C. Burnley
Charlottesville, Va.

FROSTED COFFEE COOLER

1 ½ tbsp. instant coffee
3 c. cold milk
⅓ c. chocolate syrup
2 tbsp. sugar
1 pt. vanilla ice cream

Combine coffee, milk, syrup and sugar; beat until well blended. Pour into glasses; top with a scoop of ice cream. Serve immediately. Yield: 4 servings.

Mrs. S. D. Bontrager
Scott City, Kans.

MOCHA SHAKE

1 pt. chocolate ice cream
2 c. milk
2 tbsp. instant coffee
¼ tsp. nutmeg
Whipped cream

Blend all ingredients except whipped cream in blender for 1 minute or until smooth. Pour into mugs. Top with puffs of whipped cream; garnish with additional instant coffee or nutmeg. Yield: 4 servings.

Mrs. Roy Cain
Eudora, Ark.

PLANTATION COFFEE PUNCH

¼ c. sugar
⅓ c. instant coffee
Dash of salt
1 tsp. vanilla flavoring
5 c. sweet milk
1 pt. vanilla or coffee ice cream
Whipped cream
Nutmeg

Combine sugar, instant coffee, salt, vanilla and milk; stir until sugar is dissolved. Chill until serving time. Ladle ice cream, by large spoonfuls, into punch bowl; pour coffee mixture over ice cream. Top with puffs of whipped cream; sprinkle with nutmeg. Serve in punch cups. Yield: 12 servings.

Mrs. Deats Headlee
Denton, Tex.

SOUTHERN COFFEE PUNCH

2 qt. strong cold coffee
1 pt. cold milk
2 tsp. vanilla flavoring
½ c. sugar
1 qt. vanilla ice cream
1 pt. heavy cream, whipped
Nutmeg

Combine coffee, milk, vanilla and sugar; stir until sugar is dissolved. Chill thoroughly;

pour into punch bowl. Add ice cream; top with whipped cream. Sprinkle lightly with nutmeg. Yield: 20 servings.

Mrs. Vernon E. Pepples
Punta Gorda, Fla.

SPANISH COFFEE PUNCH

6 tbsp. instant caffeine-free coffee
½ c. sugar
¼ c. dry Sherry
2 qt. cold milk
Whipped cream
Nutmeg

Blend coffee, sugar and Sherry. Add milk; beat with hand beater until blended. Chill. Before serving, stir well. Top individual servings with whipped cream; sprinkle with nutmeg. Yield: 16 servings.

Mrs. Carol A. Adams
Lackland AFB, Tex.

CREAMY CHRISTMAS EGGNOG

8 eggs, separated
12 tbsp. sugar
6 c. milk
6 tsp. vanilla, almond or rum flavoring
2 c. heavy cream
2 tsp. nutmeg

Beat egg whites until soft peaks form. Add egg yolks; beat well. Gradually add sugar, beating well. Add milk and flavoring; beat well. Whip cream; fold gently into eggnog. Sprinkle with nutmeg. NOTE: For coffee eggnog, combine 1/3 cup instant coffee with sugar and omit nutmeg. Yield: 18 cups.

Mrs. Karin Pflager
Yuma Proving Ground, Ariz.

EGGNOG

⅓ c. plus 3 tbsp. sugar
2 eggs, separated
¼ tsp. salt
4 c. milk
1 tsp. vanilla flavoring
Brandy or rum flavoring to taste
½ c. heavy cream, whipped
Nutmeg

Beat 1/3 cup sugar into egg yolks; add salt. Stir in milk. Cook over medium heat, stirring constantly, until mixture coats spoon; cool. Beat egg whites until foamy. Gradually add 3 tablespoons sugar, beating to soft peaks. Add to custard; mix thoroughly. Add flavorings; chill for 3 to 4 hours. Pour into punch bowl. Top with puffs of whipped cream; sprinkle with nutmeg. Yield: 6-8 servings.

Eva Miller
Newport, Ark.

367

EGGNOG

¾ c. sugar
3 eggs, separated
Salt
4 c. milk, scalded
½ tsp. vanilla flavoring
Freshly grated nutmeg

Beat 1/2 cup sugar into egg yolks. Add 1/4 teaspoon salt; slowly stir in milk. Cook in double boiler until mixture coats a spoon, stirring constantly; cool. Add dash of salt to egg whites; beat until stiff. Add remaining sugar; beat well. Add to custard with vanilla; mix thoroughly. Chill for 4 hours. Pile lightly into punch cups; sprinkle with nutmeg. NOTE: One tablespoon cooking Sherry may be substituted for vanilla. Yield: 6-8 servings.

Mrs. Judith Billington
Adair AFS, Oreg.

HOT PINEAPPLE EGGNOG

1 c. sugar
8 eggs, separated
6 c. pineapple juice
1 pt. cream
Grated orange rind (opt.)

Combine 1/2 cup sugar and egg yolks; beat thoroughly. Bring pineapple juice to a boil; add cream. Pour hot mixture over egg yolks, stirring constantly. Beat egg whites with remaining sugar; fold into hot mixture. Serve hot or chilled with orange rind. Yield: 12 servings.

Mrs. Spencer Medlin
Tippo, Miss.

ORANGE EGGNOG

3 eggs
3 tbsp. sugar
2 ½ c. ice water
1 12-oz. can frozen orange juice
¼ c. lemon juice
1 pt. vanilla ice cream
1 sm. bottle ginger ale

Beat eggs and sugar until light and lemon colored; add water and juices. Pour into punch bowl. Add ice cream; mix. Add ginger ale; stir well. Serve. Yield: 10 servings.

Mrs. Karl Derstein
Hutchinson, Kans.

TEETOTALLER EGGNOG

¼ c. sugar
2 eggs, separated
2 c. milk
Dash of salt
1 tbsp. vanilla flavoring
½ c. heavy cream, whipped
Ground nutmeg

Beat sugar and egg whites until stiff. Beat yolks; add to whites. Beat thoroughly. Add milk, salt and flavoring. Fold in stiffly whipped cream. Pour immediately into glasses; add dash of nutmeg to top of each. Yield: 4-5 servings.

Mrs. Carol Campbell
Belle Chasse, La.

ANNIVERSARY PUNCH

2 ¼ c. sugar
1 ½ qt. water
3 c. frozen lemon juice or juice of 18 lemons
1 No. 2 can pineapple juice
3 c. orange juice
1 qt. ginger ale

Dissolve sugar in 1 quart water; bring to a boil. Cool. Add all remaining ingredients except ginger ale; chill. Just before serving, add ginger ale and ice cubes. Yield: 25 servings.

Mrs. Edward Addleman
Pittsburgh, Pa.

APPLE-GRAPE BEVERAGE

1 qt. apple cider
1 qt. grape juice
1 qt. ginger ale

Combine juices and ginger ale; serve over ice cubes. Yield: 10 servings.

Mrs. R. W. Kidder
Belle Glade, Fla.

APRICOT NECTAR

1 c. chilled canned apricot nectar
2 tsp. lemon juice
1 tbsp. sugar
Pinch of salt
1 lge. scoop vanilla ice cream

Combine all ingredients; beat until ice cream is half melted. Serve at once. Yield: 2 servings.

Mrs. Howard Heimerdinger
New Port Richey, Fla.

APRICOT-TEA PUNCH

1 ½ c. boiling water
3 tsp. tea or 3 tea bags
⅓ c. sugar
¼ c. lemon juice
1 c. orange juice
1 12-oz. can apricot nectar
1 28-oz. bottle ginger ale

(Continued on next page)

Pour boiling water over tea. Let stand for 5 minutes; strain. Add sugar; stir until dissolved. Combine with lemon juice, orange juice and apricot nectar. Pour over ice cubes and add ginger ale just before serving. Yield: 8 servings.

Mrs. C. Stephen Wilson
Fairport, N.Y.

BANANA CRUSH

4 c. sugar
6 c. water
1 46-oz. can pineapple juice
2 12-oz. cans frozen orange juice concentrate, thawed
1 12-oz. can frozen lemonade concentrate, thawed
6 bananas, mashed
7 28-oz. bottles lemon-lime carbonated beverage

Dissolve sugar in water. Add juices and mashed bananas; stir well. Put all ingredients except lemon-lime beverage into milk cartons; freeze. Take out about 2 hours before serving. Add lemon-lime beverage. NOTE: Equal amounts of lemon juice and ginger ale may be substituted for lemon-lime carbonated beverage. Yield: 6 dozen servings.

Mrs. E. D. Adcock
Lamesa, Tex.

BANANA FROSTED

1 ripe banana
1 c. cold milk
3 tbsp. vanilla ice cream

Slice banana into bowl; beat until smooth and creamy. Add milk and ice cream; mix well. Serve immediately. Yield: 1 serving.

Mrs. Lena M. Pearson
Whiteman AFB, Mo.

BANANA PUNCH

1 ½ c. sugar
5 bananas, mashed
2 pkg. raspberry gelatin
2 c. hot water
1 lge. can orange juice
1 lge. can pineapple juice
1 ½ c. bottled lemon juice
6 c. cold water
1 qt. ginger ale

Mash sugar in bananas. Dissolve gelatin in hot water. Combine all ingredients. Mix well; chill. Serve with flavored ice cubes, if desired.

Mrs. Roy W. Giles
Granbury, Tex.

BANANA PUNCH

4 c. sugar
6 c. water
2 No. 3 cans pineapple juice
Juice of 5 oranges
Juice of 2 lemons
5 ripe bananas, mashed
2 qt. ginger ale

Combine sugar and water; cook for 3 minutes. Add pineapple juice, orange juice, lemon juice and bananas to sugar mixture; freeze. Pour ginger ale over frozen mixture; serve. Yield: 50 servings.

Mrs. Margaret Hobson
Cherryvale, Kans.

BANANA SHAKE

1 med. banana
1 tsp. lemon juice
½ tsp. vanilla flavoring
1 c. prepared dry milk, chilled
Nutmeg or cinnamon

Slice banana; beat until smooth and creamy. Blend in lemon juice and vanilla. Add milk; beat until blended. Garnish with nutmeg or cinnamon. Yield: 5 servings.

Verna Durham
Rosenhayn, N.J.

BANQUET PUNCH

⅔ c. boiling water
2 tsp. tea or 2 tea bags
1 12-oz. can unsweetened pineapple juice
1 c. unsweetened grapefruit juice
1 c. orange juice
1 c. lemon juice
1 to 2 c. sugar
2 c. ice water
1 lge. bottle ginger ale

Pour boiling water over tea; let stand for 5 minutes. Combine fruit juices and tea; add sugar. Chill; add ice water. Pour mixture over cake of ice in punch bowl. Pour ginger ale slowly down side of bowl. Yield: 2 1/2 quarts.

Mrs. Lloyd Hill
Norman, Ind.

BLACKBERRY NECTAR

12 lb. blackberries, crushed
1 qt. boiling water
5 oz. tartaric acid
Sugar

Combine crushed berries, boiling water and acid. Let mixture stand for 24 hours; strain. For each 1 cup of juice add 2 cups sugar; mix well. Store in bottles or jars. When ready to serve, mix with desired amount of cold water; pour over ice.

Mrs. Mabel Baker
Skipperville, Ala.

369

CRANBERRY FRUIT PUNCH

1 qt. cranberry juice cocktail
1 pt. orange juice
¾ c. lemon juice
1 c. pineapple juice
½ c. sugar
1 to 2 c. water

Combine all ingredients; stir thoroughly. Serve over crushed ice or ice cubes. Yield: 8-12 servings.

Photograph for this recipe above.

BRIDE'S PINK PUNCH

1 3-oz. pkg. strawberry gelatin
1 c. boiling water
1 pkg. strawberry powdered drink mix
2 qt. water
2 ½ c. sugar
1 46-oz. can pineapple juice
1 10-oz. bottle 7-Up
2 pt. pineapple sherbet

Dissolve gelatin in boiling water. Dissolve drink mix in cold water; add sugar. Stir well. Add pineapple juice and gelatin; refrigerate. Add 7-Up and sherbet just before serving. Yield: 35 servings.

Mrs. Jewel Harney
Fletcher, Okla.

CHRISTMAS PUNCH

2 pkg. red or green gelatin
3 ½ c. sugar
10 c. hot water
4 sm. cans lemon juice
3 c. canned orange juice
2 No. 2 cans pineapple juice
1 qt. ginger ale

Dissolve gelatin and sugar in hot water; cool. Add juices; chill. Add ginger ale just before serving. Yield: 50 servings.

Mrs. Bill Brooks
Siloam Springs, Ark.

COOL SUMMER DRINK

Juice of 1 lemon
Grated rind of 1 lemon
¾ c. sugar
1 c. light cream
Lemon or white carbonated beverage

Mix juice, rind, sugar and cream; put 4 tablespoons of the mixture into large glass with ice cubes. Fill glass with beverage; stir well.

Mrs. Virginia Blessinger
Racine, Wisc.

CRANBERRY PUNCH

1 qt. cranberry juice
Juice of 1 lemon
Juice of 1 orange
1 12-oz. bottle sweet soda, ginger ale or
lemon soda

Mix all ingredients; pour over ice cubes.
Let stand for a few minutes. Serve as an
appetizer or quencher. Yield: 10-12 servings.

Mrs. Donald Puls
Sparta, Wisc.

CRANBERRY PUNCH

1 qt. cranberries
2 c. sugar
2 c. water
3 sticks cinnamon
6 whole cloves
1 c. orange juice
1 c. lemon juice
2 c. chilled pineapple juice
1 qt. ginger ale
1 qt. Sauterne

Combine cranberries, sugar and water. Tie
spices in cheesecloth; drop into mixture. Boil
until cranberries are tender. Remove spice
bag; discard. Run mixture through a fine
sieve; chill. Add all remaining ingredients.
Chill before serving. Yield: 25 servings.

Georgie Kimball
Lake Charles, La.

HOLIDAY CRANBERRY PUNCH

4 1-pt. bottles cranberry juice cocktail
2 46-oz. cans pineapple juice
1 c. lemon juice
¾ c. sugar
1 28-oz. bottle ginger ale

Chill all ingredients. Combine in punch bowl.
Float holly wreath ice ring on top if desired.
Yield: 50 servings.

Mrs. Winston May
Murfreesboro, Ark.

RED COCKTAIL PUNCH

10 bottles 7-Up, chilled
1 qt. apple juice, chilled
2 pt. cranberry juice cocktail, chilled

Fill two ice trays with 7-Up; freeze until
firm. Combine juices; add remaining 7-Up.
Pour over frozen 7-Up. Yield: 35 servings.

Mrs. Ezra J. Davis
East Bend, N.C.

DIXIE FRUIT SPARKLE

5 bananas, mashed
Juice of 5 lemons
Juice of 5 oranges
5 c. sugar
7 c. water
Chilled 7-Up

Combine all ingredients except 7-Up. Mix
thoroughly. Freeze in refrigerator trays.
Fill large glasses or cups about one-third
full of frozen mixture; finish filling glasses
with cold 7-Up, using about 1 small bottle
to a glass.

Mrs. Loren Kelley
Greentown, Ind.

EASY PUNCH

3 qt. water
3 c. sugar
1 oz. granulated citric acid
1 tall can pineapple juice

Heat 1 quart water; dissolve sugar and acid.
Add remaining water and pineapple juice.
Color with food coloring if desired. Yield:
20-25 servings.

Mrs. Glenn McCommon
Wortham, Tex.

EVERGREEN PUNCH

2 c. sugar
2 qt. water
2 pkg. lime powdered drink mix
1 46-oz. can pineapple juice
1 pt. ginger ale

Dissolve sugar in water. Mix in powdered
drink mix and pineapple juice. Just before
serving, add ginger ale; pour over ice cubes.
Yield: 50 servings.

Mrs. Ernest O. Padgett
Johnston, S.C.

DELICIOUS FRUIT PUNCH

2 c. sugar
4 c. water
2 c. pineapple juice
Juice of 6 lemons
2 c. crushed pineapple
2 pt. carbonated water, ginger ale or tea
1 sm. bottle Maraschino cherries
Lemon and orange slices

Boil sugar and water for 5 minutes; cool.
Add juices and pineapple; chill. Add carbon-
ated water; pour over ice in punch bowl.
Garnish with cherries and fruit slices. NOTE:
Cherries and fruit slices may be frozen in
ice cubes.

Mrs. Gilbert J. Hess
Wynne, Ark.

FLOATING ISLAND PUNCH

½ c. sugar
1 c. water
1 6-oz. can frozen lemon juice
3 6-oz. cans frozen orange juice
1 qt. ginger ale
1 qt. sparkling water
1 4-oz. bottle Maraschino cherries and
   juice
1 orange, thinly sliced
1 pt. lemon or orange sherbet

Heat sugar and water until sugar dissolves;
cool. Combine fruit juices, ginger ale, sparkling water and fruits; add syrup. Pour into
punch bowl. Add ice cubes. Drop in sherbet
by spoonfuls or in small balls, using an
ice cream dipper. Yield: 20-25 servings.

Mrs. Miriam J. Sieron
Hill AFB, Utah

EASY FRUIT PUNCH

1 6-oz. can frozen orange juice
1 6-oz. can frozen lemonade
1 pkg. fruit punch or cherry drink powder
   mix
1 ½ c. sugar
2 ½ qt. water

Combine all ingredients; chill. Serve over
ice. Yield: 15 servings.

Minnie Lou Wilson
Greenfield, Ind.

FRUIT JUICE PUNCH

21 c. apricot juice
3 qt. orange juice
3 c. powdered sugar
4 ½ c. lemon juice
1 ½ c. lime juice
12 qt. ginger ale

Combine all ingredients except ginger ale.
Just before serving, add ginger ale; pour into
punch bowl over block of ice. NOTE: This
punch will be a golden color. An ice block
can easily be made by using a round ring
mold and adding a few Maraschino cherries
for color. Yield: 150 servings.

Mrs. Gladys Shotwell
Manton, Mich.

FRUIT PUNCH

1 qt. fresh orange juice
1 lge. can pineapple juice
1 6-oz. can frozen lemonade
2 6-oz. cans frozen limeade
1 pt. cranberry juice cocktail
1 can cranberry sauce, sieved
2 to 4 c. cold water
Sugar (opt.)
2 qt. ginger ale, chilled

Pour all juices, cranberry sauce, water and
sugar into large bowl. Stir well. Add ice
cubes. Gently pour in ginger ale just before
serving. Top with fruit ice ring and sprigs
of mint or other fruit garnish if desired.

FRUIT ICE RING:
Use any combination of lime, lemon or
orange slices. Arrange in a pattern in bottom
of 8-inch ring mold. Add water to cover
fruit. Freeze. Loosen ring by dipping bottom
of mold into warm water. Float on top of
punch. Yield: 30 servings.

Mrs. J. A. Morrison
Wadsworth, O.

FRUIT PUNCH

1 lge. can pineapple juice
2 lge. cans orange juice
2 sm. cans frozen orange juice
1 sm. can frozen lemon juice
2 envelopes lime drink powder mix
Sugar to taste
1 qt. ginger ale
Sherbet
Chipped ice

Mix fruit juices and drink powder mix. Add
sugar. When ready to serve, add ginger
ale, sherbet and chipped ice. Yield: 1 gallon.

Mabel Shobe
Chillicothe, Mo.

FRUIT PUNCH

3 qt. unsweetened pineapple juice
Juice of 8 lemons
Juice of 8 oranges
Juice of 3 limes
1 lge. can frozen orange juice
2 c. sugar
1 c. mint leaves (opt.)
4 qt. ginger ale
2 qt. soda water
1 pt. fresh strawberries, quartered

Combine fruit juices, sugar and mint leaves;
chill overnight. Just before serving, add ginger ale, soda water and strawberries; pour
over large cake of ice in punch bowl. Float
thin slices of lemon and lime for garnish.
Yield: 40 servings.

Mrs. Harold Staib
Brooks AFB, Tex.

FRUIT PUNCH

1 can frozen lemonade
1 can frozen orange juice
1 can frozen pineapple juice
¼ c. lemon juice
1 1-pt. bottle cranberry juice, chilled
1 ¼ qt. ice water
1 pt. ginger ale, chilled

(Continued on next page)

Pour juices into 6-quart bowl. Stir in ice water and ginger ale; mix well. Serve cold. Yield: 10 servings.

Mrs. Darlene S. Hickey
Burns AFS, Oreg.

FRUIT PUNCH

5 c. sugar
4 c. water
2 pkg. pink drink powder mix
1 lge. can pineapple juice
2 cans frozen pineapple juice
6 cans frozen orange juice
1 can frozen lemon juice
6 bottles 7-Up

Heat sugar and water until sugar dissolves. Mix with drink powder mix and fruit juices. Add water to taste. Just before serving, pour 7-Up into punch. Garnish with Maraschino cherries, lemon and orange slices. Yield: 50 servings.

Mrs. William A. Hare
Fillmore, Mo.

FRUIT SLUSH

3 bananas, mashed
1 sm. can crushed pineapple
1 c. orange juice
Juice of 3 lemons
3 pt. water
⅔ c. sugar
1 sm. pkg. lemon gelatin
Ginger ale or 7-Up

Combine fruits, juices, water, sugar and gelatin. Freeze mixture in ice cube tray. Place cubes in glass; fill with ginger ale. Yield: 24 servings.

Ada D. Carpenter
Cedar City, Utah

GEL-ADE

2 pkg. raspberry gelatin
3 c. hot water
1 46-oz. can pineapple juice
2 cans frozen orange juice, diluted
Juice of 3 lemons
1 bottle ginger ale

Dissolve gelatin in hot water. Add fruit juices to gelatin; chill. Add ginger ale just before serving. Yield: 40 servings.

Mrs. James C. Cripe
Delphi, Ind.

GELATIN-FRUIT PUNCH

2 c. sugar
1 pkg. black raspberry gelatin

1 6-oz. can frozen lemonade
1 6-oz. can frozen orange juice
2 ½ c. pineapple juice
2 qt. water
1 qt. ginger ale

Slowly boil sugar in 1 cup water for 10 minutes; do not stir while boiling. Dissolve gelatin in 2 cups hot water. Dilute lemonade and frozen orange juice with 1 juice can water each. Combine sugar, gelatin and all remaining ingredients. Stir well; chill and serve. NOTE: Red food coloring may be added. Yield: 6 quarts punch.

Mrs. Wilbur R. Kilmer
Monticello, Ind.

GINGER ALE PUNCH

1 c. sugar
5 c. water
Juice of 3 lemons
Juice of 3 oranges
1 c. tea
2 c. ginger ale

Heat sugar in 2 cups water to make a syrup. Add remaining ingredients; chill well. Yield: 8 servings.

Mary Cooper
Wytheville, Va.

GINGER ALE PUNCH

1 ½ qt. pineapple juice, chilled
1 ½ pt. orange juice, chilled
1 pt. lemon juice, chilled
2 qt. ginger ale
Mint leaves
Fruit slices

Combine juices with ginger ale. Add mint leaves. Decorate with fruit slices. Yield: 65 small glasses.

Mrs. Joseph Dvorchak
Warren, O.

GINGER-FRUIT MEDLEY

2 cans frozen lemonade
1 can frozen orange juice
2 c. strong tea, cold
2 28-oz. bottles ginger ale
1 pkg. frozen sliced strawberries, thawed
1 28-oz. bottle orange soda
Orange slices

Pour lemonade and orange concentrates into punch bowl over ice cubes. Add cold tea and 1 bottle of ginger ale; mix well. Add strawberries, reserving a few slices for garnish. Add orange soda and remaining ginger ale. Garnish with strawberries and orange slices. Yield: 35 servings.

Janet McGervey
Coraopolis, Pa.

GOLDEN CITRUS COOLER

1 6-oz. can frozen concentrated orange
  juice
1 6-oz. can frozen concentrated lemon
  juice
1 6-oz. can frozen concentrated limeade
1 qt. ice water
1 1-pt. 12-oz. bottle ginger ale, chilled

Pour orange juice, lemon juice and limeade
into a large pitcher. Add ice water. Refrigerate. Stir and add ginger ale just before
serving. Pour over ice in tall glasses.

Mary E. Schuman
New Castle, Ind.

GOLDEN PUNCH

2 c. sugar
3 pkg. orange gelatin
3 c. boiling water
1 12-oz. can frozen orange juice, diluted
1 lge. can pineapple juice
Juice of 3 lemons
1 ¼ bottles ginger ale

Dissolve sugar and gelatin in water. Add
diluted orange juice, pineapple and lemon
juice. Chill. Immediately before serving,
add ginger ale. Use ice containing artificial
fruits and flowers for garnish. Yield: 16
servings.

Mrs. Otto Sutton
Annapolis, Mo.

GOLDEN SUMMER PUNCH

1 6-oz. can frozen orange juice concentrate
1 6-oz. can frozen lemonade concentrate
1 12-oz. can apricot nectar
1 No. 2 ½ can pineapple juice
Sugar (opt.)

Add water to frozen concentrates as directed
on cans. Combine with apricot nectar and
pineapple juice; chill. Add sugar if needed.
Yield: 3 quarts.

Mrs. Anna Cooley
Lyford, Tex.

GRAPE COOLER

1 c. grape juice, chilled
1 tbsp. sugar
Pinch of salt
1 lge. scoop ice cream

Combine all ingredients; beat until ice cream
is half melted. Serve at once. Yield: 1 serving.

Mrs. R. C. Martin
Caswell Co., N.C.

GRAPE JUICE CRUSH

2 c. grape juice
1 c. orange juice
¼ c. lemon juice
½ c. sugar
2 c. ice water
1 qt. ginger ale, chilled

Mix fruit juices. Stir in sugar and water until
sugar is dissolved. Add ginger ale. Serve
immediately in glasses partially filled with
cracked ice. Yield: 12 servings.

Mrs. Jan Moyer
Babbitt, Nev.

MINTED GRAPE FIZZ

1 c. ice water
2 c. grape juice, chilled
2 ½ c. orange juice, chilled
2 tbsp. lemon juice
3 tbsp. sugar
2 tsp. peppermint flavoring
1 pt. lemon sherbet
6 sprigs mint

Mix all ingredients except sherbet and mint.
Pour into chilled tall glasses; top with a
spoonful of lemon sherbet and a sprig of
mint.

Mrs. R. T. Dowling, Sr.
Atlanta, Ga.

ROYAL GRAPE PUNCH

2 c. sugar
4 c. water
1 6-oz. can frozen orange juice, concentrate
1 ¼ c. lemon juice
1 1-pt. 8-oz. bottle grape juice
1 1-pt. 14-oz. can pineapple juice
1 1-pt. 12-oz. bottle ginger ale

Heat sugar and 1 cup water until sugar dissolves. Add remaining water. Prepare orange
juice as directed on can; combine with sugar
mixture. Add all remaining ingredients; chill.
Serve in glasses over ice cubes. Yield: 5 1/2
quarts.

Mrs. V. J. Danielson
El Campo, Tex.

HAWAIIAN PUNCH

1 6-oz. can frozen lemonade
1 12-oz. can apricot nectar
1 12-oz. can unsweetened pineapple juice
1 12-oz. bottle ginger ale

Combine juices; add ginger ale. Pour over
crushed ice just before serving.

Mrs. George H. Haskell
Ambridge, Pa.

HI-FI COOLER

1 ½ c. apricot nectar
1 6-oz. can frozen concentrated orange
  juice, thawed
1 ¾ c. pineapple juice
⅓ c. lemon juice
1 c. sugar
1 c. instant nonfat dry milk
1 c. ice cold water
2 qt. ginger ale, chilled
Orange and lemon slices

Mix apricot nectar and juices with sugar;
stir until dissolved. Pour mixture into trays;
freeze to a mush. Beat nonfat dry milk and
water until very stiff. Add frozen juices;
beat until well mixed. Return to trays; freeze.
Spoon mixture into punch bowl and pour in
ginger ale just before serving. Garnish with
sliced fruit. Yield: 30 servings.

Mrs. Charles D. Gross
McConnelsville, O.

HOLIDAY PUNCH

1 med. can pineapple juice
1 pkg. cherry powdered drink mix
2 c. sugar
1 sm. can frozen orange juice

Add enough water to pineapple juice to make
1 gallon liquid. Combine all ingredients in
punch bowl with colored ice cubes. Yield: 25
servings.

Mrs. M. L. Gardner
Lillington, N.C.

HOLIDAY PUNCH

3 c. sugar
3 c. water
4 c. cranberry juice cocktail
3 c. lemon juice
2 c. orange juice
2 c. unsweetened pineapple juice
2 qt. ginger ale

Combine sugar and water in saucepan; stir
over heat until sugar dissolves. Bring to
boiling point; boil, without stirring, for 7
minutes. Cool; add fruit juices. When ready
to serve pour over ice; add ginger ale. Garnish with sprigs of mint. Yield: 50 servings.

Mrs. James Molbeck
Racine, Wisc.

INDIAN PUNCH

2 c. sugar
1 qt. water
Grated rind of 3 lemons
Juice of 3 lemons
2 c. strong tea
1 tsp. vanilla flavoring
1 tsp. almond flavoring
1 lge. can pineapple juice
1 qt. ginger ale

Boil sugar, water and lemon rind for 5 minutes; cool. Add all remaining ingredients
except ginger ale. Just before serving, add
ginger ale.

Mrs. Lillian H. Danner
Boone, N.C.

JUNE FLOAT

2 c. milk
1 c. mashed ripe bananas
¼ c. honey
1 c. unsweetened pineapple juice
1 pt. vanilla ice cream

Mix milk, bananas, honey, pineapple juice
and one-half of the ice cream. Pour into
chilled tall glasses. Top with scoops of ice
cream. NOTE: Sugar may be substituted for
honey. Yield: 4 servings.

Mrs. Elmer Atwood
Dickinson, N.Y.

LEMON-LIME PUNCH

2 pkg. lemon-lime powdered drink mix
2 qt. cold water
2 c. sugar
1 lge. can pineapple juice
1 lge. bottle ginger ale

Combine powdered drink mix, water, sugar
and pineapple juice; add ginger ale when
ready to serve. Serve ice cold. Yield: 25
servings.

Mrs. Doris Stubbs
Cheraw, S.C.

LIME-GINGER PUNCH

3 ginger roots
1 gal. cold water
5 c. sugar
2 lge. cans pineapple juice
Juice of 2 doz. lemons
Juice of 1 grapefruit
1 gal. lime sherbet
1 lge. bottle ginger ale

Boil ginger roots in water for 30 minutes;
strain. Add sugar; boil for 15 minutes. Cool
syrup; add strained juices. Put sherbet into
punch bowl 30 minutes before serving; add
juice mixture. Just before serving, add
ginger ale. Yield: 45 servings.

Alma Goode
Gastonia, N.C.

MINT DELIGHT

1 c. mint jelly
1 c. boiling water
1 lge. can frozen lemonade
1 qt. ginger ale
Mint sprigs

Melt jelly in boiling water. Prepare lemonade according to directions on can; add to jelly. Stir in ginger ale. Pour over crushed ice; garnish with mint. Yield: 12 servings.

Mrs. Everette F. Jones
Roanoke, Va.

MOCK CHAMPAGNE

½ c. sugar
½ c. water
¼ c. orange juice
½ c. grapefruit juice
1 pt. ginger ale, chilled

Boil sugar and water; cool. Add all remaining ingredients except ginger ale; chill. When ready to serve, add ginger ale. Yield: 4 servings.

Eleanor Bailey
Barre, Vt.

FROSTY ORANGE PUNCH

1 c. orange juice
1 c. lemon juice
1 c. sugar
2 c. cold water
1 qt. ginger ale

Combine fruit juices, sugar and water. Pour into ice trays; freeze. Place cubes in glasses; fill with ginger ale. Garnish with orange slices. Yield: 6 servings.

Mrs. Burton H. Morris
Wytheville, Va.

PARTY PUNCH

2 qt. boiling water
8 c. sugar
½ c. mint leaves, crushed
1 qt. lemon juice
3 qt. orange juice
1 qt. pineapple juice
2 qt. iced tea
2 gal. cold water
2 qt. ginger ale
Orange and lemon slices
Mint springs

Combine boiling water and sugar; boil for 5 minutes. Add crushed mint; cool and strain. Add fruit juices, tea and cold water. Add ginger ale just before serving. Pour over ice in punch bowl. Garnish with fruit slices and mint sprigs. Yield: 100 servings.

Mrs. Dorothy Thomas
Titusville, Pa.

TEAHOUSE PINEAPPLE PUNCH

½ c. loose tea
2 bunches fresh mint
¼ c. superfine sugar
2 1-pt. 2-oz. cans pineapple juice
2 c. orange juice
2 c. lemon juice
2 c. grapefruit juice
2 sm. jars Maraschino cherries
1 qt. ginger ale
1 qt. club soda

Bring 1 quart water to full rolling boil. Remove from heat; immediately add tea. Let stand for 4 minutes. Stir and strain into container holding 3 quarts cold water. Crush mint leaves and stems in sugar with wooden spoon in large mixing bowl. Stir in fruit juices and cherries. Add tea; mix well. When ready to serve pour over ice ring in punch bowl. Carefully add ginger ale and club soda. Add more sugar if desired. Yield: 10 punch cup servings.

Photograph for this recipe on page 361.

PINK LADY PUNCH

4 c. cranberry juice cocktail
1 ½ c. sugar
1 qt. pineapple or grapefruit juice, chilled
2 qt. ginger ale, chilled

Slowly add cranberry juice to sugar; stir until sugar is dissolved. Add chilled pineapple juice. Slowly add ginger ale just before serving. Yield: 32 servings.

Eloise F. Sandy
Callao, Va.

PUNCH

5 lb. sugar
2 oz. citric acid
1 oz. tartaric acid
½ oz. epsom salts
3 pt. boiling water
Grated rind of 3 lemons
Grated rind of 3 oranges
Juice of 3 lemons
Juice of 3 oranges

Combine all ingredients except fruit rinds and juices. Stir until all solids are dissolved. Add remaining ingredients; stir well. Syrup may be stored in refrigerator and used as wanted. To prepare for serving, add three times as much water as syrup. NOTE: Addition of ginger ale makes a very tasty punch. Very good added to iced tea.

Mrs. William Stout
Alliance, O.

RASPBERRY PUNCH

2 pkg. raspberry powdered drink mix
2 pkg. strawberry powdered drink mix
4 c. sugar
6 lemons
1 46-oz. can pineapple juice
½ gal. raspberry sherbet

Combine all ingredients except sherbet. Add enough water to make 2 gallons liquid. Stir to dissolve sugar and drink mix. Chill for 5 hours. Place sherbet in punch bowl; add punch. Let stand for 20 minutes before serving. Yield: 25 servings.

Lorene Burrow
Bradford, Ark.

RUBY GRANITE PUNCH

¼ tsp. nutmeg
¼ tsp. cinnamon
¼ tsp. allspice
3 tbsp. tea
1 can jellied cranberry sauce
¾ c. sugar
½ c. orange juice
¼ c. lemon juice

Tie nutmeg, cinnamon, allspice and tea in a cheesecloth bag. Put into 2 1/2 cups boiling water; cover and steep for 5 minutes. Beat cranberry sauce with an egg beater; heat with 1 1/2 cups water. Remove spice bag; add sugar, hot cranberry liquid and fruit juices. Chill; pour over ice cubes. Serve. Yield: 6-8 servings.

Anna Mary Melhorn
York, Pa.

SOUTHERN PUNCH

3 lb. sugar
2 oz. citric acid
2 qt. hot water
1 46-oz. can orange juice
1 46-oz. can pineapple juice
3 qt. cold water

Dissolve sugar in citric acid and hot water; cool. Add all remaining ingredients; mix well. Yield: 2 gallons.

Loretta B. Britt
Troy, N.C.

SPICED CIDER PUNCH

¼ tsp. salt
Whole cloves
6 whole allspice
4 sticks cinnamon
2 qt. cider
Lemon slices
Orange slices
1 pt. ginger ale

Combine salt, 6 cloves, allspice, cinnamon and cider in saucepan. Bring to boiling point; simmer for 5 minutes. Strain. Pour strained hot cider over thin lemon slices and orange slices studded with cloves in heated punch bowl or pitcher; cool. Add ice and ginger ale. Yield: 20 servings.

Mrs. Titus M. Bush
Pease AFB, N.H.

STRAWBERRY PUNCH

3 pkg. strawberry powdered drink mix
3 c. sugar
1 lemon, thinly sliced
1 qt. ginger ale

Mix powdered drink mix and sugar with 1 quart warm water until dissolved. Add 3 quarts cold water. Add 12 ice cubes and lemon. Add ginger ale just before serving. Yield: 21 servings.

Mrs. Fred C. Johnson
Superior, Wisc.

TEA PUNCH

2 c. sugar
16 lemons, thinly sliced
4 oranges, thinly sliced
1 gal. water
2 tbsp. tea
2 qt. ginger ale
1 qt. white grape juice or pineapple juice

Add sugar to fruits; bruise fruits, stirring well. Bring water to a boil; add tea. Boil for 1 minute. Strain into fruit; allow to cool and ripen. When ready to serve, add ginger ale and grape juice. Pour over ice block so as not to dilute punch. Decorate with fruit slices or mint and strawberries, if desired. Yield: 30 servings.

Mrs. A. J. Garland
Clarendon, Tex.

YELLOW FROSTED PUNCH

1 46-oz. can pineapple juice
2 6-oz. cans frozen orange juice
1 6-oz. can frozen lemonade
1 qt. pineapple sherbet
1 qt. ginger ale, chilled

Freeze pineapple juice in can. Remove from freezer about 2 hours before serving; store in refrigerator. Have all juices reconstituted and chilled. Chop frozen pineapple juice with large knife. Place in punch bowl; add juices. Chop sherbet into small pieces; add. Pour in ginger ale. Yield: 40-48 servings.

Mrs. K. B. Holmes
Marshall, Tex.

WEDDING PUNCH

1 c. sugar
2 c. water
1 12-oz. can frozen lemonade
3 12-oz. cans frozen orange juice
4 qt. ginger ale
2 pt. pineapple sherbet

Heat sugar and water until sugar dissolves; cool. Combine fruit juices, sugar syrup and ginger ale in punch bowl. Add ice cubes; drop in sherbet by spoonfuls. Yield: 50 servings.

Mrs. Audrey True
Bentonville, Ark.

APPLE CIDER PUNCH

½ tsp. allspice
1 2-in. stick cinnamon
6 whole cloves
1 qt. apple cider
⅓ c. brown sugar
Nutmeg

Combine all ingredients except nutmeg in saucepan. Bring to boil; serve nutmeg on top. Yield: 4-6 servings.

Mrs. Howard J. Rettke
Marinette, Wisc.

SUMMERTIME COOLER

3 c. sugar
2 qt. water
1 1-qt. can apricot juice
1 1-qt. can orange juice
1 1-qt. can pineapple juice
Juice of 2 lemons
6 c. strong tea
1 No. 2 can crushed pineapple
2 qt. ginger ale, chilled

Combine sugar and water; heat until consistency of syrup. Cool. Stir in all remaining ingredients except ginger ale; chill. Just before serving, add ginger ale. Yield: 2 gallons.

Mrs. Orville J. Olson
Albany, Oreg.

SUMMER PUNCH

6 cans frozen lemonade
3 cans frozen orange juice
1 1-qt. can pineapple juice
1 No. 2 can pineapple juice
1 8-oz. jar cherries
3 1-qt. bottles soda water

Have all ingredients chilled. Dilute lemonade and orange juice, using one-half as much water as directed on can. Add all remaining ingredients. Yield: 125 servings.

Mrs. Jacob Haight Morrison
New Orleans, La.

CRANBERRY TEA

1 qt. cranberries
2 qt. plus 2 c. water
2 c. sugar
3 sticks cinnamon
2 c. orange juice

Cook cranberries in 2 quarts water until mushy; strain through cloth. Combine sugar, 2 cups water and cinnamon sticks. Simmer for 3 to 4 minutes. Add to cranberry juice and orange juice. Yield: 20 servings.

Della Stine
Nixa, Mo.

HOT SPICED GRAPE JUICE

3 c. grape juice
6 cloves
1 2-in. stick cinnamon
Sugar

Combine grape juice and spices; simmer for 5 minutes. Strain; sweeten to taste. Serve immediately. Yield: 6 servings.

Ermah C. Williams
El Dorado, Kans.

HOT CHRISTMAS PUNCH

1 can frozen orange juice
1 can frozen lemonade
2 c. sugar
1 pt. cranberry juice
1 qt. apple cider
Juice from 1 bottle cherries
Maraschino cherries

Dilute orange juice concentrate with 2 orange juice cans water; dilute lemonade concentrate with 3 lemonade cans water. Combine sugar and 2 cups water. Boil until syrupy. Add cranberry juice, cider, orange juice and lemonade; heat slightly. Add cherry juice. Place a cherry in each serving cup. Yield: 12 servings.

Mrs. Fred Bourland
Matador, Tex.

CITRUS ADE ICED TEA

2 qt. strong tea
1 ½ c. sugar
1 sm. can frozen lemonade or orangeade

Pour tea into 1-gallon container. Add sugar; stir until dissolved. Add frozen lemonade; stir until d i s s o l v e d. Add enough water to make 3 3/4 quarts liquid. Pour over ice cubes; serve. Yield: Sixteen 8-ounce glasses.

Verna J. Chedwick
Orlando, Fla.

INDEX

380

We wish to thank the following for supplying us with photographs and editorial material: Best Foods Division, Corn Products Company; California Strawberry Advisory Board; Cherry Growers and Industries Foundation; The Nestle Company, Inc.; Evaporated Milk Association; Florida Citrus Commission; American Honey Institute; United Fresh Fruit and Vegetable Association.

National Biscuit Company; National Dairy Council; Fleischmanns Yeast; Pineapple Growers Association; American Dairy Association; Beatrice Foods Company; American Molasses Company; Evaporated Milk Association; The Quaker Oats Company; The Borden Company; Farley Manning Associates, Inc.; Ruth Lundgren Company; Libby, McNeill and Libby; California Raisin Advisory Board; American Spice Trade Association; Ocean Spray Cranberries, Inc.